FAREWELL KABUL

ALSO BY CHRISTINA LAMB

Waiting for Allah: Benazir Bhutto and Pakistan

The Africa House: The True Story of an English Gentleman and His African Dream

The Sewing Circles of Herat: My Afghan Years

House of Stone: The True Story of a Family Divided in War-Torn Zimbabwe

Small Wars Permitting: Dispatches from Foreign Lands

I am Malala (with Malala Yousafzai)

CHRISTINA LAMB

FAREWELL KABUL

FROM AFGHANISTAN TO A MORE DANGEROUS WORLD

WILLIAM COLLINS

William Collins
An imprint of HarperCollins*Publishers*
1 London Bridge Street
London SE1 9GF
WilliamCollinsBooks.com

First published in Great Britain by William Collins in 2015

1

A catalogue record for this book is
available from the British Library

Hardback ISBN 978-0-00-725692-1
Trade paperback ISBN 978-0-00-725693-8

Maps by John Gilkes

Printed and bound in Great Britain by
Clays Ltd, St Ives plc

*In memory of all those who lost their
lives to terrorism – or fighting it – from
New York to London to Kandahar*

It is fatal to enter any war without
the will to win it.

General Douglas MacArthur

Contents

Contents

Maps

Afghanistan and Pakistan

TURKMENISTAN / UZB.

Mazar-i-Sharif •

• Herat

AFGHANISTAN

IRAN

Helmand

• Tarin Kowt

• Kandahar

Spin Boldak •

HELMAND PROVINCE

Quetta •

ARABIAN SEA

Karachi •

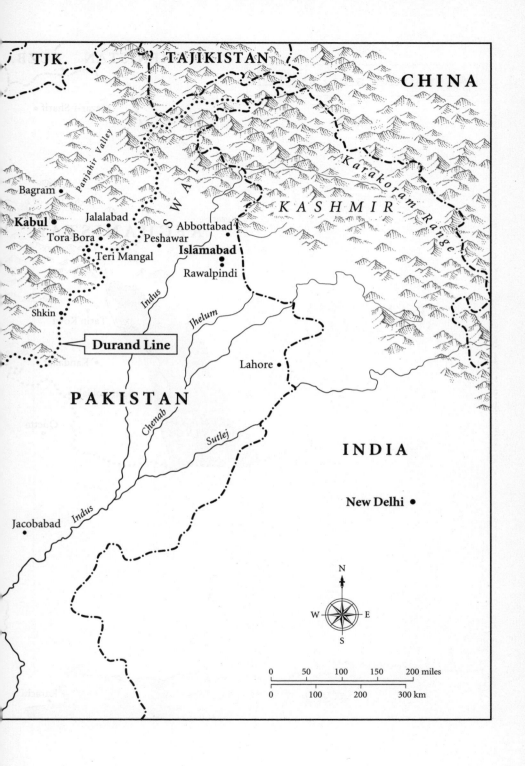

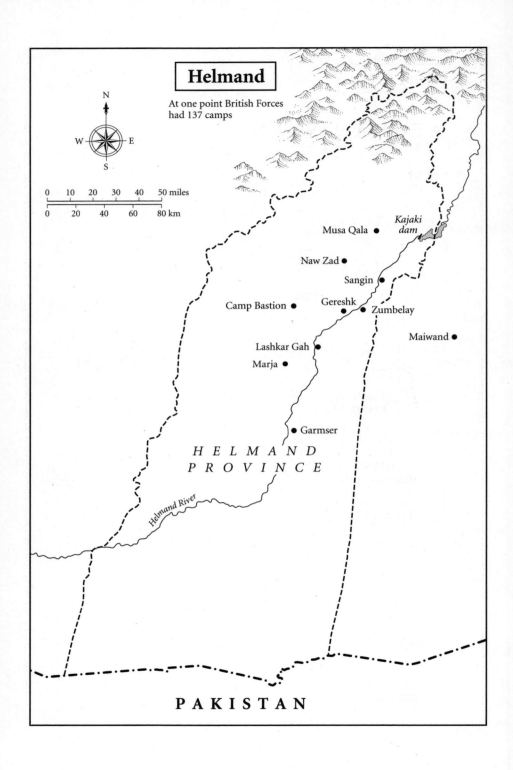

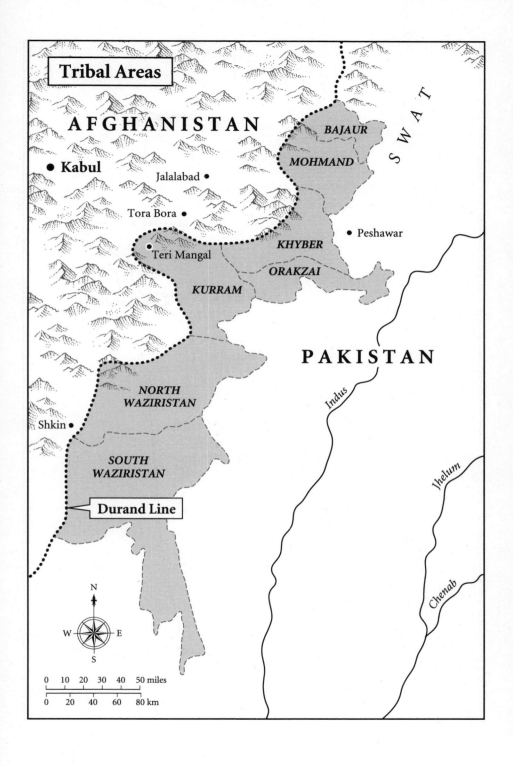

Tribal Areas

AFGHANISTAN

● Kabul

Jalalabad ●

Tora Bora ●

Teri Mangal ●

BAJAUR

MOHMAND

S W A T

● Peshawar

KHYBER

ORAKZAI

KURRAM

PAKISTAN

NORTH WAZIRISTAN

Shkin ●

Indus

SOUTH WAZIRISTAN

Durand Line

Jhelum

Chenab

N
W E
S

0 10 20 30 40 50 miles

0   20   40   60   80 km

The Leaving

Camp Bastion, Helmand, 26–27 October 2014

'LADIES AND GENTLEMEN, please take your seats for the End of Operations Ceremony!' The American voice boomed enthusiastically over the speakers as if it were the drum roll for a sporting event.

Rows of grey fold-up chairs had been arranged facing a large blast wall painted with murals marking each of the last few commands in Helmand. In front of the wall two detachments of US Marines and British troops stood to attention, flanked on either side by Afghan soldiers, who had been instructed beforehand not to hold hands. Above flew four flags – the Union Jack, the Stars and Stripes, and those of NATO and Afghanistan.

A padre read some Koranic verses, then three American generals took turns at the plinth to speak. One of them was the last commander in Helmand, Brigadier General D.D. Yoo of the US Marines, a man of Napoleonic stature both in height and personality who took the mike from the lectern to strut in front of the audience as if about to burst into song.

Phrases from the speakers, each as determinedly upbeat as the announcer, swam in the hot air like speech bubbles. No one spoke of defeat, or retreat, or withdrawal in the face of an intransigent enemy, or of publics and politicians back home who could take no more flag-draped coffins.

1

The Leaving

'This transfer is a sign of progress,' said Brigadier General Yoo. 'It is not about the coalition. It is really about the Afghans and what they have achieved over the last thirteen years.'

Helmand would now be under control of Afghan forces, commanded by Major General Sayed Malouk. 'We are ready,' Malouk insisted, even though he didn't quite look me in the eye as he said it. He had already lost almost eight hundred men that fighting season, and had himself narrowly escaped a roadside bomb in Sangin.

No British officer spoke, and Britain's eight-year role in Helmand garnered barely a mention, which seemed odd, for this had been the country's longest war in modern times, and its hardest fighting for more than half a century.

The hot sun beat down and guests swigged from bottles of mineral water as 'God Save the Queen' and 'The Star-Spangled Banner' were played and the flags were lowered. The Union Jack was carefully folded, and handed to Brigadier Rob Thomson, the last British commander. Only the Afghan flag was left fluttering as Camp Bastion came under Afghan command, and Britain's fourth war in Afghanistan officially came to an end.

Guests were taken into a cabin where a banquet lunch of smoked salmon, slow-cooked beef and chocolate fudge cake had been specially flown in. The genial Afghan army chief General Sher Mohammad Karimi presented Brigadier General Yoo with a commemorative certificate and a carpet, and both sides took souvenir photographs. It all seemed surreal.

I felt tears stinging my face. Four hundred and fifty-three British soldiers had been lost in Afghanistan, of whom 404 died in Helmand, many of them young enough to be my son. Hundreds more had lost limbs to roadside bombs or been mentally scarred for life. Tens of thousands of Afghans had lost relatives or homes, and I had met many Helmandis living as refugees in a camp in Kabul, begging for scraps of dry bread and meat fat, and burying children in the mornings who had frozen to death overnight in the winter cold.

Watching the flag come down felt like the end of everything. This fierce, turtle-shaped country had been part of my entire adult life, longer than any relationship or job. It was twenty-seven years since I'd first come to Afghanistan as a young wannabe foreign correspondent, crossing the Hindu Kush with the mujaheddin fighting the Russians, and falling unequivocally in love with this land of pomegranates and war. I'd had narrow escapes in muddy fields nearby, both with those mujaheddin who went on to become Taliban, and then with British soldiers fighting those Taliban. My first big assignment was covering the Soviet withdrawal in 1989, and never in my wildest dreams had I imagined I would be back a quarter of a century later, covering my own country's ignominious departure. Just as after the Russians had gone, everyone had lost interest in Afghanistan, now Western troops were leaving I wondered if anyone would care.

The Union Jack at Bastion was the last to come down over Helmand. Once there had been 137 British bases across the province, but over the last year these had all been bulldozed one by one and turned back to desert, home again only to scorpions and camel spiders.

Some, in places like Sangin, Musa Qala and Naw Zad, had become unlikely household names back in Britain. Many were small, primitive FOBs – Forward Operating Bases: like Camp Inkerman, which was known to everyone as Camp Incoming because it was so frequently hit. Conditions in these places were described as 'austere', which meant showers were hot bags once a week, the dust so deep that you felt it sucking at your boots, and the toilet a stinking pit that was targeted so often it was known as Tali-alley.

Bastion was where it had all started. When it opened in 2006 it was a gritty, grey, sprawling place on the edge of the Dasht-e-Margo, or Desert of Death, that had previously been used for camel-grazing, according to the agreement signed by the Defence Secretary John Reid. Over the years, like the war, it had been expanded and expanded to become Britain's biggest overseas camp since World War II, the first billion-pound base. At its height it housed more than 30,000 people with a coffee bar, Pizza Hut, Kentucky Fried Chicken, three gyms, state-of-the-art hospital and even a water-bottling plant producing 15,000 gallons of Bastion Water a day. The camp's three canteens had served a hundred million meals since 2006, getting through 66,500 eggs a week and 6,000 tubs of ice cream, all flown in. Its airfield saw so many flights a day – six or seven hundred, from jumbo jets to unmanned Reapers – that it had become Britain's third busiest airport.

Now everything had been packed up, bar-coded and sent back or destroyed. The detritus of twenty-first-century war is so vast that after more than eight years in Helmand, Lieutenant Colonel Laurence Quinn, the engineer who oversaw both its building and its dismantling, compared it to packing up 'a town the size of Aldershot with Gatwick airport bolted on'. Five thousand five hundred shipping containers had gone back, mostly by air. The hospital, the pie shop in Lashkar Gah, the air-conditioning units, the Naafi shop, the water-bottling plant had all gone, as had the tented camps, one of them ending up sheltering refugees in a new war in Iraq. The naughty posters had been stripped down and the rockery dismantled. Thousands of unspent bullets were fed into a popcorn machine to be harmlessly exploded. Fifty aircraft had been sent back, and 3,300 armoured vehicles, including Mastiffs and Wolfhounds, six-wheeled armour-caged monsters costing more than £1 million apiece, so different from the open Snatch Land Rovers in which troops had started out and that the Americans mocked as 'safari vehicles'. The security cameras and radios were stripped from the control towers, leaving the Afghans who would man them no way to keep watch on the perimeter or to communicate. Hardest of all to pack was the massive Giraffe rocket-detector. Last to go was the airport radar and a foam-dispensing fire engine. The Afghans joked sourly that the British would have taken the concrete walls if they could.

As if the foreigners were trying to erase all signs of their pres-ence, the murals had been painted over. One of the most moving sights at Bastion had been the Memorial Wall to the fallen, with 453 brass plates bearing the names of all those killed, under the lines from the First World War poet John Maxwell Edmonds: 'When you go home tell them of us and say/for your tomorrow we gave our today.' Even that had been dismantled, and there would be no monument in Helmand to British lives lost. There would be no voices calling 'We are the dead,' for the poppy fields of Helmand would be very different from those of Flanders a century earlier.

On the last night, even the electricity was switched off, a young British corporal, Sam Boswell, nervously turning off the final switch at 3.30 a.m. on Monday, 27 October. 'I double-checked and it was definitely off,' he told me afterwards. It was eerie driving around the camp in its final hours of British presence. Under the faint glimmer of a crescent moon reclining low in the sky, abandoned patches of desert stretched for miles and miles, ringed by fences of barbed wire. The only buildings left were the control tower, some giant hangars that had housed workshops or aircraft, and the line of towers around the twenty-three-mile perimeter. Adding to the apocalyptic air, a few bonfires were burning to incinerate the last remaining sensitive documents.

But the strangest thing was not the emptiness. The Bastion I knew had always hummed with the sound of large generators blasting air into each of the tented camps, and the constant take-off and landing of planes. Now there was silence. For that last night the remaining thousand or so British and American troops withdrew into a small camp by the side of the airfield. The outer perimeter towers were guarded till the end, and 'lumes', or illumination mortars, were fired off in a final expensive fireworks display meant to present a show of strength to the Taliban.

In the countdown to what was called 'H Hour', the withdrawal was coordinated from a control room facing the runway. British and American soldiers sat at a T-shaped table mounted with framed photographs of the Queen and the action-movie star Chuck Norris, and tapped away at tablets or spoke on radios. In front of them a giant screen played a feed from a Reaper somewhere overhead. The footage showed a compound just south of Bastion, where two men were clearly visible walking around outside. As we watched, the men fired off a rocket-propelled grenade. I was quickly shuffled out while the soldiers discussed whether to respond. In the end they did nothing.

For the final six hours before the withdrawal the air above us was full of Apaches, Cobras, Tornadoes and B1 bombers circling around. Nothing was left to chance. 'We don't want anything that looks like helicopters fleeing from the US Embassy roof in Saigon,' had been the instructions from Whitehall to RAF officers orchestrating the event.

The Afghan forces that the British and Americans had been talking up so highly were not being trusted to guard their exit – even the perimeter guard towers were only handed over at the last minute. The air-traffic controllers destroyed equipment in the control tower before leaving. The final wave of aircraft was guided out by an airborne control team on a Hercules.

In the end the departure was so perfectly choreographed one could almost forget it was a retreat. Fifteen waves of Hercules transport planes and a last one of choppers – four monstrous CH53s, two Hueys and two British Chinooks. It was the biggest airborne withdrawal since the Berlin Airlift. I went on one of the last waves to Kandahar, landing in time to watch the final helicopters swooping in and disgorging the troops, so cinematic that the only thing missing was a soundtrack.

The airlift went so smoothly it finished more than three hours ahead of schedule, at 11.54 a.m. on Monday, 27 October. Yet even before the soldiers had set foot back on home soil, recriminations started. There were calls for a Chilcot inquiry like that into the war in Iraq, and the country looked set for the same kind of long and bitter blame game as that which followed America's involvement in Vietnam. Lord Paddy Ashdown, the former leader of the Liberal Democrats, called it 'catastrophic'. Admiral Lord West, the former First Sea Lord, described the war as an 'abject failure', and demanded a public inquiry. Lieutenant Colonel Richard Williams, a former commander of the SAS, wrote an article in *The Times* which lambasted the lack of planning, adding, 'It is also clear to me that we did not run or command it well either.'

There would be no victory parades, for there had been no victory. Lofty aims of transforming the country were forgotten. Now it was about damage control. 'Helmand is not the Western Front; it doesn't end in a hall of mirrors in Versailles like 1918,' said Brigadier Rob Thomson. 'I don't think wars today end in defeat or victory; you set the conditions to allow other elements to come in.'

The question on everyone's lips was how long would it be till the Taliban raised their black flags instead? Already they were back in many districts, showing their presence, if not yet hoisting flags.

Brigadier Thomson would not be drawn on the future. 'There's clearly going to be a contest,' he said, 'and it would be foolish of me to make a prediction into the long term about how this will run.' The Taliban, meanwhile, had already declared victory. 'The flight of the British invaders is another proud event in the history of Afghanistan,' said their spokesman.

Locals watched and shrugged at the latest foreigners to come and leave their country. They had been surprised when the *Angrez*, as they called the British, came back, for the British Army had suffered one of the worst defeats in its history at nearby Maiwand in 1880. No one had ever really explained why they had returned, if not to avenge that. Nor had they understood what the point of killing Taliban was, when more just came over the border from Pakistan, a country which had received more than $20 billion in Western aid since 9/11, and turned out to have been hosting bin Laden.

So the farmers just got on and harvested their poppy, for it would be a record crop of more than 200,000 hectares, almost half of that in Helmand, by far the world's biggest producer. Most villages still had no jobs, no electricity, no services.

Ministry of Defence bureaucrats could spend money commissioning slick 'legacy videos', but the truth was that Britain's fourth war in Afghanistan had ended in ignominious departure. It had been the country's longest war since the Hundred Years War, longer than the Napoleonic Wars, and the most deadly since the Korean.

British officers might be lobbing accusations at each other, but Helmand was a reflection of the whole war in Afghanistan. In the thirteen years since invading Afghanistan in response to 9/11,

NATO forces had lost 3,484 troops and spent perhaps $1 trillion. For the Americans, who lost the most soldiers and footed most of the bill, it was their longest ever war. What had once been the right thing to do – what President Barack Obama called 'the good war' – had become something everyone wanted to wash their hands of.

How on earth had the might of NATO, forty-eight countries with satellites in the skies, 140,000 troops dropping missiles the price of a Porsche, not managed to defeat a group of ragtag religious students and farmers led by a one-eyed mullah his own colleagues described as 'dumb in the mouth'? And why had they even tried?

Overall, more than $3 trillion had been spent in Iraq and Afghanistan in response to a terrorist attack that cost only between $400,000 and $500,000 to mount.[1] The aim, as stated by Gordon Brown while he was Prime Minister, was that 'We fought them over there to not fight them here.' Yet it was hard to see how these wars had left the West safer. On the contrary, we had ended up with the Pakistani Taliban, who were far more dangerous than the original Afghan Taliban, and regional offshoots of al Qaeda like al Qaeda in the Arabian Peninsula (AQAP) in Yemen, al Qaeda in the Islamic Maghreb (AQIM) in North Africa, al Shabaab in Somalia and Boko Haram in Nigeria. Mullah Omar was still at large, as was Ayman al Zawahiri, Osama bin Laden's deputy, who had succeeded him as leader. Some of the original al Qaeda from Afghanistan/Pakistan that was supposed to have been incapacitated had turned up under the name Khorasan in Syria. Lastly, there was ISIS, the so-called Islamic State of Iraq and Syria, far larger and more terrifying than al Qaeda, which by the end of 2014 controlled territory the size of Britain in Iraq and Syria, as well as making inroads in Libya. ISIS had declared a Caliphate, and was vowing to extend its reign of terror and beheadings as far as Spain, prompting the US and Britain to send advisers back to Iraq, and sucking them back into their fourth war since 9/11. So many Europeans had been attracted as jihadists into its ranks that intelligence chiefs were warning an attack on British soil was 'almost inevitable'.

The Leaving

From Libya to Ukraine, around the world conflicts were springing up everywhere, like the Whack-a-Mole arcade game in which no matter how many moles are smashed with a hammer, more simply pop up elsewhere. There were more countries undergoing wars or active insurgencies than at any time since the Second World War, yet never had the major powers been wearier of intervention. What had started with hopes of a new world for Afghan women had ended with medieval black-hooded executioners, religious wars across the Middle East, and Jordan's King Abdullah warning that World War III was at hand.[2]

As for Afghanistan, schools, clinics and roads had been built across the country, yet it remained one of the poorest places on earth. By the end of 2014 the US would have spent more on Afghanistan than it had on the Marshall Plan to rebuild Europe after the Second World War. Yet poverty remained stubbornly high, with more than a third of Afghans still surviving on less than 80p a day, according to the United Nations Development Programme, and half its children having never set foot in a classroom.[3] In a land where 70 per cent of the population was under thirty, the majority had only ever known war. War against the Russians, war against each other, war between the West and al Qaeda and the Taliban. In this last, 15,000 Afghan troops had died, as well as more than 22,000 civilians, and the numbers were going up each year.

The West's relations with the country it had been trying to help, and the ruler it had installed, had deteriorated to such an extent that in President Hamid Karzai's farewell speech to his cabinet in late September 2014, there were no thanks for Britain or America. Instead he blamed America – as well as Pakistan – for not wanting peace. 'We are losing our lives in a war of foreigners,' he raged.

No one who goes to war comes back unchanged. I spent two wars in Afghanistan – the first as a recent graduate (covering the final showdown of the Cold War), the second as a new mum in the aftermath of 9/11 (covering a war involving my own country). I left a middle-aged woman who had more than used up her nine lives, with a teenage son going into a world far more ominous than that in which I grew up.

This book sets out to tell the story, by someone who lived through it, of how we turned success into defeat. It is the story of well-intentioned men and women going into a place they did not understand at all – even though, in the case of the British, there was plenty of past history. The 1915 'Field Notes on Afghanistan' given to those heading out to the Third Anglo–Afghan War are full of salutary warnings, starting right off with 'Afghans are treacherous and generally inclined towards double dealing.' Major General Dickie Davis, sent to Afghanistan in 2002, recalls how when he was briefed on the mission at military headquarters (PJHQ) before departing, he asked, 'How many hundreds of years have we got?'[4]

Anyone visiting the NATO military headquarters in Kabul might be struck by the number of saplings planted on the small green over the years – one for each commander. There had been seventeen in the course of the war. In Helmand alone Britain had had seventeen commanders, each there for just six months. They might wonder too how a war could be fought effectively when there was no real border with the neighbouring country of Pakistan, which the enemy made its safe haven.

Yet more than a military failure, this was a political failure. Just as a lack of imagination had failed to predict the possibility of using passenger aeroplanes as weapons, a lack of imagination caused us to assume people wanted the same as us, and that because our enemy were uneducated they were ignorant savages we could easily outsmart. It was a strategy that ignored tribal realities and other people's national interests, including those of our key partner. Along the way, the West lost the moral high ground by giving positions of power to those the Afghan people most blamed for the war, and by the detention and torture of prisoners, some of whom had simply been in the wrong place at the wrong time.

Over those thirteen years I watched with growing incredulity as we fought a war with our hands tied, committed too little too late, became distracted by a new war of our own making based on wrong information, and turned a blind eye as our enemy was being helped by our own ally. Yet only when Osama bin Laden was found living in a house in a Pakistani city, not far from the capital, did it seem to dawn on people that we may have been fighting the wrong war.

Throughout this period I lived in Pakistan, Afghanistan, London and Washington, as well as covering the other war and its aftermath in Iraq, and visiting Saudi Arabia, which was the birthplace of fifteen of the nineteen 9/11 hijackers. I spoke to almost all key decision-makers, including heads of state and generals, as well as embedding with American soldiers and British squaddies actually fighting the wars. Most of all I talked to people on the ground. I travelled the length and breadth of Pakistan, from the tribal areas to the mountain valleys of Swat, from the cities of Quetta, Lahore and Karachi to the jihadist recruiting grounds in madrassas and in remote villages of the Punjab. In Afghanistan my travels took me far beyond Helmand – from the caves of Tora Bora in the south to the mountainous badlands of Kunar in the east; from Herat, city of poets and minarets in the west, to the very poorest province of Samangan in the north, full of abandoned ghost villages. I also travelled to Guantánamo, met Taliban in Quetta and from the Quetta *shura*, visited jihadi camps in Pakistan, and saw bin Laden's house just after he was killed. Saddest of all, I met women whom we had made into role models and who had then been shot, raped, or forced to flee the country.

On the way I had several narrow escapes – from being ambushed by Taliban with the first British combat troops in Helmand to travelling on Benazir Bhutto's bus when it was blown up in Pakistan's biggest ever suicide bomb. I lost many friends in those years, a number of whom appear in the following pages.

I could not have lived through all this and just walked away. I have written this book because I thought it was a story that needed telling. How it ends is yet to be told.

PART I

GETTING IN

British general to Afghan tribal chief in 1842 during the
First Anglo–Afghan War: 'Why are you laughing?'

Tribal chief: 'Because I can see how easy it was for you to
get your troops in here. What I don't understand is how you
plan to get them out.'

1

Rule Number One

Kabul, Christmas Eve 2001

I SAT ON the roof of the Mustafa Hotel on the seat of an old Soviet MiG fighter jet and looked out over Kabul feeling happy. Happy endings are few and far between in my foreign correspondent world, where we fly in to report war, misery and disaster in time for our deadlines, then out again back to our comfortable lives, disturbed only by an occasional nightmare or sad memory that floods in unexpectedly to darken a moment.

The hills all around were dotted with tiny wattle houses in squares of beige and sky-blue, melding into each other like a Braque painting. There was 'Swimming Pool Hill', named after the Olympic-sized concrete pool the Russians had built on its top, long empty and last used by Taliban to push blindfolded homosexuals to their deaths off the diving tower; 'TV Mountain', with a broken antenna and littered with rocket casings from years as a major battleground for rival mujaheddin groups; and 'Cannon Hill', where until all the fighting started an old man would fire off a cannon every day at noon, a tradition begun in the nineteenth century by the 'Iron King' Abdur Rahman to give his unruly countrymen a sense of time.

Along the tops I could see remains of the old city walls picked out in relief, starting and ending at the Bala Hissar fortress, an ancient polygon of walls which crowned Lion's Gate Mountain and managed to be both crumbling and imposing. The name means 'high fort', and from this perch for centuries ruled Afghan kings (some of whom ended up in its dungeons, the Black Pit) and, long ago, some of the world's mightiest conquerors. Among them were Timur the Lame, the Tartar despot who levelled cities from Moscow to Baghdad and built towers from the skulls of their people; and Babur, the first Moghul Emperor, who adored Kabul for its gardens, where he counted thirty-two different kinds of tulips. Babur loved this city, describing it as 'the most pleasing climate in the world ... within a day's ride it is possible to reach a place where the snow never falls. But within two hours one can go where the snow never melts.'

I loved it too, even though it was a long time since Kabul had been a city of gardens. Rather it was a city of ghosts, many of whose bodies were buried in the hills. Some of them were from my own country. Britain had fought two wars with Afghanistan, losing two and perhaps drawing the third. Yet initially the country seemed so benign that when British forces first stormed Kabul Gate in 1838, to oust king Dost Mohammed and install their own king, Shah Shuja, they took with them their wives, hundreds of camels laden with provisions such as smoked salmon, cigars and port, and even packs of hounds for hunting foxes in the Hindu Kush. Wives wrote of swapping tips on growing sweet peas and geraniums with local Afghans[1] and of outings to boat on the lake or ice-skate in winter. By January 1842 the British would have fled. The king they had installed on a gilded throne under richly painted ceilings in the Great Hall of the Bala Hissar and described as "a man of great personal beauty"[2] ended up slaughtered at its gates. The defeat of what was then the most powerful nation on earth – and slaughter of thousands of its forces – by marauding tribesmen was the greatest military humiliation ever suffered by the West in the East.

Yet they went back. In the second war, the British Envoy Sir Louis Cavagnari was hacked to death in his residence inside the fort in September 1879 by tribal brigands angry at not being paid promised stipends, and at British interference in their land. In revenge the British general Frederick Roberts led a column on

Kabul called the 'Army of Retribution', and had forty-nine tribal leaders hanged from gallows inside the Bala Hissar. He ordered the fort's destruction as 'a lasting memorial of our ability to avenge our countrymen', though in the end it was left. Such was the feared reputation of the land of the Bala Hissar that in 1963 Britain's Prime Minister Harold Macmillan would declare, 'Rule number one in politics – Never Invade Afghanistan.'

I had first travelled in these valleys and mountains in the late 1980s when the Russians were being driven out, so was only too familiar with all those stories of Afghanistan as the 'Graveyard of Empires'. Indeed, Kabul still had a British cemetery, with graves going back to those killed in the First Anglo–Afghan War, if any reminder were needed.

But if we knew those things then, we were not thinking about them. If I shivered, it was because of the cold. The first snow was falling softly, and loud Bollywood music blared discordantly from the street below. On the roof were other journalists from Japan, Italy and Australia, shuffling around their satellite dishes to try to find the right angle to locate satellites in the sky so they could magically transmit their copy to their foreign desks. 'Oh for fuck's sake, bring back the Taliban!' joked one, struggling to be heard over the jarring music. I laughed, catching a snowflake on my tongue and thinking there was nowhere I would rather be.

Everything had happened so quickly it was hard to take in. On 11 September 2001 I had just moved to Portugal with my husband and two-year-old son when my sister-in-law called telling me to switch on the news. We hadn't yet got a television so we headed to a local piri-piri chicken café which had a large screen to show football matches to English tourists. Watching the planes fly through the brilliant blue sky of a Manhattan morning and smash into the iconic towers of the World Trade Center was impossible to comprehend, no matter how many times we watched.

Then we heard two other passenger planes had crashed – one into the Pentagon and one into a field in Pennsylvania. I held my son tight, for it was clear that nothing would be the same again.

GETTING IN

It wasn't long before the TV commentators were joining the dots to Saudi billionaire's son Osama bin Laden, who had vowed war on the United States. Soon they were focusing their pointers on maps of Afghanistan where the al Qaeda leader had fought in the 1980s and been living under the protection of the Taliban since 1996.

Who were the Taliban, and their mysterious one-eyed leader Mullah Omar? It was a regime about which the West knew so little that when 9/11 happened, Jonathan Powell, Chief of Staff to British Prime Minister Tony Blair, sent out his staff to buy all the books they could on the Taliban.[3] They had only been able to find one – Ahmed Rashid's *Taliban*, which had struggled to find a publisher. Now it was a best-seller and everyone had heard of the zealots who wanted to lock away Afghanistan's women and take the country back to the seventh century.

Editors who had not been in the least interested in goings on in Afghanistan suddenly could not get enough stories of the horrors of life under the Taliban. For weeks we had been writing about the women lashed for wearing nail varnish or white shoes; the men beaten with logs for not having beards as long as two fists; the sports stadiums used for amputations and executions; and the banning of everything from chess to music.

Now, just two months later, they had been driven out. In Kabul, everyone seemed to be out on the streets, hearing each other's stories, like people inspecting the damage after a massive storm. The reports we were sending were upbeat tales of life beginning again: girls' schools reopening, women casting off the blue burqas they had been made to wear. On every street there were people hammering Coke and 7 Up cans into satellite dishes. In a teahouse I came across the first meeting of a long-banned chess club; in the bookshop around the corner from the hotel was Shah Mohammad Rais, who had hidden his books to prevent the Taliban burning them. In the National Gallery I found a man with a sponge and bucket washing off the trees and lakes he had painted over faces on artworks so the Taliban would not destroy them.

Most magical of all were the kites flying from the rooftops. On the road up to the Intercontinental Hotel (that wasn't really an

Intercontinental) a parade of tiny kite shops had reopened. Inside each sat a man wrapping bamboo frames with tissue paper then pasting on shapes in bright pinks, yellows and blues like a Matisse collage and finally rolling the string onto giant reels. Each man claimed to be the most famous kite-maker in Kabul. We didn't know then that the string would be coated with ground glass, and the objective was to cut down kites of other boys (even then, we never saw girls flying kites).

The story I had written that day was of an encounter with British Royal Marines on Chicken Street, a favourite destination back in the days of the hippie trail, with all its little shops selling carpets, shawls, and lapis and garnet stones set into silver rings that would soon blacken. The soldiers were the first arrivals of the International Stabilisation Assistance Force (ISAF), which was quickly nicknamed the International Shopping Assistance Force.

The first foreign troops to enter Kabul since the Russian occupation twelve years earlier, the British were warmly welcomed by locals. After years of civil war, many Afghans saw foreigners as the only way to end the fighting so they could get on with life. The fact that of all people they were British, back for more, seemed to endear them further to the locals. The British soldiers sat on top of their armoured personnel carriers handing out sweets to Afghan children and cigarettes to the men, and all round it was smiles.

'Hello my sister, what gives?' Wais Faizi, the hotel's manager, was a thirty-one-year-old Afghan with a fast-talking New Jersey patois like the car salesman he had once been. 'The Fonz of Kabul', we called him. His family had owned the Mustafa for years, until it was seized by communists around the time of the Soviet invasion in 1979, and they had fled to America when he was just a child. They had recently returned to Afghanistan, and had been in the process of converting the Mustafa into a gemstone and money exchange when 9/11 happened and Kabul unexpectedly became the focus of world attention. So they quickly turned it back into a hotel, just in time for the flood of journalists, though with not enough time to actually make the rooms comfortable.

GETTING IN

'*Chai sabz?*' Wais handed me a mug of green tea.

'*Tashakor.*' I thanked him. It had about as much taste as old dishwater, but it was warm, tendrils of steam rising in the frigid air, and I cupped my hands gratefully around the sides.

'Still working on the espresso machine,' he apologised. He found his home country harder to get used to than we nomad journalists did, and often talked wistfully of Dunkin' Donuts and Domino's Pizza. A coffee machine would actually be useless, given how rarely we had electricity; and when it came it was in gadget-destroying bursts. But if anyone could get one, it would be Wais. He'd already turned one of the rooms into a makeshift gym, complete with some dumbbells bought from a warlord, and decorated with posters of his hero Al Pacino.

Wais had even managed to get hold of the only convertible in Kabul, a 1968 Chevy Camaro which had belonged to one of the Afghan princes before the King was deposed, and had taken me for a spin. We'd had a glorious afternoon driving around the ruins of Kabul, children waving in astonishment, carpet-beaters jumping out of the way and men wobbling on their bikes at the sight of a foreign woman in an open-top car and headscarf fancying herself as Grace Kelly.

Next he had promised us a bar, and he was organising a Christmas dinner, for, unbelievably, he had found someone in the Panjshir valley who raised turkeys. It would make a change from the past-their-date tuna ready-meals, peanut butter and white-furred bars of Cadbury's chocolate we had been living on from Chelsey (sic) Supermarket, where Osama bin Laden's Arabs used to shop.

I caught another snowflake on the tip of my tongue. 'Christina *jan*, don't eat the snow – it's full of shit!' admonished Wais. He meant it literally. Everyone in Kabul seemed to have a permanent cough, and Americans I met loved to tell me the air was full of faecal matter – waste went straight into the streets, and the smoke rising from the houses on the hills was from pats of animal dung that people burned as fuel.

'No thanks to your horrid pigeons!' I replied. Wais had recently discovered Kabul's old Bird Market, which sold anything from tiny orange-beaked finches to strutting roosters, all meant for fighting.

There, he had acquired a flock of burbling pigeons which he kept in a glass coop in the open courtyard in the centre of the hotel. Pigeon-flying was popular in Kabul, where houses had flat roofs and people trained them to take off as if by remote control then loop the loop by waving a stick called a *tor*, with a piece of black cloth on the end. As always in Afghanistan, it wasn't a benign pastime: the real aim was to try to get someone's rival flock to land on your rooftop. You could usually tell pigeon-trainers by their beak-scarred hands.

Wais claimed the pigeons reminded him of the blue mosque in the northern city of Mazar-i-Sharif, a building surrounded by so many white doves that when they take to the air it feels like being inside a just-shaken snowglobe. But to me they were completely different. Pigeons, I reminded him, had left the young Emperor Babur fatherless at thirteen, when his father fell from his dovecote. 'The pigeons and my father took flight to the next world,' he'd written in his journal.

'Why can't you fly kites instead of pigeons?' I asked.

'You of all people should like the pigeons,' Wais laughed. 'When they fly they always follow the lead of a female.'

The music stopped, its owner perhaps paid off by some exasperated journalist, and I could hear peals of children's laughter. Down on the pavement some local street kids were jumping and diving, trying to catch the snow, which was starting to fall more thickly, sending cloth-wrapped figures scurrying to their homes. Soon I would be driven inside too, to one of the freezing glass-partitioned cells with metal bars on the outside that passed for rooms at the Mustafa. But for a moment I wanted to enjoy the rare sight of children playing in this country which had seen more than twenty years of war.

The mood in Washington and Whitehall was also celebratory. Just sixty days after the first US bombing raid on Afghanistan the Taliban were gone, far quicker than Pentagon estimates. They had been driven out by a combination of American B52 bombers and Afghan fighters from the Northern Alliance, a group of mainly Tajik and Uzbek commanders who had started waging war against the Russians in the 1980s, then continued fighting against the Taliban when they took power in the 1990s.

It was an astonishing success, and seemed like a new model of war. Colin Powell, then US Secretary of State, said: 'We took a Fourth World army – the Northern Alliance – riding horses, walking, living off the land, and married them up with a First World air force. And it worked.'

The Northern Alliance certainly did not consider itself a Fourth World army, and the fact that there was already a fighting force in place well acquainted with the Taliban was a huge advantage. Based in the picturesque Panjshir valley, they were the fighters of a legendary commander, Ahmat Shah Massoud, a poetic figure with a long, aquiline nose, blue eyes and a rolled felt cap, known as the Lion of Panjshir, whom the Russians had never defeated. Under his leadership the Northern Alliance controlled around 9 per cent of Afghanistan in the north-east – the one bit of the country the Taliban had never managed to conquer.

Massoud's foreign spokesman was his close friend Dr Abdullah Abdullah, a short, dapper-suited ophthalmologist with a penchant for wide ties. His name was really only Abdullah, as like many Afghans he had just one name, but he had taken another 'Abdullah' to accommodate the need of the Western media for surnames. Dr Abdullah had repeatedly travelled to America and Britain, warning that Arab terrorists were taking over Afghanistan. He told me he had made ten trips to Washington between 1996, when the Taliban took power, and 2001 asking for help – all to no avail.[4] The Americans were not interested in Afghanistan, and had no desire to get involved with a warlord who financed his operations through the trafficking of drugs and lapis lazuli. Massoud was particularly distrusted by the State Department because he received support from Iran and Russia, and because of the fact that he was hated by Pakistan, which the US wanted to keep onside. 'They just said it was an internal ethnic conflict,' said Dr Abdullah. Massoud himself spoke at the European Parliament in April 2001, appealing for humanitarian aid for his people and warning that al Qaeda was planning an attack on US soil.

He was hardly a lone voice. George Tenet, who was Director of the CIA at the time, later testified before the 9/11 Commission that the Agency had picked up reports of possible attacks on the United States in June, and said the 'system was blinking red' from July 2001. On 12 July Tenet went to Capitol Hill to provide a top-secret briefing for Senators about the rising threat from Osama bin Laden. Only a handful of Senators turned up in S-407, the secure conference room. The CIA Director told them that an attack was not a question of *if*, but *when*.

Another warning came in the first meeting between President George W. Bush and his Russian counterpart Vladimir Putin in a Slovenian castle in July 2001, the American President was taken aback when the former KGB man suddenly raised the subject of Pakistan. 'He excoriated the Musharraf regime for its support of extremists and for the connections of the Pakistani army and intelligence services to the Taliban and al Qaeda,' recalled Condoleezza Rice, Bush's National Security Adviser, who was present. 'Those extremists were all being funded by Saudi Arabia, he said, and it was only a matter of time until it resulted in a major catastrophe.'[5]

This was written off as Soviet sour grapes for having lost in Afghanistan. No notice was taken, nor was the Northern Alliance provided with help. It says something about Massoud's charisma that without Western assistance or much hope of success, he kept his fighters together. 'He always wore a *pakoul* [wool cap], and he'd say, "Even if this *pakoul* is all that remains of Afghanistan I will fight for it,"' said Ayub Solangi, who had fought with him since the age of sixteen, and had lost all his teeth in torture in Russian prisons.

Two days before 9/11, two Tunisians posing as TV journalists came to his Panjshir headquarters to do an interview. 'Why do you hate bin Laden?' they asked him, just before their camera exploded in a blue flash. The assassination of the Taliban's biggest enemy was widely assumed to be a gift from al Qaeda to their Taliban hosts, to ensure their support as the Bush administration wreaked its inevitable revenge on Afghanistan for blowing up the Twin Towers.

2

Sixty Words

BEFORE EXACTING REVENGE, the Bush administration wanted Congressional approval, as under the United States Constitution only Congress can authorise war. So just twenty-four hours after the second plane hit the South Tower, while most people were still trying to digest what had happened, White House lawyer Timothy Flanigan was already sitting at his computer urgently typing up legal justification for action against those responsible.

The last time the US had declared war was in 1991 against Iraq, so he first cut and pasted the wording from the authorisation for that. However, the problem was that this time no one really knew who or where the enemy was, so something wider and more nebulous was needed.

By 13 September Flanigan and his colleagues had come up with the Authorisation for Use of Military Force, or AUMF, for Congress to vote on. At its core was a single sixty-word sentence: 'That the President is authorized to use all necessary and appropriate force against those nations, organizations or persons he determines planned, authorized, committed or aided the terrorist attacks that occurred on September 11, 2001, or harbored such organizations or persons in order to prevent any future acts of international terrorism against the United States by such nations, organizations or persons.'

In other words, this would be war with no restraints of time, location or means.

Sixty Words

At 10.16 a.m. on 14 September, the AUMF went to the Senate. The nation wanted action, and all ninety-eight Senators on the floor voted Yes. From there they were bussed straight to Washington's multi-spired and gargoyled National Cathedral for a noontime prayer meeting called by the White House for the victims of the attacks. It was a highly charged service, with many tears, prayers, a thundering organ and an address by President Bush, followed by the singing of 'The Battle Hymn of the Republic'. Members of Congress were then bussed to the House for their vote. One after another called for unity. Four hundred and twenty voted in favour, and just one against. Barbara Lee, a Democratic Congresswoman from California, was as heartbroken as anyone by 9/11 – her Chief of Staff had lost his cousin on one of the flights. But she worried that what she called 'those sixty horrible words' could lead to 'open-ended war with neither an exit strategy nor a focused target'. So to the outrage of her colleagues, she stood up and voted No. Her voice cracking, she cried as she asked people to 'think through the implications of our actions today so this does not spiral out of control'. She ended by echoing the words of one of the priests in the cathedral: 'As we act let us not become the evil we deplore.'

By the time of the vote, I was on a plane. International air traffic had reopened on 13 September after an unprecedented closing of the skies. Most journalists headed to northern Afghanistan to join up with the Northern Alliance, or to Peshawar in north-west Pakistan, the closest Pakistani city to the border with Afghanistan, and the headquarters of the mujaheddin during the war against the Russians. I headed further west, to the earthquake-prone town of Quetta, which was the nearest Pakistani city to Kandahar, the heartland of the Taliban, and like Peshawar had long been home to hundreds of thousands of Afghan refugees. It was also where my oldest Afghan friend, Hamid Karzai, lived.

I checked into the Serena Hotel, where there were soon so many journalists that makeshift beds were set up in the ballroom. I was happy to be back. From my window I could see hills the colour of lion-skin, populated with tribes so troublesome that the British Raj had given up trying to control them and instead given them guns and cash to leave them alone. Beyond those hills lay Afghanistan.

The town used to be on the overland route for backpackers, and in the 1980s I would see big orange double-decker buses that had come all the way from London's Victoria station. The buses did not come any more, but little else had changed. On the main Jinnah Road you could still buy a rifle or some jewelled Baluch sandals, both of which were sported by the local men who wandered around hand in hand.

I met up with commanders I had known back in the 1980s when they were young, dashing and full of hope. Now they were pot-bellied, greying and jaded, but they had been given a sudden lease of life by finding their long-forgotten country the focus of world attention. Just as in the old days we sat cross-legged on cushions on the floor drinking rounds of green tea, served with little glass dishes of boiled sweets (in place of sugar) and crunchy almonds.

The most important call of all my old contacts was Karzai, whom I had got to know when we lived near each other in Peshawar and he was spokesman for the smallest of the seven mujaheddin groups fighting the Russians. His family were prominent landowners from the grape-growing village of Karz, near Kandahar. His father had been Deputy Speaker of parliament, and his grandfather Deputy Speaker of the senate; they were from the majority Pashtun tribe, the same Popolzai branch of the royal family as the unfortunate murdered King Shah Shuja. Karzai had been at school in the Indian hill city of Simla when the Russians invaded, and would never forget the moment his schoolfriends gave him the news. 'I felt I could no longer hold my head high as a proud Afghan,' he told me. Though he was the youngest of six brothers, he became spokesman for the family as the only one to stay after the others moved to America and opened a chain of Afghan restaurants called 'Helmand' in Baltimore, Boston and San Francisco.

'If you want to understand Afghanistan you must understand the tribes,' he urged me on our very first meeting. He invited me to his home to meet elders from across southern Afghanistan who soon had me spellbound with astonishing stories that mostly involved fighting and feuding.

Karzai insisted that the key city of Afghanistan was Kandahar, where its first King, Ahmat Shah Durrani, had been crowned. He took me on my first trip there in 1988, the only time he had gone on jihad, when we rode around on motorbikes and had several narrow escapes from Soviet bombs and tanks. The group we had travelled with, the Mullahs' Front, went on to become Taliban.

A year after that trip the last Soviet soldier crossed the Oxus River out of Afghanistan, but what seemed an astonishing victory quickly soured as the Afghan mujaheddin all started fighting each other. I moved on to other stories in other countries and continents that didn't bruise my heartstrings quite as much. I still went back and forth to Pakistan, however, and had last seen Karzai in 1996, when we quarrelled bitterly in Luna Caprese, the only Italian restaurant in Islamabad after he told me he was fundraising for the Taliban.

Later he had turned against them, saying Pakistanis had taken over the Taliban and Arabs had taken over the country, and like Dr Abdullah he kept banging on offices in Whitehall and Washington with Cassandra-like warnings. For years, he too had met only closed doors. The British Foreign Office didn't even have an Afghan section, and a diplomat in the South Asia section told me Karzai would be palmed off with the most junior official, who would moan, 'Not him again.'

He moved to Quetta, to the house of his genial half-brother Ahmed Wali, who had supported him through all those years when everyone else had forgotten Afghanistan. Now, of course, everything had changed. As a fluent and eloquent English speaker he had a queue of diplomats, spies and journalists at his, or rather Ahmed Wali's, door.

Karzai greeted me warmly. His father had been assassinated in 1999 by men on motorbikes as he was walking back from prayers at the mosque around the corner from the house. Karzai blamed the Taliban and Pakistan's powerful military intelligence agency, ISI

(Inter-Services Intelligence). He had become head of the tribe after that and needed a wife, so in a betrothal arranged by his mother he married his cousin Zeenat, a gynaecologist at Quetta hospital.

He was shocked by 9/11. 'If only people had listened,' he said.'Everything will change now,' I replied.

Some things, it seemed, hadn't changed. Back in the 1980s we had endlessly discussed how ISI were pulling the wool over the eyes of the CIA, which had given them carte blanche to distribute billions of American and Saudi dollars and weapons to the mujaheddin fighting the Russians. Karzai and other Afghans had not forgiven ISI for the way they directed the vast majority to their favourites, the fundamentalist Gulbuddin Hekmatyar and Jalaluddin Haqqani, or diverted it to fund their own proxy war in Kashmir as well as build their nuclear bomb. In those days they didn't really hide this, and I'd even been to visit one of their militant training camps just outside Rawalpindi. Their openness had some limits. In 1990, when I wrote stories that Karzai had helped me research on ISI's interference and on selling arms to Iran, I had been picked up from my apartment in Islamabad, threatened and interrogated by ISI for a night, followed for a week by two cars and a red motorbike, even to a friend's wedding, then eventually deported.

Now over green tea Karzai insisted that Pakistan was again lying to the US. 'They are saying they have stopped supporting the Taliban because otherwise the US will declare them a terrorist sponsor state and bomb them too,' he said. 'The Americans told them you are either with us or against us. But you and I know it's an ideology, not just a policy. I promise you they are still supplying arms to the Taliban.'

To start with, I wasn't sure I believed him. The eyes of the world were on this region. Surely Pakistan would not be so reckless. But I did know that they had got away with it before, and how personally involved many ISI officers in the field were with some of the Taliban after more than twenty years of working with them. I'd had enough discussions with them to agree with Karzai that for many it was an ideology, not a policy – some told me they saw the

Taliban as a pure form of Islam, and would like a similar government in Pakistan.

Some strange things were happening. Shortly after 9/11, when President George W. Bush had asked Pakistan's military ruler General Pervez Musharraf for cooperation, Musharraf had asked that the US hold off any action until Pakistan had made a last try at persuading the Taliban to hand over bin Laden. General Mahmood Ahmed, the ISI chief, who had helped to organise the coup that brought Musharraf to power, led a delegation of clerics to Kandahar to personally appeal to Mullah Omar. But Mufti Jamal, one of the clerics who went with him, told me that the General made no such request. 'He shook hands very firmly with Mullah Omar and offered to help, then later even made another secret mission without Musharraf's knowledge.'

It seemed ISI had calculated that however the Americans retaliated in Afghanistan, they would eventually lose patience, and like all foreigners before them be driven out. 'We knew the Americans could not win militarily in Afghanistan,' I was told by General Ehsan ul Haq, who later replaced Mahmood as ISI chief. Pakistan would, however, still be next-door, so it was understandably hedging its bets. 'The Americans forget other people have national interests too,' said Maleeha Lodhi, then Pakistan's Ambassador to Washington.

From Quetta I went to Rawalpindi to see General Hamid Gul, who had been head of ISI when I lived in Pakistan, running the Afghan jihad. He was virulently anti-American, blaming the US for his dismissal in May 1989. It was the first time I had spoken to him since my deportation, and he insisted to me that the people who had abducted and interrogated me were 'rogue agents'. He still lived in an army house, and somehow it seemed to me that he was still involved. He had personally known bin Laden, and encouraged Arabs to come and fight against the Russians in Afghanistan, setting up reception committees, which as he said the CIA was very happy to use at the time. Indeed, on his mantelpiece was a piece of the Berlin Wall sent to him by German Chancellor Helmut Kohl. It was inscribed: 'With deepest respect to Lt Gen Hamid Gul who helped deliver the first blow.' 'You in the West think you can use these fundamentalists as cannon fodder and abandon them, but it will come back to haunt you,' he had told me in a rare interview just after the Soviet withdrawal. At the time I had not understood what he meant.

General Gul insisted that 9/11 was orchestrated not by bin Laden but Mossad, the Israeli spy agency, to set the West against Muslims and provide an excuse to launch a new Christian Crusade. 'No Jews went to work in the World Trade Center that day,' he claimed. He was dismissive about the latest foreigners to enter Afghanistan. 'The Russians lost in ten years, the Americans will lose in five,' he said. 'They are chocolate-cream soldiers, they can't take casualties. As soon as body bags start going back, all this "Go get him" type of mood will subside.'

Meanwhile, we waited. War had come to America, 3,000 people had been killed in the Twin Towers, and we knew the US administration would soon retaliate. 'My blood was boiling,' Bush later wrote in his memoir. 'We were going to find out who did this and kick their ass.' In a televised address to both houses of Congress nine days after 9/11, he told the nation that 'every necessary weapon of war' would be used to 'disrupt and defeat the global terror network'. He warned that 'Americans should not expect one battle, but a lengthy campaign unlike any other we have ever seen.'

There was one problem. When 9/11 happened, the CIA did not have a single agent in Afghanistan. Only a handful had been there in the previous decade, and they were in the north. The CIA had no contacts among Pashtuns in the south. The FBI had only one officer dedicated to bin Laden. At Fort Bragg the top US special forces continued to be taught Russian, as if the Cold War had not gone away.

While journalists quickly found their way into Northern Alliance strongholds, renting all the available cars and houses, the military took much longer to arrive. The first Americans into Afghanistan after the journalists were a CIA team headed by a man who, at fifty-nine, had thought his days in the field were long over. One of the few agents to have gone to Afghanistan in recent years, Gary Schroen had been involved with Afghanistan on and off since 1978, and had close contacts with the Northern Alliance. He was preparing for retirement when he was called up by the Counter-Terrorism Center (CTC), much to his wife's annoyance. Seventeen days after 9/11 his seven-man team were on an old Russian helicopter into the Panjshir valley to link up with the Northern Alliance.

Apart from communications equipment, the most important part of their baggage was a large black suitcase containing $3 million in cash. On the first night they gave $500,000 to Engineer Aref, intelligence chief for the Northern Alliance, followed by $1 million the next day to Marshal Fahim, who had succeeded Ahmat Shah Massoud as military commander. More money was sent, and within a month they had handed out $4.9 million.

The plan was to send teams of US special forces to join up with Afghan commanders. The Americans would then direct airstrikes using SOFLAMs (Special Operations Forces Laser Acquisition Markers) to pinpoint targets. They also had GPS systems to provide coordinates, as these could be used in all weathers. B52s would then fly over and drop 2,000-pound smart bombs, which would pulverise the target.

However, when the bombing started, almost a month after 9/11, bureaucratic delays and infighting in Washington meant there was still not a single US soldier inside Afghanistan. The only on-the-ground information was coming from Schroen's CIA team and the Afghans.

From the start there was friction. America wanted intelligence on al Qaeda safe houses and camps, and most of all they wanted the man behind 9/11. Before he had left the US, Schroen's boss Cofer Black had told him, 'I want you to cut bin Laden's head off, put it on dry ice, and send it back to me so I can show the President.' The Northern Alliance commanders were more interested in targeting Taliban front lines so they could advance on Kabul and take power.

On Friday, 7 October, President Bush stood in the Treaty Room of the White House and addressed America, announcing the launch of Operation Ultimate Justice (which was quickly renamed

Operation Enduring Freedom). A few hours earlier – night-time in Afghanistan – an awe-inspiring fleet of seventeen B1, B2 and B52 bombers had taken off from bases in Missouri and Diego Garcia to drop their bombs on one of the poorest places on earth. Alongside them were twenty-five F14 and F18 fighter jets flown off the decks of aircraft carriers USS *Enterprise* and USS *Carl Vinson* in the Arabian Sea. Fifty Tomahawk missiles were launched from American ships and a British nuclear submarine. Several had been painted with the letters 'FDNY' – Fire Department of New York – in remembrance of the firefighters who lost their lives trying to rescue victims at the Twin Towers. The heaviest bombing that night was carried out by the B52s, which rained 2,000-pound JDAMs as well as hundreds of unguided bombs aimed at taking out the Taliban air force and suspected al Qaeda training camps in eastern Afghanistan. That first night they struck thirty-one targets.[1] The US State Department sent a cable to Mullah Omar via Pakistan informing him that 'every pillar of the Taliban regime will be destroyed'.

In my hotel room in Quetta I watched on CNN the Pentagon videos of the planes setting off on the bombing raids, and the flashes as targets were hit. Taken on night-vision cameras, the footage was green, with a ticking digital timer running at the bottom, and looked like a video game. I wondered what the Americans could bomb in that country of ruins, with no real infrastructure. Soon they found themselves running out of targets. All the air power in the world was of little use when what they were really fighting was an ideology, not a conventional army.

Our own movements were curtailed by Pakistani minders. For our 'security' we were not allowed out of the hotel without the company of one of the ISI agents who frequented the lobby. I'd found a Fuji photographic shop that had a back door into the market through which I could be met by an old friend. He would whisk me off to meet tribal elders or Afghan commanders so they could speak freely while my minder was watching TV in the Fuji shop. I knew I was testing their patience, so sometimes I met people in what we called 'Nuclear Mountain Park' – its centrepiece was a model of Chagai in the Baluch hills, where Pakistan had carried out its first nuclear tests three years earlier on what was referred to as 'Yaum-e-Takbeer', or Allah's Greatness Day. Every evening people came out to walk round and round the model nuclear mountain, eating ice creams from a cart decorated with red-tipped rockets.

When the US bombing started across the border there were riots in Quetta, and anything perceived as Western was attacked. In Quetta this was not a lot – basically the cinema and the HSBC bank, which had its cashpoint ripped out of the wall, causing untold inconvenience to us correspondents, as it was the only one. The protests gave ISI an excuse to lock us in the hotel altogether, on the grounds that it was too dangerous for us to venture out.

I kept thinking of what Karzai had told me about Pakistan. Before we were locked in I managed to go to the frontier town of Chaman, where I met a chief of the Achakzai tribe, whose people lived on both sides of the border and controlled the smuggling routes in and out. He told me that trucks coming from the National Logistics Company of Pakistan's army, supposedly transporting flour, were actually full of weapons for the Taliban.

Nine days into the bombing, on 16 October, a second CIA team, Team Alpha, arrived in Afghanistan, joining General Abdul Rashid Dostum in the northern city of Mazar-i-Sharif. The choice caused consternation among the Northern Alliance leadership. The whisky-loving Uzbek and his feared Jowzjan militia were notorious for atrocities, such as driving over prisoners with tanks, and had fought alongside the Soviets during the jihad, fighting pitched battles against Ahmat Shah Massoud's forces. Dostum switched over to the mujaheddin in 1992 when the fall of the Soviet-backed President Mohammad Najibullah was imminent, and had only recently linked up with the Northern Alliance. In their view he was not to be trusted. They thought the CIA team should have been placed with their long-time commander Mohammad Ustad Atta, Dostum's rival for control of the city.

GETTING IN

The first US military to set foot in Afghanistan was special forces team ODA 555, codenamed 'Triple Nickel', which was flown in from Uzbekistan and landed on the Shomali plains north of Kabul on 19 October to join Marshal Fahim and his CIA advisers. The following day a second special forces team, ODA 595, joined General Dostum in the northern city of Mazar-i-Sharif. A third group was dropped south of Kandahar. Using SOFLAMs, they laser-guided bombs from US fighter jets onto Taliban targets with such precision that Dostum bragged on the radio to Taliban that he had a 'death ray'. They also attempted to organise the Afghan fighters, and were joined by SAS and some Australian special forces.

Back in Quetta, the nights had started to chill. We had all grown tired of the nightly lamb barbecue and fresh apple juice in the orchard. American newspapers were already talking of quagmires. It felt as if we might be there for a long time.

One day, shortly after the bombing had started, I knocked at Karzai's door to be told by his assistant, Malik, that he had gone away.

'Where has he gone?' I asked.

'Karachi,' he replied.

Malik was not a good liar. 'He's gone to Afghanistan, hasn't he?' I said.

Karzai had told me he'd been planning to go to southern Afghanistan to try to raise support. I'd begged him to take me along. 'Taking you inside is as easy as cracking this nut,' he had said, holding up an almond. 'The problem is what to do then.'

He'd always felt insecure about the fact that he hadn't actually fought in the jihad. The only time he had gone inside Afghanistan during the war against the Russians was our trip to Kandahar in 1988. If he was going to play an important role in whatever government replaced the Taliban, he needed to prove his bravery. Also, Pakistan had cancelled his visa, so if he stayed in Quetta he could be arrested.

His intention was to go and rally the southern tribes against the Taliban. He seemed to think this would be quite easy. I couldn't help remembering our own trip to Kandahar, and the way we kept almost being bombed by the Russians as he naïvely broadcast his presence everywhere by radio. Now he was heading into the Taliban's own backyard.

Ahmed Wali said he'd tried to dissuade him, but to no avail. One day Karzai told his wife he was going to visit some relatives near the border, and to pack him a toothbrush. 'If I don't come back after two days forget about me,' he had said.

He'd set off on a second-hand motorbike, accompanied by a few trusted elders. He had asked for help from the CIA, meeting with his case officer 'Casper' in Islamabad. They thought his mission was crazy, so provided him only with a satellite phone and an emergency phone number. He was so poorly equipped that he had to send someone back out to Ahmed Wali in Quetta on a motorbike with the phone batteries for charging.

Over in the east, another old friend from the jihad days had gone into Afghanistan with the same idea. Abdul Haq had been the main mujaheddin commander in the Kabul area during the Russian occupation, and had lost his right foot to a landmine. Like Karzai he was a long-time critic of ISI. He had kept fighting, but eventually left Peshawar for Dubai after his wife and son had been killed there in 1999 – he believed by ISI. After 9/11 he returned to Peshawar and began renewing his old mujaheddin networks. While Karzai headed west, Abdul Haq gathered supporters to head into his home area of eastern Afghanistan around Jalalabad, where his family were very influential, and planned to start a Pashtun uprising against the Taliban.

A charismatic man with twinkling eyes, Abdul Haq always liked to talk. Back in the eighties I had spent many afternoons with him in his house in Peshawar, eating pink ice cream and listening to his stories of the war and why it was going wrong. Predictably, he had told journalists of his plans before setting off over the border on 21 October with his nephew Izzatullah and seventeen men, mostly veterans of the jihad. They had travelled in pick-ups, crossing the border the old way near Parachinar, stopping for the night under the stars, sleeping under Orion and the Milky Way.

It was hard for Haq to walk far over the rugged mountains

because of his artificial foot, so the next morning they mounted horses in Jaji, near where bin Laden used to have a camp. They rode through the Alikhel gorge, which had been a favourite spot for ambushing Soviet convoys. But just as their own forces had cut off that road in the past, they soon found themselves cut off by the Taliban, and in the midst of a firefight.

As the bullets were flying, Izzatullah ducked behind a rock and managed to make a call to the US on the satellite phone. He telephoned Bud McFarlane, a retired CIA agent who had been a long-time backer of his uncle. McFarlane contacted the Agency headquarters at Langley, Virginia. But they could do nothing, and the men were captured and taken to Jalalabad.

On 26 October we got the news that Haq had been executed. He was forty-three. I was horrified. He seemed to me to have been one of the genuinely good people, and someone who might have been critical for Afghanistan's future. His friends believed he had been betrayed by ISI.

I was worried about Karzai.

Frustrated by not being able to report freely in Quetta, I flew to Karachi to meet Mufti Nizamuddin Shamzai, a cleric close to Mullah Omar and the Taliban who headed the Banuri complex, the city's largest madrassa. Some said it was he who had first introduced Mullah Omar and bin Laden. He laughed at the idea that Pakistan had stopped supporting the Taliban. He had personally declared a fatwa against the US.

The evening I returned to Quetta I went to Ahmed Wali's house. We spoke to Karzai on the satellite phone, and he told me some of the things he had seen crossing the border. I got back to the Serena just before the 9 p.m. curfew, planning to write my story for my paper the next day.

I am lucky to sleep well even in war zones, and was deeply asleep when around 2 a.m. I was woken by pounding on my door. Through the spyhole I could see the hotel's duty manager with a group of five men. Wearing grey *shalwar kamiz* and aviator glasses even at night, they were instantly identifiable as ISI.

'There are some guests for you,' said the duty manager.

'It's the middle of the night!' I protested. 'Tell them to come back in the morning.'

I started walking back to my bed, but the duty manager had the room key, and one of the men in grey snapped the door chain. I was shocked rather than scared. I was in pyjamas, and to have strange men barging into my room in an Islamic country where I had always thought there was respect for women was unbelievable. They snatched my mobile phone, which was charging on the side cabinet, and told me I was going with them.

They let me dress after I protested, then marched me downstairs to reception, where I was made to pay my bill before leaving. I was glad when another group of men appeared holding Justin Sutcliffe, the photographer I was working with. They tried to put us in separate vehicles, but we made so much fuss that they finally bundled us into the same jeep, and we were driven off into the night.

The streets were deserted because of the curfew, and for the first time I felt scared. They could do anything they liked with us, and nobody would know. I was relieved when we turned into a driveway rather than out into the vast Baluch desert. At the end was an abandoned bungalow. Inside, the only furniture was a bed. We were told to sleep while our nine guards sat around and watched. We later discovered this was the old rest-house of Pakistan Railways from colonial times. Fortunately Justin always travelled with spare supplies, and he whispered to me that he had managed to secrete a phone in a pocket. During the night he went to the toilet, from which he called our newspaper while I distracted the guards by pretending to be hysterical. None of our editors answered, as it was the middle of the night back in the UK, but eventually Justin managed to get hold of our Washington correspondent, David Wastell.

The next night our guards drove us to the airport, radioing colleagues with the code 'The eagle has landed.' We were put on a flight to Islamabad and handed over to the FIA, another Pakistani intelligence agency, where no one seemed to know who had ordered our arrest or why. The FIA Director was at a loss what to do, as his cells were being rebuilt, so he kindly fed us some of his own curry dinner and put us under guard in the VIP section of the departure lounge. The next day a diplomat came from the British High Commission, who unhelpfully told us the best thing in terms of our security would be if we left Pakistan. We were unceremoniously deported.

The typed expulsion notices were dated 3 November 2001, and signed by Shah Rukh Nusrat, Deputy Secretary to the government of Pakistan. Mine stated: *'Whereas Miss Christina Lamb, British national acting in manner prejudicial to the external affairs and security of Pakistan it is necessary that she may be externed from Pakistan. Now because in exercise of the powers conferred by section 3 subsection 2 clause C of the Foreigners Act the federal government is pleased to direct that the Miss shall not remain in Pakistan and should leave the country immediately.'*

The Pakistani newspapers printed a ludicrous story, fed from ISI, that we had tried to buy a plane ticket in the name of Osama bin Laden. Years later I would still get asked why we had done this.

My relationship with Pakistan had been conflicted since my previous deportation. As we were led onto the PIA plane (having been asked to pay for the ticket, which we refused to do), I vowed I would never go back.

Shortly after take-off, one of the stewardesses came and said the pilot was inviting us into the cockpit. We were astonished. This was less than two months after 9/11, and the world's airlines had all issued instructions to keep cockpits locked. I pointed out we had been deported as threats to national security, but she just smiled and led us to the front. Inside the cockpit was Captain Johnny Afridi, the plane's pilot, a Pashtun with John Lennon glasses and a long, skinny ponytail. 'Don't worry about those goons,' he laughed. 'I've been arrested too.' By the end of a very entertaining flight, sitting in the cockpit for a spectacular sunset landing at Heathrow, my resolve never to return to Pakistan was forgotten.

Back in London we were called into the Foreign Office to meet the head of the consular service. I was furious that they had done nothing to fight our case – we were from one of Britain's leading newspapers, the *Sunday Telegraph*, and had been trying to report on a war in which Britain was involved.

'You must understand Pakistan are our allies,' we were told. 'We need their support during the bombing campaign. It's a very sensitive time.' We later learned that four Pakistani bases in Sindh and Baluchistan were being used to fly some of the bombing raids.

It was a bright sunny day, but as we walked out into St James's I blinked back angry tears. It seemed my war was over before it had even started.

Meanwhile, in Afghanistan everything was suddenly happening very quickly. Since the start of November the US had agreed to all the urging from the Northern Alliance commanders, and begun pounding Taliban front lines with giant daisy-cutter bombs dropped from AC-130s. Gary Schroen and his CIA team were monitoring Taliban radio traffic, and could literally hear the fear. 'Our guys were listening to the radios and the panic, the screaming, the shouting as bunkers down the line were going up from 2,000-pound bombs,' he said. 'I mean, they were just simply devastated, and they broke.'

There was no more talk of quagmire. Mazar-i-Sharif fell to Dostum's men on 10 November. 'This whole thing might unravel like a cheap suit,' President Bush told President Putin.

The Taliban quickly realised it was no contest, and by 13 November had fled Kabul, leaving the Northern Alliance to move in. By the beginning of December they were gone from all the major cities apart from their heartland of Kandahar in the south, which they finally abandoned on 7 December. 'I think everybody was surprised (with the possible exception of [US Defense Secretary] Don Rumsfeld, who would have felt vindicated) at the result of military intervention, which was nasty, brutish and short,' said Lieutenant General Sir Robert Fry, commandant of the Royal Marines at the time, who went on to be Director of Military Operations at the Ministry of Defence. 'It was remarkably successful in that there were negligible Western casualties. You had overwhelming Western firepower, loads of CIA playing the Great Game with buckets of money, and a compliant infantry in the shape of the Northern Alliance. All of a sudden they thought they'd found the philosopher's stone of intervention.'

New technology, like laser-guided bombs, had avoided a major deployment of troops. To overthrow the Taliban the US had put on the ground fewer than five hundred men – 316 special forces and 110 CIA officers. Only four American soldiers and one CIA agent had been killed, and three of those soldiers were killed by their own bomb – in 'friendly fire'. The whole operation had cost only $3.8 billion. The CIA estimated it had spent $70 million, mostly in bribes to Afghan commanders. President Bush called it one of the biggest 'bargains' of all time.

So easy did it seem that on 21 November, while US forces were still fighting the Taliban, Bush had secretly already directed Rumsfeld to begin planning for a war with Iraq. 'Let's get started on this and get Tommy Franks looking at what it would take to protect America by removing Saddam Hussein,' he said.

General Franks, the commander of US Central Command, was sitting in his office at MacDill Air Force Base in Tampa, Florida, working on plans for Afghanistan when he got the phone call from Rumsfeld. 'Son of a bitch. No rest for the weary,' is how he recalled his reaction in his memoir. Bob Woodward's book *Plan of Attack* has a rather different account. 'Goddamn, what the fuck are they talking about?' Franks is reported as saying. 'They were in the midst of one war, Afghanistan, and now they wanted detailed planning for another?'

Back in London, Justin and I got help from an unexpected source when Iran obliged us with visas to get into Afghanistan from the west. We flew to Tehran, then to the pilgrim town of Mashad near the border, and drove into Herat the day after the Taliban left. We were helped by Ismael Khan, a warlord who looked the part, with his flowing beard and trucks of neatly clad but fearsome gunmen who accompanied him everywhere. I'd first met Ismael when I went to Herat during Russian times, and his resistance was legendary. He had been imprisoned during the Taliban after being betrayed by General Dostum's men, though he'd managed to escape. Although part of the Northern Alliance he had his own status as 'the Emir of the West', and as soon as the Taliban left he took power in his home city.

From Herat we managed to catch the first Ariana flight to Kabul, a nerve-racking experience, as I'd never before been on a plane that had to be jump-started. As we flew awfully close to mountains, the pilot told us the only instrument working was his 'vision'.

But we made it, and found ourselves in the Mustafa. It had been a complicated journey that in a way felt the culmination of years, not just months. We had hardly any electricity and little food, but we were happy. Wais even got hold of a TV so we could watch BBC World on the occasions when there was electricity.

The challenges ahead were brutally clear. There was destruction everywhere – parts of the city such as Jadi Maiwand, the old carpet bazaar, and the road to Dar ul Aman palace, resembled pictures of Dresden after the bombing of the Second World War. The once sparkling-blue Kabul River was a brown trickle clogged with evil-smelling garbage. I went to visit the Children's Hospital, where the doctors told me the power often went off in the middle of surgery, so children just died. My own son had been born more than eleven weeks premature two years earlier, and I asked a doctor what would happen to him if he were born in the hospital. The doctor looked at me as if I was mad. 'He would die of course,' he said. Afghanistan was the worst place in the world to be a mother or a child.

After I wrote of this in the *Sunday Telegraph*, generous readers raised money for a generator which the British military agreed to fly out. In what should have been a warning for the future, once it reached the hospital the generator disappeared.

Everyone was promising not to abandon Afghanistan again. It had been a model war, and the plan was for a model construction of democracy. There would be no more 'ungoverned space' which terrorists could move into and use as launching pads for attacks. 'You abandoned us last time and got bitten by a scorpion,' warned

Hamid Gilani, whose father Pir Gilani was one of the seven jihadi leaders who had raised arms against the Russians. 'If you abandon us this time you'll get bitten by a cobra.'

We all assumed foreign aid would pour in to turn Afghanistan around – a donors' conference was scheduled for Tokyo, and there was talk of billions being pledged. Already there were lots of aid agencies moving in. Kabul was the new sexy place to be, and every day more people arrived at the Mustafa, prompting effusive reunions. 'Hey, I last saw you in East Timor/Kosovo/Bosnia/Sierra Leone …!' became a common refrain.

There were French lawyers arriving to draw up a constitution. Feminists setting up gender-awareness classes, a women's bakery and a beauty school for which American beauty editors sent make-up. There would even be estate agents, as so many aid agencies coming in pushed rents sky high. Elections were planned for the following spring. But when I talked to my Afghan friends, nobody mentioned democracy or women's rights. They wanted security and food and speedy justice.

The West had its swift military success, dismantling the Taliban regime in two months. I don't think anybody spoke to ordinary Afghans about what they wanted.

3

Making – and Almost Killing – a President

THE WAR THAT would never end started in a way that it never should. US special forces captain Jason Amerine and his team from the 5th Special Forces Group were eating 'truly bad pizza' in Fortuna Pizzeria in the town of Aktogay in Kazakhstan on the evening of 11 September 2001 when his mobile rang. It was Dan Pedigor, the Defence Attaché from the local US Embassy, with startling news. A plane, he said, had flown into the World Trade Center.

Amerine's reaction was 'Oh wow.'[1] In primary school he'd read a book about air disasters, and had made a diorama of the B25 Mitchell bomber that hit the Empire State Building in thick fog in 1945. He imagined something like that.

They went back to their pizzas, talking animatedly. Many of the men were thinking about home. They were in Kazakhstan to train Kazakhs in small-unit tactics for counter-insurgency, and had just three days left. Amerine was feeling nostalgic. His divorce had come through in June, and at thirty he thought it was also time for a career change. He had dreamed of being in the special forces since he was a teenager in Hawaii and first met a Green Beret, and now he was an experienced captain, leading a team specialising in parachute insertions behind enemy lines. He knew that as an officer you only have so many opportunities to lead men in the field, then you're on the staff – and he could not imagine doing an office job. With not much going on in the world, he assumed this would be his last deployment.

Then the phone rang again, and turned everything upside down. A second plane had hit the Twin Towers. Amerine knew then that his country was at war: 'It was OK, it's an attack, and had to be al Qaeda who were operating out of Afghanistan.'

Shocked by the news, the men went back to their quarters, and called home to check on their families. Amerine and his sergeant talked late into the night about what might happen. He knew the US would go to war in Afghanistan, and had no doubt that they would be part of it.

What had not occurred to him was that they would be stuck. Although they were probably the special forces team nearest to Afghanistan, military bureaucracy meant they had to go back to base in the US to be assigned orders. However, war had come from the skies, and air traffic closed down around the world for almost a week. The men were left waiting in Almaty, the old Kazakh capital, and he tried to distract them with some sightseeing. One day they went to the World War II museum which was full of displays of big battles fought by the Soviet Union that emphasised all the deaths. One of their guides was a former Soviet officer who had served in Afghanistan fighting the US-backed mujaheddin. 'It is impossible to win in that country,' he warned them. 'Don't trust the Afghans, and just make sure you come back alive.'

It was 20 September when Amerine and his men finally got back to their base of Fort Campbell in Kentucky. He found it 'surreal' to see how everything had already changed. The airport was guarded by men with guns, and there was an Apache helicopter gunship patrolling the highway outside the gate.

Several other special forces teams had already been deployed to bases in Central Asia. Amerine's team practised live firing and basic soldiering skills while they anxiously waited to be assigned a mission. They presumed this would be to link up with Northern Alliance commanders in northern Afghanistan, and destroy al Qaeda safe havens. Finally, on 10 October, three days after the bombing of Afghanistan started, they were sent back to Central Asia. They had been chosen, along with another team, for the next deployment, and were flown to K2 airbase in Uzbekistan, where they waited.

Two teams were sent to northern Afghanistan, and eventually, after two weeks, Amerine was told that his team would be heading to south-eastern Afghanistan to link up with Abdul Haq and help him start an insurgency. Amerine knew little about him, other than that he was one of Afghanistan's best commanders from the war against the Soviets. However, within a few hours the news came that Abdul Haq had been captured by the Taliban and executed, so they were to 'stand down'. 'That kind of put into perspective the kind of risk the teams were taking,' said Amerine.

The next day they were told they were being sent to join Hamid Karzai. Nobody seemed to know anything about him, other than that he was a Pashtun, and was trying to raise some kind of Southern Alliance. The information they were given did not even include a photograph. Amerine envisaged 'some grumpy warlord, missing an eye, with a scar on his cheek who spoke no English'. He sent one of his men to the bazaar to buy a 'really big knife we could give to our warlord, and say, "We're here to fight with you, here's a knife."'

Amerine along with eleven of his Green Berets was flown to the Pakistani airbase Jacobabad, in the southern province of Sindh, which the Americans were secretly using. Karzai and his men were waiting there. They had already been into Afghanistan, but had found themselves woefully ill-equipped. 'We weren't prepared at all,' Karzai later told me. 'I went in just in a *shalwar* and vest, and we ended up sleeping on mountains. It was so cold, even curled up. We finally got to Tarin Kowt [capital of Uruzgan], but people told us there were still lots of Taliban and we should go back.'[2]

Some of the people he met up with betrayed them, and the Taliban came in pursuit. But Karzai got a message out on his CIA phone, and was luckier than Haq – helicopter-borne US Navy Seals flew in to rescue them and take them to Jacobabad.

* * *

When Amerine met the less than athletic Karzai, he was astonished. Instead of a warlord, he found an educated and dignified man speaking impeccable English. 'In some ways his total lack of military experience made it easier,' said Amerine. 'I knew immediately there would be no games, no swaggering or posturing – this was someone I'd be able to talk to.' He left what had become known as 'the BFK' (Big F—ing Knife) in his backpack.

Karzai was accompanied by seven or eight tribal leaders who also did not look as if they would be much use on a battlefield. 'Most were older, they seemed tired and a couple looked kind of frail,' recalled Amerine. 'We figured out he had no forces pretty quickly.' Only one man stood out. 'There was this guy Bari Gul with an angry scowl on his face the whole time, he looked a real fighter.'

Karzai seemed unfazed by the task ahead, despite what had happened to Abdul Haq and his own narrow escape. He told Amerine he didn't think they would have to fight at all. 'He believed we'd pretty well show up in Uruzgan, that the main town of Tarin Kowt would rise up and that would be it, the Taliban would surrender.' Amerine was less convinced. 'If it's peaceful that's great, but we'll plan for it to be a lot more difficult,' he told him.

While we in the media sat in our hotels in Quetta watching the bombing on TV, Amerine, Karzai and their men gathered around a large map of southern Afghanistan every day for a week, drinking endless cups of green tea, and formed a plan.

In Amerine's eyes the aim was to 'infiltrate, grow a force, lay siege to Tarin Kowt, then grow a bigger force and slowly make our way to Kandahar and compel the Taliban to surrender, which would be the end of them'.

Their maps were so poor that they didn't even know there was only one road between Tarin Kowt and Kandahar. Also, Amerine had never actually raised an army anywhere. Nor was he pleased to discover that he was supposed to take Karzai's CIA handler Casper and four other agents, which would mean he could take fewer of his special forces team than he wanted.

When Karzai asked Amerine about America's long-term plans for Afghanistan, he had to admit he had no idea.

There was another problem. Amerine's commander, Colonel John Mulholland, had given orders that they were not to go into Afghanistan unless Karzai had at least three hundred men on the ground. 'He meant three hundred bright smiling faces greeting us,' said Amerine. 'Karzai said there are more than three hundred men, but they won't gather unless I go in.' As it was, on the night they chose to infiltrate because the moon would be at its lowest, Amerine couldn't reach Mulholland on the phone. Mulholland's deputy told them to go ahead.

They needed to get going. The bombing campaign was having a quicker impact than expected, and by the time they set off on 14 November, Kabul had already fallen. It was around midnight when Karzai and his seven tribal elders, Captain Amerine and his eleven-man team, and the CIA agent Casper and four more spooks, climbed into five heavily armed Black Hawk helicopters which would drop them deeper behind enemy lines than any other Americans. The soldiers were in camouflage, and most sported beards grown over the previous month to help them blend in with the locals, though close up their thickly muscled builds would give them away. Apart from their weapons and personal GPS, each carried a so-called 'blood chit' with a message in seven local languages. 'I am an American and do not speak your language,' it read. 'I will not harm you. I bear no malice towards your people.'

The infiltration was a disaster. One of the helicopters was blown off course by all the dust and dropped four of Amerine's men in the wrong place, which meant the rest had to wait half the night for them to show up. When the weapons and equipment were airdropped, hundreds of Afghans appeared from the mountains and stole everything, including laptops and the SOFLAM for calling in airstrikes. The Americans were taken to a village on a bend in the Helmand River that was not the place for which they had meticulously planned and studied. It was also clear that Karzai had few people.

Even so, Amerine believed the plan could work, because they would build the force bit by bit. He estimated they would need six months to take Tarin Kowt. He had reckoned without the Afghans. After just three days he got a note from Karzai to say that the people of Tarin Kowt had risen up and taken the town from the Taliban. Amerine was flabbergasted. It turned out that the townspeople had heard that Kabul had fallen to the Northern Alliance, so they stormed the palace of the Taliban Governor of Uruzgan, dragged him out and hanged him. They then drove out the remaining Taliban and declared the town free. To Amerine, this was a disaster. The powerbase of the Taliban was the south, and Uruzgan was Mullah Omar's home province. Amerine was convinced the Taliban leader and his men would not give that up so easily.

Karzai commandeered some local pick-ups and a bus, and they moved into Tarin Kowt that evening and set up headquarters in a compound. Hours later, as they were about to eat dinner, a message came that an enormous Taliban convoy was on its way from Kandahar to retake Tarin Kowt. Eighty vehicles, they were told. Even allowing for Afghan exaggeration, Amerine was worried. 'Doing the math in my head, that was a lot of guys.'

He asked Karzai to round up all able-bodied men from the town. After half the night Karzai had managed to find only thirty men. They borrowed some vehicles and drove off, having to stop for petrol on the way. Just south of Tarin Kowt they found an ideal vantage spot from which to protect the town, a bluff that overlooked a wide valley through which the Taliban would have to pass. The men positioned themselves along the ridge, some of the Afghans smoking hashish, and Amerine's radio operator called in air cover. Soon three F18s were hovering high above at around 30,000 feet.

It was not long before one of Amerine's men spotted something glinting between the hills. It was the Taliban convoy, so long that it looked like an endless snake. Amerine's radio operator contacted the US pilots overhead and pronounced the vehicles 'cleared hot', meaning they could start bombing. The first bomb missed, but the second hit the lead vehicle, turning it to dust and flame. However, when Amerine turned around, his own Afghan fighters were all jumping in their trucks to flee. They had never witnessed American air power before. Without Karzai, who had stayed back in town, Amerine had no translator to explain to them that the airstrikes were theirs, and they should stay.

'I got really frustrated and mad,' said Amerine. 'We had no trucks of our own, and I'd been warned by one of the CIA guys to make sure we took the car keys from the guerrillas, but I hadn't done that.' The Americans had no choice but to jump in the fleeing trucks. 'It felt like we were stealing defeat from the jaws of victory,' he recalled. 'In that moment we lost Tarin Kowt. People would be slaughtered, and there wasn't anything I could do. I even thought about shooting one of the drivers to take a truck, but if I shot one of our guerrillas they'd never trust us.'

Amerine thought they would just have to grab Karzai from the town and leave. However, when they got back and told him what had happened, Karzai managed to get them two trucks and they drove back. There was not enough time to return to the bluff, but they got to the edge of town and started calling in airstrikes, having figured out that the Taliban were advancing along three paths from the valley in a three-pronged attack.

Word went out at US Central Command that a lone team of Green Berets was under attack from hundreds of Taliban, and F14s and F18s were scrambled from all over the country. 'Every available US aircraft with bombs was in Tarin Kowt to help us,' said Amerine. 'It was this incredible feeling that the might of the military was coming to assist. They knew that our lives were pretty much in their hands.'

One of the pilots looked down from overhead and radioed, 'Where are the friendly forces?'

'OK, so see the two trucks …' replied Amerine.

'That's it?' the pilot asked incredulously.

Despite the massive display of air power the bombs could not wipe out all the Taliban, and some made it into town. 'What really pushed it over the edge was the people of the town came out with guns,' said Amerine. 'At first we were shooing them away, but then we realised they were actually there to fight with us. We killed hundreds of Taliban that day.'

With Tarin Kowt won, over the next three weeks Amerine's team began moving south towards Kandahar, which was still firmly in Taliban hands. They set up a headquarters on the way at a place called Damana. From there, on 3 December they launched an attack to capture the town of Shawali Kowt and its hill, which overlooked a vital bridge over the Argandab River towards Kandahar. There was intense fighting, and the Taliban counterattacked. One of Amerine's men, Wes, was shot in the neck though luckily the bullet missed an artery. Eventually the Americans fought them off, and by the next day had taken the hill, giving them control of the bridge.

Yet when Amerine radioed the news to his headquarters, he was ordered to give up the hill. 'It was a complete foul-up,' he said. 'We'd had two days of fighting and no sleep at all. I was very angry.' The Afghans with them were baffled as they retreated, and with no interpreter it was impossible for Amerine to explain.

'What seems to have happened is that up till then in the war there were no American casualties in battle [just one from an accidental airstrike in the north],' he said. 'At that point fighting up front with the guerrillas wasn't the norm. So when I radioed that one of my men was shot, there was this shock – "What are your men doing, putting themselves in harm's way?" I think someone at some level thought there must be a safe area we could be operating from, but they didn't understand – sorry, we are behind enemy lines, and the guerrillas won't fight unless we are up front.'

The next day they were ordered to retake the hill, which they did, christening it the Alamo.

* * *

While Amerine and Karzai were battling it out with the Taliban in southern Afghanistan, 3,000 miles away in Bonn a group of twenty-five Afghans were huddled in a castle on a wooded hill overlooking the Rhine, trying to form a government. Chairing the meeting was Lakhdar Brahimi, the veteran diplomat and former Algerian Foreign Minister who was the United Nations' Special Envoy for Afghanistan. He had thought the Taliban would hold on till spring, but then cities started falling like dominoes – Mazar-i-Sharif, Kabul, Herat – so the Northern Alliance controlled more than half the country. This would not have been acceptable to Afghanistan's Pashtun majority, or indeed its neighbour Pakistan, so there was a sudden rush to come up with a more representative interim administration before it was too late.

The White House wanted to do this at Bagram airbase, but Brahimi insisted it needed to be neutral territory. The Germans offered their official guesthouse, the Petersberg Hotel, a site laden with history. It was there in 1949 that the three occupying powers, Britain, France and the US, had signed the agreement paving the way to the birth of the German Federal Republic.

The aim of the Bonn Conference was to form an interim administration which would run the country for three to six months until a *loya jirga*, a traditional gathering of elders, could be held to decide Afghanistan's future. There were four delegations – the main ones being the Northern Alliance (including representatives from General Dostum and Ismael Khan) and the Rome group (royalists loyal to the ex-king, Zahir Shah, to which Karzai belonged), then two smaller groups: the Cyprus group (intellectuals thought to have ties with Iran) and the Peshawar group (including the powerful Gilani family). No Taliban were invited, for this was a conference of victors – something that would be rued later. Most of the Afghans were dressed in suits, and aside from the Northern Alliance, many were émigrés, well-educated and Westernised. One of the few in a turban was Pacha Khan Zadran, a warlord. The meeting was opened on 27 November by German Foreign Minister Joschka Fischer, and tasked with producing a government within a week. That was the deadline because the hotel was then booked for a conference of dentists.

Even without the Taliban, getting an agreement was no easy task. The Northern Alliance felt that they should run the country having taken Kabul, and they resented being outnumbered in Bonn. In fact back in Kabul, their leader, Professor Rabbani, had already moved into the presidential palace. The Pashtuns, as Afghanistan's majority tribe, insisted they should run the government, and were highly suspicious of the Northern Alliance.

As usual in Afghanistan, the situation was complicated by outside interests. Also present in the hotel, though not inside the conference room, were a number of international observers from countries in the region or involved in the conflict, including the US, the UK, Iran, Russia, India, Pakistan, Saudi Arabia and Turkey. The atmosphere was not helped by the fact the meeting was being held during Ramadan, the holy month of fasting, during which Muslims cannot eat in the hours of daylight.

The Americans had sent James Dobbins, a former US Ambassador who had been appointed envoy to the Afghan resistance. A veteran of international conferences that were fuelled by fine food and plentiful wine, Dobbins wondered how this one would work with everyone sober, hungry and tired. Before reaching Bonn he had travelled to Tampa, Florida, to meet General Franks, and had heard the name Hamid Karzai for the first time. 'They said we've got him in a helicopter – he'd been overrun by Taliban and was being flown out to Pakistan. They didn't want another Abdul Haq incident.'[3]

A few days later in Islamabad Dobbins met the head of ISI, General Ehsan ul Haq, who was the first to suggest Karzai to him as future leader. 'He wasn't an American candidate,' said Dobbins. 'But then I went to Kabul, and Abdullah Abdullah also suggested him. I thought, gee, if ISI and the Northern Alliance are agreed, he must be something.' In Bonn he found the Russians, Indians and Iran all suggested Karzai. 'There was a clear consensus among international observers that he was the most broadly acceptable.'

The Americans had their man. The only problem was convincing the Afghans. Francesc Vendrell, the Deputy Special UN Envoy, describes the astonishment of the delegates when they sat around the big round table for the opening session and saw a microphone hanging down. They were even more surprised when they were told, 'Now we will hear from someone inside Afghanistan.' It was Karzai, speaking from Uruzgan. He told me later, 'I was in a mud hut of two rooms and had a cold. I don't know what I said. I never figured I'd be President.' The line from the satellite phone was not great, but in a way the crackling added to the atmospherics, as he made an impassioned plea for people to set aside their differences for the sake of the nation. 'This meeting is the path towards salvation,' he said.

Dobbins thought the most capable figures were from the Northern Alliance, such as the leader of its delegation, Yunus Qanuni, a small, elegantly dressed man with a slight limp. But the Pashtuns would never accept one of them. One Pashtun delegate, Abdul Haq's brother Haji Qadir, had already walked out, claiming Pashtuns were under-represented.

It was agreed then that the Rome group would choose the new leader. Supported by the Italians and some of the other Europeans, they really wanted the former King as head of state, but were persuaded by the Americans that he would not be acceptable. So they proposed Professor Abdul Sattar Siarat, an Islamic scholar who had been Justice Minister in the King's last government thirty years earlier. When it came to a vote, Siarat was the clear winner with eleven, compared to two for Karzai.

Siarat was not a Pashtun but an Uzbek, who made up less than 10 per cent of the population, and Dobbins worried that he would not get people to rally round him, nor be able to command respect from Northern Alliance warlords. But while he found none of the Afghan delegates very enthusiastic about Siarat, no one would speak out. Even Qanuni said he could not object to Siarat, as he was a respected figure and his cousin by marriage.

In the end Francesc Vendrell had to call the King in Rome and persuade him to convey to his delegation that 'rather than an Afghan of their choosing he was asking them for a *Pashtun* of their choosing'.[4] Siarat was so unhappy about the decision that he locked himself in his room, while another of their delegation, Hedayat Amin Arsala, walked out.

The chairman of the conference, Asadullah Wasifi, was furious, even though Karzai was his nephew and had studied with his son Izzatullah in Simla. 'We elected Siarat but the Americans told me, "No, we want to bring a Pashtun." I asked, "What kind of democracy is that, where *we* elect the man *you* want?" Then Khalilzad came to me and said, "What's the problem? He's your brother's son!" I said, "Yes, he is, that's why I know he won't be able to run the country."[5]

He refused to sign the document, pointing out that Karzai had never run anything. The only post he had ever held was as Deputy Foreign Minister in the ill-fated mujaheddin government which took power in 1992 after ousting the communists then quickly started fighting each other. Karzai only lasted eighteen months before having to flee to Pakistan, helped by Hekmatyar, putting him in the warlord's debt.

When Karzai later asked Wasifi why he hadn't accepted him, he replied, 'Afghanistan is a big problem and you're too small.'

The next challenge was persuading Rabbani to step aside. The Northern Alliance leader refused to allow his delegation to submit names of candidates for posts in the interim administration. Instead he called a press conference in Kabul, and announced that Afghanistan should hold direct elections for an interim council rather than abide by the decisions made at Bonn.

The Americans were terrified that the Northern Alliance would pull out of the discussions, and then it would be impossible to organise another meeting. Dobbins called Secretary of State Colin Powell to ask his advice. The answer was unequivocal. 'Do not let them break up!' he was told. 'Keep them there; lock them up if you have to!'

Powell asked Russia, which had a close relationship with the Northern Alliance, to persuade Rabbani not to break up the conference. According to Dr Abdullah, the Russians 'passed on a message that the world expects an agreement', and warned that the Northern Alliance 'shouldn't expect that without an agreement [Russian] support ... can continue'.[6]

The Iranians also played a key role. To his surprise, throughout the conference Dobbins found himself working closely with them, meeting the leader of their delegation, Jay Zarif, every morning for coffee and cakes to discuss developments.

Under such concerted pressure, the younger members of the Northern Alliance decided to mutiny and continue to participate in the Bonn Conference with or without the support of Rabbani. A strategic American rocket landing near Rabbani's house may have helped.

Even so, Northern Alliance participation came at a price. They demanded three quarters of the cabinet, including the most powerful portfolios of defence, interior and foreign, as well as control of the intelligence. Finally, after a late-night session with the Americans, Indians, Russians and Iranians, the Northern Alliance agreed a deal, with the Iranians once again playing a critical role. There would be twenty-nine ministries, far more than Afghanistan needed, of which sixteen would go to the Northern Alliance. Two women were included. The King would get the meaningless title of 'Father of the Nation', and convene the *loya jirga* the following year.

The other main argument was over who would provide security for Kabul. The Northern Alliance wanted an all-Afghan force. Others feared that a Northern Alliance-led force would carry out the same kind of abuses that had occurred after the jihadis took power in 1992, which led to the emergence of the Taliban. A small multinational force under the auspices of the UN was agreed.

Thorny issues like disarming warlords were left unresolved – proceedings needed to wrap up by dawn on 6 December so the dentists could move in.

At the time the rapidly approved administration was hailed as a 'diplomatic miracle'. The West had its military success, dismantling the Taliban regime in two months, and now it had a West-friendly interim government to replace it. Brahimi would later admit: 'The deal was reached hastily, by people who did not adequately represent all key constituencies in Afghanistan, and it ignored some core political issues.'[7]

* * *

When Amerine and his men got the news that Karzai had been named interim leader of Afghanistan they were astonished. Up until then Amerine had no idea how important Karzai was – which was not surprising, as most Afghans had never heard of him. He was glad he hadn't known. 'If I'd been told he's the future leader of the country, how do I put the guy in a convoy and try to make my way to Kandahar with three hundred guys?'

By then they were less than thirty miles from Kandahar. But they would never make it. The day after retaking the 'Alamo' hill a team of American reinforcements from headquarters flew in, this time equipped with their own trucks. They immediately started calling in airstrikes on a cave a couple of miles away which they thought might be a hiding place for Taliban.

They also brought welcome cargo – care packages from home, though not for the recently divorced Amerine. The men were on the ridge of the Alamo, reading their letters and enjoying Rice Krispies bars while Bari Gul and some of the Afghans watched the explosions, by then accustomed to the idea that these Americans could call down fire from the sky on their enemies. Amerine was sitting twenty yards away, discussing the battle plan for Kandahar with one of the staff officers who had flown in, when suddenly there was an almighty blinding flash. Amerine was tossed through the air. 'I knew the only thing it could be,' he said. 'We'd been hit by our own bomb.'

They had been struck by a JDAM, one of the satellite-guided 2,000-pound bombs that the Americans had used to decimate the Taliban. 'The person giving the coordinates to the cave accidentally gave our own coordinates,' said Amerine.

There were bodies everywhere, and people groaning – it was clear that they had been hit badly. His own thigh was ripped open by shrapnel, and both his eardrums were perforated. Three of his men were dead, as were many of the Afghans. 'Bari Gul and most of his men were killed in the explosion. My team was finished, everybody had to be medivaced.'

By sheer luck, Karzai was further along the ridge, and was only slightly wounded in the shoulder. 'Hamid couldn't believe what had happened,' said Amerine, who years later would still find it hard to talk about that day. 'We could easily have killed him too. I just didn't have it in me to tell him that our own headquarters had done it.'

Amerine later found out that just that morning, the Taliban had sent a delegation to Karzai to surrender Kandahar. 'The bomb that hit us was probably the last bomb that was dropped in that theatre ... at least in that stage of the campaign.'

It was an ominous start.

Still in shock, Karzai was flown into Kabul on 13 December. One of the first people to see him was James Dobbins, anxious to meet the man he had helped get chosen in Bonn. He was relieved, finding Karzai 'an attractive personality, warm, reasonably open. Many of the qualities we chose him for are what we would later criticise him for. A more forceful person wouldn't have been acceptable.'

Though Dobbins was happy to have formed an administration so quickly, he worried that there had been no provision for peace-keeping forces, which he was convinced would be necessary if the fledgling government were to work. He told Rumsfeld they needed 25,000 troops, but was firmly rebuffed. 'He refused even to discuss it.'

His concerns were shared by the British government, which organised a conference in London bringing together fifteen potential troop-contributing countries. But the Pentagon laid down strict conditions. First, what the Bonn agreement had termed an 'international security force' would be renamed the International Security *Assistance* Force (ISAF), to eliminate any idea that internationals would provide security, which it saw as an Afghan responsibility, even though there was no Afghan army to do this. US troops would not participate, as they 'did not consider peace-keeping a fit role for American troops'. Bush told a meeting of his National Security Council, 'We don't do police work.'[8] The US would also limit the numbers. 'We were very wary of repeating the experience of the Soviets and the Brits who ended up looking like occupiers,' Bush wrote in his memoir.[9]

GETTING IN

On 20 December the UN Security Council approved the deployment of a peacekeeping force numbering between 3,000 and 5,000 troops. It would be led by Britain, which would supply 1,500 troops, commanded by General John McColl.

Afghanistan, emerging from more than two decades of war with armed men everywhere and little effective government, would have just one peacekeeper for every 5,000 people. The last conflict in which the West had been involved was Kosovo, where it had left one peacekeeper for every forty-eight people.

It wasn't only the numbers that was a problem. The US had insisted that the peacekeepers be restricted to Kabul, giving the US forces of Operation Enduring Freedom free rein to comb the rest of the country for Osama bin Laden and al Qaeda. It was the birth of two parallel forces.

Nobody in Kabul seemed to have heard of their new president-to-be. 'Who is he?' people would ask. 'Do you have a picture?'

Few people were aware that Karzai was already in the city and had moved into the Arg, the presidential palace. Shortly after I arrived in the city I got a message from his assistant Malik, inviting me over.

It was not easy to get in. The guards on the gate were those of Burhanuddin Rabbani, the head of the Northern Alliance, who had moved into the palace as soon as Kabul had fallen, and thought he should be President, so was refusing to leave. They said they had never heard of any Hamid Karzai. Eventually Karzai's uncle Asis came out to find me and took me inside.

The driveway to the palace was lined with stone lions which had all been decapitated. 'Taliban,' explained Asis. He had been Deputy Chief of Protocol for King Zahir Shah, and knew the palace inside out. He showed us into what he called 'the Peacock Room', in which the Taliban had laboriously daubed white paint over the heads of the peacocks on the wallpaper. There was a dark patch on one wall, where Asis recalled a beautiful Gobelin tapestry of an English garden scene used to hang – a gift from Queen Victoria to King Abdur Rahman when his son visited London. 'Afghans were very confused, and asked why did the stupid king put a horrid carpet on the wall, Afghans have much more beautiful carpets on their floors,' he laughed.

Asis reminisced wistfully about Kabul in the old days. 'We had lots of clubs,' he said. 'Club 25, Club Moon, a bowling alley, dancing at night, and the wonderful Khyber restaurant by the fountain where there was better food than in Italy or France. It's like we've gone back five hundred years.'

Karzai was sitting in an armchair in another room which had a Philips freezer standing incongruously in the middle. The room was as cold as the inside of the freezer – there was just an ineffectual one-bar heater – and he looked dwarfed by the large chair. I was surprised to see him wearing a long, shiny *chapan* coat in striped green-and-blue silk, and an astrakhan hat. As long I had known him he had always been in jeans and leather jacket, or occasionally beige *shalwar kamiz*. 'I didn't have clothes so someone lent me these,' he explained. 'Everything is still in Pakistan.'

I was still cross that he hadn't taken me on his return to Afghanistan. 'The conditions were very cold and hard,' he said. 'We had to sleep in a shepherd's hut. It wasn't like when you and I went in the old days and people fed us in villages.' He looked thin. Even so he claimed that everything had gone well in Uruzgan, people all coming out to support him. He did not tell me that he had been accompanied by special forces, only that the Americans had flown him on a transport plane from there into Bagram, a military camp just north of Kabul. He had been met by Marshal Fahim, the new Defence Minister, who was astonished to see him alone. Like all warlords Fahim never went anywhere without pick-ups crammed with heavily armed men. 'Where are your militia?' he asked Karzai. 'I have no men,' Karzai replied. 'You are now my men.'

That was all very well, but they weren't his men. They were Tajiks and he was Pashtun. And how could he trust Fahim? It was Fahim who had ordered his arrest seven years earlier when Karzai was Deputy Foreign Minister, and had him interrogated for hours.

I could see his shoulder was bothering him. He told me he'd fallen over in Uruzgan, but wouldn't go into any detail. Something didn't add up. Only later did I hear the whole story.

22 December, the day of Karzai's inauguration, dawned grey. The ceremony took place at the Interior Ministry building just along the road from the Mustafa. Security was tight, roadblocks manned by soldiers and police patrolling in old Russian peaked caps decorated with red and gold braid. They were clutching an assortment of arms, including handheld rocket launchers. Alarmingly I saw one policeman drop his just outside our hotel. Fortunately it didn't go off.

A motley band in uniforms with braided gold epaulettes played a sort of monotone oompah on the only remaining brass instruments in Afghanistan as dignitaries walked along the specially flown-in red carpet. It was all quite grim, not at all like the installation of the last Western-backed ruler, Shah Shuja, in 1839, when one British soldier and artist present wrote that 'the wild grandeur of the whole pageantry baffles description'.[10]

The foreigners seemed satisfied. General Franks was there, the man who had made this all possible. Next to him was British General McColl, as well as the Foreign Ministers of Belgium, Iran, India and Pakistan, and many diplomats.

More interesting for me was watching the assortment of sworn enemies take their seats next to each other as part of the new administration after years of trying to kill each other. General Dostum was there, glowering and bearish as if he'd like to go and kill a few people. He was to be Deputy Defence Minister. Ismael Khan made an entrance by arriving late, thus outdoing Dostum, whose deputy had betrayed Ismael to the Taliban.

A Pashtun might be heading the new administration but it was clear who was dominating it. In prominent places were the Panjshiri trio – Marshal Fahim, the new Defence Minister, who still had his own army on the Shomali plains just outside Kabul; Yunus Qanuni, who was to be Interior Minister; and Abdullah Abdullah, the Foreign Minister.

Overlooking proceedings was a huge portrait of the late

Northern Alliance commander Ahmat Shah Massoud in his trade-mark pakoul. Massoud was rapidly becoming the Che Guevara of Afghanistan. His photograph was everywhere, hindering visibility on the windscreens of the ubiquitous Toyota jeeps, decorating traffic islands and shops. One of the seats in the front row was left empty in deference to him, with his picture on the back and a bunch of plastic flowers on it.

Just as when the British were impressed by Shah Shuja's appearance, Karzai was winning plaudits for his lambswool hat and green-and-blue-striped *chapan*. The fashion designer Tom Ford even called him 'the chicest man on the planet'.

What they thought was his dress sense wasn't the only reason for satisfaction among Western diplomats. They believed they had found the perfect President – a charming man who spoke immaculate English, loved English poetry and was from the majority Pashtun tribe yet was also a nationalist. And in some ways the fact that no one knew him seemed a good thing, as he was not compromised by his role in the jihad, unlike the warlords who most Afghans blamed for getting the country into such a mess.

After being sworn into office he spoke in his native Pashtu, then read a poem in Dari, one of the seven languages he speaks. He embraced Rabbani and called on Afghans to 'forget the painful past'. He was just two days away from his forty-fourth birthday, and made reference to his lack of experience. 'Oh God I am a novice so please help me.'

There was already one black cloud. A group of elaborately turbaned elders from Gardez who had come for the ceremony told us that a convoy from Khost they were supposed to be coming with had been bombed by the Americans, and as many as sixty-five elders killed.

When we journalists clustered round General Franks after the ceremony, he defended the bombing. 'Friendly forces don't fire surface-to-air missiles at you,' he said. 'We believe it was a bad convoy. We have reason to believe it was a good target.'

No surface-to-air missile had been fired. It would be the first of many such mistakes.

* * *

We should have realised then that instead of the end this was just the start. While Karzai was being sworn in as new leader of Afghanistan, a British man called Richard Reid was boarding American Airlines Flight 63 from Paris to Miami. The heels of his shoes had been hollowed out and packed with explosives.

It was the Saturday before Christmas, and the plane was packed with 185 passengers. Over the Atlantic, two hours out of Paris, some of them complained of smelling smoke. Hermis Moutardier, one of the French air hostesses, spotted Reid trying to light a match, and warned him that smoking was forbidden on the plane. He promised to stop, but a few minutes later she smelled more smoke.

To her horror she found Reid hunched in his window seat holding a lit match to one of his shoes. As she went to grab him, he pushed her away so hard she fell. 'Get him!' Moutardier screamed. Her colleague Cristina Jones rushed to the scene and threw herself at Reid, who was six feet four and snarling like an animal. He bit her hand and she screamed. Reid was not easy to control, but a small army of flight attendants and male passengers managed to hold him down, doused him with bottled water and tied him up with seatbelts, plastic handcuffs and headphone cables. A doctor on board sedated him. His shoes were then carried into the cockpit for inspection by the pilots, and only then were the fuses spotted.

The ordeal wasn't over. The crew had no idea if he had any accomplices onboard, so the remaining passengers were kept in their seats for the final nerve-racking two hours and fifty minutes until they could land at the nearest airport, which was Boston. Afterwards they found numerous spent matches. No one knew why they hadn't caught light. If they had, the shoes had more than enough explosives to blow up the plane.

Less than a week later, on 28 December, General Franks went to visit President Bush on his ranch in Crawford, Texas. Bush told reporters afterwards that they had discussed Afghanistan. In fact it was the first detailed briefing to discuss plans for a war in Iraq.

4

Ground Zero

Manhattan, New Year's Eve 2001

IT WAS THE charred smell that would most stick in my mind, a mix of jet fuel, burned carpet and ground cement. That and the fliers. Smiling faces of the missing stared out from A4 sheets on every wall and noticeboard, made all the more poignant by the fact that most of the photographs seemed to be of happy occasions – tossing a mortarboard at graduation; sitting in a boyfriend's lap; sipping colourful cocktails through a straw with friends; or laughing wind-swept on a beach with dogs or children or both. People with every-thing to live for. Underneath were brief descriptions, some printed and some handwritten, and from those few lines one could imagine a life.

'We are searching for information for our daughter who worked on 93rd floor,' read the first one I saw. 'Black hair, grey/blue eyes, kind smile, wearing white scoop neck.' The photograph showed a gentle young woman with olive skin and dark hair who looked like someone easy to confide in. Overlapping it slightly was a beaming black man: 'Patrick Adams. Age 62, Security Officer, Worked on 80th Floor, Tower 2. Wife (for 47 years): Allison Adams. Left a message on the answering machine at home informing his wife that he was trapped. 32 grandchildren and 2 great-grandchildren.' Next to that was 'Missing NYC Firefighter, former US Army Reservist', with a picture of a powerfully built white man. Several were headed 'Desaparecido'. And, faded by the wind and rain, I could just decipher a child's drawing in coloured pencils of a house with stick figures of a couple, two children and a dog. On top was the plea, 'Daddy Come Home'.

More than three months after the 9/11 attacks, these posters were still pinned all over New York. At subway stations, bus stops, walls and phone booths where once there might have been adverts for dog walkers or masseurs, instead there were 'Missing' faces. Thousands of them, interspersed with miniature Stars and Stripes flags, small wilted posies, crucifixes on strings, ribbons, teddy bears, poems and finger paintings. I realised that all that time I had been in Afghanistan and Pakistan since 9/11, unable to read Western newspapers, I had thought about the attack as an event so massive as to be impersonal, not about the individual victims. Now I read every such poster I could find.

I had gone to New York on a crazy whim. On Christmas morning I had arrived home in London from Afghanistan after three months away from my family, and I would be heading back there within weeks. I had been away so much that when I held my two-year-old son he said 'Bye-bye.'

However, in Afghanistan almost everyone I had met kept asking, 'What is this building that the planes flew into?' In a country where the tallest office building was a five-storey block in Kabul and there were no escalators, they could not conceive of towers 110 floors high. I had promised to bring back pictures of the World Trade Center.

I could have just downloaded them from the internet, or cut a picture from a magazine back in Britain, or got a friend to send some. A last-minute flight just for the New Year holiday cost a fortune. But I desperately wanted to see for myself the place at which all our lives had changed.

So, within a few days of arriving home, I left my son with my parents and dragged my bemused husband Paulo through the newly tightened security at Heathrow (laptop out; belt off, and now shoes, though not yet water bottles and cosmetics) and onto the Virgin Atlantic flight.

Ground Zero

As to so many people, New York was a special city to us – we had got engaged there five years earlier, and had always adored visiting it. But this was a very different trip.

Next morning, fortified by the espresso I had so missed in Afghanistan, we went to Grand Central Station to catch the subway downtown. A makeshift board of the missing had been set up which showed people of almost every colour, nationality and religion. Looking at names like Cohen, Greenstein and Rosenblum, I grimly remembered General Hamid Gul and countless other Pakistanis insisting to me that Mossad was behind the attack, and that no Jews had gone to work that day. Most of all I noticed that so many seemed to be thirty-something mothers and fathers, just like me and Paulo. Later I read that the age of the greatest number who died was between thirty-five and thirty-nine.

Eighteen thousand people had gone to work in the towers that day. Almost 3,000 never came home, most dead by the time they would normally be fetching a morning coffee. One hundred and forty-seven died on the planes that crashed. Three hundred and forty-three firefighters and emergency workers and sixty police who had gone to rescue the victims became victims themselves.

Friends and relatives had started putting up the missing posters the day after 9/11 in the hope that their loved ones had wandered off dazed with amnesia, or were lying unidentified in a hospital bed. In fact very few were pulled out alive after the towers had collapsed, and what had started off as pleas of hope were now poignant memorials to loss.

Almost a mile away from Ground Zero, my nostrils already twitched with the smouldering smell of burned paper and metal still in the air all these weeks after the attack. The subway stations near the Twin Towers remained closed, so we got out at Battery Park, near the bottom tip of Manhattan. A cutting wind was sweeping in from the Atlantic. There was no need to ask the way – lines of people bundled up against the cold were shuffling in the same direction. A few canvas booths had been set up along the route as prayer stations for those wishing to commune with their God.

GETTING IN

Thousands of posters fluttered from the park railings, as well as personal mementoes and 'I Love NY' postcards. One section of fence was entirely pinned with soft toys. Every so often we would pass a small shrine with candles.

There was another wall of remembrance outside St Paul's chapel, just across from where the towers had stood. A blonde woman, her face streaked with tears, was tightly clutching the hands of three angelic little blonde girls in smart brass-buttoned coats. 'Uncle Luke, we miss you', they wrote on the wall.

As we stopped to look, many people seemed to be discussing where they were when they heard the news. In that way 9/11 had already become the J.F. Kennedy assassination of my generation.

Where the towers had stood was still a crime scene, and there was yellow tape all over the place, stamped 'Police Line Do Not Cross'. We joined the queue pressed behind police barricades to shuffle slowly up the ramp to a viewing platform which had just opened. A large American flag flew overhead. There was utter silence as we reached the top and looked down.

Below was a vast chasm in the earth, far, far bigger than I had envisaged. Where once there had been two gleaming concrete-and-glass towers with 110 floors full of people just starting their working day, there was a seventy-foot-deep pit stretching for ten acres, filled with rubble, mangled steel girders and twisted bits of building. Dust was rising from diggers moving back and forth. It looked like a demolition site, or as if some monstrous force had torn the earth asunder.

Giant cranes swung their hooks across, reaching in to dig out debris and then pour it into trucks to be taken to a landfill on Staten Island. The creaking back and forth was the only sound. 1.5 million tons would be removed, and ten years later experts would still be sifting through it.

Down in the pit, workers with masks over their noses and mouths were still searching, working day and night under giant portable lights, looking for anything recognisable, and occasionally disappearing into the large white tents that dotted the site. We read in the paper the next morning that they had found ten bodies that day. However, such was the force of impact that at least a thousand bodies were pulverised beyond recognition. More than half the grieving families never even got a body part.

The North Tower, which was struck by the first plane, had stood ablaze for 102 minutes, while the South stood for fifty-six minutes. Eventually the burning beams and girders could resist no more and buckled. Each tower took just twelve seconds to fall. Later in the day a smaller third tower would collapse.

I had seen horrific photographs of people who had become known as 'the jumpers', matchstick figures throwing themselves out of the windows. More than two hundred people had died in this way, one landing on a fireman and killing him. I had read harrowing accounts of workers trying to get down stairways of flame and soot helped by heroic firemen, many of whom lost their lives.

Yet, perhaps because I was so caught up with reporting what was happening in Pakistan and Afghanistan, until I stood on that platform the full horror of what had happened did not really strike me. Years later, when the war seemed futile and it was hard to remember what it was all about, I would recall that grim, bitter morning.

It was unbelievable to think that nineteen young Arabs armed only with box-cutters had done this. They had turned four passenger planes into weapons, two hitting the towers, one smashing into the Pentagon, and the final one crashing in a field in Pennsylvania. It was thought to have been aiming for Washington DC, perhaps for the White House or Congress, but to have been brought down in a struggle between the hijackers and courageous passengers who had perhaps saved many more lives.

Standing there, looking down from the platform, my head filled with the screams on the footage and the thudding of the cameraman's feet running as the towers started crashing down. As they fell they had sent a tornado storm of ash barrelling along the streets and steel beams flying through the air to lodge into nearby office buildings. Such was the tremendous force of each tower's collapse deep into the ground that water mains, gas lines and the subway were smashed, while debris crushed cars and ambulances. Whole streets were buried under rubble.

Inside the towers, virtually every desk, chair, computer and filing cabinet was burned or smashed to bits. Somewhere among all the wreckage were the remains of a priceless collection of Rodin sculpture from Cantor Fitzgerald, the brokerage firm that lost 658 people in the attack, as well as the famous wine cellars of the Windows on the World restaurant.

It was the small personal details that most struck home. A friend who lived in a fifth-floor apartment only a few blocks away told me that for days afterwards she found charred pieces of yellow Post-it notes fluttering onto her terrace.

The workers we could see searching the rubble found very few personal effects. The most common objects to have survived were keys, some marked 'World Trade Center – Do Not Duplicate'. They did find the wallet of Robert Gscharr, a supervisor at an insurance company on the ninety-second floor of the South Tower who had last been seen between the fortieth and fiftieth floors trying to help others escape before the tower collapsed. Inside the wallet was his yellow and blue Metro pass, a few family photos and a rare $2 note with a special story. When he proposed to his wife Myrta in 1998 he had two. He gave her one, and kept the other.

On the platform people stood transfixed, although the police kept trying to move them on. Suddenly I felt like a voyeur. Other people on the platform were taking snapshots of themselves in front of the devastation, as if it were a tourist attraction. I had promised to take a photograph of the site for the Afghans, but I knew it would never convey the full scale of the devastation, or the emotional impact. Frankly, the pictures of rubble looked like much of Kabul.

'Let's go,' said Paulo, who was looking uncomfortable. Neither of us had uttered a word since we had reached the platform. Tears streamed down my face as we walked away. 'I just can't believe this was done from a cave in Afghanistan,' I said.

I had spotted a sign saying 'Kill all Muslims' among the missing posters, though there were also many white doves of peace. Back in September President Bush had described the war on terrorism as 'a crusade', though he later apologised.

I didn't want Americans to hate Afghans. As I would remind anyone who would listen, there were no Afghans involved in the attacks. Of the nineteen hijackers, fifteen were from Saudi Arabia, two from the United Arab Emirates, one from Egypt and one from Lebanon. Osama bin Laden, a Saudi whose family were originally from Yemen, had approved the plan, and applauded the attack in his videos, describing it as 'reaction to the huge criminality practised by Israel and the United States in Palestine and other Muslim countries'. Bin Laden himself said, 'There is no evidence of the involvement of the people of Afghanistan in what happened in America.' He never actually claimed credit for the attacks, and we'd later find out that though the hijackers had sworn allegiance to al Qaeda, the man behind the plot was not an al Qaeda leader at all, but a nightclubbing Pakistani who grew up in Kuwait and whose name was Khalid Sheikh Mohammad, known as 'KSM'. He was the uncle of Ramzi Yusuf, who had tried to blow up the World Trade Center in 1993, packing a Ryder rental van with 680 kilos of explosives. Yusuf's plan had been to blow up the North Tower and send it crashing into the South Tower, bringing both towers down and killing thousands of people. The plan failed, but the explosion did kill six people and injured more than a thousand.

A few days after 9/11 a gruesome motivational message was found in the luggage of one of the dead hijackers. 'Completely forget something called "this world",' it exhorted. 'Purify your soul from all unclean things. Tame your soul. Convince it. Make it understand ... remember this is a battle for the sake of God. The enemies are the allies of Satan; the brothers of the Devil. Do not fear them for the believer fears only God ... Make your final words there is no God but God.'

What sort of people could do this? Where had such hatred come from?

* * *

GETTING IN

We didn't speak much for the rest of the day. But we decided we would go to Times Square that evening to see in the New Year despite the security alert. New Yorkers had gathered to watch the giant crystal ball drop from One Times Square on the stroke of midnight every New Year since 1907, through wars and the Depression, and I was sure that they would not allow terrorists to stop them.

The roads all round the square were closed off by police barricades and patrol cars with flashing lights. There were 7,000 police around the square, more than twice the usual number. The crowds were down, but even so around half a million people came out, many clad defiantly in red, white and blue. It would be wrong to call them revellers – there was none of the usual New Year's Eve craziness. People had come out onto the streets in solidarity, and to show they would not be bowed by terror. As the ball fell complete strangers hugged and kissed each other. One of the police officers asked me where we were from, and when I said England he shook my hand. 'Thank you for being with us, ma'am,' he said.

I thought about all the faces on the missing posters. Mostly I thought about my baby son. The world he was growing up into was a very different place from the extended peace I thought he had been born into just two years earlier. I knew my own home city London was almost certainly next on the terrorists' list – officials in Pakistan had warned me their information was that the UK was full of sleeper cells. I wanted to go home.

'Afghanistan didn't do this,' I wrote in my diary. 'I don't know who or how, but I am sure this came from Pakistan.'

World Trade Center in Numbers
At 8.46 a.m. American Airlines Flight 11 hit Tower 1 (North Tower).
At 9.03 a.m United Flight 175 hit Tower 2 (South Tower).
The South Tower fell at 9.59 a.m. The North at 10.28 a.m.
Time they took to fall: twelve seconds.
Total number killed (official figure as of 9 May 2002): **2,819**
Number of firefighters and paramedics killed: **343**

Ground Zero

Number of NYPD officers killed: **23**
Number of Port Authority police officers killed: **37**
Number of WTC companies that lost people: **60**
Number of employees who died in Tower 1: **1,402**
Number of employees who died in Tower 2: **614**
Number of employees lost at Cantor Fitzgerald: **658**
Number of nations whose citizens were killed in the attacks: **115**
Number of Jews killed: estimated between **400 and 500**
Ratio of men to women who died: **3:1**
Bodies found 'intact': **289**

5

Losing bin Laden –
the Not So Great Escape

A FEW WEEKS later, Hamid Karzai also visited the ruins of the Twin Towers, and laid a wreath of yellow roses. He had been invited to America to be President Bush's special guest at the annual State of the Union speech to Congress in Washington DC. Also invited were the two American Airlines hostesses who had managed to pin down Richard Reid, the shoe bomber. It was Karzai, however, in the long striped coat that he now wore everywhere, who was the star of the occasion, nodding and smiling as he received a standing ovation from the assembled Congressmen and Senators. The man who just six months earlier couldn't get a meeting in this city was suddenly the toast of the entire Western world. The press was effusive. Nicholas Kristof in the *New York Times* called him the 'caped hero', while in an editorial in the *Washington Post*, Mary McGrory described Karzai as the 'role-model US-installed leader of Afghanistan. He is, in fact, a dream.' He'd even been nominated for the Nobel Peace Prize.

Bush was also enjoying an astonishing approval rating of 80 per cent following the quick demise of the Taliban, and his speech that night was triumphant. 'In four short months, our nation has comforted the victims, begun to rebuild New York and the Pentagon, rallied a great coalition, captured, arrested, and rid the world of thousands of terrorists, destroyed Afghanistan's terrorist training camps, saved a people from starvation, and freed a country from brutal oppression.' This boast was greeted by wild clapping

– his forty-eight-minute speech was interrupted by applause seventy-six times. However, there was one thing missing. What the US hadn't done was track down Osama bin Laden, the man because of whom they had invaded Afghanistan.

Instead they had managed to lose him completely. While I had been back home in London for Christmas, bin Laden had released another video that was clearly designed to taunt the US. Dressed in a combat jacket, with a Kalashnikov propped up next to him, he described his thirty-three-minute-long message as a review of events following 9/11, which he referred to as 'the blessed strikes against world atheism and its leader, America'.[1]

Later we'd find out that US forces had come within two miles of catching him less than two weeks earlier in the mountains between Afghanistan and Pakistan, but he had escaped over the border. It would be some years before I properly pieced together the story of what some called the greatest military blunder in recent US history.

On paper, finding bin Laden didn't look hard. The FBI Most Wanted page described the al Qaeda leader as between six foot four and six foot six tall, about 160 pounds, olive complexion, left-handed and walking with a cane. His bony, bearded face and lanky frame were distinctive and easily recognisable from his videos. He was also rumoured to be suffering from kidney disease and requiring dialysis, though his son Omar would later dismiss this, explaining that it was kidney stones.[2] And there was a $25 million reward on his head.

'I don't want bin Laden and his thugs captured. I want them dead,' Cofer Black, head of the CIA's Counter Terrorism Center, had told his agent Gary Schroen as he set off with the first team for Afghanistan on 19 September.[3] In case there were any doubt about its intent, their operation had been codenamed 'Jawbreaker'.

Shortly after the fall of Kabul on 13 November 2001, reports started coming in that bin Laden and as many as a thousand of his followers were in hiding a few hours south of the capital, in the mountainous area of Tora Bora not far from Jalalabad.

GETTING IN

I'd been to Tora Bora in the 1980s during the jihad against the Russians, and it was really just a series of caves made by rainwater dissolving the limestone in the Spin Ghar, the White Mountains that run between Pakistan and Afghanistan. Bin Laden and his Arab followers had realised that the forbidding terrain of narrow stony valleys and jagged peaks reaching 14,000 feet turned it into a natural fortress, and had used dynamite to extend the caves.

The mujaheddin I was travelling with at the time told me to hide my face as we came to a place called Jaji and passed the entrance to a cave cloaked with camouflage netting and guarded by fierce-looking men with dark skin, some of them apparently African. 'Arabs,' they whispered. 'They are crazy dangerous.'

The Afghans did not like the Arabs, who they felt looked down on them. 'They called us *ajam* – people with no tongue – because we pray in a language we can't understand [Arabic],' Karzai's elder brother Mehmud told me.

I'd never heard of bin Laden then. But later, in Peshawar, I would hear stories of the young Saudi millionaire who was bringing in bulldozers and dynamite from his father's construction company and even an engineer to blast a network of tunnels in the caves so his fighters could move unseen in the mountains. His propaganda headquarters and guesthouse in Peshawar for Arab volunteers, the 'Services Bureau', was actually just along the road from the American Club where we foreign journalists used to gather at night for Budweisers and Sloppy Joes.

The Bureau had been set up in 1984 by a man called Sheikh Abdullah Azzam, a charismatic Palestinian cleric whose book *Defense of the Muslim Lands* compared Afghanistan to a drowning child that everyone on the beach had the duty to try to save. He argued that if even just one metre of Islamic land had been occupied by *kuffar* or infidels, then all able-bodied Muslims should strive to liberate it. The foreword was written by Saudi Arabia's chief cleric, which seemed to give the book official sanction.

Azzam had studied at al-Azhar University in Cairo, which was the centre of Islamic scholarship in the Middle East, and he cut a distinctive figure with his black beard streaked with lightning forks of white, and round his neck the *keffiyeh*, the black-and-white-checked scarf favoured by Palestinian resistance fighters. In 1981 he took a job teaching Islam in the International Islamic University in Islamabad, and began spending every weekend in Peshawar where he met many Afghans fleeing the Russians or injured in bombings, and became passionate about their cause.

Among those inspired by Azzam's writings was a twenty-four-year-old Algerian imam who went by the name of Abdullah Anas. Brought up on stories of the long war for Algeria's independence from France in which his father and grandfather had fought, he'd joined the Muslim Brotherhood, the Islamist socio-political movement founded in Egypt, and thought his turn had come to take up his gun for a cause.

He flew to Mecca in 1984 to meet Azzam, who invited him to visit him in Islamabad. On his first night there, at dinner at Azzam's house, Anas was so mesmerised by his host that he barely noticed another guest, recalling only that he was 'very shy' and had a 'soft voice and handshake'.[*] It was Osama bin Laden.

Azzam talked that night, as he often did, of his frustration at the demise of the Muslim world, expounding on how back when Europe was in its Dark Ages, the rule of the Caliphates stretched from China to Spain, and it was a time of great innovation. Islamic scientists and mathematicians produced the first studies on optics and blood circulation, devised algebra, and invented astrolabes, Al Jaziri's elephant clock and even an early flying machine (which crashed). But seven centuries of expansion came to an abrupt end in 1492 when Granada fell with the capture of the Alhambra by Christians, an event celebrated in London's St Paul's Cathedral with the singing of the *Te Deum*, a hymn of thanks.

In the same way that Americans regarded Afghanistan as a Cold War battleground on which to fight the forces of communism, Azzam saw in Afghanistan, with its simple brave men fighting a mighty mechanised army, a way of motivating a billion Muslims across the world and the first step to recapturing past glory and all former Muslim lands.

GETTING IN

Galvanised by Azzam's words, Anas travelled to Peshawar and joined some mujaheddin, with whom he walked for forty days across war-torn Afghanistan. It was so hard that he lost most of his toenails, but he said afterwards: 'I felt I was reborn when I first got there ... Even though I was sick for ten days, I was so happy to be walking along with my Kalashnikov and with my brothers.'

He decided to stay in Peshawar. He married Azzam's daughter and helped him establish the Makhtab-al-Khidamat (MK), or the Services Bureau. Bin Laden had also decided to stay, and provided much of their funding as his father owned the biggest construction company in Saudi Arabia, estimated to be worth $5 billion, and gave him a yearly stipend of at least $7 million.

Right from the start the three men realised the importance of propaganda, and from those headquarters they produced a magazine called *al-Jihad*. Initially a few black-and-white pages crudely stapled together, it grew into a full-colour glossy with a circulation of 70,000 throughout Muslim communities across the world. Many were distributed in the United States, where the MK established a string of offices with a headquarters in Brooklyn.

In Washington at that time a Texan Congressman, Charlie Wilson, was pounding the corridors of the Capitol extolling the bravery of Afghan 'illiterate shepherds and tribesmen fighting with stones' in order to persuade his colleagues to commit more funds. 'I had everyone in Congress convinced that the mujahideen were a cause only slightly below Christianity,' he said.[5]

In the same way, in Muslim communities around the world, including in America, Azzam used his magazine and speeches to create the image of an almost mythical holy warrior. Those who heard him speak say he spellbound audiences with tales of flocks of birds that flew over Afghan villages to warn of approaching Soviet helicopters; of mujaheddin almost single-handedly defeating columns of Soviet tanks; and miracles such as fighters being hit by bullets yet magically not being wounded.

Such stories, combined with the idea of recapturing a glorious past, created a powerful message to frustrated young Arabs. To further motivate them they were told that if they died in jihad they would not only be rewarded with seventy-two virgins in the after-life, but would also enable seventy family members to go to heaven. Azzam went on recruiting tours, exhorting young Arabs to 'join the caravan'. Agents rounded up people, picking up recruiting bonuses for doing so. The bin Laden construction company acted as a pipeline, with Osama setting up a halfway house in Jeddah and providing a stipend to the families of fighters of $300 a month. Some were just tourists going off to jihad for a week, helped by generous discounts offered by Saudi Airlines. Others became committed jihadists.

Reception committees were set up at Pakistan's main airports. One of the greeters was Dr Umar Farooq, who at the time was a medical student at King Edward College, Lahore, and whose family was regarded as a kind of Islamist aristocracy in Pakistan. His father had set up the country's first madrassa, and his elder brother had built the first hospital for Afghan refugees in Quetta and married the daughter of the leader of Jamaat-e-Islami, Pakistan's largest religious party.

'Azzam was very impressive,' he said. 'Whoever met him became a mujahid. I would receive the Arabs at the airport. To start with they were good people, Egyptians, Yemenis, Saudis, Kuwaitis, Sudanese, Moroccans … I gave them maps with arrows pointing to show Soviet forces heading toward the Warm Water and we would send them to Peshawar and Quetta to our reception centres from where they would be sent to all the [mujaheddin] parties.'[6]

Not all came to fight. The Services Bureau provided schooling, clinics and refugee care as well as running an active propaganda division. But most came for jihad, and Azzam thought these Arab fighters should be scattered throughout Afghan groups to motivate them and teach them about Islam. The majority were sent to join Abdul Rasul Sayyaf, one of the seven Afghan mujaheddin leaders, who like Azzam was a graduate of al-Azhar and a Wahhabi. Sayyaf was very close to the Saudis, in particular the intelligence chief Prince Turki al Faisal. Not only did the Saudis provide the mujaheddin with $500 million every year, that went to a Swiss bank account controlled by the US and distributed to ISI, but Prince Turki's chief of staff Adeeb (who had once been bin Laden's biology teacher) visited Peshawar twice a month with cash for the leaders.

After a while Dr Farooq noticed a change. 'Initially the Arabs went to different groups but then they started to be diverted all one way to promote the Saudi kind of Islam, Wahhabism, and all went to near Jalalabad. Different sorts of people started coming, criminal people who grew these long beards.'

Many were fugitives, some of whom had been involved in radical Islamic movements at home. Countries such as Egypt and Saudi Arabia were only too happy to get rid of such people. In Peshawar they would adopt a new identity – often being known by where they came from, such as 'al Libbi' – the Libyan.

Milt Bearden, who was CIA station chief in Pakistan at the time, later admitted that many were criminals. 'Egypt and many other Islamic nations found Afghanistan a convenient dumping ground for home-grown troublemakers. Egypt quietly emptied its prisons of its political activists and psychotics and sent them off to the war in Afghanistan with fondest hopes that they might never return.'

Both ISI and the Americans thought it was a good idea to broaden the cause, and turned a blind eye to the backgrounds of these additional fighters. 'All we cared about then was defeating the Soviets,' admitted Richard Armitage, then the Under-Secretary of Defense. 'We weren't thinking about Osama bin Laden. Who cared what happened in Afghanistan? We had a much greater objective. Our Afghan policy was amoral in my view,' he added. 'Not immoral but amoral. We had one objective, and we didn't care what happened after that.'[7]

General Hamid Gul, who headed ISI from 1987 to 1989, esti-mated that around 3–4,000 Arabs came to join the fight. 'The Pakistan government never objected to them coming,' he said. 'Princes used to come and go inside [Afghanistan] from all over the Middle East for jihad, and this was just an extension.'

Though General Gul would send his officers to talk to bin Laden, he says he never met him when he was living in Peshawar. 'I only met him in Sudan in '93 and '94 when I was invited by him. Before that I used to hear about Osama from CIA officers – they used to admire him, romanticise him, they seemed enamoured of him.'

From 1985 bin Laden started spending less time fundraising at home in Saudi Arabia and more time inside Afghanistan. When he did go home to Medina, he spent his time studying military maps. 'I hated the Russians because they took my father away from me,' his fourth son Omar later wrote.[8] One day the five-year-old Omar tried to get his father's attention by dancing round the maps. Bin Laden was so enraged that he summoned his older sons and caned them all for allowing Omar to disturb his work.

Inside Afghanistan, bin Laden worked closely with Jalaluddin Haqqani, a powerful commander based near the south-eastern city of Khost who had become something of a folk hero. But increasingly he became convinced that what was needed was his own Arab force, rather than dispersing the Arabs among the Afghans as Azzam advocated. In 1986 a mujaheddin leader called Yunus Khalis, who was also close to Haqqani, agreed to let bin Laden set up his own camp in an area under his control. Bin Laden chose Jaji in the Tora Bora mountains, and named it al Masada, 'the Lion's Den', after his own name, which meant lion.

To the Afghans it seemed an odd choice. The camp was on a pine-clad mountain and very near a Soviet base – 'almost as if they wanted to be seen', said Khalid Khwaja, an ISI officer who went there in 1987. For four months of the year it was cut off by snow.

Accompanying bin Laden were fifty or sixty of his most fanatical followers – mostly Saudis but also Yemenis and Sudanese. In key positions he had two former Egyptian policemen: his military commander Abu Ubaidah, whose brother had been involved in the assassination of Egyptian President Anwar Sadat, and his deputy Abu Hafs.

After some initial humiliations the first major engagement of these 'Arab Afghans' came in April 1987 when they were bombed by the Russians in what became known as the Battle of Jaji. Accounts vary of whether the bombing went on for one week or three, but Osama and his men stood their ground, even against the feared Spetsnaz, or special forces, and later claimed to have shot down one of their Hind helicopter gunships.

The stories of Jaji became legendary, and led to many young Arabs wanting to join bin Laden. The once shy young man became more assertive, producing his first promotional videos. These showed him on the back of a white horse, a deliberate reference to the Prophet on his white-winged horse Burak, as well as speaking on a walkie-talkie and firing off Kalashnikovs. The tall, lanky millionaire who had given up his privileged life to fight with the Afghans became a Saudi hero. 'He'd give you the clothes off his back,' said Anas.

Bin Laden's first wife Najwa was horrified when her husband came back from Afghanistan to their home in Jeddah with 'red raised scars all over his body' and boasting he had learned to fly a helicopter. She was his cousin from Syria and they had married in 1974, when she was just fourteen and he seventeen, and she might reasonably have expected an easy life after marrying into one of the richest families in the Middle East.

Instead she found a fanatic who refused toys to his children, or to let his family have air conditioning to relieve the sweltering desert heat. Yet initially she was proud. 'Everyone was astonished that a wealthy bin Laden son actually risked death or injury on the front lines,' she later wrote. 'I heard silly talk that many people wanted to inhale the very air Osama breathed.' She was less impressed when he took their eldest son Abdullah to Jaji to experience jihad at the age of just nine.

Bin Laden became known as 'the Sheikh', and his growing reputation led to inevitable rivalry with his former mentor Azzam, though he continued to finance MK. Then one day, visiting some of his wounded fighters in the Kuwaiti Red Crescent hospital in Peshawar, bin Laden met an Egyptian eye doctor called Ayman al Zawahiri.

Bin Laden had long been anti-American, his wife Najwa complaining that his children were not allowed to have Western products such as Coca-Cola or television. But his focus had always been on expelling infidels from Afghanistan, and he had never talked of opposing the Saudi monarchy or other Arab regimes.

That changed after he met Zawahiri. At thirty-five, Zawahiri was seven years older than bin Laden and much more of an intellectual, and he gradually took Azzam's place as his mentor. The two men made an unlikely pair, one tall and lean, the other portly and bespectacled, but they found much in common. The Egyptian had grown close to Gulbuddin Hekmatyar, but was otherwise condescending about the Afghans, who he did not think knew the first thing about Islam. To him they were simply tools. He agreed with bin Laden about the need to create an all-Arab force, and had gathered around him a small cadre of well-educated doctors and engineers from Egypt, many of whom had already been imprisoned and tortured for their beliefs. By then several of bin Laden's key men were Egyptian radicals.

In May 1988 the Soviets began pulling out troops from Afghanistan in a phased withdrawal that would take nine months, and the two men began looking to the future and what they could do next. In August 1988 they officially formed an organisation called al Qaeda, which meant 'the Base', the hub for what was to be the first terrorism multinational, and whose members would pledge the *bayat*, an oath of allegiance to bin Laden.

After the defeat of the Soviet Union in 1989, and the failure of the mujaheddin to take over Afghanistan, bin Laden left Peshawar disillusioned, and eventually set up operations in Sudan. In 1996 the government there expelled him under American pressure, and he flew back to Afghanistan. He made Tora Bora his base, moving in with his three wives and twelve of his seventeen children, and joined by many al Qaeda fighters.

His son Omar hated it there, and later described surviving on eggs, rice and potatoes, with no electricity or running water – hardly the life of a Saudi millionaire. Bin Laden got to know the mountains well, taking hikes with his sons, and learning centuries-old trails used by smugglers and traders into Pakistan.

In the following years, his men stockpiled weapons and fortified an area about six miles square between the Wazir and Agam valleys. Some of their caves were reported to be concealed 350 feet inside the granite peaks. It was, in other words, an obvious hide-out and escape route.

*   *   *

Gary Berntsen, a tall man with cold blue eyes, had been in the last CIA team to go into Afghanistan before 9/11 – a trip to the Northern Alliance in 2000, though they were quickly pulled out and he ended up in Latin America. After the attack he was sent back in late October 2001, his team replacing that of the other Gary, Gary Schroen, in northern Afghanistan. By mid-November the capital had fallen, and he was running CIA operations from a Kabul guesthouse when the first reports came in that bin Laden was in Tora Bora. He went straight to Major General Dell Dailey, the US special forces commander at Bagram, and asked for an SF team to go down there together with some of his agents. When I met Berntsen afterwards, he told me Dailey had said, 'We're not going to – it's too disorganised, too dangerous, too this, too that.'[9]

Berntsen decided that if the special forces wouldn't go, he would mount his own operation. 'Bin Laden killed 3,000 Americans in my city New York, and I wanted him dead. Simple as that,' he said. 'I wasn't going to ask for permission, because I knew I wouldn't get it. I knew if I didn't do anything bin Laden would escape the country with his entire force, so I just improvised.'

He sent a small team of eight men to Jalalabad, where they began coordinating with local commanders. In late November four of them with ten Afghan guides set off into the mountains, scaling 10,000-foot peaks. Their equipment was packed onto mules (one of which was blown up when an RPG round on its back detonated). They knew they faced an enemy who outnumbered them by perhaps hundreds to one. 'I sent four guys into those mountains alone to look for a thousand people,' said Berntsen. 'It was a very, very large risk. If they'd been found they would have been tortured and killed, and I would probably have been fired.'

After two days they spotted bin Laden's camp, complete with trucks, command posts and machine-gun nests. They estimated there were between six and seven hundred people there. 'We got them,' they radioed Berntsen, who punched the air in delight. 'One word kept pounding in my head: revenge. Let's do this right and finish them off in the mountains.'

The agents mounted their laser marking devices on tripods and began lighting up targets using lasers invisible to the naked eye. To be doubly sure, one of them punched coordinates into a device that looked like a gigantic palm pilot. For the next fifty-six hours they directed strike after strike by B1 and B2 bombers and F14 Tomcats onto the al Qaeda encampment. The battle of Tora Bora had begun. But there was a fatal flaw. They might have the world's most overwhelming air power and sophisticated communications system on their side, but at the end of the day they were just four Americans against perhaps a thousand men.

As the bombardment went on, bin Laden and his men fled further into the mountains. A twelve-man special forces team was sent in, as well as some crack SAS operatives. The plan was to pin the al Qaeda fighters against the mountains, using Afghan forces to trap them in a 'kill-box' between three promontories. Three rival local commanders who between them controlled most of Jalalabad were hired – Hazrat Ali, Haji Zahir and Haji Zaman Ghamsharik – and a day rate of $100–150 per soldier agreed. 'I raised an army with a couple of million dollars,' says Berntsen. But he doubted that they were really committed.

Hazrat Ali – or 'General Ali', as he called himself – had fought the Soviets as a teenager in the 1980s, and later joined the Taliban for a time. Haji Zahir was the nephew of Abdul Haq, who had been executed by the Taliban the previous month. Haji Zaman was a wealthy drug smuggler who had also fought the Soviets, but when the Taliban came to power he went into exile in France. He had been persuaded by the United States to return to Afghanistan.

Between them they fielded a force of around 2,000 men, but there were questions from the outset about the competence and loyalties of the fighters. The warlords and their men distrusted each other, and all appeared to distrust their American allies. According to Hayatullah, head of a group called the Eastern Council whose cousin Rohatullah also had men there, Hazrat Ali and Haji Zaman each got $6 million, but then Haji Zahir said the

Americans had so much money they hadn't asked for enough, and should have demanded $100 million.[10]

Berntsen was certain bin Laden was at Tora Bora, because a second CIA team he sent in had a stroke of luck. One of the dead bodies they found was clutching a cheap Japanese walkie-talkie. Through it they could hear bin Laden exhorting his troops to keep fighting.

'We were listening to bin Laden praying, talking and giving instructions for a couple of days,' said Berntsen. 'I had a guy called Jalal, the CIA's number-one native Arabist, who'd been listening to bin Laden's voice for five years, down here listening. Anyone who says he wasn't there is a damn fool.' Berntsen sent an urgent request to General Franks at Central Command in Florida for a battalion of six to eight hundred US Army Rangers to be dropped behind the al Qaeda positions to block their escape to Pakistan. 'We need Rangers now!' he radioed repeatedly. 'The opportunity to get bin Laden and his men is slipping away!' But the answer came back, no, it should be left to the Afghans. 'The generals were afraid of casualties!' said Berntsen, still incredulous. 'Yet these guys had just killed 3,000 people in New York, and might do again. What kind of insanity is that, not sending troops?'

Only on 6 December, the eleventh day of the sixteen-day battle, did Delta Force arrive in Tora Bora and the military take control from the CIA. They set up base in an old schoolhouse, commanded by a major who uses the pseudonym 'Dalton Fury'. Yet they numbered just forty – and to Berntsen's wry amusement they had to pay bribes to their Afghan allies to be allowed through.

Because they were so few, the plan was to send the Afghan forces into the Tora Bora mountains to attack the al Qaeda positions from valleys on either side. The Americans would remain in observation posts, providing advice and air support, not lead the Afghans into battle or venture towards the forward lines.

For several days in early December, Fury's troops moved up the mountains in pairs with fighters from the Afghan militias to set up observation posts. The Americans used GPS devices and laser range-finders to pinpoint caves and pockets of enemy fighters for the bombers. But the Delta Force units were unable to hold any high ground, because the Afghans insisted on retreating to their base at the bottom of the mountains each night, leaving the Americans alone inside al Qaeda territory. In a later official account the special forces said of Hazrat Ali's forces, '[Their] fighting qualities proved remarkably poor.'[11]

Still, American aircraft were carrying out as many as a hundred airstrikes a day, and it was clear from what the US forces could see and what they were hearing in the intercepted conversations that the relentless bombing was taking its toll. A couple of times Berntsen even thought they had got bin Laden. Through the walkie-talkie they knew the al Qaeda fighters were running short of food and water, so they let them be resupplied by some local Afghans. The Afghans were paid to carry a GPS and press a button whenever they saw men or weapons. 'We delivered food and water to them so we could get a GPS on bin Laden's position then [on December 9] we dropped a Blu 82, the size of a car, and killed a whole lot.'

The 15,000-pound bomb, known as a daisy-cutter, was the largest bomb in the US inventory short of nuclear weapons, and was so huge it had to be rolled out the back of a C-130 cargo plane. It shook the mountains for miles. Before Afghanistan, the weapon had not been used since Vietnam, and to start with the Americans feared that it had made less impact than they expected. But then Fury heard al Qaeda fighters radioing for the 'red truck to move wounded', and frantic pleas from a fighter to his commander, saying, 'Cave too hot, can't reach others.'[12] A captured al Qaeda fighter who was there later told American interrogators that men deep in caves had been vaporised in what he called 'a hideous explosion'.

Late afternoon the following day, 10 December, Hazrat Ali told the Americans that his men had bin Laden surrounded. But as the Americans set off up the mountain in six Toyotas, they came across Ali leaving in a convoy. He promised that he and his men would turn round at the bottom and return, but they never did. Frustrated, the Americans called in seventeen hours of continuous airstrikes.

Fury was astonished when next day Haji Zaman asked for a twelve-hour ceasefire, saying that al Qaeda wanted to come down from the mountains and surrender. Bin Laden was heard on the radio telling his men that he had let them down and it was OK to surrender. Fury hoped the battle was over as Zaman claimed, but he was suspicious. They agreed an overnight pause in bombing, but by the next day not one surrendering fighter had appeared. Fury would later believe the message was a ruse to allow al Qaeda fighters to slip out of Tora Bora for Pakistan. As many as eight hundred are thought to have left that night.

Yet bin Laden was still in Tora Bora, and it seems he expected to die there. A copy of his will was later found, written on 14 December 2001. 'Allah commended to us that when death approaches any of us that we make a bequest to parents and next of kin and to Muslims as a whole,' he wrote. 'Allah bears witness that the love of jihad and death in the cause of Allah has dominated my life and the verses of the sword permeated every cell in my heart ... and fight the pagans all together as they fight you all together.' He instructed his wives not to remarry, and apologised to his children for devoting himself to jihad.

Berntsen kept warning everyone that they were losing the chance to get bin Laden, and needed to send troops to block off exits on the Pakistan side. But Major General Dailey said General Franks had refused, explaining that Rumsfeld wanted to keep the US presence to a 'light footprint', and he feared alienating their allies.

'I don't give a damn about offending our allies!' Berntsen shouted. 'I only care about eliminating al Qaeda and delivering bin Laden's head in a box!' Dailey said the military's position was firm, and Berntsen replied, 'Screw that!'

Back in Washington, Berntsen's boss Hank Crumpton, head of Afghan strategy for the CIA Counter-Terrorism Center, went to see Bush at the White House and warned him, 'We're going to lose our prey if we're not careful.' He recommended that Marines or other US troops be rushed to Tora Bora.

'How bad off are these Afghani forces, really?' asked Bush. 'Are they up to the job?'

'Definitely not, Mr President,' Crumpton replied. 'Definitely not.'

Yet still no more troops were forthcoming. Fury recommended sending his men to the Pakistan side of the border, but was given the thumbs down. So desperate was he that he even suggested dropping landmines to blow up the al Qaeda fighters as they came out of the tunnels.

What none of them knew was that General Franks was already busy on Iraq plans.

On 15 December Berntsen's men heard bin Laden on the radio again. The following day the al Qaeda leader is believed to have split his men into two and left with one group of two hundred Saudi and Yemeni bodyguards over the mountains to Parachinar in Pakistan's tribal area, a strip of lawless land between Afghanistan and Pakistan. Bin Laden had been helped by Pakistanis and Afghans he had paid, some of whom were also being paid by the Americans.

Fury finally managed to persuade Hazrat Ali to keep his men in the mountains, and for the next three days they went from valley to valley, but there was no more resistance. Al Qaeda had disappeared. They found 250 dead. By 17 December Hazrat Ali declared the battle over.

That same day Berntsen left Afghanistan, frustrated beyond words. Back home with his wife and two children for Christmas, he was horrified when he switched on his television to see the bearded face of his tormentor: 'I just kept thinking we could have had him.'

The Pakistani military were angered at the widespread perception that they had let bin Laden and his men through. General Ali Mohammad Jan Aurakzai, a friend of President Musharraf, had been appointed commander of the Frontier Corps shortly after 9/11. When the US started bombing Tora Bora on 8 December, he got a call from Pakistan's Director General of Military Operations. 'He asked me about the possibility of sending troops into the tribal agencies of Khyber and Kurram, as there was a possibility of bad guys coming over the border from Afghanistan. I didn't think it was a good idea, as we had no government presence, no police, no intelligence in those areas ...'

Coming from the tribal areas himself, he knew it would upset decades of delicate balance since the days of the Raj. The British had found the only way to deal with the Pashtun tribes along the frontier was by stick and carrot, giving subsidies to their chiefs or '*maliks*' and putting in representatives called Political Agents who could impose collective punishment on the whole village or tribe for any misdemeanour.[13] As long as the tribes stayed quiet, government would stay out of their affairs. The idea was they would serve as a buffer or 'prickly hedge' to guard the entrance to British India.

When Pakistan was created in 1947 this policy continued and these so-called tribal areas were left semi-autonomous, with federal control extending only a hundred yards either side of the road. The Pakistan army had never entered these areas, yet would now be doing so at the behest of *kafir* foreigners and against one of the key tribal principles of *melmastia* – providing hospitality to a guest or those who come looking for sanctuary (which of course also made it the perfect hiding place).

General Aurakzai feared this could spark a tribal uprising. 'But the Americans said if we didn't do it, there was the possibility of hot pursuit, which would have been humiliating for us, so I said we must act. It was also an opportunity to open up these inaccessible areas. We spoke to the local tribesmen and said either you allow in Pakistani troops or you will have US troops and aerial bombing, which they were very averse to. So they promised full support, as long as we were not a permanent presence, and told us they would not harbour foreign terrorists. Three days later, on 11 December, we dropped troops on the passes. There was no road, so the main body had to go on foot and equipment carried on mules. Within ten days we had arrested 240 al Qaeda and killed ten. We lost seven of our own men. It was all going well. But then unfortunately India mobilised its forces on our eastern border [in reaction to an attack on its parliament] and we had to decide what to do as we couldn't be in both places.'[14]

Berntsen was convinced that had Bush not refused the request for more soldiers, the al Qaeda leader would have been killed at Tora Bora instead of becoming a recruiting tool for jihadis, and the world would have been a different place. 'There isn't a day when I don't think "If only",' he told me. 'We didn't need much more. If we'd had six to eight hundred men we could have finished the job. Afghanistan was a flawed masterpiece.'

In 2009 a Senate report chaired by Senator John Kerry on what happened at Tora Bora would reach the same conclusion: 'The failure to finish the job represents a lost opportunity that forever altered the course of the conflict in Afghanistan and the future of international terrorism, leaving the American people more vulnerable to terrorism, laying the foundation for today's protracted Afghan insurgency and inflaming the internal strife now endangering Pakistan.'

In Jalalabad I went to see one of the three main commanders to whom the Americans had contracted out the fight, to hear his version of events.

Haji Abdul Zahir was the closest thing Afghanistan had to mujaheddin aristocracy. He was the nephew of the late Abdul Haq and the son of Haji Qadir, who had also been a commander, and was one of five Vice Presidents to Karzai and one of the few Pashtuns in the administration. In July 2002 Haji Qadir was assassinated by gunmen as he left his office in Kabul, his truck riddled with thirty-six bullets.

Haji Zahir's house was a study in warlord chic. A golden chandelier dominated the marble entrance hall, and a sweeping staircase led up to a balcony with a billiards table. Everywhere there were blown-up photographs of himself and his late father and uncle. He was waiting for me, lounging on cushions on a raised platform beneath a gilt-framed oil painting of his father with an Afghan flag.

A servant brought us glasses of fresh pomegranate juice and small bowls of almonds and pistachios, and Zahir's personal cameraman appeared to record the interview. But Zahir's words were drowned out by what I thought at first was screaming, but which he explained was the sound of birds.

'I keep hundreds of birds,' he said. 'I love birds.' I presumed he meant fighting birds – a tradition in a country where just about every hobby involves fighting – but he looked pained when I asked. 'Not fighting birds,' he pouted. 'I like them singing, it's very sweet.'[15]

Somebody was dispatched to take out the birds, and he began to talk about Tora Bora, using floor cushions to illustrate the topography. 'From the beginning the mission was not strong enough and the plan was weak,' he said. 'If you have enemies on this pillow and you don't surround it, then they will run away. So without any plan the planes were flying and bombing, but the ways were open so of course they ran away.'

Like Berntsen, he had no doubt that bin Laden was there. 'I myself caught twenty-one al Qaeda prisoners, some from Yemen, Kuwait, Saudi and Chechnya. One was a boy called Abu Bakr, and I asked him when he had last seen bin Laden. He said ten days earlier bin Laden had come to his checkpoint and sat with them for twenty minutes and drank tea and said, "Don't worry, don't lose morale, we'll be successful and I am here."'

Zahir went to join the fight after he switched on CNN one evening and saw an interview with his rival commanders Hazrat Ali and Haji Zaman. 'They were saying they were in Tora Bora with 3,000 soldiers. Then General Ali called me and asked, "Why aren't you here?" I said, "We can't just go without any plan," but then I spoke to my father who was at the Bonn Conference [to choose the interim Afghan government] and he said, "This is our fight, so prepare your things and go." I got 1,100–1,200 men ready, and we arrived there at night. The first shock was that Hazrat Ali and Haji Zaman had boasted on CNN they had all these men, but in fact there weren't even four or five hundred. They were just telling the Americans they had more to get more money.'

They had a meeting, and divided the area into three. Haji Zaman was to be in charge of Wazir valley, General Ali in charge of Milawa where bin Laden's refuge was, and Zahir in charge of Tora Bora and Girikhel village. According to Zahir, Ali was being directed by the Americans while Zaman was liaising with the British. 'There was a lot of money floating around. The US were paying $100–150 per day for each soldier, and the others claimed they had 3–5,000 men. I didn't receive anything from them, not one gun, one bullet, one dollar. I spent $40,000 of my own money.' (Later I would meet Hazrat Ali, who said Zahir had got the same as them.)

After a day of preparation they all set off up the mountains to their areas. By then the bombing of the encampment at Milawa had started. The plan had been to attack al Qaeda from the Wazir valley side, to trap them as the special forces wanted. Then, on 11 December, the evening the attack was due, Zaman, whose men were that side, said that al Qaeda had sent a radio message asking to be given till 8 o'clock the following morning, when they would surrender.

'I didn't agree,' said Zahir. 'I said, if they want to surrender, why not today? They're the enemy – why are we giving them twelve hours to run away?' But Zaman replied that they needed time to get in contact with each other, and halted the advance of his troops.

Zahir believed that Zaman had been bribed to let them disappear over the passes, and was convinced that the majority escaped. 'Supposedly there were six to eight hundred people,' he said. 'I captured twenty-one. Ali and Zaman got nine. Dead bodies were not easy to count, but around 150. That means at least four to six hundred got away. For all that money spent and energy and bombing, only thirty were caught.'

To this day he remains mystified by the Americans. 'Why weren't there more Americans in Tora Bora?' he asked. 'Even after Delta Force arrived, they weren't more than fifty or sixty. Believe me, there were more journalists than soldiers. It would have been easy to get bin Laden there. I don't know why there was no plan to block the passes.' He dismissed General Aurakzai's claim that Pakistan had apprehended people on its side of the border. 'What happened to those people? Aurakzai's men were helping them move west to Waziristan.'

* * *

Mike Scheuer, who headed the CIA's Osama bin Laden Unit from 1996 to 1999, and then became its special adviser from 2001 to 2004, probably knew more about bin Laden than any other Westerner alive. He was on the receiving end in Washington of many of the cables from Tora Bora. 'It's like many things in your life,' he said. 'If you don't do something when you have the chance, sometimes that chance doesn't come back.'[16]

Though he was frustrated by losing bin Laden at Tora Bora, he pointed out that the US had already squandered ten different opportunities to get their man back in 1998 and 1999. President Clinton had signed a secret presidential directive in 1998 authorising the CIA to kill bin Laden after al Qaeda bombed the American Embassies in Kenya and Tanzania, killing more than two hundred people. But when it came to it, said Scheuer, Clinton did not have the necessary resolve: 'Clinton was worried about European opinion. He didn't want to shoot and miss and have to explain a lot of innocent deaths. Yet the very same day [in 1999] we turned down one opportunity to kill bin Laden, our planes were dropping thousands of bombs on the Serbs from 20,000 feet. The Serbs never did anything to us.'

On one occasion that same year, the US had live video pictures of bin Laden coming in from a Predator spy plane, the only time he was actually seen. 'But the drone wasn't armed at that time, because the fools in Washington were arguing over which agency should fund the $2 million installation of the Hellfire missile. It's a very upsetting business. I got into a slanging match with Clinton on TV because he claimed that he never turned down the opportunity to kill bin Laden. That's a very clear lie, and we're all paying the price. Similarly at Tora Bora, our generals didn't want to lose a lot of our soldiers going after him. They had seen what had happened to the Russians, who lost 15,000 men in Afghanistan. So it was easier to subcontract to Hazrat Ali, Haji Zahir and Haji Zaman. At the time we said, "Look, these guys are going to be a day late and a dollar short." But they wouldn't listen.'

Although some of the CIA officers involved later blamed the fiasco on infighting between the CIA and the military, Scheuer insisted that responsibility also lay with George Tenet, the CIA Director at the time. 'Part of it was Mr Tenet's fault, because he told the President, Rumsfeld and Powell that all you have to do is spend a lot of money in Afghanistan. Everyone who was cognisant of how Afghan operations worked would have told Tenet that he was nuts. During our covert help to the mujaheddin in the fight against the Russians, we spent $6 billion between us and the Saudis, and I can't remember a single time the Afghans did anything we wanted them to do. The people we bought, the people Mr Tenet said we would own, let Osama bin Laden escape from Tora Bora into Pakistan.'

I wanted to see for myself the tunnels from which he had escaped, so I went to see the local Governor, Gul Agha Sherzai. 'Tora Bora is already a world-famous name, but we want it to be known for tourism, not terrorism,' he said. 'Long before anyone had heard of Osama, Tora Bora was known as a picnic spot, and now it can be both.' He showed me plans he'd had drawn up for a $10 million hotel development overlooking the caves. He also intended to build restaurants and to pave the road built by bin Laden leading to the mountains from Jalalabad. 'I don't just want one Tora Bora hotel,' he said. 'I want three or four!'[17]

The next morning, the chowkidar of the aid-agency guesthouse where I was staying hammered on my door in terror. 'Gunmen are asking for you,' he said. Outside were a police jeep and two pick-ups full of men with Kalashnikovs, one of whom introduced himself as Commander Lalalai, a famous old mujahid from Spin Boldak. As Tora Bora 'wasn't quite safe' Governor Sherzai had sent these guards to accompany me. I climbed into the jeep and we sped off through the streets of Jalalabad, scattering donkey carts and turbaned men on bicycles. Eventually we turned off on an unmade road towards the White Mountains. 'Tora Bora,' said the driver, Mahmood, rolling his eyes.

On either side of the track were mud-walled compounds, one of which had an actual-size model of a car on its roof. Every so often Mahmood put on a terrifying burst of speed, throwing up so much dust that we could see nothing, and I would grip the door handle.

'Al Qaeda, al Qaeda!' he explained. Occasionally the truck in front would screech to a halt, and Commander Lalalai would jump out and start berating Mahmood for not going fast enough, saying we could be killed by the 'bad guys'. I began to wonder about the Governor's plans for tourism.

After two hours we stopped at the schoolhouse that had been used by the CIA and then Delta Force as base camp during the battle for Tora Bora, and collected two more vehicles of guards. By then we had twenty-six gunmen. So much for travelling low-profile.

The road deteriorated from dust to rocky scree, making the journey even more bone-shaking. But the scenery was spectacular, swirled-toffee mountains as far as the eye could see, rising to black rock, all under a deep-blue sky. On one side of the road lay the passes to Parachinar and the tribal areas of Pakistan. Almost twenty years before I had crossed these mountains with mujaheddin coming to fight the Russians, riding a donkey laden with rockets and grenades that left my legs purple with bruises.

Eventually our convoy pulled up under a tree and everyone piled out. 'Now we walk ten minutes,' said Mahmood. I had spent enough time in Afghanistan to know to multiply any times and distances by three. Foolishly, I left my food and water in the jeep, as it was Ramadan fasting month, and I didn't want to eat in front of the others, who must let nothing pass their lips until nightfall. It was a decision I would regret.

An hour later we were still climbing the stony track along a dry riverbed and scrambling up and down scree-covered slopes, breathless from the thinning oxygen. But the guards seemed happy. They held hands, posed for photographs and kept coming to me with little offerings – some lavender they had picked, spent ammunition cartridges, and pieces of pink quartz. Every so often we passed people with donkeys or small children bearing bundles of wood – the slopes all around had been denuded of trees. The women hurriedly pulled their shawls over their faces.

Finally we stopped. The guards pointed across the gorge, shouting, 'Osama house! Osama house!' At first I could see nothing, but then I just made out a few holes and ruins on the terraced slopes. We clambered across past a burned-out tank and over some large bomb craters, and came to the ruins of some mud-walled houses.

I realised that the reason I had not seen it at first was that the site of the last great showdown between US forces and al Qaeda was not at all what I was expecting. At the time newspapers had run detailed graphics of James Bond-style hi-tech cave systems with internal hydro-electric power plants from mountain streams, elevators, ventilation ducts, loading bays, caverns big enough for tanks and trucks, and brick-lined walls.

Where was the vast network of tunnels that led to Pakistan? All I could see among the ruins was a circular hole, about three feet high, that seemed to be an entrance. I walked in, cursing myself for not having brought my torch. One of the guards had a cigarette lighter which he flicked on and off, but it was soon clear that the tunnel did not extend very far. Some of the gunmen were nervous, and stayed by the entrance blocking what light there was and giggling as if Osama was suddenly going to appear.

A combination of Afghan scavengers and US and British intelligence had scoured the caves, and nothing remained to suggest their past purpose. In one of them an SAS team had found plans for al Qaeda's next attack, in Singapore. CIA agents even scraped the sides of the cave for DNA in the hope of finding that they had killed bin Laden.

The 'light footprint' which had been such a success in toppling the Taliban with minimum American casualties had enabled the world's most wanted man to escape the net. Though bin Laden would periodically release videos which CIA agents and geologists would scrutinise to try to identify an area, there would be no more confirmed sightings. The CIA team would start referring to him as 'Elvis'. President Bush was left with the consolation argument that the al Qaeda leader and his deputy were fatally weakened, detached from their followers and unable to plan any new operations.

6

A Tale of Two Generals

BIN LADEN MAY have vanished into the mountains of the tribal areas, but his bony, bearded face was hard to avoid in Rawalpindi, where it stared out from boxes of sweets and posters on sale in the labyrinthine bazaars just a couple of miles from President Musharraf's house. Right from the start it wasn't clear whose side Pakistan was really on.

Although Pakistan had been a nominal ally of the US since Pakistan's creation in 1947, it had never really been a happy marriage. Pakistan had long been ambivalent about the United States, which had poured money and arms in when it needed something – such as help in training and arming the Afghan mujaheddin to fight the Russians during the Cold War – then was never there when Pakistan needed it, such as in its three wars against India.

I always found this combination of Pakistan's desire to be an American ally with its widespread anti-Americanism confusing. 'Pakistan's problem,' said Husain Haqqani while he was the country's Ambassador in Washington, 'is that it is trying to be Iran and South Korea at the same time.'

'America needs Pakistan more than Pakistan needs America,' Pakistan's founder Mohammad Ali Jinnah insisted to American journalist Margaret Bourke-White in an interview for *Life* magazine just one month after the country was born.

At the time that was clearly ludicrous. And indeed, during his election campaign in 2000, George W. Bush had been asked the name of the President of Pakistan, and had no idea.

But 9/11 had changed everything. Pakistan knew the Taliban better than anyone, for it had helped create them. Afghanistan was a landlocked country most easily reachable through Pakistan with its sea ports and air connections, and the two countries shared a 1,600-mile border which split Pashtun tribes living on either side, who crossed back and forth freely.

The Americans would have found it almost impossible to mount their operation to topple the Taliban regime without Pakistan. 'And they knew it,' said Richard Armitage, who was Deputy Secretary of State at the time.

In his memoir, President Musharraf recounted that Colin Powell, the US Secretary of State, phoned him on the morning after 9/11 and warned: 'You are either with us or against us.'[1]

The head of ISI, General Mahmood Ahmed, happened to be in Washington at the time, ironically to try to convince the CIA that the Taliban were 'misunderstood' and should be engaged with. On 9 September he had lunch with the Director of the CIA, George Tenet, who later wrote, 'The guy was immovable when it came to the Taliban and al Qaeda. And bloodless too.'

The day after the attack, Mahmood was called in by Powell's deputy Armitage. 'It was clear he was pretty much an Islamist,' said Armitage. '9/11 for Americans was a life-changing event, because we'd always been protected behind our two great oceans, unlike almost any other country in the world. Yet Mahmood started out trying to tell me, "You've got to understand about what our people feel." I could see he didn't get it.'[2]

Musharraf wrote in his memoir that Armitage had used the meeting to make 'a shockingly barefaced threat' to bomb Pakistan 'into the Stone Age' if Islamabad decided not to cooperate. Armitage, a big hulk of a man who admits he can be 'fearsome', insists he said no such thing. 'I'd love to have been able to,' he laughed. 'I would have needed a cigarette afterwards. I had no such authority. But we did have very strong discussions.'

As a former soldier himself, who understood the importance of honour, he did something else. 'I took Mahmood to my private office, the small room behind the ornate main office, and said, "I want to show you something." I opened a box, and inside was this Star of Pakistan I'd been awarded. "You see this?" I said. "No American would accept this ever if Pakistan is found wanting in assisting us. Ever."'

The message got through. Musharraf chose cooperation, but it was hardly enthusiastic. 'I made a dispassionate military-style analysis of our options,' he later wrote. 'I war-gamed them [the US] as an adversary. The question was if we do not join them, can we confront them and withstand the onslaught. The answer was no, we could not ... we could not endure a military confrontation with the US from any point of view.'

The first American official to meet with Musharraf after 9/11 was Wendy Chamberlin, the US Ambassador, who had only been in Pakistan two weeks. She'd met the President when she arrived in August, and he had told her his vision was to encourage foreign investment, and to do that he realised he needed to control domestic terrorism and the sectarian violence in Karachi. 'He thought Pakistan was the battleground in the proxy war between the Wahhabis and the Iranians, but didn't feel empowered or think he had the tools to really crack down,' she said.[3]

When she went in to see him on the morning of 13 September, she did not mince words. 'It was the first time anyone had said directly to him, "Are you with us or against us?" He wasn't persuaded at first.' 'It's an opportunity,' she told him. 'We can help you in ways which will empower you to help us against internal terrorists.' Musharraf was unconvinced. 'He didn't buy it. We went over and over – I said you can expect things – lifting of sanctions, the resumption of military aid, spare parts, direct assistance, grant aid ... He waffled and danced around, giving me this whole bunch of crap, and in the end I turned away and put my head down in my hands. My DCM [deputy] kept looking and asked, "Wendy, what's wrong?" I said, "I haven't heard what I need to tell my President, which is we support you unstintingly." Only then did Musharraf agree.'

'Very good,' she replied in relief.

As she walked down the long corridor out of the palace she saw CNN reporter Tom Mintier and his crew waiting. 'I thought, "Do I tell CNN before I tell my government?" and I thought, "Yes, I do, because then I lock Musharraf in" – I felt him waffling.'

That night Colin Powell called Musharraf and sealed the deal.

For the wily Musharraf this was his chance to transform his image on the world stage. Until then he had been seen as an international pariah, having seized power in a coup on 12 October 1999 and locked up the elected Prime Minister Nawaz Sharif in the old Attock Fort.

He told anyone who would listen that Sharif had tried to kill him 'and hundreds of innocent Pakistanis'. Musharraf had been in Sri Lanka attending a conference and playing some of his beloved golf when Sharif had clumsily tried to sack him as his army chief. Musharraf jumped on a PIA flight back to Karachi which Sharif then refused permission to land, even though the pilot said he had only twenty minutes of fuel left. With the plane circling over the Arabian Gulf the generals stepped in, took over the TV station, airport and key buildings, and arrested Sharif.

In Musharraf's view he had done both his country and the world a favour. 'Today we have reached a stage where our economy has crumbled, our credibility is lost, state institutions lie demolished,' he said in an address to the nation late that first night. He suspended the constitution and disbanded parliament, but to try to make the situation seem less coup-like, he did not take the usual title of Chief Martial Law Administrator. Instead he called himself 'chief executive', as if Pakistan were a business. Just like previous military rulers, he insisted: 'The armed forces have no intention to stay in charge any longer than is absolutely necessary to pave the way for true democracy.' In the case of his predecessor Zia-ul-Haq that meant staying eleven and a half years.

I was in the country within days of the coup, and it was clear that it was widely welcomed, people handing out sweets to cele-brate. Pakistanis generally viewed their politicians as corrupt and incompetent, while the army is the only really respected national institution, despite having lost every war it has fought.

I went to see Musharraf in the white-colonnaded Army House with neat rose gardens where eleven years earlier I had interviewed Pakistan's last military ruler General Zia, and he took a leaf out of the Tony Blair speech-book on Princess Diana. 'I'd like to be seen as the people's general,' he told me.

But on the eve of the millennium the international community had little stomach for coups. Another one in Pakistan seemed a retrograde step in a country that had spent half its existence under military rule. Pakistan was expelled from the Commonwealth. Even Pakistan's traditional friend Saudi Arabia was showing a cold shoulder; the Saudi royal family was close to the Sharifs, and would go on to provide them with homes in exile.

It wasn't just the way that Musharraf had seized power that caused international concern. Pakistan and India had fought three wars over the disputed province of Kashmir, and five months before his coup, the then army chief Musharraf had brought the two nations to the verge of a fourth, this time nuclear. As Musharraf liked to remind people, his background was as a commando, and in May 1999 he ordered Pakistani troops into Indian Kashmir disguised as jihadis. The plan was to seize a 15,000-foot strategic height called Kargil. The ill-conceived operation prompted a fierce reaction from India, which responded with aerial bombardments. Western intelligence picked up that the Pakistani army was preparing nuclear missiles.

The Kargil operation totally undermined Prime Minister Nawaz Sharif's efforts to make peace with India after Pakistan's nuclear tests the previous year, and he always insisted it was launched without his knowledge. He pointed out that he had just signed the Lahore Declaration with his Indian counterpart Atal Bihari Vajpayee, a bilateral treaty to normalise relations between the two countries, and that it would make no sense to then wreck it by sending troops across the agreed Line of Control which divides Kashmir. Musharraf pooh-poohed the idea that Sharif did not know, saying, 'Nothing could be farther from the truth.' He claimed the Prime Minister was briefed three times.

Either way, by July Sharif was in a panic, and flew to Washington, where he begged President Clinton to intervene to broker peace with India. Clinton insisted that before there could be any cease-fire Pakistan must withdraw all its troops. Sharif agreed, to the fury of Musharraf and the army, who saw it as a humiliating climbdown. 'We became the most sanctioned country on earth' said Chaudhry Nisar Ali, his Interior Minister, who went with him.[4] The Prime Minister's days were almost certainly numbered from that point.

'People forget how close we came to nuclear war,' said David Manning, who was foreign policy adviser to Tony Blair at the time.[5]

9/11 changed everything, making Pakistan once again crucial, just as it had been after the Soviet invasion of Afghanistan in 1979. It seemed an astonishing replay of history, for that time Pakistan had also been under military dictatorship, that of General Zia. He too had ousted an elected Prime Minister – Zulfikar Ali Bhutto – who had appointed Zia as his army chief because he thought him unintelligent and no threat, calling him 'my monkey general' and pretending to jerk him on a string like a puppet-master. It was an unwise move – Zia referred to Bhutto as 'the bastard'. A few hours after the two men attended a Fourth of July reception at the US Embassy in 1977, Zia had him arrested and seized power.

He did not stop there. Bhutto was sent to the gallows on 4 April 1979, prompting worldwide condemnation.

As a vocal defender of human rights, the US President Jimmy Carter was outraged. But Pakistan was not the only country in the region in turmoil. A seismic shift in international relations was under way as a result of Islamic revolution in neighbouring Iran, prompted by the return from exile of the Shia cleric Ayatollah Khomeini. The American-backed Shah, Reza Pahlavi, was toppled in January 1979, taking the West completely by surprise. The Shah's demise deprived the US of vital CIA listening posts to monitor its main enemy the Soviet Union. American officials looking at the map of Central Asia realised they needed Pakistan.

Yet Pakistan's relations with the US were plummeting to a new low. On 4 November 1979 Iranian revolutionary students stormed the US Embassy in Tehran and took hostage fifty-two American diplomats and citizens. While the Carter administration was consumed by this crisis, sending warships to the Gulf, on 20 November a mysterious group of Muslim fanatics seized the Grand Mosque in Mecca, the holiest site in the Islamic world, trapping thousands of pilgrims inside. The next day, with the mosque under siege, wild rumours spread across Pakistan that the US and Israel were behind the siege. Students belonging to the Islamic Jamaat-e-Islami society at Islamabad's elite Quaid-e-Azam University decided to take action. Thousands of students in government buses converged on the US Embassy, pouring over the compound walls and setting the buildings aflame. One hundred and thirty-eight people were trapped inside.

The Pakistan army headquarters was only a few miles down the road, yet it was almost four hours before General Zia dispatched a helicopter. It circled once over the burning Embassy then turned back, the army command apparently convinced no one still inside could have survived, and that it was not worth risking Pakistani troops to retrieve the bodies of dead Americans. However some Americans were still trapped inside, including an injured Marine who would probably have survived if he had received help. He died, as did another American who was beaten to death with one of his own golf clubs, as well as two Pakistani employees.

One US government auditor, who was relaxing eating a hot dog by the Embassy pool when the riot started, had been taken to a student dormitory and subjected to a mock trial by students. Afterwards he said he felt his crime in their eyes was 'simply being American'.[6] Maybe somebody should have taken notice that a country with such hatred for the US was unlikely to be its loyal ally.

A month later, just after Christmas 1979, everything changed, with the Soviet invasion of Afghanistan. Once again the Carter administration was caught unawares, perhaps not surprisingly, as many in the Soviet regime were just as shocked. Carter's hawkish

National Security Adviser Zbigniew Brzezinski immediately spotted a chance. 'The day that the Soviets officially crossed the border I wrote to President Carter, we now have the opportunity of giving to the USSR its Vietnam War,' he later recalled.

American diplomats were still sifting through the charred remains of their Embassy when their government began shipping weapons to Islamabad, though not ones that could be traced back to them. First they sent in Soviet-made ones which they had stockpiled, then later Egyptian and Chinese mortars and AK47s.

Zia was unimpressed, and dismissed an initial offer of $400 million in aid as 'peanuts'. Then in 1981 the Republicans returned to the White House in the form of Ronald Reagan. A fervent Cold War warrior, he upped the deal to $3.2 billion. General Zia would soon be gracing the doors of the White House and 10 Downing Street. The Soviet invasion became known as 'Zia's Christmas present'.

In the same way Musharraf determined to make the most of 9/11. He would get the most possible from the Americans, but he would not trust them, and he would hedge his bets.

There was, however, a major problem. Having given the Bush administration his agreement, Musharraf had to convince an army that was predisposed to take a dim view of the US, and that saw the Taliban as 'misunderstood'. As his Ambassador in Washington, Musharraf had appointed Maleeha Lodhi, a tiny, feisty woman who had been Pakistan's first female newspaper editor, but was also close to the military. She tried to defend the Taliban to Condoleezza Rice, Bush's National Security Adviser, arguing that it had cracked down on opium production (in November 2000 Mullah Omar had imposed a ban on poppy cultivation which reduced production from almost 4,000 tons that year to 185 tons in 2001). 'Yeah, Stalin also got a lot of things done,' came Rice's dry reply.

Musharraf himself was a secular, whisky-drinking general. When I interviewed him in Army House just after he took power, his wife Sebha and another couple were sitting on a sofa in a back room eating popcorn and watching an American movie. There was shock in Pakistan when he allowed himself to be photographed cradling his pet Pekingeses, Dot and Buddy, as dogs are regarded by many Muslims as unclean.

Pakistan's President had little personal sympathy for the Taliban; indeed, he found them exasperating at times, such as when they blew up the ancient Bamiyan Buddhas in March 2001 after refusing to bend to international pressure, including a mission by his own Interior Minister, General Haider, and ISI chief General Mahmood.

However, Musharraf had personally fought in two of Pakistan's wars against India, and was obsessed by trying to capture Kashmir, the former princely state which had been left divided in 1947 when India was given independence from Britain, and Pakistan was created. Thus he understood the value of a proxy force, one of Pakistan's main weapons being the militants it trained to infiltrate Kashmir, and he often differentiated between terrorism and jihad.

Other senior generals went much further. When Zia became army chief in 1977 he had introduced a programme of Islamisation. I interviewed him in 1988, just a few weeks before the mysterious plane crash in which he was killed, and asked him why it had been necessary to try to 'Islamise' a country where the overwhelming majority of the population were Muslim. 'It's what the people want,' he said. 'Education, agriculture, industrialisation – there are 101 important issues, but the fundamental issue is that this country must have the spirit of Islam.'[7]

Nowhere had he ensured this more than in the army. From the beginning, Pakistan's military leaders had seen themselves as defenders of their religion and had used Islam as a rallying cry. During the 1971 civil war which culminated in the loss of Bangladesh, Pakistan's then ruler General Yahya Khan motivated his soldiers by declaring the Mukti Bahini (the Bengali guerrillas) to be a *kafir* army against which the Pakistani army was waging a legitimate jihad. His army chief, General A.A.K. 'Tiger' Niazi, told reporters in Dhaka, 'Remember, every Muslim soldier is worth ten Hindus.' Ten days later the General was forced to surrender on Dhaka racecourse in front of crowds shouting anti-Pakistan slogans. The humiliating defeat had a major impact on Pakistan's soldiers, many of whom felt that they had lost because they were not good Muslims, and Islam began to play a greater part in military training. Musharraf, who was a commando at the time, though not involved, said he 'literally wept'.[8]

Under Zia, for the first time piety became a part of an officer's evaluation. The role of the army became not just to protect the country's geographical borders, but also its ideology as the first nation created in the name of Islam, and a particular kind of Islam. Zia changed the battle cry of the Pakistan army commandos from the Shia 'Nara e Haidry – Ya Ali' to the Sunni 'Allah Hoo Allah Hoo!' and built mosques in each garrison, appointing imams for every regiment. These were generally from the ultra-conservative Deobandi group Tableeghi Jamaat (TJ), and he encouraged soldiers and officers to spend their leave participating in its preaching missions. He was the first chief of staff to attend the huge annual gathering of TJ at Raiwind, near Lahore.

From the start Zia cultivated a close relationship with Pakistan's largest religious party, Jamaat-e-Islami, which had considerable street power. He met the JI chief for ninety minutes the night before the hanging of Bhutto, and JI members took to the streets to celebrate Bhutto's death.

During Zia's tenure as army chief, the writings of JI's founder Maulana Maudoodi, including his book *Jihad in Islam*, started to circulate in army-run educational institutions. Many officers began to openly express their support for JI's ideology. In the mosques it was as if jihad became the sixth pillar of Islam, along with the belief in one god; the *namaz* or prayers five times a day; giving alms or *zakat*; *roza*, fasting from dawn till sunset during the month of Ramadan; and *haj*, the pilgrimage to Mecca which every able-bodied Muslim was supposed to do once in their lifetime. This was encouraged by the CIA as a recruiting tool for defeating the communists in Afghanistan. Ziauddin Yousafzai, whose daughter Malala would later be shot by the Taliban, was growing up in a poor, remote village in Swat in the 1980s, during Zia's rule. He said talk of jihad was so glorified that many of his friends went across the border to fight, and he almost went too.

There were other influences at work. Several army officers posted to the Arab states around the Persian Gulf in the 1970s and 1980s came back heavily influenced by an orthodox interpretation of Islam. Zia promoted those who thought like him, and they invariably rose to occupy prominent positions in the military hierarchy. Many more officers came under religious influence as they worked directly with the Afghan mujaheddin, seeing their defeat of the Russians as a victory of Islam against an infidel superpower. It was not just a policy, but a cause they believed in.

This was reinforced when relations were cut off in 1990 and Pakistani officers had no more access to US military academies.

By 2001 those who had come through Zia's indoctrination were in senior positions. Some of the key generals who had brought Musharraf to power while his plane was circling the skies above Karachi were committed Islamists. One to whom Musharraf was particularly beholden was General Mahmood, who had been his front-line commander in the Kargil raid. At the time of the coup Mahmood was commanding 10th Corps, the key unit stationed in Rawalpindi which moved into Islamabad to detain Nawaz Sharif and secure government buildings.

The most important people for Musharraf to win over were the nine army corps commanders, the real power in the land, each controlling as many as 60,000 men. He summoned them from all over the country for a long and heated meeting in the operations room of the Pakistani Joint Chiefs of Staff. Like General Mahmood, whom he had appointed ISI chief, some were very close to the Islamic militants they had nurtured for years, and could not believe that Musharraf would ally with the unreliable US against them. As Bob Woodward wrote in *Bush at War*: 'In so many words, Powell and Armitage [were] asking Pakistan to help destroy what its intelligence service had helped create and maintain: The Taliban.'

The army which used to send many of its officers to train in the US had become virulently anti-American, furious at how Washington had cut off support once the Russians had been ousted from Afghanistan. Many of them believed the US was behind the mysterious plane crash that killed Zia in 1988 along with many senior officers.

Musharraf told his generals that Pakistan had no choice but to cooperate with the US or be declared a terrorist state, and thus also attacked. He argued that if he refused to cooperate, then the great enemy India would step in and offer its bases to the US, and Pakistan's very existence could be threatened. The US would destroy Pakistan's military forces and take the opportunity to destroy its nuclear weapons. The Taliban were 'not worth committing suicide over', he said. He cited the example of them blowing up the Buddhas to point out that 'After they came to power we lost much of the leverage we had over them.'

As always in Pakistan, even the Buddha story had two versions. According to Mullah Zaeef, the Taliban Ambassador who accompanied the Pakistan delegation, General Haider warned Mullah Omar about the risks of continuing to shelter bin Laden. 'I am up to 80 per cent certain that the Americans will attack you,' he said. As Haider talked, Zaeef said, 'Mahmood leaned towards me and whispered, "What is this silly donkey talking about?"'[9]

Three days after 9/11, Musharraf telephoned Colin Powell, agreeing to accept his list of seven demands. These included allowing overflights, cutting all arms and fuel shipments to the Taliban and al Qaeda, and publicly condemning the terrorist acts. Less publicly, he allowed American forces to use four airbases in Baluchistan and Sindh, supposedly just for logistics. It later emerged from US Central Command that over 50,000 combat missions were flown out of these.

However, Musharraf made it clear that he had agreed to the US demands against public sentiment, and would need to show Pakistan was getting some benefit in return. For a start, he wanted the removal of all the sanctions imposed because of the country's nuclear programme and the coup. He also wanted the cancellation of its $3 billion debt to the US, and some F16s for his generals.

Ambassador Wendy Chamberlin went in to see him again on 15 September to seal the details. 'Everything he promised that day he did deliver,' she said. 'He didn't get everything he wanted, but nor did we. He wanted us to support their position on Kashmir – I said no. He wanted to make sure the Indian air force didn't overfly Pakistan, which we agreed, and absolutely no US combat troops in Pakistan. He did agree the use of airbases as well as over-flight rights. He also said, "We will help take down al Qaeda and the Taliban, but if there are any Pakistani citizens involved, you can't arrest them, we'll do that." It was one of the red lines.'

Within ten days of Musharraf's agreement, and just twelve days after 9/11, Bush had waived all sanctions against Pakistan and asked Congress to reschedule old loans and agree fresh loans of more than $600 million. Japan and the EU followed suit. Over the next few years Musharraf would get billions of dollars. The man whose name Bush had forgotten would end up being known as Bush's best friend.

But the lack of trust was still there on both sides. 'With Pakistan you get part of the story, never the whole story,' said Armitage. 'There are those who would say: "How do you know when Pakistanis are lying? Their lips are moving."'

The first indication that Musharraf might not be entirely on-side came just eight days after 9/11 with his public address to the nation. By then I was in Pakistan, and I watched eagerly to see what he would say. He made clear the pressure he was under. 'Pakistan is facing a very critical time,' he said. 'If we make any mistake they can culminate in very bad ends.' Yet he did not condemn the Taliban or al Qaeda, or blame them for 9/11, as he had agreed with Powell. 'He wanted to break with the Taliban,' says Armitage. 'But at that point we didn't want him to, as they were holding two American women [among eight foreign mission-aries arrested in August] and thought Pakistan could help.'

Others say Musharraf already thought he could play a double game, and fool the Americans just as Zia and ISI had in the 1980s. 'The ISI had become a mini CIA with Afghanistan,'[10] said Husain Haqqani, who was very familiar with the agency, having worked with them in 1988 to try to stop Benazir Bhutto coming to power, then ending up working for her, eventually becoming Pakistan's Ambassador in Washington from 2008 to 2011.

Bob Grenier, who was CIA station chief in Islamabad at the time of 9/11, was not surprised. 'Right from the start, I was convinced that the Pakistanis did not want to foreclose their options. They'd seen the Americans come and go in the past. They weren't at all sure they trusted Hamid Karzai. And irrespective of how they felt about him, I think there was probably a tendency to see him as a Pashtun face of what was really a Northern Alliance government. They were very distrustful, obviously, of the Northern Alliance.'[11]

Such was the lack of trust that while the US agreed no military action would start until General Mahmood's mission to see Mullah Omar in Kandahar, the CIA sent their own mission, led by Grenier, to meet one of Mullah Omar's representatives in Quetta. It had no more success.

The Taliban leadership was outraged at Musharraf's volte-face, but not surprised. Mullah Abdul Salam Zaeef was Ambassador to Pakistan at the time of 9/11, and became known as 'the Smiling Taliban' for his jovial 4 o'clock press briefings in his garden during the US bombing campaign. He said no Afghans really trusted ISI: 'The wolf and sheep may drink water from the same stream, but since the start of the jihad the ISI extended its roots deep into Afghanistan like a cancer. Every ruler complained about it, but none could get rid of it.'

Before the bombing campaign started three top ISI officers came to Saeef's house in Islamabad to pledge their support – General Mahmood, his deputy General Jailani, and Brigadier Farooq who ran the agency's Afghan desk. 'We want to assure you that you will not be alone in this jihad against America,' they told him. 'We will be with you.' Saeef was enraged. 'You speak of jihad while the Americans are stationed in your airbases and flying through your airspace, even attacking Afghanistan based on your intelligence reports!' he shouted. 'You should be ashamed to even utter the word jihad!' When he looked at General Mahmood, 'tears were running down his face'. As for Jailani, 'He was crying out loud with his arms around my neck like a woman.'

Shortly afterwards, all three were removed from their posts in what was described officially as 'normal military procedures'. General Mahmood was retired and replaced by General Ehsan ul Haq, whose instructions were to 'weed out the beards'. Brigadier Faruq and General Jailani were both transferred. Mahmood has never spoken about these events, but his friends told me he felt totally betrayed. Once I managed to speak to his wife by phone, and asked what her husband thought of Musharraf. 'How do you think he feels?' she replied angrily.

Mullah Zaeef said he was told that before they left their posts these ISI officers had burned documents regarding Afghanistan which the Americans had requested, and had advised Mullah Omar to find safe haven.

General Zia's son Ijaz-ul-Haq, who was in close contact with senior military and Taliban because of the respect in which they held his late father, predicted the changes at the top would make little difference. 'ISI chiefs only last one or two years anyway,' he told me. 'The real people running the game are the majors and colonels lower down, and they haven't switched sides. It isn't a matter of policy for them; it's a matter of belief.'

The Interior Minister General Haider agreed. 'It cannot be ruled out that some members of the intelligence services may have their sympathies with the other side. You see, since 1979 we had been actively helping and directing the Taliban along with the Americans against the Soviets. When suddenly a U-turn is taken, your [individual] contacts will remain.'[12]

The biggest indication of how deeply ISI were still involved came after General Mahmood had been transferred, in an episode that became known as 'the Airlift of Evil'. By mid-November 2001, the US bombing had forced the Taliban and al Qaeda out of Kabul and concentrated their fighters in two main areas – Kandahar in the south and Kunduz in the north. In Kunduz, al Qaeda fighters, along with thousands of Taliban under the command of Mullah Dadullah, had been surrounded by Northern Alliance forces from two rival commanders – Atta and his Tajik forces to the south, and

Dostum and his Uzbeks to the west. But they were refusing to surrender to these commanders, who they feared would slaughter them. Instead they sent radio messages offering to surrender to the US or the UN.

There was one other problem. Trapped with them were hundreds of ISI and Frontier Corps officers who had been sent from Pakistan to help. Musharraf phoned Bush and asked for a pause in the US bombing so that the Pakistani air force could rescue them. On 15 November Northern Alliance commanders told journalists that Pakistani planes had landed at Kunduz. This was strongly denied by Donald Rumsfeld and the Pentagon, and the foreign media were distracted by reporting the fall of Kabul. In fact, for each of the next few nights there were night-time rescues, and they were flying out not just ISI but also Taliban and al Qaeda.

When Kunduz finally fell to the Northern Alliance on 24 November, so many had been flown out that only 3,300 Taliban remained, about half what the CIA had estimated. Those men had been right to be worried about what would befall them. Most of them ended up packed into shipping containers, where they suffocated.

The Northern Alliance leadership was furious that once again the Americans had allowed Pakistan to say one thing and do something else. 'I don't know how much we understood of what we were getting into,' said Armitage. 'And attention was already moving elsewhere.'

The reality was that Washington's attention had shifted elsewhere. 'We rapidly moved on to Iraq,' said Richard Armitage. 'Frankly, we didn't care much about Afghanistan. We didn't have a strategy for Afghanistan. Rumsfeld wanted to pull out of there early on. We would have been perfectly willing to let the Taliban sit it out if they'd stopped helping the Arabs.'

7

Taliban Central

THE ADDITIONAL SECRETARY Home and Tribal Affairs for Baluchistan was fed up. 'Look at all these files, it's rubbish!' he barked. 'This whole building is filled with rubbish!'

I could hardly disagree. Every available surface was covered with tottering piles of dusty files spewing out yellowing papers, and from adjoining offices came the sound of clattering typewriters churning out more. A stream of men wandered in and out, bringing files back and forth containing carbon-copied letters to be signed and placed in other files.

'You people did this,' he said, waving his hands. In fact, I suspected things hadn't really changed since colonial days, though I wasn't sure if he meant the bureaucracy, or if he was gesturing at the map on the wall. It was a large hand-drawn map of the region on which the land north of Afghanistan was marked 'Russian Dominions', while that to the west was 'Caucasia'. Some parts had been shaded in different colours, and there was an explanatory key code at the bottom: Red = Tribes in Baluchistan; Blue = Pathan in Pakistan and Afghanistan; and, confusingly, Blue [though a slightly different blue] = Miscellaneous Tribes in Iran.

A gold-lettered wooden board over the Additional Secretary's desk showed that no one stayed long in the post. Humayun Khan was the eleventh occupant in fourteen years, and that included several long periods for which the board was inscribed 'Post Vacant', as if that were a person's name.

I was trying to get something called a No Objection Certificate (NOC) to permit me to travel through the tribal areas to the Afghan border, and he was the only person who could grant one. However, he had a thick blue file which he explained was on me. 'What are these "undesirable activities"?' he asked, leafing through it. 'You are a terror! More, more undesirable activities,' he intoned. 'Undesirable activities, I suppose they are one of the great indefinables, like national interest or supreme national interest. Frankly, Mrs Lamb, I am surprised you are back in Baluchistan.'

So was I. It was less than ten weeks since my previous stay had come to an abrupt halt when I'd been woken up by ISI banging on the door of my room in the Serena Hotel at 2 a.m. Probably the last place on earth I wanted to be was back in Quetta, particularly on my own. However, I had spent the previous few weeks in Kandahar, where I learned that when the Taliban surrendered this, their final stronghold, without a shot on 7 December 2001, they had fled to the Pakistan border in their thousands. There they were met by ISI officials and Frontier Constabulary who shepherded them to camps, madrassas or houses in a suburb of Quetta known as Satellite Town, and told them to lay low. The B52s may have driven the Taliban out of Afghanistan in less than sixty days, but in their view they had only lost the battle, not the war.

Among them were most of the leadership, who would come to be known as the Quetta *shura*. My friend Dr Umar, who used to run reception committees for Arabs coming to fight in the jihad, had close connections with senior Taliban. He offered to take me for tea with some of the ministers, and I had no intention of passing up the chance. The problem was how to do it without being caught by ISI. The agency received a list of every foreigner who flew into Quetta or checked into any of the few hotels, and as a tall, blonde Englishwoman, if I took the bus from Karachi I would be very conspicuous.

My plan was to go to Quetta openly, stating that I was on my way to Kandahar, just over the border. This would also give me a chance to talk to people in the frontier towns of Chaman and Spin Boldak. I would cross over legally, then sneak back into Pakistan using the old mujaheddin trails. ISI would assume I was in Afghanistan.

It wasn't a great plan, and frankly I was terrified. It also depended on me getting an NOC, and this depended on the crotchety Additional Secretary. A series of phone calls got me nowhere, and I had been forced to check back into the Serena.

I didn't get much sleep, for there was a picture I couldn't get out of my head. Two weeks earlier, on 23 January 2002, an American reporter named Daniel Pearl from the *Wall Street Journal* had been kidnapped in Karachi while investigating links between militant groups and Richard Reid, the British shoe bomber. Just before I travelled to Quetta an email had been sent to news organisations with photos of a frightened Pearl in shackles with a gun to his head, and a warning for all American journalists in Pakistan to leave within three days.

The sender was the 'National Movement for the Restoration of Pakistani Sovereignty', a group that nobody had heard of, and they seemed to have strange demands. Apart from the release of 177 Pakistanis being held in Guantánamo, they were demanding the delivery of American F16 fighter jets purchased by Pakistan in 1989 but never handed over. I'd never heard of a terrorist group demanding F16 jets. However, anyone who had spent much time in Pakistan knew that the F16s are a national obsession. The issue was frequently raised in newspaper editorials, and the jets vied with Bollywood stars as the favourite thing to paint on the colourfully decorated Bedford trucks that transport goods around the country. Most of all they were an obsession of Pakistan's powerful generals, for whom they were a festering sore in relations with Washington.

The issue went back to the late 1980s, when Pakistan and the US had been going through a good patch in relations (or at least shared a common interest), working together to train and arm the Afghan mujaheddin to oust the Russians. In 1989 Pakistan had ordered twenty-eight F16s from the American company General Dynamics for $22 million each. But in 1990, before the planes could be shipped, the sale was cancelled by Congress because of reports that US jets bought by the military ruler General Zia in 1983 had been modified to carry nuclear warheads. The departure of the Soviet Union from Afghanistan in 1989 meant the US was no longer prepared to turn a blind eye to Pakistan's nuclear activities, and the F16s were sent to a facility in the Arizona desert known as 'the boneyard'. Not only did the US refuse to reimburse the $656 million paid by Pakistan to American defence contractors, but to add insult to injury they also charged it for storage. The episode left Pakistan's generals convinced that Americans couldn't be trusted. They only got the money reimbursed by the Clinton administration a decade later after they hired former White House lawyer Lanny Davis. But really they wanted the planes.

'It's either ISI or someone wanting to make it look like ISI,' said Umar when the kidnappers' demands circulated.

Pakistan is a land of conspiracy. Everyone I met told me that ISI had encouraged the kidnapping of Pearl to discourage other foreign journalists from investigating the country's murkier links. If that was so, they had been pretty successful. When I had last stayed in Quetta two months earlier, the Serena had been so packed with journalists that some were even paying to rent the laundry cupboard or to sleep on the floor of the ballroom. This time it was empty.

I had no intention of spending more time in Quetta than necessary. So that morning when I got into the Additional Secretary's office, I was determined that I would not leave without the NOC in my hand.

It seemed clear that the real problem was that no one wanted to take responsibility. While the Additional Secretary was complaining to me, another carbon-copied letter came down from the section officer upstairs, this time on green paper. 'Regarding Mrs Christina Lamb,' it stated. 'The NOC could be issued or otherwise.'

Mr Khan pushed it aside. 'The only reason you Britishers are successful is because of the cold weather,' he said. 'I went to Britain once, to Brighton and Blackpool. It wasn't worth it,' he added dismissively.

I had no idea which way he was leaning, when suddenly he reached for his pen. 'If no one else wants to take responsibility I suppose I'll have to use my discretion,' he said.

After a second near-sleepless night in the Serena, I couldn't believe it when I woke the next morning to snow – the first in Quetta for fifteen years. Everyone in town was happy, because it meant the end of drought. I was worried the snow would trap me in the Serena for more sleepless nights, but Umar turned up as promised with his ambulance, in which we would travel to the border. 'It's good luck for your trip,' he said, smiling. He may have spoken too soon. By the time we collected the guards assigned by Mr Khan's office and headed towards the Khojak Pass, the snow was falling quite thickly, coating the hills and making the way treacherous.

The road to the border follows the railway from Quetta to the border town of Chaman, built by the British in the 1880s, after the Second Anglo–Afghan War. The railway was clearly intended to go into Afghanistan – to the fury of King Abdur Rahman, who described it as 'like pushing a knife into my vitals', and forbade his subjects from travelling on it. It is an incredible feat of engineering, snaking in and out of the pass via tunnels through the mountains, including the longest one in South Asia, which is commemorated on Pakistan's five-rupee note.

Even without snow it is inhospitable terrain, and it was perhaps a Baluch idea of a joke to give the towns along the way inappropriate names. There is Gulistan, which means 'place of flowers' and has none; Fort Jilla, which has no fort; and Chaman, which means 'fruit garden', yet nothing grows there. Most poignant was Sheilabagh, supposedly named after the wife of the chief engineer. Apparently he'd made a bet with the engineer working from the other end of the line that the two tunnels would meet on a certain date. When they didn't, he committed suicide. The tunnels met the next day.

As we climbed above Sheilabagh the ambulance wheels started slipping and sliding. Umar had no idea how to drive on ice, and kept braking. I tried not to look over the side of the pass, with its precipitous drop. When we finally managed to slip and slide further up the road, we found the way blocked by painted trucks, one heavily overloaded with logs and the other with bright-coloured cloths and mattresses spilling out. Men were shouting unhelpful advice and occasionally pushing.

I jumped out of the ambulance, causing everything to stop, foreign women being rare in these parts, when suddenly an army jeep drove up. Inside were two Pishin Scouts, members of one of the regiments of the paramilitary Frontier Corps originally set up by the British to control smuggling and the border. They got the trucks moved, and one of the officers, Captain Mubashar, gallantly came to my rescue. 'I will take memsahib in my 4x4,' he said.

On the way he told me they had spent the night before on foot patrol in the mountains, looking for al Qaeda. It was very difficult, and so far the Pishin Scouts had caught just four Arabs. 'It's a very long and porous border and they still have lots of money to pay locals,' he explained. 'What about Taliban?' I asked. Had he seen them coming across the border when Kandahar fell? 'They have switched from black turbans to white and are tricky to spot,' he laughed.

Captain Mubashar told me that before 9/11 the Scouts' main work was stopping smuggling. When I admired a particularly elaborate painted truck, jingling with chains, he said, 'Behind the rose is a thorn.' He explained that the intricate paintings and metalwork often hide cavities in which contraband is hidden – sometimes opium, but also imported Japanese electronics, or just cloth or fruit to avoid duty. Some trucks have as many as twenty cavities. 'Once I saw a truck of goats which didn't look right,' he said. 'The goats looked too tall.' When he opened the truck he found it had a false floor, with a whole level below.

Captain Mubashar and his colleagues had been so successful in catching smugglers that the previous year they had sent 550 million rupees in duties and fines to the federal government. But the local tribesmen were furious, and revolted, blocking the road and killing three soldiers. 'It's the only industry,' he explained.

'There are no factories, and nothing grows, even the apple orchard dried up, so everyone smuggles, even children of five or six have contraband in their pockets.' In the end they decided to turn a blind eye to the small stuff. But he admitted they had little success in intercepting drugs. 'They are transported over the mountains on unmanned donkeys which are trained to be terrified of anyone dressed in dark clothes.' The Frontier Corps wear charcoal *shalwar kamiz*. 'They run like mad when we come.'

In Captain Mubashar's view, the lack of alternative sources of income, combined with the area's traditional hostility to foreigners and the Pashtunwali honour code, which means strangers must be protected, made it extremely unlikely that any local would cooperate in handing over Taliban or al Qaeda.

I heard the same in the scruffy border town of Chaman, where he left me with Nasibullah, the head of the levies, the local tribal force set up in British times. Nasibullah was sitting in a room with walls painted baby pink with a bottle-green stripe all the way round and dominated by a vast Sony TV which looked suspiciously like the smuggled goods in the trucks we had passed. Around him, their eyes glued to the screen, was a gaggle of men with orange henna-stained beards. Also on the wall were three gilt-framed black-and-white photographs – Nasibullah's late grandfather, first head of the levies; his father, who came next; and himself. 'You Britishers created us, then left us orphans,' he said.

Pashtun hospitality dictates that no visitor can leave without food, however much of a hurry they might be in. A servant laid a plastic cloth on the floor then brought in huge, steaming bowls of fatty lamb and a foot-long strip of stretchy nan bread. A plastic jug of water and a dirty towel were passed around for us to wash and dry our hands. The men then began to tear off the bread and scoop up the meat, eating lustily, with loud smacking noises. I tried to avoid the gristle and globules of fat, and to make it look as if I was eating more than I was, something I had perfected after years of practice.

Nasibullah told me that his uncle was head of the Achakzai, one of the tribes that straddles the border. I asked if they thought of themselves as Pakistanis or Afghans. 'We've been Pashtuns 5,000 years, Muslims 1,400 years, then Pakistanis just fifty years,' he replied. 'You Britishers with your Colonel Durand divided our tribe. The real Afghan border should be a hundred kilometres south of Quetta, not this fake line of Durand.'

He told me that his men had arrested three al Qaeda they had found being treated in the local hospital and taken them to the authorities in Quetta, but later heard they escaped. As for Taliban, he said that Abdul Razzaq, the Interior Minister, and other senior Taliban were sheltering in the local madrassa run by Abdul Ghani, deputy to Maulana Fazlur Rehman, head of one of Pakistan's main religious parties, Jamiat Ulema-e-Islam (JuI).

What about Osama bin Laden? 'As long as he stays in our tribal areas he will not be found, because he is protected by Pashtunwali,' he replied. But the Americans had announced a $25 million reward. Wouldn't that tempt people? I asked. 'That doesn't matter, because most people think he was fighting for Islam,' he said. 'Anyway, it's too much money. Nobody here understands what that means. They would have been better off offering a herd of goats.'

The last few miles to the border were full of people selling things by the wayside. An old man with an emerald-green turban and a long white beard was crouched on his haunches the way Pashtuns seem to be able to sit all day, with a cockerel in each hand like balancing scales.

It was almost dark when I finally reached the border post. There was a stream of bearded men blatantly walking to one side of it rather than through. Inside, a white-haired man was sitting at a desk. He looked relieved to see me. 'Ah, Christina Lamb, I have been waiting for you,' he said, unfolding a typed carbon copy, headed 'Deletion of Mrs Christina Lamb from Exit Control List'. 'I was worried you would slip over my border and I would lose my job of twenty years.'

* * *

GETTING IN

The first thing that went wrong with my plan to sneak back into Quetta was that the new border office in Spin Boldak on the Afghan side tried to take all my money in bribes. The passport office consisted of a group of men lounging on cushions in a smoky room, drinking green tea and inventing ways to extract money from the few people who passed through legally.

'$200 by order of the Governor for security,' demanded one of them.

'I don't need security,' I replied.

'It is not a choice.'

'$200 for a car,' came next.

'I've already got a car,' I protested.

'It's for the security guards,' was the reply.

'Also $50 entry fee by order of the Foreign Ministry.'

'I already have a visa,' I pointed out.

'That's for Afghanistan, not for Kandahar.'

'I'm a journalist, and this is not giving a very good impression of the new Afghanistan,' I said in exasperation.

This prompted some heated Pashto discussion which I could not follow, but I assumed they were reassessing their extortion. I was wrong.

'Journalist. $100 for press,' said one of the men. 'If you have camera and phone there will be more charges.'

'What? Where is this written?' I began to lose patience. 'Look, I'm a friend of President Hamid Karzai, and I don't think he would be very happy you are making up all these charges.'

They laughed heartily. 'Karzai, who is he?' said one.

It all took so long that when I finally got back outside my driver had disappeared. 'He's a hashish smoker and gone to the place where they smoke hashish,' the guard told me helpfully.

No wonder most people just wandered to the side of the border posts. If Afghan democracy came with endless shakedowns I began to understand why people had initially welcomed the Taliban.

* * *

Back in Quetta, this time hidden under a burqa and staying in the curtained-off purdah quarters of a friend's house, I received a coded message in a telephone call shortly after breakfast on the second day. 'The carpet has arrived,' said a voice. 'It's a very valuable one, and we can't keep it here long for security reasons.'

Haste is a relative concept in Pakistan, and it was four hours before the car arrived to pick me up. We drove past the bus station, where a man was holding a muddy pelican on a string, and through the bazaar. I was told to go inside a tailor's shop with shelves lined with giant rolls of dress material. A door at the back led out onto a rubbish-strewn alley where a man on a motor-bike was waiting. We sped down a few roads and into a small mud-walled compound, the home of a local religious leader. I was beckoned into the women's quarters, where a couple of women lifted my burqa over my head. Finally a bearded old man in a swan-white turban summoned me through the dividing curtain into a room with a large roaring fire. Inside, two men were sitting on floor cushions – the two Taliban Ministers who had agreed to meet me.

It was the strangest feeling. For most of the five months since 9/11 I had been in Pakistan and Afghanistan writing about the evil Taliban regime and meeting one after another of its victims. I had met Hazara women whose husbands had been burned to death in front of their eyes, a Kandahari footballer whose hand was cut off in a public amputation at which officials then discussed whether to also chop off a foot, and a man who had worked as a torturer and was trying to devise ever more cruel tortures.

For a moment I was taken aback. These were some of the world's most wanted men, but with their beards trimmed short, they looked surprisingly young. I knew the Taliban leadership were mostly in their thirties, but somehow I had thought of them as bigger and older – and more malevolent.

One of the pair, Maulana Abdullah Sahadi, the former Deputy Defence Minister, was only twenty-eight, and looked vulnerable and slightly scared, greeting me with a wonky Johnny Depp-like smile. He told me it was the first time he had ventured out of his hiding place since escaping Afghanistan after the fall of Kandahar two months earlier.

The other Minister, a burly man in his mid-thirties who had agreed to meet me only on condition of anonymity, was responsible for some of the acts that have most horrified the Western world, and looked defiant. After a while we were joined by the Director General of the Passport Office who had issued Afghan visas to some of the Arab fighters who were on America's most-wanted list.

'You see, we don't have two horns,' said the older Minister with a smile as he poured me tea from a golden teapot and offered me boiled sweets. 'Now anyone can say anything about us and the world will believe it. People have been saying we skinned their husbands alive and ate babies, and you people print it.'

We started off talking about how they had joined the Taliban. Maulana Sahadi told me his family had moved to a refugee camp in Quetta when he was just five after his father, a mujahid with Gulbuddin Hekmatyar's Hezb-i-Islami, was killed fighting the Russians. The family was very poor, surviving much of the time on bread begged or bought with money earned from sewing carpets, so his mother was pleased when he got a place at a madrassa at the age of eight. His food, board and books were all provided. At some point he learned to use a Kalashnikov, though he would not say at what age, claiming, 'A gun is such a thing, one day you use it, the next day you master it.'

In mid-1994 a delegation of elders and *ulema*, or religious scholars, from Pakistan came to the madrassa. 'They issued a *fatwa* telling us we must join the Taliban and fight jihad. I joined with a group of friends from the madrassa, so we were there right at the very beginning, in the first attack on Spin Boldak that October. At that time we were only about a hundred people. We were killing men and many of our companions were martyred, but we were happy because we were doing it for Islam. We were the soldiers of God.'

Sahadi went on to fight in battles all over Afghanistan, including Herat, Mazar-i-Sharif, Kunduz and Bamiyan, commanding five hundred men, then 2,500, then becoming Director of Defence. 'I would motivate my troops before fighting by telling them that if they were martyred they would go to paradise and could take with them seventy-two of their family members.' He got on well with Mullah Omar, whom he described as 'a very nice, good-natured person with good morals. He treated me like a son. Whoever came to him, he treated with respect.'

Eventually, in 1999, Sahadi became Deputy Defence Minister to Mullah Obaidullah. As such he had frequent personal contact with bin Laden, though he insisted that 'the Arabs were not controlling things. Anyone who supports Islam was welcome in our country – we had British, Americans, Australians.'

Sahadi told me how during the American bombing offensive, he and his colleagues had to keep changing houses in Kandahar to avoid being hit. But he said the Taliban leadership never contemplated handing over bin Laden to save themselves. 'He was a guest in our country, and we gave him refuge because hospitality is an important part of our code of behaviour. Besides, he was supporting us, giving us money, when no one else was.' He also complained that the Americans had not given the evidence they had asked for to show bin Laden's complicity in the 9/11 attacks: 'The Taliban leadership do not believe the Twin Towers attack was carried out by al Qaeda. According to my own opinion, the attack was wrong. It is not Islamic to kill innocent people like that.'

The other Minister interjected. 'What this war is really about is a clash between Islam and infidels. America wants to implement its own *kafir* religion in Afghanistan. We are the real defenders of Islam, not people like Gul Agha [the Governor of Kandahar] and Hamid Karzai. They are puppets of America.'

But why, then, did the Taliban collapse so easily? 'We're not broken, we're whole,' insisted Sahadi. 'We weren't defeated, we agreed to hand over rather than fight and spill blood. Our people went back to their tribes or left the country. Now we are just waiting. Karzai cannot even trust his own people to guard the presidential palace, but has to have American troops. We are regrouping. We still have arms and many supporters inside, and when the time is right we will be back.'

How had they escaped Afghanistan? 'We shaved off our beards, changed our turbans from white Taliban to Kandahari [green or black with thin white stripes], got in cars and drove on the road across the border. My beard was as long as this,' he said, gesturing down to his chest. Among those who had headed across the border were Mullah Turabi, the Justice Minister; Abdul Razzak, the Interior Minister; Qadratuallah Jamal, the Culture Minister; Mullah Obaidullah Akhund, the Defence Minister; and Mullah Baradar, deputy to Mullah Omar. The local Pakistani authorities, he claimed, not only turned a blind eye but helped.

'Thank God this war happened, because now we really know who is with us and who is against us,' added Sahadi. 'Karzai went to the other camp. Once he pretended he was with us, but now we see he just wanted power. They will all be brought before justice and punished according to Islamic law. The Americans are celebrating victory, but they have failed. They have not caught bin Laden or Mullah Omar. All they have done is oust our government. We never did anything to them. Mullah Omar is still in Afghanistan [between Uruzgan and Helmand], and will stay there making contact with those commanders unhappy with the new government. You will see Islam will win out and we will break the Americans into pieces as we did with the Russians and, *inshallah*, bring back the name of the Taliban.'

I was intrigued, but feared lingering longer in case word of my presence got back to the authorities. The nameless Taliban smiled as I left. 'You see, unlike you people, we are not in a hurry.'

A week later I was back in Kabul, and went to the headquarters of the ISAF peacekeeping forces, then under the command of the British general John McColl. I asked what they thought about Taliban living freely in Pakistan. They weren't much use, pointing out that they weren't allowed outside Kabul, and their job was 'stabilisation', not to hunt down militants – that was down to Operation Enduring Freedom, the US forces.

So I went to see the Americans. If I could find Taliban Ministers, then surely they could. Yet by that point only one senior Taliban had been arrested – Mullah Abdul Wakil Muttawakil, the Taliban's Foreign Minister; and that was only because he surrendered to Afghan officials in Kandahar. He had actually offered to cooperate with the US forces, but instead they imprisoned him in Bagram, which no doubt deterred other Taliban from coming forward.[1]

Nobody seemed interested. The Taliban was gone, as far as they were concerned. 'If these are senior Taliban officials, maybe the Pakistani authorities should be arresting them,' shrugged one US official. 'Frankly there was no great interest on the part of the Pakistanis in catching Taliban, and it wasn't our priority,' said Bob Grenier, who was CIA station chief in Pakistan at the time. 'I suppose we might have kicked and screamed and held our breath and demanded "By God you've got to get these guys," but that might actually have undermined our efforts in what was for us the greatest priority, and where we already had their active coopera-tion, which was al Qaeda. I didn't see any particular reason to do that.'

The lack of will to do anything about the Taliban was infuriat-ing President Karzai. He told me he had even given the Americans the names and addresses of Taliban in Quetta. Both he and his Foreign Minister Abdullah Abdullah had used their visit to Washington in January to ask the Bush administration to pressure Pakistan. 'I told the Americans I know the Taliban leaders are in Pakistan,' said Abdullah. 'But they were only interested in al Qaeda, and for that they believed they needed Musharraf.'

After going to Washington, Abdullah went to see Musharraf. 'He told me, "ISI is now under my control, previous governments didn't control it but I've sacked eighty people." Then he told me his brother was visiting from the US, and said he's a very free kind of person who likes to travel and wanted to go to Kabul. Musharraf said, "I told him no, it's not safe," but then said, "I'll send him in a bus with my ISI." I couldn't believe he was so blatant.'

* * *

The very week I was meeting Taliban in Pakistan, Musharraf was being fêted in Washington on his second visit since 9/11. He met Vice President Dick Cheney and had lunch with President Bush at the White House. 'President Musharraf is a leader with great courage and vision,' said Bush. 'I am proud to call him my friend.'

On 12 February 2002, while Musharraf was in Washington, the Pakistan government announced that it had arrested a British-born Pakistani called Omar Saeed Sheikh for the kidnapping of Daniel Pearl. A graduate of the London School of Economics, this was not the first time twenty-seven-year-old Sheikh had been involved in a kidnapping. He had served time in an Indian jail for the kidnap of four Western tourists in Delhi in 1994. Pretending to be a local, he had befriended the three British and one American travellers and invited them to what he said was his village. They were freed by Indian police and he was jailed till 1999, when he was released in exchange for 155 hostages on an Indian Airlines plane that had been hijacked to Kandahar.

Mysteriously, Sheikh turned out to have been staying with retired ISI brigadier Ejaz Shah for a week before being handed over to Pakistani police working with the FBI hunting for Pearl in Karachi. Nobody explained why Shah did not turn him in earlier. The CIA believed Sheikh had been working for ISI. Even once he was in police custody, it was a month before the FBI were allowed to interview him. By then it was too late. What we didn't know when Sheikh's arrest was announced was that the thirty-eight-year-old Pearl was already dead. Nine days later, on 21 February, a video was handed to the US Embassy entitled 'The Slaughter of the Spy-Journalist, the Jew Daniel Pearl'. The horrific footage, showing a knife slitting Pearl's throat and beheading him, was the first al Qaeda execution recorded on video.[2] It ended with the captors demanding the release of all Muslim prisoners at Guantánamo Bay, and warning that if their demands were not met they would repeat the scene 'again and again'.

Pakistan refused to extradite Sheikh. When asked about this, Musharraf said, 'Perhaps Daniel Pearl was over-intrusive. A media person should be aware of the dangers of getting into dangerous areas. Unfortunately he got over-involved.'

Pakistani generals were astonished that the US hadn't committed more troops to Afghanistan, and that they had allowed bin Laden and so many al Qaeda fighters to escape. Throughout 2002, ISI sent memos to Musharraf saying that the Americans were clearly not interested in Afghanistan and would soon leave, and that the Taliban should be kept as an option.

In February 2003 Mullah Omar emerged from silence with a letter faxed to a Pakistani newspaper, calling on all Afghans to rise up against the Americans and the Karzai government: 'The Afghans should abandon the ranks of America, the crusaders and their allies, and should immediately start a jihad. Vacate all offices, ministries, provinces so that the distinction between a Muslim and a crusader is made.'

A few weeks later I went back to Quetta, and found the Taliban were no longer in hiding. World attention had moved on to Iraq, where the US was poised to invade any day, and the city had become Taliban Central.

Umar took me to Mizan Chowk, a busy square. Men in black turbans, their eyes lined with black kohl, wandered about openly, exchanging the typical lengthy Pashto greetings. Newsstands openly sold Taliban CDs and tapes, including one of Mullah Omar's speech.

We visited the New Muslim Speeches Music Shop, which displayed posters and stickers depicting grenades, handheld rocket launchers and other jihadi weapons of choice, imprinted with slogans calling for youth to rise up against the West. Inside were a group of younger men with tightly wound turbans and trousers cropped way above the ankle, which was typical of Taliban. They seemed galvanised by Mullah Omar's call to arms. 'We fought before to liberate our country, and we will fight again,' said one. 'Now it is time to expel these infidels from our land.' They told us that they had been in Kandahar when the bombing started, and had come into Pakistan – white flags were flown near the border to tell them it was safe to cross.

One told us that ISI was giving them satellite phones, Toyota pick-ups and motorbikes. Once again the agency was running training camps, just as it had during the jihad in the 1980s, and bringing in arms shipments and funds from the Gulf.

I was fascinated and wanted to talk longer, but my presence was drawing attention, and Umar was growing nervous. He pointed out a car with dark-tinted windows that had stopped nearby.

Later we heard that Taliban commanders were being threatened that if they did not return to the fight, ISI would hand them over to the Americans, and they'd end up in Guantánamo.

After I wrote about what I had seen, Pakistan's Embassies started excluding Quetta when they issued visas to journalists. 'It's for your own safety,' said the smiling Press Minister at the High Commission in London. 'But I have friends in Quetta who will keep me safe,' I pleaded, to no avail. The handful of other journalists who sneaked in were beaten up or arrested, like my good friend Marc Epstein from the French magazine *L'Express* and his photographer Jean-Paul Guilloteau, who were picked up in December 2003 and held for almost a month. Their fixer Khawar Mehdi Rizvi was accused of sedition, conspiracy and impersonation of Taliban, and was tortured while in jail. He later went into exile in the US, as many Pakistanis have been forced to do.

Next time I got a visa it was stamped 'Islamabad Only'. 'No country in the world issues visas just for the capital city,' I protested.

Back home, I met up with an old friend from ISI in a south-west London bistro full of yummy mummies and ladies who lunch. 'We never had this conversation,' he said as we started our soup. 'What you have to understand is everything we do to cooperate with the Americans there are others who work in the opposite way.' He referred to what he called 'the shadow organisation' – the first time I heard about the so-called 'Sector S' – explaining that Pakistan needed to keep its options open, so ISI had an entire group of people who were officially retired, perhaps heading 'welfare organi-sations', but were still training and advising Taliban. 'It's all about deniability,' he said. If any of them were caught, they would be shrugged off as 'rogue elements'.

My soup got cold as I sat open-mouthed, wondering if Pakistan really could pull the wool over the eyes of the world's most powerful country. 'Does Mullah Omar even exist?' I asked.

'There is a man with one eye and limited intelligence called Mullah Omar, if that's what you mean,' he chuckled. 'You saw what happened to Danny Pearl,' he said, as all around us the bistro tinkled with the laughter of gossiping women and small children and sunlight. 'If I were you, I would know this: I would eat my lunch and I would investigate no further.'

8

Merchants of Ruin –
the Return of the Warlords

Jalalabad, 2002

HAZRAT ALI WAS eager to show off his new toy, a top-of-the-range Toyota Land Cruiser. He had left the factory plastic wrapping on the tan leather seats so they did not get sullied by the gunmen he always travelled with. 'Look!' he said, jolting us all in our seats as he fired the vehicle dramatically into reverse. The sensor beeped insistently as it tried to cope with warning of old men on bicycles, chickens, a stray goat, a beggar on stumps and all the usual mêlée of an Afghan street. Best of all was the flashing computer console on the dashboard, with satellite TV and GPS. The only problem was, it was programmed in Japanese, and there were no maps available for Afghanistan.

Hazrat Ali didn't care. Perhaps because their own land is so devoid of modernity and so drained of colour, Afghan commanders adore glitter and gizmos. In the days of the war against the Soviets in the 1980s it was flashing fairy lights round the windscreen, or my personal favourite, a brake pedal which when pressed intoned 'Bismillah' – In the name of Allah.

The paymaster for Hazrat Ali's latest car was the same – and as they always did back then, he had hung a sickly-sweet pine-tree air freshener from the rear-view mirror – but this was a whole new scale of warlord gadgetry. Black Toyota SUVs were the vehicle of choice of Third World militias, and he had just taken delivery of a fleet of six spanking-new ones, cementing his status as the biggest warlord in Jalalabad.

I was sitting in the restaurant of the gloomy Spinghar Hotel, staring at the one-item lunch menu – 'Chicken kerahi or not' – with my gloomy interpreter Dr Rais when we heard a vehicle roar up outside. It had a Dubai number plate, and I could tell it was one of Hazrat Ali's as it had a large poster on the back of the late Ahmat Shah Massoud, the Northern Alliance leader for whom he had fought. Out jumped five men in khakis clutching AK47s and grenade launchers, walking straight past the 'No Kalashnikovs' sign at the hotel entrance. They were my escort.

We sped through the city, which it was hard to imagine had once been the winter capital of the royal family, a place of palm trees and orange groves. The old palaces were all in ruins, but Dr Rais pointed out the tomb of King Habibullah, the son of Abdur Rahman. Like most Afghan Kings, he had been assassinated – in his case while on a hunting trip nearby in 1919. The garden was over-grown and scattered with old iron bedsteads and chairs, among which some men were scavenging for anything they might sell. 'The merchants of ruin,' sighed Dr Rais poetically.

In the distance we could see the Tora Bora mountains where Osama bin Laden had last been seen. Since then his only manifestation was on the occasional video or tape recording.

It was because of bin Laden that Hazrat Ali, at thirty-eight, and with three wives to support, was experiencing such a change in fortune. Barely able to read or write, he was from the small Pashai tribe, which was looked down on by the local Pashtuns. Behind his back they called him *'shurrhi'*, which means stupid mountain man. He didn't care. Marshal Fahim, the Defence Minister, had named him military commander for Jalalabad; he claimed to have 18,000 men under his control; and more importantly, he had the most powerful backer of all.

Back at his house, two visitors had arrived. I was shown into the living room. Hazrat Ali was sitting cross-legged on the floor, sucking salted pomegranate pips that shone like rubies in a dish and click-clacking a string of blue prayer beads, lapis from the mountains of Badakshan. Next to him was a satellite phone.

His visitors were two Americans, squatting awkwardly on the floor cushions with a black briefcase in front of them. One was pale, grey-bearded and blue-eyed, the other olive-skinned and black-bearded, with thickly muscled arms and Oakley sunglasses. I recognised the pair immediately. They had been staying in the building behind the Mustafa Hotel in Kabul which had been taken over by the CIA/special forces operations team Taskforce 121, who were looking for bin Laden.

Hazrat Ali handed them a lined A4 sheet of paper torn from a notebook. It was a list of names. In return they slid over the briefcase. He popped open the catch and allowed himself a thin smile. Inside were stacks of $100 bills.

Similar transactions were going on all over the country. In the hunt for bin Laden and al Qaeda the CIA was totally reliant on local informers. President Bush had demanded bin Laden 'dead or alive', and the Agency had $1 billion to spend, putting some 45,000 warlords on the payroll.

There was one major flaw. 'How do you know they're al Qaeda?' I asked the Americans later. 'Those names are probably just Hazrat Ali's enemies and rivals.' I had spent the previous evening at the house of Haji Zahir, a rival commander, who told me, 'If there are five houses in a Pashtun village, at least three will have feuds.' No wonder Hazrat Ali was smiling. He could get one of his enemies taken out by an American bomb, and be paid for it. There were even stories of one group of US special forces almost calling in an airstrike on another group because they were with rival warlords.

The Americans didn't seem to care. They told me his list would be entered into the big Harmony computer at Bagram. The names would also be cross-checked with what they called 'the 1267', the sacred list of bad guys they all carried around with them, which some referred to as the kill-list. Some of those on Hazrat Ali's list would end up in prison in Bagram or at Guantánamo.

Outside, his men glowered. Some were missing limbs, and several had eyes lined with kohl, and wildflowers tied onto their Kalashnikovs.

Most of them knew nothing but fighting. One told me he only went to school till the age of eight, then joined the mujaheddin. A year later, some of these men would feature in a report issued by Human Rights Watch entitled 'Killing You is Very Easy for Us'.[1] It carries interviews with people claiming that Hazrat Ali's commanders ran a reign of terror in the province, keeping secret prisons, raping young boys, making arbitrary arrests and demanding bribes to release people. It alleged that anyone who refused to do his bidding was warned that he would call down American B52s on them.

The Americans were shocked that I was travelling around on my own, and offered me a lift to Kabul. Against my better instincts I accepted. Four foreign journalists had recently been killed on the road – their names were on a plaque put up by colleagues at the Spinghar Hotel. As I climbed into the back seat I saw the glint of a Glock pistol strapped on the thigh of one of them. 'Bet you've never felt so safe,' he grinned.

Actually, I didn't. I usually travelled very low-profile, in a battered vehicle, often wearing a burqa so as not to be identifiable as a foreigner to anyone watching from the roadside. The Americans would never look like Afghans, however much facial hair they grew, and they seemed very conspicuous to me. The pistols made me uncomfortable. I almost missed my hashish-smoking driver from my last trip along this road, whom I had christened 'Easy Dent' after we had smashed into another car and he had laughed, 'No problem, easy dent.'

I never tired of this road. The tarmac had long disintegrated under columns of Soviet tanks and American bombing, and it was now almost entirely hole. But I loved the way it lulled one into a false sense of security by starting with soft painted scenes of green fields, watered by the turquoise Kabul River, papyrus grass blowing in the wind and occasional flashes of colour as young girls in pink and red passed with jugs of water on their heads, heading to mud-brick villages. On a patch of dusty ground a group of boys were playing cricket using a pile of balanced stones as a wicket. The mountains in the distance looked like crumpled paper.

Then, with the city no longer in sight in the back window, you round a corner and the landscape changes dramatically to grey, pebble-strewn mountains. The road becomes a switchback of hair-pin bends between towering granite cliffs that lean on each other, goats perched precariously on ledges. I thought about the thousands of British troops and followers retreating this way in the wintry January of 1842 at the end of the First Anglo–Afghan War and being picked off by the tribals on the hillside until only Dr Bryden was left to tell the tale.

As we bumped along, the younger of the two Americans told me, 'We've been handing out a lot of dosh to commanders. In J-bad [Americans seemed unwilling to allot more than two syllables to any Afghan town, so had abbreviated them all] this commander told us he'd captured a computer with phone numbers of all the bad guys. He asked for $100,000. It turned out to be a videophone he'd stolen from CNN. The only numbers were for their editors.'

The car lurched back and forth as the driver negotiated the remains of a bridge which had been smashed into concrete blocks propped up on two rusted, upended Soviet tanks. From nowhere a grinning man appeared at the window, waving a lot of fish on a string.

'Fucking Afghans,' said the younger American. With that he stuck on the headphones of his iPod, selected Alicia Keys' *Songs in A Minor* and tuned out Afghanistan.

To the Bush administration, contracting out the removal of the Taliban to local commanders backed by small groups of special forces and a hi-tech air force had been a highly successful new way of waging war with minimum cost or risk to its own troops. So it also seemed to make sense to contract out keeping the peace in the countryside, and the hunt for bin Laden.

The problem was, it was these very commanders or warlords whom Afghans most blamed for the destruction of their country. Kabul in particular had remained intact during the years of Soviet occupation – it was afterwards, when the mujaheddin ousted the communist-backed President Najibullah in 1992 and ran the country for four years, that their leaders all started fighting each other, turning the capital into a battlefield. You could see the damage everywhere. Kabulis would curse, '*Jangsalar*,' Dari for 'warlords', as they showed you the destruction, their eyes often wet with tears as they waxed lyrical about how their city had been a beautiful place full of rose gardens and fruit trees.

As a Deputy Minister in that administration, albeit briefly, Hamid Karzai knew this only too well. 'I'm very adamant we must finish warlordism, and will use whatever means necessary,' he had told me before his inauguration. 'It won't be like last time. The problem is, what do we do with them?' he mused. 'If only I could just chop off their heads!' We were sitting with his elder brother Qayum, who had recently returned from Baltimore, where he ran one of the family's Afghan restaurants. They joked about turning the warlords into tour guides to show visitors the part of the city they were personally responsible for destroying.

In Karzai's first month in office he called on all militias to go back to their bases: 'All people with weapons or ammunition are not allowed to walk in the streets', read the order. No one had taken the least bit of notice. Karzai exerted absolutely no power over these men.

He had, for example, promised the governorship of his home-town of Kandahar to Mullah Naqibullah, head of the Alikozai tribe, who ended the war by negotiating the Taliban surrender of the city on 7 December 2001. The two men were old friends – in 1988 I travelled with Karzai to Kandahar and we stayed at Naqib's base in Argandab, and heard stories, true or otherwise, of him shooting down three Soviet gunships with Stingers.

But while Naqib was negotiating peace, Gul Agha Sherzai, head of the rival Barakzai tribe, was driving from Quetta into Kandahar airbase, accompanied by pick-up loads of his men, including some of the Achakzai I had met at Spin Boldak, escorted by US special forces. Sherzai was one of the Pashtuns with whom the CIA had made contact after 9/11, and had already received $1 million for sending some of his men to act as target-spotters for US bombs. Karzai called him by satellite phone to instruct him to stay at the airbase, and told him he was to be commander of the base while Naqib would be Governor. Sherzai was furious. 'I don't take orders from Hamid Karzai,' he raged. 'Kandahar is mine!' He and his fighters headed into the city under cover of US air support, and moved into the Governor's Palace, next to the mausoleum of Afghanistan's founding father Ahmad Shah Durrani.

Local Kandaharis did not have fond memories of Sherzai. A giant bear of a man with dyed black hair flattened across his pate and a bristly beard, missing front teeth and an elaborate turban, he had been Governor before, from 1992 to 1994 during the mujaheddin government. Then there was so little authority that local commanders set up chains or ropes all along the highway manned by gunmen demanding bribes from everyone who passed. He had a reputation for being uncouth, blowing his nose and wiping his mouth on his turban, and had taken the name Sherzai, which means 'Son of Lion' – in fact he was the son of a dogfighter called Haji Latif.

But his new US escort gave him superpower credibility, and taking him on would mean taking on American B52s. Khalid Pashtun, Sherzai's slick Afghan-American spokesman, began spreading stories to their US friends and foreign journalists that Naqib was linked to the Taliban, and had brought them to Kandahar in the first place. Naqib unwittingly played into their hands by setting up camp across town in Mullah Omar's old headquarters, amid its fibreglass palm-tree sculptures and garishly painted rooms, from which the Taliban leader would hand out money from a tin box.

To try to resolve the issue, Karzai called a meeting between Sherzai and Naqib at the Governor's Palace. Sherzai's American friends sat on his side of the table. Karzai acted as interpreter, and when Sherzai accused Naqib of handing the city over to the Taliban in 1994, he did not intervene. Naqib had indeed handed over Kandahar to the Taliban, but it was in order to end the factional fighting, and had been at the urging of Karzai himself, who in those days was chief fundraiser for the Taliban. This was something the new President did not want to remind the Americans of.

The meeting ended with Sherzai as Governor. He quickly became one of the most powerful Governors in the country as well as one of the richest men, helped by contracts with the Americans to supply fuel and cement at exorbitant prices, and selling back the Stingers the Americans had given him in the first place.

'My motto is "Construction with corruption", that's why people like me,' he boasted to me once over a bowl of mutton soup he told me he'd cooked himself. I tried not to think about that as he tore off hunks of fatty meat which he plonked on my plate in between noisily sucking the flesh off a large bone, then wiping his mouth on the end of his turban. A British official told me that Foreign Minister Jack Straw had been incapacitated for days after lunching with him.

I survived the lunch, and next saw Sherzai in Jalalabad, where he had been transferred and had renovated the King's palace. As always, he was presiding over a long table of tribesmen chewing and slurping food. He was wearing a black *shalwar kamiz*, with a white linen cowl wrapped over his head and round his neck as a napkin. He insisted I sat next to him so he could spoon chunks of meat onto my plate while he chewed away at large bones. Also at the table were two shadowy Americans who had jumped out of big Hiluxes with blacked-out windows. They told me they were involved in 'development projects', and made sure they were out of sight whenever I took photographs. Sherzai was well known to be on the CIA payroll.

Afterwards he took me on a tour. In the audience room was a painting of the man for whom the palace had been built, King Abdur Rahman. 'My grandfather,' announced Sherzai. I looked at him in astonishment, but this was not the time for a discussion of heredity. We headed for the basement, where the Russians used to kill people and the walls were stained with blood. Sherzai had turned it into a disco room with platform, glitter ball, giant woofers and carpets to lounge on. The tour ended outside, with a final flourish of warlord kitsch – a display of coloured lights round the fountain and swimming pool. He told me he was leaving for Germany the next morning to get his teeth fixed. I loved the idea of a warlord with a sparkling CIA-funded smile.

* * *

It was a similar story all over the country. Ismael Khan had declared himself Emir of the West, in charge of five provinces. In the north, the Uzbek warlord General Dostum had added to his past atrocities by suffocating hundreds of Taliban prisoners in metal shipping containers after defeating them, and was battling it out for control with his Tajik rival Mohammad Atta. Another Tajik commander, General Daud Daud, controlled Kunduz and the north-east. The central Hazarajat region was dominated by the Shia Hazara warlords Mohammed Mohaqeq and Karim Khalili.

In Kabul and the south-east, the dominant figure was the man I found scariest of all – Abdul Rasul Sayyaf, an enormous white-bearded Wahhabi with a penchant for strange pronouncements: 'If somebody becomes kind and shows sympathy to the tiger, this will be cruel to the sheep,' was typical. Sayyaf had been the most funda-mentalist of all the seven mujaheddin leaders, the man responsible for inviting Arabs to join the fight against the Soviets, long-time critic of the Americans and patron to a veritable Who's Who of terrorists. His camps in Peshawar trained Ramzi Yusuf, who tried to blow up the World Trade Center in 1993, and the report by the 9/11 Commission named Sayyaf as 'mentor' to Yusuf's uncle Khalid Sheikh Mohammad, the mastermind of 9/11. He had been close to bin Laden since the 1980s, when he referred to him as his 'golden chicken', and was instrumental in helping him move back to Afghanistan in 1996. Without Sayyaf, 9/11 might never have happened. I wasn't sure if the Americans didn't realise that, or just didn't care. Either way, with American help he got his house back in Paghman, a beautiful valley of snowcapped mountains about an hour west of Kabul, where his gunmen were soon terrorising the local population, breaking up weddings if music was played and seizing property. Sayyaf installed his men in key positions such as police chiefs and the judiciary in Wardak and Ghazni, while his commander Mullah Taj Mohammad became Governor of Kabul. This meant his men had carte blanche to terrorise western Kabul, looting and raping, armed with Kalashnikovs and grenades.

In the east, Karzai had appointed Din Mohammad, brother of the late Abdul Haq, as Governor of Nangahar; but the real power lay with Hazrat Ali, the man with the singing birds. In neighbouring Paktia, Karzai had named a warlord, Pacha Khan Zadran, as Governor, but locals had already appointed their own man, and refused to accept him. Scores of people were killed between February and May 2002 as Pacha Khan and his men tried to fight their way into the palace in the provincial capital Gardez, unleashing rockets on the city. Eventually Karzai sent a delegation asking him to surrender. 'Who is Karzai, who is the government?' he laughed. 'Is Karzai going to come and kill me? He needs his head examined!'

Most powerful of all was Marshal Fahim, who despite being Defence Minister was clearly not the least interested in building a national army. He still kept his own militia and his options open by continuing to take money from Russia and Iran, and one only had to go an hour north of Kabul to see his tanks on the Shomali plains.

It was all mad.

Back in December 2001 the warlords had been running scared. Just before Karzai's inauguration, I attended a meeting at Kabul's dilapidated Intercontinental Hotel. One after another roared up to the front entrance, accompanied by pick-ups full of gun-toting militia. Inside the banquet hall they discussed the American bombing campaign which had enabled them to run the Taliban out of the country. They all agreed they had never seen anything like the B52s.

It was clear they thought their days were over. They were almost all on the criminal lists of human rights agencies, and when they heard about Guantánamo they feared ending up there.

Instead, the Americans had come to their rescue. Zalmay Khalilzad, an Afghan-American academic who had worked for Reagan, had been sent as US Envoy by his great buddy George W. Bush, and argued that they had no choice. 'We couldn't have cut them out – they'd been decisive,' he said. 'We had a few hundred people and an air force liberate this country – they were the ones who actually fought. When I went to my hometown of Mazar-i-Sharif they asked, "Who the hell is Karzai? It was Dostum who liberated Mazar." It was people like Dostum, Ismael Khan,

Mohaqeq, Khalili, Fahim, who were in the trenches putting their life on the line. What we hoped was, as central institutions built up, these other forces would weaken,' said Khalilzad. 'I felt these warlords were paper tigers.'

Yet Zal, as everyone called him, played his own part in undermining Karzai's authority. He soon became known as 'the Viceroy', and acted as if he was running the place, even sitting in on cabinet meetings. While Karzai rarely left the heavily guarded palace, Zal flew around the country in a US military plane resolving disputes and handing out wind-up radios, accompanied by a gaggle of attractive young female aides inevitably known as Zal's Gals.

Jonathan Powell, Tony Blair's chief of staff, also felt there was little choice but to work with warlords: 'It was impossible to find anyone with clean hands,' he said.

However, the fact that American forces continued to work with the warlords and pay them gave them new power in their communities. They intimidated local people by telling them they could call in airstrikes on their satellite phones. And to the horror of many of the Europeans, Rumsfeld and other US officials would visit them as if they were important leaders. 'There is a certain illogic in trying to boost the authority of the central government on one hand and in conniving with local warlords on the other,' complained Chris Patten, the European Union Commissioner, when he visited Kabul in May 2002. 'There are things done in the short term which are unhelpful in the long term.'

While the warlords were becoming prosperous and powerful on CIA handouts, in Kabul the government was weak and broke. Said Tayeb Jawad, who had left a lucrative job as a lawyer in San Francisco to come back to set up a private university and had ended up as Karzai's chief of staff, was shocked. 'We didn't have a single computer in the Presidency – all we had was my laptop I had brought from the US. We didn't have a printer, so I would type documents then show them to the President on the screen, or to the British or US Ambassadors, then drive across town to an office with a printer.'

Communications were equally difficult. The Presidency had a few satellite phones, but if they wanted to arrange meetings with people like Brahimi, the UN Special Representative, or his deputy Jean Arnault, they would have to send a messenger. 'There was no postal service, no fax, so our only connection with the outside world was the twice-weekly Ariana flights to Dubai,' said Jawad. 'I'd give instructions for them to call me before flying, so if I needed to get a document out they would fly it.'

I experienced this first-hand when Karzai asked me to send him cuttings about himself from British newspapers. The envelope addressed to 'President of Afghanistan, Arg Palace, Kabul' came back stamped 'Addressee Unknown'.

There was an even bigger problem. Karzai's government had so little money it could not even afford its fuel bills, let alone pay salaries. Six containers full of banknotes printed in Russia for the Taliban regime had been seized by the Northern Alliance when they entered Kabul, and they refused to hand them over. In January 2002 the representatives of sixty-one countries had gathered at a conference in Tokyo and raised an impressive-sounding $4.8 billion for Afghan reconstruction. But for a population of twenty-five million that was just $20 per head – a fraction of what was given to Bosnia, Kosovo or East Timor ($256 per head) at the end of their wars. The Americans only contributed $290 million – little more than half the $540 million provided by Iran. The money took a long time to come, much of it never arrived at all, and most countries used their contributions for projects using their own people rather than entrusting it to the Afghan government.

Meanwhile, Karzai's government had 260,000 civil servants to pay, yet only $20 million in the kitty. 'Money was a major issue,' said Jawad. 'I had to phone round begging money from different Embassies. We didn't even have a functioning toilet in the Presidency for guests coming in. We could get money for specific things like this, or vehicles, but not for running the government and paying our staff.'

They became dependent on cash handouts from the CIA which were dropped off in suitcases, rucksacks and even plastic bags. This was known as 'ghost money', because it came and left secretly. From 2003 Karzai's office was also given cash by the Iranian government, which the previous year Bush had declared part of the 'axis of evil'.

The lack of funds made it difficult to find good people to work for the government, particularly as the years of war had left the vast majority of the population with no education. The only trained administrators were those who had been taught by the Soviets during the communist regime, and who were thus regarded by many as unpalatable. In the end it would be these people the West would come to rely on most, such as Hanif Atmal, who set up the National Solidarity Programme to alleviate poverty, and Gulab Mangal, who became the Governor of Helmand.

Karzai himself had no experience of running anything. He was, said Jawad, 'hopeless with numbers, confusing billions and trillions'. Jawad found himself having to do things such as draft his own investment law. 'I did some research and found the best one was Chile's, so I just copied that, took it to cabinet and they approved it. I could feel the pressure on Karzai's shoulders,' said Khalilzad. He had no executive experience, and the challenges of rebuilding this shattered country were huge, while the capacity of people with relevant knowledge and experience was very limited. 'I remember I had to go and object to someone we thought non-desirable, and he said, "Give me some names." In fact we didn't have a lot of names. He said we foreigners didn't appreciate this.'

The international community preferred to build schools for children, which made nice photographs back home, rather than funding unsexy adult programmes to train a civil service. Yet there was one resource staring them in the face. In those early days hundreds of Afghan-Americans like Jawad were coming back to their country, eager to help. 'The international community never came up with a viable plan of mobilising the expat community,' he said. 'They were ready. All they needed was housing and a decent salary of $2,000 to $4,000 per month. International consultants were getting that a day.'

Instead, contracts were awarded to American consultancies like Bearing Point, or Adam Smith from the UK, to bring in their own people to run ministries and government departments. The Afghans themselves had little say. 'The quality of internationals was extremely poor,' complains Jawad. 'I had an adviser to my office assigned through USAID, and one day I asked him to draft three template letters in English to reply to congratulatory letters to the President, and requests we kept getting for pictures and flags. All it needed to say was "Thank you, but we don't have any." This adviser spent two days on this, and then I had to go and correct it – and it wasn't even my language. In the end I said, "You're fired."' Jawad then received an angry call from the USAID office to say they had spent $60–70,000 on hiring this man, so he could not fire him. 'I don't care,' replied Jawad. 'I don't have room for him in my office – send him to Dubai or somewhere. So much money was wasted.'

In the bazaars between the carpet merchants and burqa sellers and stalls draped with second-hand clothes it was common to see men sitting with satellite phones and calculators on which they would tap away. This was Afghanistan's banking system – *hawala* – an informal yet highly efficient way to transfer money in an entirely cash economy. I used it myself when I was running low on cash – I would hand over a cheque from my UK bank account and be magically presented with bricks of afghanis.

The *hawala* system was often used by terrorist networks, as it was hard to trace, and was thus frowned upon by international agencies. Aid agencies and embassies bringing in millions of dollars were having to physically fly it in in suitcases. There were three different currencies in circulation, and the IMF suggested switching to dollars. Karzai refused, knowing this would not go down well with Afghans.

Nobody had a clue how much it would cost to rebuild Afghanistan, but one thing was clear – its financial system would have to be built from scratch. In this the country was lucky. Ashraf Ghani, a brilliant economist and anthropologist who had studied with Khalilzad at the American University in Beirut in 1968, had worked for years at the World Bank, and was eager to help. 'The President had asked me five times to be his Interior Minister, but I believed that a functioning public finance system was the key to getting government right. That's Islamic tradition. Umar, the second Caliph, established a public purse with enormous commitment to accountability and transparency.'

At fifty-eight, Ghani had lost much of his stomach to cancer, and could not eat proper meals, instead nibbling like a bird throughout the day. Not knowing how much time he had left, all he wanted to do was to help, and as quickly as possible. He arrived with Clare Lockhart, a fiercely bright British barrister who had worked with him at the World Bank. They found the Finance Ministry had no equipment, the central heating had not worked for more than twenty years, and there were no phones or lighting. 'People were literally in the dark and the offices bare, as most of the furniture had disappeared,' he recalled. Ghani went unpaid, as did many of his staff: 'We used to joke we were the largest voluntary organisation in Afghanistan.' They worked sixteen-to-eighteen-hour days, seven days a week. Like Jawad, they quickly discovered that the biggest problem was finding competent staff. 'A limit was set of $50 a month for government employees, yet the UN and other international agencies were paying salaries twenty times as much. The net result was an exodus, with teachers and engineers becoming drivers, translators and guards for aid agencies, as they could earn more money. The international community actually led to the destruction of the government. In my view the international community actually worked against us. It took away our best people, and it dealt with and financed drug dealers and warlords.'

We journalists were equally guilty. My own interpreter, Fraidoon, was a gynaecologist, but earned more in a day with me than in a month working in the hospital. But if I hadn't hired him, one of my colleagues would have. They were all using doctors or medical students. I tried to justify it, telling myself that the money would enable him to gain extra training, and I was happy when he did eventually end up working in a clinic in Herat.

Kabul is surrounded by hills. View of the ancient walls today from the ruins of the Bala Hissar Fort, which was used as barracks by British forces in the First and Second Anglo–Afghan Wars.

An early predecessor to Camp Bastion: a British camp in Afghanistan in 1879 during the Second Anglo–Afghan War.

Britain's first experience in Afghanistan was a disaster. Ten thousand British troops entered Kabul in late 1838 to install their own King, Shah Shuja Durrani, bringing with them wives, ice skates and even a pack of hounds to hunt foxes. Within three years the British envoy, Sir Alexander Burnes, was hacked to death and the British forced to flee in January 1842. Thousands were killed as they retreated.

Shah Shuja, installed by the British in 1839, holding court on his marble throne in the Bala Hissar. Known as the puppet King, he was assassinated in 1842 when the British fled. The Taliban revelled in drawing comparisons between him and President Hamid Karzai, who is from the same tribe.

The Mehsud tribesmen on the Khyber Pass photographed in 1919 look no different to the
Pashtun tribesmen encountered by NATO troops after 9/11.

The battle of Maiwand in 1880, not far from Helmand, was one of Britain's worst ever military defeats. Every Afghan knows the story and they were astonished when the British returned to the area in 2006.

Soviet troops crossing the Oxus River to withdraw from Afghanistan in February 1989 after a ten-year war in which they lost fifteen thousand men. The international community never spoke to the Russians about their lessons.

Ahmat Shah Massoud, known as the Lion of Panjshir, was Afghanistan's most charismatic commander and leader of the Northern Alliance and his forces never surrendered to the Taliban. He was a lover of poetry and is pictured here reading a book in November 2000. He was assassinated two days before 9/11.

Pakistani Islamists in Quetta in 2002 with a poster of Osama bin Laden, protesting against US air attacks in Afghanistan. Quetta became the headquarters of the Taliban.

Osama bin Laden sweets were for sale in bazaars throughout Pakistan after 9/11.

Hamid Karzai in his trademark chapan coat, with First Lady Barbara Bush on his left, at the State of the Union speech in Washington in 2002. At that time he was admired worldwide.

Karzai in his garden at the Presidency in 2006 with his pet deer. Cut off from the outside world by many layers of security, he was mocked as the Mayor of Kabul. He told the author he was tired and lonely.

Afghan polling station in the 2004 Presidential elections in Sangisar, where Mullah Omar used to live. Wanting Karzai to win, the international community ignored the fraud in those elections.

US soldiers body-searching Afghans for weapons near Urgun in Paktika, close to the Pakistan border in 2003. Karzai repeatedly complained to the Americans that the searches were intrusive, particularly night raids in villages where soldiers entered women's purdah quarters.

Merchants of Ruin – the Return of the Warlords

'Without human capital, financial capital is useless,' Ghani would argue as he tried to persuade donors to create a school of public administration. 'Billions of dollars have been spent in Afghanistan, but not one donor was willing to put up the $120 million needed. I cajoled, begged, threatened, but they wouldn't give me.'

The government's ability to raise revenue was hindered by corruption. 'Too many people made a decision to prefer personal enrichment to public service,' Ghani said sadly. 'For someone to pay $1 in taxes they had to pay $8 in bribes, and waste a week of their life getting twenty signatures. Customs revenues were all disappearing, as provinces which had access to transit routes were taking the revenue without any legal authority. We had a payroll system where 25 per cent of salaries disappeared within ministries before they were paid, and no one had a clue how many employees there were.' Fahim's Ministry of Defence alone claimed to have 400,000 soldiers and officers. Ghani refused to give it any money any at all till Fahim agreed to reduce the number on the payroll to 100,000, then to reduce it every month on a sliding scale if accurate figures couldn't be produced. By the time Ghani left office the number on the MoD payroll was 8,000.

There were other successes. A new currency was produced after Ghani used his connections to call Paul Volcker, chairman of the Federal Reserve, who arranged a design and didn't charge a cent. Twenty-eight billion new afghani notes were printed in Germany and Britain, and distributed with the rate fixed at fifty afghanis to the dollar.

Afghanistan had no functioning telephone system, but soon everyone seemed to be carrying a mobile. Ghani asked for assistance from Tony Blair, who sent a team of telecommunications experts for six months to draw up laws and issue licences for two networks. Within a short time these new phone companies were the country's biggest taxpayers.

There was success too in health, with child mortality reduced by 15 per cent, though one in four children still died by the age of five, and Afghanistan remained the most dangerous place on earth to give birth.

Ghani became Karzai's *de facto* Prime Minister. But his intolerance for corruption, combined with his abrasive manner, won him few friends. 'It's a miracle I'm alive,' he would say. 'By all odds I should be dead.' He wasn't referring to his precarious health. 'President Karzai used to say there's a long line of people who want to shoot me.'

His experience as Finance Minister left him exasperated with the international community. There was no coordinator, so he would have to waste time repeating things in numerous meetings with different countries or agencies which would often be replicating or undermining each other. Just in dealing with the Americans, there was the Pentagon, the CIA, Khalilzad, the Embassy and USAID, each of which often had a different agenda.

Like Jawad in the Presidency, Ghani frequently lost patience with his foreign advisers. 'Technical assistance had become an unregulated industry,' he complained. 'Some things we needed help with, like the design of currency and drafting telecommunications laws. But certain American firms were paid by the number of people they put on the ground; so, for example, privatisation of public enterprises was not my priority, but one day I suddenly found an adviser on privatisation on my staff. There were others who didn't know anything, and who we had to teach. They were being paid thousands of dollars, and they became part of the problem.'

One only had to go to Kabul airport to see a classic example of the aid community helping itself rather than Afghans. The scariest part of going to Afghanistan was flying in from Dubai on the state airline Ariana. Its planes were in such bad condition that they were banned from most places on earth. Even the model plane in the sales office was held together by sticking plaster and elastic bands.

The UN has its own airline to fly staff in and out of danger spots, so it quickly began its own service from Dubai or Islamabad to Kabul. As I stood nervously fiddling with my Ariana boarding pass, I would enviously watch the foreign aid workers and diplomats boarding the shiny UN planes. What I didn't realise was that the millions of dollars to subsidise this service was coming from the money pledged to help Afghanistan. Ghani was indignant. 'The first thing the UN system provided through the $1.6 billion of donor money channelled to UN agencies in 2002 was an airline devoted to serving UN staff, and occasionally (after much lobbying) some Afghan government officials.'

While nobody would give Ariana the $100–200 million investment to turn it into a proper, commercially viable airline, Ghani believes the UN was subsidising its own airline by as much as $300 million. As the UN has never disclosed the cost of its operations, the actual figure is unknown. 'There is a clear double standard between the UN staff, who need to fly on a safe airline, and the leaders and nationals of a country, who are confined to flying with an unsafe airline,' said Ghani.

At Ghani's urging, Karzai tried to boost government revenue by demanding that warlords who had become Governors or border police chiefs hand over the customs duties they collected. According to Finance Ministry estimates, in 2002 $500 million had been collected for goods moving in and out of the landlocked country, but only $80 million handed over to the central government. As Governor of Herat, Ismael Khan was the worst culprit, with the crossing points from Iran and Turkmenistan both falling into his fiefdom, earning him as much as $1 million a day. When Karzai demanded he hand some of this money over Ismael instead sent him back a bill for development in his province.

Finally, in desperation, in May 2003 Karzai summoned a dozen of the warlords and Governors and threatened to resign if they refused to hand over the customs revenues. A few weeks later two Toyota Land Cruisers arrived at the Ministry of Finance with $20 million in cash.

Emboldened, Karzai tried to take on Ismael and appoint his own police commissioner and military chief for Herat. Ismael had 20,000 men under his command, including special forces who skinned live snakes with their teeth, and was not to be messed with. He continued to receive support from the Iranians, as he had for years. Their influence was becoming very visible in Herat, and Ismael played them off against the Americans, who also had him on their payroll.

When Karzai dismissed his men, Ismael grabbed forty of his commanders and flew to Kabul to confront him. I met them in the House of Heratis in Kabul. Ismael was disdainful of Karzai, and expressed outrage at the state of the roads in Kabul. 'Look at this mess,' he said, pointing at all the mud and potholes and endless traffic jams. In Herat, being a warlord, he had simply bulldozed homes and shops to widen the roads, and no one argued.

Ismael flew back, his men reinstated. A year later, fed up with still receiving none of the customs revenue, Karzai sacked Ismael as Governor. Angry riots broke out across Herat. Khalilzad says it was he who finally persuaded Ismael to go. 'Karzai wanted me to play the heavy guy. I had to go to Herat and hold his hand and then have a press conference saying Amir Ismael Khan has decided to move to Kabul.'

This naturally made it look even more as though Karzai had no control. Ismael was given the Ministry of Energy, where it was felt he could do less damage. As only about 6 per cent of Afghanistan had electricity, inevitably he became known as 'Minister of Darkness'.

Dostum also finally went too far that year, fighting against Karzai's chosen Governor in the northern province of Faryab, then refusing to allow newly trained soldiers from the Afghan National Army (ANA) to pass through his home area of Shabargan on their way to Herat.

'If you send them there we will put them all in body bags. We'll make it worse for you than Vietnam,' he told Khalilzad.

'Do you understand there are Americans with ANA, so an attack on the ANA is an attack on Americans?' replied Khalilzad. 'This is a bridge once you cross, you can't come back.'

Dostum would not listen. 'He was clearly drunk,' said Khalilzad. 'I told him, "You need to drink lots of tea and coffee, then we'll talk when you're sober." Instead he phoned Karzai to complain that I was the worst of the Americans. When he called me a couple of hours later he still refused to let the troops through. So I got B1s to fly from Diego Garcia over his house repeatedly, breaking the sound barrier.'

The show of force was something Dostum understood. When he called again, Khalilzad told him to move to Kabul and stop causing trouble. He moved into a house in Wazir Akbar Khan, the city's most affluent suburb, favoured by warlords and aid agencies, and named after the Afghan hero who had captured the garrison from the British. Dostum had the house painted lavender, and set up his own TV station called Ayna, which means 'mirror'. A TV station had clearly become the latest warlord accessory – Sayyaf also had one.

Meanwhile, trapped inside his palace, Karzai had become mockingly known as 'the Mayor of Kabul'. His weakness was evident when he tried to stop warlords bringing their own armies into the Presidency. 'They were coming for meetings with private militia of anywhere between six and sixty undisciplined, untrained people carrying very dangerous heavy weapons,' said Jawad. But when in 2003 the palace imposed a rule that only a few guards could come into meetings with the President, it was met with outrage. 'What do you mean?' they'd say. 'I'm a resistance leader. I fought the Soviets. Nobody stops me!'

'We had people drawing guns at the palace guards,' recalled Jawad, 'and got very close to shooting.'

Yet Khalilzad believes Karzai had much more power than he himself imagined. 'He got himself into this situation. I told him, "Can you imagine Dostum going back to the mountains? They are all too fat and rich." I just don't think Karzai ever got comfortable with using the military, with the shadow effect of force.'

Jawad argues it was not so easy. 'Should Karzai have challenged the warlords? Maybe. But I think he knew that he didn't have enough resources and forces to take them on, and he didn't have support from outside. The Americans talked about promising support, but when it came to take decisive action against spoilers they'd back off, using this term "We don't want to be involved in a green on green confrontation." The warlords were getting a lot more than we were, so how could he take a stronger stand? Even his own personal bodyguards were Fahim's men, then later on Americans.'

It was Fahim who was behind a scheme that prompted Karzai's greatest anger with the warlords. With all the people coming back to Afghanistan and all the foreign agencies that had moved in, Kabul had a major shortage of real estate, and property prices were booming. Just a couple of miles down the road from the palace, on the edge of affluent Wazir Akbar Khan, was an area called Shirpur. Fahim came up with a plan to distribute plots to military officers and cabinet colleagues for just $1,000 each. Not only were the plots actually worth at least $100,000 each, but there were more than thirty families living on the land, in houses they had been in for twenty-five years. In September 2003, when they ignored requests to leave, the Kabul police chief sent in bulldozers and men with sticks. According to the Afghan Independent Human Rights Commission all but four of the thirty-two cabinet Ministers had accepted a plot, as well as many senior military officers.

The story soon got round town, the area becoming known as Shirchoor, which means 'lion-grabbing'. The UN Envoy Brahimi denounced it as 'wrong and unacceptable', adding, 'You don't destroy homes on the heads of women and children inside.' When Karzai heard of what had happened he was livid. He stormed out of a cabinet meeting after calling his Ministers thieves and murderers. 'Haven't you spilled enough blood of this country?' he demanded.

The one person to stand up to the warlords was someone with no power or weapons, and who did so in the unlikely venue of a German beer tent.

One of the main priorities of Karzai's Western backers was a new constitution so that elections could be held. This was to be agreed through a *loya jirga*, or grand assembly of tribal elders, the traditional Afghan way of making important decisions which can go on for days or weeks. In 1747 one was held in Kandahar to choose the first King, Ahmat Shah Durrani, known as 'Pearl of Pearls' for his trademark dangling pearl earring.

Merchants of Ruin – the Return of the Warlords

For the constitutional *loya jirga* of 2003, delegates were chosen from every province, 502 in total including fifty-two nominated by Karzai. There was no building big enough to accommodate them all amid the ruins of Kabul, particularly as there were also press and international observers, so someone had come up with the idea of flying over a marquee from a Rhineland Oktoberfest.

After a series of delays caused by the sheer difficulty of delegates reaching the capital from remote provinces cut off by winter snows and with no roads, the meeting finally opened on 14 December 2003. It was a bitterly cold day, and gunmen and tanks lined the approach to the tent in the grounds of Kabul Polytechnic. Inside, the tent was filled with elders, or 'whitebeards', the Pashtuns wearing large turbans, the Tajiks in flat woollen caps, Hazaras and Uzbeks in smaller, more colourful turbans and some technocrats in Western suits. Many of Karzai's nominees were the old jihadi leaders, who sat in the front row. To show that this was the new Afghanistan there was one major difference from such gatherings in the past – a hundred women.

The first task was to choose a chairman. Karzai proposed one of the jihadi leaders Sibghatullah Mojadeddi, his old boss when I first knew him in Peshawar, a bumbling character with a grey beard and large plastic-rimmed glasses.

The *loya jirga*'s main objective was to agree on a system under which elections would be held the following year. I hadn't met a single Afghan who thought elections were a priority – what they wanted was security, roads, water and electricity. But the Bush administration was desperate to have a success in Afghanistan and declare it a democracy before going into its own presidential election the following November.

Endless discussions began inside the heated tent, which still carried a slight yeasty smell of hops. But the real negotiations went on outside, with the usual Afghan wheeler-dealing, everyone trying to get something. Delegates told me of being given mobile phones, pick-up trucks and dinners at the palace if they voted the right way. But there were greater gifts on offer. Dostum got the recognition of Uzbek as an official language, in return for dropping opposition to the presidential system. Sayyaf agreed to shelve his demand for implementing Sharia law in return for his pick for chief justice and the supreme court – he also got 'Islamic' included in the official title of the government.

The interminable speeches inside the tent seemed irrelevant. Then, on the fourth day, a young girl in a striped white coat and black headscarf appeared from nowhere to step up to the microphone. Her name was Malalai Joya, she ran a clinic in the western province of Farah, she stood just five feet tall, and at twenty-five she was the youngest delegate. In a small but determined voice she denounced the 'criminals and warlords' who stole from 'barefoot Afghans', and demanded, 'Why do we allow those whose hands are still wet with blood to speak?'

'I could take it no more,' she told me afterwards, her words coming in great bursts. 'I was shocked and appalled to see warlords and other well-known war criminals in the front row pretending to be democrats for the cameras of the West. All my life I had heard of the horrible things they had done, and seen some with my own eyes. In the refugee camps where I grew up stories of their savagery were commonplace, and in my home province of Farah the orphanage I ran was full of children who had lost their parents to these men and their allies.'

As she spoke the crowd stiffened, then sat up in stunned silence. 'They have to be condemned internationally,' she continued. 'They have to be taken to the world court.'

The mujaheddin leaders jumped up from their seats, shouting and waving their fists. 'Sister, look what you have done!' shouted Mojadeddi furiously. 'You have upset everybody here!' Malalai's microphone was switched off, leaving her mouthing silently like a goldfish. Insults were hurled at her, many calling her a communist. In fact, she told me afterwards, her father had lost his leg fighting the Russians. One of the angriest was Sayyaf, yelling in his great booming voice, 'The mujaheddin who liberated this country are heroes! When you call them criminals this speech is a crime itself!'

Mojadeddi summoned security, and guards hustled Malalai out of the tent. Fearful of the savagery of the crowd, UN officials provided a car to take her away, and four guards, as well as a safe house to sleep in. It was just as well. That night a mob forced their way into the Kabul University hall of residence where she had been staying. 'Where is that whore?' they demanded, brandishing sticks with which to beat her.

Malalai would pay for her ninety-second speech with endless death threats, that meant she could not stay in one place for more than a couple of nights ever after. But her words had struck a chord. The proceedings had been broadcast live on Radio Kabul, and people began calling in to the station in support, with their own stories of commanders gang-raping and looting with impunity. Many compared her to her namesake Malalai of Maiwand, a young woman who had picked up a flag and inspired Afghan forces back into battle against the British in the Second Anglo–Afghan War in 1880. This tiny woman had stood up to the people the President had not dared to.

9

Theatre of War

Wagah border, March 2003

I COULD HEAR the roar even before I got out of the car. 'Pakistan Zindabad!' snarled the crowd, seething back and forth like a predatory animal. 'Long Live Pakistan!' Packed into a concrete grandstand, they looked like highly agitated sports fans – only there were no signs of any teams or goals, just a dusty parade ground with a pair of gates, beyond which was another noisy grandstand.

As the sun started to disappear below the horizon the lone note of a horn sounded, and the gates opened. One was marked 'Pakistan', the other 'India'. Two high-kicking Pakistani soldiers appeared, both with handlebar moustaches, black-kohl-rimmed eyes, white sashes, and headdresses that fanned out like peacock tails. They curled their lips with utter contempt and began quickmarching their way towards the border, rifles gleaming on their backs. On the other side two equally elaborately uniformed Indian soldiers did the same.

On either side of the gate the audiences waved flags and raucously cheered on their respective sides. 'Jai Hind!', 'Long Live India!' came from one side; 'Pakistan Zindabad!' and 'Allahu Akbar!' from the other. Men and women were separated on Pakistan's side, just as they were at weddings, but as a sort of third-sex foreigner I could wander at will. A man near me banged over and over on a large wooden drum, and several people beeped horns. Hawkers

154

passed through the crowd selling paper cones of monkey nuts or trays of *paan*, dark-green betel leaf tightly furled around a mix of tobacco and lime that everyone chewed and spat, staining their teeth. Most of my friends in Lahore seemed to think an evening incomplete without going out to get *paan*, but I found it too bitter.

Around me the crowd shifted impatiently, like a barely contained wild beast, as the soldiers reached the border. Once they had got so close to their counterparts that they were almost eyeball to eyeball they came to an abrupt halt, hands on hips, glowered and rolled their eyes ferociously. If ever looks could kill, it was here, on what was called the zero line. It was like a cross between a tribal dance ritual and a comedy routine (though I seemed to be the only one who found it funny), each side trying to outdo the other with ever higher kicks and more savage expressions.

The men swirled around, did a few more high kicks then straightened their headgear in exaggerated fashion before giving one final glare, then pulled a string to lower their nation's flag. It all seemed carefully choreographed to make sure the crescent of Pakistan and the Indian tricolour with its Gandhi spinning-wheel motif came down at exactly the same time.

The Wagah border point lies midway between the Pakistani city of Lahore and the Indian city of Amritsar, around fifteen miles from each, and is the only crossing on the entire 1,900-mile border between the two countries. This 'Beating the Retreat' ceremony happens at dusk, and is like a mini war every day.

The performance ended with the furious clanging shut of the border gates, at which point each country's flag was carefully folded and carried to a room for safekeeping overnight. By then the crowds had been whipped up into a terrifying frenzy, and I wondered what they might do. They stayed for a bit, jeering at each other, then drifted away into the falling Punjab night. Soon the only sound was the lowing of buffalo and the occasional croak of a frog in the rice paddies.

Afterwards I met the Pakistani commander-cum-choreographer, Captain Rauf. He had been in the army more than eleven years, and had come to Wagah to mock-fight Indians after more than a year of actually fighting them up on the Siachen glacier, the world's highest battlefield.

He was shaking his head. 'It wasn't good today,' he apologised. 'It was our second division. They have problems with their feet, most of them.'

'I thought they were very impressive,' I said.

'No, no!' he protested. 'If you saw our main guard I think you would agree it will be completely stunning.'

He told me that to join the special guard, a soldier had to be able to kick so high that his feet touched his turban. The soldiers practise pulling warlike faces in front of the mirror over and over each day. Captain Rauf was proud of his innovations. 'I don't know if you noticed, we wrap our flag five times, while the Indians just do three. The Indians are still doing the same steps, but I have heard they are desperately trying to think up new steps. I wanted a more attractive ceremony, because it's a show of pomp, so we want as much pomp as possible, and we want as many people as possible to come to generate more feeling. I think you will agree it's simple and elegant, yet also instils fear.' To Captain Rauf it was much more than just a show. 'We're facing an adversary who is much bigger and stronger than us, but as you can see here, nobody in Pakistan is afraid of India.'

The stadium had been built two years earlier, in 2001, but so many people were coming to watch the ceremony each evening that an extension was already planned. I thought it had been packed that day, but Captain Rauf claimed there were often far more people, 'particularly when relations are very hostile, as they were in December'.

One of the last to leave that evening was an old man in green with a long white beard and carrying a large Pakistani flag, who had acted as a kind of unofficial cheerleader. 'I lost two sons fighting those bloody Hindus,' he told me. 'I will come every day till I die.'

For behind all the comical theatrics lay real hatred. India and Pakistan had fought three wars in less than sixty years, and spent money they couldn't afford on vast armies and arsenals of nuclear bombs. They were in fact still fighting on what must be the world's most hostile (and costly) battlefield, the glacier 19,000 feet up in the Himalayas where Captain Rauf had been posted and where more soldiers succumbed to weather than gunfire.

To understand the anger you needed to go back to the origins of Pakistan, for few nations have had such a bloody beginning. Created at the stroke of midnight on 14 August 1947, it was the world's first separate homeland for Muslims, carved out of what had been British India by an act known as Partition, which divided India while giving it independence. It was almost entirely the obsession of one man.

A towering minaret called Minar e Pakistan in a dusty park in the centre of Lahore marks the place where Pakistan's founder Mohammad Ali Jinnah first proposed the Two Nation theory in 1940, defining Hindus and Muslims as two distinct nations that could not exist as one state. It had become a favourite suicide spot.

Jinnah was a lawyer trained at Lincoln's Inn in London, married to a Parsee, and something of a dandy if the museum next to his mausoleum in Karachi is anything to go by. Inside one glass cabinet is a collection of spivvy two-tone shoes with their own special travelling box, and another of bow ties, which he only ordered from a particular tailor in Paris. There is also a collection of his speeches, including one to the first Constituent Assembly of Pakistan which many people seemed to be forgetting, in which he promised, 'You are free to go to your temples, you are free to go to your mosques or to any other place of worship. You may belong to any religion or caste or creed, that has nothing to do with the business of the state.'

Some believe Jinnah never actually intended the division of British India into two countries, but simply wanted a better deal for Muslims within a federal India. Pakistan's creation had been resisted by the British negotiating the independence of the subcontinent they had ruled for a century. Up until the last minute, Lord Mountbatten, the last Viceroy, was still calling Pakistan 'an impossible dream'. He described Partition as 'the worst service I could do to India if I were her enemy or completely indifferent to her fate'. The US President Franklin D. Roosevelt said the idea 'sounded terrible'.

But Jinnah was persistent. In the end Mountbatten agreed to what Jinnah referred to dismissively as a 'truncated' or 'moth-eaten' Pakistan. Drawn up by British lawyer Cyril Radcliffe, it was a bizarre country divided into two parts, East and West, with a thousand miles of hostile Hindu-dominated India in between.

Even the name was made up. 'Pakistan' means 'Land of the Pure', and was a clever acronym formed by students at Cambridge University from the names of the provinces **P**unjab, **A**fghania [North-West Frontier Province], **K**ashmir, **S**indh and Baluchi**stan**.

When the deed was done, Jinnah was already dying, his body riddled with TB and lung cancer, but his doctors kept silent about the fatal shadows on his lungs. Many years later Mountbatten confessed that, had he known, he would have delayed matters until Jinnah was dead, and there would have been no Pakistan.

Occasionally I met people who could remember Partition, and there was anguish in their eyes, for it was the largest and bloodiest human migration in history. More than ten million people packed up their homes. Muslims headed for Pakistan, while Hindus and Sikhs made their way in the opposite direction. The religious hatreds unleashed between people who had once lived peacefully side by side saw around one million people killed.

Nowhere had suffered more than the area around Lahore, which is perhaps why feelings run particularly high in that region. The province of Punjab was divided, and no one knew which side Lahore would end up on until the final maps of the boundaries between the two nations were released just hours before Partition. In the end the city went to Pakistan. Almost immediately riots broke out among Muslims, Sikhs and Hindus, causing many deaths as well as damage to historic Moghul buildings including the Lahore Fort and the Badshahi Mosque.

The mass exodus of people at Partition would have been impossible without the railways; and it was on the railways that much of the worst violence took place. Streets literally ran with blood as thousands of Hindus and Sikhs fought their way to Lahore station to flee to India on trains like the Bombay Express. At the same time, train after train was arriving from south of the border, carrying hundreds of thousands of Muslims to their new homeland. Lahore station became a battleground, railway staff grimly hosing down pools of blood and carrying away piles of corpses on luggage trolleys for mass burial. Those who made it off the trains said the whole of Punjab seemed to be ablaze.

Syed Shahid Hussein,[1] who was sixteen at the time of Partition and living in Hyderabad, in India, was one of millions of Pakistanis whose families lost their homes and had to start from scratch in the new Pakistan. 'Jinnah clearly hadn't thought about what would happen,' he said. 'When the first trains came with the dead bodies we were astonished.' Even for those born long afterwards, stories were passed down by grandparents or neighbours, and this bloody separation had been imprinted on the national consciousness.

Pakistan also felt cheated, as it found itself with fewer resources than the one-sixth share it had been promised. The ill feeling was not helped by the fact that while India consolidated itself as the world's largest democracy, Pakistan's first Prime Minister was assassinated, and by 1958 the country was a military dictatorship, having got through seven Prime Ministers in its first decade. Pakistan then lurched between ill-fated experiments with democracy and spells of military rule, and in 1971 it suffered another trauma when its eastern flank seceded to become Bangladesh.

When I first lived in Pakistan in the late 1980s, Pakistanis consoled themselves with economics – they had the better standard of living. Even this would change. By 2003 India was a powerful economy with a burgeoning middle class. Pakistan, meanwhile, would end up being overtaken by Bangladesh on the UN Human Development index.

India became the convenient bogeyman. Frequent power cuts and water shortages were blamed on India's control of the headlands of Pakistan's main river, even though far-sighted diplomats who realised the importance of dividing up water as well as land had struck the Indus Water Treaty in 1960. In my first year living in Pakistan one of the military's prized F16s was destroyed at Karachi airport in a freak accident when a wild pig ran into the engine on take-off. Pakistani newspapers carried stories claiming the Indian intelligence agency RAW was training wild pigs to sabotage the country's air force.

Like the Wagah ceremony, it would be comical had the two countries not already fought three wars, and were it not the excuse for Pakistan having an enormous army of almost 600,000 men, devouring 16 per cent of the budget (fourteen times as much as the miserly 1.2 per cent spent on education) and so politically powerful that it had ruled the country for more than half its existence. It was the justification, too, for amassing nuclear weapons, which Pakistani officials freely talked of using to take out an Indian city, the only question being whether it was acceptable to take out five million people or ten. School textbooks demonised Indians while glorifying Pakistan as Fortress Islam and neglecting to mention Pakistan's own atrocities in Bangladesh. At least 200,000 women were reportedly raped by Pakistan's forces, and supporting militias, during the war for independence.[2] Apart from the costs of maintaining a country in a perpetual state of near war, blocking trade with the vast market next door also carried a price. The tea I drank everywhere in Pakistan, for example, was imported from Kenya, rather than from the Indian tea warehouses just twenty miles across the border.

The biggest flashpoint between Pakistan and India could not have appeared a more peaceful spot. The valley of Kashmir looks like a real-life Shangri La, an idyllic place high in the Himalayas of snowy mountains and blue lakes floating with lilies. Kashmir was the largest of a number of princely states that had to decide which way to go when India was divided. Though the population was predominantly Muslim, they were ruled by a Hindu maharajah, Hari Singh. He was still deciding which side to opt for when the state was invaded by tribesmen from Pakistan's north-west frontier, backed by the Pakistan army, sparking off the first Indo–Pak war. Panicked, Maharajah Singh decided to go with India, and the United Nations intervened to halt the fighting, creating the ceasefire line known as the Line of Control (LoC), which divided Kashmir into Pakistan- and Indian-controlled parts. A UN resolution was passed, promising a referendum for the people of Kashmir to decide which country they wanted to belong to. But this was never held.

To Pakistan, Kashmir staying part of India undermined its own raison d'être as a country. How could there be more Muslims in India than in Pakistan, the Muslim state? Similarly, for India to lose Kashmir would undermine its status as the world's largest secular democracy.

When Americans asked for his help against the Soviet invasion of Afghanistan, General Zia spotted an opportunity not just to improve his international image. Pakistan and Afghanistan had never had good relations – Afghanistan had been the only country to vote against Pakistan being admitted into the United Nations. The Afghans refused to recognise the Durand Line, and the Pakistanis suspected that Afghan monarchists still harboured dreams of a greater Pashtunistan, bringing in all Pashtun tribal areas, including Waziristan, as it had once been under King Ahmat Shah Durrani. As if as a reminder he had even left in Lahore his gun 'Zam Zammah', on which Rudyard Kipling's famous orphan boy Kim played king of the castle.

For a country always nervous about its eastern border with India, a friendly Afghanistan, or even better a satellite state, would secure Pakistan's western flank. The Generals called this concept 'strategic depth'. At the same time, Zia decided he could copy exactly what the Americans were doing in using Afghans to fight their real enemy, the Soviet Union, and train his own proxies as 'strategic assets'.

A year after the Soviet invasion of Afghanistan, General Zia summoned the Kashmiri cleric Maulana Abdul Bari to meet him in Rawalpindi. Bari was a veteran jihadi who had participated in the 1947 war in Kashmir. He had close links to the Saudi establishment, and in 1974 had set up the Azad Jammu and Kashmir branch of Jamaat-e-Islami, Zia's favoured political party. Bari later said that Zia told him the war in Afghanistan could be a smokescreen behind which Pakistan could prepare for a battle for Kashmir.

When Bari expressed scepticism, Zia retorted, 'How can the Americans stop us from waging jihad in Kashmir when they are waging jihad in Afghanistan?'

Zia explained that the costs of financial support to the Afghans from the CIA and the Saudis were highly inflated, and the profit, as well as some of the guns and ammunition, would be diverted to Kashmir. As Bari got up to leave he asked, 'Who in the Afghan jihad will receive the biggest share of international arms and American money?' Zia smiled and replied, 'Whoever trains the boys from Kashmir.'[3]

Over the next few years a series of meetings took place between ISI officers and Kashmiri activist leaders, using the cover of the *haj* pilgrimage in Saudi Arabia to escape the notice of Indian intelligence. The Kashmiris were sceptical, but eventually agreed, and from 1983 began to send men across the border for training. Their numbers multiplied after state elections in Kashmir in 1987, which were widely thought to have been rigged to deprive the newly formed Muslim United Front of seats. Inspired by the Palestinian struggle and the Afghan jihad, many young Kashmiris felt their only alternative was to take up guns. Groups such as Harkat-ul-Jihad-al-Islami[4] and Lashkar-e-Toiba, or 'Army of the Pure', were created. A recruitment drive got under way on both sides of the Line of Control, and the armed struggle was formally launched in July 1988, with a series of bombings and attacks on Indian officials and police. By then the training wasn't exactly clandestine. I was taken with a few Pakistani journalists to see a training camp by Sheikh Rashid, a Rawalpindi politician who lived in a wonderful crumbling old *haweli* in the centre of the old city and was close to General Zia. 'What will you do with these people afterwards?' I asked.

Zia's sudden death a month later, after a crate of mangoes apparently exploded on his plane, did not halt the activity. The subsequent elections saw Benazir Bhutto become the first female Prime Minister in the Islamic world, and the world's youngest at just thirty-five. Even at her inauguration it was clear who was calling the shots. A hijacked Soviet plane was allowed to land in Pakistan that day without her even being consulted. Among the conditions she'd had to agree with the military was leaving them in control of policy on Kashmir and Afghanistan, as well as the nuclear programme. 'I am in office but not in power,' she told me at the time. 'Zia's men are everywhere.'

In the winter of 1989, by the time of Bhutto's first anniversary in power, the Kashmir insurgency had become a full-scale uprising against the Indian government. Kashmiris poured into the streets to demand *azadi*, or freedom. Curfew was imposed, and hundreds of young men dragged out of their homes by Indian paramilitaries. This only prompted more protests, and sent many more young men over the Line of Control for training.

On 21 January 1990, tens of thousands of Kashmiris took to the narrow streets of Srinagar for a massive anti-India rally. The police reacted violently, firing indiscriminately into the crowd, killing more than a hundred people. It was the opportunity for which Pakistan's military had been waiting. General Aslam Beg, the army chief, told Bhutto he wanted to launch what he called an 'offensive defence operation', using ISI-trained militants such as the ones I had met. By then there were more than thirty militant training camps in Pakistan.

'They informed me that 100,000 battle-hardened mujahideen were willing to go into Kashmir to assist the Kashmir freedom movement, and were somehow confident of defeating the much larger Indian army,' recalled Bhutto. 'General Beg told me, "Prime Minister, you just give the order and your men will take Srinagar and you will wear the crown of victory and glory." I thought he had lost all sense of reality.'[5] She firmly vetoed the idea, and instructed the army and the ISI leadership that no Afghan mujaheddin be allowed to cross the LoC.

She agreed only to a low-level insurgency. They asked for money to fund it, suggesting that they could raise cash by selling Pakistan's nuclear technology. Beg flew to Iran as the guest of the Revolutionary Guard, and offered to provide them with uranium-enrichment technology in return for hard cash to fund the Kashmiri jihad.[6]

Bhutto had just been to Washington, where she had been humiliatingly caught out over Pakistan's nuclear programme. In an address to Congress she had confidently declared: 'We do not possess nor do we intend to make a nuclear device.' The following day she was confronted by CIA Director William Webster, who showed her exactly what kind of bomb her nuclear scientists had made, including photographs and a mock-up model. 'Benazir was shocked,' said her close friend and lobbyist Mark Siegel. 'She had no idea.' She assured the Bush administration that her scientists would stop weaponising uranium, and the US agreed to continue to give Pakistan its third largest foreign-aid package.

But when Bhutto got back home, Beg instead gave the order to step up production at the nuclear-research facility at Kahuta. The Americans were horrified. Ambassador Robert Oakley warned Bhutto that the US would have no choice but to cut off aid. However, when she tried to schedule a meeting with the President, Ghulam Ishaq, and A.Q. Khan, the head of Pakistan's nuclear programme, to find out what was going on, they kept proffering excuses to delay, cancelling three times.

I was living in Pakistan at that time, reporting for the *Financial Times* and *Time* magazine. One day I met A.Q. Khan at a wedding at which he was the much-honoured guest. He invited me to his house for tea to boast of Pakistan's nuclear prowess. Then, in May 1990, I was deported after I wrote a story saying the army was planning to move against Bhutto. The deportation notice accused me of 'trying to jeopardise Pakistan's fragile democratic institutions'. I didn't think Pakistan needed any help in that respect. On my way to the airport I saw some graffiti on a wall: 'We apologise for this democratic interruption – normal martial law will be resumed shortly.'

A few months later, on 6 August 1990, President Ishaq announced to the nation that he had dismissed Bhutto, accusing her of corruption and incompetence.

The timing was well chosen. Saddam Hussein had just invaded Kuwait, and the world's attention was elsewhere. Distracted by the prospect of war in the Persian Gulf, Washington had no interest in protesting against the dismissal of a Prime Minister who had failed to stop her Generals making bombs. It was, the US said, an 'internal matter' for Pakistan.

The Russian defeat in Afghanistan had been a victory beyond the Americans' wildest dreams, triggering a collapse of the Iron Curtain, with communist regimes being kicked out across Eastern Europe and the fall of the Berlin Wall amid jubilant scenes of East and West Germans crossing back and forth. Pakistan may have been the crucial staging ground for the mujaheddin to deliver the crucial blow to Moscow, but with the communists out, it was no longer needed.

On 1 October 1990 President Bush announced that he could no longer certify that Pakistan did not possess nuclear weapons. A $564 million aid programme to Pakistan that had already been approved by Congress was frozen, and the twenty-eight F16s Pakistan had ordered from General Dynamics were suspended.

New elections were called for November. This time ISI was taking no chances. It brokered a deal among all political parties opposed to Bhutto's Pakistan People's Party so that in most constituencies only one candidate stood against it. It also distributed huge amounts of money through a slush fund of 150 million rupees provided by BCCI, the bank whose criminal doings would be revealed a few years later. The then ISI chief Lieutenant General Asad Durrani later admitted that he handed out sixty million rupees to twenty anti-Bhutto politicians. Bhutto was depicted in the media as unpatriotic, and leaflets dropped by ISI called her and her mother 'gangsters in bangles' who had danced bare-armed in the White House and would sell out Pakistan's security interests to 'the Indo-Zionist lobby' in the US. The mastermind of all this was General Gul, then a corps commander, using his former subordinates at ISI. As the election results came in, he even called Pakistani media commentators and asked them to describe the vote as a rebuff to the US.[7]

The new Prime Minister was General Zia's chubby-faced protégé Nawaz Sharif, a wealthy industrialist who had been Chief Minister of Punjab. I didn't hold out a lot of hope. I had spent a day on the campaign trail with him and watched him breakfast on whole chickens. To every question I asked him, he responded, 'I don't know. What do you think?'

As his Ambassador to Washington he sent Abida Hussain, one of Pakistan's first female MPs, who was unique as a woman in ruling over feudal lands in Jhang, Punjab. America, she said, had no more interest in Pakistan than Pakistan had in the Maldives.

Throughout the 1990s, as power swung to and fro between Nawaz Sharif and Benazir Bhutto, and then back to the military under Musharraf, the jihadi programme continued unabated. By the time of 9/11, a bewildering array of organisations existed. Even then, after agreeing to help the Americans, Musharraf told colleagues he could 'compartmentalise' – go after al Qaeda, but still allow the home-grown jihadis to operate. He turned a blind eye when a cleric called Sufi Mohammad travelled round Swat after 9/11, rallying thousands of young men to go and fight in Afghanistan.

'We didn't see eye to eye on the jihadi groups from the get-go,' said Wendy Chamberlin, the US Ambassador. 'We continually asked them to shut down the Kashmir groups. They continually asked in return for us to give them tariff breaks on textiles, knowing full well our Congress would not agree.'

Initially the Americans presumed these groups were all separate. However, the CIA was soon getting reports that LeT members had smuggled the al Qaeda logistics chief Abu Zubayda out of Afghanistan, taking advantage of the fact that the border police never stopped their distinctive Land Cruisers with their tinted windows and 'Free Kashmir' numberplates.

Then they went too far. In December 2001 Jaish-e-Mohammad and LeT were behind a suicide-bomb attack on the Indian parliament in which fourteen people were killed. They had apparently planned to murder a number of India's top politicians, but both houses had just adjourned, and the guards reacted promptly, killing all five bombers. An attack on the parliament of the world's biggest democracy was not going to go without a response. A week later India deployed almost a million troops to the borders in Kashmir and Punjab, the largest military mobilisation since the 1971 Indo–Pak war.

'We were near nuclear war,' said Chamberlin. 'Colin Powell, along with the British, did a wonderful job with the Indians getting them to back off. This was partly in return for us saying we'd push Musharraf on stopping these groups going across – I pushed quite hard. I was very clear he had to make a very sharp statement removing support from jihadis.'

On 12 January 2002, General Musharraf gave an address to the nation announcing that he was banning a number of jihadi groups: Lashkar-e-Toiba, Jaish-e-Mohammad, Harkat-ul-Mujaheddin, Sipah-e-Sahaba, TNSM and Tehrik-e-Jafaria. He had arrested hundreds of their members, including their leaders, raided their offices, frozen their bank accounts, and ordered an end to infiltration into Kashmir, their main cause. He even tackled the madrassas, the religious schools where many jihadis were trained and recruited, saying they must be registered by March. 'The writ of the government is being challenged,' he said. 'Pakistan has been made a soft state. The situation cannot be tolerated any longer.' Within minutes an ecstatic Wendy Chamberlin was on the phone to Colin Powell to say Musharraf had done all they had asked for.

More than 2,000 people had been rounded up. But 1,800 were soon released. After lying low for a while, the organisations simply changed their names, opened new websites, and shed the ostentatious black balaclavas and heavier weapons of their bodyguards. The frozen bank accounts turned out to have little money in them.

Not only were the jihadis freed, but some were even helped in the 2002 elections. Just as ISI had once brought parties together to stop Benazir Bhutto being re-elected back in 1990, this time it encouraged six religious parties to come together to stop mainstream secular parties. They formed the Muttahida Majlis-e-Amal, or MMA, known by everyone as the 'Mullah Military Alliance'.

Pakistan's religious parties were always good at getting people out on the streets, but they never did well in elections. This time, with ISI help, they won sixty-eight seats in the national assembly – almost 20 per cent – and swept to power in both border provinces, NWFP and Baluchistan. This meant ISI had a free hand for its activities in those provinces, as training grounds for militants and Taliban. Major General Ehtisham Zameer Jafferi, head of the ISI political cell, who had manipulated the whole thing, later went public.

One of those elected was a jihadi leader, Maulana Azam Tariq, head of the banned Sipah-e-Sahaba. He attended the wedding of the daughter of Musharraf's National Security Adviser despite facing at least fourteen charges of being involved in murders. Another leader, Hafiz Saeed, a retired engineering professor on a state pension, was touring the country stirring up support for his organisation Jamaat-al-Dawa, the new name for Lashkar-e-Toiba. In a typical speech in February 2003 in Rawalpindi, he railed, 'Allah has told us to make atom bombs. America is telling us not to. Who should we listen to, oh Muslims, Allah or America?'

'We released them because we had no evidence against them,' said Musharraf's spokesman General Rashid Qureshi when I went to see him in his office in Rawalpindi with its banks of TVs. 'Yes, they yell and they shout a lot, but that's not a crime.'

There was another view. 'Musharraf wants to have his jihadi cake and eat it,' complained a British diplomat I spoke to in Islamabad. 'He tricked the West, saying, "Pakistan is plagued by all these mullahs and jihadis, and I'm the only secular leader who can save you." But in fact he's thriving on these groups. Imagine if they weren't operating. Why should anyone need him to stay on?'

Many believed the leaders were freed because of what they might reveal in court about ISI.

One evening in March 2003, just as a purplish dusk was settling, I drove with my old friend Umar east of the city through lush paddy fields. Small boys were leading buffaloes home for the night, throwing up clouds of dust.

'That's it,' said Umar suddenly. Off to the right hundreds of strip-lights surrounded a field. It looked like a vast prison camp. 'That's Muridke.'

Silently we took the turn-off and drove up to a gatehouse. Bearded men with Kalashnikovs and camouflage jackets appeared, guarding the entrance surrounded by barbed wire and protected from view by tall trees. 'No visitors,' said one of the guards barring the way. 'It's just a school.' It wasn't. The sign at the entrance was for Lashkar-e-Toiba, the Army of the Pure, one of Pakistan's biggest jihadi groups.

Inside the 190-acre camp, aside from a school there was a bakery and a fish farm. The hundreds of teenage boys these fed spent their days listening to lectures glorifying jihad, or holy war. They would later write or record their death-wishes before heading off to fight, in the belief that they would be rewarded by beautiful virgins in paradise.

In central Lahore, LeT was building a large new mosque and office complex near the old Moghul fort of Chanpuri, under its new name Jamaat-al-Dawa.

I met the party's spokesman Yahya Mujahid in a room down an alley at the back of Temple Street, surrounded by guards with beards as long as bin Laden's and dressed in camouflage. On the wall was written, 'There is no Deity only Allah'. 'We are a common party like any other,' he said. 'We are working for preaching of Islam and we have madrassas and ambulances and clinics.'

Outside, thunder and rain had started, and I could hear doors banging and crows cawing. When I asked about the ban, he smiled patiently. 'Work is not stopped by banning organisations. When our leader calls, hundreds of thousands of people gather.' More would gather soon, he said, if the US invaded Iraq. 'We consider Allah to be a superpower, but America thinks it's a superpower.'

He told me that anger with what America was doing in Afghanistan had seen recruitment rise to record levels. In villages I had seen poor families distributing sweets to celebrate their sons being selected to go to camps like Muridke and to fight jihad, regarding it as an honour as well as meaning they would get free board and lodging and education. Although collecting money for jihad was officially banned, collection boxes had reappeared in shops and teahouses. During the Eid festival the previous month, when animals are sacrificed and their skins donated to charities to sell to shoe and bag factories, the banned parties were openly collecting animal hides. Mujahid told me it had been the best ever collection, with Jamaat-al-Dawa collecting 1.2 million hides, more than any other charity. He insisted, 'We are not a terrorist organisation but a common party like any other party. We have no fighting wing, only political ambitions and support for the Kashmir cause.'

But something had changed. In the past, collections had been for jihad in places like Afghanistan, Chechnya and Kashmir. This time many were calling it '*darul harab*', or war at home. Defence specialists estimated that there were more than 200,000 jihadis in Pakistan – a frightening number of armed and trained young men if they had nothing to do. 'They are a strategic asset,' said an army colonel. 'If we ever go to war in Kashmir we would need them.'

Their numbers had been bolstered by growing anti-Western sentiment in Pakistan, particularly among young people, which had been whipped up in the mosques since the bombing of Afghanistan. Over the previous ten years, since the scandal over BCCI, I had watched Pakistan becoming more and more anti-American. I'd been astonished after 9/11 at the number of Pakistani friends who insisted to me that Mossad had carried out the attack to blacken the image of Muslims.

Another new motivating factor had emerged in 2002 with the publication of shocking photographs from 'Camp X-Ray' at Guantánamo. These showed manacled inmates in cages, wearing orange hooded uniforms with earmuffs and blacked-out goggles, kneeling on the ground like dogs. Any moral high ground the US had for fighting the war in Afghanistan was lost at that point.

More than forty jihadi publications had sprung up after that, including a magazine called *Allah's Army* and a daily newspaper called *Islam*. Mehmood Shaam, editor of *Jang*, Pakistan's biggest-selling paper, told me that within a year *Islam* had become the second biggest-selling, with an estimated 200,000 readers. Page after page was devoted to photographs of 'martyrs', young men who had died in jihad, and accounts of their 'glorious' afterlife, as well as proud tributes from their mothers and sisters, stories of outrages from Guantánamo and of American guards kicking Korans. A typical editorial in *Zerb Momin* claimed, 'America wants to occupy all resources of the Muslim world. Its actual agenda is to crush the economic, military and atomic capabilities of the Islamic world. Now it has become imperative for the Muslim Ummah to step onto the battlefield and thwart America's evil designs.'

In 2002 Pakistan had seen its first suicide bombs, in Shaam's hometown of Karachi – one at the Sheraton Hotel in May in which fifteen people were killed, including eleven French naval engineers, and one in June at the American consulate, killing twelve Pakistanis. Afterwards Shaam wrote an article in *Jang* entitled 'Letter to a Suicide Bomber'. He urged the nation's youth to follow the peaceful way of its founder Mohammad Ali Jinnah and the poet Iqbal instead of choosing militancy. The response shocked him. 'I got hundreds of threatening letters saying, "We are on the right track, who are you to question us?" Even political leaders contacted me, saying, "You should not discourage this tendency."'

You only had to visit a madrassa to see what a Frankenstein's monster Pakistan had created. Madrassas were not a new phenomenon – like church schools in England, for centuries they had been the major sources of learning in the Islamic world. But during the Afghan jihad against the Soviet Union, madrassas in Pakistan mushroomed, funded by Saudi money and organisations promoting Wahhabism, and many of them became less concerned with scholarship and more concerned with making war on infidels.

Madrassas not only provide free education, but also free board and lodging. President Musharraf told CNN after 9/11 that they were 'the biggest welfare organisation' operating anywhere in the world. Millions of Pakistani families had no alternative but to send their children to madrassas if they wanted any form of education. Pakistan was one of only twelve countries in the world to spend less than 2 per cent of its GDP on education. Less than half the population are literate, and many poor families end up sending their children into bonded labour, making bricks or sewing footballs used on Western playing fields.

However, aside from teaching the Koran, memorising all 77,934 words of it, some madrassas added how to use a Kalashnikov to their curriculum, something I first witnessed at a religious school for young boys in Baluchistan back in 1988. When the Taliban movement emerged in the 1990s, these so-called 'universities of jihad' provided thousands of footsoldiers. One madrassa director, Maulana Sami-ul-Haq, boasted how he would declare holidays and send his students off to fight whenever he got the call from Mullah Omar. Encouraged by the state, others went to Kashmir to fight Pakistan's proxy war with India. 'Our educational institutes have become nurseries for all these militants,' said Anwar Ahmad Zia, Assistant Secretary for Education for Sind province. 'If we really want to eradicate them, that's where we must start.'

Lack of regulation meant no one even knew how many madrassas there were in Pakistan. Most estimates put their number at 13–20,000, educating between 1.5 and two million students. Only 1 per cent were registered. The former Minister for Religious Affairs, Mehmood Ahmed Ghazi, said he believed that only 1 per cent of them were involved in any kind of violence. That would still mean at least 130 schools, and thousands of students.

At first the US had not cared about the jihadis or madrassas or suicide bombers in Pakistan, because their focus was on al Qaeda, not the Taliban or any of these other groups. That missed the point: they were all connected. The main objective of these other groups may have been Kashmir, but global jihadists were training in Jamiat Ulema-e-Islam madrassas, using LeT camps, and being provided safe houses by people from Jamaat-e-Islami. 'We in the West made the mistake of seeing all these different Islamic organisations as hermetically sealed,' one Western diplomat told me. 'But in fact they all know each other, personnel and individuals shift around and help each other.'

Once they realised this, American and British officials didn't know what to do. They all seemed scared of destabilising

Musharraf, pointing at the 2002 elections as evidence that without him, the mullahs would take over. A destabilised Pakistan, with its growing nuclear arsenal falling into the hands of the mullahs, was the West's worst nightmare. Others argued that was precisely what Musharraf wanted them to think.

Few knew the inner workings of power in Pakistan as well as Husain Haqqani, himself a former Jamaat-e-Islami youth leader who had gone on to be a journalist, then an adviser for both military and non-military rulers. His book *Pakistan: Between Mosque and Military* looks at how the country's military rulers fomented and used Islamic militant groups for their own devices. 'Musharraf has been very good at convincing the West that his hands are tied, pleading *"Après moi, les islamistes,"*' he said. 'But there is no evidence for that. The real reason for his inaction is that these extremist groups were protégés of the state, just as it was the military that radicalised some of the madrassas and used them for recruitment of militants to send into Afghanistan and Kashmir. You can't use the same people who started the fire to put it out. It's very difficult for an intelligence agency to turn on its own.'

US officials feared that if they pushed too much on shutting down the jihadis they would lose Pakistan's help with hunting al Qaeda, particularly as bin Laden and his deputy Zawahiri were still at large. As early as autumn 2003 Rumsfeld questioned in a leaked memo if that was really the main priority. 'Is the US capturing, killing or deterring and dissuading more terrorists than the madrassas and radical Muslim clerics are recruiting, training and deploying against America?' he asked.

'It's better to have some cooperation than none,' Admiral Mike Mullen would later explain to me while he was President Obama's top military adviser. And the Pakistanis were clever, said Richard Armitage, 'because they have the ability to give just enough'.

*　*　*

As he pointed out, whenever a senior US official visited Pakistan to chew their ears off, a major al Qaeda figure would suddenly be caught. The biggest catch of all came in March 2003, just after I had visited the Muridke training camp. The war in Iraq was about to start, and I was supposed to be flying to Kuwait, but a trusted old contact told me to stay on, as something big was about to happen.

On the evening of Saturday, 1 March I was at a friend's house in Zaman Park, having filed my story for the week about the militant camps. He had just poured me a generous gin and tonic (alcohol may be banned in Pakistan, but the country's elite keep their bars well stocked) when my mobile rang. It was Sheikh Rashid, the Information Minister. 'We have caught a big fish,' he said.

'Osama?' I asked, sitting up alert.

'No,' he laughed. 'You know he is the golden goose.'

'OK. Al Zawahiri?' I ventured.

'No, no …'

I started working my way mentally through the list. Could it be the mastermind of 9/11 who had brazenly given an interview to the new Qatari TV station, al Jazeera, a few months earlier from Karachi? 'Khalid Sheikh Mohammad?' I suggested. 'No comment,' he replied.

'Wow! So it's him,' I exclaimed. 'Where? How?'

'No comment.'

'But the others you denied. This time you said "No comment."'

'Yes. No comment.'

The Pakistani government produced a photo of KSM looking wild-eyed and dishevelled, his hair all mussed up and a paunch hanging over the waistband of his pyjamas. It was hard to believe this man could mastermind anything, or that he'd had a $25 million price on his head.

Next morning I flew to Rawalpindi and took a cab to 18a Nisar Road, where KSM had been picked up in his pyjamas in a 2 a.m. raid. The house was slap bang in the military area, just a mile from Army House, where Musharraf lived. On the porch, I found two women in tears. One was Mahlaqa Khanum, who said she lived there with her husband Dr Abdul Qadoos, a microbiologist; the other was her daughter-in-law, married to their son Ahmed. They also lived in the house with their two children, Aisha, twelve, and Bilal, eight.

Mrs Khanum and her husband had been away for the weekend at a wedding in Lahore, so only Ahmed and his family were there, sleeping in a downstairs room. 'We were woken at 2 a.m. by a loud bang,' said Mrs Qadoos. The front door was forced open and twenty-five Pakistani police and ISI burst through. 'We were petrified,' she said. Her husband was arrested, and she and the children were bundled into a spare room and told to remain silent, guarded by an armed policeman, while for more than an hour officers ransacked the house.

The CIA had been tipped off about KSM's presence by one of his acquaintances, who had been on their payroll for months and was later flown out to the US under protective custody and with a hefty reward.

In an upstairs room the police found KSM fast asleep, having taken sleeping tablets. He tried to bribe them, but to no avail, and they dragged him out and arrested him. There was an unexpected bonus. Also staying there was a Saudi whom the CIA later discovered was Mustafa al Hawsawi, the al Qaeda moneyman who had organised transfers to the 9/11 hijackers.

The women insisted to me that they were all innocent, no one had been staying at the house, and that Ahmed had been kidnapped. 'I'm so worried for him,' said his mother. 'He was taken in his vest with no shoes, nothing – and he had flu.' She showed me a large cage of blue and green budgerigars on the terrace. 'These are his life,' she said. 'Ahmed is a very simple person. He had no job, he hardly went out, just to the mosque to pray. He never travelled and his main thing was pets. He loved pets. We wouldn't let him have a dog because we're an Islamic family, but he loved his budgies.' She told me that he would watch the army dog-training centre behind the house for hours.

She went inside and came back with a file of papers. Among them was a medical report describing Ahmed as a 'low IQ person'. 'You see, he is a simpleton not a terrorist,' she said.

GETTING IN

Their neighbour, Colonel Shahida, then popped by, and told a similar story. 'Ahmed can't be a terrorist,' he laughed. 'He's a goof. Once he shot himself in the hand because he was cleaning a gun with the barrel against his palm. They are a purdah-observing household. We never saw anyone strange enter the house.'

But it later emerged that Ahmed's mother was a leading member of the women's wing of Jamaat-e-Islami. The family had been housing al Hawsawi since January. Their other son, Adil, an army major, was also arrested. American and Pakistani intelligence officials said they had seized a laptop computer, a satellite phone, letters, cassettes of Osama bin Laden and documents.

'That's ridiculous,' protested Mrs Khanum. 'They took my diaries and address book, a box of family photographs, tapes of the Koran that I like listening to, and a computer we bought last month for the children.' Her granddaughter Aisha chimed in: 'It was our computer. We didn't even have the internet. It just had some games – Aladdin and The Lion King.'

The odd thing was that the photograph released of KSM supposedly just after his capture had him standing against a wall that didn't match anywhere in the house. I wondered if the whole thing had been some kind of set-up, particularly when ISI later held its first ever press conference. They screened a video, supposed to be of the raid, but which was so obviously a staged reconstruction that journalists started laughing.

Not everything in Pakistan is a conspiracy. It later turned out that the CIA back in Langley had decided the photos of KSM taken in the house were too flattering, so they had got their agents to take a new one once he was in detention, looking far more dishevelled.

Nobody could deny he was an impressive catch. 'It's hard to overstate how significant this is,' said Ari Fleischer, the White House spokesman. KSM was the fifth leading al Qaeda operative to be arrested in Pakistan in a year. 'No one can criticise Pakistan's commitment to the war on terror,' insisted Faisal Saleh Hayat, the Interior Minister. 'No one has done more than us. We have arrested more than 440 al Qaeda suspects'.

This was hard to verify, as no one would give names or details. And there was a disconcerting fact. None of the so-called high-value targets actually seemed to have been hiding. They had all been picked up in different Pakistani cities, all sheltered by local families. 'Pakistan is the key to solving the war on terrorism,' President Karzai kept insisting. 'We know Taliban are gathering openly. You can't play a double game in terrorism.'

From Rawalpindi, I went to Kabul. It was a flying visit, as the war in Iraq was about to start any day, and I was supposed to be in Kuwait. Karzai joked he would close the airport so I couldn't leave. I almost wished he would. 'You know the world will forget us now,' he said.

10

A Tale of Two Wars

Shkin, Paktika, Afghan–Pakistan border, September 2003

WHEN AN AMERICAN army officer describes somewhere as 'the most evil place on earth', it is a foregone conclusion that journalists will want to go there, or their editors will send them. So when Colonel Rodney Davis, spokesman for the US forces in Afghanistan, used this phrase to describe Shkin in south-eastern Afghanistan, I knew I would end up there.

I had just come back from a long, hot summer in Baghdad. The battle for Fallujah was kicking off, and the UN headquarters in Iraq had just been blown up, killing twenty-two people including the hugely popular Brazilian Special Representative Sérgio Vieira de Mello.

Like that of Afghanistan, the invasion of Iraq initially seemed quick and successful. Unlike Afghanistan, this time the Bush administration sent ground troops – 245,000 of them, along with 45,000 British, 2,000 Australians and a few hundred Poles: the so-called 'coalition of the willing'. Operation Iraqi Freedom kicked off in the early hours of 20 March 2003, with 'shock and awe' airstrikes on targets across Baghdad in a massive display of pyrotechnics. I watched on CNN from the Kuwait Hilton, which had become the hotel for US officials and journalists waiting for war, and felt the familiar skin-crawling of fear and anticipation. Later that day I would cross the border into southern Iraq behind endless columns of US troops.

Within just three weeks, the huge bronze statue of Saddam Hussein in Baghdad's Firdous Square had been toppled by cheering crowds, an emblematic end to twenty-four years of Saddam's rule. Back in the Kuwait Hilton, US officials were doing high fives and talking 'Iran next'. On 1 May, President Bush jumped out of a fighter jet onto the deck of the aircraft carrier the USS *Abraham Lincoln* and stood under a 'Mission Accomplished' banner as he declared the war over.

The toppling of Saddam's statue later turned out to have been staged by US Marines, which seemed to sum the whole thing up. I thought Iraq was a disaster. I'd spent the war in the south covering the British forces tasked with capturing Basra, and seen how they were not welcomed with flowers and waves, but by sullen faces, even stones.

As soon as Basra fell, half the city seemed to turn out to loot everything from the banks to the museum. The streets were full of streams of people carrying air-conditioning units, office chairs, microscopes from the university, even hospital beds. The British forces made no attempt to stop them – only the oil installations were guarded.

When my newspaper held an end-of-war party in London for those of us who had covered it, I refused to go. It was the first time in my journalistic career that I had reported on a war my own country was involved in which I felt very strongly was the wrong thing to do. I'd never been convinced of any connection between the Saddam regime and al Qaeda or 9/11, despite the efforts of the British intelligence services to leak stories of contacts between them, and of Iraqis training al Qaeda in bomb-making. On the contrary, it was clear from conversations during my trip to Pakistan on the eve of the war that the attack on Iraq would be a rallying point for even more anti-Western sentiment.

The main pretext for the invasion had of course been Saddam's much-vaunted weapons of mass destruction (WMD), which Bush and Blair were still insisting would be found. The summer after

Baghdad fell, I watched the many teams searching for them get nowhere. I spent a day following them: they swooped into a site identified from satellite pictures as suspect, bursting into a locked room only to find a cupboard full of vacuum cleaners. Sensitive documents that they picked up turned out to be someone's high-school biology project.

I also met Iraqi chemical-weapons scientists, including Brigadier General Ala Saeed, the head of quality control, who told me he had done a doctorate at Sussex University and missed Brighton, where he still had an account at the Nat West bank. He took me deep into the desert to al Muthanna, the regime's main chemical-weapons complex. There he showed me bombed-out laboratories where Iraq had once produced deadly nerve agents like sarin and mustard gas, used on the Kurds to terrible effect in Halabja in 1988, killing at least 5,000 people, and tried to develop VX, which needs only one droplet on the skin to kill. The complex had been bombed in the first Gulf War in 1991, and Saeed insisted that all production and bulk agents had been destroyed by 1994. All that was left was what he called the 'forbidden programme', a small operation run by the Mukhabarat intelligence service in the basements of houses. Saeed had been responsible for the reports to UN weapons inspectors, so I asked why on earth, if they didn't have any WMD, hadn't they let them have access to everything? He said it was a question of face, an important issue in the Arab world. No scientist wanted to be the one to tell Saddam that they were not managing to produce anything, nor was Saddam about to reveal any weakness. Had we gone to war for hubris on both sides?

In the run-up to the war, at Foreign Office press briefings in Whitehall, I'd asked several times about the plan for afterwards – how to replace the regime. They were very vague, and I'd assumed they were being secretive. But once Saddam was gone, it quickly became clear there was no plan at all. Many Iraqis had been left without water or power by the bombing, and there seemed to be a complete inability to restore basic services. Nothing illustrated the chaos more clearly than the fact that one of the world's biggest oil producers suddenly had enormous queues at petrol stations.

The Bush administration had not yet found a Hamid Karzai to run Iraq, so they set up something called the CPA – the Coalition Provisional Authority. This was based in a high-walled complex on the Tigris where Saddam had built a series of palaces in classic dictator chic, all marble floors, gold taps and giant chandeliers, and stocked with plentiful supplies of Cuban cigars. It became known as the Green Zone. The CPA seemed to be staffed by young Republicans with clipboards who kept talking about 'Free Iraq'. They had just seventeen Arabic-speakers for 6,000 staff, and added more and more concrete barriers, ever higher razor wire and Hesco sacks, and parked tanks at the gate, with the result that they gradually became more and more cut off from the rest of the country.

The Green Zone was such a cloud cuckoo land that while bombs were going off on the streets outside, one American was drawing up a new Iraqi traffic code. He based it on that of the state of Maryland, which he had downloaded from the internet, and it included the advice that 'Pedestrians walking during cloudy weather should wear light or reflective clothing.'

The CPA's first official act would have rather more far-reaching impact. Order Number 1 on 16 May 2003 decreed the de-Ba'athification of Iraqi society, to purge all members of Saddam's ruling party from the state and disband the entire 450,000-strong army. It was immediately clear that this was a really bad idea. At Al Kindy hospital I met Dr Osama Saleh, head of the orthopaedic department, who had just finished his twentieth operation that week. One of only twenty orthopaedic surgeons in Iraq, he was about to lose his job because he was a senior Ba'ath Party member, even though he pointed out that under the Saddam regime you had to be a party member to get a government job.

Even more worryingly, along the roadside one day I got talking to a man selling cigarettes and fizzy drinks who turned out to be an army major. His name was Haider Ali Said Khusan, and he invited me to his home to meet his wife and three pretty young daughters. He told me he had been in the army for nineteen years, and had fought three wars for his country – one against Iran and two against the US – yet he was now forced to hawk things on the street to feed his family. He called some other officers over to meet me. All said they had only ever been following orders, were happy to see Saddam go, and had expected to serve whoever took over, not to lose their livelihoods. 'Our loyalty as soldiers was to Iraq, whoever was running it,' said Major Khusan. Hundreds of thousands of disaffected, well-trained soldiers from the past regime with nothing to do – and lots of weapons – was a bad thing.

Iraq was a country replete with place-names from my school history books. That hot summer before the violence kicked off, I managed to go to Babylon, of hanging gardens fame, which Saddam had spoilt by rebuilding them with his name stamped on bricks; to Samarra, where I climbed the ziggurat of the great golden-domed mosque, a spiral minaret that reminded me of one of those retractable children's telescopes; to Uruk, the first city in the world, of which Gilgamesh was King; and best of all to the Tree of Knowledge. Who knew that was an actual thing? An Iraqi from the southern marshes took me one afternoon to al Qurnah, where the Euphrates and Tigris rivers meet before emptying into the Persian Gulf. There, in a dusty garden by the waterside, was an ancient tree with a small concrete plaque describing it as 'Adam's Tree', the very place where Eve ate the forbidden fruit. The tree looked dead.

It would have been more thrilling to visit these places if there weren't American soldiers everywhere. They were very jumpy after a spate of suicide bombs at checkpoints, and suspicious of the local people, whom they referred to as 'Eye-rakis' or 'hajis'. It got to the stage that whenever we approached a checkpoint, my colleagues made me poke my blonde head out of the vehicle's window so we wouldn't get shot at. Vast prison camps had been set up under a female brigadier who had no experience of managing prisons, and just as in Afghanistan, there were reports of innocent people being detained and of prisoners being abused.

I had always been sceptical of reports of links between al Qaeda and Saddam Hussein, but the US-led invasion had created links where there had been none. In 2002 it wasn't just George W. Bush who was preparing for Iraq. Abu Musab al-Zarqawi, a Jordanian former gangster who had once worked in a video-hire shop, from which he had been sacked, moved from Afghanistan, where he had been working with Osama bin Laden, to Iraq, to create the al Qaeda franchise there. Bin Laden publicly urged jihadists to go and join it. It was al-Zarqawi who was behind the attack on the UN headquarters at the Canal Hotel, and targeting US soldiers.

All the time I was in Iraq, Hamid Karzai's words were ringing in my ears: 'No one will care about us now.'

I was happy to be back in Afghanistan, even if it meant flying Ariana, or 'Scaryana', as we called it. The plane to Kabul the previous day had lost its front wheel, and circled round and round to offload fuel before making an emergency landing on its belly.

Kabul airport was as chaotic as usual. A baggage belt had appeared, but it did not go round. Some bemused-looking grey-haired and grey-suited British men were wandering around, and I asked them what they were doing there. 'We're customs officers,' replied one. 'We've come to teach the Afghans how to use the green and red channels.' I looked at all the Afghans grabbing cases, boxes of food, plastic containers of holy water from Mecca and electronic gadgets from Dubai. They were all swarming out of the exit, completely ignoring the channels. These people had fought twenty-three years of war, and been locked away under one of the world's most repressive Islamic regimes. Now the West had liberated them and given them customs channels. 'Good luck,' I said.

Besides, with that year's opium crop the biggest ever at 3,600 tons, it occurred to me that it might be more important to stop things going out than coming in. Bill Rammell, the Parliamentary Under-Secretary of State at the Foreign Office with responsibility for the drug trade, told me that 95 per cent of the heroin sold on UK streets came from Afghanistan. But I had long ago given up trying to understand Western priorities in Afghanistan. No one was going to bother now. Afghanistan was already yesterday's war.

The Mustafa Hotel was deserted. Its manager Wais Faizi was sitting brooding in his room in his leather jacket. There were pots of pills on his desk. Afghanistan wasn't working out as he had imagined, and he was missing New Jersey. He said he was being asked for bribes the whole time, and that the Northern Alliance was trying to kill him.

He was very happy to see me, however, and took me on a guided tour of all his latest innovations. He had tried to make a downstairs coffee bar, and had bought an espresso machine, but it had blown up in a power surge. He'd lost the spacious room that had been his office to his white-bearded father, who had also come back from America, and who sat there all day with other bearded friends drinking tea, clinking amber worry beads and shaking their heads like nodding dogs.

Much to his father's disapproval, Wais had kept his promise to open a bar. To enter it meant opening a heavy vault door with a giant combination lock. Inside was all pink marble floors and mirrored ceilings, and the Four Horsemen of the Apocalypse protruded from one wall. There was a snooker table where a group of Americans were pulling out flick-knives to see who had the biggest blade, and a drunk Belgian photographer tried to show me snaps he had taken of women's cleavages. The bar was lined with bottles of Johnnie Walker, and there was a dancing Osama bin Laden doll on the counter. You could order a Tora Bora Sunrise (vodka and pomegranate) or a Green Goddess (Heineken) from a barman with a dotted line tattooed on his neck over the words 'Cut Here'. There were bullet-holes in the ceiling from shoot-outs, and in one corner was a giant-screen TV with a DVD playing *Apocalypse Now*. It looked exactly the sort of place Hollywood might dream up for a war zone.

I was put as usual on the fifth floor, which Wais called 'the private floor'. It felt rather too private, as I was the only guest, which made me feel a bit vulnerable. The lights were very dim – Wais's refusal to pay bribes meant the hotel often had no power. 'We are an island of darkness in a sea of light,' I complained to him one night. Not only was this uncomfortable, but it made it hard to work. There were lots of new guesthouses with power, internet connections, proper rooms instead of glass cubicles, showers instead of buckets, and rose gardens instead of pigeon coops. I could see that in future I was going to have to stay elsewhere, and I would feel horrible about it. Wais always called me his sister.

The roads in Kabul were as potholed as ever, and the traffic much worse, with lots of Afghan refugees having come back from Pakistan and Iran. There was one very positive change as far as we foreigners were concerned – in the affluent suburb of Wazir Akbar Khan, where many NGOs and warlords were based, an enterprising Thai divorcee named Lalita Thongngamkam had opened a restaurant called Lal Thai, with spicy green chicken curry and beer and wine served by Thai waitresses with pistols in their garters. She told me she specialised in what she called 'post-conflict restaurants', and so far had opened them in Vietnam, Laos, Rwanda, Kosovo and East Timor. Her next plan was Baghdad. The prices were outrageous – a meal cost the average annual salary for an Afghan – but I could see it was a good idea, with Kabul full of UN workers and consultants on huge salaries and nothing to spend them on. As Lalita said, 'People still have to eat, and there's not much competition.'

On 1 May, hours before President Bush landed on the deck of the *Abraham Lincoln* and stood under the 'Mission Accomplished' banner, his Defense Secretary Donald Rumsfeld was in Kabul making a similar declaration at a press conference in Hamid Karzai's palace. 'We clearly have moved from major combat activity to a period of stability and stabilisation and reconstruction activities,' he said. 'The bulk of the country today is permissive, it's secure.'

The reality on the ground was rather different. Government workers had not been paid for months, because Karzai had no money, and indeed three weeks after Rumsfeld's declaration he publicly threatened to resign.

As for the security, when I went to see Nick Downie, the security coordinator for all the aid agencies based in Kabul, he painted a less optimistic picture. While everyone was focused on Iraq, the Taliban were coming back in the south and east of Afghanistan, he said, and were not just attacking the US troops. Aid workers had also become targets – both foreigners and local staff for working with the 'infidel'. Attacks were taking place on aid workers almost every day, he said, with eight killed in the past sixteen days. There were reports of training camps reopening in Pakistan near the Afghan border.

The ISAF peacekeeping troops were still confined to Kabul, and numbered a paltry 5,000. The new Afghan army the US was supposed to be training had attracted only 2,000 recruits. In August NATO had taken over command of ISAF, the first time the Alliance had mounted a theatre outside Europe, and there were finally plans to expand outside the capital, as Karzai had been pleading for. The idea was to start with the north – which seemed perverse, as that was the most peaceful part of Afghanistan. But the US still had around 11,000 troops roaming the country in their parallel Operation Enduring Freedom, looking for bin Laden, even though everyone I talked to said he was in Pakistan. They did not want ISAF troops in their way.

To try to see for myself what was going on, there seemed nowhere better to head than south-east to Shkin, the place that had been described as the most evil on earth.

I arranged an embed with the US Army, and drove with photographer Paul Hackett through spitting rain up to Bagram, the US headquarters in Afghanistan, about an hour north of Kabul. Once a Soviet base, it was a vast site, about 6,000 acres, on a plain looking towards the snow-capped mountains of the Hindu Kush. I was amazed how it had grown since my previous visit more than a year earlier. Tents were being replaced by plywood structures called 'B Huts', and a food plaza was being built which I was told would have a burger joint, a Pizza Hut and a Subway sandwich bar. There was already a Green Bean coffee and muffin bar. Lots of gravel had been trucked in to try to keep down the endless dust, and it crunched under our boots as we walked. Someone with a sense of humour had named the main street 'Disney Drive'. It looked as if the Americans were planning to be there for some time.

A Tale of Two Wars

A large hangar served as a makeshift prison for Afghans picked up on the battlefield, many of whom had simply been in the wrong place at the wrong time, or were victims of false information from enemies. The inmates were rumoured to include Aafia Siddiqui, a Pakistani scientist dubbed 'Lady al Qaeda' who had been missing since March, when she was last seen getting in a taxi in Karachi with her three children and heading for the station. No one knew, as no one had access. Hundreds of people were detained for years without trial or any contact with family or lawyers.

Later I'd meet people who had been inside, and who would confirm disturbing reports of prisoners being stripped naked, hooded and kept standing in perpetual light with music blasting. Two detainees had died the previous December from torture and beatings. One of them was a twenty-two-year-old taxi driver called Dilawar from Khost, a father of two who had been picked up driving near a US base after a rocket attack and found to be carrying a passenger with a walkie-talkie. The *New York Times* reported in March 2003 that the US military death certificates for both of the deceased gave the cause of death as 'homicide'. Everyone was too wrapped up in the impending war in Iraq to take much notice. By the time I went there the Bagram military interrogators responsible had been redeployed to another prison – Abu Ghraib in Baghdad, where their methods would soon be known worldwide.

I met Colonel Davis, or 'Colonel D' as everyone called him, for a briefing in a large hangar by the airfield. A long-limbed man from Virginia, he had a Southern drawl in which he said things like, 'We're here to kill, to put a line of red dots on foreheads,' then spat over his shoulder and hooted with laughter. He confirmed that where we were headed was currently the most dangerous place in Afghanistan. 'Yes, ma'am!' he said. 'It's real Mad Max territory.' I felt relieved, then I realised how warped that was.

Shkin was right on the border with Pakistan, and most of the attacks were hit-and-runs from the other side, the tribal area of Waziristan, where it was thought al Qaeda had fled after escaping Tora Bora. Two American soldiers had been killed a few days earlier, and the base came under daily rocket fire. Some of the encounters were ending up on al Qaeda recruitment videos.

Like most military, Colonel D spoke in acronyms. He talked of frequent 'TIC's, which meant troops in contact – attacks, in plain English – and told me I could not report what I saw in the 'TOC', the tactical operations centre. Helicopters he referred to as 'birds', and all the clocks were set on something called 'Zulu time', which was an hour behind the UK, and four and a half hours behind local time. He warned me I might have to wait at Bagram for days before I got a bird, as journalists were pretty low down on their priority list – in fact last.

I asked if we could visit the prison while we were waiting, and his shoulders shook with laughter. 'What prison?'

Bagram blacked out at night to reduce the chances of an attack, so Colonel D told us we needed to buy blue or red filters for our torches, as well as goggles against the dust in the day, which he said was even worse at Shkin than at Bagram. This gave us an excuse to go to the PX, the army shop where you could buy Dime bars, Dr Pepper drinks, protein muscle-building powders, and all manner of cool gadgets and war souvenirs like T-shirts and mugs with an OEF slogan and the American eagle, though there was nothing to rival the Saddam watches from Iraq. There was an array of DVDs and Xbox games, mostly involving shooting, which was apparently how the soldiers spent their downtime. I bought mini LED blue and red torches, a camouflage bandanna and some Snickers bars. Then we went to the chow hall, where we feasted on bacon cheeseburgers and sloppy joes, chopped iceberg lettuce, tomatoes, croutons and dressings from the salad bar, ice cream with toppings and Oreo cookies from a special counter, and Forest Dew and Snapple drinks from huge fridges. It was as if we weren't in Afghanistan at all.

Colonel D handed us over to Major Richard Sater, an air force reservist whose job back home was as a classical-music announcer for public radio. He had spent a year as a Mormon missionary in Newcastle, and professed a fondness for the British. He took us to the press tent, which they had christened 'Pressmenistan'. We unrolled our sleeping bags on fold-out army cots and lay listening to the scurrying of little mice looking for biscuit crumbs.

Perhaps Colonel Davis was worried about us wandering around the prison, as the Mormon music announcer woke us at 3.30 a.m. to say there was a bird going to Shkin, and to hurry. Flights with the military were always at ungodly hours. Blearily I put on my flak jacket, my helmet on which my blood group was scrawled, and my new goggles and bandanna, and we rushed to the airfield. So many helicopters were coming and going it was like Heathrow, but there was no sign of ours. First light cast a pink glow on the snow-topped mountains, and brought out joggers who started running along the perimeter road round the airfield. Dawn came and went. Travelling with the army was all about hurry-up-and-wait. All around me soldiers lay on their packs reading Harry Potter or Dan Brown's *Da Vinci Code*. Few people spoke. I longed for a coffee.

I kept thinking about something Major Sater had told me about the commander of Bagram, General John Vines. All military wear a dogtag stamped with their name, blood group and service, and the General told his troops he had also stamped his with 'Infidel'. This, he said, was 'to remind myself how they think of us'.

It was 8.30 a.m. when we were finally called. I ran into the Chinook, laughed at for ducking under the whirring rotors. Inside, I was handed a pair of squashy yellow earplugs. In the corner, somewhat disconcertingly, was a pile of boxes marked 'Blood for Shkin'. It was cold, and the gunner took pity on me and gave me his sweatshirt to wrap around my hands. Strangely, though I can rarely sleep on passenger jets, on noisy, juddering Chinooks I often fall asleep instantly.

When I awoke a couple of hours later we were over the mountainous border province of Paktika. Pashtuns say that after Allah created the earth he had a pile of rocks left from which he created Afghanistan, and it certainly looked like it. It was hard to imagine anywhere as hostile to man's presence as this moonscape of pewter and beige. No vegetation seemed to grow but thorny bushes; there was nothing green or soft on the eye. In summer there was no shade from the harsh 120°F sun, while in winter sub-zero winds seemed to pierce the bone. I wondered how on earth people lived there, or what they did.

The helicopter was almost hugging the scree-covered hillside, climbing and descending as one mountain range after another rose jaggedly from the ground like scales along the spine of a giant dragon. So close to the ground were we that we could count the goats and make out the brightly coloured clothing of a few Kuchi nomads, and it felt as if we could touch the rocks from the open sides where the gunners sat. The pilot explained that we flew so low to make it harder for anyone to fix a bearing on us. Even so we were fired on as we landed in a wide valley with fudge-coloured mountains all around.

Orgun E was the last base before Shkin, just fifteen miles away, and we were told the helicopter would go no further, as Shkin was under attack. It looked down on a village which was actually called Urgun, a small, very poor place of mud-walled houses and cupboard-sized shops. The base had been there just over a year and a half, and had about three hundred soldiers, mostly from the 10th Mountain Division and special forces, of whom just three were women. Conditions were better than I expected – there were showers and closed WCs, and wooden shacks with cots. We stayed in the room of Airman Sergeant Osborne, who coordinated the helicopters in and out and always had a radio pack on his back and an antenna sticking up behind his head, reminding me of the cartoon character Rolie Polie Olie, who my little boy loved.

A patrol was about to go out to search for illegal weapons, and we managed to ride along. We set off in three open vehicles and one Humvee. I was directed to the Humvee, which was very uncomfortable in my heavy flak jacket, bumping over the ruts, but less dusty than it was for the men on the open vehicles, who were quickly coated in grey. There were large piles of potatoes along the side of the road, which were presumably the local crop, though it was hard to believe anything could grow in this rocky terrain. A few children waved then ran away. I wondered what the soldiers must look like to them, bristling with arms and wearing Oakley sunglasses or goggles under their helmets, like some kind of aliens. It was like the twenty-first century coming face to face with the Middle Ages.

The road was just a rough single track along the base of the valley. The area around Orgun E was inhabited by some of the fiercest tribesmen on earth – the Wazirs and Mahsuds, who all carried weapons and lived by the extreme honour code of Pashtunwali, which called for an eye for an eye.

Winston Churchill, who started his career as a war correspondent and a soldier with British forces fighting Pashtun tribesmen along these borders in 1897, accused his fellow Brits of romanticising Pashtunwali. To him it was 'a system of ethics which regards treachery and violence as virtues rather than vices'.

Blood feuds carried down generations, and some of the adobe forts dotted about on the hillsides had watchtowers so a lookout could be kept for enemies. 'How do you know if they're good or bad guys?' I asked Captain Opladen, the patrol commander, as we passed another fort. 'Trial and error,' he replied. 'If they shoot at us we know they're bad guys.' This was not reassuring. He also told me the vehicles were always breaking down, which was even less reassuring.

The real problem in these borderlands, however, was that only the Americans seemed to take any notice of the border. The Wazirs and Mahsuds lived on both sides of it, and crossed back and forth at will. Like many Pashtun tribes they had been split by the drawing of the Durand Line by the British in 1893. On a map the Durand Line might officially run the 1,610 miles between Afghanistan and Pakistan, but it wasn't a border you could physically see – locals described it as 'drawn on water'.

Sir Henry Mortimer Durand, the civil servant with monocle, top hat and cane after whom it was named, appeared to have just drawn a pencil line along the mountains, separating pasture from villages and in some places even cutting villages in two. The Afghans never recognised the line, feeling they had been tricked into it – and the agreement had anyway expired after a hundred years. Nobody knew exactly, but there were about twenty-six million Pashtuns on the Pakistan side and about fourteen million in Afghanistan, all able to cross the border as they pleased.

On the other side of the border, just beyond Shkin, was South Waziristan, the tribal area where it was believed Osama bin Laden and his men had gone after escaping Tora Bora.

After a while I realised that the road was not really a road, but a dried-up riverbed. Some way along we stopped and set up a checkpoint. The soldiers jumped out of the vehicles and crouched by their sides, guns at the ready – 'locked and loaded'.

It was surprising how much traffic passed through on this non-road in the middle of nowhere. Soon we had a queue of Toyota pick-ups, all packed with Afghans – 'ragheads', the soldiers called them. We had no interpreter, so the men had some difficulty explaining what they wanted. The Afghans came out of their vehicles, hands in the air. Some looked scared. Everyone had heard stories of the Americans raiding houses, going into women's quarters in the middle of the night, and sending people to Guantánamo. The proud tribesmen clearly did not like being patted down by foreign soldiers.

To start with the Americans only found AK47s. Every Afghan is allowed one AK47. Then one young soldier shouted, 'Hey, I found anthrax!'

Everyone rushed over and stared at the small glass vial he was holding up. It was labelled 'Anthrax spore vaccine'. The turbaned man in whose pocket it had been found kept saying '*Wuz,*' which was Pashto for goat. Finally the soldiers decided the anthrax must be for his flock, though I had never heard of an Afghan injecting his animals. On the other hand, it seemed unlikely that a farmer in a remote village would be planning an anthrax attack.

After checking for weapons, the soldiers asked questions. 'Have you seen any al Qaeda?' The Afghans looked blank.

'Al Qaeda? Al Qaeda?'

They shook their heads. '*Wo, wo.*' No.

'Osama bin Laden?'

'*Wo.*'

It all seemed a bit pointless. Was someone really going to say, 'Oh yes, he came for tea yesterday'?

We got back to the base in time for lunch. It was 'surf 'n' turf' day, the last thing I'd expected in Paktika, with ribs as well as lobster tails flown in from Florida, brought in on my flight apparently, along with the blood. On the TV there was nothing but Iraq.

Behind some netting and a large satellite dish was the TOC, or control room, which we were invited to after lunch to meet the commander. Inside, officers pored over maps marked 'Classified', monitored radio frequencies used by al Qaeda, studied satellite images coming in and downloaded intelligence gleaned from recently captured prisoners, some of whom were in cages outside.

We weren't allowed to call them prisoners – they were PUCs, or 'persons under control' – and I was told I wasn't allowed to write about them, as it would be 'prisoner exploitation'. That seemed to be the least of their worries. I could see that they were being made to wear snorkel masks, and were kept standing. One of the soldiers guarding them told me this was to try to break them down, and that sometimes they 'cried like babies' at night.

Sitting at a desk, drinking black coffee from a paper cup, small lines of tiredness etched around his eyes, was Lieutenant Colonel Michael Howard, a thoughtful and surprisingly soft-spoken man who commanded all 1,050 troops at four firebases in the border area.

Here in Orgun E nobody talked about that other war 1,400 miles to the west. Many of the men in the control room had seen some of the heaviest fighting of the whole war in Afghanistan.

'This is the real front line in the war against terror,' Howard told us. The last few months had seen much more activity, and he said that every day there were 'skirmishes'. The word reminded me of the old books I had read in the India Office papers in the British Library. A number of al Qaeda had settled across the border in Waziristan, he said, Arabs and Chechens, perhaps marrying into the local tribes and radicalising them. Their fighters were going back and forth across the border from a country that was supposed to be one of America's main allies in the war on terror.

'The fighting is on their terms,' shrugged the Colonel. 'We have to wait for them to come to us. Then when we attack back they run across the border and come back to fight another day. It's very frustrating.'

While we waited to go to Shkin, we wandered round the base. There was a makeshift gym, and on its wall someone had painted: 'The More You Sweat In Training The Less You Will Bleed In Combat'. We ended up in the internet room, which soldiers could sign up to use. Mostly they seemed to be trying to buy Mustangs and Dodgers on credit at exorbitant interest rates.

I got talking to a Sergeant with large Austin Powers glasses. His name was Don Kenitzer, and he told me he was an artilleryman, just as his father had been in the Korean War, and was in his ninth year in the army. 'It's the first time I've had people shooting at me,' he said, recounting how a few days before he had to dive to the ground between tents as 107mm rockets pounded the base. 'In two months here we've had seventeen rocket attacks. Thank God they're not accurate. What gets me is, why would anyone fight over this place? Nothing grows here but terrorists and rocks.'

We were joined by Specialist Beau Hawkins, who looked just out of school but told me he was twenty-five, with a five-year-old daughter back home in Washington State. He spoke like James Dean. 'Before I came here I'd never been shot at,' he drawled. 'Now I've been in twenty-five ambushes.' He had just come from Shkin after one ambush that was almost too many, and was bored at Orgun E. He was spending his days writing endless letters to outdoor-equipment companies, asking them to sponsor his unit and to send telescopes. So far he had received nothing in response but a catalogue. That day he planned to write to Hugh Hefner asking for a night at the Playboy Mansion for his unit when they got out of Afghanistan.

'I want to get sent to Iraq next,' he said. As a father, didn't he fear for his life, I asked. 'Of course you're scared,' he admitted. 'But after the rounds have gone off just over your head a couple of times you get beyond fear, you've got to get your men back alive. Besides, this guy Osama bin Laden is waging a holy war against America, and it's my job to put an end to it so my daughter can grow up safely.'

American soldiers openly spoke of God and avenging 9/11. Many of them wore crucifixes round their necks. Given President Bush's unfortunate use of the word 'crusade' in describing the war on terrorism, I could see how this could be taken the wrong way by Muslims, who saw it as an invocation of Christian holy war which had seen thousands of unarmed Muslims slaughtered in the capture of Jerusalem nine hundred years earlier, following the call of a Pope promising his warriors a passport to heaven. In his videos bin Laden would repeatedly talk of the 'crusader war against the Islamic world'.[1]

In the evening I went out with a night patrol. It was so cold that even with woolly tights under my trousers, a fleece, a jumper, a windproof Gore-Tex jacket and thermal mittens I'd borrowed from my mum, I was still freezing.

We drove without lights. The moon was very full and large, casting a pinky glow on the mountains. We went back to the river-bed and set up another checkpoint where the soldiers started checking what they called 'acid-trip trucks' – the colourful jingle trucks I had seen in Pakistan. They were all laden high with wood from the remaining border forests, which was being taken to be sold in the main town of Ghazni. It was probably illegal, if Afghanistan had any environmental laws. I told the soldiers about the secret compartments and false floors the Pakistani frontier guards in Baluchistan had explained to me, but it was far too complicated to get anyone here to unload all the logs to check. Then a Toyota pick-up full of bearded men with weapons and a small boy drove up at speed. Everyone got very excited and trained their guns on them, till the men presented a torn sheet from an exercise book stating 'we Afghan police go Surobi'.

The Americans were about to wave them on. 'How do you know

they're Afghan police?' I asked. 'It's just a bit of paper anyone could have written.'

Fortunately, this time we had an interpreter. His name was Qulbuddin, but the Americans called him 'Q', or 'the Terp', as they said his name was too complicated. He wore dark glasses even though it was night, and a scarf wrapped round his head and most of his face. 'People will kill me,' he explained to me. He told me he kept getting 'night letters' – papers pinned on his door at night warning that he and his family would be killed if he did not stop working for the infidels. I noticed he didn't bother to translate much of what was said.

By the time we got back to camp I could no longer feel my toes or fingers, and the chow hall had stopped serving dinner. The only food we could find was 'compressed wheat substitute rolls' and dry Froot Loops from the cereal dispenser. Everyone was in a bad mood.

The most interesting part of the camp was supposed to be off-limits. This was where the special forces were based – immediately identifiable as they were not in uniform, had bulky muscles from endless workouts, wore Oakleys and baseball caps over their sunburnt faces, and grew beards to try to look like Afghans, which they didn't at all. They had 'gators', or quad bikes, which they used to zoom around the camp. There were also some even more shadowy people from the CIA 'special activities division', which we weren't supposed to know existed.

Some of the SF were quite chatty, and one, who said his name was 'Brad', took me for a ride around the camp on his quad bike. None of them seemed very optimistic about the future of Afghanistan. 'These people switch allegiance like the change in the moon,' said one.

They were supposed to be finding bin Laden and al Qaeda, but they admitted that the trail for bin Laden had gone cold. This was not helped by the fact that many of their Delta Force colleagues in Task Force 121 had been pulled out and sent to Iraq, where they were busy trying to find Saddam Hussein. One of them, whom I'd got to know quite well, had ended up escorting Ahmed Chalabi, one of the leading Iraqi exiles, to Baghdad, much to his irritation. Meanwhile all the leads he had painstakingly built in Afghanistan and Pakistan melted away.

'Brad' didn't seem to think their departure had made much difference. 'What we're doing searching for the top guys is futile,' he said. 'Unless we do something at grassroots and make it secure so there can be development, then the bad guys will always have recruits.' He told me that al Qaeda had put a $1,000 bounty on the head of each interpreter, and $5,000 for killing an American.

'Three major problems,' he said. 'One – Pakistan. Two – Pakistan. And three – no one believes we will stick around.' He told me he had recently given some sweets to a ten-year-old boy and told him, 'We'll be back.' The boy replied, 'Oh no you won't. You never come back.'

Finally a helicopter was going to Shkin, and we were told we could go on it. Helicopters only flew to Shkin in pairs, and never turned off their engines but hovered just long enough to disgorge one lot of American troops and load another. All the time a smaller Black Hawk patrolled the skies above them.

The Americans had taken over a mud fortress perched on a desolate rock-strewn hill, surrounded by coiled barbed wire, and with a US flag fluttering from a pole. It looked like something from the Wild West, and very exposed. 'Welcome to Shkin' read a hand-painted sign as the Chinook touched ground, churning up thick clouds of dust with its whirring blades.

'Trust me, you don't want to be here,' said one man who was waiting to jump on as we jumped off. He said his name was Bruce Capehart, and he was a combat psychiatrist. I told him I'd never heard of such a thing. 'Wait till you've been to Shkin,' he replied.

It was a desolate place, so primitive that soldiers there sometimes went days without water. Gritty dust coated everything, getting in the mouth, eyes, ears and under fingernails, so all the soldiers seemed to have grey complexions and eyelashes, and at night they kept me awake with their hacking coughs.

The Pakistan border post was clearly visible on a pine ridge on the mountain facing us. Beyond that was South Waziristan and the village of Angor Adda, where bin Laden may or may not have been hiding, but which US officials described as the capital of al Qaeda. Eight men had recently been found dead with their ears cut off and dollars stuffed in their pockets, apparently a warning of what happens to informers.

The most recent fighting had begun on 27 August, with an ambush of US troops who included Specialist Beau Hawkins, who I met at Orgun E.

'It was the day after my twenty-fifth birthday,' he told me. 'I was driving the second of two vehicles. Our strategy was that we'd often go into combat areas in two trucks as bait to try and lure the enemy, but that time we were in what was supposed to be a nice area. As we were coming over the hill, our first truck started receiving fire from the hill, then before we could react they were firing on us too, using AK47s with armour-piercing rounds. We kept trying to push through, but the enemy knows our battle drill and it was non-stop bullets. We were on a narrow road in a valley near the Pakistan border so we couldn't turn round. In the end we got into an overwatch position about half a kilometre away where we could see the enemy, and we were going to call in 105 artillery, but then the enemy pushed out four or five women in front. We didn't know if they were fighters dressed as women or what, but they know we can't call in artillery if there are civilians present. So we called in the Quick Reaction Force, who came in vehicles, but they got hit really badly so we had to get back into the firefight to pull them out. The enemy were firing RPGs on us and we were trapped, so in the end we called in air support. RAF Harriers flew in and dropped a thousand-pound bomb on them, and that was that.'

Hawkins was lucky. Four days later his two best friends, Specialist Thomas and PFC Fuller, both snipers, were ambushed in the same area, now known as 'Ambush Alley', and killed. 'After that some of our guys went to try and find the guys who had done it, and a guy walked out from behind the tree and they shot at him. But before they could get him, he'd unpinned a hand grenade and blown himself up. There were body parts flying everywhere.'

The man was identified as a Chechen – also Muslims, Chechens had been training with al Qaeda in Peshawar and Afghanistan since the 1990s for their own fight for independence against Russian domination, and had been behind the siege in a Moscow theatre which I had covered in 2002, and the attack on a school in Beslan in 2004. A video camera was found where the man had been hiding. On it was footage of fighters praying in mosques before launching an ambush, attacks on American troops, and alarmingly close-up shots of the US base at Shkin. Many of the fighters on the film were Chechens.

'Chechens are the hard guys,' said Hawkins. 'And they pick up their bodies, like us – they believe that if they don't bury their men before dark they go to hell. So we try to blow up their bodies so they can't bury them.'

Since then the attacks on the Americans had been relentless, rockets on the base often seeming to be timed for when the troops were eating chow, which they christened 'Rocket Hour', and becoming more accurate than before, even hitting the control room. Apart from mortars and RPGs, the al Qaeda fighters around Shkin were using remote-controlled landmines, Russian Dishka machine guns, and new Chinese 122mm combustion rockets, which were silent.

The fighting was so much more disciplined and sophisticated than anything the Americans had encountered before as to convince them that there must be a high-level al Qaeda official organising it, perhaps bin Laden's Egyptian deputy Ayman al Zawahiri. Locals had told the soldiers that the former doctor was regularly in Urgun before the American bombing of Afghanistan started in 2001. 'It was the first time we'd seen anything of that complexity,' said Captain Tom McCarron. 'Someone had to be in charge down there to synchronise it.'

It was clear who they really blamed. Some of the shooting had come directly from Pakistani border posts manned by the Waziri Scouts. They had watched as Pakistani army trucks delivered Taliban fighters to the border then collected them a few days later, even giving them covering fire while they crossed over. At Bagram there were often wireless intercepts between Taliban commanders and Pakistan army officers. Taliban would speak to officers at border checkpoints asking for safe passage.

The soldiers told me that in the most recent attacks on Shkin the fighters had been wearing US Army uniforms. 'They were wearing our uniforms, our ponchos, and swigging from Snapple bottles as if to taunt us,' said Second Lieutenant Eric Schwartz. 'Others had cloaks covering their bandoleers of bullets so we'd think they were civilians. They were Chechens and Waziris, and they fight dirty. You know, a lot of people think the war here in Afghanistan is over, but we're on the ground, and I'm telling you, this is where the war on terrorism really is, and it's getting harder.'

I wasn't allowed to stay long in Shkin, as an operation was about to get under way, so I was transferred back to the relative safety of Orgun E. I went out on one last patrol with Captain Opladen's men and 'Q', this time handing out schoolbooks and accompanied by a medic vaccinating children.

It was clear that the soldiers meant well. Afghanistan was an alien culture which they struggled to comprehend, a land where people sold their children, men with guns held hands and older men were entertained by young tea boys. But they were shocked by the poverty, and wanted to help. Some of them used their own money to buy sweets or pens for the children, and got people back home to send things. But they were never going to win hearts and minds while the special forces were carrying out night raids on villages, or airstrikes that sometimes killed civilians.

To every local he encountered, Captain Opladen said, 'Any problems, come to the base.' That seemed very unlikely. He admitted that none had ever come.

I said to a local man, 'These Americans are building you a clinic, bringing you things which you accept. Yet every night you rocket them.'

'It is very simple,' he replied. 'They will go and the bad guys will still be here.'

11

Voting With Mullah Omar

Sangisar, October 2004

I SPENT THE night before Afghanistan's first ever presidential election sleeping next to a ballot box in the village where Mullah Omar used to preach.

Sangisar, twenty-five miles south-west of Kandahar, had not seen rain for seven years. The houses, flat-roofed and with walls of hard-packed mud, were so bleached and baked by the fierce sun that they appeared to be dissolving into the desert. Afghans are on a different calendar to the West, so to them this was the year 1383, but the village looked like something from Biblical times.

I was the guest of Haji Ahmat Shah Lakokhel, a senior elder from the village whom I had met a few days earlier at the house of Hamid Karzai's brother and campaign manager Ahmed Wali. There could hardly be anywhere more symbolic than the place where the Taliban was founded.

His house was a small fort. He led me into a guest room shaped like a barrel, with a domed roof and no windows, so it would stay cool in the burning summers. 'Haji' is the honorific every man gets once he has been on the annual Haj pilgrimage, and a shiny poster of Mecca was the only decoration. There were cushions scattered around, and a white plastic crate in pride of place which he explained was the ballot box. A boy brought green tea and boiled sweets, and we sat talking by the flickering light of a kerosene lamp.

Haji gave me a potted history of the village. Although it looked ancient, he told me most of the houses were less than fifteen years old, as the original village had been completely destroyed by bombing during the Russian occupation. He himself had narrowly escaped with his life, sheltering from a bombing raid under a roof with three other people, who had all been killed. Like more than three million Afghans, he had spent the rest of the war in Pakistan. On the way into the village I had seen the sprawling cemetery of stones and tattered coloured flags, reminders of death all over a country which saw almost a tenth of its population killed in that war.

About three hundred people lived in the village, and like much of Afghanistan it was completely neglected by the government. There was no school – the nearest was an hour away by bicycle. They had no electricity, no TV, no running water. Once they had grown wheat and barley, but the seven years of drought had put an end to that. Anyway, Haji said, aid organisations like the World Food Programme had brought in wheat, which destroyed prices. Now all they had left were grapes, and they risked losing those too, as even the deep wells were drying. All the wells dug for drinking water had dried up except one. Many of the men had gone back to Pakistan to work on road-building to send back money.

It was a grim and hard life. Yet Haji seemed quite excited about the election, and said everyone would vote for Karzai. 'How do you know?' I asked. 'We had a meeting and decided,' he replied. 'Also, they will give us irrigation and maybe money.'

That wasn't exactly how the new democracy was supposed to work. President Karzai himself had told people a few days earlier, 'If someone comes and tells you, "I will give you money to vote for me," if someone uses force to tell you to vote for me, don't vote for me.'

It seemed to me that Afghanistan had a lot of other priorities than costly elections. The presidential election had already been delayed twice, and parliamentary elections, which were supposed to happen simultaneously, had been postponed till the following year. However, in June President Bush had described Afghanistan as the first victory in the war on terror, and with the situation in

Iraq deteriorating every day, the White House was eager to trum-
pet the birth of Afghan democracy. 'Votes instead of guns' was the
message it wanted to convey.

I asked Haji if the women of Sangisar would vote, and he
laughed. 'No women will vote here,' he said. He told me his wife,
Mariam, had wanted to register, but he and his mother were horrified, telling her she would bring shame on the family. 'Also, it will
be dangerous for us in the future if the Taliban find she got a card.'

Haji took me across a courtyard and through a curtained-off
doorway to meet his mother and his wife, who like all rural Pashtun
women were in purdah, and his seven children. I had brought some
of my son's old toys, including a cuddly penguin and a tower of
plastic building blocks. The penguin was put on the shelf next to
the Koran, like a prized ornament. Mariam gave each child a plastic
block which they used for their food. We ate after the men had
finished and sent us out their leftovers. It was nan bread with a
fatty mutton stew, followed by yoghurt curd floating unappetis-
ingly in water.

After we had eaten Haji took me back to the guest room, where
some men with long grey beards, sun-wrinkled faces and silky
turbans had arrived. They were chewing opium paste. They all said
they planned to vote, despite threats from the Taliban to disrupt
the elections. 'I heard on the radio that the Americans asked
Pakistan to stop the Taliban attacking the elections,' said one man.
Was it that easy? 'Yes,' said Haji. 'It is ISI training people and sending them to destroy villages and kill people. Pakistanis keep coming
here, they killed and wounded twenty-two people nearby, but they
are not here now.' He was not happy about the American forces.
'They arrest people and keep them naked, which is very shameful
for us. At night they go into women's quarters. Some people may
take revenge.'

The men had never talked to a foreign woman, and one asked if
he could put some questions to me. I could hardly say no. But after
so many years of going to Afghanistan, I might have known what
was coming.

'In your land, Inglistan, do you have arranged marriages or love marriages?' he asked.

'Love,' I replied.

'So how do you know who to marry?'

'You fall in love.'

The turbaned men looked at me blankly. Bollywood movies had yet to arrive in Sangisar.

'How many wives can your men take?'

'One.'

'What about in times of war?'

'Still just one.'

This was baffling to them. They could have four even in peacetime.

'How much is a wife?' asked another man.

I laughed. 'Wives are very expensive.'

'What is the exact price, say for your sister?'

'I meant expensive to maintain,' I replied. 'We don't pay for wives!'

To that they grunted in approval. 'Here they are expensive, 3 to 400,000 afghanis for a satisfactory one.'

That was £4,000, which seemed an astronomical sum.

'Can you marry your cousin?' they asked. 'That way the money stays in the family.'

It was already midnight and I was tiring of this Afghan Twenty Questions, so I told Haji I would like to sleep. The turbaned men were also staying. We would sleep on the cushions in our clothes. As Haji unrolled the eiderdowns for each of us to lie under, there was one last question. 'Why does your husband let you wander round alone like this?'

We didn't sleep much. It was cold on the mud floor even on the cushions, and at 4 a.m. the men got up to pray, spitting noisily into a bowl.

By 7 a.m. polling was due to begin, and a crowd of other men arrived, emerging from the dust, dark-cloaked figures against the morning chill. Some were on donkeys; others had brought small flocks of goats. Haji carried the ballot box to the courtyard where voting would take place. The only problem was that there was no sign of the election officials.

While we were waiting, one man took me to see the rubble of the small mosque they called the White Mosque, in which Mullah Omar used to preach. This was where the founding meeting of the Taliban was held in the autumn of 1994, when forty or fifty mullahs gathered to agree to cleanse the region of armed mujaheddin who were robbing and raping people, and chose Mullah Omar as their leader.[1] 'He lived here with his wife and they had a child,' said my guide, who like Haji told me he knew nothing of the meeting. 'He was not a bright man.' Nobody seemed to want to talk about Mullah Omar. They obviously didn't want to be known as the Taliban village.

Around 8.30 a.m. a couple of police were dropped off by a pick-up. They were carrying RPGs, which they promptly dropped. Then an election official arrived. A white sheet was draped over some poles to make a polling booth in the corner of Haji's court-yard, and a trestle table was set up. The first voter had his registra-tion card punched and his thumb dipped in purple ink so he could not vote twice. He was given a long green ballot paper with the photos and names and symbols of eighteen candidates.

The man took his ballot paper to the polling booth and stared at it. Like most of the people in the village he couldn't read, so he looked at the pictures. There was one woman, much to his aston-ishment; at least one warlord, General Dostum; Abdul Sattar Siarat, the original choice for President of the Bonn Conference; Yunus Qanuni of the Northern Alliance; and a number of others.

'Who do I pick?' he asked me. I tried to explain that he should vote for whoever he thought best for the country. It turned out to be an easy choice. Haji had taken up a position by the booth, and pointed to the box to tick next to Hamid Karzai, whose symbol was the scales of justice.

This was not exactly democracy as the Bush administration envisaged it, but everyone seemed happy. One of the men with goats, Mohammad Rahim, waved his purple thumb and told me he was so happy he felt like dancing. 'We are illiterate people, we don't really know what this voting means, but we heard it was good,' he said.

Indeed, it was so good they asked me if I'd like to vote too. I was tempted. If I voted it would have a huge impact on their voting statistics. Just to check, I had gone to the other end of the village, to the clinic that was being used as the women's polling centre. It had been chosen so women could say they were going to the doctor rather than voting. Not a single woman had cast a vote.

The Americans had clearly been expecting trouble, as the vote-counting centre in Kandahar looked as well-guarded as Guantánamo. Presumably for symbolic reasons, they had chosen as the venue the old stadium where the Taliban used to execute people and amputate limbs. A ring of shipping containers had been positioned around the counting tents, then sniper trenches, then more shipping containers, surrounded by barbed wire. Next to it was a large military encampment with US, Romanian and Afghan troops. In a surreal touch, next door to that was the new fairground, with a pink and green neon ferris wheel.

The day before the election I went out on a dawn patrol with a US Army pys-ops team – the people responsible for psychological warfare, or propaganda. The aim of the patrol was to reassure people not to be scared of the Taliban, and to come out and vote. To do this we set off in Humvees with a speaker on top broadcasting one of twelve messages such as, 'This is the ANA and the US Army. We are here to help and bring peace. Do not listen to the Taliban.' I wasn't sure if the people of Kandahar really appreciated that at 5 o'clock in the morning.

'This is the best job in the army. We get to drive around being nice to people,' said Captain Lowe, who was next to me in the Humvee. His feelings weren't exactly reciprocated. They had been in Afghanistan a year, and told me they'd had their windscreens shot out more times than they cared to remember, particularly further west in Uruzgan, where they had been handing out 'wanted' posters featuring Osama bin Laden, Mullah Omar and Ayman al

Zawahiri. The posters asked for people to come forward with information, and promised a $10 million reward. Not a single person came forward.

In between the 'Go vote' messages, Captain Lowe put on a Norah Jones CD. 'Norah got us through this deployment,' he said. It was bizarre driving through the streets of Kandahar blasting Norah Jones as the city was coming to life and people began appearing pushing carts piled high with onions or pomegranates.

Our destination was a small mud-walled outskirt of Kandahar called Dand district, and once we arrived, some of us got out and walked. The men handed out what they jokingly referred to as 'Afghan porn' – leaflets showing Afghan women voting with their faces uncovered. This was a presence patrol to show people that the US Army were around and they could vote safely. 'In this society guns and money talk,' said Major Flynn, the press officer, 'and we got the monopoly on both.'

They didn't have much sense of direction, however. The plan was for the vehicles to drive around the village, and meet those of us who were on foot at the other end. The Humvees and jeeps started bumping along narrow tracks between mud walls. But after crossing narrow bridges and manoeuvring around tight corners which one of the soldiers described as 'great ambush country' they came to a dead end, the vehicles nearly crashing into each other. It was almost impossible to turn round, and there was chaos. While I stood watching, a bemused man in a mint-green *shalwar* asked, 'When you've finished surveying this village, can you come and survey ours?'

The election seemed to be the great success the international community had hoped for. More than eight million Afghans voted – nearly 80 per cent of the electorate. When Bush heard from his own National Security Adviser, Condi Rice, about the long queues which had led to polling stations extending their hours, he was delighted. 'History shows that when given the chance, people of every race and religion take extraordinary risks for liberty,' he wrote in his memoir.

Afghanistan is a vast country with few roads and many remote valleys, some of which are only accessible by donkey, and it took two weeks to collect all the votes and count them. After my experience in Sangisar it was no surprise to me that when the results came in Karzai had won easily, with 55.4 per cent. That was more than three times as much as the second-placed Qanuni, with 16.3 per cent, so there would be no second round. Twelve candidates, including the woman, got less than 1 per cent.

Almost all the losing candidates cried fraud. They pointed out that people had voted several times, as the special UN ink could be washed off with soap and water, and that many people had registered twice. A three-man UN panel was set up, and found that there had been fraud, particularly ballot-box stuffing, and as many as 15 per cent of people had registered twice, but that the fraud was not limited to one candidate, and was therefore apparently acceptable. 'There were fewer problems on election day than many experts had anticipated,' concluded Craig Jenness, one of the panel members. In other words, this was Afghanistan, the West had wanted Karzai to win, and no one outside really minded if he'd had a little help. The margin of victory was such that Karzai would no doubt have won anyway, but ignoring the fraud was a decision that would come back to haunt future elections.

Tony Blair was the first to congratulate him. 'I am sure the whole House will join me in sending congratulations to President Karzai,' he told the House of Commons. Bush liked Karzai, flattering his ego with weekly video conferences and folksy advice, but he was not particularly interested in Afghanistan. The brave American soldiers I had embedded with the previous year in Shkin complained to me in an email that there was more coverage of Janet Jackson's 'wardrobe malfunction' when she inadvertently revealed a breast at the Superbowl half-time show than of their derring-do in the hostile borderlands.

The truth was that the Bush administration had its hands full with Iraq. Saddam Hussein had been captured and executed, but there was a mounting insurgency by his fellow Sunni Arabs, who only made up a fifth of the population but who had ruled the Shia majority for centuries. There were shoot-outs and bombs across the country. A survey by the medical journal the *Lancet* had put the number of Iraqis killed already at more than 100,000.[2]

The US was losing one soldier a day in Iraq, compared to one a week in Afghanistan. The priorities were clear – there were 138,000 US soldiers in Iraq, and just 20,000 international forces in Afghanistan, and the US military was spending $4 billion a month on operations in Iraq, compared to $900 million a month on Afghanistan, even though the two countries had similar-sized populations, and Afghanistan was half as big again as Iraq.

General David Barno, the US commander in Afghanistan, did not feel he needed more troops. 'There was a duckboard theory among some people that Taliban were like hornets under a duck-board, so if you don't go walking in those areas you don't run into them,' he said. 'But the election argued otherwise – we were in every province, and they didn't come out and attack us.' Every day he got violence figures for the two theatres. 'By early 2005 Afghanistan was zero to three insurgent incidents per day, which was just background noise really, while Iraq was ten times that and rising, and would soon be two hundred.'[3]

Bush admitted that he had made a 'miscalculation' of what conditions would be in post-war Iraq. That was not the only 'miscalculation'. The original argument for invading Afghanistan and then Iraq had been to win the 'war on terror', and make sure there was no base for al Qaeda. But contrary to reports issued before the war in Iraq, al Qaeda had never been present in that country. Then, on 23 October 2004, two weeks after the Afghan election, Iraq experienced its most horrific attack yet. A group of fifty newly trained Iraqi soldiers were heading home on leave in three minibuses when they were ambushed at a fake checkpoint north of Baghdad. They were made to lie down, and shot dead one by one. A new group, al Qaeda in Mesopotamia (later al Qaeda in Iraq), led by the Jordanian al-Zarqawi, claimed responsibility. Terror was spreading.

* * *

Afghanistan was nation-building on the cheap, and mostly it looked like it. What money came in was spent on Western priorities like the elections and gender-awareness training, and even animals for the zoo. Meanwhile, even in the capital many people were living in bombed-out buildings with no roofs or windows, while the river that ran through the centre was a cesspit of garbage.

Every Afghan I met complained about being asked for bribes by officials to do anything. The growing corruption was hindering foreign investment. In my guesthouse I was invited to share some salami and rye bread with a group of disappointed German businessmen who had spent the last two years trying to set up Afghanistan's first sugar factory. It sounded like a good idea in a country which uses so much sugar with its tea, but imports it all. They had invested fifteen million euros, making it the biggest private investment in the country so far. They had made six trips back and forth, and all had been arranged for the grand inauguration ceremony, to which they'd invited 1,500 people. But when they arrived the Finance Minister told them it was cancelled because they 'hadn't followed proper procedures'. It soon became clear that this meant they hadn't bribed the right people. On top of that, their licence had been granted by the Minister of Light Industries, and he and the Finance Minister were not on speaking terms.

Afghans complained particularly about the courts and the police. In some parts of Kabul the police, most of them former mujaheddin, were terrorising neighbourhoods, looting homes.

One day I went to the Kabul Police Academy to watch a session of riot-control training by the Americans. It was hilarious. The police were holding their riot shields like knights of old, and waving their batons as if they were conducting orchestras. When they were told to turn, they all crashed into each other and fell over. The earnest press officer from Missouri was keen for me to report that among them were four women. 'This is a historic day for Afghanistan,' she said. The policewomen were in full chador, which was not ideal for a riot-control exercise, as they could not see very well. Underneath hers, one of them was wearing fishnet tights and high, spangly sandals she could hardly walk in. When I spoke to the women it turned out they had all been police during Russian times, but had been sent home under the Taliban. I asked the lady from Missouri if it might not be more useful training the police how to carry RPGs, as everywhere I went I saw them dropping them, but she looked bemused.

At the end the police were presented certificates, which they all stared at. It was clear that most of them could not read. Afterwards one of them came up to me and blatantly asked for dollars. 'What kind of example are you setting?' I asked him, crossly. He explained that they were not being paid, and he needed to feed his family. 'We are human too,' he said. Their official salary was $30 a month, but as no one in Afghanistan had a bank account, this was supposed to be distributed by their commander. Some months he gave them $5, sometimes nothing. This was alarming, as foreign NGOs were paying their guards more per day than his monthly salary, which hardly encouraged good people to stay in the police. When I asked the earnest press lady about it, she said, 'Ma'am, that's an Afghan matter.'

A British friend working out of a shipping container in Karzai's palace to help create a National Security Directorate told me that of the $112 million estimated to be needed for the first two years of the Law and Order Trust Fund to create a police force, only $11.5 million had been received. 'If you don't do simple things like paying the police then you are on a hiding to nothing,' he said. 'What's the point in training them if they have to go and steal bread?'

My unpaid policeman later became a Deputy Inspector in Kandahar, and I visited him at his office. He had placed his riot shield on top of his filing cabinet with plastic flowers around it as an ornament.

Kabul was like a different country from Sangisar. I didn't stay at the Mustafa this time but at the Gandamack, Kabul's most convivial guesthouse, which had been opened by Peter Jouvenal, a British TV cameraman and former soldier, who I had known years before back in Peshawar. Decorated with Peter's collection of Victorian rifles, the Gandamack quickly became a favourite for journalists with its 'no rice zone' menu that instead offered British favourites like shepherd's pie and breakfast of bacon and eggs. He'd even opened a cellar pub called the Hare and Hounds, complete with beermats and a dartboard.

On a pre-election trip to Kabul in August 2004, Donald Rumsfeld had said, 'Every time I come I notice the amazing progress that's being made ... energy on the streets, the new stores, kiosks, cars ...' I wasn't sure this was quite what he had in mind. Indeed, all sorts of unlikely places were springing up in post-liberation Kabul. Down a long alley by the side of the Chinese Embassy, two young British men whose father ran one of the many private security agencies in Kabul had opened a sea-green-and-chrome lounge bar called the Elbow Room. 'Like Soho in Kabul,' someone said. Except the music had to compete with the constant hum of Apaches and Chinooks overhead. The Elbow Room made great margaritas and also offered club steaks for $19, which I tucked into happily until I thought about the unpaid policeman.

That wasn't all. There was a Hot and Sizzling steakhouse; the Deutsche Hof Bierhaus offering pork chops and sauerkraut; and a number of Chinese massage parlours offering all sorts of things. The latest opening, a French restaurant, l'Atmosphère, which everyone called Latmo, even had a swimming pool. I had never thought of taking a bikini to Kabul. Outside all these places the streets were crowded with the Land Cruisers of foreign aid workers and consultants. Not only were the restaurants way beyond the pay of the locals who actually lived in Kabul, most of them had signs saying 'No Afghans allowed'.

One day I even met a British tour group. Admittedly, there were only two in the group, the rest having dropped out when the Minister of Tourism, who had written them a welcome letter, had been assassinated. The pair admitted that this had put them off slightly. Benedict Jenks said his friends told him he was 'absolutely mad' to go to Afghanistan. However, when I ran into them in Emperor Babur's Garden, they were clearly enjoying themselves.

'The best things always involve risk,' said Peter Lowes, a seventy-seven-year-old grandfather of ten. 'I might as well die stepping on a landmine in Afghanistan as in an old people's home in England.'

My friend Dominic, who was helping to set up Afghanistan's first private radio station, took me to a new Croatian restaurant that served prosciutto, cold beer and fried calamari. There was so much going on that he'd started a magazine, *Afghan Scene*, which had *Hello*-style social pages and in its first edition boasted a fashion article entitled 'I Can't Believe I'm Buying a Tube Top in Kabul'. He told me that at the Mustafa someone had recently borrowed a monkey from the zoo and taken it into the bar, and the guests had all been photographing it holding a Kalashnikov. The place was becoming seriously weird.

Hamid Karzai was in chipper mood after the elections. He invited me for coffee at the palace, which was easier said than done, as there were layers of x-ray machines and sniffer dogs to get through, and his office was guarded by burly men with wraparound mirrored sunglasses and M4 rifles with telescopic sights. The man who on first arriving in Kabul had told Marshal Fahim 'Your men will be my guards' had ended up being guarded by Americans. Initially these were US special forces, who had saved him from an assassination attempt in Kandahar that left him badly rattled and rarely leaving the palace. At the end of 2002 the responsibility was handed over to the American private security company DynCorp. They referred to Karzai as 'Roadrunner', and were incredibly aggressive to visitors.

To get into the palace that day I had to pass through three body checks, four bag checks and two dog checks. Inside, Karzai was meeting with tribal elders as he did every afternoon at around four, after prayers, and just as he had at his house in Peshawar when I first met him. He might have been a bad manager, but he was very good at tribal politics, and so far he had kept the fractious country together. The palace garden by the mosque was full of men in baggy pyjamas, pinstriped waistcoats and elaborate turbans. The men from DynCorp watched them suspiciously. When one of them suddenly got up and started speaking, their guns followed his every move. 'What's with that dude?' one of them asked me. 'He's reading a poem,' I explained. The suspicion was mutual. It was clear the tribal elders visiting didn't appreciate being patted down by Americans. Many of them had come to see the President to complain about American forces raiding their villages, going into their women's quarters or bringing in dogs. Nor did it seem to send a great message to Afghans that the President didn't trust them to look after his security.

Election day had been the most violent day of the year, but Karzai was clearly relieved that the disruption had been less than feared. 'I am very happy,' he said. 'The Taliban are finished, both as a political organisation which will stop people going to vote or a military one that can threaten them. They are just terrorists, with a leadership of maybe a hundred. The others are footsoldiers, trapped or forced to fight by the Pakistanis because they are told otherwise they will be handed over to the Americans.'

But he didn't want to talk politics. He wanted to reminisce about the 1980s in Peshawar, and the trip we had taken into Kandahar during the jihad. 'I never imagined I'd be President then,' he said. 'Do you remember in that orchard in Argandab, eating fish and pomegranates?'

Mostly I remembered being bombed.

'We were young then,' he sighed.

A few days later I went back to do an interview. As elected President, he said, he was holding out an olive branch to the Taliban to end their life on the run. His aim was to split what he called good and bad Taliban. 'There are probably fifty to a hundred who have committed crimes against Afghan people who still continue to hobnob with AQ and terrorists. They are not welcome. But for the rest, for thousands of them, this is their country like it's my country, and they are welcome to come and live and contribute to its economic prosperity.'

Afterwards I chatted with his National Security Adviser, the soft-spoken Zulmay Rassoul, who was always the subject of palace gossip as he was unmarried, unusually for an Afghan, and believed to have a great love affair in Rome. Rassoul said he thought it was the moment to act decisively to finish off the job that should have been done three years earlier, when the Taliban were on the run. 'What we need is major cooperation with Pakistan to stop production of new Taliban in madrassas and the training and support of old ones,' he said. 'We need realism from Pakistan that terrorism isn't something for others. And we need realism from the US that ISI are part of terrorism – you can't separate the man doing the act from the men promoting the act and giving logistical support.'

For a while it seemed as if Pakistan had realised this. The tiger that General Musharraf had been riding, of nurturing some militants while helping the US go after others (for which the US was paying handsome rewards), was starting to get out of control.

By then Musharraf had had two narrow escapes. The first was on 14 December 2003, the day Saddam Hussein was found by US special forces of Taskforce 121 in a 'rathole', the dark cellar of a small farmhouse on the banks of the Tigris. Musharraf had just heard the news, and was travelling back to Army House in Rawalpindi when a bomb blew up a bridge thirty seconds after he had crossed it. The blast was so powerful that it sent his three-ton armour-plated Mercedes into the air. Eleven days later, on Christmas Day, two suicide bombers drove vans at his motorcade in the same area and detonated their bombs, killing fourteen people including themselves, and injuring many others. 'As my car became airborne I was staring terrorism in the face,' Musharraf later wrote. His wife Sehba, hearing the nearby blasts, was hysterical. Musharraf went on television looking shaken. 'I am the target,' he said. 'These blasts have given new strength to my resolve to eliminate terrorists and extremists from the country.'

After each attack the surrounding areas were sealed and scoured for clues. Musharraf put the investigation in the hands of General Ashfaq Kayani, the Rawalpindi corps commander. Ghoulishly, the head of one of the bombers was found on a roof, and the face was reconstructed and found to match the picture on a charred identity card also discovered at the scene. The mobile phone of one of the bombers had also blown onto a roof, and although the terrorists were switching SIM cards, if they used the same physical phone they could still be traced.

Musharraf's US allies kept offering help, and eventually ISI asked for their technical assistance with identifying explosives. After four weeks when they were presented with the US report, Musharraf complained it was 'nothing we didn't know'. 'That was the help we got from our friends,' he wrote sourly.[4]

Kayani's investigation led to an alarming discovery. The first attack had involved six members of the Pakistan Air Force (PAF), working with the jihadi group Jaish-e-Mohammad and al Qaeda. The second had involved members of the army's elite Special Services Brigade of commandos, Musharraf's own regiment, as well as of the security guard of his Vice Chief of Staff. Pakistan's powerful military had been infiltrated by Islamic militants. Musharraf shrugged this off. 'It is almost impossible to guard against extremists indoctrinating the lower ranks in any armed forces,' he wrote in his memoir.

One of the PAF officials arrested was Flight Engineer Adnan Rasheed. Though he was given the death penalty, he continued to have access to phones in jail, regularly posted on social media, and eventually escaped to become a Taliban commander. He would later claim that there was a secret organisation inside the Pakistan military called Idara tul Pakistan (the Institution of Pakistan), linked to Jaish-e-Mohammad, which was aimed at nurturing jihadist networks. 'We are soldiers in uniform and they are soldiers without uniform,' he said of JeM, 'and we are all reporting to ISI.'

The West's two most important leaders on the ground in the war on terror had both had narrow escapes within just over a year. For the US, Musharraf's near-misses had a positive outcome. His investigators traced the assassination plots back to Waziristan, and three months later, in March 2004, Pakistan sent large numbers of troops into the tribal areas for the first time.

Across the border from Shkin, where I had been embedded the previous year, 7,000 troops were sent into the rugged mountains and valleys of South Waziristan – more than the international forces had in Kabul. General Barno, the US commander, said he hoped that Pakistan operations on one side and the US on the other would create a 'hammer and anvil effect' to flush out al Qaeda fighters who had settled there.

Apart from clearing out the foreign fighters, the aim of the Pakistan troops was to go after Nek Mohammad, a Waziri tribesman with long black hair who was the main facilitator for al Qaeda in the area. He had been a car thief as a teenager, and had joined the Taliban in 1993, when he was just eighteen. The military's plan was to use the old British method of punishing tribes collectively by demolishing the houses of those who sheltered the militants. However, the Pakistani soldiers were unprepared for the resistance they encountered. 'We were shocked by the response,' said General Aurakzai, commander of the Frontier Corps. 'We thought they must be protecting someone important.'

A bloody battle ensued, with Pakistani helicopter gunships and heavy artillery pounding the area. The Pakistani military claimed they had surrounded Ayman al Zawahiri, but later said he had 'slipped the net', and then that he wasn't there at all.

Many of the foreign fighters in the region were from the Islamic Movement of Uzbekistan (IMU), led by Tahir Yuldashev, and were dug into tunnels, while their hosts, the Pashtun tribesmen, rallied under Nek Mohammad and Baitullah Mehsud. The Pakistani army sustained heavy casualties and the tribesmen took twenty soldiers hostage, of whom they left eight in a ditch, shot in the head. After just twelve days the Pakistanis agreed to withdraw, in order to secure the release of the remaining hostages. A peace agreement was signed on 24 April 2004 between Nek Mohammad and General Safdar Hussain, the Pakistani commander. Under this deal the foreign fighters were allowed to stay in South Waziristan, but were supposed to 'register' with the authorities. The government promised funding to local Taliban so they could pay 'debts' to al Qaeda.

The stiff resistance made clear that many tribesmen had been radicalised by their al Qaeda guests. Yet rather than fearing the implications of this for itself, Pakistan still thought in terms of proxies and how these could be used against the Americans in Afghanistan, who ISI reported were increasingly bogged down.

The foreign fighters never registered. Nek Mohammad boasted to journalists that the Pakistani commander had been forced to capitulate to him, and the peace deal broke down. A couple of months later, in June, he was giving an interview on his satellite phone when he heard a metallic whirring above and asked a follower what it was. The next day a Hellfire missile slammed into his compound, blowing off one of his legs and killing him and four others, including two boys of ten and sixteen. At the time Pakistan's military spokesman Major General Shaukat Sultan told the press that Pakistani forces had rocketed the compound. In fact Nek Mohammad had been killed by a CIA Predator drone, the first in what would become the world's biggest secret assassination programme.

It was a deal that Pakistan would deny for years. The Americans had taken out one of Pakistan's enemies in return for the CIA using Pakistani airspace to kill its own enemies. Musharraf reportedly told one CIA officer it wouldn't be hard to hide. 'In Pakistan things fall out of the sky all the time,' he said. Not only would Pakistan deny giving consent for the drone programme, but would endlessly criticise the Americans for 'violating its sovereignty' and encouage its media to do the same, whipping up more anti-Americanism.

Pakistan did send more troops into the tribal areas, 74,000 by the end of the year, which as it pointed out far outnumbered the international forces in Afghanistan. 'On the other side there were just 16,000 troops,' said General Aurakzai. He said his men were shocked when they entered the tribal areas: 'It was like the Stone Age.' The fighting was heavy. 'We arrested 656 terrorists and killed 302 and we lost 221 men,' he said. The Pakistanis claimed to have set up 637 checkpoints, but the cross-border infiltration continued, and rather than take on militant tribals, the army signed a series of peace deals.

Some sympathised with Musharraf's plight. India's military leadership had been alarmed at how long it took to mobilise their troops on the border after the attack on their parliament in 2001.

The word was that their defence planners had come up with a new strategy called 'Coldstart', aimed at being able to deal Pakistan's army a rapid and decisive blow before the international community could intervene.

When the UK Parliamentary Select Committee on Foreign Affairs questioned Pakistan's lack of will to take on extremists, Dr Gary Samore from the International Institute on Strategic Studies responded, 'President Musharraf cannot fight on all fronts at once, he has got to pick his battles.'

What Pakistan saw as 'hedging', the West would see as playing a double game. In October 2004 Musharraf moved his friend General Kayani to head ISI. Kayani had attended US Army staff college at Fort Leavenworth and Fort Benning, was a keen golfer, and such a chain smoker that he would light one up while smoking another. No one seemed to know much more than that about him. 'A soldier's soldier,' people said, whatever that meant. The US thought he was a good man, on their side. This seemed largely based on the facts that he had no beard and was fond of whisky.

I was uncomfortably reminded of something Benazir Bhutto had told me. In June 1989, when she was Prime Minister for the first time, she had gone on a state visit to Washington. It was a month after the last Russian left Afghanistan, and she was given a thunderous reception when she addressed Congress. At the White House she had a private meeting with President George Bush, at which she told him she was worried about her army's backing of fundamentalists. 'I mentioned that in our common zeal to most effectively combat the Soviets in Afghanistan our countries made a strategic decision to empower the most fanatical elements of the mujaheddin that might later prove to be uncontrollable,' she said. 'Mr President,' she told him, 'I am afraid we have created a Frankenstein that could come back to haunt us in the future.'

The Americans, she said, never took this seriously. Shortly after that, one of her generals told her, 'Your army has defeated the Soviets, and with a call from you we can defeat the US.' Bhutto sent a message to the US Ambassador. 'That cannot be true, that guy drinks alcohol,' came the response. Bhutto was shocked. 'I realised that drinking alcohol somehow had become the yardstick by which the West determined who stood where on the Islamic spectrum.'

Under the watch of Kayani, 'the soldier's soldier' with a fondness for fine malt, the Taliban would expand beyond recognition.

Karzai continued to ask for more peacekeepers. On 10 February 2005, NATO announced that ISAF would be further expanded in 2006, into the west and south-west of Afghanistan, going for the first time into the Taliban heartland of Uruzgan and Helmand.

The Afghan government was delighted. 'Afghanistan is unique in that the presence of coalition forces is extremely well perceived,' said Karzai's National Security Adviser, Rassoul. 'Any time people come to us they ask for more forces. If we can just add more reconstruction, roads, dams to provide electricity, irrigation and more police, that would cement this wall.'

The plan was that in 2006 Canada would take charge of the key city of Kandahar, and the Dutch would run remote Uruzgan. Tony Blair volunteered British troops to take control of Helmand, as the UK still had responsibility for counter-narcotics, and this was the province responsible for producing most of Afghanistan's opium.

In May 2005 General Barno came to the end of his tour as US commander in Afghanistan. He was confident he was leaving the country in a good state. 'When I got on the plane I absolutely thought things were going in the right direction,' he said. 'I thought the enemy was flat on its back. My headquarters in Bagram made a chart, "How do you know your enemy is defeated?", and we checked off half the boxes. Violence – very low; election – very successful; civilian–military relations – very good. All the pieces were in place for this to be a success. The enemy was broken, looking to come out of the cold. I left Afghanistan fully expecting that this would have a happy ending.'

PART II

WAR

First they ring the bells, then they wring
their hands.

Robert Walpole

12

Ambush

'HAVE YOU EVER used a pistol?' yelled Sergeant Major Mick Bolton, amid Kalashnikov fire and bursts from a machine gun as we ran across the baked-mud field and dived into a ditch for cover. 'If it comes down to it, everyone's going to have to fight.'

I'm a journalist – I don't use weapons, I wanted to say. But the firing started again, a different sound now, a thump and a whistle. They were mortaring our ditch, and soldiers were shouting at me to 'Get out!' I couldn't breathe, I couldn't think, I just knew I had to keep running. And keep down, down. My blue flak jacket with big white letters proclaiming 'PRESS' was way too visible in the bleached Afghan landscape.

Round after round fizzed past our ears, sending up clouds of dust. My mouth was furry – I had no water bottle, and the temperature in Helmand in the middle of summer was 55°C. My heart was thudding crazily against my flak jacket, my breath coming in short rasping pants like that of an animal. The sounds of my body were so loud, the war was almost like background noise. Then the whoosh of a rocket-propelled grenade close enough to lift the hairs off the back of my neck was followed by a sunburst of orange flame as it landed nearby. I hurled myself into another irrigation ditch and crouched amid the tall reeds, the soil just above me flying up as bullets landed all around. The Taliban had us from all sides.

Justin, the photographer, and I were with the elite of the British Army – forty-eight men of C Company, the 3rd Battalion of the Parachute Regiment – with a Ranger platoon from the Royal Irish Regiment and a few Military Police, facing a bunch of Afghans in rubber sandals. We could not see them, but we knew they were less than a hundred yards away.

The grey-haired sergeant major had kept us amused for days with his wisecracks, behind which was a touching concern for his soldiers, who called him 'the Silver Fox', as well as adoration for his fiancée Lizzie, whose photos he had shown me. Now this veteran of two tours in Iraq and six in Northern Ireland was telling us we were the closest he had ever come to being 'rolled up'.

'If we get overrun I'll save the last bullet for myself,' said Private Kyle Deerans, a handsome South African of twenty-three who had dived into the same ditch. With his poetic black floppy hair, I was sure he had broken a string of hearts.

As I stared at them in horror, it dawned on me what had been wrong about Zumbelay, the village we had just visited on a hearts-and-minds mission with soft hats and promises of development projects. I should have noticed there were no children around – you always saw them in Afghan villages asking for candy and baksheesh.

There was no time to think about that as something whistled and a mortar landed nearby. 'Get out of the ditch!' screamed someone. The ditch was deep, and I wanted to stay in, hiding. 'No, no, it's not safe!' shouted Leigh Carpenter, a military policeman attached to the unit, tugging me away.

I clawed my way up the slippery bank, oblivious to the thorns ripping my hands and legs. The most terrifying part was as I got to the top, climbing over the high earth mound, which felt so exposed – surely the Taliban would get me. I rolled down the other side. 'Keep down, keep down!' came another shout. As I flattened myself I heard a crump and saw a flash – a mortar landed just where I had been crouching.

For the next two hours we were under relentless fire. The muddy ditches we kept jumping into felt like trenches in a First World War movie. I couldn't imagine how we could ever get out.

Ambush

Every direction we ran, we seemed to run into fire. 'Hails of bullets' – I never understood what that meant before. The worst thing was that when I looked at the men, I could see they were scared too. We were all thinking the same thing – this was no 'peace support mission', this was war.

The Paras had been in lively mood earlier that day when we left Camp Price, the British base at Gereshk, which was Helmand's second biggest town, a sprawling place of mud-walled compounds, two bridges and a bazaar of open-fronted shops. Around 3,600 British troops had arrived in Helmand since April, of whom around a third were the 3 Para Battle Group. There were three companies – A, B and C – and while A Company, under Major Will Pike, and B Company, under Major Giles Timms, had already been busy on operations, C Company kept being stood down. Some of the soldiers had not been out of the camp, and had been getting bored.

The trip to Zumbelay was the furthest they had ventured. The plan was to meet the villagers and discuss their needs, then camp for the night before stopping at another village on the way back. It was called a familiarisation patrol – part of winning Afghan hearts and minds.

The soldiers didn't seem to know much about what they would encounter. Before we left, Captain Alex McKenzie, commander of the Fire Support Group, told me, 'We've never been out to those villages, and want to see what kind of a reaction we get.' He said they'd had US intelligence reports that there were half a dozen or so medium-level Taliban commanders in the valley less than a mile to the north.

'If you ask me, what we'll get is a Taliban attack,' I had said to Justin.

As we set off with cold drinks and Pringles we had bought in the small Naafi hut, we joked about going on a picnic. 'Aggressive camping is what I call it,' said Colour Sergeant Michael Whordley. They laughed at me in my local dress of *shalwar kamiz* worn with desert boots and a flak jacket.

We were in a convoy of fifteen vehicles. An assortment of Snatches, lightly armoured Land Rovers which had caused controversy in Iraq over their vulnerability to roadside bombs, and Pinzgauer trucks that were sort of open troop-carriers, escorted by a Fire Support Group in WMIKs (weapon-mounted installation kits), similar to the Snatch Land Rovers, only with a heavy machine gun on top that fired half-inch bullets capable of cutting a man in half.

As we drove out of Gereshk, some of the men 'dicked' – or spotted – a man in a black turban who pulled out on a motorbike and followed alongside us for a while. To be honest, anyone could see us, sending up clouds of dust visible for miles as we travelled east through the desert into a landscape of undulating sand and gullies.

The afternoon was clear for once – most days, after lunch, sand and dust whipped up, part of the annual 'Hundred Days Wind' which locals say is hot enough to grill a fish on an upturned palm. At the British headquarters in Camp Bastion, where I had been before Gereshk, Lieutenant Colonel Stuart Tootal, the commander of 3 Para, told me many of his men were getting eye infections.

We arrived near Zumbelay late afternoon – that special time of day when fingers of fading sunlight trap the dust being churned up by men returning to their villages with herds of shaggy goats. Most of Helmand is scorched brown desert stretching south to the border with Pakistan, but Zumbelay was in what the soldiers called the Green Zone, a thin strip of irrigated land either side of the Helmand River that cuts diagonally from north-east to south-west. Zumbelay is a small oasis. A wide canal runs through one side, with deep irrigation ditches leading off between fields. Bedouin tents and mud-walled houses, some with courtyards of flowers, are dotted about a patchwork of fields of tall green grass and dried poppy stalks.

The convoy stopped about a mile from the village. The Fire Support Group, who would provide firepower in case of trouble, drove off in the WMIKs with a mortar team to take up a secure position beyond a high ridge from where they could protect us.

The rest of us removed our helmets, I covered my head with a scarf, and we walked towards the village, crossing a field where a few camels gazed at us. We had to jump over the canal, and I caused hilarity by falling in and emerging covered in mud. A kingfisher swooped low over the water in a flash of bright green, and everyone commented on how quiet and bucolic the village seemed. 'All it needs is a nice pub where we could enjoy a cold pint,' joked Major Blair.

Even the name had a certain ring to it. Zumbelay made me think of Manderley, from Daphne du Maurier's *Rebecca*. Of course Manderley had a dark secret, and in retrospect the quiet of Zumbelay was also suspicious. We sat on a raised bank at the edge of the field under a mulberry tree along with a few local men, one of whom seemed to be glaring at us from under his sparkly prayer cap. Their suspicion was not surprising. The last foreigners they would have seen in these parts were the Russians. They had probably heard stories on the radio of American forces breaking down doors or bombing wedding parties.

'We are British, not Americans,' explained the commander, Major Paddy Blair, a wiry Irishman, through the interpreter we had brought along. 'We come at the invitation of your government as friends and brothers to help you and find out what you need.'

I mentioned to Major Blair that there didn't seem to be many elders there, so he asked where the others were. An old man with a white beard who seemed to be in charge said they were at the mosque for prayers. Later we would realise it was not prayer time. The old man told us the village had no problems, they had definitely seen no Taliban, and suggested we came back two days later, on Thursday, for tea at 10 a.m., when everybody would be around. As we took our leave, he pointed in the opposite direction to the way we had come. 'If you go that way there is a bridge,' he said.

Afghans are the most hospitable people, offering everything to visitors even when they have nothing. It seemed odd to me that we hadn't been offered at least tea. But Major Blair was happy. 'I think that went well – they seemed friendly,' he said as we walked away.

I was just jotting that in my notebook when a burst of gunfire rang out from the ridge to the left where the Fire Support Group had gone. Blair's radio crackled into life. 'We've had a contact,' came McKenzie's voice.

About a dozen armed men dressed in black had appeared on the ridge. Two of the Support Group's vehicles had peeled off to try to intercept them, but as they did so the first RPG landed by the vehicles, then a whole rain of them, followed by small-arms fire.

For a moment we stood staring up at the ridge listening to the gunfire and explosions. Then we started walking again, looking for the bridge. Within seconds we heard the staccato crack of Kalashnikovs. 'Helmets on!' shouted someone. 'Put your fucking helmets on!' Suddenly we were running for our lives across the fields. The ground had been ploughed weeks before, and baked hard into treacherous ridges. We stumbled over the furrows, with bullets and loud explosions all around.

I threw myself into a ditch as bullets whizzed overhead. As I did so I dropped my notebook in the undergrowth. In nineteen years as a journalist I had never lost a notebook, so I tried to reach up to get it. An RPG whistled just past my ear, and I jumped back down. All around me was shouting and yelling. The two platoons had been scattered by the ferocity of the ambush. In the deep ditches their radios were not working.

I had no idea where Justin was. He had lost his footing and fallen on his back as he ploughed into the ground. As he looked up an RPG flew about ten feet above his head, bursting in the field near a group of Paras who had made the sprint in better time. He struggled to his knees in time to see the first mortar round land exactly where he had been only half a minute earlier. The troops returned fire. A prolonged burst of rapid machine-gun and rifle fire followed. Then, using red phosphorus grenades to set off white smoke as cover, they moved left to take up firing positions behind the ridge. They dived to the ground to avoid incoming fire, but this time it was coming from the left as well as from the original direction. It was impossible to know whether the firing was ours or theirs. The soldiers started releasing canisters of red or green smoke to show each other their positions, but this revealed them to the Taliban too.

The firing came again and again, wave after wave of it, with hardly any break. The eight-foot-deep irrigation ditches that criss-crossed the fields had turned into trenches. In and out of them we stumbled, slipping and falling in the muddy water as the Paras tried to regroup. People yelled instructions like 'Go Firm!' which I didn't understand but means stay still.

'When I shout "Rapid fire," run!' yelled Corporal Matt D'Arcy as we crouched in yet another ditch. 'Rapid fire!' he screamed. There was a clatter of heavy fire. Was it ours or theirs? I didn't know. The Afghan interpreter stayed praying and moaning in the ditch until Private Deerans, the handsome South African, grabbed him by the collar and kicked him out of it.

Ears ringing, I forced myself to climb out of the trench and run under the hail of covering bullets. I couldn't imagine how we would ever get out, and I could see that many of the Paras thought the same. In the nineteenth century thousands of Englishmen spilt their blood on fields like this, and I didn't want to join them. Rudyard Kipling had written a famous poem, 'The Young British Soldier', after the Second Anglo–Afghan War, which saw 2,500 British dead. A couple of lines from it would soon be much quoted: 'When you're wounded and left on Afghanistan's plains ... Jest roll to your rifle and blow out your brains.'

I really, really didn't want to die from a Taliban bullet in this muddy field in Helmand. I thought about my husband and our six-year-old son back home in south-west London. On Sunday it would be his birthday, and we were supposed to be holding a World Cup party for a bunch of six- and seven-year-olds. In my belt pouch were some of his toy cars and pens, which he had given me for 'the poor children of Afghanistan'. The image of his face kept me running and jumping into trench after trench.

Frantically I looked round for Justin. We had worked together on and off for years, surviving escapades all over the world. He too had a wife and a young son who were expecting him to come home. I couldn't see him anywhere.

Major Blair, who had just got his radio to work, was yelling into it to British headquarters at Camp Bastion. 'Where's the fucking air support?'

'Two A-10s ten minutes away from you can be with you for twenty minutes,' came the response. But ten minutes later we were still running, and nothing had arrived.

'We need air support. Where's the air support?' Major Blair radioed again after sliding on his back in another trench, pulled down by the fifty-kilogram kit they all carried. The message came back that the A-10s had been called off to Sangin, a village to the north where two British special forces soldiers had just been killed. No other planes were available, because fighting was still going on in the Sangin valley. Why the troops there were more important than us was unclear.

Blair realised at that point that we were going to have to get out of this on our own. He checked the grenades on his belt. 'I was counting them because I thought the fight would get down to twenty-five yards,' he told me later.

It began to feel as if the Taliban were toying with us, like a cat with its prey. At one point we ran back towards the village, only to be fired on from that direction. 'They're playing with us like chess pieces!' shouted Corporal Matt D'Arcy, the leader of the group I was with. The Taliban clearly had someone on the ridge to the right of us directing movements, for they were constantly changing position. They were using the ditches as rat runs to get around the fields without being seen, pop up, take a shot, then go down again. Unlike us, they knew the territory.

I ran again, and found myself in a trench with the platoon snipers, including Private Deerans. Some had .338 Magnum rifles, which sounded like cannon. Others were armed with Minimi 5.56s, the army's lightweight machine gun. Something whistled right next to me. 'Zip zip zip means it's bloody close,' said Private Deerans.

'Look, two at 2 o'clock behind that white mound!' shouted Sergeant Whordley, who at thirty-nine was almost as old as me.

The other guys called him the Buzzard, as he usually did the air control for the helicopters coming in and out of the camp, but he had begged to go along on this patrol, as it was his last year of service. 'In twenty-two years in the army I've never been in anything like this,' he said.

No one had. In entire tours in Northern Ireland they had fired less than they did that afternoon. I was beginning to realise I had seen more action as a war correspondent than most of the soldiers.

'Slotted!' shouted Private Deerans as a man with a short beard in a blue *shalwar kamiz* popped out from behind the mound and straight into his sights, to be hit in the chest. 'I fucking killed him!'

'Happy days!' shouted Corporal D'Arcy. I looked at him incredulously. This was the worst day of my life by an awfully long way.

Before the British troops arrived in Helmand, I had gone to a lunch briefing at the Old Admiralty Building in Whitehall for a few columnists and 'opinion-makers' hosted by John Reid, the Defence Secretary. I was the only woman there, and the only journalist to have been to Helmand. I was astonished at the breezy way the deployment was presented as a 'reconstruction' mission. Reid famously said, 'We would be perfectly happy to leave in three years and without firing a single shot.' Justin later went to photograph Reid for a profile and, spotting a rather grand globe in his office, asked him to point to Afghanistan for the picture. He couldn't find it.

Whatever had made these people think the Afghans would not fight? Over the centuries they had seen off every superpower that had tried to conquer them.

In fact the British understood so little that when Colonel Stuart Tootal went to a planning meeting and presented his proposal in the event of being attacked, he was taken aside by a Royal Marines colonel from Permanent Joint Headquarters (PJHQ), which was overseeing the deployment. The colonel told him not to worry, as he 'didn't anticipate there being any trouble from the Taliban in Helmand'.[1]

* * *

The firing had been going on for almost two hours, and I was finding it harder and harder to run. I had thrown off everything I was carrying, including, unwisely, my water bottle, and was gasping from thirst. Leigh, the military policeman, saw my plight, and thrust the straw from his Camelpak into my mouth, urging 'Drink!' before pushing me to run again. My helmet was almost falling off because of the broken strap I had never got round to fixing.

It was relentless. AK47s, RPGs, mortars and a Dushka, a heavy Russian machine gun – they were throwing everything at us.

I thought about all the things undone, the words left unsaid or unwritten. Most of all I thought of my gorgeous little boy with his big blue eyes and curly hair, and I just wanted it to stop.

'How much ammo have you got left?' Corporal D'Arcy called to the snipers. Were we running out? And where was the promised air support?

'Targets at 10 o'clock! Targets at 10 o'clock!' someone shouted.

'Don't shoot, they're civvies!' yelled Corporal D'Arcy.

'How can we fucking tell?' screamed someone else.

I found Justin just as the battle started to turn. We hugged each other in relief, then dived, as there was a sudden massive burst of fire from the ridge on our right.

'That's ours,' said someone.

Captain McKenzie and the Fire Support Group had managed to beat off their attackers, drive their vehicles to the south, where they were more secure, and then come back along the ridge to our aid. Now they were using everything they had.

'We could see the group of ten to fifteen men who engaged us moving towards the houses down below,' said Captain McKenzie later, 'so we let rip with 50-cal heavy guns. The force of the blast from those guns is so powerful it can rip off your arm without hitting you. All that was left of those guys was pink mist.'

Down below we managed to get away from the fields of trenches, past a farm where a bale of hay was blazing orange, and onto open hillside. I felt terribly exposed, but the Paras were much happier here because they had 'good optics'. Then came the worst part. 'Single file with good spaces in between so no one can fix a target,' barked Sergeant Major Bolton. 'Single file.' I tried to stay near a Para. 'This isn't fucking Club Med you know!'

By that time it was 8.30 p.m., and the light was fading. Only then came the reassuring rumble of the Apaches, almost three hours after Major Blair had requested them. We knew that the Taliban hated the Apaches. With these overhead, firing their 30mm cannons to give us cover, we reached the vehicles. Sergeant Major Bolton did a quick head-count. Everyone was safe and sound.

However, the battle was not over. There was only one way back to Camp Price, and only one bridge over the Helmand River, which the Taliban knew we had to cross. Major Blair was convinced they would lay an IED or ambush us there. We could not go back. Instead we drove south into the desert. At least we had air support. I was in Major Blair's Land Rover, and all the time his radio operator was in touch with the planes overhead.

On and on we drove through the bumpy sand, deeper into the desert, until the pilot assured us there were no ACM (anti-coalition militia) within a mile or so of us. We pulled the vehicles into a herringbone formation with guards round the edge, then all tumbled out and started talking at top speed, pumped up with adrenaline at having survived. As Churchill wrote, 'It's exhilarating to be fired at without effect.' But I didn't want to repeat the experience.

'I've never been in anything as intense as that,' said Major Blair. 'That was a 360-degree battle.' Later, he described it to his commander Colonel Tootal as 'a bit cheeky'.

None of us could believe we had escaped unscathed. Blair told me that if one of us had been wounded and we'd had to slow down, he thought we might all have been killed.

Everyone was stunned at how quickly the Taliban had organised themselves and how coordinated they had been. From the time we had walked into the village to the start of the ambush was less than an hour, though some of us remembered the man with the black turban on the motorbike. They had also been undeterred by our array of hardware. 'That's as bold as it comes,' said Captain McKenzie, shaking his head in awe. 'The Taliban are quite ingenious, but they've probably got twenty-five dead blokes and we've got none, and that speaks volumes.'

His gunners had got through three or four boxes of ammunition. It turned out they had begged and borrowed rounds from other NATO forces, as the British-issued ammo had poor machine work on the brass cases and often stuck after firing one or two rounds. If they'd had to use those it might have been a very different outcome.

We had been saved by the bravery and expertise of the Paras when their training kicked in, but also because, just as in the old days when I had travelled with the mujaheddin, the Taliban were not good shots. Private Deerans said, 'We don't tend to think the Taliban can fight as well as us, but they're fighting for something they really believe in and they have the advantage of local terrain. They're world-class at getting rounds down but fortunately their shooting was crap. Still, it was close enough for me. They had the advantage from the beginning and I don't know how none of us got shot.'

Sergeant Major Bolton realised he had forgotten to take his wedding ring that day. 'I have Lizzie's ring on a string and it's the first time I've gone on an operation without it,' he said. I looked at my own bare finger. Checking in for my flight at Heathrow three weeks earlier, I realised I had left the two rings I always wear in the oyster shell by the side of my bed.

The big question was whether the villagers were in on the ambush. It seemed clear to me that they had directed us straight into it, and there must have been locals among the fighters for them to have organised so quickly. 'Maybe they were coerced by the Taliban,' said Major Blair. It seemed more likely to me that they feared the British had come to take away their main source of income – poppy.

While we were discussing this, another volley of gunfire rang out. Surely we were not under attack again? 'Hush,' warned the sergeant major. 'Everyone still and quiet. It's not over yet.' We still had to get back across the bridge at Gereshk, and we needed air support.

I lay on the warm sand staring up at the flickering canopy of stars. Unlike back home, with all our towns and street lights, here the darkness was complete and constellations innumerable. I picked out the bluish tinge of Sirius, the brightest of all stars, and down close to the horizon the yellowish Canopus. I remembered being astonished by the thousand-star skies in Afghanistan on my very first trip, lying on a roof on a mountaintop in Paktika, and one of the mujaheddin telling me every star was a dead mujahid.

In the distance were flashes I first thought were shooting stars, until someone told me it was the fighting at Sangin. Tracer bullets were lighting up the sky. Whatever was going on there was bad.

I looked at my watch. It was after midnight Afghan time, mid-evening back in London. Something brushed my ankle and I jumped. I hoped it wasn't one of the huge camel spiders that live in the sand, and that some of the soldiers would collect to fight against each other. I hated spiders.

For the next two hours Camp Bastion kept telling us that 'all air assets' were tied up in Sangin. A snatch raid on four Taliban commanders had succeeded in getting two of them before descending into a bloody firefight, and Harriers, Apaches and A-10s had all been called in. Surely they weren't just going to abandon us to get back on our own.

In between his radio pleas for air support, Captain McKenzie and I discovered we grew up near each other, and used to frequent the same Surrey pubs.

It was after 1.30 a.m. when we finally got the nod for air support, only to find that three of our Snatches had got bogged down in the sand and wouldn't budge. Amid all the stars we could just see the lights of the A-10s, anti-tank aircraft of awesome firepower.

'How long have we got air for?' radioed Major Blair as his men pulled out spades and started digging around the tyres.

'Forty more minutes,' came back the pilot's broad American drawl. After that they would have to refuel. Major Blair checked his watch. Even once we got the Snatches out, it was going to take a good half-hour to get to the bridge.

I remembered chatting to Corporal Robert Jones, an American Humvee driver, who had expressed horror at how exposed the British vehicles were. He had told me that if any American vehicle got bogged down in Helmand for more than five minutes it was abandoned. 'We hate going west from Kandahar,' he said. 'It's all IEDs, RPGs, Taliban, al Qaeda. We call it Hell-land.'

Eventually the vehicles were pulled out and we were on the road back to the bridge. We reached it just before the planes had to leave to refuel. 'Please don't let there be an IED,' I prayed.

'Do you guys want me to give a show of force?' asked the American pilot. 'Could drop to 5,000 feet and scatter some flares.'

'That would be kind, many thanks,' replied our controller. The American laughed at his very British accent, and we laughed too, in relief as we crossed the bridge safely, white flares dropping all around like exploding eggs.

It was first light as we drove into Camp Price to be greeted by those who had been left behind. They had followed the desperate pleas for air support on the radio, and were waiting half-anxious, half-envious.

We were all exhausted, but first there had to be a debrief of all the men. 'Well, that definitely reinforced the old adage "Never underestimate your enemy"!' began Major Blair. 'It's fair to say I'm going to have to review our approach to villages,' he told me afterwards. 'We're going to have to go in with far more security. It's pretty annoying to think we were sitting there offering things and having a laugh and a joke with villagers who knew that five minutes later we'd be attacked and might be killed.'

A few days later some Zumbelay farmers came to the camp and asked for compensation for blowing up their fields and goats. Major Blair sent them away.

13

Bringing Dolphins to Helmand

Gereshk, summer 2006

THE PROJECTOR WHIRRED, and images of whales and dolphins swam across the wall, part of the BBC nature series *Blue Planet.* Thirty or forty tribal elders with long beards and strings of worry beads stared in complete bafflement. Frankly, I was baffled too. I had seen a lot of odd things in my years as a foreign correspondent, but I had never seen anything like this. The elders from across Helmand had been waiting all day for their first meeting with the British. They had sat in a corridor in a school in Gereshk in stifling heat with no fan and no refreshments as hours passed and the British did not come.

Finally, three hours late, there was the sound of a helicopter. Colonel Charlie Knaggs, the tall Irish guardsman who was commander of the British troops in Helmand, jumped out followed by a number of other soldiers, and two British women in long shirts and scarves who were clearly not quite sure how to dress for the local culture.

Knaggs spoke first. 'We come here as our fathers and forefathers did in the 1880s, but this time as friends and brothers at the invitation of your government,' he began.

The Afghans muttered as his remark was translated into Pashto. It seemed an odd thing to say – after all, we lost the war in the 1880s, as everyone I met in Helmand was keen to remind us, and most claimed their ancestors had fought in it. Moreover, when the Russians occupied Afghanistan, they also came saying they had been invited by the Afghan government to bring security and development.

Then the two women introduced themselves – Susan Crombie from the Foreign Office and Wendy Phillips from DFID, the British development agency. This was the so-called 'Triumvirate', intended to show that the British mission was not just about a military show of force, but was also bringing development and 'extending the writ of government' – turning Helmand into a model for the rest of Afghanistan.

The elders did not know where to look. Helmand was very conservative, and their women were kept in purdah. I wondered whose idea it had been to send women. To make things worse, Wendy Phillips said 'We respect your culture,' then began talking about gender rights. The men jiggled their worry beads noisily. One cleaned out his ear with a cotton bud. Then a man with a beard 'as long as a lantern' (the Taliban's minimum length requirement) got up and accused the women of being spies. 'If your government was really serious about ending insecurity here it would do something about Pakistan where all the terrorists come from,' he said. 'You are trying to stop water from a hose without turning off the tap.'

Others muttered agreement. 'You have been to Mars, why can't you find Osama?' demanded one.

The men were becoming very agitated, so Colonel Knaggs told them he had something to show them. They were led into a class-room, where Major Blair's men had set up a projector. In a stunning indication of the enormous chasm between thinking in London and the reality of Helmand on the ground, someone had come up with the idea of making a film to show locals, comprising five-minute segments of *Blue Planet*, the familiar voice of David Attenborough talking about the world's oceans, interspersed with goodwill messages from the Governor of Helmand and Commander Knaggs.

None of them could understand what it meant. A few had been to Quetta, but none had ever seen the sea. The British were back after more than a century, and projecting monsters on their walls. This was not a good sign.

'Let's turn this off, shall we?' said Major Blair in embarrassment after the first segment.

'Why have they come here?' asked the man with the longest beard as we drifted out. 'Afghanistan has many provinces.'

From the start the British seemed unable to explain why they were in Helmand, either to the Afghans or to themselves. They were coming for three years, they said. But was it to hunt Taliban, or to be hunted? Clearly they had no idea what they were going into, and as I would learn, they had inadvertently made things worse for themselves before they even arrived.

Not only could no one understand why the British had chosen to go into Helmand; no one admitted responsibility for taking the decision. General David Judd says he remembers hearing the news from NATO and calling colleagues. 'We were astonished,' he said. Brigadier Ed Butler, who commanded the first Helmand Taskforce, described it to me later as 'the billion-dollar question'.[1]

It was in 2004 that President Bush had asked for other NATO countries to take responsibility for south-west Afghanistan as part of an anti-clockwise spread of peacekeeping forces around the country, since the US was committed in Iraq. Keen to cosy up to its US allies, Britain readily agreed, its own generals believing at the time that the war in Iraq would soon be winding down, and wanting some other adventure to prove the necessity for a larger army and thus avoid budget cuts. Instead, of course, the situation in Iraq deteriorated, leaving British forces unable to withdraw as speedily as planned.

The key place to secure in southern Afghanistan was Kandahar, as the biggest city, the place that had crowned the country's first King, and the heartland of the Taliban which Mullah Omar made his capital. As the main contributor of troops after the US, Britain should have had first dibs. Instead, it seems that when the south-west was divided up the Canadians simply got there first, snapping up Kandahar because it had a ready-made American base, while the British were still dithering about troop numbers. The Dutch took responsibility for little-known Uruzgan.

General Mike Jackson, who at that time was Chief of the General Staff, told his opposite numbers it was the UK politicians who had 'volunteered for the Guardsroom'. Senior military figures felt that taking responsibility for Helmand had been a macho gesture by Prime Minister Tony Blair because it was the most difficult place. Also, as Britain was lead country on counter-narcotics, however ineffectively, it made sense to go into the province with by far the biggest output. In 2006, 93 per cent of the world's opium came from Afghanistan, of which more than a quarter came from Helmand. Ninety per cent of the heroin on British streets came from Afghanistan. Sorting out Helmand fitted perfectly with Blair's 'war on drugs'.

However, Britain had a history in the area. I remembered how Hamid Karzai had laughed as he asked me, 'Don't they remember Maiwand?' when it was announced that British troops would be going there.

I suspected that few people did, though it was one of the biggest defeats in British military history. In July 1880 during the Second Anglo–Afghan War, a British detachment led by General George Burrows had arrived in Gereshk, then capital of Helmand, only to find itself 'in the midst of people openly hostile from which no supplies could be obtained'. It was decided to fall back towards Kandahar. Near the small town of Maiwand, the two brigades of around 2,000 British and Indian soldiers were set upon by 15,000 tribesmen under the command of Ayub Khan, a pretender to the Afghan throne.

Every Afghan knows the story of the ensuing battle, for it produced one of their greatest legends. Watching it was a shepherd's daughter called Malalai who had gone with other women to carry water and tend the wounded. Her father and her fiancé were both fighting. The Afghans were losing, and when their flag-bearer was slain, Malalai ran onto the battlefield with her veil lifted high over her head. 'Young love!' she shouted. 'If you do not fall in the battle of Maiwand then by God someone is saving you as a symbol of shame.'

She was killed by British fire, but shame is the greatest insult for a Pashtun, and her bravery rallied the men to turn the battle around and defeat the foreigners. Though the British were armed with nine-pound cannons, their infantry flanks collapsed in the face of the rush of tribesmen and 971 British soldiers – almost half of Burrows' men – were killed, as well as 786 followers and drivers and 201 horses.[2]

In Victorian times British schoolchildren grew up with the story of Maiwand. It was so much part of popular culture that Arthur Conan Doyle, the creator of Sherlock Holmes, had Dr Watson wounded there before becoming the partner of the great detective. But Britain had fought two world wars since then, and other battles had become more famous.

For the Afghans, it remained their most evocative battle. Afghanistan's last King built a Maiwand victory memorial in the centre of Kabul, which had become a busy traffic roundabout. Throughout Afghanistan many girls' schools are named after Malalai, and the young educational activist Malala Yousafzai, who was shot by the Taliban in Pakistan, was named in her honour.

When I went to Helmand I found that many people didn't know about 9/11, yet locals talked about Maiwand as if it had happened yesterday. Afghanistan's population might be largely illiterate, but it has a rich tradition of oral history, and the story has been passed down and much embroidered. The arrival of 3,300 British troops in Helmand in April 2006 was the largest British deployment to Afghanistan since that time.

To get some sense of what awaited them I had travelled to Helmand in late January, a few months before the deployment. When I told Afghan friends where I was going, most tried to dissuade me. Mirwais Yassini, who had quit the thankless job of Director General of the Ministry of Counter-Narcotics and been elected as an MP, described it as 'the Fallujah of Afghanistan, only bigger'. When I collected my Afghan visa in London, the Defence Attaché at the Embassy put my chances of being abducted at 25 per cent.

Hamid Karzai's half-brother Ahmed Wali lent a pick-up load of armed men to accompany me from Kandahar, but as we headed along Highway One towards Helmand, it was hard not to think of these warnings. Part of it was the inhospitable landscape – a stony desert in shades of beige and grey, full of dips and culverts where bandits might lurk, under a flat yellow sky. The road passed through Maiwand, and my guards told me that locals still found the bones of dead British soldiers in fields and irrigation channels.

When we got to Helmand there was no more paved road, because the Taliban kept killing the construction workers trying to build one, as well as the police guarding them. Tracks snaked back and forth across the barren plains, and the few vehicles threw up clouds of dust. Occasionally we passed crouching men in black turbans with guns on their backs, waiting and watching for who knew what.

Suddenly I heard a rattle of gunfire and crouched down, to the hilarity of the men squashed with me in the cab of the pick-up. 'Desert chickens,' said one of them. He explained that they had spotted some of the bustards Arab sheikhs used to come here to hunt. I had a feeling they just liked firing their guns.

As we entered the capital, Lashkar Gah, the driver pointed out a school where the caretaker and a pupil had been killed the previous month. 'Neat' is not a word usually associated with Afghanistan, so it was unexpected to find the town laid out on a grid system. It turned out that the British were not the first to try to turn Helmand into a model – the Americans had been there before them. World War II had provided an unlikely boon for Afghanistan, as the Nazi Holocaust had driven Jewish furriers out of Europe to New York, where they needed a new source of pelts for a growing Western craze for astrakhan coats. They found it in the fat-tailed Persian sheep which Afghanistan had in abundance, unexpectedly boosting the Afghan treasury. By 1946 the Afghan government had $100 million in its exchequer and the young King Zahir Shah decided to use some of the windfall to hire an American engineering firm for Afghanistan's biggest ever modernisation programme, the Helmand and Argandab River Valley Project, intended to create 'a new world in the desert'. The plan was to construct a network of irrigation canals and build a model town complete with tree-lined streets, a mixed high school and a community swimming pool, all powered by electricity fed from a generator at the huge Kajaki dam that would be built upriver. The King had an ulterior motive: he believed that if he created a utopia in southern Afghanistan it would catch the eye of Pashtuns across the border in Pakistan and they would wish to be part of this, thus creating his much-dreamed-of Pashtunistan.

The American company hired by the King was Morrison Knudsen, which had carried out mega projects in the US, including the Hoover Dam and the San Francisco Bay Bridge. However, bringing in expensive American contractors and equipment meant the $20 million provided by the King ran out with little to show for it. The US government stepped in with a further $80 million, fearing that if they did not, the Russians would take their place.

In the 1950s and 60s the area became known as 'Little America', the breadbasket of Afghanistan, famous for watermelons, pomegranates and grapes, and home to many foreigners and well-educated Afghans. There was a cinema and tennis courts. Girls studied in mixed schools and did not wear headscarves, and young Americans came as Peace Corps volunteers. Kajaki dam and the canals doubled the amount of irrigated land and drew in immigrants from other parts of Afghanistan. They grew wheat and also cotton, which was processed in a British-built gin and exported. However, the area never took off as the King had envisaged. The soil was shallow, and the Afghans tended to overwater their land so pools formed and salt built up. The ditches farmers were supposed to dig to drain the fields rarely materialised. They did not have roads to take produce to market.

The experiment ended in 1978 when all the Americans pulled out following the communist coup. Years of fighting after that, first against Russians, then against each other, destroyed much of the irrigation system and the dam. Many people fled to Pakistan as refugees, and those who stayed survived on subsistence agriculture – or opium poppy, which starting in northern Helmand had spread across the province from the 1980s.

When the Taliban came in 1994 they brought order but not development or repair, and never won the people over. Nor had there been any sign of development since the Taliban left. There were more than a thousand aid agencies in Kabul, but only five in Helmand, because the UN considered it a no-go area, marked red on its security maps. One of those aid agencies, a Bangladeshi organisation, had recently had an engineer shot in the mosque in Lashkar Gah.

Until 2005 the only international troops to enter the province had been US special forces hunting for al Qaeda. The Americans then set up a Provincial Reconstruction Taskforce, or PRT, in Lashkar Gah. This consisted of about ninety engineers and reservists protected by thirty Spanish-speaking Texas Guards, and they lived behind high walls under heavy guard, venturing out only rarely and at high speed.

I wandered around the bazaar. There was little to buy other than Lux soap, fly-covered meat, second-hand clothes and fighting quails with speckled feathers and smaller than a fist. I didn't feel threatened, but the peace was uneasy. As well as the engineer killed in the mosque, Lashkar Gah had recently had its first suicide bombing. Shopkeepers I spoke to said it was fine in the daytime, but no one travelled on the roads after sunset. The Taliban, they told me, were focusing on 'soft targets' such as teachers and engineers. Many schools had closed after 'night letters' had been posted on their doors warning that anyone who sent their children to school would die. Three schools had been burned down in the previous fortnight, and a teacher at one had been pulled in front of his class and killed. Fewer than half of the province's estimated 7,000 pupils were thought to be at school. The latest night letters warned about the impending British arrival. 'Don't listen to the infidels,' they read. 'They are lying, anyone who cooperates with them we will kill.'

'Taliban have cast a black shadow,' said one shopkeeper. 'They are waiting among us like frozen snakes and scorpions.'

* * *

That didn't mean locals wanted the *Angrez*. Not only did the British have a history in the area, but they had unwittingly upset Helmand's delicate tribal balance even before the first troops set foot there. Helmand has five main tribes – the Alizai, who fought against the British in the First and Second Anglo–Afghan wars and were part of the Durrani clan of Afghanistan's first King; the Barakzai, another Durrani clan, from which all Afghanistan's subsequent monarchs heralded; and then the Alikozai, Noorzai and Ishaqzai.

The Alizai dominated northern Helmand along with the Alikozai, while the rival Barakzai were based around Gereshk and the Helmand River valley. The balance was mostly held by the Noorzai, headquartered in the southern town of Garmser, which literally means 'hot place', and also clustered on the way in and out of the province on Highway One.[3] The Ishaqzai were powerful in Sangin but were otherwise looked down on, as were smaller tribes such as the Baluch and the Kharoti, which along with others had come in with the irrigation project, further complicating the tribal dynamic. They never really had much place in the system, so they often tended to be labelled Taliban, which sometimes became a self-fulfilling prophecy.

The Ishaqzai had turned against the coalition early on, after an American operation killed one of their prominent elders. In May 2002, US special forces had descended by Chinook one night on the small village of Bandi Temur, west of Kandahar, a smuggling crossroads whose headman was Haji Berget, a mujaheddin leader who had once been a backer of Mullah Omar. By this time he was extremely old – eighty-five, said some, or even a hundred. When he heard the helicopters he fled to the mosque, where the Americans shot him in the head then took his body away, as well as more than fifty men. Villagers said they stormed compounds and even searched under the burqas of the women, and a three-year-old girl was so terrified that she fled and fell down a well to her death. I happened to be in Kandahar, admiring the plastic-flower arrangements in the office of the new head of police, when a delegation turned up from the furious tribe, threatening to storm the

Governor's office and demanding the body returned and their men released. From then on the Ishaqzai became deadly opponents of the coalition, and when the Taliban came back some of their men would join them.

That wasn't all. One of Hamid Karzai's first acts as President had been to name as Governor of Helmand Sher Mohammad Akhundzada, leader of the Alizai, as he wanted a strong man of his own in the region to counterbalance the warlord Gul Agha Sherzai in Kandahar. Akhundzada, or 'SMA', as he was known by the British, was a fellow Durrani, vaguely related to Karzai by marriage: his sister was married to General Mirwais Noorzai, the brother of Arif Noorzai, the Tribal Affairs Minister who had tried to sell me a prisoner in his garden. Noorzai's sister was married to Karzai's half-brother Ahmed Wali.

Sher Mohammad's late father, Rassoul, and his uncle, Mullah Nasim, had been very active in the jihad against the Soviets, and also pioneered the poppy business in Helmand. Nasim had even issued a *fatwa* legalising opium-growing in Helmand. Sher Mohammad had continued the family business. In June 2005, nine tons of opium was found in his office by SAS operating in the province. This was awkward for the British, who were nominally responsible for Afghanistan's anti-drugs programme, even if it was highly ineffective, and they told Karzai they would not send their troops to Helmand unless SMA was removed as Governor.

This was directly counter to advice from Lieutenant Colonel Richard Williams, who had been on SAS operations in Helmand in late 2001 and returned in command in 2005. Though he regarded SMA as a gangster, he found 'a significantly improved province that was mainly peaceful run by an infuriatingly corrupt and piratical Governor who maintained his position by juggling the need to conform to the will of Kabul with keeping the complex balance of local power from becoming unstable. In this way he made sure everything was basically peaceful.'[4]

When a planning team came out from London, which to Williams' surprise was led by a submarine officer from the Royal Navy, he told them, 'Don't challenge the status quo.' Though himself a former Para, he warned, 'No amount of fighting spirit and enthusiasm would secure a peace if the fragile balance of power was reduced or the Governor replaced.'

His advice was ignored, and the British insisted SMA must go. Karzai was furious, but eventually in December 2005 he agreed and appointed the British choice, but made Akhundzada's brother Amir Mohammad ('AMA') Deputy Governor, so the family retained their influence.

However, the British had made a powerful enemy. SMA instructed his men to fight them, and they were many. Karzai was so bitter about it that every time I met him afterwards, even eight years later, he always brought it up.

Being Governor of Helmand was one of the most dangerous jobs in the country. It was particularly dangerous for someone like Engineer Mohammad Daud, who was a water engineer who had been living in Kabul working in the British-funded National Security Council, and not skilled in the arts of tribal politics.

We met in January 2006 at the Bost guesthouse overlooking the Helmand River, where we were both staying in rooms painted pink and mint green with lacy curtains. He was not a happy man. Security was tight, as a suicide bomber had got into his office compound the previous month while he was meeting the local US commander. The man was shot by American soldiers before he could blow himself up. They found that his car was also packed with explosives.

Daud told me he had not wanted the job, but had been urged to do it by Karzai, with the promise that British troops would be arriving in support. He'd been assured they were coming in January, but that had been delayed to April. 'If we have the British here we can tell teachers and students, "Don't close your schools, we have thousands of friends here,"' he said. 'But right now our hands are empty. Meanwhile the enemy are not sleeping. They are simple, uneducated people, they have not seen the world, they think the British are delaying because they are scared to come.'

From what he said, it was clear he had virtually no control of the province. Helmand is Afghanistan's largest province – around 23,000 square miles, the size of Wales, but one of the most sparsely populated, with somewhere between one million and 1.4 million people depending who you talked to. There were mountains in the north and desert in the south stretching down to a southern border of more than a hundred miles with Pakistan, part of the Durand Line, which Taliban crossed freely.

The Taliban forces for the whole south-west, from Kandahar to Zabul, were all under the control of a veteran jihadi in Quetta known as Mullah Dadullah Lang. He had lost a leg stepping on a landmine during the fight against the Soviets, acquiring the moniker 'Lang', which meant lame, like Timur Lang or Tamerlane, the Tartar conqueror who had wreaked havoc across Iran and Afghanistan in the fourteenth century. Stories abounded of his ruthlessness: he was said to have once tied five prisoners to cars facing opposite directions which at his command drove off, dismembering the men.

With SMA out of the way and the British expected shortly, the Taliban had been sending mullahs into Helmand to preach against the Karzai government and encourage young men to join jihad against the infidels. Each of Helmand's fourteen districts had an assigned Taliban commander, such as Mullah Malik in Gereshk and Mullah Dad Mohammad in Garmser, most of whom were thought to have only between thirty and forty-five men. The overall commander Mullah Dadullah had toured Waziristan recruiting fighters to go to Helmand to take on the British, and they, as well as ISI officers, were being sent to train the local recruits.

'The Pakistanis are sending many men across our border to try and fool the British and the international community that the problem is in Afghanistan,' said Daud. 'It's very difficult to count how many as we have no regular border police and no way of monitoring. But we have reports that hundreds and hundreds are coming over and gathering in mountainous areas in the north and at night the mullahs are calling on people to participate in holy war. Residents of those areas are very concerned and keep coming to me asking to increase security of villages because they don't have any protection.' A Taliban spokesman had warned, 'We will fight any foreign infidel force. We are just waiting for the order to go.'

Yet Daud insisted that the real problem was not Taliban, but drugs. He said more than 90 per cent of the agricultural land of the province was covered in poppies – twice as much as the previous year. Most of this was taken to the market of Baram Chah near the border with Pakistan, a former staging post of the mujaheddin. From there it was moved on to Pakistan or Iran to be processed into heroin, and smuggled through Iran to Turkey then on to Europe, much of it ending up on the streets of London. Daud believed that an astonishing two thirds of Helmand's population was dependent on poppy-growing. 'Everyone is involved and at harvest time schools close while teachers and pupils go to the fields. It's become a cultural thing, not just economic.' Even 25,000 acres of government-owned land leased to farmers was being used to grow opium.

To deal with all this he had only a hundred recently arrived soldiers from the nascent Afghan army and 540 police, most of whom seemed to work for tribal militias, including 180 border guards he said collaborated with the Taliban. His counter-narcotics police were only thirty strong. 'Everything here is a tribal set-up not a government set-up. So if a Chief of Police is from one tribe, 90 per cent of his men will be from the same and will not act against their tribe.'

As he described it, the government was just one player in a system of tribal leaders. Most disputes were resolved through tribal *shuras*, and each tribal leader exacted local taxes and fielded his own militia. Even if police cooperated with government, there was little they could do. 'Our police have Russian jeeps that go only at 30 mph while smugglers have Land Cruisers that go faster than 90,' he complained.

As a water engineer, Daud suggested that the north, south and central areas needed to be treated differently. Central Helmand, or the Green Zone, used water from the Helmand River or from the irrigation scheme built by the US. But in the north the only irrigation was a traditional system of wells which had been affected by years of drought, leaving the people there with not even water to drink without paying. They had no choice but to grow opium to survive, because other crops were not sufficient for a livelihood and there were no job opportunities. 'Those vulnerable areas must be assisted to provide alternative livelihoods. And in the short term they must be given cash and food assistance. If we don't do that we are forcing people to fight against us.'

Drugs weren't just a problem in Helmand. Afghanistan had been a major player on the world opium market for years, producing about a quarter of the world's total between 1990 and 2000. Poppy production had stopped in 2000 when it was prohibited by the Taliban. The Karzai government had also banned the production, cultivation and trafficking of opium. However, amid all the insecurity of the US-led invasion in 2001, poppy was the easiest crop to grow, being high-value and low-weight, and requiring little effort on land parched by years of drought. Most crucially, it was easy to get credit to grow from the traffickers. Moreover, in 2002 the British started paying people to eradicate their poppy fields, or promising them development, which only encouraged more people to grow. Soon I was seeing vast fields of purple and pink poppies in places that had never produced it before, such as Badakshan or just off the highway in Jalalabad.

The UK had spent £70 million over the first three years, and pledged to eliminate 75 per cent of poppy production in five years. Instead, in 2004 the area under poppy cultivation across Afghanistan increased by 64 per cent to a record 320,000 acres, and expanded from eighteen provinces to all thirty-two.[5] All around Kabul were giant billboards with a picture of a poppy and the message 'By growing poppy you are digging your own graves'. No one took any notice. People joked that counter-narcotics was the most successful agricultural programme in Afghanistan.

The Americans thought the answer was total eradication of the crop, and advocated chemical spraying, as had been done in Colombia. However, this was sensitive in a country so poor that people had few other ways to make a living. As one farmer explained to me, 'We have no jobs and no factories to process anything so we produce wheat but import flour, we produce fruit and import jam.' Moreover, provincial Governors were often involved in the drug trade themselves, so simply directed the limited eradication forces against rival tribes.

Before going into Helmand, the British government boasted in Parliament that in 2005, for the first time since the fall of the Taliban, the area under cultivation in Afghanistan had declined – by an impressive-sounding 21 per cent, with much of the fall in Helmand. However, the amount of actual opium produced had declined less – it only fell from 4,135 tons to 4,035 – and that was due to factors that had little to do with its counter-narcotics strategy. The Counter-Narcotics Minister Habibullah Qaderi told me that for all their effort, little more than 4 per cent of the land under opium had been eradicated in 2005 – just 11,000 acres of a total 256,000 – because there were too many powerful people involved. His office was full of brand-new Dell computers still in their packing, paid for by the Foreign Office, and highly paid British consultants, and he had a gaggle of security guards. 'I'm not very happy to do this job,' he admitted. 'I couldn't sleep for fifteen days after I was offered it. But I know if we can't solve this problem, we might as well give up on Afghanistan.' Even if anyone was caught, he said, it was impossible to prosecute them: 'We don't have a system or mechanism for prosecuting warlords.'

One of the names that came up repeatedly was the President's half-brother Ahmed Wali Karzai. Diplomats in Kabul were full of the story that an American checkpoint had found a huge stash of opium in one of his vehicles. 'The Americans keep telling me this but I ask them, where's the evidence?' said Hamid Karzai when I asked him, the tic under his left eye twitching furiously as it always did when he was annoyed. 'It's a smear campaign against my family.' He was outraged when the Americans had suggested he send Ahmed Wali overseas as an Ambassador.

One day at his house in Kandahar, I asked Ahmed Wali directly if he was involved. He was impassioned in his response. 'Christina, we're old friends. You have to believe me,' he insisted, taking my hand. He picked a pistachio from a bowl and held it up. 'I swear on my son's life I've never sold even this much opium. I'm prepared to take not just one polygraph but ten or even a hundred. If I was a drug dealer I would have money, but I don't have a bank account or any money or houses,' he protested. 'What happens is because I'm the representative of the tribe here, I meet every day tribal leaders who are opium farmers. Also I live in the house of a drug dealer but so do the UN, Pakistan and Indian Embassies because drug dealers are the only ones who have money.'

In 2009 the *New York Times* would report that Ahmed Wali had been getting regular payments from the CIA since 2001 for help-ing to provide fighters for a paramilitary group known as the Kandahar Strike Force and allowing them to use Mullah Omar's former compound as their base. American radio journalist Sarah Chayes, who had moved to Kandahar to run a soap factory for another of Karzai's brothers, Qayum, and later became an adviser to the US military, said she personally witnessed Ahmed Wali receive tin cans of cash. One section of the Americans had been paying him while another was trying to get rid of him. Nothing was as it seemed in Afghanistan.

'It's a farce,' said Anthony Fitzherbert, an agricultural specialist who had been going to Helmand for years. He explained that poppy cultivation only went down in Helmand in 2005 because there was a large stock, and also the previous year there had been too much land under poppy, causing a lot of disease and poor yield, so farm-ers went north to Farah and Balkh, or west to Herat, where they rented land to grow poppy. 'Now they are back and their land rested,' he said. 'Really they've danced rings round the interna-tional community.' He was right – in 2006 that reduction was reversed, and production rocketed to 6,100 tons. Between 2005 and 2006 the area under opium cultivation in Helmand almost trebled, from 65,500 to 171,300 acres.

Bringing Dolphins to Helmand

Everyone involved in counter-narcotics talked about providing 'alternative livelihoods', but seemed able to come up only with saffron or rosewater, and had no idea where this would be sold. Governor Daud told me that a Helmandi had reopened the old British cotton gin and encouraged farmers to grow cottonseed instead of poppy, giving them fertilisers as an incentive. Many farmers grew cottonseed and took it to the factory, but five or six months on they still had not been paid, and were going every day to the factory and to the Governor's office. 'I told the factory owner to borrow money to pay them but he said he couldn't get a loan from anyone,' said Daud. 'If DFID provided a loan to this factory it would help thousands of farmers.'

There were other things that could make a difference. Helmand had no cold-storage unit, so apples produced there in the summer would be taken across the border to Pakistan, where there was cold storage, then sold back to Helmand in the winter.

Mercy Corps had come up with the idea of growing mushrooms, a project that DFID was funding. They wanted women to be trained in their cultivation, so sent fifteen of them to Peshawar, each taking a male chaperone. But people in Helmand had never seen mushrooms, so when they started producing them and putting them on stalls, people laughed hysterically, asking 'What are these?' This meant the agency was faced with either conducting an education campaign on mushrooms across the province or trying to transport them to Kabul, which was not economic.

They weren't alone. The US Agricultural Department spent $34.4 million trying to create a market for soya beans, which Afghans had never eaten, and which like the mushrooms they had no idea how to cook.

The scale of the challenge was apparent when I met the chief of Helmand's narcotics police, Colonel Faisal Ahmed. He was sitting in a new office built by Americans, with a computer which he said was 'karab', or didn't work, probably because he had no electricity. Nor did he have a phone. 'We also need cars and walkie-talkies and modern guns,' he said.

His force was only thirty men. He earned $80 a month and his men $60 for what he said was very risky work. Recently border guards had tried to take control of Baram Chah, the main opium bazaar, and lost sixty-five soldiers. The Taliban basically controlled Baram Chah, he told me. 'Fighting against terrorism we're only fighting al Qaeda and Taliban, but fighting against drugs we're not just facing Taliban but our own people. If the government or the foreigners go there to demolish farms people will fight against them.' He and his men had toured around holding meetings with elders, warning them that growing poppy was illegal and anyone who grew it was a criminal, so they should stop. 'They didn't take us seriously.'

According to Colonel Faisal, the amount of cultivation had spiralled because the Taliban were sending out night letters encouraging people to grow poppy. The Taliban, who had once prohibited opium growing, had a quid pro quo with drug smugglers whereby the Taliban gave them protection and in return the smugglers would provide resources. So, for example, one of the biggest drug smugglers in Sangin, Fatah Mohammad, gave generously to the Gailani hospital in Quetta, which was used by the Taliban to treat their wounded. The Taliban benefited financially in two ways – local mullahs exacted a levy from farmers which they passed up to the leadership, then another tax was taken from those selling the paste in the bazaar.

Faisal pointed out that it wasn't just the Taliban who were encouraging opium growing, but also district chiefs who in theory worked for the government yet either trafficked drugs themselves or took cuts: 'They are basically warlords, and police commanders in the districts don't help the government but their district chiefs – they are almost like their family police.' According to Colonel Faisal some very big dealers were living in Helmand, and were protected by the government. He claimed that more than 80 per cent of government officials were growing poppy.

Some of the very people the US special forces had been working with to provide them with security or information were the biggest drug dealers. The West's total lack of understanding about tribal dynamics meant it was easy for often illiterate tribesmen to manipulate them, simultaneously gaining bounty money and having their enemies picked up by claiming they were al Qaeda. Twenty-two Helmandis had ended up in Guantánamo, and one died in Camp Price, the US base in Gereshk, before even leaving Helmand. This also made people angry.

The real cost of opium was brought home to me the next day when I met Parwin, a fifteen-year-old girl with eyes of limpid green who was in hiding from the sixty-four-year-old man to whom her own family had sold her. Her hands twisted over and over in her lap, she had pockmarked skin, and her eyes were downcast, so when she suddenly fixed her gaze on me it was all the more startling. 'Death is better than life with him,' she said.

She explained that the man was the most powerful drug smuggler in her area, and her father had borrowed around $2,000 from him that had been supposed to be repaid with twenty-four kilos of opium at harvest time. But the harvest had been poor because of disease. Other farmers had gone to northern provinces and rented land, but her father had prayed for the poppy to be plentiful. When the stalks were high, tractors had come and demolished the crop, apparently because they were in an area controlled by a rival to SMA, who was still Governor at the time. This left Parwin's father unable either to feed his family or to pay his debt. The smuggler demanded Parwin as repayment.

Parwin was what's known as an opium bride. 'I was ready to do this for my family,' she said. But the man already had two wives, who looked down on her because she was Baluch and cursed her and treated her like a slave, while the man himself beat her with his belt. 'One night while they were all sleeping I just followed the stars,' she told me. She disguised herself in man's clothes and escaped to Lashkar Gah, where she'd heard there was a shelter. 'I was shaking the whole way.'

Her story was common in Helmand, according to Fauzia Ulumi, who ran the shelter. 'A lot of girls who come to me are victims of drug traffickers. Farmers who have been paid in advance for poppy but then cannot honour the debt because the crop was eradicated will give their daughters.'

Fauzia had been a headmistress before the Taliban came and closed the schools, and her recently set-up women's centre was the only one in Helmand. Aside from the shelter, it offered vocational training and work such as crafting jewellery out of tiny pewter-coloured beads, and fabric dolls in brightly embroidered dresses, a couple of which sit on my bookshelf.

To Fauzia's fury, the Minister for Women refused to attend the centre's inauguration on the grounds that it was too dangerous. Fauzia herself received regular death threats, mostly through Taliban night letters warning they would kill those who sent women out to work. 'The government in Kabul talks about equality for women but here in Helmand women have no value,' she shrugged. She called girls like Parwin 'loan brides' or 'opium flowers' – marriageable daughters who could be sold off if a crop failed or there was a family emergency.

The Governor had told me he knew of hundreds and hundreds of cases in which families had lost their daughters because of loans. 'The West needs to understand that if we eradicate, many farmers can't discharge their loans and families will have to sell their children,' he said.

The next day Fauzia was going to take me to Gereshk to meet some farmers, so I could understand why so many people were growing poppy. As we were about to leave we heard that two road police had just been blown up there, so the Governor sent us eleven guards armed with Kalashnikovs and RPGs for the ninety-minute journey. Throughout the ride they scanned the desert for white Toyota Corollas, the vehicle of choice for suicide bombers. White Toyota Corollas were about the only vehicles we saw.

In Gereshk we stopped at a house full of yellow-dyed nightingales to pick up Fauzia's friend Razia Baluch, a member of the provincial council who told me she had been married at the age of eleven and a mother by twelve. She had a horrible story to recount. A few weeks earlier an entire family of ten in her district had been massacred because they refused to let one of their daughters become a smuggler's bride. The family had gone into hiding only for the prospective bridegroom to turn up one night with his militia, gun down the mother, father, brothers and sisters, and take away the girl.

'Opium not Taliban is behind women's problems and insecurity in this province,' said Razia. She took us to the village of Abazan, where all the fields were full of green poppy, not yet flowering. I had been warned that we needed to be in and out quickly so we could be back in Lashkar Gah by sundown, but that reckoned without Afghan hospitality. Before we could do anything we had to be served lunch with some elders – less-than-appetising-looking fish from the less-than-clean-looking Helmand River.

'Why are the *Angrez* coming back here?' the elders wanted to know. 'Will you burn our bazaars again?' Everyone laughed, but I couldn't help notice one man had his black-eyed gaze fixed on me suspiciously.

The fish disposed of, we headed into the fields. No one grew anything apart from poppy. The first farmer I met was Jan Mohammad, a recently widowed father of three with a sorry tale. He and his family had been refugees in Iran, and after moving back to Helmand his wife Salima's brother had been jailed, so another brother asked Salima to take poppies from Afghanistan across the border to Iran under her burqa to raise money to free him. On the way she was caught by police and imprisoned. When she finally came back with neither opium nor money, the buyer accused her of selling the narcotics elsewhere and keeping the cash. Village elders came to mediate, and the man promised he would not hurt her. Three days later the man went to their house and gunned Salima down in front of their children while she was saying prayers. 'I tried to go to court but the man is a powerful drug smuggler and has a lot of money,' said Jan Mohammad. 'Who will listen to a poor man in Afghanistan?'

He showed me how during harvest he would scratch vertical lines in the bulbs of the flowers, out of which oozed a white sap that would be collected and sold to dealers who came to the village. He was hoping to get 100,000 afghanis – about £1,300. If he had any extra he would keep it in bricks as an easily transportable asset, just like a gold necklace from a woman's dowry. 'I heard on the radio they will destroy the poppy, but if they do how will we eat?' he asked. 'The government can say it's illegal but I need to feed my three children.'

In another bone-dry field was Mohammad Gul Barahawi, an old man from the Baluch tribe with a grey turban and a beard, with a gaggle of dusty-faced children scampering around in bare feet. He told me he'd switched from wheat to poppy three years ago, and explained the economics of it. 'Most families here have only a small piece of land so have no choice but to grow poppy because it is high-value. I have half a *jareeb* [about a quarter of an acre] and sell in the bazaar five kilos for 35,000 afghanis [£450]. If I grew wheat I would only get 2,000 afghanis [£65], and also have to pay for seed and fertiliser. I wouldn't even be able to feed two members of my family, let alone fifteen.'

He had heard on the radio about the British coming. 'Let me say this,' he said. 'The one who comes as brother will be treated as such. Those who come to betray us will be sent away, we will drive them out. My grandfather and great grandfather kicked the British out of this country with their swords.' As he spoke he waved his scythe around. 'Only if we kick out the Pakistanis will we progress. As long as Pakistanis are active in Afghanistan then it doesn't matter if Brits, Americans, anyone comes, we cannot have peace and security. You need to go to the source of the *dushman* [enemy].'

Everyone said the same. What was the point of fighting Taliban in Helmand if you did nothing about all the recruiting and training over the border?

'This is not a local insurgency,' said a British intelligence officer in Helmand. 'It's all about Pakistan. Unless you hit the supply chain you're going to be fighting this for generations, and that's in Pakistan.'

Everyone told me how Pakistan had helped the Taliban take Helmand in January 1995. When listening to Afghan stories you always have to allow for exaggeration, but people told me that the ISI had sent in hundreds of Toyota Hiluxes for the Taliban, as well as providing army artillery fire and helicopters to fight off Ismael Khan's forces, which had come from Herat to defend the province along with some Kandahari commanders. Now they believed they would do the same again, just a little more discreetly.

Yet according to Governor Daud, Karzai believed that sending British troops to Helmand would stop the Pakistanis backing attacks. 'It was the President who forced me to go to Helmand,' he said. 'He told me he agreed that the British should go to Helmand because it has a long border with Pakistan and the Brits and Pakistanis are very close friends and allies, so the Pakistanis will not want people from Pakistan to kill British soldiers in Helmand.'[6]

No one else seemed to share that optimism. Anthony Fitzherbert, the agronomist, told me that just before the troops arrived he had been in Quetta, where he found 'the Taliban are really in your face. They have almost unlimited resources to go on bothering across the border. The more troops the West sends, the more they raise the ante.'

Before the Helmand deployment, Afghanistan's Foreign Minister Dr Abdullah Abdullah went to London to meet his British counterpart Jack Straw and other officials. 'In every meeting my main point is "You must do something about Pakistan,"' he told me at the time. 'At the beginning they looked at me as if I was mad, and asked "Where's the hard evidence?" as if we had videotape of Pakistan sheltering Mullah Omar. Now they understand but they don't do anything. I will raise this with Mr Straw again and again.'

Yet at the lunch briefing I had attended at the Admiralty Building with John Reid, the Defence Minister, my questions about Pakistan were brushed off. 'What is the point of sending our troops into Helmand if we don't do anything about Pakistan?' I asked, pointing out that I had personally seen the Taliban recruiting in Quetta and there were reports of ISI officers in Helmand.

Reid looked at me as if I was mad or stupid. 'Pakistan is our ally,' he said. 'We have good cooperation with them on the border.'

I was stunned. Pakistani forces were not only turning a blind eye, but facilitating Taliban crossing the border. Either the British didn't know what was going on or they were wilfully ignoring it. I wasn't sure which was worse.

'I think we didn't appreciate the scale of the capability that was there,' said Brigadier Ed Butler, the commander of 16 Air Assault Brigade, who were the first British troops to go to Helmand.

Yet the Americans on the ground knew what was going on. In March 2006 President Bush made his first visit to Afghanistan, flying in under tight security and describing it as 'a thrill to come to a country which is dedicating itself to the dignity of every person who lives here'. 'People all over the world are watching the experience here in Afghanistan,' he added.

After meeting Karzai, who complained to him about Pakistan, he was flown up to Bagram to meet US troops. In a separate meeting with special forces, Bush asked, 'Are you guys getting everything you need?'

One Navy Seal raised his hand. 'Mr President, we need permission to go kick some ass inside Pakistan.'

As far as I could discover, the British took only one step. General Sir Mike Walker, the Chief of the Defence Staff, went to Pakistan in February 2006 with Colonel Alan Richmond to see President Musharraf with the message, 'We are going into Afghanistan, and lay off our guys in Helmand' – no doubt phrased a little more diplomatically. Musharraf responded by insisting that ISI was 'fully under' his control, and was not up to any such thing. On his way back from Army House in Rawalpindi to Islamabad, riots broke out over cartoons depicting the Prophet which had been published in a Danish newspaper, and Britain's top soldier ended up taking shelter in the French Embassy.

At the American PRT in Lashkar Gah I met Lieutenant Colonel Henry Worsley, a tall, tanned officer from the Royal Green Jackets who had been there since November to prepare for the arrival of the troops. He confessed to me he didn't even have his own vehicle, and had to hitch rides with the Americans. When I asked him what he was expecting, he said, 'We are coming to a place where there has been no military presence at all, and with so many problems we are bound to draw fire – it really is like poking a stick in a hornets' nest. I don't accept reports of Falklands-scale casualties' – 252 British were killed in the war against Argentina. 'But the Taliban are a major threat and we're under no illusions at all that they'll have a go at us. I don't single out the Taliban. There is such a blurring at the edges of drugs, gangsters, tribal spats. This is not a place where the enemy wears a uniform.'

When the 'hornets' nest' comment was published back in the UK, Worsley was ticked off by his superiors. Yet it was to prove an enormous understatement.

On my return to the UK I went to speak to 3 Para at their regimental headquarters in Colchester about their forthcoming deployment, and was struck by how little they seemed to know about what lay ahead.

They had been told it was a 'peace support' mission to extend the writ of the Afghan government. However, anyone who knew Afghanistan could see a major flaw with this. Steve Shaulis from the Central Asia Development Group, who had been in Helmand since 1997, pointed out, 'Here are Brits extending the writ of the Afghan government, but people hate the Afghan government. The police are 99 per cent corrupt, so the Brits are going in to back corrupt and unpopular police against the Taliban and jihadis from Pakistan.'

It also raised the question, if they were not planning on fighting, why send a regiment as 'kinetic' as the Paras? As I was told when I went to Colchester, they had seen no major action since the Falklands in 1982, when they won key victories and came back to be garlanded with medals. Since then they had mostly had the grind of Northern Ireland and had been disappointed with their limited role in the war in Iraq. They were clearly up for a fight.

The truth was that the military top brass was still so focused on Iraq, where the situation had continued to deteriorate, that they had given little of the thought and planning that should have gone into Afghanistan. 'We were totally fixated militarily and politically on Iraq,' said Brigadier Ed Butler. 'We'd known since 2004, when Blair said we were going into Afghanistan in 2006. There were all these signposts. Yet no one was doing the good old military "What, where are the resources, who will be giving military the directions, how do you define success?"'

He himself had been in southern Afghanistan with the SAS in 2001, and knew only too well how challenging the terrain could be. 'If you'd thought about it, in 2005 we were just coming out of the Balkans after ten years; we'd already been three or four in Iraq, and look how that was going badly wrong; we were in Northern Ireland thirty-five years, so it was clear this would take some time; yet DFID and the Treasury were saying we could sort Helmand in three years. A chairman or CEO would be sacked or their shareholders have them out if they took that kind of strategic decision.' Major General Andrew Mackay would later tell *The Times* that Britain had gone into Helmand with its 'eyes shut and fingers crossed'.

The Paras told me they'd been briefed that there were just a few hundred Taliban in Helmand. Many senior figures seemed to think the Taliban would simply be frightened off by the British arrival. General David Richards said, 'The Americans had just 130 people, we're putting in more than 3,000 and a huge cross-government effort, if you were Taliban you'd think this could spell curtains.' He told me that '80 per cent of Afghans' were 'floating voters' who could be convinced either way. I had no idea where they got this figure, yet I would hear it over and over.

As Colonel Worsley later admitted to me, they had no intelligence. 'You go in somewhere like Helmand, you need to know what's going on, who the enemy are, where they are, but there was nothing. We had no idea what was going on in these districts. We were going somewhere we didn't know anything about.' As for the threat from across the border, he said, 'Pakistan didn't feature at all in our planning for Helmand. Not at all.' When he travelled around the province telling people about the forthcoming British arrival, he said, 'To a man people told me, "You do realise they'll be waiting for you, there will be trouble this summer."' But he admitted: 'We never imagined the severity of the reception party.'

As it was, the timing of the British arrival could not have been worse. In March, shortly before the first troops arrived, the Afghan government launched a major drug-eradication campaign. Nothing could have been more guaranteed to fuel resentment. As it got under way Worsley did not hide his concern. 'I'm afraid the eradication has started too late. There is no system in place to help poor farmers make up for the loss of their poppy crops. The main point we want to drive home is that British soldiers are not involved.'

Yet initially the Helmand mission was presented to the British public as aimed at ending the cultivation of opium poppies. The confusion of policy was summed up by Colonel Gordon Messenger's statement to a *shura* of provincial councillors and mullahs in Lashkar Gah on 19 March 2006: 'No UK military personnel will be eradicating poppy; however part of the UK mission is to support the [Afghan] government in its counter-narcotic efforts.'[7]

Certainly everyone in Helmand believed the British were coming in to wipe out their livelihood. 'It was very hard to convince people we weren't coming in to eradicate poppy,' said Worsley. 'That's what they thought, everywhere I went. They envisaged helicopters and lines of troops destroying their crops. But that wasn't the reason we were there, it never featured in our planning. It just happened that the Paras were arriving at the same time as harvest.'

On the ground, commanders quickly realised they had enough to deal with without worrying about drugs. When they came across stashes of opium during operations they mostly ignored them. They even began broadcasting radio messages announcing that they were not there to destroy drugs.

Colonel Stuart Tootal, the commander of 3 Para, said he was told their job was 'peace support – reconstruction and extending the writ of government'. Later he would say there had been a lot of 'wishful thinking ... we should have thought more about what we were getting into'.[8]

'We confused ourselves and the public that this was a peace support mission but that presupposes parties signing up to a peace deal,' he said. 'The Taliban had signed up to nothing.'

I never found out who was behind the *Blue Planet* video mission statement, but nothing better illustrated the confusion of the mission in Helmand.

'War should be the politics of last resort,' said Tony Blair's Chief of Staff Jonathan Powell. 'And when we go to war we should have a purpose that our people understand and support.'

The first thing the British soldiers saw when they arrived in Afghanistan was a place that was incredibly poor. 'Post-medieval' was the description of General David Richards, who arrived in Kabul in May 2006 to command ISAF. Five years after 9/11, Afghanistan was still at the bottom of the world list for access to water or electricity, and was one of the most dangerous places to have a child in terms of both infant and maternal mortality.

Ed Butler believes the troops should have gone into Helmand with engineers and power companies. 'We could have taken in huge generators in containers that straight away give people lights, air conditioning, mobile-phone chargers ... imagine if we'd turned on the lights on 30 April, something the Taliban can never do.'

Instead, despite being told their mission was about winning over hearts and minds, the military was thwarted from even small immediate ways they saw they could make a difference. On his first patrol of Gereshk on 29 April 2006, Major Pike visited the hospital along with the unit medical officer Captain Harvey Prynn and Major Chris Warhurst, squadron commander of the engineers. They were given a short tour by the hospital administrator, who spoke excellent English and told them he had a severe shortage of medicines. Having noticed the soiled sheets on the wards they were surprised to see a large industrial washing machine in a corridor, still in its plastic wrapping. The doctor explained that it had been given to them by USAID but they had not installed it. Major Warhurst said his men could get it working, and Captain Prynn also offered to provide some drugs from his stocks.

Major Pike wrote up a proposal to organise a proper recce of the hospital to see what they could do. When he got it Colonel Tootal was pleased: 'This was the kind of quick-impact project that would make a small but immediate difference to the lives of locals.'

They had reckoned without DFID. Back at Camp Bastion they were informed that it was not UK policy for the Battle Group to get involved with such issues. These were matters to be left to the development agency or NGOs, not the military. 'We got banned by DFID from going into the hospital again and any other medical facility in the province,' said Pike. But DFID never went beyond Lashkar Gah, and NGOs had stopped working in Helmand because of security. Two months later DFID left altogether. 'We weren't allowed to do it, but no one else would do it either,' said Tootal. 'That washing machine became a symbol of all we couldn't offer.'

Nor were they allowed to deliver footballs to the school. Major Pike was so angry that he wrote a formal report. 'We British claim to be masters of COIN [counter-insurgency] but do not practise what we preach and cannot even serve simple requirements,' he wrote in his diary that evening, 7 May. 'V.v.frustrating.'

It also baffled the Afghans, who had expected the British to continue what the Americans had started the previous year. American commanders had access to something called CERPs – Commanders' Emergency Response Program – and according to Colonel Worsley, the head of the Amercian PRT had 'something like $500,000 in cash in a safe in his office'. There was, he said, 'no filtering process, just a queue of people outside the front gate of the PRT saying "We'd love a new school," and whoever shouted loudest got. A lot of it was unbelievable waste of money, like a public loo. But it was almost instantaneous, and Afghans saw things happening, so the level of expectations when we came was very high.'

By contrast, Colonel Tootal had just £250 a month. 'Later I lost even that,' he said, 'but I could expend millions of pounds' worth of ammunition in a single day. Just one Javelin missile cost £60–70,000, and we were firing off loads. I could have achieved a lot more if I'd been empowered to have that money in bags of gold.'

Anything done by DFID had to go through the Ministry of Rural Rehabilitation in Kabul, because they wanted it to be seen as delivered by Afghans. This might have been a good idea in a functioning country, but in Afghanistan it meant it was very slow, and left lots of scope for corruption.

Like Major Pike, when he moved into Gereshk Major Blair was very frustrated to be stopped from renovating the hospital or repairing water pumps. 'Our credibility is at stake here,' he said. 'After a while people are going to start saying, "You came and promised to help us, but what have you actually done?" The other problem is when I ask locals what they need they don't come up with projects. Mostly they ask for things like mobile phones, laptops and motorbikes.' It took the local head of education just ten minutes into their first conversation to remind him of Maiwand.

14

Tethered Goats

Sangin, summer 2006

THE THRUMMING OF Chinook rotor-blades had already become the soundtrack of the war, for helicopter was the only way to travel between British bases avoiding the risk of ambush, if not yet the IEDs or roadside bombs which the Taliban would soon begin to copy from Iraq. I sat trussed up in flak jacket and helmet, the squidgy yellow RAF-issue earplugs blocking out only part of the noise. Through the open hatch of the gunner who was scouring the parched land, gun trained on anything that moved, I followed our dark shadow crossing the desert. The sand was pinky ochre and almost alluring in the morning sun, and on the horizon was a camel train, perhaps carrying the poppy paste that would end up as heroin on British streets.

A flash of movement caught the gunner's eye and I followed his gaze towards a goatherd with his small shaggy flock. As we swooped low, like a giant dark insect bearing down from the skies, I wondered what he must think – another foreigner come to fight some battles who would eventually leave like all the others.

We were following the Helmand River north to Sangin. One of the airmen held up two fingers to indicate that we were just two minutes from the LZ, or landing zone. Around me the men checked their weapons and ammunition belts, or made last-minute adjustments to their kit. I put on my goggles and pulled my bandanna over my mouth, though I knew the dust would get through anyway, for it was as fine as talcum powder.

Then we were on the ground and running off the tail ramp through the furnace-like blast of hot dust in the downdraught of the Chinook, urged along by an airman. I always hated that moment – the helicopter was a big, noisy target that attracted RPGs and small arms, and though I kept my head down there would be another blast of grit and dust as it swiftly took off again.

There were Paras with guns crouched all around securing the area. One of them ran ahead and we followed along a line of trees and irrigation channels to a small, fast-moving canal, over which a metal pipe acted as a footbridge. I couldn't imagine crossing it in my heavy boots, but there was no time or choice.

On the other side was a walled compound surrounded by sandbags. This was the district centre, a whitewashed one-storey building with a covered patio overlooking a dusty courtyard with a couple of mulberry trees, a few colourful flowers and some outbuildings. Waiting for us was Major Pike, commander of A Company, who was the brother of a good friend and had hosted me in Colchester. He was from impeccable Para stock – his father Hew Pike had commanded 3 Para in their glory days in the Falklands, and he was widely expected to follow. He was dusty and unshaven, as were all his men, like soldiers in a war movie. He explained that they had come for a two-hour rescue operation with just day-packs, and were still there four days later, so they didn't even have spare socks. They were living under what they called 'hard routine', and what water they had was for drinking.

We sat on plastic garden chairs under the tree which was the only respite from the already pounding heat – in Lashkar Gah the previous day I had watched the thermometer reach 55C. Everything was very basic. The main building was made of mud bricks, and there was no running water or electricity. The only furniture was the garden chairs. There were no beds, and the men were sleeping on the floor in makeshift dormitories that smelt powerfully of sweaty bodies. There was an ops room with a radio and a satellite phone, and another room had been converted into a first-aid post.

Across the courtyard was an unfinished, taller building which they had turned into their guard post. Major Pike took me up the concrete steps to the flat roof, where men were on stag – guard duty – manning machine guns and Javelin missile launchers. The district centre was at the edge of the small town. From the roof it looked nothing out of the ordinary, though it was known in Helmand as an important crossroads of the opium trade. When I dictated my copy to my newspaper later that day I had to spell 'Sangin', yet within weeks it would be a household name.

The bazaar was only a few hundred yards away, and Major Pike said I could accompany some of his men on foot patrol. The stalls were empty and all the shops shuttered except for a butcher's with meat hanging from hooks, turning blue and rank in the hot sun, and one man selling motorbikes stamped with the trademark 'Hodna'.

The place had an uneasy feel, not at all friendly. As usual there were no women to be seen, and the few men glared. 'We don't know if people are friend or foe until they fire,' said Corporal Tam McDermott, who I was walking with. The patrol had no interpreter, so had no idea what was being said about them.

We passed an irrigation ditch where some local men were bathing. They scowled as British snipers took up position on the bank.

A small group of turbaned men had gathered on a corner in front of a pharmacy, and were looking towards us. 'We definitely have a sense that we're being watched,' said Lieutenant Tom Fehey, the platoon commander. He pointed out that the same motorcycle had already passed our patrol three times.

I began to walk quicker as we headed downhill to the end of the bazaar and a flat open area, a kind of river wadi where some Kuchi nomads were selling goats. Suddenly a white Toyota Corolla packed with people came to a halt. 'He's got a weapon in the front!' shouted Corporal McDermott.

Several paratroopers spread out and took position on the stony ground. The rest of us headed quickly back to the district centre.

Nothing happened – most Pashtuns carry guns. But the soldiers' nervousness was understandable. Only twelve days earlier, on 11 June, British troops had lost their first man in Helmand – twenty-nine-year-old Jim Philippson – at a ferry crossing just down the Helmand River. Philippson was a highly popular captain in 7 Para Royal Horse Artillery, and had been mentoring a group of Afghan Army (ANA) recruits at a base called FOB Robinson just five miles from Sangin. They had sent a patrol to retrieve a small remote-controlled plane (UAV) called a Desert Hawk that had crashed while doing surveillance on the other side of the river. The patrol had used a local ferry to cross the river, but could not find the Desert Hawk and returned the same way. Just after crossing they were ambushed on a levee track and one of the men was shot in the chest, so they radioed for help.

Philippson was part of the twenty-man relief force hastily scrambled to go to their aid. By the time they arrived it was night, and they were surrounded by gunmen hiding in the darkness. He was hit by Taliban fire and killed instantly as he crossed a field towards the ambush site. A second relief force to rescue them also came under fire, and Sergeant Major Andy Stockton had his arm severed by an RPG. In the end a casevac helicopter flew in to extract the men.

Philippson had made a video diary in which he talked about some of his frustrations over the inadequacies of his equipment, and a coroner would later describe his death as unlawful killing, blaming the lack of night-vision goggles and machine guns. 'They were defeated not by the terrorists but by the lack of basic equipment,' said Oxford assistant coroner Andrew Walker. 'To send soldiers into a combat zone without basic equipment is unforgivable, inexcusable and a breach of trust between the soldiers and those who govern them.'[1]

Back at the district centre, behind our sandbags, one of the men pointed out the ferry crossing from the roof. Down below the mortar people were digging trenches, and men were filling more sandbags. But with just a breeze-block wall between us and the outside, it felt very exposed.

I had spent more than enough time in Afghanistan to be aware that Sangin was a bad place. 'We know they will try and take us on, and we're ready,' said Pike. I couldn't help thinking about his wife and small children, whose pictures I had seen in his office in Colchester.

Within days Pike and his men would be under siege, and Sangin would become a symbol of all that had gone wrong with the Brtish engagement in Afghanistan. It would end up seeing the fiercest fighting any British forces had been involved in for fifty years. More soldiers would die in this small, flyblown town than in any other place in the war.

The reason for sending troops into Sangin was indicative of how little the British understood of local tribal dynamics, and would have raised eyebrows among the British public had they known.

What had happened was that in mid-June the former District Governor, Gul Mohammad, was ambushed by Taliban and killed, along with four of his guards. When his family set out to retrieve the body they were also attacked, and around thirty-two people killed. Among the wounded was the fourteen-year-old son of the current district chief.

Gul Mohammad's brother Dad Mohammad was an MP and a powerful local figure from the Alikozai tribe who had been a commander during the jihad, and more recently had provided militias for the US special forces in the area. He demanded that his remaining family members be rescued from the Taliban and the boy flown for medical treatment. Later it would emerge that the 'Taliban' were from the rival Ishaqzai, the tribe whose elder had been shot dead in a mosque by US special forces a few years earlier. They were competitors to Dad Mohammad in the drugs business, and were fed up with being harassed by his American-backed militias.

Nor was it just Dad Mohammad's family who were asking to be rescued. The district police chief Mohammad Khan, also an Alikozai, was accused of raping a young girl and had been besieged in the police station by locals wanting to kill him. He also demanded to be extracted. Mohammad Khan was hated by the community, who said he ran a regime of rape and abduction of boys and girls.

Governor Daud told the Helmand Taskforce commander, Charlie Knaggs, that Sangin was about to be overrun by Taliban, and insisted that the British deploy to extract the wounded boy and the besieged police chief. The same message came from President Karzai.

Colonel Tootal was uneasy about this – sending in his men to rescue a rapist seemed the antithesis of winning hearts and minds. Moreover, with reports of Taliban activity in the area, he feared having a helicopter packed with fifty Paras shot down. However, the brigade commander Ed Butler told him that Daud was saying the district centre was about to fall, and it was politically important to preserve the Afghan government writ in town.

So, in the early hours of 21 June, Tootal set off with four Chinooks bearing 116 Paras of A Company to extract the family members and the injured boy as well as the police chief. They expected to land under fire, but instead it was surprisingly quiet. The men ran the four hundred yards to the district centre building, where they were welcomed by the district chief and his men, who told them there were Taliban 'all over the area'. One thorny issue was resolved when they discovered the community had already driven the police chief out of town.

The Paras set up a cordon between the district centre and the edge of town, and took up positions around the compound. The District Governor's son was examined by the medical officer, Harvey Prynn, who found him 'very, very stable, just needing pain relief and fluids'. He was flown to Bastion. It seemed a lot of fuss, but the Paras were then told that instead of going back to base they would stay in Sangin for another forty-eight hours. A Company would end up being there for three weeks, and the 3 Para Battle Group for most of the tour.

Pike started off by calling a *shura* of local elders. To his surprise about sixty men turned up. They told him in no uncertain terms that they would rather the British left, because there were many

Taliban around, and 'You staying will mean bringing fighting with the Taliban into our town.'

Pike replied, 'We are here at the invitation of your government and we're staying here to further governance and bring you, the people of Sangin, an opportunity to develop things and have a better tomorrow.' He admitted afterwards: 'It sounded a bit crass, because I was aware nobody had done anything for them in the past four years since the Taliban had gone.' The elders were not impressed. '"We've seen this all before," was the general reaction,' said Pike. He thought there were probably Taliban at the meeting, casing them out.

A few days later Charlie Knaggs and Governor Daud flew to Sangin to hold another *shura*, and I went along. Around fifty bearded men were sitting cross-legged under the mulberry tree in the district centre. Voices were soon raised. The main complaints were over lack of development. 'Look at this place, we have nothing!' complained one tribal elder, Mohammad Safir. 'We need clinics and bridges.'

'I can't understand all this political talking,' said Haji Azizullah, a senior tribal leader. 'I just understand how to grow poppy, and we're worried the British want to destroy that and then we can't feed our families.'

Others nodded in agreement. 'We don't want you here' was the clear message. At the end Governor Daud gave them three days to decide whether they would support the Taliban or the government. He was worried that only fifty men had come from such a large district. 'They're scared. They feel the British will go and the bad guys still be there.' He added that there had definitely been Taliban at the *shura*. He was even more unhappy than he had been when I'd met him a few months earlier. 'It's no good having meetings like this in a compound when the reality is you can't go one kilometre down the road either way,' he said. He told me that the town of Garmser in the south had already been taken by Taliban who had come across the border from Pakistan. 'They [the British] are not doing enough to save districts,' he complained.

Not only had the British troops arrived three months later than he had expected, but there were fewer of them. What he hadn't understood, and in this I sympathised, was that 3,300 troops didn't mean 3,300 fighting men. A modern army like the British has a long tail, and much of this was support – logistics, communications, engineers, administration, and all the other things needed to keep them in the field thousands of miles from home. There were only about four hundred actual fighting men – basically three rifle companies and the heavy-weapons groups from 3 Para and some from the Royal Irish Regiment and Gurkhas – to defend a province the size of Wales that was turning into the world's biggest narco-state.

Being in Sangin hadn't been part of the original plan at all. A few months before the deployment, at Christmas 2005, General Richards and Colonel Tootal had met and agreed that with a limited number of troops it made no sense to have them spread thinly around the province. Instead they would stay narrowly focused on a 'lozenge' around Lashkar Gah, within which they would create something called Afghan Development Zones, or ADZs.

The Helmand Plan, as it had been explained to me, was for the troops to stay in a small area of central Helmand – from Bastion to Lashkar Gah twenty-five miles to the south, and Gereshk twenty-five miles to the east. Though this was only a sixth of the province it contained the main population areas, and was pretty much the only part of Helmand where the provincial government had any control.

Before going to Helmand I had interviewed General Richards in Kabul. He had explained, 'The thinking was you couldn't be everywhere at once, so you had to concentrate your military forces. The vision is to go into a number of key areas, have a *shura* with elders and work out what they want, then within a short time they see the thing happening, and people outside say, "We want some of that, not the hopeless future the Taliban is offering."' There would, he said, be a particular focus on road-building.

The plan was modelled on the 'ink spot' strategy of Field Marshal Gerald Templer, the British commander widely credited with defeating the insurgency in Malaya in the 1950s, which seemed to be the only successful counter-insurgency anyone could think of. Richards explained: 'So the army secures an "ink spot" allowing DFID to start development. The FCO [Foreign Office] then help Afghans govern themselves and drive counter-narcotics then spread out from there. My aim is the creation of a feel-good environment. We want to create a situation where people have no excuse to grow poppy.' He even said Helmand would be 'a model for the whole country'.

General Richards was a man of little self-doubt, but I thought he was a good thing for Afghanistan. He had become known in Britain for turning around the civil war in Sierra Leone, where he had been supposed to just extract the foreigners, but was so appalled by the sight of children with their hands cut off by the rebels that he led his men against them. He seemed to genuinely care about Afghanistan, unlike some of the ISAF commanders before him, and was clearly shocked that there had not been more progress after nearly five years of Western presence since ousting the Taliban.

However, even if they had stuck to the plan, officers on the ground pointed out that just that area would have been too big for four hundred troops. Moreover, the Templer plan had taken twelve years, whereas the British had said they would only be in Helmand for three years. It had also involved the use of Agent Orange, which no one ever seemed to mention.

Just as the name of the Helmand mission, Operation Herrick, had been computer-generated, the Helmand Plan seemed a computer-generated plan that bore no relation to realities on the ground. What might have made sense in PowerPoint presentations in Whitehall or Colchester all started to unravel pretty quickly in Helmand. The first problem was of our own making. While Templer had control of everything in Malaya – both military and civilian – in Helmand it was hard to understand who was really in command. There had always been the confusion of the two parallel operations – the Americans of Operation Enduring Freedom (OEF) hunting for al Qaeda who reported to one General in Tampa, and the ISAF peacekeepers with all their multinational NATO masters including a large number of American troops who reported to a different General. As one civil-military adviser from ISAF described it to me, 'Our job is to put the locks back on and repair the doors after OEF troops smash them.'

Helmand was a whole new scale of confusion. At the headquarters in Lashkar Gah was Colonel Charlie Knaggs, who was officially the Helmand Taskforce commander. He answered to a Canadian brigadier, David Fraser in Kandahar, who controlled the whole south-west. Then there was Brigadier Ed Butler, described as commander of British forces in Afghanistan, who was Knaggs' superior and normally in charge of 16 Air Assault Brigade, but had no tactical control in Helmand. He was based in Kabul, and answered to Permanent Joint Head Quarters (PJHQ) in north London. Then there was General David Richards, who was the most senior British officer in the country and in charge of all the NATO troops except for those in the south-west, which he would take over in September 2006.

To start with I thought the reason I found all this incomprehensible was my own lack of understanding about the military. But later Tootal (who was based in Bastion) confirmed that it was in fact complete confusion: 'In effect I was answering to three bosses. Butler, because he was my normal boss and the most senior British officer; Fraser, because he was the multinational commander; and Knaggs, because he was my immediate superior.' To make things worse, Fraser reserved the right to give Tootal direct orders, but Tootal would still have to clear them with Butler, who then cleared them with PJHQ. It turned out that Knaggs had been inserted for protocol reasons, so that a British brigadier didn't end up subordinate to a Canadian of the same rank.

As if that wasn't complicated enough, there was also an American Major General, Ben Freakley, who was head of Combined Joint Taskforce 76 responsible for counter-terrorism operations in Afghanistan. As such he was superior to Fraser, so could also call on the British to do things. He told Tootal he wanted the British to go on raids against so-called 'high-value targets' believed to be hiding in southern Helmand, but most times, after lengthy preparations, the forces would be stood down.

Freakley had no time for the British 'ink-spot' approach. 'Everything about him suggests resentment and absolute focus on kinetic solutions,' wrote General Richards in his diary. 'He thinks we can defeat the Taliban principally through killing more of them.'

Freakley's masterplan was Operation Mountain Thrust, aimed at clearing Taliban from Helmand and making it easier for the British troops, using massive air power and search-and-sweep operations. Launched in mid-May, this ended up having the opposite effect, creating enormous resentment among the local people, reminding them of Soviet operations.

The whole set-up led to confusion and different people giving orders, so the British high command hadn't even known of patrols going out, such as that in which Captain Philippson was killed. Colonel Tootal said afterwards, 'It was questionable whether the risk of searching for the UAV [remote-controlled plane] was worth the life of a brave and popular officer.'[2]

It made for an awkward situation for the gentlemanly Knaggs, who was a less forceful personality than Butler or Tootal. General Richards quickly decided he would remove him once Helmand came under his responsibility. Knaggs was 'not proving up to the job and needs his span of command reduced', he wrote in his diary on 10 June.

It was also very frustrating for Butler, who was the only one of the British command with experience of Afghanistan, having been there twice in 2001–02 when he was in the SAS. A dashing Old Etonian with a sharp brain he didn't hide, his personality didn't help. 'Ed is very capable but wears his talent on his sleeve,' was Richards' description. 'He is the sort of competent but slightly arrogant British officer that upset the US in the Second World War.'[3] He so irritated Freakley that the American told colleagues he'd wanted to 'punch that guy's lights out'.

* * *

Meanwhile there were political masters not just in the UK, but in Afghanistan. Governor Daud, having been put in place by the British, then been annoyed by the delay in the troops arriving, assumed the British forces would be his private army, and endlessly harangued Knaggs over green tea to do more. As Daud pointed out, the Taliban were not just sitting back and waiting. Baghran in the north was the first place to fall, at the end of April, while the troops were still arriving.

By 17 May reports were coming in that another northern district, Musa Qala, was under attack by Taliban from Baghran, and the district chief Mohammad Wali needed help. To Daud's fury, the British prevaricated. 'I told them there was fighting in Musa Qala and six to seven hundred Taliban had attacked, a hundred police managed to defend, and they didn't believe me that there were so many Taliban – Americans were telling them they had information from the air and couldn't see any signs of Taliban.' He shook his head. 'It's very difficult for foreigners to distinguish between Taliban and non-Taliban – the Taliban have no special dress, no uniform, they look like local people.'

Eventually Butler sent only a thirty-strong UK Pathfinder platoon, the brigade's elite reconnaissance unit, which helped the pro-government militia of the Deputy Governor Amir Mohammad Akhundzada secure the town. To show who was boss, they dropped a 20,000-pound bomb on a nearby hillside.

Daud had complained, 'The British are very new here so have no good connections to find out realities on the ground.' Yet, as they would later discover, the district chief, Wali, whom they had gone in to rescue had a brother, Bismillah, at Guantánamo, suspected of links with al Qaeda. Wali was close to the ex-Governor of Helmand, Sher Mohammad Akhundzada, and rather than a Taliban attack, the whole episode had been part of a feud with an old enemy in Baghran.

A few days later Governor Daud called Knaggs again. This time he said another northern town, called Naw Zad, was about to fall. Tootal was summoned to an emergency meeting with Knaggs and Butler in Lashkar Gah. Knaggs told Tootal it was politically important to be seen to support Daud, so he should establish a platoon house of thirty soldiers in Naw Zad. Tootal pointed out that it would need more than that, which would stretch his forces and helicopters. In the end, on 22 May B Company under Major Giles Timms was sent to Naw Zad. Timms found a bustling small town, and no real evidence that the Taliban had tried to take the place. The local police told him, 'We're glad you are here so we can sleep now.' In fact the real problem in Naw Zad seemed to be that it was run by a barbaric chief of police who was widely hated, and whom the British were now seen as supporting. Timms secured the town and departed a few days later on 2 June, leaving it protected by a small group of Gurkhas who were supposed to be guarding Camp Bastion.

This was the first of a series of calls from the Governor to rescue supporters claiming to be surrounded by Taliban. Sangin was next. Each time, Daud demanded that the British deploy to stop the Taliban capturing the district and raising a black flag. If they did nothing he would call President Karzai, who would then call the American commander Lieutenant General Karl Eikenberry to complain about the British. Daud also threatened to resign. 'We were becoming increasingly reactive to events,' said Tootal. 'I wondered whether we had got too closely into bed with the Governor and were in danger of chasing shadows.' It was serious mission creep. By the end of June British troops had been deployed to Musa Qala, Naw Zad, Sangin, Kajaki and Garmser at the behest of the Governor.

There was no direction from Whitehall. In early May 2006 John Reid had been succeeded as Defence Minister by Des Browne, as part of a cabinet reshuffle. Browne later told a parliamentary committee that the decision to redeploy forces to the north of Helmand was made without his involvement. 'It was all briefed to me retrospectively,' he said. 'It has been subsequently described by those who were in command in military terms as an operational decision, and that is how I perceived it.'[4]

The problem was that there were not enough troops to keep everyone in those positions, and they ended up being spread too thinly – exactly what Tootal and Richards said they had wanted to avoid. Apart from Sangin, where A Company was deployed, the other places had just a platoon of men each. Resupply was very difficult with only six Chinooks, particularly as two were generally in service and two were always ring-fenced for medical evacuations, leaving only two for use on a day-to-day basis. Travel by road was extremely dangerous, with the Snatches vulnerable to ambush. In many cases, such as in Sangin, the soldiers were sharing a compound with the local police (ANP), whom they didn't trust, and believed might be passing information to the Taliban. The men ended up trapped in platoon houses under siege, with the Taliban dug in only two hundred yards away. It became known as the 'tethered goats' strategy.

'The ideal was we occupy every town in Helmand and had lots of money to spend and employ locals, but we didn't,' said Major Pike. 'We only had so many people. I don't think there's any question we were overextended. Because Tootal and Butler couldn't say no, we went "off script" from the start. We had one battalion doing Sangin, Musa Qala, Naw Zad, Garmser and Kajaki as well as Lashkar Gah and Gereshk. One battalion only has three manoeuvre companies, so if you have seven or eight locations that simply doesn't work.'

Even before the troops first came under serious attack on 4 June, Pike and Hew Williams, the battalion deputy commander, had discussed all the things wrong with the mission. On 22 May Pike listed in his diary five problems, from 'No unity of command' to 'Not enough troops', adding, 'If we cannot resource properly we shouldn't be doing it.'

Just as I had seen in Sangin, when the British went into these districts they didn't know who were Taliban or not, had no idea of tribal politics, and upset local people by bringing fighting and none of the promised reconstruction. They basically created a local insurgency where there had been none.

Mike Martin, a young British Army captain who spoke Pashto, and set up the army's terrain-mapping team to study what was driving the conflict, wrote an official history of the war, sponsored by the MoD, which then tried to ban it. The book is full of instances in which the troops were exploited by tribal feuds.[5] He describes how he was taken to see a school in Shin Kalay, in Nad e Ali, which he was told had been bulldozed by the Taliban. He later learned that the perpetrators were actually a local militia. In fact the school was built by a friend of mine, Mohammad Kharoti, and he told me it was destroyed by people from a rival tribe who were jealous of it, even taking the chairs to sell in the bazaar. It was the Taliban who offered him protection when he rebuilt it. 'We did not understand what was going on,' concluded Martin. 'In my view the Taliban were not the main drivers for the conflict.'

It didn't help that the ISAF press releases sent out to the media labelled every attack as Taliban. The Taliban were of course never going to deny anything, as it made them look more powerful than they actually were.

Whether it was Mullah Omar or ISI, the Taliban propaganda machine was always more effective than that of the MoD. If the British public didn't understand what our troops were doing in Helmand, the Afghans were even more confused. Most thought they were there to destroy the poppy, but one man even told me he knew they were there to 'get uranium for their chemical weapons'.

Meanwhile, the Taliban message was very clear. 'The Taliban had a very effective PR campaign,' said Ed Butler. 'Their fathers and forefathers are scratching in their graves to see off the infidel for the fourth or fifth time. Some of our people just dismissed that, saying most Helmandi were on the fence. They were always well over the fence. I'm not sure how close we ever got to the fence.' It was a message that was also being spread in the mosques by mullahs who got their salaries from the Afghan government, and therefore from those same foreign 'infidels' they were preaching against.

After the ambush I was involved in with 3 Para at Zumbelay, on 27 June 2006, the Taliban put out a press release claiming to have killed ten infidels, though they had killed none. The ISAF press office put out nothing, though the British had killed at least ten Taliban. By the time of that ambush, things were already going badly wrong. It turned out that similar things were going on all over Helmand. On Sunday, 2 July every British position apart from Camp Bastion came under fire.

The reason no helicopters had been available to rescue us at Zumbelay was that they were occupied in a firefight just a few miles south of Sangin, where a US-led raid to capture a Taliban commander had gone awry and two soldiers had been killed. A reaction force of Gurkhas was sent to rescue them and ended up in a three-hour gun battle, calling in artillery and air support.

The attack seemed to act as a catalyst for fighting in Sangin. After the battle local elders went to the district centre and again asked Pike to leave. That night the first attacks began. They started with a volley of automatic fire and RPG rounds from some compounds to the north and the row of shops. Initially the firing was sporadic and just at night. Then the attacks started to come in the day too, mortars and Chinese 107mm rockets. But the Taliban were completely outgunned by the Paras on the roof with their Minimi machine guns, 50-calibre machine guns and Javelin anti-tank guns. 'They weren't very clever,' said Pike. 'They attacked us from places where we could apply devastating fire back at them.'

Yet the Taliban attacks became bolder. One day they even attempted a blatant frontal assault on the district centre which was decisively repelled when the Paras called in a 500-pound precision-guided JDAM as well as Apaches with cannon fire and mortars.

Everyone has their worst moment in a war, and for Pike, his was without question on Saturday, 1 July. He had gone to FOB Robinson for a meeting with its commander and Stuart Tootal. Flying back at last light, the Chinook dropped him in the wrong place. 'I'm in the back so I can't see, but you trust the pilot to put you in the right place. I felt a bit nervous on my own. When the dust cleared I could see two Afghans in pick-ups and some compounds and real-ised I wasn't by the district centre. The helicopter had gone and I turned on my 349 radio, which was useless as it was too far out of range.' He started to run towards the river to try to work out where he was. 'I could feel these Afghans watching me. I knew I could be captured or worse. I said "Fuck" quite a lot, and tried to get as much distance as possible between myself and the compound.' Fortunately Major Andy Cash, who was flying the escorting Chinook, had spotted that the other helicopter hadn't landed where it was supposed to, and noticed the dust cloud to the south. After what seemed an interminably long time to Pike, but was probably about twenty minutes, the Chinook came back to rescue him. When he got on, one of the airmen asked how he was. 'How the fuck do you think?' he replied.

That wasn't the end of the day. Back at the district centre he was in his ops room hoping for a quiet night when at about 9.30 p.m. there was a 'God-almighty explosion, much louder than anything we'd heard before'. Outside they saw the top of the main building ablaze with smoke and flame. A 107mm rocket had slammed into the roof, and on top they found a scene of devastation. Three men had been killed – two signallers, Lance Corporal Jabron Hasmi, twenty-four, and Corporal Peter Thorpe, twenty-seven, along with their interpreter Daoud – and others wounded.

It was too dangerous to send in a helicopter at night, so the body bags were laid out under the tree of the *shura*, which meant the men had to keep passing them. Pike took the deaths of his men particularly hard, as he had moved them to their new position on the roof just that night.

When Tootal flew in the next morning on a helicopter to take out the casualties and the bodies, he saw exhaustion etched on the men's faces. Their combat fatigues were filthy, some caked in the blood of their dead comrades. Pike 'had the look of a man who had not slept in days; his face was gaunt and hair matted with sweat'. He told Tootal that the district centre was dangerously exposed, and that more men would die if they stayed there.

It was clear the men were questioning the point of being there at all. Although Pike said there was never any chance the Taliban would take the centre, the 'idea of development had become laughable'. At the start he'd brought in a local man to measure up to build a wall, thinking he'd provide some employment – and income – to townspeople. The wall was never built. 'We were not doing anything but force protection, securing ourselves. We were killing quite a lot of people so they didn't kill us.'

It was a similar situation in all the platoon houses where British troops were holed up in police stations in town centres, so vulnerable that they were drawing comparisons to the Alamo or Rorke's Drift. Musa Qala, for example, was besieged for eight weeks. The only way to get supplies in was by helicopter, but the fighting was so intense that Chinooks were only able to land in Musa Qala six times. General Richard Dannatt, the army chief, was visiting Afghanistan in early September when one Chinook had to abort a landing at Musa Qala after nearly being hit by two RPGs, and small-arms fire damaged a wing blade. He became seriously worried that a helicopter might be shot down, or that a platoon could be 'cut off and potentially massacred'.

To defend themselves the troops were forced to call in hundreds of air and artillery strikes on the towns they had gone in to protect, turning them into war zones and their residents into refugees.

At Bastion, waiting for the helicopter to Kabul, I met a bearded soldier from the Scots Guards with intense eyes. His name was Captain Leo Docherty, he told me he had been aide de camp to Knaggs, and he was angry. 'We've deviated spectacularly from the original plan,' he said. He criticised the FCO and DFID for not using the initial window of peace to carry out some of the promised development. 'Now the ground has been lost and all we're doing in places like Sangin is surviving. It's completely barking mad! We're now scattered in a shallow, meaningless way across northern towns where the only way for troops to survive is to increase the level of violence so more people get killed. It's not something I want to be part of.' A month later he would resign, and become the first army officer to speak out publicly against the British mission.

Yet back in Whitehall there was so little understanding of what was going on that when Des Browne made his first visit to Helmand as the new Defence Secretary, he asked Tootal why he was planning strike operations instead of development. 'Because, sir, this is Afghanistan and we are in the middle of a vicious counter-insurgency. The Taliban are trying to kill my soldiers, which is why we are conducting strike operations when resources permit.' Afterwards Tootal was so incensed he spoke to one of Browne's special advisers and asked if the Minister had any idea what they were experiencing.

Back in Kabul I was invited to dinner at ISAF headquarters by General Richards. I recounted what had happened at Zumbelay. After my narrow escape I couldn't stop talking, and I knew it. Richards let me prattle on, but it was clear he was angry about the 'tethered goats' strategy. 'We're stretched too far,' he said. 'There is little reconstruction and development happening. We need to bring ourselves back into areas which are defendable and start the psychological battle of hearts and minds.'

I had a question for him. In some of the district centres where the British troops were pinned down, those attacking them were speaking Urdu, prompting the Gurkhas in Naw Zad to dub one area 'Pakistani Alley'. I knew General Richards had recently visited Pakistan and been encouraged by President Karzai to pressure it to stop backing the Taliban. Yet it seemed he shared the institutional blind spot. On his trip he had met Major Pasha, then the Director General of Military Operations, who later became head of the ISI. 'He explained confidentially and reasonably why Pakistan did not [take on] the Taliban in Quetta,' Richards wrote in his diary on 6 June. 'It risked upsetting 2.5 million Afghan Pashtuns [in refugee camps], turning them into violent enemies of President Musharraf ... he admitted it was just not in their interest at this stage to try to crack down heavily. However they [ISI] did not support or incite trouble in Afghanistan whatever the position might have been even five years ago. I accepted much of it though he agreed he could not account completely for some elements of the ISI.' He added that Pasha had frankly questioned whether the British knew their enemy. 'We could kill hundreds but if we did not know even how many there were or what really motivated them what was the point?'[6]

*　*　*

After three weeks in Sangin, Will Pike's A Company was replaced by Giles Timms's B Company, then Paddy Blair's C Company. They too came under constant attack from RPGs, 107mm rockets and small arms. By the end of August twelve men had been killed in the town. On 6 September a group were hit by a mortar as they gathered for a briefing by the mulberry trees in the compound. Two were badly injured, one of them dying before reaching Bastion. To my horror, I learned that it was Corporal Luke McCulloch, a twenty-one-year-old from the Royal Irish Regiment who had been with me that day at Zumbelay, and whose cheerful banter had helped keep us running. His friends nailed a clover-shaped memorial to the tree where he was hit, and his heartbroken father posted a poem online, 'Killed in Sangin in the Compound While Eating Lunch', wishing his son would walk back through the door.

I desperately wanted to return to Helmand, but the MoD was having none of it. In London I met up with Captain Al McKenzie, the platoon commander who used to frequent the same Surrey pubs as me, and who was home for mid-tour R&R. By then C Company had been in Sangin a month. He told me that morale in Sangin was very high despite the casualties. So much so that when the Taliban came back after a lull in fighting for a couple of days, cheers went up. The Paras had reinforced the walls around the district centre, yet they were being attacked sometimes as many as seven times a day. 'I've been really surprised by their commitment and numbers,' he said. 'By the end it was third-division Taliban – guys creeping up we just took out.'

He was concerned for another reason: 'It's not reconstruction, it's deconstruction.' He told me they were using astonishing amounts of firepower – even Javelins, which he referred to as 'fire and forget' missiles. 'I never thought we'd use any, as they are anti-tank missiles, but one day there were four guys on the roof and one of our guys, Buck Rogers, said let's try and take them out with a Javelin. I didn't think it would work but it did, and since then we've used fifteen of them at £60,000 a pop.'

There was not much of Sangin left. 'At one point I looked at all the roof and bazaar burning, all this black smoke like *Black Hawk Down*, and I thought this isn't really hearts and minds.' Major Giles Timms felt the same way. When he went back to Musa Qala later that summer he found it unrecognisable – 'It looked like a war zone.'

It was the same story in Naw Zad. Twenty-five airstrikes had been called in on the town that summer, dropping 18,000 pounds of explosives, flattening the bazaar. Many of the residents had fled, some of them ending up in a refugee camp in Kabul. 'In Naw Zad and Musa Qala there are no people left,' said McKenzie. 'We could end up taking a piece of ground where there are no people. How many of those displaced people are going to think kindly about us?'

On 4 September Lieutenant General Nick Houghton, the UK's Chief of Joint Operations, called General Richards to say that after all this, the UK was thinking of withdrawing from Musa Qala and Naw Zad. Richards was furious. 'I gave Nick the works, explaining what a balls-up the UK had made of things,' he wrote in his diary that night. 'Far from setting the agenda in terms of security and development they were in danger of becoming ISAF's laughing stock.'

Afterwards, when the blame game started, many people blamed Ed Butler, saying he was too gung-ho and the Paras were too up for a fight. 'That's naïve in the extreme,' he said to me, arguing that they had had little choice and had bought time. 'We were under enormous pressure to do something. There were huge expectations from Karzai down to Daud that we'd come in December 2005, but we didn't actually turn up till April then dribbled in and didn't have a fighting force till July, and even then it was only really six hundred people.'

The delay had given the Taliban the chance to move in. 'We were sitting in Bastion and could see this advancing tide of Taliban going down through northern Helmand gaining control, then when the Governor or Karzai rang up and said, "What are you going to do about it?" we said nothing. The constant message from Karzai and Daud was, "If the black flag of Mullah Omar flies over any centre of population then we've lost, so go home. You turn up late, you haven't got the numbers you said, so go home and leave us." This battle raged for weeks, got more and more heated, and there was no strategic direction from London because they didn't understand, so we took the decision to defend the flags and see. People suggesting that if 16 Air Assault Brigade hadn't gone to the platoon houses we wouldn't be in the situation we were, is naïvety beyond belief. If all northern Helmand had fallen we'd have been fighting round Gereshk and Lashkar Gah, which had 30,000 people. Six hundred Paras couldn't have protected all those people. They wouldn't have just sat in Musa Qala and Sangin, they would have been straight down the main highway. You can war-game this to death and still get the same result. Of course, what happened is we created forts, and Afghans love attacking forts. The fact is we hadn't got enough resources and we expended a huge amount of ammo but we gained six months and handed over a slightly better understanding.' He believes things might have been different if DFID had actually started development quickly in places that weren't under attack: 'Stuart could have done his plumbing.'

Others questioned whether there really was a wave of Taliban coming down from the north. 'Taliban were already all over the province,' said Major Pike. 'We just stirred them all up, and everyone else that didn't want us to be there.'

Back in the UK the British public was horrified by the news coming out of Helmand. My report from Zumbelay had made it clear that this was war, not reconstruction. Questions were asked everywhere from Parliament to breakfast TV shows. Eventually the government agreed to send more helicopters and more troops.

The story had also made other journalists keen to experience some action themselves. The MoD tried to cover up what was happening by blocking media access, which of course simply made cynical journalists more suspicious. Some claimed it was for safety reasons, which seemed ludicrous, as we were after all war correspondents. 'It is very dangerous to write the truth in war and the truth is very dangerous to come by,' wrote our hero Ernest Hemingway.

Yet after my return I was invited for lunch to PJHQ, where officers tried to get me to say that Helmand had been too dangerous, and that my presence had risked soldiers' lives, as they might have had to slow down to help me. This showed a complete ignorance of what we'd actually been through – it was every man and woman for themself. Either way, I wasn't allowed back for two years.

In fact there was a complete media blackout for several months after Zumbelay. This frustrated commanders on the ground like Tootal, who wanted coverage of the bravery of their soldiers. 'You've been responsible for the single biggest media disaster since World War II,' Mark Laity, the ISAF spokesman, told me that October. 'After your report the MoD just shut down. They said all reports must focus on reconstruction, but there was no reconstruction. By not allowing journalists the media started turning on the whole mission, and the soldiers on the ground started feeling the government was hiding what they were doing because they were ashamed, so they too began questioning.'

There were acts of extraordinary bravery which no media were there to report. In Sangin, one hundred Paras fought off forty-four attacks in twenty-five days. In Kajaki, eight British soldiers and twenty-four Afghans repelled thirty attacks in ten days. At Naw Zad, forty Gurkhas held off twenty-eight assaults in two weeks.

All this happened out of the public eye. But the MoD bureaucrats, or 'suits' as the army referred to them, had forgotten one crucial thing – twenty-first-century soldiers had smartphones and the internet. I was contacted by the parents of a corporal in Sangin who in the five-minute phone call he was allowed once a week had told them they had been under siege for six days, the helicopters wouldn't fly in, they'd run out of supplies and were hunting for scraps of food. 'He described it as like the Alamo,' said his father. 'It was the most disturbing call for a father to take.' 'It's an absolute disgrace,' his mother said. 'They are getting two attacks a day and he said it's as if sometimes we're just forgotten.'

Other such calls followed. 'Lions led by donkeys' was the phrase I heard repeatedly, referring to the famous First World War description of incompetent Generals sending brave infantrymen to their death. With casualties mounting and no media access to the courageous men on the ground and their derring-do, people inevitably began to question the whole mission.

By the end of that summer of 2006, there had been 498 contacts. Thirty-three British soldiers had been killed and around a hundred injured in the most intense fighting involving British forces since the Korean War.

Far from John Reid's single bullet, by the end of their six-month tour the Paras had used 479,236 rounds. Subsequent tours would more than double and quadruple that figure – it almost became a competition to see who could use the most. The second tour, from October 2006 to March 2007, fired 1.295 million bullets. The next, from April to September 2007, got through 2.474 million.

And yet when General Richards returned to London in February 2007, although he was rewarded with a knighthood, he was astonished not to be asked to brief the service chiefs on Afghanistan. Instead he found 'a widespread feeling that the war was little more than a passing distraction. At a certain level and above, some officers were in denial that Afghanistan was a proper war.'

Major Pike, who had been expected to follow his father's footsteps into commanding 3 Para, was so disillusioned that he left the army on his return to Britain. 'It was all so amateur and incompetent as a national effort,' he said. 'My very strong view is that the whole British chain of command in Helmand, Afghanistan, PJHQ and London were complicit in wilfully ignoring very sound principles of counter-insurgency and unwilling to say no to things. The result was they led us on an ever-expanding dance of destruction and death all over the province that led to extreme overextension and meant people like me had no choice but to use extreme violence in order to keep my soldiers alive. I regret enormously that this chain of command placed companies like mine in that position, which was devastating for us, the campaign, and most importantly the Afghans we were supposed to be helping.'

15

The President in His Bloody Palace

The Arg Palace, Kabul, October 2006

IT LOOKED MORE like a medieval court than a presidency. Men with elaborate silken turbans and long beards, whose craggy faces bore testament to their war-scarred land, scooped handfuls of mutton rice from plates piled high and washed them down with fresh pomegranate juice. At the centre Hamid Karzai was in his element, boisterously hailing everyone with hugs and long exchanges of Pashto greetings that seemed to involve enquiring after every known relative. Just as when I first knew him in Peshawar and he handed out weapons and food to fighters, these days he could offer roads, clinics and wells, though just as then it was paid for with the money of some foreign power.

However, the men weren't happy. They were Helmandis from the small town of Musa Qala, north of Sangin. The name means 'Fort of Moses' – some believe the Pashtuns to be descended from the exiled lost tribes of Israel – and it was one of the places British forces had moved into that summer and found themselves under siege. The local people had ended up caught between the rocket fire of the Taliban and airstrikes called in by the British, and many had lost their homes or had family members killed in the bombings. They were fed up. Many of the town's 30,000 inhabitants had fled.

They pointed out to Karzai that they had voted for him, and expected better. 'We have suffered a long time from bad police looting us and abducting our children, and now the British are working with them,' said Haji Shaha Agha, one of the elders. 'We don't want British troops there. We can guarantee the security of Musa Qala. We will not allow Taliban into the centre.'

They explained that they had held a *shura* the previous month and agreed a ceasefire with the Taliban, who they claimed were also tired of fighting after the son of their senior commander had been killed and their ammunition had run short. Now the elders wanted the British to leave, or they said the Taliban would end the ceasefire. Their plan was to form a militia from fifty or sixty of their own sons to defend the town. General David Richards, the ISAF commander, now had the British troops under his control, and as a critic of the platoon houses, saw the truce as a way to extricate them. The Americans, however, were horrified at the idea of doing deals with the Taliban.

After a while the Musa Qala elders were shepherded out and a new group of turbaned men brought in – the Governors of the southern provinces Kandahar, Helmand, Uruzgan and Nimroz. All of them said the Taliban were back in force in their areas, setting up checkpoints and killing local officials, particularly in Kandahar, which the Taliban had launched a concerted effort to recapture. They joshed each other over who had the most dangerous job.

Among them was my friend Engineer Daud, Governor of Helmand. I asked what he thought about the Musa Qala deal. 'The Brits are asking me to leave the district but I'm telling them if we leave and don't have police the enemy will capture it,' he said.

The Governors all complained about insurgents crossing from Pakistan. 'The enemy is increasing every day,' said Daud. 'I don't know why the British are not monitoring the border in Helmand. We don't have any checkpoints in the whole hundred miles. If the door is open, how can you stop intruders?'

I pointed out that from what I had seen in Zumbelay and Sangin, local people were also fighting. 'We must admit some local people are fighting, but their commanders and employers are coming from Pakistan,' he replied. 'Where are they receiving medical treatment?

From where are they procuring bombs? If the world can somehow not see this, they will be fighting for eternity.'

None of this fighting had any point, of course, if people thought the Taliban were a better option for running the country than the Afghan government.

It wasn't just in Helmand and the south that the fighting had increased. 2006 had seen a Taliban resurgence throughout the country, catching everyone by surprise, popping up in areas they had not been before and in larger numbers. The US focus, however, was on Iraq, which was engulfed in sectarian violence worse than anything before. That February insurgents had bombed the Al Askari mosque in Samarra, one of the world's holiest Shia sites, destroying its golden dome, next to the ziggurat where only three years earlier I had picnicked. The attack was masterminded by Abu Musab al-Zarqawi, the leader of al Qaeda in Iraq, who had vowed to plunge Iraq into a civil war between the Sunni and the majority Shia. That June al-Zarqawi was tracked down to a safe house by what was known as 'Death Star', the shadowy special forces of JSOC led by General Stanley McChrystal, and two 500-pound bombs were dropped on it in a US airstrike. But even after his death the violence he had unleashed continued to spiral. Over 50,000 Iraqis would be killed in 2006 and 2007.

Yet suddenly it had become nearly as dangerous statistically to serve as an American soldier in Afghanistan as in Iraq. Copying from Iraq, the Taliban had also unleashed a campaign of roadside bombings, or IEDs, as well as suicide bombs – which had formerly been almost unheard of in Afghanistan. Suicide bombings had gone from just five between 2001 and 2005 to 123 in 2006 – one every two or three days, many of them at markets or other crowded places, to create maximum deaths and damage. I started trying to avoid meetings that meant driving through busy roundabouts at rush hour. Kabul was on 'White City' – the United Nations code for lockdown – so UN staff, diplomats and many other foreigners were not allowed out of their compounds, which at least reduced the traffic a bit.

The President in His Bloody Palace

The problem wasn't just the Taliban stepping up their campaign. In August 2006 the US Defense Secretary Donald Rumsfeld sent an adviser, Marin Strmecki from the Defense Policy Board, to Afghanistan for two weeks to assess what was going on. His report warned of a 'deteriorating security situation' and blamed it on 'the decision by the Taliban and its external supporters to escalate the scope and character of enemy operations; and weak or bad govern-ance that created a vacuum of power into which the enemy moved'. In particular he highlighted corruption by 'ineffective Governors and incompetent police'.[1]

Every Afghan I spoke to complained about having to pay bribes to do anything from registering a case with the police to applying for a driver's licence. I kept hearing disturbing reports from friends who had worked in the palace that Karzai was surrounding himself with sycophants. Anyone who spoke the truth was either moved on, usually to some ambassadorial post overseas, or quit in frustra-tion. Of all Karzai's old friends only the loyal Zia Mojadedi was still there, and he was depressed. 'The insurgency is spreading,' he told me. 'The Taliban are not strong. But we are weak.' General Karl Eikenberry, commander of the US forces in Afghanistan, made the same point: 'The challenge we face is not of a military nature. The critical task at this stage is strengthening the govern-ment of Afghanistan, developing the economy and building Afghan society.'

Yet no one did anything about it, and other Western officials were still sending rosy assessments back to their capitals. To see what it was like for myself, I asked Karzai if I could spend a week as a fly on the wall in his palace, the Arg-e-Shahi, or Citadel of the King. It had been built by King Abdur Rahman when he took power in 1880, at the end of the Second Anglo–Afghan War, when the Bala Hissar had been partially destroyed by the British. Every Afghan King and President since had lived there, apart from Mullah Omar, who preferred to stay in Kandahar. As its name implied, the Arg was more of a fortress than a palace, a large square enclosure surrounded by grey crenellated walls with a gateway in the middle and an outer wall, between which there was once a moat. As you entered there was the old treasury on one side and the armoury on the other. The central driveway led into a grassy courtyard planted with trees and roses. There was a mosque, and a *darbar* or audience chamber in the centre, and Karzai's office to the right. The compound stretched for eighty-three acres and was scattered with buildings including an army barracks, a jail and several palaces, some of which were in ruins.

The security to get inside the Arg was tighter than ever. My handbag was x-rayed and sniffed by dogs brought on golf carts, and I went through a series of x-rays and 'lady checks'. The bane of foreign women in Afghanistan, a 'lady check' means being hustled into a curtained-off cubicle where a stout woman made up like a doll sits with a kettle and a small fuzzy-pictured TV waiting to do a pat-down so vigorous that in most places it might be called a grope. Apart from my phone, this time they confiscated pens and even my lipstick. I mused whether there had ever been a lipstick bomb. Only my notebook got through, and I was provided a pencil.

Karzai worked out of the rather poetic-sounding Gul Khana, or 'House of Flowers', named for its large conservatory at the front which has floor-to-ceiling windows and used to have colourful flowerbeds, wooden cages of canaries and a fish tank. The flowers, birds and fish were long gone, and the palace was a gloomy place. Moreover, I had clearly chosen a bad time. It was the annual Ramadan fasting month when people cannot eat or drink in the hours of daylight, so they were breakfasting at 3 a.m. and everyone was moody. The atmosphere in the palace was nervous, and the President's staff told me he had been on edge ever since riots had engulfed the city on 29 May after the brakes had failed on a United States military truck, sending it ploughing into rush-hour traffic, killing three Afghans and injuring many more. Many Afghans had long felt bitter about the Americans and foreigners because of what they saw as the trampling of their culture during night raids in villages and the killing of their civilians in bombings. In Kabul they resented the concrete anti-blast blocks that were put up around foreign organisations which cut off roads and led to more traffic, and the feeling that billions of dollars were coming into the country yet ordinary Afghans were seeing nothing.

The accident happened in the working-class district of Khairkhana, where many people were out of work, and Afghans had begun pelting the US vehicles with stones. Terrified of being trapped, the Americans fired into the air not just with pistols but with large-calibre machine guns. Just as during the First Anglo–Afghan War rumours had swept through teahouses and bazaars that the British were interfering with Afghan women, provoking an uprising in November 1841 that took the British by surprise, news of the car crash spread round Kabul, and was quickly exaggerated into a massacre by drunken American soldiers.

Afghans rampaged through the city, shouting 'Death to Karzai!' and 'Death to America!' and setting fire to buildings, attacking anything with English-language signs, from aid organisations to a pizza parlour. The police were nowhere to be seen as the riots raged for hours. A British brigadier, Nick Pope at ISAF, organised the rescue of some of the foreigners under siege, such as the EU delegation.

All the time Karzai was pacing around his office as the reports came in, terrified that the rioters would breach his walls and storm the palace. Afghan Kings and Presidents almost always met grisly ends – most recently in September 1996 when the Taliban had entered Kabul and President Najibullah, who had taken refuge in the UN compound, was dragged out, tied to a Toyota Land Cruiser and hung from a lamppost on the street outside, with money stuffed into his fingers, cigarettes in his nose and his severed penis stuffed in his mouth.

The rioting went on for six hours, leaving several dead and hundreds wounded. Finally, after urging from ISAF command, the Defence Minister deployed troops. Karzai ordered a curfew and went on TV to reassure the nation that everything was under control.

He could not have felt less in control. The riots had made him realise how vulnerable and alone he was. His Chief of Staff Jawed Luddin told me he kept watching footage of the riots over and over, as if searching for a clue. Khairkhana, where the rioting began, is mostly populated by northerners, and Karzai was convinced that the Northern Alliance was behind them, particularly Marshal Fahim, who was angry because he had been removed as Vice President and Defence Minister, and Yunus Qanuni, the Speaker of parliament. Seeing enemies inside and out, he also suspected his own intelligence chief, Amrullah Saleh, who had once been Fahim's interpreter.

Karzai summoned the US Ambassador Ronald Neumann, as well as the CIA station chief, whom he had known for years and who had been with him in Uruzgan when he went to try to raise an army against the Taliban. He asked them if they believed the riots were really spontaneous. When they said that they believed they were, he replied, 'Then it's clear people don't want you here and don't want me, and I want to leave.' That, said the Americans, was not an option.

My week as a fly on the wall started with the dinner for the elders from Musa Qala, at which Karzai was in a jovial mood. The next morning was very different. I'd just sent an email to my foreign editor describing Kabul as 'quite relaxed' when there was a loud bang. A bicycle bomb had blown up a police bus just two blocks from the Park Palace guesthouse where I was staying. Soon there were sirens and roadblocks all over the city, so I arrived late at the Arg. When I finally got through security to arrive at the media office, the staff were all watching Tom and Jerry cartoons. They took me through to see Karzai, but he was brooding at his desk. 'Do you want me in a good mood or a bad mood?' he asked. 'If you want me in a good mood let's start this tomorrow. Today I'm in a bad mood.'

I decided to go and visit my friend Colonel Karim, who was Director of Training at the Defence Ministry. He complained about the deteriorating security situation, and said he had been very worried that morning, as his son was a policeman and he hadn't been able to get through to him for two hours. Colonel Karim had joined the army in the 1970s and been sent to Sandhurst, graduating in summer 1979, just a few months before the Russians invaded. He became Chief of Staff of a division, and later Deputy Commander of the Quick Reaction Regiment. He had taken part in the battle for Jalalabad in 1989, when I had been with the mujaheddin on the other side. 'Lucky we were not better shots,' he always teased me.

When the mujaheddin took power in 1992, what they saw as the communist army was sent home. Karim ended up scraping a living as a trader, then becoming a pharmacist under the Taliban. But his name was still on a list as a trainer at the military academy, and when Karzai took over someone found out he spoke English, so he was made liaison officer to the NATO HQ.

'In the Najibullah days we had a very good army of around 100,000 men and a very good air force with heroic pilots,' he told me. 'Now ... well, let me show you.' He took me out to a parade ground where a shambolic group of Afghan recruits were trying to do star jumps, apparently unable to coordinate their arms and legs. I tried not to giggle as the baffled American trainer kept repeating the demonstration. When the task of building the new Afghanistan was divvied up back in 2002, the Americans took responsibility for the army, but they had always seemed a bit half-hearted about the task, and some of it had been contracted out to DynCorps, the American private security company which also provided Karzai's guards. One trainer told me his recruits had asked him if he liked cats, after seeing him stroking a local stray. He said yes, and a few days later a recruit had proudly turned up at his office with something wrapped inside a cloth. When he opened it, there was a painting of Afghan scenery with a dead black-and-white cat pinned to it.

Karim told me that although the ANA had 35,000 men on paper, in reality it was much smaller. 'The problem is soldiers keep escaping and deserting, so many of our battalions are empty,' he shrugged. 'Every time a new battalion graduates it gets split up to fill in holes in others.' He explained that many recruits came for only two or three months to earn some money – they received $80 a month. Others deserted because of 'lack of training and low morale, and also they don't have effective weapons, only Russian

Kalashnikovs from 1948 so they just go home. All we have is all these expired guns and one heavy machine gun,' he complained. 'It's as if the foreigners don't trust the ANA. If they don't they shouldn't promise to help us, they should spend their time on other conversations. Most people in Afghanistan are disappointed that foreigners promised them facilities but didn't give them, so some call the foreigners liars and even go to the other side. It's like if there's a baby and you promise her something but don't give, the baby will be angry and not like to come and sit near you.' The other problem was that very few of the recruits were Pashtuns, and nobody wanted to be sent to the south. To get soldiers to go to Helmand they had to be blindfolded.

He had a paradox for me. 'We also don't understand – that Pakistan is running the Taliban is as bright as the sun in the sky, and protecting Osama. Without ISI it's impossible for him to spend even one week in Pakistan. Yet your countries keep giving them money.'

Next morning I was back at the Arg bright and early. The internet server was down, so the palace was cut off from the outside world. Karzai was back to being Mr Jovial. 'Have you had breakfast?' he boomed as he welcomed me at the top of the stairs, his guards looking on suspiciously. 'Come, I have interesting people for you to meet.'

The long reception room leading to his office was the most palatial part of the Arg, with large chandeliers reflected in gilt-edged mirrors. At one end was a fireplace over which was a double-headed eagle, the seal of the former King. Along either side was a line of sofas on which guests waited. Karzai's big-tent approach meant I would often find jihadi leaders sitting alongside former communists and even the occasional ex-Taliban. Finally the jihadi leaders had been stopped from bringing in their gunmen.

That morning two Pashtun men stood nervously by the mantelpiece, next to a tall vase of pink gladioli. They were dressed humbly, with dirty plastic sandals and silver-sequined prayer caps. Karzai greeted them effusively. They were from his hometown of Kandahar and had come, he said, with news of the fighting in the district of Panjwayi, where NATO forces had been carrying out their biggest ever offensive against the Taliban, Operation Medusa.

The pair were cousins, and introduced themselves as Abdul Waheed and Faiz Mohammad from Gheljan village, in Panjwayi. The President's brother Ahmed Wali had arranged for them to come to the palace. Their news was alarming. 'An aircraft bombed my house and killed seventeen of my family including my wife and children, even our seven-month-old baby,' said Abdul Waheed. 'They also killed my brothers. I'm the only one left.'

He explained that he had been in the mosque praying around 3 o'clock one afternoon when he heard bombing. 'They gave no warning. I came out and saw my home destroyed and all the bodies. There were no Taliban in our area, the place where Taliban were was twenty kilometres away. A lot of civilians were killed and I don't think the bombs killed a single Taliban. I will never forget and forgive the foreign troops.'

Karzai kept clucking his tongue, and I saw there were tears in his eyes. 'You see?' he said to me. 'A seven-month-old baby killed by ISAF. This is what I'm trying to explain to them has to stop.'

One of his staff handed him a medal, which he pinned to Abdul Waheed's waistcoat and then shook his hand. Abdul Waheed looked overwhelmed. 'It's the Wazir Akbar Khan medal,' Karzai told me with a grin. 'One of the heroes of the First Anglo–Afghan War who helped defeat you British. Do you know who is Wazir Akbar Khan?' he asked the man, who shook his head. 'No!' exclaimed Karzai. 'Our kids today don't know anything, that's why they burn our schools.' He presented the men with certificates which they couldn't read but which entitled them to compensation of 20,000 afghanis – about £650.

Afterwards he took me into his inner office. 'So that's how things are,' he said, shaking his head. 'The people don't like the foreign forces, but they like the government.' I wasn't quite sure how he had reached that conclusion. He sat in a winged leather armchair beneath a watercolour of the Minaret of Jam. On the shelves were a clock mounted on silver camels which I presumed was a gift from some

Middle Eastern potentate, a photograph of the King, and another of a young man. 'This is the Shia boy who saved my life in Kandahar in 2002,' he said, noticing me looking at it. 'He was shaking my hand in the car when I saw the gun behind him and heard the shots. He turned like a lion or tiger and ran at the shooter, pushing the gun upwards so he could not shoot us. My security fired and unfortunately he was killed. His mother told me he was eighteen.'

Karzai looked weary. He dropped a vitamin C tablet into some water and watched it fizz. I'd last seen him at the beginning of the year, but he looked much older. 'What's going on around town?' he asked. 'I suppose people are nervous because of the suicide bombings?'

'Yes, and the riots of course,' I said.

The tic under his left eye seemed much more exaggerated. 'It was terrible,' he said. 'I could not understand the reason. Why would people come out and destroy their own country? Why? Who was behind it?'

It was not surprising that Karzai was nervous. The Arg's first inhabitant, Abdur Rahman, always complained, 'The weakness of the kingdom of Afghanistan was so great that whenever the King went a few miles out of his capital he used to find someone else King on his return.'

Abdur Rahman ruled so firmly he was known as 'the Iron Amir', but he left nothing to chance. He had a taster even for his tea, and, convinced that most treachery happened at night, he slept during the day then worked till 4 a.m. He kept horses saddled, and was said to always have a pistol and some bread in his pockets to be able to make a quick escape if there was an uprising. It was he who signed the Durand Line, which he claimed to have been tricked into, a move that provoked outrage. He managed to survive by fighting numerous small wars to keep down the tribes. He died in 1901, after handing over power to his eldest son Habibullah Khan. Since then all of Afghanistan's Kings and Presidents had either been assassinated or forced to abdicate, and most had been killed off in extremely brutal manner.

The President in His Bloody Palace

On my third day in the palace we heard that workmen carrying out repairs on the roof of one of the palace buildings had discovered some skeletons. They were of a man, a woman and a child, and it was thought – mistakenly, as it turned out – that they might be those of one of Karzai's predecessors, Mohammad Daoud, and members of his family, who were murdered in the communist coup of 1978. Their bodies had never been found. The news of the discovery led to a heated discussion in the office of Karzai's Chief of Staff over which of the counry's rulers had suffered the most gruesome death. Most thought it was between Daoud and Najibullah.

'This is a very bloody palace,' said Sher Khan, Karzai's media adviser. One afternoon he and Khaleeq Ahmad, Karzai's debonair young foreign-press spokesman, took me on what they called the 'assassination tour'. It seemed hard to find a place where a President had not been killed. We started by walking past a tall brick clock tower that had had a chunk taken out of its top by a rocket, and through some overgrown gardens to the ruined Dilkusha Palace, or 'Palace of the Heart's Desire'. The crest over the door was that of King Amanullah, and the palace had something of the feel of a gingerbread house – Sher Khan said it had been designed by a German architect, though others said he was British. It had wrought-iron balconies, an old lift and a vast sweeping staircase, much of which was broken. We managed to make our way up to a bathroom with an old claw-foot bath and a steam cubicle overlooking the gardens. A storage room was chockful of the stuffed heads of giant curly-horned Marco Polo sheep, Bactrian deer and other wildlife hunted by the Kings of old.

'Afghan Kings love killing things,' said Sher Khan. He said that Abdur Rahman's successor King Habibullah was hunting near Jalalabad when he was assassinated. Habibullah had angered many of his anti-British countrymen by keeping Afghanistan neutral in the First World War, which they saw as pandering to their long-time foe. He managed to stay in power by taking a wife or concubine from almost every region or major tribe, and was said to have had thirty-five sons, but eventually he was shot dead in February 1919.

Some pointed the finger at his ambitious third son, Amanullah, who they said was spurred on by his mother. Initially Habibullah's brother Nasrullah, who had been a constant threat during his reign, took the throne, but after just six days Amanullah ousted him and threw him in jail. Then, possibly as a diversionary tactic, he mobilised forces to move down the Khyber Pass for a surprise attack on British forces on the frontier, declaring the Third Anglo–Afghan War. From Peshawar he called for a jihad to get back land lost when the Durand Line was drawn. The British were exhausted by the First World War, and hardly relished the prospect of getting involved with Afghanistan again, and many of their local Pashtun troops deserted to join the Afghans. However, they managed to bring the fighting to a swift end by sending RAF pilots in Sopwith Camels and a Handley Page over the mountains of eastern Afghanistan to carry out the first air raid in South Asia, bombing Jalalabad and Kabul, hitting the tomb of Abdur Rahman. One of those pilots was Arthur Harris, who would become famous in the Second World War as 'Bomber' Harris. The war was ended after a few months when Britain signed the Treaty of Rawalpindi, agreeing to stop interfering in Afghanistan.

Amanullah was a fervent admirer of the Turkish moderniser Kemal Atatürk, and with the fighting out of the way he set about trying to modernise his own backward country. However, his reforms were far too radical for his times. He opened co-educational schools and a secular law school to replace Islamic law, and introduced a minimum marriage age of eighteen. As one of the first Afghan Kings to travel in Europe he changed dress codes, banning turbans and astrakhans at court, to be replaced by bowler hats and homburgs worn with Western suits. He was said to have walked about with a pair of shears to cut off the clothes of anyone who did not follow the new rules, and held a *loya jirga* at which he made tribal elders wear morning suits.

Conservative Afghanistan was not at all ready for such change. The first uprising came in 1924, and Amanullah managed to put it down. But when pictures were published from his trip to Europe in 1928 showing his Queen Soraya in a low-cut evening gown with bare arms, the mullahs used this to incite another uprising. As various tribes advanced on the Arg from the north and south, Amanullah fled in the middle of the night in his Rolls-Royce, handing over power to his brother Inyatullah. He drove to Kandahar, hoping to raise an army with which to return.

So worried by the chaos were the British that between Christmas 1928 and New Year 1929 they organised an airlift first of their women and children then of all personnel, the first large-scale air evacuation in history. In January 1929 Inyatullah was deposed and the Arg was seized by the illiterate Tajik son of a water-carrier who would be known as Bacha Saqao, or 'the Bandit King'.

Sher Khan did not know which palace he had lived in. 'Perhaps Palace Number 8,' he said — several of the palaces had numbers rather than names. But he was sure of some things: 'He found lots of British pounds in the treasury which he handed out to his tribes so they would not topple him. Then he dug up all the flowers in the Arg and planted vegetables instead.'

That sounded to me like typical Pashtun contempt for a Tajik. While the Bandit King was supposedly pulling up the roses, Nadir Shah, one of Amanullah's generals and distant cousins from the Barakzai tribe, had returned from exile on the French Riviera to Dean's Hotel in Peshawar and begun raising an army of Pashtun tribes. After a few anarchic months Bacha Saqao's days were numbered. He barricaded himself in the Gul Khana Palace, but Nadir Shah bombed it. Bacha Saqao was dragged out and executed by firing squad in November 1929, along with his brother and supporters, and their bodies put on display.

Instead of bringing back King Amanullah, Nadir Shah predictably took the throne himself, and Amanullah ended up in exile in Italy. Four years later, in November 1933, King Nadir Shah also met an untimely end. Sher Khan took me along the path to the Kushan Palace: 'This is where the King was walking through his guard of honour to hand out awards to high-school students when he was shot dead by a Hazara teenager from the German School.'

Nadir Shah's shy nineteen-year-old son Zahir Shah was sworn in within a few hours of the assassination, before anyone else could make a move. Initially assisted by a council of elders, King Zahir Shah's reign lasted forty years, until 1973, and is now remembered nostalgically as peaceful, given what followed. However, at the time many people were frustrated by the cautious pace of reform. In 1965 a group of students and writers formed the country's first communist party, the People's Democratic Party of Afghanistan (PDPA), which quickly split into two rival factions – the Khalq (People), which was mostly rural, and the Parcham (Banner), which drew its support from the cities.

Zahir Shah's reign was also brought to an abrupt end. He was in Italy, recuperating from an eye operation, when his cousin and brother-in-law Sardar Mohammad Daoud, whom he had sacked as Prime Minister, took advantage of his absence to seize power and declare a republic. Zahir Shah was taking a mud bath in Ischia when he got the news. Rather than fly back and battle it out, he abdicated. The rest of his family was in the palace preparing for the wedding of his daughter Princess Homaira when they were surrounded by tanks in the middle of the night. They were held for a week. The women and children were flown out, but the men were tortured and imprisoned.

Five years later, Daoud was in the middle of a cabinet meeting when a column of tanks arrived and the first shell was fired. He told his Ministers to flee to save their lives. By the evening troops loyal to the PDPA had seized key points around the city, and aircraft began bombing the palace. A group of commandos broke in, and in the ensuing firefight Daoud and every member of his family were killed. 'They never found the bodies, but there is still an old retainer who walks round the room rather than straight across because he says it is where Daoud was killed,' said Sher Khan, showing me the spot.* It remains unclear whether the Russians were behind the PDPA putsch, or only

---

* On 28 June 2008 two mass graves were found near Pul-i-Charkhi. Sixteen bodies were in one, and twelve in the other. Mohammad Daoud's body was identified on the basis of teeth moulds and a small golden Koran which had been given to him by the King of Saudi Arabia. On 17 March 2009 he was given a state funeral.

found out about it afterwards, as Soviet leader Leonid Brezhnev claimed.

The new President was Nur Mohammad Taraki, who had been editor of the communist newspaper. He renamed the Arg 'the House of the People', and threw thousands of intellectuals, political opponents and Islamists in the Pul-i-Charkhi prison, where many of them were executed. He launched a programme of radical changes such as land redistribution and women's liberation, for the first time giving a woman a top position, as Minister of Social Affairs. When violent resistance to the regime spread through the country he flew to Moscow and begged for troops, but was turned down.

Taraki did not last long. Next, Sher and Khaleeq took me to the 'Kuti-e-Baghtscha', or Garden Mansion, where he had lived. Though it was derelict, all broken glass and timbers and peeling walls, I could see it had once been exquisitely beautiful, its high-domed ceilings painted with flowers and birds, and inset with gold and lapis. 'It makes me feel heartbroken to see all this history,' said Khaleeq. 'They built this beautiful place sixty years ago, and now we don't have the skills, we went back to the Stone Age.'

It was eerily quiet, the only sound birdsong from the shady garden. They led me through the wreckage to the first floor, and the room at the back. This was where Taraki was suffocated in October 1979, smothered with a pillow on the orders of his deputy Hafizullah Amin, who claimed Taraki had tried to shoot him.

Under Amin the repression continued – according to some reports between 27,000 and 50,000 people were executed in Pul-i-Charkhi prison between the communist coup and the Soviet invasion. Many Afghans I met had lost relatives in those years. Amin had studied at Columbia University in New York, and some accused him of having links with the CIA though he kept a picture of Stalin on his desk. The Soviets grew increasingly concerned at the unrest in Afghanistan and his overtures towards the West, and at a Politburo meeting on 12 December 1979 the decision was taken to send in troops.

Moscow wanted a pliant government in Kabul, so the KGB secretly flew Babrak Karmal from the rival Parcham faction of the party into Bagram and began plotting to seize the Arg. An attempt to get Amin out of the way by poisoning him with doctored Pepsi-Cola failed. On Christmas Eve, Soviet aircraft began flying in troops almost non-stop for forty-eight hours until Boxing Day, when they began coming in by land from Tajikistan across the bridge over the Oxus River. Amin had moved out of the Arg to the Taj Beg Palace, where the army was headquartered, presumably assuming it was safer. On 26 December he held a lunch party for members of his Politburo at which he told them the Soviets were at last sending troops to protect him. This time the KGB had succeeded in poisoning the meal, and before it was over Amin and several guests lost consciousness. Ironically he was revived by Soviet doctors who were not privy to the plan to kill him. He still had drips in his arms when the palace came under fire that evening and was stormed by Soviet special forces. Hundreds were killed, including Amin and his five-year-old son.

Karmal moved into the Arg and was more responsive to Soviet wishes, but was otherwise little improvement on his predecessors. Within weeks of sending the Red Army into Afghanistan the Politburo in Moscow was already talking about getting them out. Instead the USSR found itself becoming further sucked in, sending more and more troops to prop up a President who was weak, indecisive and often drunk. Eventually a young reformer called Mikhail Gorbachev came to power in Moscow in March 1985. Determined to find a way out of Afghanistan, he installed a more energetic leader – Mohammed Najibullah, head of the notorious KHAD secret police. Karmal was sent into exile in Moscow, where he died ten years later. 'His bones were brought back but the Taliban threw them in the river so he couldn't even be buried in peace,' said Sher Khan. 'The thing about Afghanistan is to know when to get out,' he added.

After the assassination tour, I could see why Karzai was nervous. Moreover, in a country where anyone that mattered had their own militia, he had no one. What had seemed an advantage at the start was clearly now a disadvantage.

The President in His Bloody Palace

I saw the fear every afternoon when he went for his daily walk from his office to his house behind it. It was a short distance, just a few hundred yards, but he was accompanied by ten guards with three Land Cruisers following behind, there were snipers on the rooftops, and no one was allowed to move inside the palace grounds while he was walking. A Land Cruiser was always kept outside the palace with its engine running for a quick escape – a modern-day equivalent of Abdur Rahman's horses.

The ever-ready getaway vehicle was not the only way in which Karzai copied the Iron Amir. Conscious of how the KGB had tried to bump off Amin, he also had a team of official tasters. The chief taster was Ghulam Habib, known as 'Doctor'. Always smartly dressed in a grey suit with a silk tie, he told me he had been a doctor at Kabul's Central Hospital when he got a call summoning him to the palace. With a team of three, he tasted everything, from the kabuli rice to the green tea. I followed him as cooks laid out all the plates on a table in the kitchen about an hour before the meal, then watched him sample a bit of each. Providing he hadn't dropped dead, the dishes were taken by security guards to the dining hall.

'It's very risky,' he said. 'I'm always worried when I taste. I tell my wife and children, "This is my job. If I die in it, don't worry, for if I die it's not a big deal, but if the President dies it's a big thing."' He told me he had sent back the President's food many times, but not because it was poisonous, rather because he thought it was unhealthy.

That evening we shared the pre-tasted food with more elders from the south. Holding court among them, apparently deciding who could speak to Karzai, was a short man who to my astonishment turned out to be Sher Mohammad Akhundzada, the ousted Governor of Helmand, now a Senator. Karzai's staff told me he was a frequent visitor. I asked him about the allegations that he was involved in drug trafficking. He replied that the British had planted opium in his office to frame him. He had been lobbying General Richards to try to get his job back, or at least to raise a militia. 'I know the tribes of Helmand and how to control them,' he said.

'Within three months I could reduce violence by 60 per cent. I don't know what it is with the British. Do I have blood on my hands like Dostum or Fahim?'

He swept away, and I found myself talking to a white-bearded old man with thick black caterpillars of eyebrows who introduced himself as Haji Wakil Ghulam Ali from Maruf district in Kandahar. He told me his thirty-five-year-old son had been in the border police, and had recently been killed defending the village from Taliban. 'The Taliban wanted me to surrender – they asked for my weapon, and said they would make me chief of the area, but I refused. So they attacked. They attacked us three times, and on the third my son was killed by an IED as he was taking wounded colleagues to hospital. They are not really Taliban. They are poor people from cities in Pakistan being paid 30,000 rupees a month to fight. Pakistan is throwing dust in the eyes of the world.'

Haji Wakil told me he used to be an MP during Daoud Khan's time. 'I didn't have a beard then,' he said. 'I knew the President's father, he was Deputy Speaker of parliament. I've known the President since he was this high, he has kissed my hand many times. I don't know why he looks old, he is a young guy. To be President of a country is too much responsibility. You need even to know the conditions in a remote place. It is better to be a free man. I say, "Why have 1,200 turbans when you can have twenty?"'

Not everyone was a fan of Karzai. 'He is not like his father,' muttered several elders. He spent so much of his time in gatherings like this that a friend of mine who worked in the palace described them as, 'Oh Vizier, they killed my lamb.' Yet I could see that it was through such meetings that Karzai kept the country together. Balancing all of Afghanistan's competing tribes and ethnic groups was a tricky business that we foreigners couldn't begin to fathom. Everyone wanted something – money, the release of a tribesman from jail or NATO custody. Earlier in the day Karzai had received a delegation of Uzbek parliamentarians who had come to complain that there were not enough Uzbeks in the bureaucracy. 'They're right,' he told me afterwards. 'How many Uzbeks are they? Six per cent? Ten per cent? Then tomorrow the Barakzai are coming with the same complaint ... Too many foreign visitors, parliamentarians, mujaheddin leaders, not to mention the elders.' He shook his head. 'I'm their President, and they have to ask for things. When they are sick they come to me, when there's any injustice they come to me, and they have that right. Every day letters come addressed to me. Even on music request shows on the radio, people call for a request, then instead of asking for a record they say, "My request is, tell Karzai this or that is wrong." My job is to build this country with a stable future, to reverse the past which was inclusivity for one group, exclusivity for another. I want to make an Afghanistan for all Afghans, and that's what I've done.' He sighed. 'There are so very many people to see. Somehow they persuade the guards to get in, then they wait for me in mosque and when I pray they say, "Can I just have a minute?"'

It wasn't hard to work out how they got in. 'They give us presents,' the guards at the palace entrance told me one day.

Next morning the mood in the office was tense. A portly man in a suit had appeared, and was sitting on a chair outside Karzai's office reading *Le Monde*. He had flown in from Paris, and said he had come to be the President's Chief of Staff. The problem was, the President already had a Chief of Staff, Jawed Luddin. 'The man is claiming the President has promised him a job,' said Khaleeq. 'But no one here knows anything.'

I went to talk to him. His name was Akram. 'I have come to be Chief of Staff,' he said.

'The President already has a Chief of Staff,' I said.

'No matter,' he replied. 'I have come and I will wait.'

No one sent him away. He sat there all day and the next day and the day after reading his paper. Eventually he was made Head of Protocol. Said Jawad, Karzai's first Chief of Staff, who had gone to be Ambassador in the US, later told me that Akram's father had been a friend of Karzai's mother.

This was typical of how the Arg was run. People turned up and got jobs for which they were completely unqualified. One day I met an elder from Uruzgan who had been put in charge of the national archive. He told me he was completely illiterate. 'He has already broken two computers,' said Khaleeq. Another man wandered into the Chief of Staff's office. He had been fired from the protocol department but still hung around, I was told.

Apart from cabinet meetings, Karzai seemed to spend most of his time signing decrees – mostly awarding compensation from some kind of slush fund he seemed to have, or jobs. He signed off on petrol for government vehicles, he even chose school headmasters.

General Richards was so horrified by the chaos both in Karzai's administration and among the foreigners who were supposed to be helping that he came up with the idea of a Policy Action Group, or PAG, a kind of war cabinet to try to coordinate everyone. Karzai agreed, but saw it as a slur on him, and as soon as Richards left, it ended.

I never saw Karzai meet any kind of advisers, use a computer, or read any reports other than the daily press clippings from local and foreign media, which he seemed obsessed by. The US Defense Secretary Robert Gates noticed the same thing. 'Wholly dependent upon the largesse and protection of foreign governments and troops, he was exceptionally sensitive about any foreign commentary,' he wrote. 'He tracked foreign press zealously, and once showed me an article critical of him in the *Irish Times*. I thought to myself, who in the hell reads the *Irish Times* outside Ireland?'[2]

The clippings often put Karzai in a fury, sometimes for quite spurious reasons. 'Look!' he said to me one day, waving a copy of the *Kabul Times*. 'Look at this photograph of me in the paper.' On the front page was a picture of him meeting MPs from Wardak province. I looked, and could see nothing wrong. 'The photo is not even of the event, and there is a refrigerator in it!' he shouted. 'Why?'

Karzai's moods were a common theme of discussion among his staff. 'He gets very angry,' said Khaleeq. 'Sometimes the waiters are so scared to serve the tea the cups are rattling. When Ismael Khan was being removed [as Governor of Herat] and eighty of his supporters came to protest to the President, he was really shouting at them.'

Increasingly, that anger seemed directed at the international community. Every day Karzai complained to me about the civilian casualties they caused, and their failure to understand the tribes.

On the Saturday morning Karzai met the US commander General Karl Eikenberry, and berated him in front of me because ISAF forces in Uruzgan had arrested a man called Haji Sharang. 'This is as disastrous as anything you've done. It will turn the whole province against you!' shouted Karzai.

Eikenberry started to explain that the man had been caught with opium, and was believed by ISAF to be helping insurgents.

Karzai exploded. 'So deal with it straight away!'

Eikenberry left. I was astonished to see Karzai speak to one of America's top generals like that.

'It was a terrible thing to go and arrest one of our best supporters. People will lose faith,' he said. He explained to me that the man in question had helped him when he was in Uruzgan in 2001. 'He was the person who cleared the space to make helipads for the Americans. And when I went in the first time, he led me over the mountains, he knew the whole way. We got to the village then when they didn't invite us in the first houses he knew something was wrong and said we had to go back. I said, "We've walked twenty-four hours, we're tired and sick, we need to rest," but he said, "No we must go back." He saved my life. Even if he betrayed me a thousand times I would still support him.'

Like Helmand, Uruzgan was a sore point between the NATO forces and Karzai. When he became President, he had appointed as Governor an old one-eyed jihadi commander called Jan Mohammad Khan from the Durrani tribe who had been so close to Karzai's father that the Karzai sons called him 'agha', or father. A former wrestler, 'JMK', as the foreigners called him, was staunchly anti-Taliban, having been imprisoned by them. But as Governor he had given jobs only to his tribe and the Popalzai of Karzai, and used his power to settle old scores, getting the US special forces to go after his enemies by labelling them al Qaeda. This had turned other important tribes against the government and towards the insurgents. Moreover, like Akhundzada he had been found with a huge stock of opium. The Dutch wanted him replaced before they took control of security for the province. As he had done in Helmand, Karzai removed his man, but he was not happy about it, and believed the security situation in the province worsened as a result.

Haji Sharang wasn't the only man from Uruzgan whom Karzai had demanded that ISAF release. He told me they had also recently arrested someone from his tribe, the brother of a man he had sent to contact senior Taliban leaders. He had been picked up while fighting against the coalition. When Karzai found out, he ordered his release then summoned him to his office to ask what had happened. Karzai told me the man was afraid the coalition might arrest him because of his family contacts with the Taliban, so he had gone to Pakistan. Within a month he was picked up by ISI and thrown into the notorious Mach jail outside Quetta. 'After three months they told him, "You are al Qaeda, we can either send you to Guantánamo or we give you weapons and send you to Afghanistan to fight." He had no choice. So he went and conducted four operations, and on the fifth he was arrested. This is how things are.'

Karzai's normal working day started at 8 a.m. Three times a week the first meeting was a security briefing from his intelligence chief Amrullah Saleh, his National Security Council adviser Zulmay Rassoul, and Defence Minister General Rahim Wardak. This always began with 'Report from Pakistan'. In particular he was getting briefings on the situation in the Swat valley, where a radical mullah called Maulana Fazlullah had set up a radio station and was broadcasting Taliban propaganda, warning people to stop listening to music or sending their daughters to school.

They also discussed General Richards' recent visit to Pakistan. Karzai was upset with Richards, whom he had believed to be an ally and had expected to confront Musharraf on the issue of ISI's support for the Taliban. Instead Richards had come back with the usual line that Pakistan was doing what it could. 'Pakistan had got itself into a situation it couldn't get out of,' he told me later.[3]

Britain was in a complicated position. With its own Pakistani population of more than a million, many of whom flew back and forth between the two countries, the UK needed to maintain good relations with ISI for intelligence. The 7/7 attack in 2005 had brought that home sharply when fifty-two people were killed and hundreds injured by four suicide bombers blowing up three tube trains and a bus in central London. Three of the bombers were Britons of Pakistani descent who had gone to Pakistan for training.

Karzai's aides told him Richards had not discussed Afghanistan at all with the Pakistanis, and he became convinced that Britain was in cahoots with Pakistan. Robert Gates later remarked, 'Distrust and dislike of the British, who famously failed to pacify Afghanistan in the nineteenth century, was in his DNA.'[4]

Whenever the subject of Pakistan came up – which was frequently – Karzai became like a dog with a bone: 'There is an open campaign in Pakistan against Afghanistan and the presence of the Western troops here. I told you the story from Uruzgan. This is what ISI do, they recruit in the refugee camps and they threaten people with Guantánamo. I've been telling everyone we have to address the places where they get trained or we will keep suffering terrorist attacks all round the world.'

'People want to see evidence,' I said.

'Look,' he replied, 'we had someone come from Karachi last summer, a labourer in an Afghan leather factory, whose son was studying at a madrassa and disappeared one day. After three months of searching they found him and he explained that one day some mullahs had come to the class and asked, "Who is the best student?" The teacher pointed to him, so he was taken away to a place where they told him there is a war of crusaders continuing and Afghanistan has become the base for the anti-Muslims and if he went and killed anyone there he would go to heaven instantly with all the good things heaven offers. These are not stories – they are people I have actually met.'

As he often did, he went back to the past. 'You know how radicalism was promoted during those years of jihad. The more you became radical the more you received in assistance. Until Pakistan stops relying on promoting extremism as an instrument of policy, we will all keep suffering. When you and I would go with the mujaheddin inside Afghanistan, the group we were with later became Taliban, yet did you see any extremism or bias in them? Mullah Mohammad Rabbani, who you met and who became deputy to Mullah Omar, was a sensible man – so what happened? Suddenly some very good mujaheddin became the worst enemies of everything a decent human being would be seeking – a good house, a good education, a good country. And lots of them, the good ones like Mullah Rabbani, were later mysteriously killed. Why would a simple countryside movement of religious students suddenly turn into an extremist organisation of hatred against their own people and against the world? These are questions the West did not ask. Someone was trying to turn them into evil extremists, and that's the reason we're all in trouble today and the Twin Towers fell and the 7/7 attack in London. You know, a cousin of mine who was working for a demining agency in Quetta and often used to come to my house for dinner back in those days said to me one day in 2000, a young Taliban of fifteen or sixteen had come to his office that day and said, "I wish I had a skirt full of bombs to throw at New York City." How would an Afghan country boy know New York, and if he did it would be with the desire to go there. So who was teaching this young mind this hatred? Until we end the system promoting that, we will not succeed in stopping them, and they will not stop at Afghanistan.'

Karzai hated the fact that people mocked him as 'the Mayor of Kabul', yet as my week in the palace passed I realised that even that was an overstatement. In his walled fortress behind the dogs and the lady checks he was astonishingly cut off. 'When you come to power your eyes go blind, your ears go deaf and you don't know anything any more,' was an Afghan saying.

Every Monday was his cabinet meeting. Later the day was changed to Thursdays, to stop the Ministers all flying off for the weekend to Dubai, where many had acquired property worth far in excess of anything they could afford on their salaries.

Twenty-five Ministers and three advisers filed into the room, and the meeting started with a long prayer sung by a young mullah.

The President in His Bloody Palace

The Ministers were all male, apart from the Minister for Women's Affairs, who was completely ignored. Karzai proudly told foreigners of his support for equal rights for women, which he had enshrined in the constitution, and he kept telling me had lots of female staff – but apart from the lady-check police, I didn't see any. When I pressed him he said, 'I wanted more women in the cabinet but I haven't managed it. We have a senior lady, Sharifa, who will take up a post. We have lots of women in the press department, not in my immediate office. I just appointed a female Ambassador to Bulgaria. The Red Crescent is headed by a woman. We have a female Governor.'

Whenever I asked to meet his wife, he said she was away in India.

One day we drove just up the road to ISAF headquarters for a change-of-command ceremony. It was very hot, and a number of soldiers fainted during the proceedings. Afterwards Karzai was taken, with me in his wake, for a rare visit to the control room. It was full of people sitting at computers, with more screens all around showing footage from unmanned planes, all the intelligence that was coming in, the locations of all 31,000 foreign troops, and any TICs, or 'troops in contact'. It was fascinating, and I was bursting with questions.

Karzai seemed completely uninterested. 'Do you get tea and coffee in here?' and 'Does this really stay open twenty-four hours?' were his only questions.

One evening he had dinner with two visiting American Senators, both from the Democratic Party: Jack Reed from Rhode Island and Richard Durbin of Illinois. It was a classic Karzai performance – charming and disarming them. They wanted to talk about problems with governance and narcotics. He offered them pumpkin, asked them about Halloween in the US, and commented on the wild wind.

I remembered the words of the Danish Ambassador Franz-Michael Melbin, who went on to be the EU Special Representative.

'Whenever we have Ministers or politicians going to see him I always warn them before going in, "He will distract you – try to think of two main points you want to raise, and make sure you get them out."'[5]

Though I spent a lot of time with Karzai that week I found it hard to pin him down on anything serious. All he wanted to do was reminisce about the past.

One day after a counter-narcotics meeting, I asked how he felt about his country becoming a narco-state. He laughed. 'As long as we produce poppy the world will be interested in us,' he said. Then he became serious. 'Remember in Argandab sitting under the pomegranate trees and someone came with a big cloak which he threw near our feet to sit on? That orchard, that beautiful environment is now a poppy field. What would it take for that family to turn that beautiful pomegranate orchard into a poppy field?'

I asked about the widespread allegations that his own brother Ahmed Wali was trafficking opium. 'Yes, they say that,' he said. 'I've called him here, he's met with the international community, and they've not given any evidence. I've called in the Brits, the Americans, and asked them repeatedly, repeatedly, for evidence, and there is nothing. It's political, people trying to get at me by defaming him.'

The story I had heard was that when Karzai confronted him, Ahmed Wali retorted, 'At least I'm only ruining Kandahar. You're ruining the whole country.'

'Are you absolutely sure he's not involved?' I asked.

'Yes, to the extent he tells me repeatedly he's not, yes I am.'

His facial twitch worked away.

The next day he was in exuberant mood. He came out of his office with a long green-and-blue-striped *chapan* over his shoulders against the autumn chill. In his hands was a big sheaf of papers with sections highlighted in yellow. 'Christina, we're going to be rich!' he boomed. It was a report from the Council of Foreign

Talented poet Nadia Anjuman risked her life to write secretly under the Taliban. In 2005 she was killed by her husband. Her grave in Herat is now a shrine for women.

British soldiers from the 3rd Battalion of the Parachute Regiment and the author talking to elders in the Helmand village of Zumbelay in June 2006, just a few minutes before being ambushed.

Surrounded by Taliban on all sides, British soldiers fighting their way out of the ambush. Amazingly no one was killed. The commander, Major Paddy Blair, was awarded a DSO.

ISI Colonel Imam (real name Brigadier General Amir Sultan Tarar) headed the training of Afghan mujaheddin to fight the Russians from 1979–89, training ninety-five thousand men, including many of those who went on to be Taliban. He told the author in Rawalpindi in 2009 that he was continuing to help them.

US Major Larry Bauguess Jr was shot dead by a Pakistani soldier at a border meeting in May 2007. At the time he was reported as having been killed by enemy fire. The last photograph he took (later found on his camera by his wife) was of the Pakistani who shot him (second left, wearing helmet).

The triumphant return of former Prime Minister Benazir Bhutto to Pakistan on 18 October 2007 after almost nine years in exile. Her return was part of a US/British-backed deal to keep General Pervez Musharraf as President which could never have worked.

Bhutto talking to the author on top of her bus minutes before it was blown up in Pakistan's worst ever suicide bombing, killing more than 140 people. Many were students and youths who had formed a human chain round the bus.

Whoever wanted to kill Bhutto did not stop there. Ten weeks later, on 27 December 2007, she was killed in Rawalpindi after leaving an election rally.

General David Petraeus, seen here visiting a base in Kandahar, former heartland of the Taliban, became commander of ISAF troops in 2010 after his success leading the surge in Iraq. He was criticised in Afghanistan for ramping up airstrikes and trying to 'kill his way to victory'.

Osama bin Laden lived for five years in this house in Abbottabad, just a mile from Pakistan's prestigious Military Academy.

Obama's first pledge when he became President in January 2009 was to close the prison at Guantánamo. It remains open with 122 prisoners.

Prisoners often went on hunger strike as their only form of protest and were force-fed through rubber tubes.

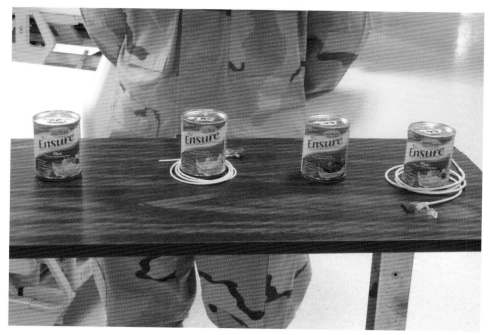

President Karzai and President Barack Obama at the White House
in January 2013. The two men never got on.

Relations on Afghanistan's mineral wealth, referring to reserves of 3.2 billion barrels of oil and gas.

He told me to come to his house with him. It was weird walking along, surrounded by all the gunmen. 'Guards follow me everywhere,' he shrugged. 'I long to get out. Sometimes I do. I have been out five or six times. I was planning to sneak out today with you but they stopped me.'

His house was a grim-looking two-storey building in grey concrete with white pillars and a large concrete blast wall in front of the windows. Before we went in he showed me the garden. There were plenty of roses, which he stopped to sniff, and a fountain that did not look as if it had worked for years. What had been an indoor swimming pool by the side of the house had been turned into a garage. 'I like to swim, but we're a poor country so we use it as a garage,' he said. On the other side was a tennis court with towels hanging from the net, which seemed to be used as a washing line. 'I'm banned from here!' he said.

Grazing on the lawn were four deer. Karzai smiled as they came towards him. 'These are my deer – mother, father and two babies. They were a gift from Uruzgan and Shiberghan. I like my deer, sometimes they feed from my hands.'

Standing there with his deer in front of his walled-in house, he looked like the loneliest man in the world.

Inside the house, the ground floor was lined with wooden shelves full of books. 'These are all my favourites,' said Karzai. 'My English poets – Keats, Poe, Shelley and Tennyson, my most favourite of all.'

The house was very 1970s. It had been built for Najibullah, he explained, the Soviets putting up the blast wall when they left as bombproof protection. During the Taliban times it was lived in by Mullah Rabbani. Karzai led me up an open wooden staircase to the family room. 'This is the room I like best and am in least, unfortunately,' he said. In it stood a leather saddle on a wooden stand. 'This was a present from President Bush with my name carved on the top. I will use it one day when I will have horses. He had it made for me in Texas. I didn't realise they made good saddles there. It's very soft.'

The shelves and walls were covered with photographs and certificates, reminders of how, to begin with, he was fêted all over the world. 'All the honours I've received,' he said. 'The best of course from the British Queen!' There were photographs of him with the Queen of Jordan, the Emperor of Japan, the Chancellor of Germany Helmut Schroeder, and of course with President Bush. That one was signed 'To Hamid, Best always, respectfully George'.

There were also albums of overseas visits. He pulled out one from Tajikistan and the latest, from China. 'They played our national anthem very nicely,' he said. He leafed through the pictures. 'Look, that's me trying to make a point – "You guys don't understand!" And this one of me looking very arrogant, I like that.' The next album was of a trip to Britain in 2005. 'Look, there's Prince Charles and Camilla!' he exclaimed happily. 'The Prince hosted me twice for dinner. You know, my favourite country is the UK, particularly the countryside for walking. I love to walk.' He had taken the trip after the 7/7 bombing, and there was a photograph of him and Tony Blair at the memorial site. 'Tony is a good man. I can tell him anything I want, and he does too.' I tried to imagine him and Blair swapping confidences, but it didn't quite work. 'He's aged a lot,' he added. 'Why's that? All the stress over Iraq?'

'You've aged too,' I said, undiplomatically.

'Yes,' he agreed. 'I don't notice until I see myself on TV, and then I'm shocked how bad I look – weak. You know I always looked older than my age, but now I look so old I think it's taking a toll on me. Sometimes I'm very sick, I feel very tired. In the morning I feel unwell, but when I look at schedule there's no way I can change it.'

I didn't know what to say, so I commented on the bowls of dried flowers that were everywhere. 'They are all from the garden,' he said. 'My wife does it. I keep asking her why.'

Maybe she's bored, I suggested. After all, she had been a working woman, a gynaecologist in a Quetta hospital, before they got married. Since he became President she had been hidden away –

never photographed or seen in public, and all the times I had been at the palace I had never met her. 'She wanted to work here but it was impossible as she would have had to have security,' he said.

'Why don't you take your wife on the trips?' I asked.

'She's having a baby,' he replied unexpectedly. She was pregnant with their first child. I congratulated him.

He ignored me, and pulled out an exquisite black-and-red-painted box. 'I have this from President Khatami, and it doesn't open. There is something inside here, but I don't know what – maybe Iranian music? The Iranians have been very helpful to us.'

I had wondered where the money came from for the slush fund he seemed to have from which to hand out compensation and gifts to the elders. It turned out that once or twice a year the Iranians gave 'bags of money', sometimes as much as 700,000 euros. The CIA was doing the same thing.

On the coffee table were large photographic books of *National Geographic* and Bollywood. 'I like Indian movies,' he said. 'But my favourites are English. I like *The English Patient* and all those with Peter O'Toole, particularly *Man of la Mancha* and *Goodbye, Mr Chips*. So that's life. That's my life.'

Downstairs was a locked room which he opened up. Inside were dark ebony walls. 'This is for my most formal meetings,' he told me. The cabinets were full of gifts. 'This is my most precious gift,' he said, pointing at a beautiful carved wooden ship on a stand. 'It was made by His Majesty, the Father of the Nation, when he was seventeen. When we came back we found it lying in the same place despite all the wars, the communists, the mujaheddin, the Taliban. It was still intact. Take it. I wish I could build something like that, but I'm bad in art.'

The concrete wall just outside made the room incredibly dark, like living in a bunker. 'I want to remove it, even just a bit, but the security don't agree. I can't see my deer, and I'd like to see even just a bit of the sky. In winter when it snows I want to be able to sit there watching.'

*   *   *

Journalists are supposed to be objective. I am not sure that is ever possible – perhaps the best we can hope is to be fair and to present all the facts – and in any case I was way too involved in Afghanistan to be objective about it. I was so saddened by what I had seen during my week in the palace that I didn't write the story, fearing the outside world would see Karzai as a madman.

A few weeks later, in November 2006, Tony Blair made a flying visit to Kabul to mark five years from the fall of the Taliban. He admitted that Western leaders had underestimated the size of the task in Afghanistan: 'I think we are wiser now to the fact that this is a generation-long struggle.' He had a short private meeting with Daud, and told Karzai, 'We strongly support Engineer Daud.' That was like the kiss of death. The following day at the National Security Council meeting where Blair's trip was discussed, people questioned why a mere Governor had met the Prime Minister alone. Karzai said, 'Yes, this is bad, this Governor is not our Governor, he is the Governor of the British,' and promptly sacked him. Jawed Luddin, his Chief of Staff, tried to defend Daud, to no avail. Jawed had studied in London, and at the start of the new year he was also removed, accused of being too close to the British. He was sent off as Ambassador to Norway. His replacement was Umer Daudzai, a former close ally of Gulbuddin Hekmatyar, who had helped Karzai escape Kabul in 1996 when he was arrested by Marshal Fahim. More old debts.

I was on holiday in Mozambique with my family over Christmas 2006, trying to forget about Afghanistan for a while, when my phone rang. My old friend Wais, the manager of the Mustafa Hotel, had been found dead in the bathroom. He had apparently committed suicide, though one friend who had spoken to him the previous day said he had just bought a plane ticket to India, and was upbeat. He was buried next day in freezing snow at the foot of TV Mountain in a plot overlooking the city. It felt like the end of an era, and the start of very bad things.

16

Whose Side Are You On?

On the Durand Line, 2006–07

'BROTHERS, THE WEATHER has turned bad,' warned the voice over the radio. 'The skies are cloudy; you need to stop and come back home.'

The American special forces soldiers raised their eyebrows as the message was interpreted. It was a beautiful, clear-blue day. The instructions to the Taliban were coming from a Pakistani military post near the border with Afghanistan.

Lieutenant Colonel Michael Waltz was on his second tour of Afghanistan commanding special forces along the border, staying in a small mud-walled base called FOB Lilley that looked like a mini Fort Alamo. That day they had gone to visit a nearby Afghan border post which had been fired upon when they heard the high-pitched whoosh of rockets and somebody shouted 'Incoming!'

'We saw the white smoke of the rocket trail coming from a base on a hill just below the Pakistani border post, Post 28,' said Waltz. 'There was no way the Pakistanis could have missed it.' After a series of rockets from the same place, he called in an airstrike. 'The local commander denied us permission, because he was looking at the maps and could see the location was so close to the Pakistani military post. I overrode him and we got a tremendous explosion dropped from a B1, destroyed the rocket position and killed several militants.'

Waltz and his men then went up to investigate, carrying out what they call BDA, or battle damage assessment, taking pictures so they could respond to any Taliban counterclaim. They started out in a heavy armoured MRAP, then when the terrain got too difficult they climbed by foot, up and down through steep wadis, everyone conscious of Post 28 just above.

'The Afghan border police with us were really nervous and told us if we had not been with them the Pakistanis would have fired on them with their heavy machine guns,' said Waltz. 'When we got to the site we found several IEDs surrounding it and seven rockets put on a timer which we stopped from launching on our base. All this within gunshot distance of the Pakistani post.'

They knew the insurgents used walkie-talkies, so had bought their own at the bazaar, and got the interpreter to scan channels until they found the one the enemy were using. 'We heard the Pakistani army post giving directions to the insurgents on where we were going and how to ambush us. It was in a Punjabi Pashto accent.'

Waltz called for air support. That was when the weather message came from the Pakistani soldiers to the insurgents, warning them off so they would not be hit. 'We saw this operational complicity between the Pakistani military and the insurgents again and again,' Waltz told me a few years later. 'It could be turning a blind eye as insurgents launched rockets at our bases – we regularly had insurgents launching rockets at us within firing distance of the Paks, and they did nothing. It could be allowing them passage right under their noses. It could be even aiding and working with insurgents to know what times to cross the border, telling them when our patrols or the Afghan patrols were coming. It certainly didn't feel like they were on our side.'

Yet the US was giving Musharraf around $100 million a month in aid.

*　*　*

In October 2006 I travelled by Chinook, following the turquoise ribbon of the Kunar River to a place called Naray, the remotest base of the coalition, in the mountainous province of Kunar high up in the Hindu Kush, where Pakistan once again lay just across the mountains. The small encampment of rows of tents on gravel surrounded by razor wire and sandbags had been a special forces post until a few months earlier, when US troops from 10th Mountain Division had arrived.

It was heartstoppingly beautiful, a land of tall mountains cloaked with pine and cedar forests, and ice-cold rivers of the clearest blue. It was also deadly – the regiment I was with had already lost their popular commander Joseph Fenty back in May (just a month after his wife had given birth to a daughter) along with nine other men when their Chinook came down during combat, and a reconstruction team had been killed in June. They would lose a total of thirty-nine men during that deployment, making them the hardest-hit US division in the whole Afghan theatre. The following year US troops there would come under attack 973 times. Yet when their families back home told people where they were, the usual response was, 'At least it's not Iraq.'

I was met off the helicopter by First Lieutenant Joe Lang, who told me he headed the Information Operations Cell and had read my piece about being ambushed at Zumbelay in Helmand with the British soldiers. 'We really loved your article,' he said. 'I hope we can show you some action up here.' I smiled, but my heart sank. The last thing I wanted was another narrow escape.

He took me straight into the chow hall for a breakfast of powdered scrambled eggs. The camp was pretty basic – most of the food was MREs, ready-to-eat meals in packets, to which you added water which magically heats them. There was a television showing American Forces TV which switched between baseball games and pictures of Afghan or Iraqi women and children superimposed with inspirational messages such as 'Your sacrifice ensures their freedom'.

Back outside, looking up at the towering black mountains all around, which the Americans had dotted with lonely observation posts, I could see the place was a natural fortress. On the other side of the mountains was Bajaur, the most northern of Pakistan's tribal areas – or 'Paksville', as the guys in the chow hall called it. No one had succeeded in conquering this area right back to Alexander the Great, who in his quest to conquer the entire known world invaded Kunar in the fourth century BC. Locals burned their houses and launched ambushes to drive the Macedonians away. Many centuries later they joined fellow Pashtuns in Bajaur across the invisible border to fight the British in the 1940s, armed with Mausers and Enfield rifles. During the fight against the Soviets, Kunar was a no-go area. The main commander, Jamil Ur Rahman, was a Salafist who attracted many Arab fighters, some of whom stayed and married local women, and much of the population adheres to Wahabbism. After 9/11 locals helped Taliban and al Qaeda escape across the border into Pakistan.

The Arab presence in Kunar led to regular rumours that Osama bin Laden and his deputy Ayman al Zawahiri were there, or further up the valley in even more remote Nuristan. In Pakistan I often spoke to Hamid Mir, a Pakistani journalist who was the only person to have interviewed bin Laden after 9/11, and who wore a black Casio watch that had been a gift from the al Qaeda leader. He told me he believed bin Laden had found refuge in the Pech valley leading up to Nuristan, crossing into it from Chitral in northern Pakistan.

According to Mir, it was in Kunar, in the first week of March 2003, that bin Laden held his first meeting with all his commanders since 9/11, taking advantage of the US distraction with Iraq. 'He told them, "The bad patch is over and we'll have a new breeding ground in Iraq," and assigned Saif al Adel [an Egyptian former army officer believed to have been behind the 1998 US Embassy bombings] to go to Iran and meet Abu Zarqawi then establish training camps.'[1]

A video dropped at the Pakistan office of the Qatari TV station al Jazeera in September 2003 showed bin Laden and al Zawahiri scrambling down scree-covered slopes similar to those in Kunar and Nuristan. Since then the al Qaeda leadership was believed to have moved back into Pakistan, but the valley had remained a murderous place. My first night at Naray I was kept awake by the heavy boom of a howitzer firing out, sending shudders through the whole camp, punctuated by the pop of smaller arms, insurgents firing down from a ridge. The soldiers told me that happened almost every night.

Just as I had seen in other places, some of the fighting here was nothing to do with the Taliban. Mostly illiterate and cut off from the outside world, with not even a TV signal from Kabul, the locals saw the Americans as infidels. It was a feeling reinforced when a local elder, Abdul Wali from Ganjgal, was picked up by the coalition forces in June 2002 and died in mysterious circumstances. That was not all. The main business in the valley was timber smuggling, and the Americans had earned the wrath of one of the major smugglers by working with one of his rivals.

In the convoluted manner of things in Afghanistan, many of the fighters were from the Hezb-i-Islami of Gulbuddin Hekmatyar, the fundamentalist warlord who had been the biggest recipient of CIA funds for the fight against the Soviets back in the 1980s. It was also his men with whom President Karzai had surrounded himself in the palace since the Kabul riots.

The Americans in Naray had no doubt who they were really fighting. 'We know the enemy is not from here,' said Private Zak Schultz of Charlie Company. Fighters simply disappeared across the border. 'I gotta tell you, ma'am, it's like chasing shadows up there,' he added, pointing up at the mountains. 'If we could go just ten miles the other side we could finish this.'

His commander was more circumspect. It was Lieutenant Colonel Michael Howard, the same soft-spoken man I had met in Shkin three years earlier, and he now looked even more war-weary. 'The enemy is not a home-grown enemy,' he said. When I pressed him about his frustration, he simply replied, 'My country is in a strategic partnership with that country.'

In the meantime they were trying to enlist the help of the local population. Kunar and Nuristan were poor and forgotten even by the standards of Afghanistan, where more than a third of the population live on less than 75 pence a day. 'These people have nothing – you can go out and see them making bricks just like in Moses' day,' said Captain Todd Polk, the Charlie Company commander. He told me they had a $50,000-per-month fund. In between all the fighting at night, they were trying to win over the population by day, providing them with things like potable water, bridges, roads and electricity from micro-hydro turbines.

'We're no longer breaking people's doors down – that was a mistake,' said First Lieutenant Lang. Instead they had set up a radio station built from scratch in a wooden cabin to broadcast messages, and handed out wind-up solar-powered radios. Before starting they asked local people what they wanted to hear, and were surprised to be told science, poetry and history.

These Americans in the east might have had far more money to splash around than the British troops I'd been with far to the south-west in Helmand, but they seemed to me to be engaged in an equally impossible task. 'The problem is you do a school in one village, then next day a guy comes from another village saying, "This village got one, why can't we have one?"' said Captain Polk. 'I've been reading a book about a guy from England who came here in the 1800s, and it was the same thing – people came down from the mountains to see who he was and what they could get.'

The biggest problem was that almost every time a team went out to see how they could help, it was attacked. The roads were incredibly dangerous. Not only was it hard to manoeuvre among all the rocks and boulders, but they were single-track along the floors of narrow valleys surrounded by high mountains from which it was easy to launch an ambush. However, there was little alternative, as the insurgents were also shooting at helicopters.

A mullah who supported the Americans had been beheaded, and his decapitated body left with a warning message attached. So had a contractor, Haji Yunus, who had been working with the Americans.

Next afternoon the howitzers started pounding again, and then two B1 bombers appeared overhead. Yet again one of the convoys coming back to camp from Kamdesh had been ambushed. Polk told me they had been measuring a road for widening, then had rounded a bend to see a little girl standing there. About fifty yards further on, they were ambushed with 'the whole works' – rockets, RPGs, machine guns and small arms. They managed to push their way through and got to a safe area, then 'put eyes' on the enemy and called in air support in the form of two 2,000-pound bombs and the guns of Naray. They reckoned ten to twelve insurgents were killed. The others just fled across the border as usual. No one saw what happened to the little girl.

'We're showing we're guests, we're not here to occupy, but at the same time that doesn't mean being prissy when you're shot at,' said Captain Polk.

My own fears of being caught in another ambush, this time on a narrow mountain road instead of in the middle of a hot desert, were put to an end when the photographer I was with took pictures of some of the Americans training Afghans. They turned out to be Afghan special forces we weren't supposed to see. He quickly deleted them from his digital card, but the Americans were furious, and told us we were being 'dis-embedded'.

I couldn't believe it. It was typical of the crazed life of a war correspondent that I could go straight from being worried about being shot at to being worried about not being shot at. I was also suspicious. It was clear that they were preparing for an operation, and I couldn't help thinking something was going on that they didn't want us to be around for.

While American soldiers on the ground like Colonel Waltz, or the ones I had been embedded with in Shkin and Naray, were frustrated by what they could clearly see, the line from Washington and Whitehall had always been that Musharraf was doing what he could.

The first public admission of frustration came in spring 2005 when Zalmay Khalilzad, the US Ambassador to Afghanistan, was transferred to Baghdad. Before leaving he gave an interview on Afghan television in which he questioned Pakistan's claim that it did not know where the Taliban were. He pointed out that Pakistani journalists had recently interviewed senior Taliban commanders in Pakistan. 'If a TV station can get in touch with them, how can the intelligence service of a country which has nuclear bombs and a lot of security and military forces not find them?' he asked.

His buddy President Bush told aides he worried that 'old school ties' between Pakistan's intelligence and the Taliban remained. But nothing changed. 'The problem was the vast American machine was way too invested in Pakistan,' said Nigel Inkster, who was head of operations for MI6 at the time. 'There was little we could do – their intelligence budget is $80 billion a year compared to our $3 billion, and we had the problem of our own Pakistani diaspora.'

'I spend more time on Pakistan than any other issue,' Karzai complained to me over and over again.

In February 2006 he travelled to Pakistan, and warned Musharraf that encouraging extremism would backfire. 'If anyone thinks he can train a snake to bite another person he should know that it is possible at any time for that snake to turn and bite his trainer,' he said.

With him went his intelligence chief Amrullah Saleh. 'We handed over a dossier of addresses for members of al Qaeda and Taliban,' said Saleh. Among them was intelligence that al Qaeda was using safe houses in Mansehra, not far from the Pakistani capital (and near Abbottabad). He also told Musharraf that Osama bin Laden was living under protection in a Pakistani army cantonment (though he didn't know which).

Musharraf was furious. 'Am I President of a banana republic?' he demanded. One of his interior ministry officials was derisive about Saleh when I spoke to him. 'He is a thirty-three-year-old boy while our ISI chief General Kayani has thirty years of experience,' he snorted.

When I spent my week in the palace six months later, Karzai and his advisers said Pakistan had not acted on any of the intelligence they had provided. 'They haven't arrested a single Taliban figure,' said Zulmay Rassoul, the National Security Adviser. 'We've had a series of addresses and phone numbers of Taliban *shura* in Quetta which we gave to Pakistan, and they just say it's outdated.' Nigel Inkster had a similar experience: 'When we gave ISI locations of Taliban – say, they were living on this street, in the blue house – it was as if they had a Dulux colour chart: they'd come back and say, "It's not that shade of blue."'

Dr David Kilcullen, a former Australian special forces officer and an expert on counter-insurgency who had been seconded to the US State Department as Chief Strategist on Counter-Terrorism, told me that, 'very much against the objections of the CIA', his office had handed over to ISI a list of names and addresses of around two hundred wanted Taliban. 'Within forty-eight hours they had all been moved.'

Indeed, the former Foreign Minister Abdullah Abdullah told me, 'We have stopped giving information to Pakistan as they use it the wrong way.'

Rassoul gave a more horrific example. Shocked by the sudden spate of suicide bombing, they had focused efforts on finding the bombers' handlers, and tracked some down to Shamshatoo refugee camp, just outside Peshawar, in Pakistan. 'We had an informer so we gave ISI names of ten people involved and their phone numbers, all except our own man. Then a few days later a garbage bag was found with our informer's body chopped up in six pieces and a note attached saying, "Anybody that helps government of Afghanistan this is what happens to you."'

President Bush continued to tell people who asked about Musharraf, 'He's one of my best friends.' However, he worried that in every conversation he had with Karzai the Afghan President was obsessed with Pakistan, while Musharraf obsessed with India. In March 2006 Bush went to India to sign a deal on nuclear cooperation which basically accepted Pakistan's great enemy as a nuclear power. Knowing such a deal would send off alarm bells in Islamabad, Bush agreed to stop off there on his way home to appease Musharraf. His Ambassador Ryan Crocker suggested he should stay overnight, something no US President had done since Richard Nixon thirty-seven years earlier. This was a nightmare for

Bush's Secret Service. Such were the security fears that a decoy motorcade drove from the airport while the President and First Lady flew in secretly on a Black Hawk.

Bush's meeting with Musharraf had two main objectives – internal and external. The hypocrisy of preaching democracy in Iraq and Afghanistan while supporting a military regime in Pakistan had not gone unnoticed. It was something that infuriated liberal Pakistanis. 'In the eyes of a growing number of Pakistanis Bush was all for democracy except in the second largest Muslim country in the world, their homeland,' said former CIA officer Bruce Riedel. As Riedel points out in his book about the US–Pakistan relationship, *Deadly Embrace*, America had endorsed every Pakistani military dictator, even when they started wars with India, built nuclear bombs and moved their country ever deeper into bed with jihadists.

John F. Kennedy hosted the first dictator, General Ayub Khan, and his wife at Mount Vernon for the only state dinner ever held at the home of America's first President. Richard Nixon turned a blind eye to the murder of hundreds of thousands of Bangladeshis in order to keep his friends in Pakistan's army in power (though this ultimately failed). Ronald Reagan entertained General Zia even as Zia was building a nuclear bomb and welcoming in Arab jihadists who would become al Qaeda.

In the same way, the Bush administration were giving billions of dollars to a man who gave Taliban a sanctuary from which to kill American soldiers in Afghanistan. They had done nothing to press Musharraf to allow a return to democracy, and had complained only half-heartedly when the 2002 elections had been rigged in favour of Islamic parties. Musharraf was still serving as both President and army chief, even though this was unconstitutional. The country's two main political leaders, Benazir Bhutto and Nawaz Sharif, were still in exile. Yet in 2004 Pakistan had been named by Bush as a 'major non-NATO ally'.

The UK was equally hypocritical. When Musharraf seized power in 1999 Pakistan had been suspended from the Commonwealth. Yet in June 2003 red carpets were rolled out for

Musharraf for a state visit, with dinners hosted by Prince Charles and the Lord Chancellor Lord Falconer. The following year Pakistan had been readmitted into the Commonwealth. Then in November 2006 Prince Charles made his first ever visit to Pakistan, a five-day tour with his new wife Camilla. 'Britain has deeper, more complex relations with Pakistan than anyone,' said Richard Codrington, who was head of Afghanistan at the Foreign Office at the time. 'The fact that the heir to the throne went there for almost a week was a clear signal of what we think of Pakistan.'[2]

Benazir Bhutto was so concerned that Britain was in bed with Musharraf and might start handing over information about her that she took her children out of school in London and moved from her flat in Kensington to Dubai. There they lived inside a gated community in a pink villa surrounded by palm trees with her mother Nusrat, who was descending into Alzheimer's.

During Bush's 2006 visit to Islamabad he urged Musharraf to shed his military affiliation and govern as a civilian. 'He promised to do it,' Bush wrote in his memoir. 'But he wasn't in much of a hurry.'[3] Bush also stressed the importance of the fight against extremists. 'We've got to keep those guys from slipping into your country and back into Afghanistan,' he told Musharraf, who assured him they were doing all they could. 'We are totally on board,' he said.

A few months later the Pakistani military agreed another peace deal in Waziristan, which would lead to spiralling violence in Afghanistan. Like the previous deals, this one, signed in early September 2006, committed Pakistani forces to withdrawing from the area, while tribal leaders pledged to stop al Qaeda and Taliban from using Waziristan or infiltrating over the border. Pakistan agreed to hand over seized weapons and to release over 130 detainees suspected of being al Qaeda, and also paid an unknown sum of money. Bill Roggio, the widely respected editor of the *Long War Journal*, described it as 'abject surrender'.

The signing ceremony was held at a football stadium over which flew the al Raya, the black flag of al Qaeda, and the agreement referred to the area as the Islamic Emirate of Waziristan. Among those attending was Jalaluddin Haqqani, head of the Haqqani network, and Tahir Yuldashev, commander of the Islamic Movement of Uzbekistan. After the Pakistani delegation left, Taliban openly paraded in the streets of Miranshah, the capital of North Waziristan. Some estimates indicated that the flow of Taliban fighters into Afghanistan increased fourfold after the deal. US army figures showed the number of attacks in the border area going up by 300 per cent.

Karzai was furious about the deal. As Musharraf and Karzai continued to trade insults, Bush became so worried about his two main partners in the fight against terror that he invited them both to Washington in September 2006 for a peacemaking dinner at the White House.

The visit started with a welcome from Bush in the Rose Garden which was supposed to show unity in front of the cameras. Instead it had the opposite effect when the pair refused to shake hands or even look at each other. When they sat down for a light supper of soup, sea bass and salad in the Old Family Dining Room, the situation did not improve. 'Cheney, Condi, Steve Hadley and I watched as Karzai and Musharraf traded barbs,' wrote Bush. A White House statement later described the dinner as a 'constructive exchange'. In fact Karzai had accused Musharraf of harbouring Taliban, while Musharraf retaliated by calling him 'an ostrich' for refusing to accept the problems within Afghanistan. An alarmed Bush told the pair that the stakes were 'too high for personal bickering', and kept the dinner going for two and a half hours to try to 'help them find common ground'.

A couple of months after that, in November 2006, I went to Pakistan to hear its side of the story. In October Musharraf had admitted for the first time that 'retired ISI operatives' could be abetting the Taliban. Others told me they were not really retired at all, this just provided convenient deniability.

Fearful of big hotels with ISI spies pretending to read newspapers in the lobby, I stayed at the Chancery guesthouse, which had a rather alarming fish tank containing three of the fattest goldfish I had ever seen. The room was brown-carpeted and brown-bed-covered, with only a tiny window and a sign on a cupboard that said 'Prayer Mat and Holly [sic] Books Inside', as well as a handy arrow nailed on showing the direction of Mecca.

December is the main wedding month in Pakistan, so the tailors were busy with women looking at rolls of intricately embroidered material, and the jewellers crowded with women buying gold bangles for their dowry. Along the roadsides were groups of men in amber-coloured robes and bright-blue sashes, some with elaborate matching blue turbans, hoping to be hired as wedding singers.

There was only one topic of discussion among my friends in Pakistan. On 30 October, while Prince Charles was at a reception hosted by the British High Commissioner in Islamabad attended by the cream of Pakistan society, including the politician and former cricketer Imran Khan, a madrassa had been blown up in Bajaur, just on the Pakistani side of the border from Naray, where I had been with the American soldiers. Eighty-two people were killed, including children, and locals said body parts had been scattered everywhere. They said the explosion had been caused by a missile from a US Predator. I couldn't help wondering if there was any connection with my hurried expulsion from Naray just a few days earlier.

The Americans later revealed that they had acted on intelligence that the deputy al Qaeda leader Ayman al Zawahiri was visiting the madrassa. However Pakistan initially claimed responsibility. General Shaukat Sultan, the military spokesman, called it 'an army strike led by helicopters' acting on information that seventy to eighty militants were hiding there, preparing suicide bombs. 'It was done purely by the Pakistan authorities,' he insisted. 'There was no American involvement.'

An old friend, Ayesha Siddiqa, who bravely tracked Pakistan's military, had recently published a book, *Military Inc.*, showing how the army had amassed a £10 billion private business empire involved in everything from producing cereals to running bakeries and petrol stations through vast 'welfare foundations'. She thought assuming responsibility was a foolish strategy. 'By whitewashing America's crimes on this territory just to prove he's in control Musharraf is creating double trouble for himself,' she told me.

A Pakistani newspaper, *The News*, published the names of sixty-nine children killed at the madrassa in Bajaur. People were angry, and the reaction was swift. Just nine days later, on 8 November, a suicide bomber wrapped in a shawl rushed onto a parade ground where soldiers were being drilled in Dargai, Northwest Frontier Province, killing forty-two. It was the biggest ever single attack on the Pakistan army.

To try to make sense of what was going on, I arranged to go back and see General Ali Jan Aurakzai, the former commander of the Peshawar Corps, which includes the paramilitary Frontier Corps who had spearheaded Pakistan's first deployment of forces into the tribal areas. He had retired in 2004, but retirement for Musharraf's generals meant being rewarded with university chancellorships, heading a quango like the Post Office or being given the governorship of one of the four provinces. General Aurakzai had been made Governor of Northwest Frontier Province.

Peshawar had become much easier to get to since my days in the late 1980s of chugging up the Grand Trunk Road in my little blue Suzuki. Nawaz Sharif may not have done much as Prime Minister in the 1990s, but he had built motorways. 'I love motorways,' he would tell people. It was the first one I'd ever driven on with a sign over it warning 'No camels No carts No donkeys'.

General Aurakzai was a pale-faced man with pale eyes and moustache and liver-spotted skin. He was wearing a dark pinstripe suit, and he was, he said, fed up with everyone blaming Pakistan for harbouring and training Taliban. He told me he had gone to Kabul with Musharraf in September, and they had been shocked by what they had encountered. 'Karzai is living in a big bunker. The President and the parliament are besieged in Kabul and have no control over Afghanistan. The Afghans are trying to cover their own weaknesses by blaming Pakistan. They say there are terrorists being trained then launched into Afghanistan, they say Mullah

Whose Side Are You On?

Omar is sitting in Serena Hotel, Quetta. I would say, "Where was bin Laden before 9/11? In Afghanistan! Who is Mullah Omar – is he Pakistani or Afghan? Who are the Taliban?" The problem is there – they should be fighting rather than complaining.'

I told him what I had witnessed in Naray and Shkin. 'I'm not saying there is no cross-border activity,' he replied, 'but the Taliban were in small groups in 2002–03. To say ISI are training Taliban couldn't be any more ridiculous remark. First, the Afghans have been fighting for the last twenty-eight years, so hardly need training. Secondly, is it in our interest that Afghanistan should be bleeding and in a state of turmoil? If they are, so are we. We'd be out of our minds to do any such thing.'

'Their numbers have swelled because moderate elements are gravitating towards them because of the war in Iraq, because wedding parties are being bombed and mosques bombed and children killed by NATO forces, and the lack of development so people are frustrated. It's now a nationalist movement, a war of resistance. None of these factors are to do with us. The NATO forces are making allegations against Pakistan to hide their own weaknesses. Dammit, why don't they monitor their own side of the border and fight like men instead of sitting in their bases?'

He pointed out that Pakistan had twice as many soldiers as NATO in border areas. 'We're doing far more than the entire coalition – they have 31,000 troops in Afghanistan, we have 80,000, and we have lost 750 men, three times more than the entire coalition suffered in five years. In just one incident – the suicide bomb at Dargai barracks last week – we lost forty-two soldiers, as many as Britain in the whole year.' He was warming to his theme. 'I say to the Americans, "You bring 50,000 more troops and fight ten more years in Afghanistan and you won't resolve it, and I stand by that – there will be no military solution. You can ask the Soviet Union, but you Britishers know the history better than anyone else. Look at the First Anglo–Afghan War: initially it was celebration – they built a cantonment, installed a puppet King, brought their wives and sweethearts from Delhi, their man Alexander Burnes cabling back all's well. In the meantime the Afghans started getting organised, and a day later his head is on a pole. This is exactly what the Afghans are doing today – it's a repeat of the First Anglo–Afghan War.'

On the way back down to Islamabad I stopped at Akora Khattak to visit Darul Uloom Haqqania, the madrassa where Mullah Omar had studied, along with 90 per cent of the Taliban leadership, their names on the roll of honour. One of the graduates was Jalaluddin Haqqani, head of the Haqqani network based in North Waziristan, which ran its own transport mafia and had close links to al Qaeda, arranging places to stay for those who came over the border after 9/11.

Most of the boarding houses were empty – like all Pakistani madrassas, Haqqania closed for two months every winter, supposedly for students to go and visit their families, although some said it was to go and fight in Afghanistan.

The school's director, Maulana Sami-ul-Haq, was a Senator, and leader of his own faction of the JUI, a religious party that was part of the MMA alliance that had swept into power in NWFP in 2002. With his long bushy beard and heavy spectacles, he always reminded me of Jim Royle, the layabout dad from the British sitcom *The Royle Family*, but lounging on floor cushions instead of a sofa. He was friendly, despite the fact that the last time I had gone to see him, in 2001 with photographer Justin Sutcliffe, we had accidentally knocked down his front wall.

He repeated the same old story, that the Jews were behind 9/11, and insisted that the war in Afghanistan was all part of a Western plot to establish bases in the region, occupy Pakistan and seize its nuclear assets. 'The Taliban are very wise and can foresee the US future objectives. They think that America's problem is not Osama bin Laden, but instead it aims at a long-term plan of staying in Afghanistan by finishing Taliban and installing a puppet government to exploit the markets of the surrounding countries. They will turn Afghanistan into a big cantonment and a base for policing China, USSR, Tibet, Iran, Pakistan and Central Asian states.'[4]

He also claimed the Americans were trying to 'turn Pakistan into a mercenary', with the aim of discrediting and weakening the army, enabling India to move in and destroy Pakistan. 'The next target for the US will be nuclear Pakistan,' he said. 'The US is working on plans to de-Islamise and de-link Pakistan army from the people so that the people of Pakistan lose confidence in their army. I fear if the US succeeds in disgracing the Pakistan army their fighting ability will be weakened. Pakistan army will be forced to deploy maximum of its standing army on western frontiers [with Afghanistan]. There will be less force on the eastern border and India may attack Pakistan in conspiracy with the US. By cooperation with the US we are heading towards an unimaginably dangerous situation.'

Before I left he offered the same final warning as General Aurakzai. 'My sincere advice to the US is that they should go back from Afghanistan as soon as possible. Afghan people will never rest unless they kick the last US soldier out.'

For their part, the Afghans believed Pakistan was behind everything. In their view Islamabad, or rather Rawalpindi, where the military was headquartered, was determined to give the Americans a bloody nose and force them out of Afghanistan then control it themselves.

'The reality is Pakistan is a lethal deceptive terrorist-sponsoring state,' insisted Amrullah Saleh, the Afghan intelligence chief. 'Without Pakistan's support Taliban don't exist for a day. NATO is fighting a Pakistan proxy. It's like the US for whatever reason is financing both sides of the war.'

With the situation in Afghanistan deteriorating, Britain decided to expand its Embassy, making it one of its biggest in the world, and send one of its most flamboyant and high-powered diplomats, Sherard Cowper-Coles, who had been Ambassador in Saudi Arabia. He arrived in Kabul in May 2007 and was shocked to find that 'Karzai saw a Pakistani hand almost everywhere ... and worse, believed Britain was in league with Pakistan.' Every time they met, Karzai steered the conversation round to Pakistan. 'Once getting very excited Karzai told me that if Musharraf did not accede to some particular demand he would personally head a Pashtun march on the Attock bridge across the Indus and lead an attack into the Punjab.'[5]

There was, after all, some justification. A report in September 2006 by Britain's Defence Academy, which is run by the MoD, stated: 'ISI has been supporting terrorism and extremism whether in London on 7/7 or Afghanistan or Iraq.' It added that 'US/UK cannot begin to turn the tide [in Afghanistan] until they identify the real enemies.'

A cable from ISAF headquarters on 21 May 2007, later revealed by WikiLeaks, reported that members of the Taliban and Haqqani networks had recently returned to Logar after five months' training in Pakistan in IEDs and propaganda. It also stated that ISI had provided a thousand motorbikes to Jalaluddin Haqqani to be used for suicide attacks in Afghanistan.[6]

That year the UN mission to Afghanistan (UNAMA) commissioned a study by American academic Christine Fair on who was carrying out the suicide bombings. Her report found that they 'appear to be young (sometimes children), poor, uneducated, easily influenced by recruiters and draw heavily from madrassas in Pakistan'. Some were schoolchildren, 'lured with promises of adventure or material gain such as motorbikes and cell phones'; others had been abducted outright. Some were Afghan refugees settled in Pakistan.

I'd heard the story of children being recruited from madrassas from many bereaved families in Pakistan, though they were always too fearful to give their names. As in the story Karzai told me from the Afghan in Karachi, it seemed there were jihadi talent-spotters who went to madrassas and took selected students off for 'extra tuition'. This meant training at camps run by militant groups such as Jaish-e-Mohammad and Harkat-ul-Mujaheddin, which Musharraf had told the US Ambassador Wendy Chamberlin he would not close. Often families didn't know their children had any involvement in such activities until they got a call saying, 'Congratulations, your son carried out a successful martyr mission.' People also talked of middlemen being paid to scout villages for recruits.

Whose Side Are You On?

Chris Alexander, a brilliant young Canadian who was deputy head of UNAMA at the time, and who later became an MP, sent me a copy of their suicide-bombing report, and told me it had been hushed up. However, Fair cautioned that the interview subjects were provided by Amrullah Saleh. Even so, she said there was no doubt most suicide bombers were coming from Pakistan. She herself had met a failed suicide bomber in Herat who had come from the southern province of Sindh intent on blowing up Americans only to find the soldiers there were Italians, whom he was unsure whether were *kafir* or not.[7] Many came from the camps – there were still 2.6 million Afghan refugees in Pakistan. Less than a quarter of school-age Afghans in refugee camps in Pakistan go to school, according to UNHCR.

When the report was published in September 2007, the Pakistanis were outraged. 'They went ballistic,' said Fair. Pakistan's Ambassador to the UN went to the Secretary General's office and pointed out that Pakistan had long been the number-one contributor to UN peacekeeping forces, threatening that it would withdraw its soldiers unless whoever was responsible for the report was fired. Pakistani forces had been involved in forty-one UN missions, had lost 128 men and were providing more than 10,600 troops – almost 13 per cent of the worldwide total. The suicide-bomb study was taken off the UN website, and Fair went home.[8]

Back in Washington the leadership of the war was changing, and with it there was renewed attention on Afghanistan. At the start of 2007 Robert Gates, who had replaced Donald Rumsfeld as Defense Secretary, made his first trip to Afghanistan. He had already told President Bush he believed the war in Afghanistan was being neglected, and his opinion was confirmed by what he saw. He heard the same story from everyone he met: 2006 had been the bloodiest year since 2001, suicide attacks and roadside bombs were up,[9] 191 coalition troops had been killed, and the number of direct attacks had almost trebled, from 1,558 to 4,542. The Taliban insurgency was growing, their safe havens in Pakistan a big problem. A CIA analysis warned that the Karzai government was losing control.

'The war in Afghanistan as in Iraq was clearly headed in the wrong direction,' said Gates. 'In Afghanistan as in Iraq from early on we had underestimated the resilience and determination of our adversaries and failed to adjust our strategy and resources as the situation on the ground changed for the worse.'[10]

Recognising that the situation was going downhill, Bush had ordered what he called a 'silent surge', increasing the number of US troops from 21,000 to 31,000 over two years, particularly reinforcing their numbers along the border with Pakistan. He had also doubled the funding for reconstruction and increased the number of military civilian teams. 'We face a thinking enemy,' he said. 'And we face a tough enemy – they watch our actions, they adjust their tactics.'

Gates thought more troops were needed, and faster. General Eikenberry asked for the battalion of 10th Mountain Division (around 1,200 men), who I had been with in Kunar, to have their stay extended by six months to see them through the forthcoming spring offensive.

Colonel John 'Mick' Nicholson, their commander, a thoughtful and likeable man who would end up involved in Afghanistan longer than almost any American officer, had to pass on the news. 'We'd just done a year, and then get told, "Now you do another six months." I remember getting on the VTC [video conference] with the families and it was not good. But we needed more troops, no one knew the area better than we did, and we were the right ones to be extended, so after the first forty-eight hours of banging our heads, we redoubled our efforts to get after the enemy.'

Gates also accelerated the deployment of the 82nd Airborne, which along with 10th Mountain provided an extra 3,200 troops, bringing the total to 25,000.

The problem was that on 10 January 2007 President Bush had announced an extra 30,000 troops for Iraq, the so-called 'surge'. With 160,000 troops there, the US Army didn't have capacity to spare for Afghanistan. 'I realised I couldn't deliver in both places at once,' said Gates. Admiral Mullen, Chairman of the Joint Chiefs of Staff, in testimony to the House Armed Services Committee in December 2007, described Afghanistan as an 'economy of force' operation: 'In Afghanistan we do what we can, in Iraq we do what we must.'

While he was in Afghanistan, Gates travelled by helicopter to the east of the country to visit FOB Tillman, a fortified outpost 6,000 feet up in the mountains, just a few miles from the Pakistan border and on one of the major infiltration routes. There he saw the problem at first hand.

Looking across into Pakistan, he reflected how just over twenty years earlier, as Deputy Director of the CIA, he had been on the other side of that border, looking into Afghanistan and 'doing business with some of the very people we were fighting now … it was a stark reminder to me of our limited ability to look into the future or to foresee the unintended consequences of our actions'.[11] As he told me a few years later, 'We have skin in the game.' This complicated dealings with Pakistan.

Any meeting with Pakistani military officers usually involved them complaining about how the US had used them and dropped them the moment the Russians were driven from Afghanistan. They were convinced the same thing would happen again the moment bin Laden was captured. One Pakistani officer wrote a paper entitled 'The Coming Betrayal', which he presented to Colonel Nicholson.

As commander of one of the brigades on the border, Colonel Nicholson had been sceptical about the peace agreement from the start. Before signing it, some Pakistani officers had travelled to FOB Salerno in Khost in May 2006 to brief coalition officers, showing what Nicholson called the 'Give Peace a Chance' PowerPoint.

Over the following months his worst fears were realised. 'Under what the Pakistanis described to us as the conditions of treaty the militants were essentially given freedom of movement to mount large attacks. They drove right up to the border.'

'Were the Pakistanis helping them?' I asked.

'The point is it didn't require them to give any help other than passively not to interfere,' he replied. Soon it was happening all the time. After a couple of particularly big fights on the border, the Americans called meetings to discuss the situation. 'We'd say, "Why are you not intercepting these guys as they come to attack us? Or why when they attack us and they are crossing back to your side, we are calling you and you are not doing anything."' He laughed as he recounted that the Pakistanis replied that the attacks were emanating from the Afghan side.

The Americans became so frustrated that they would film the attacks, and in the case of indirect fire they would use radar to plot exactly where the shots emanated from.

Once Nicholson brought his opposite number from Pakistan, Brigade Commander Rizwan, over from North Waziristan to demonstrate. 'His local battalion commander had been bitterly complaining we'd been shooting into his space and endangering his troops, he was really upset about it. He claimed all these mortars we were receiving were coming from our side of the border and we were firing back on his side of the border. So we brought him over, sat him down in front of our counterfire radar, and said, "I'll show you how accurate this is." He had a mortar set up outside and got someone to fire it as he instructed the brigadier to watch the radar screen. We fired the mortar – phow! – and he looked at the radar and the plot was very precise.' Nicholson then said, '"Now let me show you every single firing," and I replayed all the data back to show where all the mortars fired from – all from inside Pakistan. The brigade commander, to his credit, went out to his guy and had a conversation in Urdu where he scuffed him up for all the false reports he'd been sending in. But it didn't really change anything, they didn't intercede or interfere.'

The following January, just after Gates' visit, came the most blatant incident of all. 'We traced five truckloads of militants coming from North Waziristan, driving to the border on trucks then walking straight in to attack a combat outpost we had just constructed in Marghan in Paktika, on a major infiltration route near Shkin. There were about two hundred of them, all armed and pretty well organised, and split in two groups.'

They had passed several Frontier Corps posts in the vicinity, which had failed to report any enemy activity. When Nicholson's men called in with the specific location, they replied that they were woodcutters' trucks. 'Well, we saw what we saw,' he said. The Americans then spent a couple of hours confirming with the Pakistani military that this was not a Pakistani army unit which had unintentionally crossed the border. Once that was confirmed they called in an airstrike, dropping two massive bombs to kill the militants.

Next day, Governor Pahwa called local people in, laid out the bodies and weapons, and asked, 'Are these your sons?' They replied, 'No, they are from our tribe but from across the border.' The report was passed on to the Pakistanis, but the border crossings continued. 'It was as if we were living in alternate realities,' said Nicholson. 'We were saying, "Look, they're attacking up here, we're killing them by the dozens, yet you are saying you are not hearing anything, not seeing anything. Are you kidding me?" It was surreal.'

Gates recognised the need to get Pakistan to do more to end safe havens and stop infiltration. However, in his five years as Defense Secretary he travelled there only twice. 'I quickly realised my civilian counterpart had zero clout in defence matters,' he said.

On his first trip, on 12 February 2007, he was given the usual story that Afghanistan was the problem, and Pakistan 'the victim of the export of Afghan Taliban'. As General Aurakzai had told me, the Pakistanis pointed out that the number of soldiers they had lost fighting in the tribal areas was more than the total lost by NATO.

However, the US Congress had just passed a measure linking future military aid to White House certification that Pakistan was 'making all possible efforts to prevent the Taliban from operating in areas under its sovereign control'.

Gates met Musharraf privately in a small room where the Pakistani President acknowledged 'Pakistani failures on the border', but asked what a lone Pakistani border sentry could do if he saw thirty or forty Taliban moving towards the Afghan border. 'You should permit the sentry to warn us, and we will ambush the Taliban,' said Gates. 'I like ambushes, we ought to be setting them daily,' replied Musharraf. If only, thought Gates.

Gates gave him a list of specific actions the US wanted taken. These included capturing three named Taliban, giving the US expanded authority to take action against specific Taliban and al Qaeda leaders in Pakistan, dismantling insurgent and terrorist camps, shutting down Taliban headquarters in Quetta and Peshawar, disrupting certain major infiltration routes on the border, and allowing expanded intelligence flights over Pakistan.

'Musharraf kept a straight face and pretended to take all this seriously,' wrote Gates. 'We'd still be asking for virtually all these same actions years later.'

Musharraf had other things to worry about. In March 2007 he suspended the Chief Justice Iftikhar Mohammad Chaudhry, fearing he would rule that Musharraf was violating the constitution by serving as both President and army chief. Chaudhry had made himself awkward by ruling that ISI was complicit in the forced 'disappearances' of around four hundred people since 9/11, and ordering them to produce the people in court.

Chaudhry's dismissal prompted huge street demonstrations and the launch of what became known as the Lawyers' Movement. The protests were shown live on all the new private TV channels Musharraf had allowed to open. More than forty people were killed and hundreds arrested in a police crackdown. Chaudhry became a national hero.

I even started to hear grumblings from within Pakistan's usually hierarchical army. Musharraf's long tenure as army chief meant no one else in the top echelons could be promoted (and therefore receive more plots of land). Senior officers also worried that his actions were bringing the armed forces into disrepute.

Bush made his first public criticism of Musharraf, warning that he needed to do more to hunt down terrorists. 'Pressure mounted on me to cut ties with Musharraf,' he wrote later. 'I worried that throwing him overboard would add to the chaos.'

Then something shocking happened that, had it been made public at the time, would have provoked outrage in the US.

In an effort to cope with the increased flow of militants from Pakistan since the peace deal, the Afghans started to build more border posts. One of these was at a place called Gawi, in Jaji district, which was one of the main crossing points. The Pakistanis objected, claiming it was inside Pakistan, and occupied it by force, killing thirteen Afghans. Dozens more were killed over the following days as both sides traded mortar rounds and rocketed each other.

As Pakistan, Afghanistan and the US were theoretically all on the same side, whenever matters got out of hand, so-called 'flag meetings' were arranged to try to de-escalate tension. On Monday, 14 May 2007 one was held in Teri Mangal in Pakistan. Americans from the 82nd Airborne flew across the border with a dozen Afghans including Rahmatullah Rahmat, the Governor of Paktia, to meet their Pakistani counterparts, a mix of Frontier Corps and regular military officers. Among the Americans was Major Larry Bauguess Jr, the operations officer. A thirty-six-year-old father of two from North Carolina, he kept in touch with his small daughters by playing tic-tac-toe with them over email, sending them his moves on a PowerPoint slide then getting theirs back the next day.

The meeting took place in a local school, and went on for five hours. The atmosphere was difficult at first, the Afghans and Pakistanis both hurling accusations and the Americans describing it like 'refereeing children'. However, it ended in an apparently 'cordial' atmosphere, with everyone sitting down to lunch together and taking pictures. The US soldiers then began loading up pick-ups for the ride to the helicopter landing zone where they would be collected.

They were saying goodbye when one of the Pakistani Frontier Corps soldiers walked up to Major Bauguess, lifted up his AK47 and began firing, pumping multiple rounds into his chest. His horrified colleagues returned fire, killing the gunman, and the Pakistanis started shooting back from inside the classrooms. After a real shoot-out the Americans and Afghans fought their way to the helicopter, carrying their casualties. Bauguess had been killed almost instantly. Two other US soldiers had been badly injured, along with their interpreter. The men described the Black Hawk in which they flew off as 'blood-soaked'.

At the time it was reported on the official ISAF press release that Major Bauguess had been killed by 'enemy small arms fire'. His wife Wesley was told he had been shot in the head boarding a helicopter. 'I knew that couldn't be right,' she said.[12] He had phoned her the previous day saying, 'Tomorrow will be a good day,' which was their code to mean he was going on an operation. The first time she realised he had been killed in Pakistan was when she met one of his fellow soldiers who had been wounded. She filed for a freedom of information report, but when it came it was mostly blank or redacted pages. It would be four years before the Pentagon acknowledged publicly that he had been killed by America's supposed ally, and almost five before Mrs Bauguess got a report. When she was sent her late husband's possessions, she found the camera he had had with him that day. The last photograph he had taken was of a group of Pakistanis, including the man who killed him.

The Pakistanis initially blamed the attack on militants, then when pressed to investigate said it was a 'rogue troop'.

Even when the official Pentagon report was published in September 2011 it said 'the initial shooter caused all casualties incurred on coalition forces'. However, it added that 'some of [the coalition forces] reported seeing other Pakistani military personnel shooting at them from the building'. Pakistan later claimed they were firing at the gunman.

One day before the killing of Major Bauguess, his brigade commander Colonel Rick Kaiser also crossed into Pakistan for a meeting with his Pakistani counterpart Colonel Qaiser at Torkham border. 'When we crossed over there were clear signs something was wrong,' he said. 'Our meeting was diverted from going up to the headquarters of the Khyber Rifles, but just stayed at a small house by the gate. Colonel Qaiser was very nervous and not himself. He refused to allow my guards outside. There were other odd signs, so when I returned I reported something was wrong. In hindsight it is clear there was a plan to kidnap a senior US officer, and I'm glad it didn't happen to me that day, but so sad we weren't able to piece it together before that meeting.'

'It wasn't a spontaneous thing, it was obviously planned,' said Colonel Nicholson. 'It could have been a lot worse – we believe the Pakistanis had planned to take hostages. But the Americans reacted well, fought back, and killed some of the Frontier Corps. Obviously it set things back a lot in terms of trust.'

17

The Snake Bites Back

Mingora, Swat valley, 2007

'WELCOME TO PARADISE' read the sign as we drove into Swat. The tranquil mountain valley of meadows and waterfalls in northern Pakistan was a holiday destination for affluent Pakistanis. Years before, I had spent a blissful couple of weeks there myself with an old university friend, paddling in its clear rivers, eating trout and wandering in its mountains looking at old Buddhist stupas and carvings from the time when the valley rang with temple bells. It even had Pakistan's only ski resort.

The former princely state that used to be ruled by the wonderfully titled Wali of Swat was an unlikely place for the start of Pakistan's own Taliban. But on 8 October 2005 a devastating earthquake shattered the peace of the valley, killing more than 73,000 people, including 18,000 children, across northern Pakistan. Most of the roads and bridges were wiped out, making it difficult to reach victims, so the initial help came from the army in helicopters as well as local volunteers from the Tehrik-e-Nifaz-e-Sharia-e-Mohammadi (TNSM), or Movement for the Enforcement of Islamic Law, a group that had sent men to fight in Afghanistan after 9/11 and whose leader Sufi Mohammad had been in jail since 2002. Soon came Jamaat-al-Dawa, the welfare wing of Lashkar-e-Toiba, one of the militant groups that Musharraf had supposedly banned in 2002 under pressure from the Americans. They set up hospitals and took some of the orphans to their madrassas. Their mullahs preached that the earthquake was a warning from Allah that Islam was not being followed properly in the valley.

Shortly after this, a new radio station started operating. For two hours morning and evening a man called Maulana Fazlullah came over the airwaves on an illegal FM wavelength, instructing listeners how to follow Islam. He was a twenty-eight-year-old high-school dropout who made a living operating a pulley box to cross the Swat River and had married the daughter of Sufi Mohammad, then taken over his TNSM. Soon almost everyone was listening, and he quickly became known as 'Radio Mullah'. 'In my staff room Fazlullah was all anyone talked about,' said Ziauddin Yousafzai, who ran a large school in Mingora and whose daughter Malala later began writing a blog about life under the Taliban.

People liked Fazlullah's practical advice on Islam, and his talk of social justice appealed to many in an area where locals felt frustrated by the continuing feudal power of the khans and the slow and corrupt justice system. When he asked for money, women came forward with their wedding gold, and he built a large mosque and headquarters by the Swat River in Iman Deri, with many local people providing free labour. There he set up his own Islamic courts offering to speedily resolve disputes, and sometimes appeared galloping on a big horse. He began issuing decrees banning music and television, closing beauty parlours and requiring men to grow beards longer than two fists. These were enforced by his followers, who like the Afghan Taliban sported camouflage vests with trousers well above their ankles, and became known as the 'Tor Patka', or black-turbaned brigade for the turbans they wore over their long straggly hair.

Black smoke could be seen all over the province as CDs and DVDs were incinerated in huge fires. Next Fazlullah announced that women should not go to market or girls to school. His men also tried to dynamite the valley's ancient Buddhas. It was a copy of what the world had seen and condemned in Afghanistan.

Then they began taking over districts, killing police, beheading local politicians, activists and dancers. The main square in Mingora where they often hanged their victims became known as Bloody Chowk. Soon Fazlullah controlled much of the valley.

Pakistanis further south were stunned by the stories of such terror in a place they associated with holidays and peace. Yet nobody arrested Fazlullah or shut down his illegal radio station. The state not only seemed powerless, but its most senior official in Swat, the Deputy Commissioner, Syed Javid, regularly prayed at Fazlullah's mosque.

It should have been clear how out of hand Pakistan was getting when from early 2007 female vigilante gangs known as 'Burqa Brigades' began terrorising the streets of its capital. The girls were students from Jamia Hafsa, the biggest female madrassa in the country, which was part of Lal Masjid or the Red Mosque, right in the heart of Islamabad.

Dressed in black burqas and armed with sticks, they attacked the city's pirate DVD and CD shops, shutting them down and burning their goods on bonfires. They held a sit-in at a children's library to protest at the demolition of some mosques, and raided beauty salons which they claimed were being used as massage parlours.

When friends in Islamabad told me about this, I found it hard to believe. Islamabad had always been a sleepy place, a purpose-built capital to twin with the army headquarters of Rawalpindi, laid out with colonnaded white government buildings based on those in Washington surrounded by a backdrop of smudgy blue-green hills. The town was neatly laid out on a grid, its addresses in Orwellian letters and numbers giving it an order far removed from the violence of Karachi or the cacophony of Lahore. Yet the government and the police seemed frozen.

The Red Mosque got its name from its red walls and stood just a few blocks from parliament and around the corner from ISI headquarters. Many government officials and military used to pray there. It stood squarely on Pakistan's military–jihadi nexus. The mosque's founder Maulana Abdullah Ghazi had been close to General Zia, and its madrassas were used for training jihadis to fight in Afghanistan and Kashmir. I'd been taken inside it myself in the 1980s. Maulana Ghazi was also friends with Osama bin Laden, and had visited him and Mullah Omar in Kandahar in 1998. He was assassinated shortly after that trip and the mosque taken over by his two sons, Maulana Abdul Aziz, the chief cleric, famed for his fiery sermons, and Abdul Rashid Ghazi, who oversaw the administration. The female madrassa was run by Umme Hasan, the wife of Abdul Aziz.

After 9/11, when Musharraf agreed to help America in the war on terror, the mosque broke off its long links with the military and became a centre of protest. Abdul Rashid was even accused of being part of a plot to blow up Musharraf's convoy in December 2003. Investigators said the explosives had been stored in the mosque, though Abdul Rashid was later cleared.

When Musharraf sent troops into Waziristan in 2004, the Red Mosque brothers led a campaign denouncing the action as un-Islamic. They had their own website and, like Fazlullah, started a pirate FM radio station to spread their message. Umme Hasan announced that she had trained many female suicide bombers and would launch them if the government dared to do anything. These students then kidnapped members of the police and some Chinese women who they claimed were running a brothel.

The Chinese government, which was among Pakistan's few friends, lodged a furious protest. Perhaps it was this that finally prompted Musharraf to act after months of inactivity. On 3 July 2007, Special Services Group (SSG) commandos in tanks and armoured personnel carriers surrounded the mosque. The electricity was cut off, and as dusk fell there was a burst of gunfire and explosions as the tanks blasted holes in the walls. Helicopter gunships hovered overhead and messages broadcast through loudhailers called on the girls to surrender.

Inside the mosque, however, the mullahs were coming over the loudspeakers urging students to 'destroy your enemies'. Many of the militants had fought in Afghanistan and Kashmir, and took up sandbagged positions, armed with rockets and assault rifles, while others barricaded themselves in.

So began an extraordinary siege. Worried parents from across the country gathered outside calling their daughters on mobiles and begging them to come out. The next evening a small group of girls emerged. Hidden among them, disguised in a burqa, was the chief imam Abdul Aziz. He was caught and paraded in front of TV cameras.

The majority stayed inside. Negotiations began to try to end the standoff. Then, on the sixth day, a sniper in one of the minarets killed the commander of the SSG assault group.

That was when the military lost patience. The following day the commandos launched Operation Silence to storm the compound. Gunfire and blasts echoed throughout the capital as commandos descended from helicopters and fought from room to room. The militants retaliated with petrol bombs in Sprite bottles and grenades, or even by hurling themselves at the soldiers in suicide vests. Eventually the military trapped Abdul Rashid and his followers in a basement, where they fought to the death. They found more than fifty women and girls hiding in bricked-up spaces under stairs. When the siege was finally over more than a hundred people had been killed, including ten commandos. The television news showed shocking pictures of pools of blood, broken glass, wreckage and bodies.

Though the authorities talked of how the mosque had been turned into an arsenal, people were horrified. How could such carnage happen in a mosque, and right in the middle of the capital?

Chaudhry Shujat, a veteran politician close to a number of Islamic leaders, had been one of the negotiators. He said he had managed to get Abdul Rashid to agree to a deal under which he would leave the mosque in return for safe passage to his home village, but the military had stormed the mosque regardless. Tears spilled from his eyes as he told me, 'There were women and children in there. We could have got them out but the military would not let us.'

* * *

Reaction was swift across the country. In Swat, the Taliban leader-cum-radio-star Maulana Fazlullah declared war on the Pakistani state. There was an enormous protest in Bajaur agency, where local people were still angry about the drone attack on the madrassa the year before. A wave of suicide bombings began across Pakistan – a fivefold increase on the previous year.

That September, Fazlullah and thirty-nine other militant and tribal leaders from across the tribal areas met in South Waziristan to form a united front. Having supported the Afghan Taliban as what it called 'strategic depth' to protect its western border, while also upsetting decades-long balance in the tribal areas by sending in troops, Pakistan had ended up with its own Taliban. They called themselves the Tehrik-i-Taliban-Pakistan, or TTP, and chose as leader Baitullah Mehsud, a charismatic long-haired man in his late thirties from the powerful Mehsud tribe. He had fought in Afghanistan, and had close contacts with ISI even though he was officially branded a dangerous criminal.

On the morning of 24 November a suicide bomber driving a car packed with explosives rammed into a seventy-two-seater bus carrying ISI officials to work at Hamza Camp on Murree Road in Rawalpindi. Hamza Camp had formerly been known as Ojheri Camp, and during the Soviet occupation of Afghanistan it was where ISI had stocked CIA-supplied weapons for the mujaheddin. The blast was so powerful that seventeen people were killed, some of their bodies being burned beyond recognition. Less than half an hour later another suicide bomber tried to drive into the main army headquarters (GCHQ) in Rawalpindi, and killed two guards.

Was this the snake biting back, as Karzai had warned? Had Pakistan's military lost control of their proxies?

Something else should have set off alarm bells. A poll conducted in September 2007 for the American organisation Terror Free Tomorrow by the Pakistan Institute for Public Opinion found that Osama bin Laden was far more popular among Pakistanis than Musharraf, and five times more popular than President Bush, despite all the US aid pouring in. Al Qaeda enjoyed a 46 per cent approval rating, while Musharraf was on 36 and Bush only 9. 'We have conducted twenty-three polls across the Muslim world and this is the most disturbing,' said Ken Ballen, the head of Terror Free Tomorrow. 'Pakistan is the one Muslim nation that has nuclear weapons, and the people who want to use them against us like the Taliban and al Qaeda are more popular than our allies like Musharraf.'

Yet Western leaders still feared that Pakistan would be more dangerous to them without Musharraf, apparently convinced by his argument that only he was holding off the Islamists waiting at the gate.

With Musharraf in trouble, Western policymakers came up with what on paper in Washington and Whitehall presumably seemed a bright idea, their own version of 'hedging'. To try to keep their man in power and to soften the face of his regime, they would forge a deal between him and the country's most electable politician, Benazir Bhutto. As they saw it, she would provide him with legitimacy and he would provide her with power.

But anyone who knew the two of them realised that it couldn't work, for they loathed each other. The first time I interviewed Musharraf, just after he took power in 1999, he told me, 'You're a friend of Benazir – tell her as long as I am here she is never coming back.' In December 2004 he had released her husband Asif Zardari from jail, where he had spent eight years on corruption charges. It might have looked like an olive branch, but Zardari later told me the military had offered him the premiership if his wife would agree to stay out of politics. (That wasn't the first time – senior military officers had approached him before, when she was Prime Minister, saying they could not salute to a woman.)

Britain's High Commissioner in Islamabad, Mark Lyall Grant, began conveying messages to Bhutto that Musharraf might be prepared to let her back. The contact was encouraged by the White House, particularly Condoleezza Rice, Bush's National Security Adviser, and Richard Boucher, the Assistant Secretary of State, as well as by the British Foreign Office under Jack Straw. In 2005–06 a series of meetings were held between Tariq Asis, Musharraf's National Security Adviser, and Rehman Malik, a former intelligence chief who had become one of Bhutto's closest advisers.

So unlikely was the idea of Musharraf and Bhutto working together that when I was initially told of the contacts I didn't believe it. However, Bhutto had been in exile since 1999, and was desperate to return home and get back into politics, a life she missed so much that she often resorted to self-help books and tubs of Ben & Jerry's caramel fudge ice cream. As for Musharraf, he was desperate to cling on to power.

In 2006 Musharraf and Bhutto met secretly in the UAE. After protracted negotiations, he agreed to drop corruption charges against her, her husband and senior party officials, so she could contest elections. For her part she agreed that her party would then support him as President – a position elected by MPs.

'We might as well have painted a bull's-eye target on her forehead,' said Mark Malloch Brown, who was Junior Foreign Minister at the time.

Pakistan's other leading political figure and twice former Prime Minister, Nawaz Sharif, was furious. He and Bhutto had mended fences and signed a 'charter for democracy' to work together; he had even sent her flowers for her birthday – and now she was doing a deal with a dictator. Not any dictator, but the very one who had ousted him from power and thrown him into Attock jail. He decided that if she was returning to Pakistan, he would go back too, which was not at all part of the US/UK plan.

I met Bhutto in London just before her return, at a town house just off the Edgware Road that belonged to Rehman Malik. There was a chaotic press conference in his ornate sitting room dominated by a garish painting of the Last Supper. Party officials jostled to sit next to Bhutto on the gilt-edged sofa so they would be in the photographs. Afterwards she was going to Oxford to say goodbye to her son Bilawal, who was studying at Christ Church College. Before leaving, she whisked me upstairs for a chat. She told me she'd had a series of assassination threats.

Despite these threats, in the weeks before her return to Pakistan, Bhutto remained characteristically outspoken. At a gathering in Washington she spoke out against militants, and even broached the touchy subject of Dr A.Q. Khan, the father of Pakistan's nuclear programme, who had been under house arrest since 2004, when the US had confronted the government with evidence that he had been running a nuclear proliferation network supplying Libya, North Korea and Iran. Pakistan had refused any international access to question him, and many suspected that such an operation must have been officially sanctioned, particularly as military planes had allegedly been used to transport the materials. Bhutto suggested that if she were elected she would provide this access.

Such comments on Pakistan's taboo subjects were almost certainly unwise. Her close friends begged her not to go back. Mark Siegel, a Democratic strategist who was one of Bhutto's oldest friends, bade farewell to her in the lobby of the Ritz-Carlton in Washington. As he turned back to wave, he recalled the scene in *The Graduate* in which a rain-soaked Anne Bancroft stands bereft after realising that her lover Dustin Hoffman is in love with her daughter. 'I had this terrible feeling,' he said.

Just before Bhutto's return, a militant called Qari Saifullah Akhtar was released from three years of ISI protective custody. He had been implicated in a coup attempt against her back in 1995, and was an associate of bin Laden and Mullah Omar as well as closely connected to ISI.

In Dubai Bhutto got a message from Hamid Karzai that his intelligence service had picked up talk of a plot to kill her. The UAE authorities also warned her. Yet there was no changing her mind. 'The time of life is written and the time of death is written,' she insisted.

A few weeks before going back, Bhutto had lunch with Britain's Shadow Defence Secretary Liam Fox in her favourite Persian restaurant in Dubai, ordering what she told him was 'the best feta cheese in Dubai, imported from Denmark'.

'You know they will try to kill me, don't you?' she told him.

'Who?' he asked.

'The ISI. They want me dead.'

She was emphatic about who her enemies were. 'What the army knows the ISI knows,' she said. 'They are effectively one and the same.'

Fox asked why on earth she was going back, given the risks. 'The country needs me,' she replied. 'Being killed is part of the risk you take in Pakistan. It's how we operate.'[1]

And so, on 18 October 2007, Bhutto said goodbye to her husband and two teenage daughters in the VIP lounge at Dubai airport and boarded a plane to Karachi. 'This is the beginning of a long journey for Pakistan back to democracy and I hope my going back is a catalyst for change,' she said before leaving. 'We must believe that miracles do happen.'

The Emirates flight was packed with noisy supporters, some of whom had come from as far as Canada. They couldn't restrain their enthusiasm, and availed themselves freely of the drinks en route. By the time we landed they were in a state of near hysteria. The pilot refused to taxi off the runway until they quietened down, and Bhutto herself had to speak over the PA to calm them. Finally we came to a halt and the doors opened. The media were allowed off first so they could have the cameras ready as Bhutto descended the steps. She looked stunning, dressed in emerald green with a floaty white dupatta, the colours of the Pakistani flag, and garlanded with amulets. As she reached the ground she almost stumbled, and tears fell from her eyes. 'I was just so emotional to be home,' she told me later. 'It felt like this huge burden off my shoulders after so many years.'

I had decided I wouldn't travel with her to the rally, but behind, on the media bus. I'd had too many narrow escapes. It was only a year since I'd been ambushed by the Taliban in Helmand, and in the meantime I'd also been at a hotel which was suicide bombed. Yet when I saw Bhutto on top of her open-top bus just outside the gates of the airport with all the crowds around, I knew I had to be there. 'You've followed us from the start,' she had said to me in London. I couldn't miss it now. So I pushed my way through the crowds, elbows at right angles against the groping men who cannot resist a Western bottom, and got Bhutto's colleagues to whisk me up.

Once I was on top I saw an amazing spectacle. Supporters had come out in their tens of thousands to welcome her home. There was literally a sea of people, waving red, black and green banners and flags, cheering, dancing, and holding up pictures of Bhutto and her late father. Car horns blared and music played. Somebody even released a flock of white doves. One of them fell to the floor of the bus and hurt its foot. Bhutto cradled it and put it on her shoulder, where it perched for hours as she waved to the crowds.

The atmosphere was electric – I had forgotten how much fun Pakistan's politics could be. Bhutto's face was lit up with exhilaration. It also felt incredibly exposed. The bus might have armoured sides and a bulletproof Perspex box that Bhutto was supposed to stand in, but she was standing in front of it and we were all out in the open. Moreover, we were travelling at a snail's pace because of the crowds. There were people everywhere on the streets, on roofs, up trees and clinging to lampposts, some of them so close that their hands brushed ours.

'How can you possibly secure this?' I asked one of the police officers. He looked at the heavens and shrugged his shoulders. 'It's in God's hands,' he replied.

Our destination was the mausoleum of Pakistan's founder Mohammad Ali Jinnah, and the chosen route passed under fifteen footbridges and flyovers, from which it would be easy for someone to take a potshot. Musharraf was supposed to have provided the police with jammers to intercept any remote-controlled device. If they had them they clearly weren't working, as we were all managing to use our mobile phones.

Watching from Dubai on TV, Bhutto's husband Zardari was horrified. He called his best friend Agha Siraj Durrani, who was on top of the bus and supposed to be coordinating Benazir's security. 'For God's sake get her behind the screen!' he pleaded. But she wouldn't go. 'I must be with my people,' she insisted.

The only protection we had was human. A group of young men in black T-shirts who called themselves 'Martyrs for Benazir' had formed a human chain around our bus to stop anyone from coming too near, while others were keeping watch among the crowds or on the bridges. After a while we all forgot about the security fears. We had been on the bus for hours. Then, as darkness fell, Bhutto called me over.

'Have you noticed something?' she asked. As we drove, the street lights ahead were going off section by section, leaving us like a bright ship in the darkness. A shiver ran across my shoulders. I knew what that meant. Over the years I had covered many unexplained attacks in Karachi, and always the street lights had gone off just beforehand.

Suddenly there was a crack. I ducked, thinking it was gunfire. It turned out to be a firecracker, and I got up embarrassed.

Then at about 10 p.m. the bus lurched perilously to one side, and my heart skipped another beat. This time it was because there were too many people on board and we had a flat tyre. After that Agha Siraj Durrani sent many people off the top, but he let me stay. As we stopped for the tyre to be changed someone brought burgers and Pepsis on board. The food was welcome. After more than seven hours we were not even halfway along the ten-mile route, and we joked that we would have to order in breakfast.

Finally we got under way again. Once again we forgot our fears in all the euphoria. There were women and children in the crowd, and one man even tried to pass up a baby. From the top the three policemen on board swept the crowds with searchlights looking for potential suicide bombers or gunmen.

'Aren't you tired?' I asked Bhutto around 11 p.m. 'Not at all,' she replied. 'It's incredible. More people than when I came back from exile before in 1986. How must Musharraf be feeling seeing this?'

The bus had a special armoured compartment downstairs, and she told me she was going down there with her secretary Naheed to work on her speech.

I was talking to Aitzaz Ahsan, a brilliant lawyer who was part of the Lawyers' Movement against Musharraf and had once been a close ally of Bhutto, when I heard the first boom, a low sound like someone scraping a metal door against concrete. We threw ourselves to the floor. As we got up there was a second, much louder blast, and everything around us seemed to be on fire. For a moment there was silence, then the screaming and the sirens started.

'They blew up the bus.' I could hardly get out the words. 'They blew up the bus.' My heart was pounding, my head full of images of blood and body parts and cheap rubber sandals scattered across the road, and trees aflame. The blast had hit the left side of the bus. Aitzaz and I had been standing in the middle. As we scrabbled to get up, dazed but unscathed, there was one thought in my head. 'The petrol tank!' I shouted. 'We've got to get off before it explodes!' We ran to the back, passing two bodies that were clearly dead, and jumped down, helped by people. Then I had run, desperate to blot the scenes of carnage from my eyes. My *shalwar kamiz* was spattered with blood.

Somehow a group of us ended up at a nearby house which belonged to the elderly father of a colonel in the Pakistani army. The colonel gave us sweet tea, and we charged our phones so we could tell our families we were safe. We hugged each other as, one after another, stunned survivors wandered in – Farooq Naik, Bhutto's lawyer; Makhdoom Amin Fahim, who had led the party while Bhutto in exile; and Rehman Malik, her purple-haired security adviser.

'Benazir?' I asked nervously.

'They got her out straight away. She's fine,' said Malik. 'They've taken her to Bilawal House.'

Once we had drunk our tea, the colonel kindly drove us there. Named after Bhutto's first child, born back when she was Prime Minister for the first time in 1989, Bilawal House was the high-walled home she hadn't seen for nine years. Inside, she was sitting with Naheed and a few others, red-eyed, watching BBC World TV. She hugged me and sat me down next to her. We stared at the screen, mesmerised by the burned-out bus and the devastation all around it. The numbers of the dead flashed up on the screen. First they said fifteen. We knew it was far more than that, for the street had been packed. Suddenly it shot up to eighty-nine, then more than a hundred. It was Pakistan's worst ever terrorist attack. Three of the fifteen of us on top of the bus had been killed. The rest of us had been saved by the young men who took much of the brunt of the blast.

Bhutto told me she had not wanted to come to the house: 'I thought they would target this too and be waiting, knowing if I escaped I would come here.' After a while she went upstairs to wash her face. As she came back down she stopped at a group of black-and-white photographs of her three children on the wall. She touched them with her hand as if wondering whether she would see them again.

The next morning she phoned Musharraf to complain about the lack of security. 'I warned you not to come back until after the elections,' he replied.

In the afternoon she held a press conference, a typical bravura performance at which she angrily announced that she had written a letter to Musharraf naming those she believed responsible for the attack. They were General Hamid Gul, the former head of ISI; Brigadier Ejaz Shah, the former head of the Intelligence Bureau, another of Pakistan's intelligence agencies; and Pervez Elahi, the Chief Minister of Punjab, who blamed his own father's assassination on Bhutto's late father.

Afterwards I sat with her in her small book-lined study. Dressed in sombre grey silk with a black armband, she told me she had had less than four hours' sleep, and had woken with blood in her ears from the effect of the blast. 'I haven't felt weepy yet, but it suddenly hit me about 5.30 a.m. that maybe I wouldn't have made it,' she said. 'I kept thinking of the noise, the light and the place littered with dead bodies. Everything seemed lit up.'

On the wall of the study was an old spelling certificate that had been awarded to her youngest daughter Aseefa, then fourteen. She told me it had been hard talking to her children that morning. 'They kept saying, "Mummy, are you OK? Mummy, are you OK?" The worst thing is hurting them, making them fearful. Losing my father was the worst thing that ever happened to me, and I was twenty-five when he was killed – they are much smaller. It meant

I had no choices [her brothers were overseas, so she had taken over running his party], and I don't want that to happen to them.'

Yet it was clear that whoever had done this would try again. Bhutto knew that. But if she went back to Dubai it would seem that she had run away, and courage was the last thing she lacked. So she continued campaigning. 'People need to see their leaders,' she said.

However, instead of stepping up her security, the authorities had it reduced. She emailed Mark Siegel: 'Nothing will Godwilling happen. Just wanted u to know if it does I will hold Musharraf responsible.'

She complained to the Americans and British who had encouraged her return, and begged them to provide security. They refused. She told me the US Ambassador Anne Patterson warned her, 'You must not talk against Musharraf.'

A few weeks later she took a brief trip to Dubai to see her daughters. They believe she knew she wouldn't see them again. 'It was going to be my eighteenth birthday in January,' said the eldest, Bakhtawar. 'She said she wanted to wish me happy birthday in advance. I said, "Don't wish me in advance, wish me then."'

Next morning, after Bhutto left to return to Pakistan, Bakhtawar found a beribboned box containing a silver pendant with a jaguar head and a note: 'Happy birthday, all my love Mummy.'

I was spending Christmas in Portugal with my family when I got the call. It was the afternoon of 27 December, and I was with my husband, son and parents in the medieval castle town of Óbidos, a chocolate-box place which had been turned into a Christmas village complete with fake snow and elves proffering cups of local cherry brandy. Then my phone rang. Benazir had been hurt after coming out of a rally. She had been shot, it was a suicide bombing – the information was confused. I knew immediately that she was dead. The rally had been at the very same park where Pakistan's first Prime Minister, Liaquat Ali Khan, was assassinated in 1951. I batted away the elves, desperate to escape from the festivities.

Of course I flew back to Pakistan. I headed to Bhutto's ancestral village of Naudero, driving past canals, water buffalo and mango fields, and sat in the old family house among the stunned friends and family giving their condolences to Zardari. I also went to the mausoleum she had built for her father and two brothers. It wasn't even finished, and now her body lay there too, covered in rose petals and wept over by wailing villagers.

The big question was, who had done this? Everyone I spoke to had a theory, and nobody expected to find out. Right back to the shooting of its first Prime Minister, Pakistan's history was dotted with unexplained political assassinations. In the early hours of the morning before the rally Benazir had been visited by General Nadeem Taj, the head of ISI, but no one knew what they had discussed.

Musharraf said it was Bhutto's own fault for standing up through the sunroof of her armoured car to wave to the crowds after the rally. Moments later she was dead, blood gushing from a wound to her temple as a suicide bomber exploded himself in the crowd. 'Responsibility is hers,' he said. 'For standing up outside the car I think she was to blame.'

All those who had been in the car with her, like her secretary Naheed, and her spokesperson Sherry Rehman, who was in the car behind, insist she fell down before the bomb went off, and they heard cracks of gunfire.

Less than twenty-four hours after her death, Brigadier Javed Cheema, the Interior Ministry spokesman, called a press conference and said she had died from a fractured skull caused by hitting her head on the lever of the sunroof. He also announced that intelligence agencies had intercepted a call from Baitullah Mehsud, head of the Pakistan Taliban, proving he was behind it. A transcript was later made available – though no audio tape – on which the militant leader appears to be congratulating one of his men for carrying out the attack. A week later the British and American Embassies both told the press that MI6 and the CIA had authenticated the tape. It all seemed very odd. When I spoke to Imran Khan, the former Pakistan cricket captain turned politician, he was incredulous. 'The day after the murder they produce a tape of Baitullah saying, "I'm sitting here, tomorrow I'll be having breakfast. Well done, boys." Is this a joke? The guy is on the run, being hunted down. Everyone knows the phones are intercepted. Would he talk like that?'

Baitullah himself insisted he was not involved. 'I strongly deny it,' he said through his spokesman Maulvi Omar. 'Tribal people have their own customs. We don't strike down women.'

In years of reporting al Qaeda and the Taliban, I had never known them not to take responsibility for an attack. Moreover, Bhutto told me after the bus had been blown up that when some suggested that Baitullah had been involved he sent her a message saying, 'Identify your enemy. I'm not your foe.'

Meanwhile, footage had emerged of a clean-shaven man in dark glasses calmly firing three shots. A TV station showed pictures of bullets on the ground. Some witnesses said they had seen snipers on a roof. Other film showed Bhutto's chief bodyguard Khalid Shahenshah gesticulating strangely from the stage as Bhutto left the rally, and making a sign of a cut throat.

Whether or not there was an officially sanctioned cover-up, it certainly looked like it. Within an hour of the attack the scene was washed down with high-pressure hoses, wiping out almost all the evidence. This was in stark contrast to what had happened after the assassination attempts on Musharraf in the same city, when the streets were sealed off for days while the security forces went over them with a fine-tooth comb for any scrap of a clue. Saud Aziz, who was chief of the Rawalpindi police, said he issued the orders to hose the streets after receiving a phone call from a close associate of Musharraf. The Interior Ministry said it was worried about 'vultures picking up body parts'. I had never seen a vulture in Rawalpindi.

When I tried to investigate, everyone warned me off. I went ahead anyway. Benazir Bhutto had changed my life by inviting me to her wedding in Karachi in 1987, and starting in me a lifelong fascination with Pakistan. The least I owed her was to find out who had killed her.

My first stop was the spot where she had been killed, on the Liaquat Road in Rawalpindi. A small shrine had been erected, with a garish painting of Bhutto surrounded by what looked like pink bathroom tiles. There was a barricade in front, guarded by a cabin in which five policemen sat drinking tea under a lightbulb that dangled from a wire. When I tried to take photographs they became animated, telling me to go away. They noted down my driver's numberplate, spooking him so much that he drove off, leaving me to depend on taxis.

At the police headquarters I discovered that Saud Aziz had been transferred, as had others who were on duty that day. The new police chief, Rao Iqbal, told me it was a government agency that had ordered the hosing, and admitted that his men had collected only twenty-three pieces of evidence, when normally there would be thousands. One piece was the car in which Bhutto was travelling, and that had also been washed.

Doctors at Rawalpindi General Hospital, where they had tried to save Bhutto's life, refused to speak on the record. However, they said they had been stopped from performing an autopsy, and one told me, 'We all thought she had been shot.' The government claimed it was Zardari who had prevented an autopsy, which he regarded as undignified for a former Prime Minister.

Then I went to Karachi, where I found no investigation was under way into the bus bombing. I also learned that Bhutto's chief bodyguard, Khalid Shahenshah, had been murdered a few months after the assassination in another of those unexplained shootings in Karachi.

When the UN was later called in to send a three-man commission of investigation, they described themselves as 'mystified by the efforts of certain high-ranking government authorities to obstruct access'. Their emails were hacked, and when they arrived in Pakistan in 2009 they found that everyone knew their agenda in advance, and even when they changed their arrangements at the last minute, they would arrive to find the press waiting. The Interior Minister had already written their report for them.

They concluded that ISI had deliberately destroyed evidence, and when they got access to Saud Aziz he kept changing his story. They found that 'the failure of the police to investigate effectively was deliberate', lambasted Musharraf for not providing Bhutto with the protection necessary for a former Prime Minister, and described the government protection as 'fatally insufficient'. The head of the commission was the Chilean Ambassador to the UN Heraldo Muñoz. He was so perturbed by the experience that he wrote a book about it, entitled *Getting Away With Murder*.

The most unlikely outcome of Bhutto's alliance with Musharraf was that her husband Asif Zardari ended up in power. In the early hours of the morning after her death he flew back to Pakistan with their children, so that in keeping with Muslim tradition she could be buried that day. Two days later he summoned a meeting of the Pakistan People's Party's central executive in Naudero. There he asked his son Bilawal to read out a handwritten will by Bhutto which stated, 'I would like my husband Asif Ali Zardari to lead you in this interim period until you and he decide what is best.'

I had never heard of a political party being bequeathed. Zardari told me a strange story about people who had come from Dubai with the note just after Benazir's death. He said he did not know who they were. None of her close associates knew anything about the note. It was dated 16 October, two days before her return from Pakistan. Naheed, who had been her secretary for twenty years, was dumbfounded.

Zardari said that he and Bilawal would be co-chairmen of the party, though at nineteen Bilawal was too young to enter politics in Pakistan. Musharraf went ahead with elections in 2008, and the PPP predictably won a massive sympathy vote. Once it had control of parliament, it could choose the President, and Zardari was chosen to replace Musharraf.

Zardari was a liberal, with no time for militants. His family had owned the Bambino cinema in Karachi, and as a youth he used to frequent the city's discos. He even told me once that as a young man he liked to go to Kabul to drink wine. His main interest was playing polo. Yet with him in power, the Afghan Taliban continued to operate from Pakistan just as freely as before. Perhaps, as his wife had found when she was Prime Minister, Zardari didn't really have power. Certainly when in July 2008 his government announced that it was bringing ISI under the control of the Interior Ministry, within twenty-four hours it had to reverse the decision, issuing a notification that the earlier announcement had been 'misunderstood'. The military spokesman, Major General Athar Abbas, said the army had not been taken into the government's confidence. 'When we realised the decision had been taken we discussed the issue with the government and are thankful that there was a realisation of ground realities and our position was accepted.'

Normal order was restored.

Rehman Malik, who had become Zardari's Interior Minister, tried to defend Pakistan's position in the usual manner, which was to point a finger at India. 'RAW [Indian intelligence] and Afghan intelligence are one, so ISI has no option but to counter that,' he insisted to me. 'We're being pushed into a corner.' As a former intelligence agent himself, he added, 'Besides, just as CIA keeps contacts with terrorists, ISI kept them with Taliban to extract information.'

18

The Weathermen of Kandahar

Lashkar Gah, Helmand, October 2008

'WHAT WE'RE DOING here is cutting-edge experimental,' said Hugh Powell as I stared at him in astonishment. On the walls of his office in the British headquarters for Helmand were glossy photographs of smiling children and projects with names like 'Avenue of Hope' and 'Eid Park'. There was a poster of a proposed Lashkar Gah Industrial Park, complete with grassy lawns on which for some reason there wandered a well-fed pet cat while overhead flew a passenger jet. It did not look anything like Afghanistan. A glass cabinet displayed pomegranates, chilli peppers and wheat, which the happy population of Helmand were supposed to grow instead of opium.

So enthused was he that it seemed churlish to mention that so far instead of reconstruction, the British had turned parts of Helmand to rubble by dropping laser-guided JDAMs on them. As for the opium crop, that now covered 255,700 acres – almost four times what it had been in 2005 before the British arrived in the province, and two thirds of the total for the whole of Afghanistan. Oh, and just seven miles away, in Nad Ali, the Taliban were in control.

It had taken me two years to get the Ministry of Defence to allow me on another embed with British troops in Helmand, and in that time the British HQ at Lashkar Gah had been transformed. Instead of tents there were air-conditioned pods with carpets, wi-fi and even nice cotton duvets, and they were peopled by numerous diplomats and advisers on everything from women to prisons, as well as something nebulous called 'stability'. There was even an ad up for Friday-night movie nights, while in the middle of a bed of rosebushes was a wooden gazebo nicknamed 'the bus stop', which people used as a hangout.

Lashkar Gah had become one of the most bizarre outposts of the Foreign Office, with its 140 diplomats making it bigger than many Embassies, and also one of the costliest. Most of the staff never left the base. Those who did occasionally brave the five-minute drive to the Governor's compound did so in armed convoys, surrounded by bodyguards and travelling at high speed.

As the person overseeing this Whitehall fantasyland, Hugh Powell had impeccable diplomatic credentials. His father Charles had been foreign-policy adviser to Margaret Thatcher, and his uncle Jonathan was Chief of Staff to Tony Blair. On top of that he was an Old Etonian who pronounced his surname as if saying 'pole' while eating a plum. I could not resist dubbing Powell the Viceroy of Helmandshire.

The British soldiers who shared the base snorted at what they called 'Powell's folly'. After all, not far away their fellow troops from 2 Para were engaged in heavy fighting. It didn't help that while the military served six months with only one two-week break, the diplomats got two weeks' home leave every six weeks.

No one seemed eager for me to actually see Helmand. Instead a series of earnest people from Powell's team showed me a series of PowerPoints, and shared their 152 six-month objectives on how they planned to transform the province into a model. Lilypads and ink spots had been replaced by 'Clear, Hold, Build' and the 'Helmand Roadmap'.

One of the team's key priorities was justice, as this was always a major selling point for the Taliban, who offered speedy justice when they took over areas, compared to the slow pace and corruption of the government system. 'Our challenge is to provide something that has all the speed of the Taliban but none of the excesses,' said Fraser Hearst, who headed the rule-of-law department.

WAR

As a first step the British had managed to secure the removal of the Chief Justice of Helmand, who was notorious for accepting bribes to release kidnappers and murderers. However, they were finding themselves tangled up in all sorts of cultural dilemmas. In recent months three children had turned up at British bases. One was a ten-year-old girl who had been married off in a tribal deal and was being badly beaten. Then there was an eleven-year-old boy who had been sold as sex slave to a local warlord, and a nine-year-old boy raped by an Afghan policeman. The problem was, many Afghan police thought it perfectly normal to keep 'tea-boys' for their entertainment, and handing over daughters was the traditional way to settle tribal feuds. Hearst had set up a 'women and children's justice group' to resolve such cases. 'We've had a fabulous start,' he told me, before admitting that one of the women appointed to the group had been shot in Lashkar Gah the previous week. It was as if twenty-first-century legal experts were advising medieval burghers.

I couldn't help being reminded of a propaganda tour that had been organised for me by the Russians in the dying days of their occupation in the late 1980s. They had taken me to various cities to meet tribal elders with whom they were working and to demonstrate how they controlled everywhere, even though of course if they really did, they would not have been leaving. As we ate lunch in Herat, I knew the mujaheddin of Ismael Khan controlled the area just a few streets away, as I had been with them only weeks earlier. The Russians had told me how they were training locals as surgeons, engineers and administrators, and boasted that they had even trained Afghanistan's first astronaut. That sounded mad, but sure enough that same year, 1988, Abdul Ahad Mohmand was rocketed into space.

Twenty years later, NATO forces were finding that the best local administrators were those Soviet-trained commissars. One of them was Gulab Mangal, who had recently become the third Governor of Helmand since the British arrival. The local community was not overjoyed to find themselves governed by a former communist, but the British found him far more effective than his predecessors. They had little choice. While NATO countries fell over themselves to build schools in Afghanistan, for reasons I failed to understand they had introduced no public-administration course for Afghans.

When I asked Powell for evidence that Britain was improving life in Helmand, he told me there was now a girls' school with a headmistress. I explained that before our troops arrived in 2006 there had already been girls' schools with headmistresses, one of whom I had interviewed.

Next he cited 'the bustling bazaar' in Lashkar Gah. Again I pointed out that there had already been a flourishing bazaar, which I had been able to walk around freely. He looked at me disbelievingly.

I began to feel quite irritated. It was as if these people were in some kind of a cult, blind to the reality outside, and that to them history had only started when they had arrived a few months earlier.

Indeed, one of the problems in Helmand was that each commander came for only six months, so the next one had to start anew, and each seemed to treat it as his own war.

I kept asking to see something where they had made a difference – and to actually go outside the wire. Eventually one day they agreed that I could go and see the bazaar they kept talking about. To my amusement we set off at high speed in a convoy of armoured vehicles driven by heavily armed soldiers. There were cracks on the windscreen. When I asked the soldiers about these they shrugged. 'It's the locals,' they said. 'They always throw stones at us.'

I don't know if it was coincidence or a reflection of the enduring power of the British class system, but Britain's military commander in Helmand was also an Old Etonian. Indeed, Afghanistan seemed to have been invaded by Old Etonians. And as it had been for me and others back in the 1980s, Afghanistan had again become the place from which to launch a freelance career, and most of the news being sent back to the British public was from a group of young men working for *The Times*, the *Financial Times* and the *Sunday Times* who were all Old Etonians, apart from one Old Stoic.

Brigadier Mark Carleton-Smith was commander of 16 Air Assault Brigade, and just coming to the end of his six-month tour in Helmand. He had a shock of sandy hair, a patrician nose and fierce blue eyes that made it clear he was not to be messed with. He had been described to me by his men as the bravest man in the British Army. He was also the first commander in Helmand to have had anything like a proper fighting force. Altogether he had 7,800 troops, more than double the 3,300 there had been in 2006, and four combat battalions instead of the few hundred fighters of 3 Para, as well as a new array of spy-in-the-sky kit like unmanned Reapers.

The security situation, however, had worsened. Officers might claim it was due to desperation on the part of the Taliban that they were increasingly using the roadside bombs employed to such lethal effect in Iraq, but casualties were rocketing. The influx of fighters from Pakistan and the disillusionment of local people with the Afghan government had swelled their ranks. 'Retired' ISI officers had been spotted directing fighting. The Governor told me that half the province was controlled by Taliban. In their six months in Helmand, Carleton-Smith's men had sustained heavy losses, with thirty-two killed and 170 wounded.

Over a dinner of turkey cutlets and chips washed down with Ribena, the Brigadier gave a rather less rose-tinted view than Hugh Powell. The British public, he told me, should not expect a 'decisive military victory': 'We're not going to win this war. It's about reducing it to a manageable level of insurgency that's not a strategic threat and can be managed by the Afghan army. We may well leave with there still being a low but steady ebb of rural insurgency ... I don't think we should expect that when we go there won't be roaming bands of armed men in this part of the world. That would be unrealistic and probably incredible.'

It was the first time I had heard a senior military officer, or indeed any official, admit this publicly. What he was saying was staring us all in the face, but it was refreshing to finally hear some honesty. Yet for years generals would keep asking for more troops and talk of the war as something that could be won.

Carleton-Smith argued that the only way to end the conflict was political, just as it had been in Northern Ireland, and that people should accept the possibility of doing a deal with the Taliban: 'We want to change the nature of the debate to one resolved by negotiations rather than the barrel of a gun.'

Though our conversation was on the record and I was taping his words, I wondered if they would ever see the light of day. As journalists, when we embedded with British troops we signed something called 'The Green Book', which obliged us to submit all our copy, photographs, TV reports or whatever to be vetted by the MoD press office. It was supposed to be for what they call 'opsec' – operational security – but it smacked of censorship, and no other Western force imposed such a condition. They had used it before to stop me writing about the vulnerability of the Snatch Land Rovers to IEDs, as if the Taliban needed to read the *Sunday Times* to realise that.

I was pleasantly surprised, then, when the copy was given the green light. My editor put it on the front page under the headline 'War on Taliban Can't be Won, Says Army Chief', and the reaction was immediate. Both the French army chief and the UN Special Representative said they agreed. Yet within two days the US Defense Secretary Robert Gates had denounced Carleton-Smith for 'defeatism'. 'While we face significant challenges in Afghanistan, there certainly is no reason to be defeatist or to underestimate the opportunities to be successful in the long run,' he told reporters on his plane en route to a meeting of NATO Defence Ministers in Budapest.[1]

Gates was travelling there to ask other countries to send more troops to Afghanistan, so the timing of the Brigadier's comments was hardly ideal. However, there may have been another reason, from another theatre of operations, for the Defense Secretary's public putdown of America's closest ally. Every senior US military officer I had met over the past year had expressed astonishment at what they saw as a British retreat from Basra. The initial British arrogance in Iraq, based on their belief that unlike the Americans they knew how to deal with peacekeeping because of long experience in Northern Ireland, had long faded as they found themselves locked in battle with the Mahdi army, the murderous followers of the radical Shiite cleric Moktada al-Sadr, and other extremist militias. Without enough troops to deal with the situation they had ended up making a secret deal with the Mahdis to be able to withdraw in peace. On 2 September 2007 British troops left Basra Palace, their last base in the city, for the airport in a retreat described by one officer as 'utter humiliation'. The city was left to the mercy of the Mahdis, who terrorised the population with kidnappings, death squads and sectarian attacks against Sunnis and Christians, as well as attacks on shops selling alcohol or music, and on women not wearing headscarves.

Eventually the Iraqi government of Prime Minister Nour al-Maliki, himself a Shia, launched an operation on March 2008, somewhat grandly named 'the Charge of the Knights', to try to regain control of the city. The 30,000 Iraqi forces met such fierce resistance that more than a thousand deserted, and the Mahdis ridiculed it as the Charge of the Mice. The situation only turned after Iranian intervention to help strike a deal with the Sadrists, when more Iraqi forces were sent in with US Marines as advisers, launching airstrikes to help out beleaguered government troops.

Although a British officer had helped draw up the operation, the British were caught by surprise by its timing. Initially the 4,000 British troops stayed cocooned in the airport, to the derision of the Americans. Eventually they got involved and the operation was a success, but it seemed to the Americans that the British had both caused the situation and had to be dragged in to help. They had been astounded to learn that the British commander was away on a mid-tour skiing holiday. Plans for a further reduction of the British garrison in Iraq to free up more troops for Helmand had to be postponed. Basra would become a black mark besmirching the good name of the British Army, and talk of deals in Afghanistan must have set off alarm bells.

*   *   *

The US military was also growing increasingly concerned about what the British were doing in Helmand. The first British commander in Afghanistan, General David Richards, had been replaced in February 2007 by an American, General Dan McNeill. A veteran of Vietnam, Korea and Iraq, he had commanded in Afghanistan before, back in 2002, when the international force was much smaller and returned as the first US four-star commander dedicated to Afghanistan.

He lost no time in making clear what he thought. The civilian spokesman for ISAF during McNeill's command was Nicholas Lunt, a debonair former officer in the 16th/5th the Queen's Royal Lancers. Before taking up his post, Lunt travelled to Brussels to meet the NATO Secretary General. He was taken afterwards without warning into a room of senior NATO staff. On the far wall was a giant screen on which appeared McNeill in combat trousers and T-shirt with his feet up on his desk and a large bottle of water, which he swigged from.

'So, Mr Lunt, you sound like a boy who went to a boarding house,' he began.

'I think you mean a boarding school, sir,' replied Lunt. 'A boarding house is a bit different – it's for people who can't really afford a holiday on the south coast of England.'

As he spoke, Lunt could see all these people looking at him with a 'Don't correct a four-star general' expression.

McNeill questioned him about his background, and whether he'd been to Afghanistan before. Then suddenly he asked, 'So what do you think of General Richards' policy of the platoon houses?'

Lunt could feel the NATO officials in the room stiffening. 'General, I'm not qualified to comment on David Richards' policy,' he replied.

'I'll tell you, Mr Lunt, there's no way I'll be doing any more of that,' said McNeill. 'It's been a major disaster and I'll be reversing it.'

McNeill was particularly angry over the deal the British had done in Musa Qala in October 2006 when, under siege and on the verge of complete withdrawal, they made an agreement with the Taliban to hand over security to local elders.

General Richards would defend the strategy to the end as an 'early experiment in what became mainstream in Iraq under Petraeus and a model for what will probably happen more widely in south and east Afghanistan'.[2] But the Americans were horrified. To add to the ignominy, when the British soldiers left Musa Qala it was on the jingle trucks of local elders, as helicopters were thought too risky, and the whole thing had been filmed by the Taliban in a victorious video, widely available in Quetta. Some of the men wondered what the point of all that sacrifice had been – of the sixty sent there the Royal Irish had lost three men dead and seventeen had been wounded.

Whatever one's point of view, the deal collapsed within less than four months, in February 2007, just as Richards stepped down as commander of ISAF. In an April 2007 cable later released by WikiLeaks, General McNeill wrote: 'They [the British] had made a mess of things in Helmand, their tactics were wrong, and the deal that London cut on Musa Qala had failed.'

Lunt arrived in Kabul just before General Richards departed: 'I knew David Richards and his team,' he said, 'and they were definitely leaving feeling they were on a high. We had champagne – he was in no two minds he'd done a great job.' Indeed, Richards describes cracking open a bottle of his favourite Pol Roger on the plane home.

Then McNeill arrived with his team, and within twenty-four hours the mood had changed dramatically. After a few days there was a presentation by the 'legacy' team to explain the strategy they'd left McNeill with. 'It was the usual "Death by PowerPoint",' said Lunt. 'There were lots of Brits on the team, and the room was packed with ISAF people.'

After the presentation McNeill stood up. 'That's all very well,' he said, 'but we're going to change strategy. The bad guys are all up in the north-east, and we're going to kill them. We're going to stack them up like cordwood.' The room went absolutely quiet, and there was a collective intake of breath at McNeill's unexpected public destruction of his predecessor. Lunt watched as civilians rushed back to their pods and tapped out messages to various

European capitals saying, 'We've got a fucking lunatic who wants to go round killing people.'

McNeill was soon known as 'Bomber' McNeill. Karzai would later tell me he traced it all back to him when things started to go wrong.

The first problem with trying to kill your way to victory was that there wasn't a finite number of Taliban. No one knew how many of them there were. Estimates ranged from 15,000 to 30,000 full-time, much more if you factored in part-timers. Over the years various Western officials and commanders had tried to differentiate between them. We had 'Good Taliban' and 'Bad Taliban'. 'Old Taliban' and 'New Taliban'. 'Moderate Taliban' and 'Hardline Taliban'. 'Tier 1', 'Tier 2' and 'Tier 3 Taliban'. 'Ten-dollar-a-day Taliban'. The idea was that there was a minority of ideologues, then a mass of fighters who didn't really want to be Taliban but were unemployed or disaffected, and that those could somehow be peeled off.

Maybe. Certainly by labelling everything 'Taliban', as ISAF did, they made them seem more powerful than they probably were. 'I think we're in danger of mythologising the Taliban into some kind of unbeatable force,' said George Noel-Clarke, who had worked as an adviser to the British in Helmand (and who also happened to be an Old Etonian). 'When I was in Lashkar Gah we'd get radio messages in the control room saying twenty-five Taliban killed. I'd say, "How do you know?" and they'd say, "They were wearing turbans and carrying Kalashnikovs and shooting at us." I'd say, "Well, they're Pashtuns, that's what they do."' He cited the example of Uruzgan, where there had been fourteen suicide-bombing attempts on the Governor, none of them anything to do with the Taliban, but instead because of a dispute with his nephew who was out for revenge.

What I knew was that there was an endless supply of fighters from the madrassas in Pakistan, and no one was tackling that. Pakistan's Interior Ministry estimated that there were at least 20,000 madrassas, almost ten times the 2,861 that had existed twenty years earlier.[3] Of these, 11,000 belonged to the Deobandi sect and were deemed 'sensitive'. It wasn't just the madrassas that fed the conflict. The textbooks in state schools in Pakistan demonised Hindus and taught such a warped form of history that one would think Pakistan had never lost a war. The US gave $50 million to the Ministry of Religious Affairs for registration of madrassas and curriculum reform, but according to the *Friday Times* it disappeared on modern offices and swanky new SUVs.

Moreover, while a strategy of targeted killing of mid-level commanders might make sense from a military perspective, the result was that these were being replaced by younger, more radical jihadis. The old Quetta *shura* Taliban were only interested in retaking Afghanistan, but some of these new people were global jihadists. And if you killed the wrong people, you were only creating more enemies. In the culture of Pashtunwali, the Pashtun honour code demands revenge – literally an eye for an eye. Killing one civilian would recruit their entire family against you.

To be fair, it was hard to differentiate between Taliban and non-Taliban, as most Pashtun men carried Kalashnikovs and the Taliban deliberately hid among civilians. 'We were caught in between,' said Rahmatullah, a forty-two-year-old farmer from Mianrody village north of Sangin in Helmand, who told me how he not only lost his house in an airstrike, but his three-year-old son after Taliban had commandeered his house for bomb-making. 'The Taliban had been using my home to make IEDs. When I told them to stop, because my family could be destroyed, they asked, "What are you, an infidel?" Then we were bombed. The planes don't differentiate between civilians and Taliban.'

Rahmatullah hid in a hole, and ten days after the bombing he managed to find a way out and escaped with his wife, four daughters and two remaining sons. They ended up fleeing to Kabul, to a miserable camp in the western outskirts where I met him and a number of other Helmandis who had all lost their homes and were living in mud houses and tents, begging for bread. A strip of meat fat someone had thrown out was hanging on the wall as a treat. 'Life was better under the Taliban,' he said. 'There were no thieves and we could just grow our poppy in peace.'

Each time I went to Kabul the camp had expanded. Under McNeill the number of airstrikes increased so much that more civilians were killed in 2007 by Western forces than by Taliban.

It was just too easy to call in an airstrike. Soldiers on the ground in hostile territory had an array of formidable air power at the touch of a button if they got into trouble. Human rights groups complained that 2,000-pound bombs were dropped instead of 500-pound, which cause far less collateral damage, and that airstrikes were being called in even when troops were no longer in danger. Villagers said the bombers destroyed several houses in pursuit of one fighter. Sometimes the information they were working on was wrong.

The numbers were vague. As if the war was not really about Afghans, there was no official tracking of civilian casualties. UNAMA tried to keep a tally, but it was hard to get accurate information from the Afghans, who always exaggerated, or from the military, particularly as many of the operations were carried out by special forces. Only in 2008 did ISAF start a Civilian Casualty Tracker Cell, and by 2009 the British colonel appointed to lead it had been marched out in handcuffs and accused of breaching the UK Official Secrets Act by leaking information about civilian casualties to Rachel Reid of Human Rights Watch.

In fact, said Reid, Colonel Owen McNally didn't leak any vital secrets but had given her information on the wording of General McNeill's Tactical Directive, which showed two intelligence sources were supposed to be required. He was eventually exonerated, but not before the MOD tried to tar Reid and another woman who worked on civilian casualties with unfounded rumours that they'd had affairs with McNally, who was about to get married. The story was splashed across the British tabloids. 'Some in ISAF implied to me he had been singled out perhaps to send a lesson about leaks,' said Reid.

WikiLeaks would later publish documents that put the lie to the military's long-held refrain that 'We don't do body counts.' In July 2010 the so-called Afghan War Logs were published; they demonstrated that the US military secretly maintained files relating to

4,024 Afghan civilian war deaths between January 2004 and December 2009.

From inside the Arg, Karzai watched the body count mount with growing dismay. Then on 23 June 2007 he got a phone call from Helmand saying that at least twenty-five civilians had been killed in airstrikes in De Adam Khan, a village nine miles north of Lashkar Gah. The provincial police chief said the deaths included the mullah of the local mosque, nine women and three babies, as well as twenty suspected militants.

Karzai was furious, and ignoring pleas from his advisers to wait to find out the full details, he called a press conference to denounce what he called the 'extreme' use of force by NATO. 'Innocent people are becoming victims of reckless operations,' he said angrily. 'You don't fight a terrorist by firing a field gun thirty-seven kilometres away into a target. That's definitely surely bound to cause civilian casualties.' He said that ninety civilians had been killed by airstrikes over the previous ten days in Helmand and Uruzgan: 'Afghan life is not cheap and it should not be treated as such.'

Lunt watched Karzai's outburst live on TV in his office. He immediately rang NATO headquarters in Brussels and said they needed to respond. They agreed. Lunt went on CNN, al Jazeera and the BBC to say that ISAF obviously did not target civilians. However, he said, possibly something had gone wrong, and if it had, then 'President Karzai has a right to be disappointed and angry. We need to do better.'

The next morning Lunt was sitting at his desk when the door burst open and in stormed McNeill in uniform. 'He came across my desk and put his face in my face,' said Lunt. 'It was very intimidating. I stood up and stared him down. He told me, "You had no right to say President Karzai had reason to be upset, he has no right to be upset, we are here on a mission and the only person I report to is the US President."'

The two men barely spoke again. 'I felt if you go round killing large numbers of Afghans you're really setting yourself up for failure,' said Lunt.

McNeill argued that as an insurgency was in and among the people, civilians would inevitably be killed. And while NATO tried its utmost to avoid civilian casualties, the Taliban had shown a blatant disregard for civilians, planting tens of thousands of improvised explosive devices along roadways, setting off suicide bombs in crowded marketplaces, and assassinating countless local officials, tribal leaders and teachers. He invited Karzai or any of his representatives to accompany him to Uruzgan to talk to the affected community. None of them took up the offer.

McNeill later recounted that when he went to Uruzgan he met a local who told him, 'You killed Hakim, and he was a civilian.' 'My question was, "What was Hakim doing?" said McNeill. '[The man] pointed towards a wall. He said, "Hakim was there shooting his Kalashnikov." And I asked, "Who was he shooting at?" He said, "He was shooting at you." And I said, "How can you call Hakim a civilian?" He said the Arabs – and I'm using his expression, and that's an Afghan expression for anybody that's not an Afghan – came into his house, pulled him out, said, "Hakim, fight with us or we'll kill you. And after we kill you, we'll go in and kill your family."

'My friend, you and I have a different view,' McNeill told him. 'Hakim perhaps was a civilian, but he certainly was not a non-combatant.'[4]

Less than a week after Karzai's outburst, on 29 June 2007, NATO airstrikes killed another lot of civilians in Helmand. The village of Haderabad, ten miles north-east of Gereshk, was bombed for two hours, destroying five or six houses. Locals said 150 civilians had been killed, including people fleeing on tractors.

Lieutenant Colonel Charlie Mayo, the spokesman for British forces in Helmand at the time, was initially alerted by the local BBC stringer, and called in what was known as the 'Tiger Team', heads of departments, for a meeting. 'After forty-five minutes we had no information,' he said. 'We were baffled. We hadn't flown any flights, had any IDF [indirect fire] or any contacts in that area.'[5]

British helicopters and drones were sent up to overfly the village, but they could see none of the usual signs of an air raid, such as buildings demolished with crowds around them, or tractors taking people to be buried. Yet photographs appeared on the internet of injured children in Lashkar Gah hospital. It turned out that the village was in a different place than on the British maps. 'We knew it wasn't us,' said Mayo. 'So we contacted the Americans, and it turned out that OEF [Operation Enduring Freedom] had been doing a patrol in the area which got in contact, and they called in an airstrike.'

Astonishingly, six years into the war there were still two parallel military operations going on – ISAF, under the command of McNeill, which included about two thirds of all American forces; and OEF, which included special forces and shadowy other forces, and reported to a separate general and separate command in Tampa, Florida. Gates later wrote, 'This jerry-rigged arrangement violated every principle of unity and command.' One reason for the arrangement was that OEF also carried out covert or black ops, and had these been put under one NATO umbrella, the publics of some European countries might have objected.

Ordinary Afghans, of course, did not differentiate between the two outfits. The victims in Helmand blamed the British. 'This was always the issue,' said Mayo. 'The Americans of OEF would be operating in Helmand and we didn't know anything about it. As far as the locals were concerned, it was they are white, foreign soldiers, speaking English and in Helmand, so they must be Brits. We persuaded the Americans to come out and say they'd been in contact but the damage was done.'

The number of civilian casualties was, as always, contested. The Afghan government report said forty-five, ISAF said twelve. It was too dangerous for foreigners to go to the affected village, so the head of the local Afghan army brigade went to Gereshk to meet the Mayor and tribal elders, and worked out that twenty-five to thirty people had been killed. President Karzai sent a team with a large amount of money to pay off the affected families. I couldn't help wondering if victims of American bombing were being paid from his Iranian slush fund.

Despite his frustration with the Americans, Mayo admitted that it was hard to completely avoid killing ordinary Afghans: 'The problem we had was you put down your weapon and you're a civilian, pick it up and you're a Taliban.' He also pointed out that the Taliban used people as shields. He gave me an example where the British went into a village in upper Gereshk and announced over loudspeakers that everyone should leave, as they planned an operation. 'The commander called in an airstrike then when they went through the village discovered we had killed five civilians. I had a BBC journalist with me, so I was furious. "How the hell did that happen?" I asked. It turned out the Taliban had forced the people to stay.'

The number of civilian casualties had gone up so much that at the end of June 2007 McNeill issued ISAF's first Tactical Directive focused on shielding civilians. This document called for using small arms instead of airstrikes whenever feasible, and limited attacks on compounds to situations in which coalition forces 'were taking fire from the compound or there was an imminent threat from the compound, and when there were no other options available to the ground force commander to protect the force and accomplish the mission'. Commanders were supposed to keep 'eyes on' the area even after the raid, so they could establish any damage.

Larry Lewis, research scientist at the Center for Naval Analyses in Virginia, carried out a study of this tactical directive for the Pentagon, and said it had a limited effect. 'You can see the command was already acknowledging this is detrimental to the mission back in 2007,' he says. 'But they were trying to do it in just kind of a "Hey, we know this is bad, so we better put out some guidance and hopefully that will help." And it really didn't help.'[6]

Civilian casualties in airstrikes almost tripled from 2006 to 2007, rising from 116 to 321, according to Human Rights Watch.

On my trip to Helmand in 2008 I got stuck as usual for a few days at KAF, the Kandahar airbase, waiting for a helicopter to fly me on. Like all the main bases it had expanded enormously, with aircraft coming in and out non-stop. Sometimes they even brought celebrities – TV duo Ant & Dec had just been there to present an award to British medics. They'd had to dive for cover from the rockets which were occasionally fired at the base, prompting a *Daily Mirror* front page headlined 'Ant & Duck'.

One of the must-sees for any visitor to KAF was the boardwalk built by the Canadians when they took control in Kandahar in 2006. This was a wooden-planked walkway around a hockey field, illuminated at night and lined with fast-food outlets. These included Burger King, Pizza Hut, Subway and the Green Bean coffee bar as well as the French Bakery complete with painted Eiffel tower, and a couple of Afghan shops selling pirated DVDs and souvenir carpets. It was weird sitting on the walkway with a raspberry smoothie, double-dipped chocolate ice cream or cinnamon doughnut watching a hockey game, only a few miles from the war. Nearby was a series of military shops from different nations – the German one sold a 'Terror Chess' set featuring George W. Bush and the Statue of Liberty as king and queen against the Taliban – and the American PX, which even had a Harley-Davidson concession.

I wanted to meet one of those responsible for coordinating close air support to find out if things had changed in terms of use of airstrikes. My press minder was far more interested in Ant & Dec and setting up a visit for the *Sun*, which is known as the squaddies' paper, than the *Sunday Times*. However, to keep me occupied he agreed that I could spend an afternoon at the airfield operation centre, better known as 'the Taliban Last Stand', or TLS. This was where the coalition had finally cleared the airfield of Taliban by dropping a large bomb. The resulting crater now formed a court-yard in the centre of the building.

I was taken to see Group Captain Ed Stringer, who was senior RAF commander in Afghanistan and air adviser to Brigadier Carleton-Smith. He was quite clear in his view. 'The more bombs we drop in Afghanistan the worse things are getting,' he said. 'No one thinks we're going to bomb our way to victory. My priorities don't involve dropping bombs. We need air mobility so we can be everywhere, but it's as much about intelligence, understanding, weaving forty pieces of gossip and twenty-eight perceptions.' He gave the example of IEDs. 'It's not about the guy laying the bomb, but who is providing the material, financing and training.'

The Weathermen of Kandahar

He was surprisingly intellectual in his approach, and had assembled an interesting team. When I heard there was a submariner wandering around Helmand I thought it was a joke. But Lieutenant Commander Jeeves Toor of the Royal Navy was a principal warfare officer on submarines, which meant he was a trained meteorologist, and when he arrived at Kandahar airbase to take up a NATO post he found himself doing weather forecasts. Submariners use a plotting device which maps tides, lunar cycles, fishing-fleet noise, etc. to spot patterns. Out of personal curiosity, or perhaps boredom, he did the same for Taliban/insurgent activity, and found very predictable patterns, suggesting they followed lunar cycles and other natural phases. He also had local connections. A Sikh who had grown up in Britain, he had family in Lashkar Gah, and mocked the army cultural training for Afghanistan as 'Salamaleckum mate, now where's Terry?'

Stringer was impressed, and secured him for his team. 'He got to parts of Helmand that 2 Para didn't reach – he won the confidence of locals and for a while did very good work.' This came to an end when Toor's meteorological boss, a Canadian, insisted that he return to his NATO post. As Stringer pointed out, there were seven different met offices in Kandahar, all working for different organisations and all producing the same forecasts in a region where the weather hardly ever changed. 'It was well, sod me, it's clear skies and 40 degrees again. But people were more interested in protecting their fiefdoms than thinking outside the box.'

In Kabul, I often dropped by the Pakistan Embassy. It occupied the old British Embassy, a grand white stucco building commissioned in 1919 after the Third Anglo–Afghan War by then Foreign Secretary Lord Curzon, who famously declared that he wanted the British Ambassador to be 'the best-housed man in Asia'. It was a beautiful place, with rose gardens and the only sprung dance floor in the capital. The British had abandoned it in 1989 when the Soviets left and civil war broke out. The Pakistanis took it over, and an old retainer guarded the silver and china till 2001 when the British returned. However, for security reasons the British then moved to what had been the old Bulgarian Chancery, an ugly concrete block in Wazir Akbar Khan, surrounded by sandbags and checkpoints.

It was always good to talk to the Pakistanis, as no one knew the area better. An estimated 50,000 people a week crossed between the two countries, after all. Pakistan's chargé d'affaires, Asif Durrani, was himself a Pashtun, from the same tribe as Karzai. Yet so few people went to see them that the press officer had installed a ping-pong table to keep staff entertained. Durrani said that what the British were trying to do in Helmand was impossible. 'To understand this problem you need centuries of living with these people, the British need to read their own gazetteers and Olaf Caroe [the last British Governor of Frontier Province, and author of a classic book, *The Pathans*]. There are 1,162 Pashtun tribes and sub-tribes; how can they know?'

Instead, each brigade used more ammunition, called in more airstrikes, and took more casualties. 'I got a hard time for having five bases for 3,000 men,' complained Brigadier Ed Butler, who had commanded in Helmand in 2006. 'But in 2008 there were over fifty FOB bases and an operating area of just six hundred metres out – that's all they could cover.'

It was ironic then that one of the Westerners who best understood the tribes caused the biggest fight between Karzai and the British.

It all went back to Musa Qala, which seemed to have become a symbol of British problems in Helmand, and had fallen to the Taliban in February 2007. Ten months later, in December of that year, Karzai told the British he had been contacted by a Taliban commander called Mullah Abdul Salam who was apparently ready to switch sides. The British identified this man and reached out to him, and decided it was time to act to retake the town. To prepare the way there was a concerted effort to kill intransigent Taliban commanders, while the Afghan intelligence service (NDS) persuaded others not to fight so Mullah Salam could become district chief. The operation was successful, the British and Afghans occupying the town and Mullah Salam duly installed as District Governor. A wild figure with a bushy black beard and silver embroidered slippers, he told a local *shura*: 'Three weeks ago I was doing bad things but I am on board now.'

There was just one problem. The people of Musa Qala were a bit surprised by the choice. It turned out there were three Mullah Salams in Helmand. The one who had just been installed was a petty local commander from an Alizai sub-tribe in a nearby village with just twenty or thirty men. The one Karzai thought was a major commander was also an Alizai whose brother Zakir, a class-mate of Sher Mohammad Akhundzada, had been in Guantánamo and was released on the day Musa Qala fell, which seemed more than coincidence. The last one, a Noorzai, had been Taliban commander for Herat during the Taliban regime.

There was another issue. Several hundred Taliban had been persuaded to stay out of the fight, and they needed somewhere to go. Although President Karzai talked a lot about reconciliation, and various countries had provided funds, there was no real systematic programme to bring Taliban over. His office claimed to have brought over four or five thousand, but no one I spoke to thought these numbers at all credible, or the converts really Taliban.

One of the few Westerners to really understand the tribes was Michael Semple, an Irishman who was deputy to the EU Special Representative. Fluent in Pashto, he thought it was important to create some kind of political space for Pashtun nationalism so it didn't become a recruiting cause for the Taliban. Semple began working with Mervyn Patterson, head of the political office at UNAMA, on a project proposed by a former Afghan general called Naqib to retrain and resettle several hundred of the former Taliban from Musa Qala. He suggested setting up a camp for them where they would take a six-week 'life skills' course, learning about the Afghan constitution, human rights and even hygiene. Afghan officials were keen. The British Ambassador Cowper-Coles – who referred to it as 'boy scout' camp – said it had been authorised in writing by the Interior Ministry and Karzai's office.

On Christmas Day 2007 the Ambassador was back in the UK and had just finished breakfast at his mother-in-law's in

Nottinghamshire when the phone rang. It was his deputy Andrew Patrick, calling from Kabul. Patrick told him that Semple and Patterson had been detained in Helmand the previous day. Karzai had ordered them out of the country by nightfall on Boxing Day, accusing them of being British spies even though Semple was Irish.

The story was confused, but the two men had been called, along with General Naqib, to the residence of the Governor, whom they had asked about potential sites for the camp. The Governor at that time was Asadullah Wafa, who had replaced Engineer Daud, whom Karzai had sacked for being too close to the British. The men sat down on the sofas to wait. As it was evening they assumed they were going to be served dinner. Instead, Wafa shouted to his guard, 'Arrest these men!' The British version was that he was annoyed that he was not getting a cut of the large sums of money involved in setting up the camp.

Whatever the reason, Wafa called Karzai to say, 'The Brits are back down here, up to their old tricks without your knowledge, part of the old Great Game,' and that they were setting up a training camp for Taliban. Karzai was furious, and demanded that Semple and Patterson be thrown out of the country within forty-eight hours.

Cowper-Coles broke off his Christmas holiday to fly back, and finally got in to see Karzai on Saturday, 29 December. The Afghan President was waiting for him with half the cabinet, and started 'a litany of complaints about interference in Afghanistan by Britain in general and by Michael Semple in particular'.

The Ambassador countered by showing him papers signed by Karzai's own officials authorising the project. It didn't matter. The damage was done. Semple and Patterson left. When General Naqib was finally released he decided to leave the country too.

A few weeks later at the annual conference of the World Economic Forum at Davos, Karzai was unsparing in his criticism of the British in Helmand. As usual he complained about the removal of Sher Mohammad Akhundzada. 'When our Governor was there, we were fully in charge,' he said. Then he cited the example of Musa Qala. 'It took us a year and a half to take back Musa Qala,' he said. 'This was not a failure but a mistake.'

The Americans were just as critical. 'You Brits have been screwing things up in Afghanistan for 160 years and Michael Semple is the latest most spectacular example,' said Chris Dell, their Deputy Ambassador, when I went to see him.

General McNeill watched all this from ISAF headquarters in Kabul with growing impatience. He became convinced that the British were losing control. On 20 April 2008 he sent Marines in to the town of Garmser in southern Helmand, which was known as a gateway for fighters. The 24th Marine Expeditionary Unit, pronounced 'Two-four mu', was commanded by Colonel Peter Petronzio, and the message McNeill sent him was 'Stir it up in Garmser – stick around – and get some defeating done.' More than an entire battalion – 1,200 men – was sent to focus on an area five miles by seven – as many troops as the Canadians had for the whole of Kandahar. Nowhere in Afghanistan had seen such a concentration of men and firepower, and all day and night helicopters fired missiles, aircraft bombs, artillery and mortars. In the first thirty-five days they fought 170 firefights, many lasting several hours. By the time the Marines had cleared Garmser they estimated they had killed 450 to five hundred Taliban. Others fled to Pakistan.

US diplomatic correspondence later released by WikiLeaks reveals some of the frustrations felt by both the Americans and the Afghans. At a meeting in December 2008 with US Senator John McCain, Karzai was reported as saying he was relieved that US Marines were being sent to help, and 'related an anecdote in which a woman from Helmand asked him to "take the British away and give us back the Americans"'. The Americans were sympathetic. A cable from the US Embassy in Kabul, dated December 2008, said: 'We and Karzai agree the British are not up to the task of securing Helmand.'

Soon there would be more Marines than British in Helmand, and it would come to be known as 'Marineistan'.

* * *

Along with the British in Helmand there were a small number of Danes and Estonians. In November 2008, Ambassador Cowper-Coles travelled to Naw Zad in Helmand with an Estonian colleague, Harri Tiido, the Under-Secretary at the Estonian Foreign Ministry and non-resident Ambassador. Tiido had actually been to Helmand in the last war as a conscript in the Soviet Fortieth Army. Estonians were stationed in Naw Zad, which had once been a town of 30,000 people, but the population had now fled the bombing. The town was deserted, with the two sides dug into First World War-type trenches with their lines three hundred yards apart. The diplomats were briefed on the situation by the Estonian commanding officer with the usual PowerPoints. At the end he asked if they had any questions. 'I have only one,' said Harri. 'What the fuck are we doing here?'

19

We'll Always Have Kabul

Kabul, November 2008

ONE EVENING IN Kabul I lay on cushions under the stars in the garden of the house of a friend who worked at the World Bank, drinking a Chilean merlot that tasted of late blackberries and watching *Indiana Jones and the Kingdom of the Crystal Skull* projected onto the back wall. Two fires burning in copper urns kept us warm, while all around the garden were Kalashnikov-toting guards to keep us safe. It felt very surreal. We were after all in the middle of a war zone.

The streets of Kabul were always deserted by around 10 p.m., empty even of the beseeching street children and begging widows in tattered burqas, and usually I walked back to my guesthouse at night or called a local cab. That night the Canadian Ambassador gave me a lift in his armoured car. The door was so heavy that I could barely close it, and we drove at such speed, with the guards constantly radioing to another security car behind, that by time I got to the Gandamack I felt nervous about the enemy out there in a way I never had before.

For it wasn't just in Helmand that the situation was deteriorating. Across the country it was the same. I had flown to Afghanistan with Justin on a new airline called Safi. 'Have you had any crashes?' he asked its check-in lady at Dubai Terminal 2, from which departed all the flights to dodgy places. 'No, because we're new,' she replied, as if it were a reasonable question.

Safi seemed like a normal airline, with a proper meal instead of the coffee sachet, boiled sweet and piece of nan bread provided by Ariana. To our surprise there was also a new terminal at Kabul, though the plane taxied straight past it to the old ramshackle one.

I was always happy to land in Kabul, perhaps out of relief at a safe landing, because it was hard to think of another airport with more hassle. Unless you had wangled a VIP pass you had to lug all your belongings through a series of car parks and kiosks offering money-change, warm Pepsis and Iranian biscuits until you got to Car Park C. But the crisp Himalayan air and snow-capped mountains always lifted my spirits. This time, however, it was a blank, drizzly day, more like London, with a grey smudge of clouds obscuring the mountains, and the mood in Kabul seemed one of dread.

On my first afternoon I went to see my friend Maryam at the Afghan Women's Resource Centre, who told me a story that illustrated this new fear. 'There was a lunar eclipse at around 1 a.m. a few weeks ago, and in our Islamic tradition people had come out in the streets to pray,' she said. The noise woke her up. 'This is it,' she thought. 'The Taliban have come back into the city.'

In theory, Afghanistan should have felt safer by now. NATO had increased its presence to 71,000 troops, of whom 40,000 were American – more than three times the number there had been three years earlier.

Yet in those same three years, between 2005 and 2008, the Taliban had recaptured much of southern Afghanistan. They were popping up in the north and the west and creeping ever closer to Kabul, including the adjoining provinces of Logar and Wardak. The Governor of Logar, just half an hour away, had been assassinated.

One day in Kabul I met a long-faced man called Ahmed Bachar who ran an orphanage in Logar. He told me that for fifteen years he had looked after children who had lost their parents or whose fathers had lost legs or eyes in the war that had gone on for three decades. Bachar made sure they got to school, and had something to eat and somewhere to sleep at night. It had always been a struggle, so he was happy when after the fall of the Taliban he started receiving international aid money. This enabled him to arrange a proper building, books, clothes, and occasionally even balloons or kites for the children to play with. I nodded at that, for this was a country where children were more likely to have seen someone killed than ever to have possessed a toy.

Then one night in summer a group of masked Taliban came to his house and accused him of working with foreigners. They threatened to kill him if he did not stop. 'I was terrified,' he said. 'But I look after two hundred children aged five to sixteen, and didn't know what would happen to them if I stopped.' So he went to the mosque and told the local community. It was a risk. Among those gathered for prayer were local shopkeepers and farmers he knew donned masks at night and joined the Taliban patrolling the streets. The Eid holiday collection of fifty afghanis per head which usually goes to the poor had been commandeered by the Taliban. But the people beseeched him to stay. 'We need you to look after our children,' they said. 'We will talk to the Taliban and ask them to let you continue.'

A few nights later the Taliban came to his house again, and said they knew he did important work, and that he could stay as long as he broke off all connection with foreigners. He was not convinced. 'Maybe 80 per cent they leave me alone, but 20 per cent they kill me. The problem is I cannot trust the government forces to protect me. The police only want bribes from us. We are caught between the two.' Tears spilled from his eyes. 'I have sacrificed the orphans for the safety of my own children.'

Bachar's view of the police was widespread – in most cases they were the last thing anyone wanted. One of the biggest failings of the international community was its failure to create an effective police force. At a Congressional subcommittee on national security in June 2008, US Congressman John Tierney gave a grim summary of findings on the 433 Afghan national police units that had been created. 'Zero are fully capable, 3 per cent are capable with coalition support, 4 per cent are only partially capable, 77 per cent are not capable at all, and 68 per cent are not formed or not reporting.'

The problem started with recruitment. The literacy rate among recruits was about 5 per cent, so there was no hope of reports being written. Around a third were drug addicts. The force was incredibly top-heavy, with thousands of officers – more than 20,000 of them commanding 36,000 police on the beat. Not only was their $80-a-month salary far less than what they could make as a guard for an international office, but often the government failed to pay them at all. Even if they did, there was no banking system, so the wages were paid in cash through their superiors, who often siphoned some off. Only later, when a system of paying through mobile phones to agents was installed, did this change.

Then there was the issue of equipment. A *New York Times* investigation found that the Pentagon had awarded a $298 million contract to supply ammunition to the Afghan security services to a twenty-two-year-old with a forged driver's licence and a history of violence operating from an unmarked office in Miami Beach. AEY Inc. was described by the *Times* as 'a fledgling company led by a 22-year-old man whose Vice President was a licensed masseur'. The ammunition it supplied included 100 million Chinese cartridges, some of them forty years old and in decomposing packaging so unsafe that NATO and the US ended up having to pay to have them safely destroyed.

Another problem was getting the police to places. The RAF Captain Ed Stringer had realised this, and offered the RAF's services to police trainers in the south. 'They looked at us in a bemused way and said, "Sir, we don't drop bombs on people."' He left his card, and a month later they called in a panic to say a new training programme was starting, and they could not get the recruits to the training centres. 'So we came up with an "airline schedule".' Using a C130 Hercules, they looped the recruits to Herat and the graduates back to Kandahar and Helmand nine weeks later. The scheme was very successful, but when PJHQ in London found out they were not impressed: 'I was not using my aircraft to directly help the "fight" in Helmand.'

While the police and army were poorly manned and ill-equipped, the Taliban were upping their activity. Adrian Edwards, the spokesman at UNAMA, told me that the number of attacks had gone from seven hundred a month in 2007 to between nine hundred and a thousand. In June and July the Americans had lost more troops in Afghanistan than in Iraq.

The Taliban didn't need to attack to spread fear. 'They're whispering in people's ears,' said Maryam. 'They are like the bogeyman – they don't even need to be there to generate an impression.'

I asked Bachar why people in his village had joined the Taliban, as it didn't seem to be offering anything positive. He said it was partly fear, but also that people felt the government was doing nothing but making money.

'The Taliban are mining in a sea of acquiescence, a sullen, frightened acquiescence,' said British Ambassador Sherard Cowper-Coles. 'If you ask they don't want Taliban, but if it's a choice between them and corrupt, predatory government they prefer Taliban.' He told me that planners in London wanted to come up with a Plan B in case the current strategy didn't work. The trouble was, nobody could think of one.

'It's all gone to rats,' wrote Richard Codrington, who headed the Afghan group at the Foreign Office, in a memo.

Throughout the war Kabul had always been a safe haven. People called it 'Kabubble'. As often among expat communities on the edge of a war zone there was a raucous social life fuelled by illicit alcohol, cheap hash and the adrenaline of fear.

The foreigners in Kabul were a motley crowd, many of whom seemed to be men with Palestinian *keffiyeh* scarves and wraparound shades – gem dealers, bounty hunters, those engaged in black ops or just generally shady figures in some twilight world, like the American known as 'Tora Bora Jack' who kept his own prison and had ended up going to jail.[1] There were the Old Etonians, not just the journalists but a colourful character called Rory Stewart who had tutored Princes William and Harry and was living in a mud-walled fort running a foundation inspired by Prince Charles to revive traditional crafts. In 2010 he would be elected to Parliament as a Tory MP.

Then there were earnest young people with programmes to change the lives of Afghans through teaching them circus skills, skateboarding, or holding music festivals. It often seemed that you could get international funding for anything. I met endless feminist groups holding workshops on gender empowerment, and consultants with large paycheques and little to do. More than one diplomat, military commander or aid worker, including a Canadian General and a British Defence Attaché, ended up going astray and being sent home in disgrace.[2]

Though alcohol was illegal in Afghanistan, places that catered to Westerners were allowed to serve it to non-Muslims. Such restaurants had no signs and heavy steel doors with sandbags around them, manned by gunmen, so going into one of them was like entering a bunker. Inside, however, you could dine on foie gras and chablis at astronomical prices. Crazy things went on. One night someone rode a motorbike through the Elbow Room bar.

You could learn to shoot a Kalashnikov at a private range, or play golf amid burned-out tanks on a former minefield. Some hardy British and French expats even went skiing – driving north from Kabul up to the Salang Pass for what they christened the Salang Ski Club. No chairlifts, of course: it was an hour's walk up for two exhilarating minutes down on a slope they christened 'the Entente Cordiale'.

Then there were the parties. Some of the drug lords had invested in building large houses in wedding-confection style known as 'narcitecture' or 'bling houses', and these were perfect for parties. 'Tarts and Taliban' was a common theme, while the DFID team hosted a 'Graveyard of Empires' party. Any excuse was enough for a gathering. People celebrated things they wouldn't dream of back home, such as the annual black-tie dinner for Trafalgar Day, Burns Night suppers and the Queen's Birthday. The British Embassy had a pub known as the Inn Fidel, and held an annual pantomime. All this carousing was clearly creating resentment among locals, who heard about billions of dollars being given to their country yet saw roads in a state of disrepair, and a river still choked and filthy, while few of them had electricity or running water. Some of the imams at Friday prayers railed against Western debauchery. When Eckart Schiewek, head of security for UNAMA, collected the phones of all the Afghan staff for random inspection in 2007, it was found that almost every one contained anti-Western videos or songs.

Then, in January 2008, shortly after the assassination of Benazir Bhutto, the Taliban began hitting right in the heart of the Afghan capital with a series of headline-grabbing attacks, or 'spectaculars'.

The first took place at the Kabul Serena, Afghanistan's only five-star hotel. I had never stayed there, as it was beyond my newspaper's budget and clearly a target, though I often popped in for decent coffee. However, it was supposed to have good security, and dignitaries always stayed there. The Norwegian Foreign Minister was among its guests when two suicide bombers in police uniform got in. One of them blew himself up at the gate, distracting everyone while the second ran into the lobby. There he fired on guests and staff, then went down the corridor to the gym and fired on more. Throughout the attack the gunman was on the phone to his controllers in Pakistan, making fourteen calls in total.

Then on 27 April there was another assassination attempt on Karzai, the fourth one. The President was appearing at an open-air ceremony to commemorate the sixteenth anniversary of the fall of the communist government to the mujaheddin, and had told his eight-hundred-strong security staff he was worried. They assured him it was safe, but as he took his place on the parade-ground stand to the strains of the national anthem, the crack of rifle-fire broke out and all hell broke loose. Government Ministers and Ambassadors, including the British and American, ran for cover as a gunfight ensued. The gunmen had hidden for days in a nearby city hotel room, and opened fire from the window with a heavy machine gun while another group fired mortars and RPGs from a restaurant. The dead included an MP and a ten-year-old girl. Mobile phones found afterwards revealed the gunmen texting their commander in Pakistan and him urging them on.

The most deadly attack came on 7 July, when in the morning rush hour a suicide bomber drove up to the gates of the Indian Embassy in an explosive-packed Toyota Camry and detonated it. The Embassy was in the centre of the city, across the street from the Interior Ministry and just along from the Mustafa Hotel. The explosion was so massive it could be heard miles away. Fifty-eight people were killed, including the Indian Defence Attaché and another diplomat, as well as many Afghans who were queuing for visas.

While the Taliban might have wanted to create instability in Kabul so the foreigners would leave, a direct attack on India seemed to be straight from the playbook of Pakistan's ISI. Investigators discovered the bomber's cell phone in the wreckage of the car, and tracked down the facilitator in Kabul who had arranged the logistics of the attack. US intelligence found calls between him and a high-level ISI official from Pakistan's 324 Military Intelligence Battalion, based in Peshawar. This evidence was too strong to ignore. President Bush warned Pakistan's recently elected Prime Minister Yousuf Raza Gilani that if anything else happened he would have to take 'serious action'.

Before the attack the CIA had picked up calls from ISI officials planning something in Kabul, and had sent Deputy Director Stephen Kappes to Islamabad. By the time he got there the attack had happened. He urged Musharraf to remove General Nadeem Taj, the Director General of ISI. But Taj had been with Musharraf when his plane was denied permission to land at Karachi by Nawaz Sharif in 1999, and again during the assassination attempts in 2003. Instead of being sacked he was promoted that October to be commander of Triple X Corps in Gujranwala, one of the dozen men who control the Pakistani army.

Most of the attacks were carried out by the Haqqani network, and were traced back to Miranshah, the capital of North Waziristan, where they were based. The Haqqani network had always been close to ISI. Amrullah Saleh, the Afghan intelligence chief, said the CIA had even identified a specific individual, Tajmir Jawad. 'More than a dozen times we told ISI, "This guy is not hiding in the mountains. He is either in Peshawar or he is in this specific address with this phone number." They never arrested Tajmir, because he is their man.'

The Indian Embassy attack changed things. The US could no longer ignore what its ally was up to.

Brigadier General Mick Nicholson, who had witnessed first-hand the problem on the border when he commanded forces in 2006–07, returned to Kandahar in 2008, then became Director of the Pakistan/Afghan Coordination Cell at the Pentagon. He said it was a salutary lesson. 'Because they [the Pakistani military] can attend our schools, speak English and talk to us in the same idiom we assume a common mindset, but of course there's not. We learned the hard way. There are so many dimensions to this. We Westerners tend to look at things in isolation, and thought we were clever because we were playing three-dimensional chess. The Pakistanis were playing ten-dimensional chess, and we were not even showing up or aware of the chessboards they were playing on.'

Nicholson said we should have learned from the 1980s, when Pakistan managed to build the bomb while lying to the US and taking its money. 'It was incredible, how these people can be so clever. They built a nuclear programme out of nothing, literally stole the blueprints, all under our noses while we in the US were saying "They can never do that." It's shocking how blinded we were by our condescension.'

Ambassador Cowper-Coles agreed. 'We were naïve about ISI, that it was just "rogue elements". All along they hadn't moved once against the Quetta *shura*, which we thought would be relatively simple. The Pakistanis had a policy of wanting Americans bogged down here to keep the US away from their bomb.'

Yet even knowing this, the US did not know how to act on Pakistan. 'At the end of the day we needed them,' said Nicholson. 'We needed them to be active that side of the border, to apply what-ever pressure they could on insurgents even if it was less than we wanted. You just look at the map and the number of madrassas and the number of youth in those madrassas. If they recruit just 10 per cent of those into the insurgency, we lose. So regardless of how difficult it was we had to work with them and get whatever degree of unity of effort we could get.'

Back in Washington, President Bush became increasingly determined to do something. 'I understood the urgency of the threat and wanted to do something about it,' he wrote in his memoir.

His old buddy Musharraf was forced to step down as President in August 2008 to avoid impeachment, defending his record in an emotional hour-long television address. His resignation was followed by celebrations, just as there had been when he seized power. Afterwards Condoleezza Rice, the US Secretary of State, praised him as 'a friend to the United States and one of the world's most committed partners in the war against terrorism'.

Whether or not the timing was coincidental, within a few weeks of Musharraf going, the US carried out its first reported ground action in Pakistan. On 3 September American special forces landed by helicopter in Angor Adda in South Waziristan, and began shooting. There was predictable outrage in Pakistan. 'US Commandos Attack Pakistan Sovereignty' ran the headline across the front page of *The Nation* the following day. Its report stated that twenty people had been killed, including three women and children, when US troops in three helicopter gunships 'opened indiscriminate firing on the occupants of a house'. Both Pakistan's national assembly and senate passed unanimous resolutions condemning the US action. 'Such acts of aggression do not serve the common cause of fighting terrorism and militancy in the area,' read the official protest.

Pakistan responded by blocking the supply route by which fuel was taken to NATO troops in landlocked Afghanistan. Most supplies came by ship to Karachi and up through Pakistan, giving Islamabad yet another powerful bit of leverage – except for one thing: the trucking companies carrying the goods were owned by Pakistani generals, who had no desire to lose an extremely lucrative source of income.

* * *

Pakistan soon had other problems. Just twelve days after Bhutto's widower Asif Zardari replaced Musharraf as President, the capital suffered its worst ever terrorist attack.

On 20 September 2008, the Marriott Hotel was packed with Saturday-evening diners and guests when a dumper truck packed with explosives tried to drive through the barrier then detonated. The bomb set off a gas explosion, engulfing the five-storey hotel in flames and killing fifty-six people, including the Czech Ambassador, two American soldiers and a Danish intelligence agent, and injuring 280. The blast was so huge it left a sixty-foot-deep crater. This had happened in what was a supposedly secure zone, just across the road from the hostels for MPs and near the ministries and parliament. People called the attack Pakistan's 9/11.

I was in London when I heard the news, and felt a shudder. The Marriott wasn't just any hotel, but a symbol of Pakistan. When I'd lived in Islamabad from 1989 to 1990 the building had been a Holiday Inn, for years the only luxury hotel in Islamabad, and its Nadia coffee shop was the favourite meeting place for politicians, foreign visitors and journalists. Whenever I was in Pakistan and needed to catch up with what was going on I headed for the Marriott, sometimes sitting there all afternoon sifting through the latest rumours and conspiracy theories.

I should have been staying there when the attack happened. I'd been booked in, but had changed my dates. I hadn't stayed there for years, seeing such landmark hotels as targets, but on my last trip in July I had dined in its Chinese restaurant with British diplomats who assured me they saw it as secure. I had ended up moving to the Marriott, as it was one of the only places you could order food during Ramadan.

The owner of the hotel was an old friend, Sadruddin Hashwani, one of Pakistan's leading businessmen. He moved to Dubai after the attack, and when I met him there he insisted that it had been carried out with the collaboration of the authorities. The dumper truck, he claimed, had been escorted through the high-security zone by a car of the intelligence agencies. He also said that after the attack he was called by Zardari's office and asked to say the President had been the real target, as he was supposed to be hosting a dinner at the hotel for the country's top leadership, a story that then appeared in foreign press. 'It was completely untrue,' said Hashwani. 'No such dinner was booked. He wanted to present himself as a victim of terrorism just before his first visit to the US.'

Three suspected terrorists were picked up a month later, but then acquitted. The Taliban denied involvement. Instead, a group calling itself Fedayeen Islam, or 'Islamic Commandos', contacted the local correspondent of al Arabiya TV claiming responsibility. The group's demands included that Pakistan stop cooperation with the US.

Foreigners living in Islamabad and Kabul upped their security after the attacks of 2008. Islamabad had a so-called Diplomatic Enclave, where all the Embassies were, and a high-security Red Zone which comprised the government buildings and parliament. In Kabul, however, everything was scattered around the city. There was no Green Zone as in Baghdad, so to protect themselves foreigners in Embassies and organisations surrounded their buildings with concrete blocks, Hesco sacks and concertina wire, and basically cut off entire roads. In a city with a population nearing five million and an infrastructure meant for one tenth of that,[3] this made traffic impossible and further fuelled resentment among locals. Since the 2006 riots Karzai had issued a number of decrees demanding that these blocks be removed, but no one took any notice. When police removed barriers from around the offices of the Asian Development Bank, the bank simply closed its doors and said it would not reopen until they were replaced. After the 2008 attacks the march of the concrete blocks increased. The foreigners weren't the only culprits: warlords like Marshal Fahim and General Dostum had done the same.

* * *

Among all the concrete blocks and gaudy new drug-money houses, it sometimes seemed hard to find any vestiges of the old Kabul. Perhaps ironically, considering all the damage the British had caused in the past, such as the destruction of the historic covered bazaar in 1842 by the Army of Retribution, two British men were on the front line of trying to save what was left: Jolyon Leslie of the Aga Khan Foundation and Rory Stewart.

Rory was always entertaining company, and one of the few foreigners I knew who liked to walk around the city. Indeed, he had walked across Afghanistan for three weeks, and written a wonderful book about it. Occasionally I went for walks with him, he every inch the eccentric Brit in a long velvet coat.

One day we walked to Murad Khane, the oldest surviving part of the city, an area on the north bank of the Kabul River not far from the presidential palace which had been built in the eighteenth century by Ahmad Shah Durrani, the first King of Afghanistan, to house members of his court from the Qizilbash tribe. These days it was one of the poorest areas. You could identify it from far off by the black smoke rising from a line of blacksmiths and tyre shops, and people shaping rubber buckets. As part of his Turquoise Mountain Foundation, Rory wanted to restore the area. He pointed out some carved cedarwood panels on the mud-walled houses, and an old hammam, or bath house, where a djinn, or spirit, was said to live.

At first it was hard to detect the charm of Murad Khane, for what looked like decades of garbage had piled so high that residents had to burrow through them to get to their doors. Like much of the city the area had no electricity or sewerage system, and no running water. We passed a man squatting in the open to relieve himself, and a trio of goats nosing through vegetable peelings. The river was still brown and stinking, and as on every visit to Kabul I wondered why none of that foreign aid could be used to clean it.

Yet when I looked more closely I could see that the wooden panels Rory had drawn my attention to were intricately carved, with designs of lotus flowers, climbing vines and the tulips that Emperor Babur so loved, and that no two were alike. Once you got through the rubbish, some of the houses had enclosed courtyards with ornate plaster arches. This had indeed once been a place of palaces.

The area has five shrines, and we stopped at one known as 'the Shrine of the Padlocks'. We were greeted by its keeper, Pahlawan Asis, a large man with cauliflower ears who told us he had been champion wrestler of Kabul in 1963 during King Zahir Shah's time. He produced from his pocket a black-and-white picture of himself next to his Russian coach.

Though it was a Shia shrine, he said many of the visitors were Sunnis, and that miracles often occurred there. He had succeeded his father and grandfather before him as guardian of the shrine, and had stayed guarding it even during the civil war when the area was on the front line between Dostum and the government. It had been rocketed so much, he told us, that he and an old woman were the only ones who stayed. 'I defended this place with my arms,' he said, displaying impressive biceps.

When the Taliban took over they closed the shrine. 'They arrested me ten times, made us pray their way,' he said. 'Now we've got our freedom, but have lost our security.' Moreover, having survived all the fighting, the new city authorities wanted to bull-doze the area and put up concrete apartment buildings. 'Foreigners come to our land and rarely talk to the poor people, the real people of Kabul, just those in power,' he complained. 'That's why they spend lots of money but have made little difference, so most of our boys are jobless and the river is still full of sewage.'

Afghanistan was filled with stories, and sometimes it felt as if my head would burst with the weight of all its woes.

It was on one of those days that a friend took me for tea to the home of Masood Khalili, in the west of the city. It was a most beautiful house, built by King Zahir Shah for Masood's father Khalilullah Khalili, a well-known poet, and had somehow survived all the wars.

Khalili, who was then Afghanistan's Ambassador to Turkey, welcomed us inside and led us through to a circular room he described as his meditation room. The ceiling was painted with flowers, and verses by the thirteenth-century Persian poet Rumi had been painted all around the walls by his artist wife. We sat cross-legged on cushions on the floor and closed our eyes as he took a wooden mallet and traced it along the rim of a Buddhist singing bowl, a kind of upside-down bell. A soft ringing sound filled the room, and he began to read his father's poetry from a book entitled *An Assembly of Moths*.

I could only understand the occasional word, but it didn't matter, because he had such a mellifluous voice it washed over us, soothing all outside cares. Outside, the light started to fade. I wanted the moment never to end. Afterwards he talked of how poetry was so important to Afghans that people use the prefix 'sha'er mega', which means 'the poet says ...' to substantiate an argument.

On a shelf was a photograph of the late Northern Alliance commander Ahmat Shah Massoud reading a book on board a helicopter. 'That is perhaps the last photograph of Massoud,' said Khalili. 'I had the film in my pocket when the bomb went off.' The two men had been close friends, and Khalili was with him when he was killed – the attack had left him blind in one eye and deaf in one ear.

Massoud loved poetry, Khalili said, and on the night before his assassination they had talked till the early hours of the morning by the light of a small lantern. Massoud had taken a book of poems by the great Persian poet Hafiz off a shelf and said, 'Let's open the book and see what will happen.'

'In Afghanistan we often open his book and see what will happen in the future,' Khalili explained. 'I opened it and it was on a verse which read "Take out from your heart all the siblings of enmity, plant the tree and seed of love ... oh you two who are sitting together treasure this night ... you two will not be able to see each other again." We were both quiet a few minutes after that.'

The next morning Massoud came to Khalili's room at about 10 o'clock. Khalili's passport was lying on the bed, and Massoud told him to put it in his shirt pocket. 'Then we went to the Amu Darya [known in English as the Oxus], the river that divides Afghanistan from Central Asia. He told me two Arabs had come for an interview and I was to interpret. We went in and he was on my left, the cameraman in front.' After a brief chat, Massoud told them to start their camera. The reporter asked, 'Why are you against bin Laden?' then everything exploded. 'There was a blue flash and burning smell, and I felt a hand on my wrist.'

The attack left Khalili badly burned, and his body peppered with shrapnel. He said his wife found eight pieces embedded in the passport Massoud had told him to put in his shirt pocket. 'The passport stopped the shrapnel entering my heart and so saved my life.'

We were silent after that, for there were no words. Then Khalili said he would read a quatrain from his father. First he spoke in Farsi, then in English. 'Never ever allow the candle of hope to slip from your palm and heart. As long as you have a hope you win the world.'

20

Death of a Poet

Herat, May 2009

MASOOD KHALILI HAD talked of poetry and hope. Yet I think the first time I realised just how much Afghanistan was going wrong it was because of a poet, this time a woman, who was brutally killed at the age of just twenty-four.

People often ask if it is difficult working in Islamic countries like Afghanistan as a female reporter. Usually I reply that it is an advantage, for I can meet half the population who are largely inaccessible to my male colleagues. Among the most interesting women I had encountered were a group of writers and poets in Herat who had risked their lives under the Taliban to keep writing.

From far off, Herat's field of crooked minarets looked like brick chimneys all leaning in different directions. The ground around was scattered with white and lapis faience that had once covered the walls. Above the city is the ancient citadel, and down below what Heratis call the Big Mosque, on a square where boys sell peacock feathers and fight with boiled eggs, and old Sultan Hamidy shuffles around his dusty shop of ancient coins, bright magenta silks and other treasures, its windows full of misshapen glass the colours of the sea.

I'd gone to Herat both with Ismael Khan's mujaheddin and the communist regime during the late 1980s. Then, after 9/11, when ISI abducted me from my Quetta hotel room and deported me, I

411

ended up entering Afghanistan through Iran. The day after the Taliban were driven from Herat, Ismael Khan sent one of his men to meet me at the border – a majestic character called Ayubi who was wrapped in a cloak and wearing a large ruby ring. 'Welcome my Afghanistan,' he said.

Those days in November 2001, after the fall of the Taliban, were so bitterly cold that in a refugee camp outside Herat called Maslakh, which means slaughterhouse, every morning women were burying babies who had frozen to death in the night. Yet they were also days of exuberance and new-found freedom. I was walking along Cinema Street in Herat, enjoying the atmosphere, when a sign caught my eye. Written in English and Persian it said 'Herat Literary Society', and beyond it was a path leading to a small white bungalow.

I stared at it, intrigued. Herat had long been regarded as Afghanistan's cultural capital. First settled five thousand years ago, and desecrated by Genghis Khan who levelled the town in 1221 leaving only forty people alive, it went on to become one of the world's greatest centres of medieval Islamic learning. In the city's heyday in the fifteenth century, when the minarets were in their full glory, it was ruled by a famous Queen, Gowhar Shad, who filled her court with the most talented Persian miniaturists, poets, calligraphers and architects. So renowned was it for its arts that Emperor Babur joked that in Herat 'you couldn't stretch a leg without kicking a poet'.

That was long ago. Since then Herat had been desecrated many more times, most recently by the Soviets in the 1980s, who mortared its minarets, then by the Taliban in the 1990s, who burned its books, smashed its sculptures and kept its women prisoners inside their homes. It was hard to imagine that any artistic spirit had survived.

And yet I could see the door of the Literary Society, enticingly ajar. Inside seemed even colder than out, and the first rooms I came to were empty. I stamped my feet to try to bring feeling back to my frozen toes. Then I noticed a pair of scuffed sandals by a door. Beyond, sitting at a desk, was a man with a short dark beard, black poloneck, glowering dark eyes and a passing resemblance to Robert De Niro. He introduced himself as Ahmed Said Haqiqi, the society's President, and invited me to sit down. He told me about burying books so the Taliban wouldn't burn them, and how hard life had been for the city's writers under the Taliban, risking torture and death to keep on writing.

I asked if the society had any female members, and he beckoned me to follow. We walked along the muddy road, past the jangling horse carts and laughing traffic policeman to Flower Crossroads, where he told me he had one day counted eighteen bodies hanging, victims of Taliban brutality. He turned down a small alley between mud-walled compounds, and stopped outside one. On the wall by the door was a small sign: 'Golden Needle, Ladies Sewing Classes'.

Under the Taliban women had been banned from working, studying, wearing lipstick or white shoes, or even laughing out loud. Herat's female writers had racked their brains and realised that the only thing that they were still allowed to do was to sew. So it was that three times a week, six young women in blue shuttlecock burqas would shuffle up to this doorway like walking shrouds. In their handbags, beneath material, scissors and threads, were notebooks and pens. Had the authorities investigated, they would have discovered that the sewing students never made any clothes. Once inside the school, a courageous literature professor from Herat University would take out his bust of Pushkin and talk to them about Shakespeare, Dostoevsky, James Joyce and other banned writers. Under a regime where even teaching a daughter to read was a crime, had they been caught, they might have been hanged. The bravery of these women and their commitment to literature was completely humbling.

I met two of them that day – Leila Razeqi and Maria Tanha. It was Leila who had first come up with the idea of the secret classes, and for the first two years they were held at her home. She paid the professor with food and money raised by selling the family's carpets. 'It was a big risk but I was determined to be educated,' she told me, adding that she used to stay up till the early hours doing calculus because she so feared her brain would atrophy under the

Taliban. 'Life for women under the Taliban was no more than being cows in sheds,' she complained.

A few days later I was invited to a local hotel for the first mixed meeting of the Herat Literary Society in twenty years. There, Leila introduced me to two more of the group – Homeira Naderi and a raven-haired young poetess called Nadia Anjuman, who they all agreed was the most talented. She was only twenty, but she was secretly turning out wonderful poems about love, the situation of women, and attempts to silence their voices. In 1999, when there seemed no end of Taliban oppression in sight, she had written a poem entitled 'Don't Greet the Night', with the defiant lines:

> Laugh at the morning
> Shut the door on the night.

After the Taliban had gone it seemed the long years of darkness for Afghanistan's women were over. Leila, Nadia and their friends bubbled with excitement about the future. Girls' schools were reopening, Herat University would once again allow female students, and all of them imagined glittering careers as writers, doctors and professors.

Taliban repression of women had after all been one of the main reasons given by the West for ousting the regime. In London Cherie Blair hosted a gathering at 10 Downing Street to call for moves to 'give back a voice' to Afghan women. President Bush triumphantly declared in his 2002 State of the Union address: 'The mothers and daughters of Afghanistan were captives in their own homes … Today women are free.' Like other journalists I wrote breathless stories about beauty schools, the first female driving school, women TV presenters and girls' football teams, though I did notice the latter were practising at dawn in secret.

The new constitution guaranteed equal rights for women, and reserved them 25 per cent of the seats in parliament – more female representation than in the US Congress (20 per cent) or the British Parliament (23 per cent). Representatives of the international community repeated like a mantra that two million Afghan girls were now in school.

Though the government appointed only one woman Minister, for Women's Affairs, and Hamid Karzai's own wife, Zinat, never appeared in public, for a while the situation did improve. However, from 2005 I watched the situation for women deteriorate. For me it started with the killing of Shaima Rezayee, a lively twenty-four-year-old who had hosted a popular MTV-style television show. She was shot in the head in her house in Kabul after being criticised by the Ulema *shura*, the government council of religious scholars.

Then, at the end of 2005 I had a shocking phone call from Herat. The young poet Nadia Anjuman had been killed. The information was confused, but it seemed she had been beaten to death by her own husband.

The killings continued. Just of women I had met, in 2007 Zakia Zaki, a headmistress who ran a US-funded radio station called Peace Radio, was killed just north of Kabul, shot seven times as she slept next to her eight-month-old son. In September 2008 Kandahar's top policewoman, Malalai Kakar, was gunned down in her car with her teenage son as she was leaving for work. She had become internationally known after killing three would-be assassins in a shoot-out. Were we making these women targets by writing about them?

Many of the new girls' schools were destroyed. According to the Education Ministry, 122 school buildings were blown up or burned down in 2008, and another 651 schools forced to close because of a lack of security. There were cases of acid being thrown in the face of girls going to school in Kandahar, and of the poisoning of their school meals.

One day I had a call from an American friend who had helped put on performances of Shakespeare in Kabul. He told me that one of his group's stars, Parween Mustakhel, was in danger and needed to get out of the country. Parween was one of Afghanistan's leading actresses, and had been the first woman to appear on TV after the Taliban fell. 'Others were scared, but I thought it was good to show the way,' she had told me. Her own family had disagreed. Her sisters had cut her off. 'Being an actress in this country is like being a whore,' they said. After she appeared in *Love's Labour's Lost* in summer 2008 she began to get death threats. Men in turbans came past on motorbikes warning, 'Don't act or you'll be killed!' Her husband was also threatened. 'You pimp, letting your wife on TV,' they told him. 'If you're a real man you'll beat her and kick her and take her back to Khost.'

One night as Parween prepared dinner, her husband went out for firewood. She thought she heard shots, but because there were lots of fireworks going off, she took little notice. By 11 p.m. he still had not returned. 'I did not sleep all night. I knew something had happened.' The next morning as she set off for the police station she saw her husband's bullet-riddled body just two hundred yards from their house. When she tried to register the case with the police, they asked for a bribe. She took her children into hiding, and spent three months trying to get help. Eventually she ended up at the National Security Directorate, where they warned her off. That was when my friend the director called me. We helped her get to Pakistan, and from there she eventually managed to get asylum in Canada.

Malalai Joya, the young woman MP who had dared to speak out about warlords at the *loya jirga* in December 2003, had been suspended from parliament in 2007 after comparing her fellow MPs to barnyard animals, and forced to live in hiding. She told a shocked audience in London in November 2008 that the situation for women in Afghanistan was worse than it had been under the Taliban. Karzai had even considered approving a law that would legalise rape within marriage and forbid women from going to the doctor or leaving their home without their husband's protection. Only international outrage had changed his mind.

So I decided to go back to Herat and find out exactly how Nadia had died, and what had happened to Leila and the other brave women writers, and all those hopes they had back in 2001.

* * *

Death of a Poet

The obvious place to start was the Literary Society. At first I thought it had gone, as I walked past it twice before realising it had been spruced up and extended, with bookshops on either side.

I had arranged to meet Nadia's elder brother Mohammad Shafi. A thin, intense man who looked too young to be professor of fine art at the university, he shook with emotion as he told me that he still could not believe he had lost his beloved sister. 'There was only two years' difference between us, and we were like best friends. Before the Taliban came we went to school together and she was so bright we were in the same year.'

He showed me a shrine to Nadia on the wall, and introduced me to the society's current president, Mohammad Mehsud Rajazi. He had been Nadia's professor for four years, and told me that her death had dealt them a huge blow. 'Nadia was a pioneer. She was the best living female poet in Herat, and she was expected to have a very successful career.' From the shelf he took down her first book, *Dark Flower*, published the year before she was killed. It had been reprinted three times and sold 3,000 copies, he told me, impressive for poetry anywhere, but incredible in a country where only a quarter of the population was literate.

He opened the book and read me a couple of lines.

> My wings are closed and I cannot fly.
> I am an Afghan woman and so must wail.

'Her poetry was full of feelings and emotions, especially about women,' he said. 'You couldn't read it and not know the writer was a woman. But she wasn't a feminist – she respected traditions.'

One person who hadn't liked this was her husband. 'He was jealous,' said Shafi. 'He used to say, "Why do people know you and not me? I'm the man. Why do invitations come in your name and not mine?"'

Nadia had started writing poetry at the age of ten, inspired by an incident at school. 'She had come home from school in tears,' recalled her brother. 'When my mother asked what was wrong, Nadia said, "It's not fair! My history teacher lowered my grade because I'm younger than the rest of the students, even though I answered all the questions correctly! And then he raised the grade of one of the lazy boys in the class – the one who is his nephew." I'd never seen Nadia so serious. My mother tried to cheer her up, and promised to go to the school the next day, but instead Nadia used the incident as the subject for her first poem. At school the next day, she read it aloud in front of the headmaster. He immediately recognised Nadia's talent, and also confronted her teacher about the grading. This was all the motivation Nadia needed to write more poems. From then on she read her poetry at all school ceremonies.'

She was fifteen when the Taliban took over Herat and closed the gates of the girls' schools. Nadia, however, did not stop writing poetry. 'She never stopped studying,' said Shafi. 'I remember her in the kitchen, cooking, always with an open book in front of her. My father bought her a small radio which she always kept nearby. During the dark times of the Taliban, while the rest of us secretly watched Indian movies as there was nothing else to do, Nadia would be listening to the BBC. She especially liked the midday and cultural programmes. And at midnight, when we were all sleeping, she would perform a private ceremony with paper and pen: composing her thoughts through Dari poetry.'

Nadia's life changed when she met Leila Razeqi and heard about the Golden Needle. Despite the huge risk, she began going several times a week to the secret classes at the house of Professor Rahiyab. Under his mentoring, her poetry gained colour and strength. Finally in 2001, when Nadia was twenty and Shafi in his final year at university, the Taliban were driven out. After I met her she took the entrance examination for the university, and was admitted as a gifted student to the Literature Department. 'I remember that time as being the happiest of Nadia's life,' said Shafi. 'It was as though she'd been handed the whole world.'

Not only was Nadia talented, she was kind-natured, always carrying sweets for the local children, and she was soon attracting marriage proposals. In her first year at university she caught the eye of Farid Ahmad Majid Neia, one of the department administrators. He sent her mother a bunch of flowers to announce his intentions. Nadia insisted that she never wanted to marry, as marriage would impede her development as a writer. More flowers arrived, but Nadia was resolute.

Just as she had been in school, Nadia was top of her class at university. 'I was very proud of her,' said Shafi, who by then had become a professor. 'She accumulated successes like university scholarships and fellowships and got to travel to Iran, where she met many poets and writers.'

Farid Neia was determined she would be his prize too. During Nadia's third year at university he began a second round of proposals, and this time he would not be deterred. 'Nadia tried to avoid an obligation to him, but when he sent her the Holy Koran she could not refuse,' said Shafi. 'I will never forget the day we gave them their answer: yes. Tears never left her eyes and Nadia kept repeating, "It's a pity. I will waste away for his sake. I do not deserve this."' After a six-month engagement they were married in a simple ceremony. Nadia appeared to be happy, but Shafi and her friends later realised it was only a pretence. One of her poems from that time is entitled 'False Smile'.

Like most Afghan brides she had to live with her mother-in-law, who told her just two days after the wedding, 'I will never love you.' According to Shafi, Nadia was never allowed to make decisions in the household and could do no right in her mother-in-law's eyes. She complained about Nadia's cooking and cleaning, and would beat her if she caught her writing poetry. Once again Nadia found herself writing in secret. 'Her mother-in-law was a selfish old woman,' said Shafi. 'She would tell Nadia, "This house is my property. Farid is the one who has brought you here and he's the one who will have to find a different place for you." But Farid refused to intercede on his wife's behalf.'

To start with, Nadia suffered in silence. Her father was old and frail, and she didn't want to distress him. But her friends saw how she had been stopped from attending Literary Society meetings by her husband, and she confided in her mother about the abuse she received from her mother-in-law. Her mother advised Nadia to be patient, telling her, 'Every marriage has problems at the beginning. They will pass soon. Your mother-in-law only has one son, you understand.'

Then in her last year of studies Nadia gave birth to a son. Bahram Saeed was a boisterous boy who was very much loved by his mother. But instead of improving things with her mother-in-law, the baby's birth seemed to inflame the situation. Furious that Nadia continued to attend university, his grandmother refused to look after the boy and never touched him, nor would she allow his father to pick him up. Nadia had to take her son to her own mother's house when she went to classes. When Shafi asked her about it, she would silence him by saying, 'It's not a problem.' 'She didn't want to worry the family,' he said.

The last time her brother saw her alive was on 5 November 2005, the third day of the annual Eid holiday. He called over to her house just after lunch. 'I rarely went to her house and she was very happy to see me. She was alone, waiting for her husband to arrive. Farid was going to take her to a relative's house and then to the house of a close friend who had recently lost her father.' It is a custom in Afghanistan when someone dies for people to gather at his or her house on the third day of Eid following the death. Nadia served Shafi some cake she had made for the Eid celebration. 'It was delicious,' he said. 'We talked for an hour about many things, including my own marriage – I was single and she had various friends in mind. She showed me their pictures from her album. Then we watched the film of her own wedding so she could point them out.'

At that time Bahram Saeed was five months old, and had just learned to sit up. He reached for Shafi as he was leaving. Shafi rode off on his motorbike back to his parents' house, and passed Farid, who was heading home.

At five past midnight, when everyone was asleep, the phone rang. Someone was calling from the hospital's emergency room: 'Do you know Nadia? She has died. Please come to the hospital as soon as possible.'

'It was the bitterest news we had ever received,' said Shafi. 'No one could believe it. That night was a hundred times darker than other nights. My brother, father and I rushed to the hospital. We were crying. We saw Nadia lying dead on a bed in the emergency room. On the right side of her face there was a big black bruise – the doctors told us she had been hit by something with great force.' Farid was crying and shouting. 'When we asked him how Nadia had died, he said, "We argued while on the way to Nadia's friend's house and, finally, I slapped her."'

By the next day, it seemed that everyone in Herat had heard the terrible news. 'People came to our house in tears, offering their condolences – there were university professors, students, prominent people in the arts, scholars, authors, journalists, relatives and friends.'

Farid was arrested, but insisted that Nadia had committed suicide by drinking poison. However, the medical report stated that she had been killed by a heavy blow. Although the fight had taken place at 7.30 p.m., Farid had only taken her to hospital after 11 p.m., more than three and a half hours later. The rickshaw driver said that when he loaded Nadia on the back to take her to hospital she was already dead.

'If he didn't murder Nadia and didn't want her to die, why didn't he take her to hospital before?' asked Shafi.

Afghanistan's legal system is notoriously slow and corrupt, but the publicity attracted by the case forced the courts to take action, and Farid was convicted of murder. However, according to Shafi, his father was put under great pressure. 'Tribal elders kept coming to our house, asking for forgiveness and threatening him.' Finally, after five months he relented. 'We consulted with prosecutors as to what would happen, and they said even if you forgive him he will get five years' jail, so we thought, that's OK. Unfortunately because of the corruption of our legal system he was released after one month. My father was so angry he died.' Farid returned to his old job at the university, and retained custody of his son. When I contacted him he refused to speak to me.

Nadia's family moved home, because their old place held so many memories. Shafi took me for dinner one day at the new apartment he shared with his mother Nasrin, his sister and his new wife.

There were pictures of Nadia everywhere. Nasrin's eyes filled with tears as she showed them to me. 'I will never forgive myself for encouraging the match,' she said. 'If he didn't kill her directly he killed her indirectly. He was the cause of her death. He was a very restricted man with a lot of limitations. My daughter was a poet, she wanted to be famous, to work among people, but he didn't want that.'

Nadia's fellow writers from the Golden Needle told me they had no doubt that their friend was murdered because of her poems. 'I think he killed her on purpose,' said Leila Razeqi. 'The husband didn't like her writing poetry or their subject. He never let her attend our meetings. When you look at her poems and writing after her wedding you can see the hidden sorrow and grief in her words.'

Leila had invited me to her house, which was large and comfortable, with children's bicycles scattered about the yard. Although friendly, she was nervous about a foreigner being seen entering the home, and shepherded me quickly inside and into a large drawing room cluttered with sofas and glass tables laden with dishes of sultanas, salted pistachio nuts and sesame-seed brittle. Smartly dressed in a black jacket and long black skirt with a flowery blue scarf tied tightly under her chin Iranian-style, she had married well, to a man who worked for a Dutch aid agency, and had three lovely small daughters who kept popping their heads through the door and giggling at the strange sight of a foreigner. Yet her face was sad, and she looked far older than thirty-six. I would not have recognised her as the bubbly long-haired girl I had met seven years before, full of plans and hopes for the future.

As if reading my mind, she referred to that meeting. 'We were very excited at the time of the end of the Taliban,' she said.

'Have things been as you expected?' I asked.

She shook her head vehemently. 'No, not at all. At that time we really wanted to serve our people. I dreamed of being a university professor, of our group becoming a cultural association for the city's women. Unfortunately everything went wrong. Nadia was killed … Nadia had great spirit and forgave everything, but we could see she was facing problems. She complained a lot about her mother-in-law, and when she went to university she didn't dare leave her child with the grandmother. But she was trapped.'

Nadia's few poems from that time talk of her as 'a bird without wings', just as she had been under the Taliban. 'I remain, but remain a broken pen,' ends one.

'If I was to say the situation of women is better that would be untrue,' said Leila. 'The conservative mindset continues, and is not going away with a wave of a magic wand. Women are not given proper rights. Only if she has relatives in power can she get to a higher position, otherwise she'll just be like me. I'm only a teacher; I didn't want to be an ordinary teacher.'

'Are you still writing?' I asked.

She looked down at her lap. 'Unfortunately no, none of us are. I teach half the day then spend the rest looking after the house and children.' She could see my surprise. 'You know it was very bad under the Taliban, and I would be crying, "Why can't we study?" I was lucky that my father was very high-minded and believed women should be educated. What we did was a great risk. Yet somehow it gave us strength. The most tragic story of women in Afghanistan was Nadia's death. She was the most talented of all of us. Since then everything is broken and we're no longer a collective. I believe strongly her husband should be in jail. If someone kills he should be killed. If the Taliban were here now they would have punished him, and maybe that would be better.'

Leila's own mother-in-law was due back, and she was clearly anxious for me to leave. I felt sorry that I had awoken difficult memories. In my bag I had brought some beautiful notebooks and pens for her, but I suddenly felt it would be a mistake to bring them out. Before I left she hugged me. 'You are very lucky,' she whispered. 'I wish I could move about like you. Maybe one day my daughters will ...'

* * *

Nadia's death wasn't the only reason the group broke up. Another of the six, Homeira Naderi, got married and moved to Iran. But there had been a further tragedy. Leila had told me some other shocking news. Maria Tanha, who I had met with her on that very first day, was also dead. Leila told me she had been in a car accident with her boyfriend, but did not seem to want to say more.

I discovered why when I went to visit Khaleda Khorsand, then twenty-seven, who had been the youngest of the Golden Needle women. I remembered her as a great fan of Virginia Woolf, smuggling her books in from Iran at great risk. Originally from Kabul, her family had moved to Herat a year after the Taliban took power, and when she heard about the Golden Needle she jumped at the chance. She was extremely prolific, and had written sixty stories. 'It was very dangerous but I wanted to feel alive,' she told me. 'Fear was with us all the time as the Taliban were always watching the movement of women and we heard stories of private schools being found and the girls being whipped with cables.'

Khaleda had married a doctor, and was living in a small but immaculate apartment with twin five-year-old daughters whose giant teddy bear took pride of place on the red-and-black leather furniture. Everything looked so perfect I almost had a sense that she was playing house. She poured me green tea and placed glass bowls of shiny wrapped toffees in front of me, then sat down and told me about Maria.

'Maria was not married, and had gone secretly for a picnic with a boyfriend. People say she was driving, so they attacked the car and turned it over and she was hurt. Her brother-in-law was a dentist and worried about his reputation, so did not want her to be taken to hospital because of the shame it would bring on the family. So they kept her at home and then she died. If they'd taken her to hospital maybe she would have survived.

'You know, the Taliban didn't come from nowhere,' she explained. 'They have roots among traditional people. Now they have gone, but their culture hasn't, and is still infecting minds of people. Mullahs are still dominating everything. Commanders, warlords, mullahs, they are all the same.'

Death of a Poet

I was happy to see the room was lined with well-stocked book-shelves and a laptop was open on the table, so I asked about her own writing. She shook her head. 'When the Taliban left it was a wonderful feeling but those long years of Taliban put a strange feeling in our mind, a bitterness that we had wasted many years. When journalists like you came to the Literary Society we didn't know how to express what we felt. Afterwards most of us started going to the literature faculty like Nadia. But it wasn't like we imagined. We were segregated from the boys and couldn't even swap books with them. The first Governor of Herat, Ismael Khan, was a narrow dark-minded man who didn't accept freedom for women. Once I was walking with my fiancé and we were stopped six times by police.'

Khaleda was in her third year at the literature faculty and work-ing part-time for a human rights network, but even though her husband Nasir Ahmed was an educated man, she admitted it had been a long struggle getting him to allow her to work. It was an arranged marriage. The first time they met was on the day of their engagement. 'He was chosen by my parents, but I thought as an educated man he would be liberated. In fact he is like other men and for the first years of our marriage I spent all my energies convincing him these principles are part of my life. Now he lets me go out but it's difficult for a Herati man. I think all the changes for women in Afghanistan are just on the surface. We might have a great number of women in parliament and rights in constitution, but this is useless when most people think women should only be allowed out to bazaar to buy food for their family. So for example there is no law to say we must wear burqas but we do so we don't get insults from people. I'm very pessimistic.'

When I asked about Nadia, tears spilled from her eyes. 'Nadia's death was a very sad event for me,' she said. 'I can never forget her, we shared a lot. Her death was not that of an ordinary woman, she was an exceptional woman who should have been a role model for Afghan women.'

*　　*　　*

Round the corner from the Literary Society was a place I had been putting off visiting, a place where Afghan women end up when they are desperate to escape an abusive marriage like Nadia's, yet have no words to express their despair.

The Herat Burns Unit is one of the most shocking places on earth. I had been there once before, when the patients were crammed together in a dirty annexe at the end of a corridor, swarming with flies. Now it was in a new white-tiled building built by a French aid agency which was modern and sterile, and I was given plastic slips to go over my shoes. Bright sunshine streamed through the wards, but there was no hiding the smell of charred flesh and the cries of pain, and the fact that this was where women ended up when hope ran out.

The first room I entered had four beds, each bearing a young woman wrapped in bandages like a mummy. I steeled myself as the nurse lifted the sheets, but nothing could have prepared me for what looked like raw pink meat bubbling up from their pelvises to their necks and under their arms. I could hardly bear to look as the nurse pulled away a dressing on one and I saw unspeakable agony in the girl's eyes.

All of them were young wives who had set themselves alight in suicide attempts. One said hers was an accident, but the nurse told me, 'They all say that.' Next to her was Anar Gul, a girl of just twenty whose name meant 'Pomegranate Blossom' and whose beautiful face no longer seemed to belong to the badly disfigured body. By her side her mother Shirin sat hunched and weeping silently. Anar told me that her family was very poor, and she never went to school. Her father died when she was a baby, leaving only a little patch of land with no water where nothing would grow. Her mother earned a few afghanis cleaning and washing clothes, which just about fed them, but when it came to the time of her brother wanting to marry there was no money to buy a bride.

Anar's beauty had attracted some attention, and when she was fifteen her brother entered a deal. In exchange for the girl he wanted as his bride, Anar would go to Iran to be married to the girl's brother, Ghulam Sabir. 'We had never met, but they told us he was a good man with sheep and goats,' said Anar. 'I didn't hope for much. I just thought I may have a reasonable life, have a couple of children and look after them and my husband.'

Even those modest hopes were dashed. 'From the beginning he would beat me and hit me on the face with his big ring. He was very bad-tempered, criticising everything – my cooking, my clothes, my relatives coming.' He was angry too that after three years she had given birth to two daughters, but not a son. Anar became increasingly desperate. 'I never told my family what was happening. I'd been married for four years and one day I just couldn't stand it any more. He'd been beating me for a week and I didn't know what I was doing. In our tradition when a girl is married she should only leave as a dead body. So I poured fuel on my clothes and lit the match.'

Anar's cousin happened to be visiting the village, and when he heard he took her in his car to hospital. By then more than 45 per cent of her body was deeply burned. She had already had three skin grafts in the four months she had been in hospital, and would be disfigured for life.

Dr Mohammed Aref Jalali, the hospital administrator, told me, 'She will survive, but what then?'

Her husband had promised not to beat her again, but Dr Jalali looked sceptical. Anar said she had no alternative but to go back to him. 'I didn't want to survive,' she said. 'When I burned myself I wanted to die.'

Sadly, such stories are common. 'There is no happiness in this country,' the words of Isabella, a nurse at the Emergency Hospital in Kabul, came into my head. According to Dr Soraya Zobhrang, Director of Women's Rights for the Afghan Independent Human Rights Commission, 60 per cent of marriages were forced marriages. Self-immolation of women occurs across Afghanistan, yet its incidence is highest in Herat. Some attribute this to the city's history as a cultural centre clashing with the social conservatism that has been brought in from the villages; others that it is simply more reported.

Dr Jalali told me his hospital had treated eighty-one cases over the last year, almost all women aged thirteen to twenty-five. Of these, fifty-nine had died. Since the new sterile unit had opened in 2007 there were fewer secondary infections, and more women were surviving. But Dr Jalali's uncertainty about what would happen to the survivors hung like a question mark in the air.

It would be wrong to say that things were as bad for women as during the Taliban, but those who tried to break through traditional barriers clearly faced tremendous challenges that we Westerners had not begun to imagine.

One day in Herat I met a twenty-seven-year-old woman who was literally risking her life to make jam. Her name, appropriately, was Mariam Jami, and she asked me to meet her at the Istiqlal Hotel. When I arrived there were so many police gathered outside, I assumed there must be a Minister visiting. In fact they were guarding a Women's Day exhibition of arts and crafts. 'Lots of people don't like these women displaying themselves,' explained one of the police.

Inside, Mrs Jami proudly showed me her stand of jams, pickles and tomato paste, all neatly labelled 'Made by Women of Herat'. She told me she had begun making jam five years earlier in her village in Gozara district, fifteen miles from Herat, using local fruit and vegetables. It was so successful she soon had twenty women working for her. 'Everyone seemed to like it and I realised I could produce much more if I could get a loan for machinery, so I went to USAID, but they said you don't have any organisation.'

Then she saw adverts for entrepreneurs to come forward to compete for investment in an Afghan version of *Dragons' Den* on Tolo TV, the country's biggest private television channel. 'I thought, why not?' she laughs. Knowing local people would not approve of a woman going on television, she wore full *hijab* and dark glasses as she made her pitch. She was so impressive that she came second, winning $14,000 – an enormous amount in a country where police are paid less than $100 a month.

'As I handed over the cheque, I thought we are really changing this woman's life,' said David Elliott from USAID, which was partly sponsoring the show. 'I just didn't realise how.'

By the time Mrs Jami got back to her village, men had attacked her house and beaten up her brother and husband. They had been sent by local commander Ghulam Akbari, who had been working as Minister of Public Works in the Herat government but had left in 2008 and joined forces with the Taliban. 'They threatened me not to go on TV again and demanded part of the prize money,' she said. 'They told me if we find out you're doing any work with foreign NGOs we will kill you.'

Mrs Jami was not to be deterred. She wrote Akbari a letter saying: 'You claim you're fighting for the country but you're destroying the country and killing people while I'm trying to build the agriculture of my country, for my village.'

Brave as she was, she realised her family could not stay in the village, so she fled to the city where she had rented a house, using one of the rooms for jam-making. She took me to see. Inside, women in white aprons and caps giggled as they showed me the giant metal vat bubbling with carrot jam. Mrs Jami had twenty women working for her, working alternate weeks so she could provide more employment. She still bought her fruits and vegetables from her home village, even though she had not been able to go back since the Afghan *Dragons' Den*.

'I'm determined. I'm not scared,' she says. 'I don't regret what I've done. I'm proud of being on TV. I want to sell my jams all over Afghanistan, maybe even the world!'

If Herati men objected to a woman running a jam company, I could only begin to imagine the risks being taken by the woman who was the city's Chief Prosecutor.

Maria Bashir, a thirty-eight-year-old mother of three, was the first female prosecutor in all of Afghanistan. I went to see her in her office, which was being kept warm by a huge old-fashioned stove with a clunking pipe. On her desk was a letter that had just arrived, warning: 'Suicide bombers have come to Herat and you are the target.'

She had been appointed in 2006, and was considered such a target that the US Justice Department paid for six armed bodyguards. Even so, her house had been set on fire and then bombed, killing one bodyguard. For their own safety her eldest child had been sent abroad, and the other two had to be home-schooled. 'We have women who are working, and we need to persuade others to come forward,' she said. 'It shouldn't be just a few symbolic women, but the security situation is making it very difficult. Security for women is really, really bad and has worsened in the last two and a half years, and some like me have to risk their lives.'

Barely a day went by for her without death threats. She reeled off her list of enemies: 'They might be insurgents, might also be people who we've prosecuted – killers, thieves, kidnappers ... The problem is we have good written laws, but they are not implemented. I'm trying to change that. If a man beats his wife and she has a hospital report I will sentence that man to jail. People don't like that.' Like Mrs Jami, she insisted that she won't give in. 'From childhood I always felt I could do anything. But if I had known the problem this would cause my children maybe I wouldn't have taken the job.'

Maria Bashir was not yet prosecutor when the Nadia Anjuman case came up, and she was furious that the husband had been released. 'What kind of an example does that give? It undermines all we're trying to do.'

Back in Kabul I went to visit the woman who had described the situation as worse than under the Taliban. Perhaps Afghanistan's bravest woman of all, certainly its most outspoken, twenty-nine-year-old Malalai Joya was not easy to find. She received so many death threats that she moved house every few days.

She gave me instructions to drive to a particular address. There a white-bearded man in a long woollen cloak appeared and gave me directions to another spot down a narrow, muddy lane. He then reappeared magically, and led me to a corrugated iron door. Inside, five guards wielding AK47s stood in front of a narrow staircase. At the top I passed three more guards, then entered a room where

Joya was lounging on colourful floor cushions in front of a wood-burner, holding court to a few women. They were the owners of the house – Joya had not received any salary since being expelled from parliament two years earlier, and relied on the kindness of supporters.

'Most of those MPs are warlords, drug lords and criminals,' she said. It was comments like this that had led to her being labelled a 'prostitute' and an 'infidel' by her fellow MPs, some of whom had physically attacked her. She was expelled after giving a TV interview in which she said parliament was 'worse than a stable', going on to add that 'A stable is better, for there you have a donkey that carries a load and a cow that provides milk.'

Once we got onto the subject of women, Joya's words came in an almost non-stop torrent of outrage. She showed me a densely written A4 notebook in which she had catalogued one shocking case after another, including that of Nadia Anjuman. There was the MP who killed two small children by putting stones in their pockets and drowning them; Anisa, a twelve-year-old girl gang-raped by five men in Sarpul province; Bashira, fourteen, gang-raped in 2008 by three men in the same province, one of them the son of a local MP; fourteen-year-old Mariam, whose parents cut her baby out of her stomach after she was gang-raped … On and on she went, till I pleaded with her to stop.

None of these cases ever came to court, either because the families were ashamed or because they were threatened by local authorities. But there was one that did, with the perpetrators being successfully prosecuted – that of a woman known as Sara, gang-raped in 2005 by a local commander and his men in Samargan. After two years of struggle she and her family succeeded in getting three of the men convicted. To Sara's horror, within a year the men had reappeared in the village. 'Look!' said Joya. She produced a photocopy of a presidential pardon signed by Karzai. 'Doesn't this show everything? After 9/11 the main reason the US occupied Afghanistan was in the name of women's rights. Now we're as far from those values as 2001.'

*　*　*

On my last day in Herat I went to visit Nadia Anjuman's grave. It was a Friday, the Islamic holiday, and many families were wandering on the stony hillside overlooking the city which is dotted with the graves of its most illustrious citizens. In the summer it was a popular picnic spot, perhaps because after thirty years of war the city had seen so much tragedy that death was taken as a matter of course.

That morning a chill wind was blowing. It was easy to find Nadia's grave, for it seemed to have become a shrine for local women, and every so often one would stop and genuflect in front of it, or lay a small stone. The flowery Persian engraving describes Nadia as a poet who risked her life to keep writing under the Taliban. It doesn't say what happened then.

'What happened to Nadia should make the world bow its head in shame,' said her friend Leila Razeqi. 'Your Prime Ministers and Presidents promised freedom to us Afghan women. That someone like Nadia is under the soil and her husband walks free should make you ask what is really going on here.'

21

Meeting Colonel Imam

Rawalpindi, June 2009

I WAS DEPRESSED by my war. Everything I covered in Afghanistan and Pakistan seemed to be going in the wrong direction. Wars were supposed to have definitive ends and have identifiable enemies, like the twentieth-century wars I'd grown up hearing about. Instead we now seemed to be locked in some kind of forever war. And it was becoming harder to report them. Places I had travelled to freely in both countries had become no-go areas. Afghanistan was more violent; Pakistan more anti-Western. Peshawar, which had been such a friendly place to live in my early twenties, had grown so hostile I felt as if I was the only Westerner there. Women I'd written about were being killed. Hotels I'd stayed at were being bombed. Friends had been taken hostage. Late-night discussions with fellow journalists had become macabre – instead of the old gossip of who was sleeping with whom, we talked about whether we'd prefer to be killed by suicide bomb or a knife at our throats. I started actually reading the fire instructions in hotel rooms and checking out the exits everywhere I went. An old Taliban contact on the Quetta *shura* offered me an interview and I had to decline because we couldn't find a way to meet safely. It was becoming impossible to do the job in the way I always had. My heart sank when I had to give a 'proof of life' question and answer to my newsdesk before I went on assignment. Even the sunlight in Kabul seemed brittle.

Then one day an email pinged into my inbox informing me that our Washington correspondent was coming back to London. Would I be interested in the job? I was about to press the delete button. My whole career had been covering developing countries. I couldn't imagine not regularly jumping on planes to Afghanistan or Pakistan. Then my finger hovered. America had just elected Barack Obama, its first black President. Like so many people I had been fascinated by the campaign which propelled the little-known Senator from Illinois to the most powerful office on earth, and would never forget the excitement of election night, which I had spent with friends at a party in London organised by the Black Caucus of MPs. Obama had promised to change America's relationship with the world, to end the wars and close Guantánamo. People were talking of his as a transformational presidency. Most of the decisions that affected the places I covered were made in Washington, and much of the time I found them baffling. If I lived there and covered American politics, maybe, just maybe, I would understand.

I asked for advice from my friend James, who as spokesman for NATO had to defend its Afghan policy, which meant we often ended up on panels together taking opposite positions then agreeing in the pub afterwards. 'Do it!' he said. 'How long will you be there? Three, four years? Take my word for it, Afghanistan and Pakistan will still be a train wreck when you come back.'

Before I moved, there was one person I wanted to see.

'Look for the man who looks like a Taliban,' he had said on the phone. I sat in the coffee shop sipping a cappuccino and toying nervously with a slice of chocolate cake that had looked better in the display cabinet, and surveyed the room.

There were plenty of men with beards, but none who quite looked Taliban. A Muzak version of the theme from *Love Story* was being piped over the sound system. The Front Page Café in the Pearl Continental Hotel, Rawalpindi, was an odd choice of venue. I guessed he'd chosen it because of the name or the location, just down the road from the headquarters of Pakistan's army, which had ruled the country for more than half its existence. At the entrance a towering Pathan in scarlet uniform with golden epaulettes slid my bag through an x-ray machine to check for weapons, and as I walked through the lobby several heads popped up over newspapers as if jerked to attention by some invisible puppetmaster. I knew that if I came back four hours later they would still be reading the same papers – Pakistan's hotels were filled with these men in grey *shalwar kamiz* who spied for one or more of the country's intelligence services.

Five minutes turned to half an hour, one coffee became two, and fear turned to disappointment as I tried not to keep looking at my watch. I'd been trying to meet this man for twenty years. Now he had finally agreed, it seemed he was not going to turn up.

The man I was waiting for was Colonel Imam – at least, that was his *nom de guerre*. His real name was Amir Sultan Tarar, and his real rank Brigadier General, and he was a legendary figure among Afghans, revered by some, hated by others.

When I lived in Peshawar in the 1980s he had run the ISI training programme for the Afghan resistance fighting the Soviet Union which had invaded their country. Ninety-five thousand Afghans had been through his camps, including warlords like Gulbuddin Hekmatyar and Jalaluddin Haqqani, and Taliban leader Mullah Omar, and he called them all 'my boys'. In those days we called them 'freedom fighters'. When Osama bin Laden arrived in Peshawar in 1984 and began funding a wave of Arabs to join the fight, Colonel Imam welcomed them even though many were renegades in their own countries.

In those days my Afghan friends spoke of Colonel Imam in hushed tones. The CIA support to the Afghan mujaheddin was the biggest covert programme in history, yet also the one over which the Agency had least control, as all distribution of arms and funds went through ISI. Colonel Imam literally determined the fate of Afghan commanders by deciding who got what. After the Russians were driven out the Americans had given him five gallantry awards. The White House presented him with a piece of the Berlin Wall with a bronze plaque inscribed 'To the one who dealt the first blow' like the one General Gul had received.

After 9/11, however, he was on the other side. Or the West was on the other side, depending on which way you looked at it. Although by 1990 the Americans had cut off all their funding to the Afghans, Imam continued working with his boys even as they started fighting against each other.

It is not entirely true to say I had never met him. He had been involved in the planning for the battle for Jalalabad in 1989, the disastrous attempt by the mujaheddin to capture a city from the communist government after the departure of the Russians. Trapped between the rockets of the mujaheddin coming into the city and the bombs of the Afghan air force on the roads around, some 10,000 civilians were killed in the single worst week of the entire war. ISI had closed the border, and I was one of the only reporters to get to the front line to see what was happening. With bodies dropping all around us, one of the Afghan fighters I was with had suddenly stiffened and pointed out Colonel Imam directing operations. The group's commander, Rahim Wardak, had confronted him angrily, demanding, 'How dare you who have never won a war give orders to us who have never lost one?'

When the Taliban emerged as a new force in southern Afghanistan promising to restore law and order and curb the warlords who were making life a misery for millions of Afghans, Colonel Imam quickly spotted their potential and helped organise them. After they had launched their first offensive at Spin Boldak in April 1994, a cable from the US Embassy in Islamabad to Washington reported that the attack 'was preceded by artillery shelling of the base from Pakistan Frontier Corps positions' inside Pakistan. It also noted: 'coordination was provided by Pakistani officers on the scene'.[1]

They travelled in gleaming new Toyota pick-ups purchased by the Saudis and shipped to Karachi then fitted with machine guns, rocket launchers and anti-aircraft guns. The mobility these provided would be critical to Taliban success.

Imam and another ISI major had been on board a thirty-truck convoy with military escort sent by Pakistan from Quetta in November 1994, ostensibly to deliver foreign aid to Herat. Its real objective, however, was to capture Kandahar and install Mullah Omar in power. Not far across the border their way was blocked by a mujaheddin commander, Mansour Achakzai, and his militia, who were notorious for raping and abducting people. Achakzai pulled at Imam's beard and demanded, 'Why have you come to our country without our permission?' Then he impounded the convoy.

Taking on ISI was an unwise move. When they heard what had happened the Taliban mobilised fighters, helped by Pakistani commandos in plain clothes, and began battling for the city. The then Governor, Gul Agha, who had often dealt with Imam during the jihad, left for Pakistan. The local military commander Mullah Naqib also chose not to resist. Achakzai was captured and his body dangled from the gun of a tank in front of Kandahar airport as a warning. After capturing Kandahar, the Taliban swept north. An intercepted cable from Imam boasted, 'My boys and I are riding into Mazar-i-Sharif.'

Yet to the outside world Pakistan insisted it was not involved. On a visit to Washington in February 1996, Foreign Minister Assef Ali met the Deputy Secretary of State Strobe Talbott and 'categorically denied' that Pakistan was giving assistance to the Taliban. ISI Director General Nasim Rana insisted 'not one bullet' had been provided to them.

Just over six months later, in September 1996, with Kabul under siege from the Taliban, ISI launched a major offensive into Afghanistan. An armoured column headed up the Grand Trunk Road from Peshawar, captured Jalalabad and closed in on Kabul. 'The two-week massive well-coordinated armor, air and infantry attack across the Durand Line could not have been planned and executed by Taliban's barefoot mullahs,' said Peter Tomsen, the American diplomat who was Ambassador to the Afghan resistance from 1989 to 1992.

The mujaheddin government crumbled under the attack. On 26 September Ahmat Shah Massoud, who was its Defence Minister, issued orders to evacuate to Panjshir. Before leaving he went to the French Embassy, which adjoins the UN compound where Mohammad Najibullah had been living since being deposed as

President. The two old enemies met at a door at the end of the Embassy garden, and Massoud offered to fly his former nemesis to safety. Najibullah refused, and so sealed his fate.

In 1997 Pakistan became one of only three countries to recognise the Taliban, followed by Saudi Arabia and UAE. According to Tomsen: 'ISI officers were stationed in every ministry. In the provinces ISI established about eight bases manned by active-duty and retired ISI colonels and brigadiers.' Major militant groups linked to ISI – Lashkar-e-Toiba, Jaish-e-Mohammad and Harkat-ul-Mujaheddin – all ran training camps inside Afghanistan.

At the time of 9/11 Imam was officially Pakistan's consul-general in Herat. He told me he was outraged when he heard that President Musharraf, faced with the threat of US retribution, had agreed to switch sides. He refused orders to leave Afghanistan and come home. Finally Musharraf sent him a message demanding, 'What are you doing?' I arrived in Herat just after the Taliban fell in November 2001, and was told he had driven out with them.

When Imam got back to Pakistan he warned Musharraf he was making a mistake siding with the Americans: 'I told him I spent eighteen years with these people, and they cannot be defeated.' He also went to see Mullah Zaeef, the Taliban Ambassador in Islamabad. Tears ran down Imam's face as he told Zaeef, 'Almighty Allah might have decided what is to take place in Afghanistan but Pakistan is to blame. How much cruelty it has done to its neighbour! And how much more will come.'[2]

Whether officially or otherwise, Imam became part of a double game that Pakistan was playing with the West. According to UN reports, Colonel Imam and other ISI colleagues had been spotted directing operations inside the southern Afghan provinces of Uruzgan and Helmand. 'Rogue elements' was how Musharraf shrugged them off when confronted by evidence. Others said they were not rogue at all but working for S Sector of ISI, whose main aim was to drive the Americans out of Afghanistan. Later Richard Armitage, the former US Assistant Secretary of State, would tell me Imam had even been in Marja, a small town in Helmand, in 2010, just before Western forces launched a massive operation to capture it from the Taliban. 'He warned me we'd fail,' he said.

It seemed to me that if anyone knew what role Pakistan was really playing, it was Imam. Ever since he'd left Herat I had been trying to meet him. I had gone to apartments where curtains jerked closed as I rang the bell, dialled endless mobile numbers only for male voices at the other end to claim not to know him, and sent messages through intermediaries.

Finally, after a series of phone conversations, he had suddenly agreed to meet. I'd be lying if I didn't admit I was nervous. ISI regularly 'disappeared' people. Pakistan had become one of the most dangerous places in the world to be a journalist. I couldn't help fearing it was a set-up. The fact that the meeting was in a public place was no reassurance: when ISI picked me up in Quetta it was from my room in a four-star hotel packed with the world's media. Frightening as war zones like Iraq and Afghanistan could be, in my mind Pakistan was worse, as you didn't know who was the enemy – it might be the state itself.

I had just decided he wasn't coming when a shadow loomed over my table. 'Lamb to the slaughter,' boomed a voice. Two men stood there, one of whom did indeed look like a Taliban. Dressed in a white *shalwar kamiz*, Colonel Imam was tall and lanky, with a long white beard and deep-set brown eyes, and clacking a string of wooden worry beads. I knew he was sixty-five, but he looked younger. I had always thought he was a Pathan, and he looked like one, but on the phone he had told me he came from central Punjab. He introduced his friend as Brigadier Pervez, which may or may not have been his name, and told me they both worked on Afghanistan.

They sat down and ordered black tea and cold water. 'Good enough,' said Colonel Imam, an expression which was to punctuate the next couple of hours of conversation. Whenever he wanted to express exasperation he said 'My foot,' part of a quaint old-fashioned English that seemed to belong on the pages of Kipling but still appeared in some Pakistani newspapers, where buses 'turned turtle', 'miscreants escaped under cover of darkness' and journalists referred to themselves as 'this scribe'.

'What I am about to tell you has not come in any newspaper or book,' he began. 'This great tragedy all goes back more than thirty years.'

Imam told me that as a boy growing up he had dreamed of going to America, and was overjoyed when as a young army major in 1974 he had been selected to go for officer training to Fort Bragg in North Carolina, where the US trains its special forces. 'One of our instructors explained this course is to teach people to topple down a legal government,' he said. 'I got very interested and attained the leading position.'

Back in Pakistan he was posted to Peshawar as commandant of the parachute school, which at that time was the country's only special forces operation. 'When I got there I picked up some gossip in the teashops that the Russians were coming into Afghanistan with lots of money and supporting the two communist parties, Khalq [the masses] and Parcham [banner]. Sardar Daud, one of the leading politicians, had recently toppled his brother-in-law, King Zahir Shah, and the Russians saw an opportunity. Naturally people were very perturbed in Peshawar. We also heard there was some agitation among the students in Kabul, and that when it became violent Daud came with an iron hand and started arresting university students and professors. They arrested Professor Abdul Rasul Sayyaf from the Islamic law faculty, and another professor, Burhanuddin Rabbani, went underground with a large number of students and began creeping towards Pakistan. This was very scary, as the government of Pakistan and the government of Afghanistan have not enjoyed good relations since our creation in 1947 – Afghanistan was the first government in the entire world not to recognise Pakistan, and we knew they had designs on our territory. But when those Afghans came to Peshawar, as Pashtuns are very good at extending hospitality, they were accommodated.'

Pakistan's Prime Minister at that time was Zulfikar Ali Bhutto, the country's first democratically elected leader. His relations with the US were strained because of his open determination to build the first Islamic bomb. 'We will eat grass to have the atom bomb,' he had pledged after India carried out nuclear tests in 1974. His words prompted a warning from US Secretary of State Henry Kissinger, who visited Islamabad in 1976 with the message 'We will make a horrible example of you.'

Just like the British long before, Bhutto worried about Russian expansionism creeping south. So he asked Brigadier Nasirullah Babar, who was in Peshawar heading the paramilitary forces, to get hold of the Afghan rebels and organise them.

'At that time there were just thirty or thirty-five students, but they were very brilliant and bright,' said Imam. 'They told Babar, we need training to face the communist forces in Kabul – what they needed was guerrilla warfare. The army special forces said there is a major in Peshawar who recently trained in America and he could do the job. That's how I got sucked in. It's very difficult to organise Afghans – something like counting frogs in a muddy pond', he huffed. 'It took months but finally we made a political party, Jamaat-e-Islami [Islamic Society], with Professor Rabbani as head and Yunus Khalis, another Islamic scholar, as deputy. That was the first foundation of an anti-Russia movement.'

At this point Brigadier Pervez stepped in. 'You have read in your British history how the Russians were always creeping towards the south and east towards your Indian empire, and only British influence in Afghanistan stopped them, and the line of your Mr Durand. We knew their real plan was to push through Baluchistan towards the Arabian Sea; their target was the Persian Gulf oil. Afghanistan itself doesn't have any economic attraction, it's only a foothold.' He almost spat the last words. 'So anyone running Pakistan, whether Bhutto or an Islamist, would have done the same, just like you British had in the nineteenth century. It wasn't about Islam, it was about stopping Russians, and we didn't get any help. Americans and Europeans had written off Afghanistan – to them Pakistan was the buffer between the free world and the communist world.'

Imam picked up the narrative. 'From 1975 to 1977 it was silent training. It was very difficult – maybe thirteen or fifteen men would come from Afghanistan for a month or two and we'd run a camp then they would go back. Then they would train others.

They were very smart. The naughtiest student was Hekmatyar. As far as fighting [Ahmat Shah] Massoud was the best but he could not organise, he failed in politics. Another good fighter was Khalis. Although he had a small party his people were very dedicated, totally born to taking out Russians. We used to give them old World War II rifles, .303 single-barrel guns. Then they would go to the tribal areas and buy more. Whatever we had in our old arsenals we gave them and they made improvised Molotov cocktails to hit Russian tanks.'

The programme came to a halt in July 1977 when General Zia-ul-Haq seized power in a coup, imprisoning Zulfikar Ali Bhutto. The following year there were also dramatic changes across the border. Afghan President Daud was killed in spring 1978 along with many of his family, and replaced by the more hardline communist government of Nur Mohammad Taraki, who began rounding up and killing thousands of intellectuals and Islamists. Hundreds of thousands more Afghans fled into Pakistan, many of whom wanted to fight the communists. 'General Zia decided they were fellow brother Muslims and we should support them,' said Imam. 'He heard there had been some training, so he gathered all of us and said, OK, you start up again.'

There seemed little hope of outside support. As leader of a nation traumatised by Vietnam and Watergate, US President Jimmy Carter had launched a purge of the CIA aimed at ending dirty tricks and secret wars and had cut off all economic and military aid to Pakistan in response to the coup. 'The Americans were cautioning us not to interfere,' said Brigadier Pervez. 'The Carter administration took it for granted that Afghanistan was gone.'

In December 1979 everything changed when the Russians sent their army into Afghanistan, turning the country into a Cold War battleground. The US began secretly sending weapons to the mujaheddin. Imam and his team really got going when a year later Ronald Reagan was elected and millions became billions. 'When Reagan came things really changed,' said Imam. 'Although he was a film star he had a very good idea. William Casey, the CIA chief, came and said, "We'll give you anything you want, we want the

Russians to be defeated."' Zia saw his chance. 'Our President made one condition,' said Imam. 'He said, "OK, but you Americans won't interfere in any of our conduct, our operations, our training." Everything was to go through us in ISI. The CIA agreed, they were very happy. They were just monitoring on the basis of the information we gave them. It was marvellous conduct and in ten years the Soviet Union was defeated and then ceased to exist. Total cost to the Americans – $5 billion and no American lives. Now the Americans have been bogged down in Afghanistan eight years, lost more than a thousand lives, and what is the expenditure? $100 billion per year! My foot!'

Initially, Washington's objective in arming the Afghan rebels was to mire the Soviets in the Afghan bog. Some, like Carter's National Security Adviser Zbigniew Brzezinski, saw it more personally, as a chance to kill Russians as payback for their support to the Viet Cong, who had killed 58,000 Americans. It was only later that they became convinced that this motley group of Afghans could actually defeat the Red Army.

One of the most passionate about the cause was a colourful Texan Congressman with a penchant for beauty queens with names like Snowflake. Charlie Wilson was on the powerful House Appropriations Committee, and under his campaigning the US went from supplying Lee Enfield rifles to AK47s and surface-to-air missiles.

American financial assistance rocketed from tens of millions of dollars to hundreds of millions, all of which was matched by the Saudis. Arms were shipped to Karachi or flown to Rawalpindi, then placed under ISI control. The CIA bought ISI a fleet of trucks which I used to see plying up and down the Grand Trunk Road with khaki tarpaulins over their tops to hide the weapons. CIA headquarters back in leafy Langley even sent in Tennessee mules for the Afghans to transport the weapons over the mountains. Wilson was a frequent visitor to the Pearl Continental in Peshawar. By the time Milt Bearden arrived in Islamabad as CIA station chief in 1986 his instructions from his boss William Casey were unambiguous. 'We're in it to win,' he was told.

It was the proxy war to end all proxy wars – paying one nation to train another to fight – and was to become the largest covert operation in CIA history. As Imam explained, the entire enterprise was outsourced to Pakistan. ISI maintained control over the Afghans through the divide-and-rule method of their old British masters, by creating seven parties. The leaders' influence depended on their having weapons and largesse to distribute, and for this they were dependent on ISI. No American official was allowed to meet commanders or mujaheddin leaders without ISI being present. Even General Zia never got to meet one alone.

In Imam's role as chief instructor, he trained more than 95,000 fighters between 1979 and 1989. 'I had a team of two hundred officers, and we had twelve teams working day and night. About two hundred mujaheddin would come for a ten-to-fifteen-day course on a weapon system then go back.' Charlie Wilson and then Deputy CIA Director Robert Gates were regular visitors to these camps. 'When Charlie Wilson used to see Afghans training he would dance with happiness,' said Imam.

He found his students to be fast learners. 'The Afghan is a very cunning soldier. He picks up very quickly. As unit commander I'd be training recruits for six months and get 70 per cent success; in Afghanistan teenagers would come for a few days and the result would be 100 per cent. Once I only had three days to train a group of teenagers on an RD7 anti-tank rocket launcher, which is a very difficult weapon, before Charlie Wilson came to visit, and I was worried they wouldn't give a good show, but they were so good that Charlie was dancing.'

As I had seen for myself at the battle of Jalalabad, ISI had done more than train. 'I used to be on the ground all the time,' said Imam. 'My officers were with them, without that they would not have been successful. Afghans do not know strategy, just fighting. All the hard work was done by the Pakistan army.'

By the mid-1980s weapons were coming from all over the world, everywhere from France to China, and Imam's team carried out trials to decide which were most suitable. The British were reluctant to provide weapons, though they were funding the resistance.

'They didn't want their weapon systems being used as they didn't want Russians to know they were involved, but the Americans wanted them to be so they sent Blowpipes.'

Imam didn't think much of the Blowpipe, a portable surface-to-air missile which had been used in the Falklands War then withdrawn because it had proved so hard to aim. One British officer compared using it to 'trying to shoot pheasants with a drainpipe', and the official report on the war said it had managed only two hits. It was some of these mothballed units that were sent to the mujaheddin. 'It was a useless weapon I rejected,' said Imam. 'The missile came and it wasn't hitting. We were firing this way and it was going that way. But my Director General said no, you take it, we took it just as a sign to show to Kabul that the Britishers were also involved.'

All of this training and distribution of weapons made ISI the real puppet-master of the war. It had been a small, neglected part of the armed forces until the war in Afghanistan, when the American and Saudi support turned it into the most powerful organisation in Pakistan, with 10,000 officers and many more informants. American diplomats regularly told me that they considered ISI to be the most effective intelligence agency in the Third World.

'We gave them everything,' said one. In the process they turned ISI into a monster that would soon not be satisfied with running the Afghan war but would train militants for its own proxy war in Kashmir, interfere in Pakistan's politics, stoking sectarian violence, even creating a political party, and determine election results.

I sat there listening to Imam's account in horror. In the background coffee cups were clinking and the Muzak had switched up-tempo to Michael Jackson's 'Thriller'.

'Can I have permission to light up a cigarette?' he asked.

'By all means,' I replied. I felt like one myself.

Of course, living in Peshawar in the late 1980s, I had known what was going on. But we were all so busy reporting the war on the ground day to day that I had not appreciated the scale, nor how cynically the Pakistanis had misled the Americans. My Afghan friends were always complaining about ISI depriving them of weapons if they didn't do its bidding, and giving all the weapons to the fundamentalists. Of the seven mujaheddin leaders Imam and his ISI colleagues played off against each other their clear favourite was Hekmatyar. At one point he was receiving 90 per cent of the arms.

Meanwhile Massoud, the Lion of the Panjshir, who was regarded by many of us reporters as the most effective and impressive commander, received only a tiny fraction of the American largesse. ISI regarded Tajiks as sissies, joking, 'When a Pashtun wants to make love to a woman his first choice is a Tajik man.' Massoud had to develop his own sources in Iran and France. After the war, when the CIA tried to buy back the Stinger surface-to-air missiles they had provided, they sent their agent Gary Schroen to Massoud. Schroen told him the US had supplied 2,000 Stingers to ISI for the resistance. 'Do you know how many I received?' asked Massoud. 'Eight.'

Yet Hekmatyar was vehemently anti-Western. At his press conferences I was amazed by the anti-American slogans – didn't he know where his money was coming from? He also despised women. Even though I covered myself from head to foot, I was once bundled out of an interview with him because one of his aides told me, 'Engineer Hekmatyar can see your ankles.' In the vast Shamshatoo refugee camp, where Hekmatyar held sway, women teachers had acid thrown in their faces. His men were also behind a campaign of assassinations of Afghan intellectuals.

One of the most popular stops for us journalists in Peshawar was the office of Professor Sayyid Bahauddin Majrooh, a floppy-haired poet who ran the Afghan Information Centre, the only independent Afghan source of news. In 1987 his organisation carried out a survey among Afghan refugees which revealed that 70 per cent of them wanted King Zahir Shah as their future ruler rather than any of the seven mujaheddin leaders, particularly Hekmatyar. Many of us reported it. A few months later, in

February 1988, Professor Majrooh's doorbell rang just as dusk was falling. He opened the door and was gunned down by Kalashnikov fire.

I remember realising for the first time what ISI was really up to. At that time I had an American boyfriend who was also a journalist, Mark Fineman from the *Los Angeles Times*, and he was over from Delhi where he was based, and staying in the Holiday Inn. I burst into his room one evening and laid out the whole thing. We sat up till the early hours piecing it together.

ISI was not just distributing arms, but directing operations and providing the Americans with intelligence to serve its own interests. ISI's Director, General Hamid Gul, and the leader of its Afghan cell, Brigadier Afzal Janjua, were committed Islamists, members of the Muslim Brotherhood, as were the second-tier officers on the ground like Colonel Imam. Their aim was to install a client fundamentalist regime in Kabul that would recognise the Durand Line as the border and serve as a bulwark against Pakistan's real enemy, India.

The Americans had little independent information, and ISI officers used codes when they talked to each other on the phone and swept their offices for bugs. So successful was ISI in fooling its backers that Milt Bearden, the CIA station chief, openly professed his admiration for Hamid Gul, presenting him with an American cavalry sword and helping him find an American university for his son. He recalls telling the US Ambassador Arne Raphael, 'Why do I look at Hamid Gul and see a plucky little general who might one day take over the country?' From then on they both referred to Gul affectionately as 'PLG'.

The Americans all seemed to accept ISI's argument that the radical jihadists like Hekmatyar and Sayyaf were the best fighters, and therefore deserved more arms. 'That's what we used to tell them,' said Imam with a thin smile. In 1985 President Reagan even invited the muhajeddin leaders to the White House. In a bizarre photo-call he sat surrounded by these bearded men on sofas and declared to the press, 'These gentlemen are the moral equivalent of the Founding Fathers.'

By 1986 the CIA was spending 70 per cent of its entire operations budget funding a Muslim jihad to kill Russians. The whole
campaign was managed by a bunch of Islamists who were giving
the lion's share of the US money and weapons to people who
wanted to kill Americans.

The US was happy to use Islam as a rallying cry. The CIA
funded the printing of Korans to be distributed throughout the
region, and the University of Nebraska produced primary-school
textbooks, known as 'the ABC of Jihad', which taught children the
alphabet and to count with Kalashnikovs and swords instead of
apples and oranges, and were filled with images of Islamic
warriors.

Alphabet song
A is for Allah. Allah is One.
B is for Father [*bab*]. Father goes to the mosque.
D is for religion [*din*]. Our religion is Islam. The
    Russians are the enemies of Islam.
J is for jihad. Jihad is an obligation.

Far from being disturbed by these developments, the Americans
were delighted to see the Afghan jihad become a cause across the
Middle East. By the mid-1980s the Afghan fighters in Peshawar
were joined by Arabs, coming in such numbers that special reception committees were set up at Pakistan's airports. One of them
was Osama bin Laden. 'The Americans used to be very happy about
this,' said Imam. 'I'm witness. When bin Laden came they were
very happy. This rich man using his own money to dig tunnels.'

The first American official to openly question what was going on
was a slightly-built, bespectacled fellow called Ed McWilliams
who arrived at the Embassy in Islamabad in spring 1988 to be US
Special Envoy to the Afghans. A hardline Cold Warrior who had
started his career in Vietnam interrogating Viet Cong prisoners,
he seemed an unlikely maverick. However, he had lived in Moscow,
where he had got used to operating under the radar screen, away

from the eyes of the KGB, and he spoke fluent Dari. He managed to visit Peshawar and Quetta without escorts, and was shocked at what he heard. All the Afghans he met told him the same story – Hekmatyar and ISI, backed by Pakistan's biggest religious party Jamaat-e-Islami, were trying to wipe out their rivals.

McWilliams was appalled that the CIA was collaborating with ISI in promoting an anti-American movement. When he tried to raise the issue at the Embassy, he found himself silenced. Finally, in desperation, in October 1988 he wrote a cable laying out his fears. Knowing it would not be cleared by the Ambassador, he sent it direct to the State Department, CIA headquarters and the National Security Council.

Shortly afterwards I spent an evening at his house in Islamabad along with Mark Fineman, ostensibly to watch *Casablanca*, one of my favourite movies. As Humphrey Bogart and Ingrid Bergman played out their tortured love affair in the background, Ed told us what he had done. We looked at him with astonished respect. While we had just endlessly talked about what ISI was doing, he had risked his career. The US Ambassador Robert Oakley was furious, and a whispering campaign would soon begin to besmirch Ed's name. The only support he got was from some MI6 officers who were worried about the same issue. That was little help – their CIA counterparts drily pointed out that Britain had already lost at least two wars in Afghanistan.

No one wanted to know. This was a Good War, and it was not easy to report anything against the prevailing mood. When I reported some of the mujaheddin's more barbaric behaviour I was denounced as a communist by a group of American journalists in Peshawar in a loud argument at Dean's Hotel. When I questioned the battle for Jalalabad and ISI's role, I was blackballed from the American Club, the only place for Westerners to hang out, eat burgers and drink alcohol. In the spring of 1989 Ed McWilliams was sent home. His replacement, Peter Tomsen, was more on-message, talking of how he was planning to ride on the back of a tank into free Kabul – though he too would leave as a critic of ISI. When I wrote about ISI smuggling arms, I was questioned, threatened and told that I should leave the country. When I didn't, I was deported.

In the wake of 9/11 and what had happened subsequently in Afghanistan, all of this had taken on chilling significance.

Charlie Wilson never forgot his first visit to a Peshawar hospital, when he had asked a wounded Afghan how he could help, and the man had asked for something with which to shoot down Soviet helicopters. It was largely his lobbying that led to the mujaheddin being given the Stinger missiles in 1986 which really turned the war around. The Afghans loved the shoulder-fired, heat-seeking missiles in their long, black cylindrical tubes. They were light, easy to carry and very accurate, and meant that for the first time they had a weapon to counteract the Soviet advantage of air power. The arrival of the Stingers also made the role of the Americans public for the first time. On each weapon case was inscribed 'General Dynamics'.

'Stingers made a lot of difference in terminal stages, you could say it was the last straw which broke the camel's back,' said Imam. 'The Russians lost a few hundred helicopters which was very decisive in their decision to withdraw.'

By April 1988 the Russians had signed the Geneva Accords to start pulling out troops. It was an astonishing defeat, which played a major part in the collapse of the Soviet Union. 'Afghanistan has been the graveyard of empires for centuries,' said Imam. 'History confirms they don't like foreigners. It's nothing to do with Islam, it's the Afghan psyche, tribes like the Alizai and Noorzai are addicted to fighting – I used to love them. I tell you very frankly, until such time that you kill the last Alizai they will keep fighting. For the last three hundred years whoever came there, they were never subjugated. Even Alexander the Great, after defeating the Persian Empire, got stuck in Afghanistan within six weeks of entering. The same with Tamerlane, King of all Kings, he ended up having to pay passage tax to get out. And you British went three times, look what happened. But the Russians thought, we're the biggest army in the world, we're just across the border, we are a superpower. They thought the Americans are tied up with Iran because of their Embassy problem so they came here, wanting to get to the warm-water ports, and got stuck. We knew they wouldn't succeed. Even so, we never thought they'd be exhausted in ten years. I was thinking it would take thirty years or so. It was a surprise for us, and the Afghans weren't ready.'

Imam saw the Geneva Accords as the start of all the problems. 'Till then we in Pakistan, the Afghan mujaheddin and America were aligned to defeat the Soviet Union, but we all had different motives. The Americans wanted to take revenge and break the Soviet Union. The Afghans wanted to get the Russians out and form their own Islamic government. Pakistan felt they are brother Muslims, we must help them. And secure our own border.'

On 15 February 1989 the last column of the Soviet 40th Army crossed the Friendship Bridge over the Oxus River, led by their commander General Boris Gromov, ending 3,331 days of senseless war. From the CIA station in Islamabad Milt Bearden sent a two-word cable to his headquarters in Langley. 'WE WON', it said, in giant letters made from Xs. That night, for the first time in three years, he turned the light off in his office before leaving. His office faced that of his Soviet counterpart, and he had liked them to think he was working all night to defeat them.

At CIA headquarters in Langley the new Director, William Webster, hosted a champagne celebration. The US Embassy in Islamabad also threw a party.

'I wasn't invited, but I wouldn't have gone,' said Colonel Imam. For Imam and his ISI colleagues there seemed little to celebrate. Najibullah was still President in Kabul, and relations between ISI and the Americans were rapidly turning sour. 'After the Geneva Accords everything changed. Those CIA people who'd been working with us for ten years were excellent. They'd give us things without asking. If they knew I was going inside they would give me photographs, maps, gadgetry, communications gear, etc. After the Geneva Accords new people came who treated us as if we were the corrupt police of a Third World country.'

He makes no secret of his anger. 'For the Americans this was a huge success. Before the Russians came into Afghanistan it was a bipolar world. The Americans used to shit in their Embassy shelters because of the Soviet threat. These Afghans, by sacrificing 1.5 million people, finished off that threat, making it a unipolar world, and saved billions and billions off the US defence budget. It was a big prize for the Americans, scored by the Afghans. What did the Afghans get in return? Their whole country was destroyed. They had no infrastructure, no agriculture, no industry ... At least the Americans should have helped them live like a decent animal. They could have spent $5 billion over five years. That was not done, they forgot Afghanistan – it was a great selfishness.'

I thought that perhaps the Americans had naïvely assumed the mujaheddin were on their way to victory. After all, in March 1988 the CIA had produced a National Intelligence Estimate predicting 'the Najibullah regime will not long survive the completion of Soviet withdrawal even with continued Soviet assistance. The regime may fall before withdrawal is complete.'

But Richard Armitage laughed at the idea. 'We thought within days of the Russians leaving they would fall in on each other. Everyone who went to Peshawar and beyond knew it. They hated each other, and their common enemy was gone. Did we envision full-scale civil war? Well, we figured warring tribes or groups.'

Imam and his colleagues at ISI could not believe what they were seeing. 'This America had been happy to use Islam to make the mujaheddin fight, but did not want that these mujaheddin make their Islamic government, so they stopped their support and abandoned them. Net result: they started fighting each other.'

Many commanders became more focused on making money than on winning the war. In Kandahar, for example, Gul Agha Sherzai made a deal with the Governor, General Nur-al Haq Ulumi, who had been sent there after playing a critical role in defeating the mujaheddin at Jalalabad. Gul Agha's men would stage fake attacks of rockets and light weapons near the airport to keep ISI happy, and Ulumi's men would set oil drums on fire to make them look authentic. In return for keeping the peace Ulumi let Gul Agha sell ISI-provided American wheat inside Kandahar and pocket the profits. Gul Agha would then submit voucher requests to ISI for more money and ammunition to replace that used in airport 'operations'.

When Charlie Wilson visited Pakistan after the Geneva Accords, Imam complained that the Americans were abandoning the Afghans.

'What is the problem?' asked Wilson.

'They need financial support for rehabilitation,' replied Imam.

'Colonel Imam, dollars don't grow on trees,' was the Congressman's response.

'Do Afghan youth grow on trees?' asked Imam. 'One and a half million Afghans have died. What are you saying?'

Listening to Colonel Imam made me realise that men like him had been working towards an Islamist government in Afghanistan for thirty-five years – almost his whole professional life. And he was just one of many. It was clear that just as the fundamentalists had never gone away, neither had the infrastructure of ISI. Maybe its operatives were retired and off the books, maybe they were officially sanctioned, or maybe they were the beneficiaries of a large blind eye. Often they worked through fronts masquerading as welfare organisations.

An old friend of mine went to Azad Kashmir to be Chief Secretary, the most senior government official in the province. He told me that on his first day he was taken to lunch by the local ISI chief and told in no uncertain terms, 'We run Kashmir.'

The scariest thing was that the views of Colonel Imam and his colleagues were no longer held only by a minority. Now when I visited Pakistan it seemed it was the moderate views that were in the minority. Dr Pervez Hoodbhoy, a nuclear physics professor, showed me a photograph of his chemistry class standing on a balcony at Quaid-i-Azam University in Islamabad in 1985, then one of the same department in 2008. The first picture showed girls in colourful clothes, some in jeans, some in *shalwar kamiz*, their heads uncovered. In the second all were in *hijab*, with only the eyes visible. 'They look like clones,' he said. 'All of this goes back to General Zia and the way that the army went from defending our borders to transforming our society. What was once a kind of lunatic fringe is becoming the majority view.'

On the way to meet Colonel Imam, I had driven past the Red Mosque. Abdul Aziz, the preacher, had been freed on bail two months earlier, in April 2009. He was greeted by thousands of supporters who hoisted him on their shoulders chanting 'Jihad, jihad!' and carried him to the remains of the mosque. There in a fiery speech he vowed revenge. 'The blood of those who were martyred here will usher in an Islamic revolution,' he warned. Outside, rows of women in identical black burqas chanted support. The government had just signed a peace deal in Swat with the Taliban agreeing to bring in Islamic Sharia law, as well as similar deals in the tribal agencies of Bajaur and Mohmand. 'Now Islam will not remain confined to Swat,' thundered Abdul Aziz victoriously. 'It will spread all over Pakistan then all over the world!'

PART III

THE GOOD WAR

I think we need to be very clear about what we're trying to do in Afghanistan. Frankly, we're not trying to create the perfect democracy. We're never going to create some ideal society. We are simply there for our own national security.

Prime Minister David Cameron, 2010

22

The View From Washington

West Point Academy, New York, 1 December 2009

THE OBAMA CAMPAIGN had been the most media-savvy anyone could remember, and for his first big war speech as President, broadcast live at prime time, he had chosen one of America's most iconic military backdrops. The imposing grey granite towers of the country's most prestigious military academy sit on a hilly bend in the Hudson River where during the American Revolution George Washington's army placed a 150-ton iron chain supported by huge logs to block British naval advances. In 1779 the General moved his headquarters there, calling it 'the key to America'.

What was then a fortress became the elite West Point academy, alma mater to many of America's top generals, including Eisenhower, Patton and MacArthur. The campus was dotted with monuments to the greatest battles in US history, and a large stone plaque inscribed with the words 'In War There is No Substitute for Victory' from an address by MacArthur to cadets in 1962.

Yet the young Democratic President who flew in to West Point on Marine One helicopter on Tuesday, 1 December 2009 had been elected not to win wars, but to get out of them. That, it turned out, was not so easy. One of Obama's first announcements in office was the withdrawal of all American troops from Iraq by the end of 2011. But in Afghanistan he had already sent one batch, and was about to announce a whole lot more.

At exactly one minute past 8 p.m., Obama strode onto the stage of the Eisenhower Hall and looked out at a sea of more than 4,000 cadets in grey uniforms, their young faces staring up intently. What he was about to announce would put many of them in combat.

Yet the former constitutional-law professor and community organiser could not have been a less warlike President. The following week he would fly to Oslo to collect the Nobel Peace Prize. There he would say, 'I'm responsible for the deployment of thousands of young Americans to battle in a distant land. Some will kill and some will be killed. And so I come here ... filled with difficult questions about the relationship between war and peace.'

Perhaps as moral support the President had taken with him some heavyweight Ministers from what he called his 'team of rivals'. In the front row sat Hillary Clinton, against whom he had fought a bitter campaign for the presidency, yet who had been his surprise choice for Secretary of State, and Robert Gates, whom he had kept on as Defense Secretary from the Bush administration.

The President started by reminding the audience of 9/11 – the reason America had gone into Afghanistan. 'We did not ask for this fight,' he said. He also reminded them of the almost unanimous support there had been in Congress for the AUMF authorising action against al Qaeda, and how for the first time in history NATO had invoked its Article 5, which states that an attack on one member nation is an attack on all.

'Afghanistan is not lost,' he said, 'but for several years it has moved backwards.' He talked of how while US resources and attention had been diverted to Iraq, the situation in Afghanistan had 'deteriorated' and the Taliban had 'gained momentum'. He also spoke of how Pakistan was part of the problem: 'There have been those in Pakistan who have argued that the struggle against extremism is not their fight and that Pakistan is better off doing little or seeking accommodation with those who use violence. We have made it clear that we cannot tolerate a safe haven for terrorists whose location is known.'

Earlier that year I had interviewed David Cameron, then British opposition leader, and he told me he envied what he called Obama's 'soaring oratory'. Yet for all that I had heard of Obama's incredible eloquence during the election campaign, there was little passion in this thirty-three-minute speech, for this was a President with no appetite for war. When he talked of how more than any other nation the US had 'underwritten global security for over six decades', it was with a sense of weariness.

Robert Gates would later remark on this in his autobiography: 'One quality I missed in Obama was passion, especially when it came to the two wars.' While President Bush would often shed tears when meeting families of dead soldiers, he wrote, 'I worked for Obama longer than Bush and I never saw his eyes well up.'[1]

Obama pointed out at West Point that by the time he took office the wars had cost America $1 trillion. He had inherited 161,000 troops in Iraq and 38,000 in Afghanistan. He did not mention that he had already sent 21,000 more to Afghanistan. Yet now he was sending another 30,000 for a surge similar to that in Iraq in 2007, which he had opposed at the time, but which was believed to have turned the war round there. 'Our security is at stake,' he stressed. The decision wasn't a surprise – there had been leaks and speculation in the press for months. But then he added something that made me start: 'After eighteen months our troops will begin to come home.'

The rapid surge would be followed by rapid withdrawal. 'Hard and fast' were his instructions to the military command. In practice he was telling his enemies that if they just hung on another two years, the Americans would be gone. For people fighting on as long a timescale as the Taliban, that was nothing.

This made no military sense. It was all about domestic politics, which as I was starting to understand, determined everything in the US. In 2012 Obama would be facing re-election, and he wanted all the troops back home by then. 'I can't let this be a war without end, and I can't lose the whole Democratic Party,' he later told the Republican Senator Lindsey Graham, who had expressed concern at the idea of being locked into a fixed withdrawal date.

David Kilcullen, the counter-insurgency expert at the State Department, was one of a number of Afghanistan experts invited to a meeting at the White House before the speech, along with Antony Cordesman and John Nagl. 'I thought it was to get our advice on Afghanistan so was surprised it was being held in the communications office. When I walked in there were people there from Code Pink, Green organisations and the Lesbian Coalition. I realised this was all about the speech, not the strategy – it was a kind of focus group. So a lot of the things added late to the speech like the timeline of withdrawal were added by White House comms people.'

The resultant mix of retreat and advance made for a half-hearted surge. Nor was there any explanation of strategy, of how this would work. Obama did not talk of winning the war, but of 'a transition to Afghan responsibility'. Indeed, in a meeting in the Oval Office with his national security staff the previous Wednesday, at which he'd told them he was 'inclined to go with the 30,000', he added, 'This needs to be a plan about how we're going to hand it off and get out of Afghanistan.'[2]

After the speech cadets clambered over chairs to reach him and shake hands, but the officers looked grim-faced. The headline in the next day's *New York Times* read 'Obama Adds Troops But Maps Exit Plan'.

It reminded me of what Gorbachev had done when he came to power in 1985 as a reformist President six years into the Soviet occupation of Afghanistan. Determined to extricate his nation from the quagmire and to put an end to the mounting casualties and the letters from parents of dead soldiers, he gave his generals extra forces and one year to win the war. Throughout that year they launched a number of major offensives, but they failed to defeat the resistance. Calling Afghanistan 'a bleeding wound', by 1987 Gorbachev was negotiating a political settlement for withdrawal. Meanwhile he took steps to strengthen the Afghan government, replacing President Babrak Karmal with the more dynamic Mohammad Najibullah, who had headed the secret police, and giving the Afghan army and police better weapons. The Russians also paid off insurgents to stop fighting, set up tribal militias and paid them to defend their villages against the mujaheddin.

To me, Obama's surge seemed too little too late. The former commander in Afghanistan, General Dan McNeill, had told Sherard Cowper-Coles the previous year, 'I could do this if I had 500,000 troops.' Cowper-Coles was tempted to add, 'And fifty years.'[3]

At this point another 30,000 troops was never going to be enough. We had ended up locked into a war with the Taliban, who weren't our enemy and were nothing to do with 9/11, and what's more we were doing it with one hand tied behind our backs, because our supposed ally Pakistan was swinging both ways.

Having once thought there weren't enough troops, in my last few trips to Afghanistan before moving to Washington I had become convinced that the more troops we sent, the worse we made the situation. This was particularly the case in the south, where we had failed to explain to people why we were there, and lost the narrative to the Taliban with their mobilisation of the mullahs and evocative talk of foreign occupiers.

In a dinner with two Afghan Ministers at the British Ambassador's residence in Kabul in November 2009, Britain's Foreign Secretary David Miliband asked how long they thought Afghan government authorities would stay in the Helmand capital of Lashkar Gah after Western forces left. 'Twenty-four hours,' came the reply.[4]

We had lost the propaganda war at home too. By summer 2009, 184 British soldiers had been killed in Afghanistan, overtaking the 179 lost in Iraq. Yet Prime Minister Gordon Brown insisted we were winning. On 11 July, after eight soldiers had been killed within twenty-four hours, he had written a letter to senior MPs assuring them that 'current operations [against the Taliban] are succeeding in their objectives'.

At the end of that week I saw Hamid Karzai in Kabul to say goodbye before I moved to Washington. As usual I went through five security checks, at which everything from my lipstick to a packet of paracetamol was confiscated. He wanted once again to talk about civilian casualties. 'We need a new contract with the international community where the sanctity of Afghan homes and families is respected,' he said. 'We don't accept bombardment any more. I never wanted bad relations with the British and Americans but I had to speak my mind about issues that were not right. They knew very well that the war on Taliban was not in Afghan villages but it was elsewhere. To go and bomb an Afghan village for an unknown Talib and cause so many casualties was totally out of the mind. To enter a home, blast doors and fight with families – that was not a partnership. This is what's wrong with the international community – they want us to behave like robots. We're not, this is our country.'

He ranted into my tape recorder about how the British had made things worse. 'When Mullah Sher Akhundzada was Governor of Helmand there were 180,000 boys and girls going to school. Today what do we have? With all those troops, there is more than four times as much drug production and no boy going to school there!'[5]

The previous ten days had been Britain's worst in Helmand, with fifteen soldiers killed. I could see that Karzai's comments would make it onto the British front pages and outrage a nation already tired of the war. His spokesman, who had sat in on the interview, could see the same thing. Afterwards he called me and put Karzai on the line, who begged me not to use those quotes 'in respect of our long friendship'. I did not use them, though I pointed out that it had been an on-the-record interview.

However, there were already stirrings back home. That September saw the resignation of Eric Joyce MP, a former army major, from his position as a Parliamentary Private Secretary in protest at Afghan strategy. 'I do not think the public will accept for much longer that our losses can be justified by simply referring to the risk of greater terrorism on our streets,' he wrote.

British troops had already been in Helmand far longer than the three years originally planned. Horrified by the casualties and the lack of progress, public support was clearly waning. Unexpectedly, a small market town in Wiltshire called Wootton Bassett came to symbolise the nation's anguish. The bodies of soldiers killed in Afghanistan were flown back to nearby base RAF Lyneham and driven through the town, and parades of townspeople were turning out to solemnly salute them. It had all started in 2007 with a man called Percy Miles, a former Mayor, who was out shopping with his wife when someone mentioned that there was a cortège coming through. He ran home to put on his mayoral robes and stood to attention as it passed. That small act of respect started something. Soon hundreds of people were lining the streets. By 2009 the whole town was turning out, standing by the town hall singing, and stopping as the tenor church bell rang. When I went there I found people from outside the town too, including a group of leather-clad Hell's Angels.[6] It was a moving sight. When I told people I had been to Helmand they all had the same question: 'What are we actually achieving?'

Brown agreed to increase the troop strength to 10,000, but the public was turning against a war which no politician could or would explain. On Remembrance Sunday I went to London to look at the poppy wreaths on the Cenotaph, and far more people had turned out than usual. As we all went quiet to recall the moment when the guns of Europe fell silent, I wondered how many more would die.

The war remained more popular in the US. America is a remarkably patriotic nation, where people stand hand on heart and belt out the national anthem at sporting events and political rallies, and I often saw the Stars and Stripes flying in people's gardens, and 'Support Our Troops' banners and bumper stickers. There was no Wootton Bassett, and the Pentagon had long banned photographs of flag-draped caskets arriving at Dover Airbase, as such images were thought to have helped turn US public opinion against the Vietnam War. Obama decided to lift this ban as part of greater transparency, leaving it up to families to choose if they gave permission.

However, something had happened to fundamentally change the situation in both countries. Anger against the wars might have created the anti-Bush wave which propelled Obama to the limelight (Obama was not a Senator at the time of the vote on Iraq, and called it 'a dumb war'), but it was the financial meltdown, starting with the collapse of Lehman Brothers in September 2008, which had sealed his election victory. Taxpayer-funded bailouts saved the banking industry, but the resulting credit crunch meant that as President he had inherited the worst recession since the Great Depression of the 1930s.

The government budget deficit was soaring – by the time of Obama's West Point speech the national-debt clock in New York's Times Square had passed $12 trillion. The loss of millions of jobs and the closures of many companies meant that one in eight Americans were on food stamps – a record number. In such a situation it was not easy to justify sending more men to an expensive war. It cost a staggering $1 million per year per soldier in Afghanistan, what with all the kit and logistics. Obama put a $30 billion additional price tag on the first year of his 30,000 surge – the overall cost for the year would be $120 billion. As for nation-building, building schools in Afghanistan was hard to justify when people were hungry and jobless at home.

Sending more troops, then, had not been an easy decision. As a presidential candidate Obama had called Afghanistan 'the good war', in contrast to the war in Iraq, which he told a rally in Pennsylvania in April 2008 'has not made us more safe but has distracted us from the task in hand in Afghanistan'. One of his first acts as President, in February 2009, was to announce that all US combat troops would be withdrawn from Iraq by the end of 2011. At the same time he agreed 4,000 more troops for Afghanistan, on top of 17,000 already earmarked by Bush. Shortly after that he told the Sunday-morning CBS show *Face the Nation* that he thought the previous seven years had been lost: 'What we want to do now is refocus attention on al Qaeda.' He also spoke of Pakistan, emphasising, 'We have to hold them much more accountable.'[7] That same morning Secretary Gates went on *Fox News Sunday* and said that ISI had had links with extremists 'for a long time as a hedge against what might happen in Afghanistan'. He added, 'They can count on us and don't need that hedge.'

It was clear that if the situation was going to turn around the war needed a new direction. Indeed, the Bush administration had realised that, and ordered a group of twenty-four public servants from across government to work on a review of AfPak to brief the incoming President. One of them was David Kilcullen. 'From September to November 2008 we worked day and night and came up with our best guess on what needed to be done. The Obama people came in and totally ignored that.'

Instead Obama commissioned his own review, headed by former CIA analyst Bruce Riedel. He also appointed a new commander. McNeill had been replaced in Kabul by General Dave McKiernan, and Gates told Obama he felt he was the wrong man. When McKiernan refused to step down, Obama sacked him. The military was shocked. It was the first time a wartime commander had been sacked since President Truman fired MacArthur in 1951, during the Korean War.

In June Obama announced as his new commander in Afghanistan General Stanley McChrystal, from the shadowy world of special operations. He had spent the previous five years heading Joint Special Operations Command, or JSOC (pronounced Jay-sock), a unit so clandestine that for years the Pentagon even refused to acknowledge its existence, and had led hunter-killer teams in Iraq, including that which killed Abu Musab al-Zarqawi, the leader of al Qaeda in Iraq.

McChrystal was a fitness obsessive, so lean that his skin seemed tightly pulled across his skeleton. He slept little and lived on just one meal a day, snacking for the rest from a Tupperware box of salted German pretzels. Work was his life, and his social skills so lacking that when Obama cracked a joke on their first meeting he remained rigid and unsmiling. Afterwards Obama told Gates, 'He's very … focused.'

The sense of disconnect was mutual. Like many American generals McChrystal had his close team who moved with him, and one of these would later describe that first meeting to a *Rolling Stone* reporter as 'a ten-minute photo-op … Obama clearly didn't know anything about him. Here's the guy who's going to run his fucking war but he didn't seem very engaged.'

Obama told his new commander to carry out a sixty-day assessment and come up with a plan. When McChrystal came back from

Afghanistan his assessment was bleak. The situation, he said, was much worse than they had realised, and if they did not halt Taliban momentum within a year the war would be unwinnable. This, he believed, would need at least 40,000 more troops. Gates was incredulous. 'I nearly fell off my chair,' he wrote. 'Did he really believe the President would approve that massive an increase so soon after agreeing an additional 21,000?'[8]

Gates was the only senior official who had also been in the administration during the Soviet occupation, and he worried that with so many troops, the Americans would also be regarded as occupiers rather than allies. Polling commissioned by the US Embassy in Kabul showed that the number of Afghans who saw the US as partners had fallen from 80 per cent to 60 per cent over the previous three years.

Obama had kept on Admiral Mike Mullen as the nation's top military commander, and hired General Jim Jones as his National Security Adviser. However, by far the most influential military figure at the time was General David Petraeus, who had come back from leading the surge in Iraq to be commander of US Central Command, which oversees the wars in Afghanistan and Iraq.

He had returned as a hero, credited for turning the situation around, using counter-insurgency doctrine, or COIN as it was known, that he had developed for the US Army. This meant focusing on securing the local population rather than focusing on the enemy you want to kill. In Iraq he dispersed troops in small outposts in local neighbourhoods, instead of holing them up far away on large bases, and also helped form a local militia dubbed 'Sons of Iraq' which put 100,000 gunmen, mostly former Sunni insurgents, on the payroll. For the first three months this had seemed a disaster – April to June 2007 were the bloodiest three months of the war. Then the mayhem subsided, and by the end of the year the violence had dropped 60 per cent, and former enemies were working together.

The turnaround made Petraeus a household name in the US. Intrigued, when I moved to Washington I went to hear him give a lecture at the Wilson Center for International Relations. I'd never seen such an awed reception for a general – back home in Britain, I doubted most people even knew the name of our army chief. People called him 'St David', and asked him if he was planning to run for President. He was undoubtedly impressive. Often referred to as a warrior-scholar, he had a doctorate in international relations from Princeton. Like McChrystal he was superfit, starting each day with a five-mile run after just four hours' sleep, and challenging his favourite reporters to run alongside, for he was a shameless self-promoter.

Frankly, I was a bit confused by all the hero-worship. I had gone to Iraq in 2008 and seen for myself how the situation had improved with the surge. However, it seemed to me it had succeeded because of other factors, principally the so-called 'Anbar Awakening', when local Sunni sheikhs disillusioned with the insurgency that was tearing their country apart signed a series of truces with the government against whom they had been fighting, and the American occupiers. That left the Americans free to turn their guns on the Shiite militias.

Napoleon is said to have remarked, 'I have plenty of clever generals. Just give me a lucky one.' If Petraeus was a lucky general, well, Afghanistan needed some luck.

Petraeus thought he could replicate the success of Iraq in Afghanistan. He argued that what was needed was his new counter-insurgency strategy rather than counter-terrorism. The plan was to send in thousands of troops to the south and east to try to reverse the Taliban tide. He believed that if American and Afghan troops could establish themselves in villages the Taliban would fade away.

Gates called the new commander for Afghanistan, Stan McChrystal, 'the most lethal and successful practitioner of counter-terrorism in the world'. Yet, obviously under the influence of Petraeus, the plan he drew up for Afghanistan was based on counter-insurgency. He submitted it to Petraeus, Mullen and Gates in August, then to Obama on 2 September. It presented Obama with three options – 85,000 new troops, which was clearly impossible; 40,000, which was what he hoped to get; and 11,000, which he said would not be enough. As Obama said, really they had given him only one option.

Then the lobbying began. Two days after Obama received the plan Petraeus gave an interview to the *Washington Post* in which he made clear where he stood. While there was no guarantee that sending more troops would fix Afghanistan, he warned, 'It won't work out if we don't.' Less than three weeks later another story appeared in the *Washington Post*, this time under America's most renowned byline: Bob Woodward, of Watergate fame. It was a leak of the McChrystal plan under the headline 'More Forces or Mission Failure', and it came with the General's entire sixty-six-page secret assessment online.[9]

Rumours started surfacing that McChrystal would quit if he did not get his way. Obama and his political team, concerned at the financial and political cost, wanted to send as few troops as possible, but they felt the military was trying to force their hand. Vice President Joe Biden questioned whether the Taliban were actually a threat to American national security at all, and argued that dealing with Pakistan should be the priority, as that after all was where al Qaeda was based. He advocated a strategy using 20,000 extra troops (half for special forces raids and half for training), which became known as 'counter-terrorism plus'.

Over the next three months, starting on Sunday, 13 September, Obama would spend twenty-five hours in meetings about the plan. To the military these often felt like academic seminars, looking at CIA maps showing the march of the Taliban, and interminably discussing pros and cons. A book Obama mentioned on the Vietnam War called *Lessons in Disaster* became a must-read in the West Wing.

Obama questioned McChrystal's numbers, suggesting a compromise of 20,000 new troops. Petraeus insisted that this was not a serious option, as it would only provide enough men to move through the country trying to capture bad guys, and they would then leave, alienating the population without inflicting serious damage on the enemy. He told Obama he had war-gamed the scenario, and it had failed. Bob Woodward later claimed that the war game Petraeus had referred to, codenamed 'Poignant Vision', had been designed for conventional warfare, and had actually been inconclusive.[10]

In the end Obama agreed a revised second option of 30,000 troops, with a 3,000 reserve which Gates could send if there were exceptional circumstances. He also approved a CIA request to greatly expand operations in Pakistan.

The military had got almost all they wanted, but it had been a painful process. The rift with the White House, where both sides had marshalled information against the other, left a bad taste on both sides, hardly an ideal base for expanding a war.

When Obama announced his final decision in the Oval Office, he and Biden shocked the military by describing it as 'an order'. This, said Gates, 'demonstrated the complete unfamiliarity of both men with the American military culture'. It was 'unnecessary and insulting, proof positive of the depth of the Obama White House's distrust of the nation's military leadership'.

The decision would dramatically scale up the war. Over thirteen months Obama sent more than 50,000 extra troops – by 2010 there would be more than 100,000 in Afghanistan, almost as many as the Soviets had had. That would inevitably mean more casualties, something that was brought home to Obama on a bitterly cold Veterans' Day when he drove across the Potomac River from the White House to visit Section 60 of Arlington National Cemetery, the final resting place of many of those killed in Iraq and Afghanistan. Under a steely grey sky dribbling with rain, new graves were being dug to add to line after line of chalky white stones at which people had left beads, flowers, balloons and, most poignantly, children's drawings for their lost fathers. Obama left looking sombre.

He also visited wounded soldiers at Walter Reed Army Hospital in Washington, many of whom had lost arms, legs or both to IEDs. Afterwards he told his staff, 'I don't want to be going to Walter Reed for another eight years.'

23

All About the Politics

THE PROBLEM, AS I saw it, was that the focus was still on a military solution when it was clear on the ground that the real problem was political. Many Afghans simply didn't like their government, which they saw as inefficient, unable to protect them and corrupt. By 2009 Afghanistan was the fifth most corrupt nation on earth, according to Transparency International (it would end up second only to Somalia). US officials estimated that more than $1 billion a year was leaving the country through Kabul airport alone, around a tenth of Afghanistan's GDP. Cash declaration forms for July and August 2009 showed $180 million being taken out to Dubai in just those two months. Far more was presumably going undeclared. One Afghan who was stopped and searched had more than $5 million in his briefcase in US dollars and Saudi riyals. Much more probably went out through the VIP section, where officials could pass through without being searched.

Ashraf Ghani, Karzai's former Finance Minister, who contested the 2009 elections, denounced the ruling family as a mafia he called 'Karzai Incorporated'. He complained to me, 'Two individuals in the Interior Ministry have just declared assets of $21 million and $35 million. In what country can you gain that in four years?' In his West Point speech Obama pointedly said, 'The days of providing a blank cheque are over.'

Umer Daudzai, Karzai's Chief of Staff, blamed the West. 'Of course there's corruption. Show me one post-conflict society without. It all goes back to trying to spread democracy. Once we had a parliament, Ministers had to pay money to MPs to get the votes to be confirmed in their posts, so then of course they need to make money to recoup this. The day the first Minister paid a bribe it started.' Moreover, as Karzai argued, Afghans were not the only ones making money. 'I know there is corruption in the Afghan government but I also know there is vast corruption in the distribution of international funds to the Afghan government and we want that corrected too,' he told me.

Gates agreed that the US and the international community had to take some of the blame. 'For all our handwringing and hectoring on corruption we seemed oblivious to how much we were contributing to it and on a scale that dwarfed the drugs trade. Tens of billions of dollars were flooding into Afghanistan from the US and our partners and we turned a blind eye or simply were ignorant of how regularly some portion was going to payoffs, bribes and bank accounts in Dubai.'

The US government had appointed its own Special Inspector General for Afghanistan (SIGAR), who kept filling my email inbox with astonishing reports of misspent funds. Schools that fell apart; a $457,000 police training centre that 'melted'; and my personal favourite, more than $3 million on patrol boats that ended up languishing unused in a Virginia warehouse, as Afghanistan has no coastline. Somehow each of the eight boats had cost $375,000 – far more than the $50,000 usual price tag – before anyone realised they were of no use.

Corruption was just part of the problem. As Petraeus knew, one of the first principles of a successful counter-insurgency campaign is to have credible local partners. Instead they had Karzai in Afghanistan and Zardari in Pakistan.

Before his inauguration in January 2009, Obama sent Biden to visit both countries. The six-term Senator had been Chairman of the Senate Foreign Relations Committee and, unlike Obama, was well versed in foreign affairs. To make the trip bipartisan he took a Republican colleague, Lindsey Graham. Their first stop was

Islamabad. The CIA had advised them that the Afghan Taliban and Haqqani networks had virtual immunity in Pakistan. Biden told President Zardari that these safe havens needed to end. Zardari assured him he would clean up ISI and 'get out of these games'. He said the problem was that the extremists had money and the government didn't.

The Americans were unimpressed. 'The whole fucking place is burning down here, pal!' was Graham's view.

Next they flew to Kabul. Karzai had enjoyed a close relationship with Bush, who indulged him with fortnightly or even weekly video conferences in which the American President imparted folksy advice. So cosy were these that sometimes Karzai held his small son on his lap during them. Obama had no intention of doing such a thing – indeed, there was no world leader with whom he cultivated close relations, and certainly not the quixotic Karzai, who according to his CIA reports was manic depressive and 'off his meds'.

Sometimes the fates misalign, and the two key leaders for America's longest war could not have been more ill-suited. Karzai was volatile and highly strung, Obama so cold and unemotional that he was nicknamed 'Spock'. As one British Ambassador said to me, 'If you take the Myers-Briggs scale for personalities, they're at opposite ends.'

Karzai had told me he was looking forward to a new way of doing things with the new President. 'We've all made mistakes from the beginning,' he said. 'It's not about more troops. We have to rethink the way we do things.'

Obama thought the same. But not at all in the way the Afghan President was expecting. 'Things have got to change,' Biden informed Karzai. 'No more picking up the phone calling the President.'

Karzai had arranged dinner for the two Americans with much of his cabinet. As the Kabuli rice and mutton was served Biden warned him that he needed to get a handle on corruption. He added that they had seen the ornate homes of officials near the palace, no doubt paid for with American taxpayers' money. He also needed to stop being just Mayor of Kabul, and get out into the provinces. Senator Graham then moved on to the subject of Karzai's brother Ahmed Wali and the allegations of drug trafficking. The mood quickly chilled.

As usual, Karzai demanded evidence. He then brought up the issue of civilian casualties. The Americans told him it would be more helpful if he went to them, rather than holding press conferences denouncing the US and NATO. Karzai felt they were acting as if Afghan deaths didn't matter, and were belittling him in front of his own cabinet. 'We're just poor Afghans,' he wheedled. 'I know no one cares about us ...'

Biden had had enough. 'President Karzai, you're making a mistake,' he said, put down his napkin and left. The dinner had lasted just nine minutes.

Among those present was Karzai's Chief of Staff, Umer Daudzai. He said that wasn't the first time Biden had walked out of dinner with Karzai. The previous year during the American presidential campaign he had come to Kabul with Democratic Senator Joe Lieberman and encouraged Karzai to speak against Bush and the Republicans, to say they messed up in Afghanistan when they shifted their focus to Iraq. Karzai refused. 'Look, Senator Biden,' he said, 'we Afghans, when we shake the hand of friendship we don't run over it.'

'What happened later was like revenge, that's how we saw it,' said Daudzai, 'raising allegations of corruption, left and right. We have it all on record at the palace so the next generation will know. The President had had very good relations with President Bush, and to switch from that was very hard.'[1]

That first meeting with the new administration was an indication of things to come. As part of the new focus on the region Obama named veteran diplomat Richard Holbrooke as his Special Representative for Afghanistan and Pakistan. The sixty-seven-year-old Holbrooke was best known for resolving the Bosnian War in 1995, as well as for having an outsize ego, and his appointment was so resented by the State Department that his office was a ghetto in the basement next to the canteen. Kilcullen said, 'Holbrooke acted as if Afghanistan was a moderately difficult problem that the Bush administration had screwed up, and with his personality and experience from Bosnia he would turn it around.'

Karzai disliked Holbrooke from the start. He was convinced he was being fed propaganda by Pakistan. Relations worsened much more with the August 2009 presidential elections. Forty candidates entered the race, most with no hope of being elected, instead with the aim of getting something from other candidates by stepping down in their favour. Karzai managed to persuade several to withdraw, including Gul Agha Sherzai, arguing that Pashtuns should stick together.

The US made no secret of the fact that it would like someone else rather than Karzai, but realistically there was no serious challenger. What heavyweights there were might have had a hope if they had rallied behind a single candidate, but in Afghanistan everyone wants to be King, and they all wanted to stand. The only real threat to Karzai was Dr Abdullah Abdullah, his former Foreign Minister and the confidant of Ahmat Shah Massoud, but he was from the minority Tajik tribe and the Pashtuns would always unite against him. In fact, as he kept telling people, his father was Pashtun, but this made little impact as he had so long been associated with the Tajiks.

Even so, Holbrooke and General Karl Eikenberry, who had returned to Afghanistan as Ambassador, kept meeting other candidates, being photographed with them and even attending their rallies. From the palace, Karzai watched all this in fury. 'Holbrooke had been doing his best to bring about the defeat of Karzai,' wrote Gates.

To ensure his victory, the Afghan President turned to the warlords he had once vowed to eliminate. To the horror of Western diplomats, he chose as his running mate Marshal Fahim, who was at the top of their lists both for human rights violations, past and present, and for making a fortune since 2001. Brad Adams, Asia Director of Human Rights Watch, described him as 'one of the most notorious warlords in Afghanistan, with the blood of many

Afghans on his hands from the civil war and widely believed to be still involved in many illegal activities including running armed militias'. According to CIA reports he had a Soviet cargo plane which he used for transporting heroin through Russia.

Karzai also secured the endorsement of another serial human rights abuser, General Dostum, the man who had allegedly asphyxiated hundreds of Taliban prisoners in shipping containers in 2001. Karzai had allowed Dostum back from exile in Turkey, where he had been drying out from his fondness for Johnnie Walker Red Label. He had immediately got himself in trouble, storming the house of a former aide, Akbar Bhai, badly beating him and his son as well as killing two guards and kidnapping another man. When police arrived at Dostum's lavender-painted house he went up to the rooftop, beat his chest like a gorilla and hurled insults at them till they went away. Whatever his sins, he still commanded the Uzbek vote – as much as 10 per cent of the population – so Karzai gave him the symbolic post of Chief of Defence for Life, and got his support.

When I asked Karzai how he could work with such men, he snorted. 'The Americans were very happy to work with these people when it was about getting rid of al Qaeda. There is a problem in the West with this – when they need someone he's good, when they don't need him he's bad. Well that's not how we behave. Fahim has been working well for this government since 2001. General Dostum was voted for by one million Afghans when he stood for elections [in 2004], the UN let him, the West helped him. I cannot call Dostum bad when the Western press calls him bad and good when a certain Western country likes him.'

Holding elections in the middle of a full-blown war was a recipe for disaster. The security situation in the south was so bad that few turned out to vote. The Taliban had threatened to cut off the fingers of anyone who voted, and observers estimated that the turnout in the south had been less than 15 per cent.

The day after the elections, with counting only just getting under way, a process that would take weeks, with ballot papers transported from remote places by donkey, Holbrooke and Eikenberry went to see Karzai. They asked about his plans if he were re-elected. 'I have been re-elected!' he told them. They reminded him that this was just the first round, that the votes would take a couple of weeks to be counted, and that then if no candidate got 50 per cent there would be a runoff.

Karzai was furious. 'That's not possible,' he said. 'I know what the people chose.' As soon as the Americans had left he called the State Department and demanded to speak to Hillary Clinton or Obama. Neither took his calls. Two days later Eikenberry and Holbrooke again went to see him. 'You guys are opposing me,' he complained. 'It's a British–American plot.'

Soon reports were coming in of massive fraud. UN officials said that officials loyal to Ahmed Wali Karzai had forged hundreds of thousands of votes, many from 'ghost' polling stations that never opened because of lack of security. Peter Galbraith, a close ally of Holbrooke who had recently arrived in Kabul to be deputy head of the UN office, said that as many as one in three of Karzai's votes were fraudulent.

Yet as I had witnessed, the 2004 elections had also been flawed, and the international community had not complained, because that time the result suited them. Indeed, Galbraith claimed that his boss Kai Eide instructed UN staff to stay mum this time. He was fired after writing a scathing letter accusing Eide of trying to cover up the fraud.

The Finance Minister announced early results, which put Karzai on 54.6 per cent. However, the evidence of wrongdoing mounted, as did the international outcry. Eventually in October the Election Commission cancelled 1.3 million of the votes for Karzai. This meant he had only 49.7 per cent, and there would thus be a second round against his nearest challenger, Abdullah Abdullah.

Karzai was outraged. Senator John Kerry happened to be in Afghanistan visiting American troops, and was sent to reason with him. He ended up spending twenty hours in talks with Karzai over five days, walking round and round the palace garden trying to persuade him to accept a second round. 'Sometimes there are tough things,' he said, as he talked of his own bruising experience of losing to George W. Bush in the 2004 US presidential election.

Karzai ultimately agreed in an uncomfortable press conference that he would submit to a second round. Abdullah Abdullah then saved the day by saying the process was too flawed, and that he was withdrawing from the contest. Karzai was sworn in for a second term, but he would not forgive the Americans for what he saw as a public humiliation.

Ali Jalali, the former Interior Minister, was teaching at the National Defense University in Washington, and had contemplated running for President himself until he was told he would have to give up his US passport. He told me the outcome was a disaster. 'The US has ended up with the worst of all worlds. They still have Karzai but he knows they tried to get rid of him. It's like running over someone with a bus then them surviving.' Robert Gates agreed: 'It was all ugly; our partner the President of Afghanistan was tainted and our hands were dirty as well.'

Karzai's relationship with the US would never recover. He began referring to the Taliban as 'brothers' to deliberately annoy the Americans. The feeling was mutual. 'Obama couldn't stand Karzai,' Gates would later write in his memoir. *New York Times* columnist Maureen Dowd, who had once written glowingly of Karzai, started referring to him as 'the caped capo' and 'the corrupt coxcomb'. Later she described him as 'our runaway fruitcake'.

In the end the Obama administration realised that this was no way to run a war. Karzai was invited to Washington in May 2010 for a love-in. Meanwhile he carried on needling the White House, claiming the election fraud had been carried out by foreigners who wanted a 'puppet government', and then even publicly threatening to join the Taliban. The US pointedly stopped referring to him as a partner or ally, and his invitation was almost rescinded. In the end the visit went ahead, including a red-carpet reception at the White House, a dinner hosted by Vice President Joe Biden, and a walk with Hillary Clinton. He was also taken by Gates and Admiral Mike Mullen to both Walter Reed Hospital and Section 60 of

Arlington National Cemetery, with the idea of reminding him of the sacrifices Americans were making for his country. One of the frustrations of Karzai's Western backers was how he never visited troops in Afghanistan.

It was all too late. I met him one evening at the Willard Hotel, where he was enjoying keeping Holbrooke waiting. 'They complain about me but I never know which US I am meeting,' he said.

'Ultimately the fault is our own,' said Sherard Cowper-Coles. 'Like Shah Shuja we put him on the throne and thrust upon him notions of European politics but left all his enemies intact.'

Of all America's military commanders, surprisingly it was the veteran special ops operative Stanley McChrystal who endeared himself to Karzai, by imposing new rules restricting the use of airstrikes in an attempt to reduce civilian casualties. McChrystal had come to believe that one innocent death creates ten insurgents, and in July 2009 he revised the tactical directive issued by McNeill and instructed that 'The use of air-to-ground munitions and indirect fires against residential compounds is only authorised under very limited and prescribed conditions.' If there were any mistakes, he always called Karzai personally.

The new rules, known as 'cautious restraint', led to a 28 per cent reduction in civilian casualties. But they were not always popular with ISAF troops, especially those who felt they had lost comrades because of the restrictions.

That wasn't the only way McChrystal made himself unpopular with the troops. First he closed the bar at the ISAF headquarters in Kabul. Then he turned his attention to the Kandahar boardwalk, and announced that he would shut down Burger King, Pizza Hut, Dairy Queen and the Military Car Sales outlet. 'This is a war zone, not an amusement park,' read the announcement by his Command Sergeant Major Michael Hall, adding that the closure would help the alliance 'get refocused on the mission at hand'.

Ironically for someone so tight-buttoned, McChrystal was himself undone in June 2010 by some loose talk – helped by the eruption of an unpronounceable Icelandic volcano. The resulting ash cloud grounded flights around the world, leaving the General and his team stranded in Paris, then travelling on a bus to Germany with a reporter from *Rolling Stone* magazine who was writing a profile of McChrystal. What should have been a short interview turned into a two-week odyssey. In that time McChrystal's team made disparaging remarks about Biden, Eikenberry and Obama, all of which appeared in a cover profile entitled 'The Runaway General'. When the article was published no one in Washington's corridors of power could talk of anything else. Robert Gates could not believe his eyes. He phoned McChrystal and demanded, 'What the fuck were you thinking?'

Gates could not see how McChrystal could stay in his post. Yet equally he warned Obama that if he was sacked they would lose the war, as it would take months for a new commander to become *au fait* with the situation. Obama suggested that there was one man who could save the day – General David Petraeus. This may have been a shrewd political move, as it would mean Petraeus was out of the way for the next elections, when he might have been a threat to Obama if he secured the Republican nomination. So Obama sacked his second commander within just over a year, called in Petraeus and appealed to his ego. So quickly was the appointment announced that Petraeus hadn't even spoken to his wife.

Another tree was planted on the green at ISAF headquarters to mark its thirteenth commander. Meanwhile in Pakistan, Mullah Omar and the same people kept working with the Taliban. Just as the Russians had, it seemed clear to them that the Americans were losing patience.

24

The Butcher of Mumbai

Mumbai, 26 November 2008

IF WORKING WITH Afghanistan was problematic, Pakistan was a
whole new order of difficult. 'Dealing with ISI will break your
heart,' warned Mike McConnell, Director of National Intelligence,
in his first intelligence briefing to Obama on 6 November 2008,
just two days after the US election. He told him about 'Directorate
S', which financed and nurtured the very Taliban terrorist groups
America was fighting against.

It was thought that with Obama as President the situation with
Pakistan might improve. His closest friends at college had been
from Pakistan, and he had visited their country, learning to cook
keema, spicy mince with peas, and dhal, a lentil curry. He had also
been a great admirer of Benazir Bhutto, whose husband Asif
Zardari was now in power. His Pakistani friends had helped organise his first fundraiser in Chicago to be a Senator.

In his intelligence briefing McConnell explained that Pakistan
was paranoid that the US would abandon it, as it had after the
Soviet withdrawal in 1989, and leave them to the mercy of India.
He advised trying to somehow broker peace between India and
Pakistan.

Any chances of that were blown out of the water less than four
weeks after Obama's election by one of the most chilling terrorist
attacks the world had seen, ten gunmen laying siege to the city of

Afghans are famed as warriors and almost all their hobbies involve fighting.
Bird-fighting is a favourite pastime.

By 2014 Karzai's relations with the US were so bad that he blamed
America for the war and accused it of murder.

Instead of removing the warlords, the international community helped them get
back in power. One of Afghanistan's most powerful warlords is Ismael Khan,
here receiving elders at his home in Herat in 2014.

The 2014 Presidential elections were once again marred by fraud. The results were never released and a deal struck by which rivals Ashraf Ghani (right) and Abdullah Abdullah (left) became President and chief executive. They looked uncomfortable at their swearing-in on 29 September 2014.

New President Ashraf Ghani (centre) and, on his right, Vice President General Abdul Rashid Dostum, one of the country's most notorious warlords.

One of Afghanistan's first female rappers performs at an arts festival in Kabul in May 2013. Many women who expressed their freedom in similar ways now live in hiding, fearing for their lives.

Under the Taliban regime (1996–2001), girls were banned from going to school and women from working. Schools reopened in 2002 and there are now 3 million girls at school in Afghanistan.

Colonel Jamila Bayaz inspects her forces at District 1 Police Station in Kabul's old city. In January 2014 she became Afghanistan's first female police chief. Less than 1 per cent of the police are women.

Sultan Hamidy in his glass shop in Herat. His family has been blowing glass the same way for more than a century.

There are now 18 million mobile phones in Afghanistan. Even in the remotest villages such as this one in the poorest province of Samangan, elders are on Facebook. They can now check wheat prices so they are not cheated by middlemen.

Britain's last commander in Helmand, Brigadier Rob Thomson, handing over Camp Bastion to Afghan general Sayed Malouk in October 2014.

The last British soldiers leaving Helmand – and Afghanistan – after Britain's longest war since the Hundred Years War. 453 British soldiers were killed and hundreds badly injured and mentally scarred.

Sheikh Abdullah, guide at the Jihad Museum in Herat, is actually a Russian soldier, Khakimov Bakhretdin, who went to Afghanistan in the 1980s to fight. One of around thirty Russians who were taken prisoner or stayed behind, he was tracked down in 2014 but refused to go home.

The graphic sound-and-light show at the Jihad Museum is a grisly reminder of the perils of invading Afghanistan.

Mumbai for three days with multiple attacks while the whole thing played out to a horrified world audience on TV screens.

The attack unfolded in five locations across the city – Café Leopold, a favourite watering hole for tourists; the main railway terminus; a Jewish cultural centre; and two luxury waterfront hotels, including the Taj, which had played host to Frank Sinatra and Sophia Loren as well as a host of world leaders.

I was at a reception for some visiting Pakistani Ministers to London at the palatial Hampstead residence of Pakistan's High Commissioner Wajid Shamsul Hasan as the news was coming in on the first evening. 'They're Bangladeshi,' insisted one official. 'I hope to God they are not ours,' said Sherry Rehman, the Information Minister.

Pakistan's Foreign Minister Shah Mehmud Qureshi was in India at the time, in Delhi as part of attempts by Zardari to restart the peace process. It was a classic tactic for some kind of military or paramilitary action to be launched at the same time in order to derail everything, though usually it was confined to shooting across the disputed border; never had there been an attack of this magnitude.

Inevitably the gunmen did turn out to be Pakistani, poor young men from villages in the Punjab. One of them survived, twenty-one-year-old Ajmal Amir Kasab, whose surname ironically meant 'butcher'. He told prosecutors at his trial in Mumbai that he and his nine comrades had been recruited by Lashkar-e-Toiba (LeT). They had been trained for thirteen months, first at the organisation's Muridke headquarters in Lahore, then at other camps, including one near Muzzaffarabad in Pakistan-administered Kashmir, where they had also received training from retired and allegedly active duty members of Pakistan special forces and ISI. Though the camp was run by LeT, it was near a military base, was guarded by Pakistani troops, and provided with weapons and ammunition by the army. They received ideological indoctrination, training in how to use weapons and carry out assaults, and enacted role-play on hostage-taking as well as practising amphibious assault using inflatable boats on Mangla Dam. Ten trainees were selected from an initial batch of thirty-two, some of whom had run away. They were then taken to Karachi, from where the attack would allegedly be controlled by 'Major Iqbal', an ISI officer, and Zaki Rehman Lakhvi, a veteran of the jihad in Afghanistan who was the chief military commander of LeT and known to the recruits as 'chacha', or uncle. Before sending them off to their deaths he is said to have assured them, 'Your names will be etched in gold and every Pakistani will praise you.'

At dawn on 22 November 2008 the men boarded a small boat in Karachi and set sail into the Arabian Sea for the thirty-six-hour journey to Mumbai. Each had a backpack packed with an AK56 assault rifle (a Chinese version of the Kalashnikov), a Pakistani copy of a Colt pistol, ten hand grenades and hundreds of rounds of ammunition. Some had RDX explosive. They also had mobile phones, GPS, and supplies of water and energy bars, as well as steroids to help them stay awake.

On the second afternoon they hijacked an Indian fishing trawler in open sea and ordered the captain to sail to Mumbai. Once they were near it they slit his throat and boarded inflatable dinghies to land in two separate locations in the city's coastal slums. Two pairs set off by foot, and three by taxi, to their assigned targets. They were in touch by Skype and text with their controllers in the Karachi safe house, who used phones registered in Austria, US and Italy. Their instructions were to maim and kill as many people as possible from America, the UK and Israel. The first attack took place at 9.35 p.m. on the Leopold Café, a popular hangout for tourists, where two of them killed eleven diners by throwing grenades and firing randomly. That pair then headed for the Taj Hotel, firing en route and killing another thirteen people.

A second pair joined them at the Taj, while a third went to the Oberoi Trident Hotel and another to a Jewish cultural centre. The last, Kasab and his partner Abu Dera Ismael Khan, headed to the city's old Victoria railway terminus, where they hurled grenades into the busy ticket hall and started firing, creating mass panic. Khan and Kasab then headed to a hospital, where the staff managed to block their entry. As they fled they killed a policeman, who turned out to be Hemant Karkare, the city's most senior counter-terrorism officer. They were then stopped at a roadblock where Khan was killed and Kasab captured.

Meanwhile, two pairs of gunmen had burst their way into the grand marble reception of the Taj, shot staff, then headed into the restaurants, where they killed diners. They then began seizing hostages and herding them up to the nineteenth floor, moving from room to room, opening the doors and killing guests. Some tied sheets together and jumped out of windows. Others hid in bathrooms and wardrobes. Staff managed to evacuate about 250 guests to a private area called the Chambers Club, but some of these started to call relatives and to tweet, which led the media to report their whereabouts. The LeT control room in Karachi was watching everything on TV and social media, and quickly passed this information on to the terrorists.

Similar killing sprees were under way at the Oberoi and the Jewish centre, where six American Jews were among those murdered. The siege at the Taj went on the longest. Trapped in the hotel, the guests assumed they would soon be rescued, but only eight police arrived with bolt-action rifles and quickly retreated, realising they were far outgunned. It would be twelve hours before Black Cat commandos mobilised. The combination of chaos, bureaucracy and ill-equipped police meant the siege of the Taj would end up lasting sixty hours.

In all the terrorists killed 166 people, including twenty-two foreigners, sixteen police and twenty-seven hotel staff. Kasab said they had been instructed to 'Kill until your last breath.'

For Indians, this was their 9/11. Once again India and Pakistan were on the brink of war. Initially Pakistan refused to admit that the terrorists were Pakistanis, then when the evidence became overwhelming it resorted to its usual argument that these were 'non-state actors'. Afterwards it took huge restraint on the part of the Indians – and persuasion by the US and Britain – to stop India from retaliating, particularly as the role of ISI in the attack became clearer.

Some Pakistani journalists from *Dawn* newspaper tracked down Kasab's home village of Faridkot, a small, dusty place of mud-brick houses surrounded by water buffaloes and fields of rice. Locals told them that Kasab had left school at eleven after his father became ill and couldn't work, and earned money selling fried pakoras from a handcart in the square, but had then disappeared to Lahore. In a house with a green door they found Kasab's parents, two sisters and younger brother. The father sobbed as he admitted that Kasab was their son.

And then the family disappeared. Other journalists who went to the village were met with hostility, and told 'We don't know who Ajmal Kasab is.' When people tracked down the home villages of the nine dead terrorists, they found that their families too had disappeared.

In his testimony Kasab said he'd been promised that if he was successful in his operation his family would be given 150,000 rupees – about £1,000. He was sentenced to death and executed.

More incriminating information on Pakistan's role emerged almost a year after the attack when a tall, middle-aged American man with a blond ponytail was arrested at Chicago's O'Hare Airport as he was about to board a flight to Pakistan.

His name was David Headley, and he had been born in Washington DC in 1960 as Daood Gilani. His father was a well-known Pakistani broadcaster and his mother a rebellious heiress from Maryland. The couple had divorced, and Headley first lived with his father in Lahore and attended Cadet College, then at sixteen moved to Philadelphia to live with his mum above her bar, the Khyber Pass. He reportedly became an agent for the US Drug Enforcement Agency after being caught smuggling heroin in 1997 and serving several months in jail. Some time after that, on a trip to Lahore he became involved with LeT.

His arrest in October 2009 came after a tip-off from MI6. Initially he was charged with travelling to Copenhagen to scout the building of the Danish newspaper *Jyllands-Posten*, which had published cartoons said to lampoon the Prophet, for a terrorist attack. Then the FBI accused him of conspiring to bomb targets in Mumbai and providing material support to LeT, to which he pleaded guilty.

At his trial he told how he had been recruited by 'Major Iqbal' from ISI while on a trip to Pakistan in 2006 and given money to travel back to the US and apply for a passport with an anglicised name. He was given training from an army officer on ISI surveillance techniques. Major Iqbal then gave him $25,000 to open an office in Mumbai, where he made friends who nicknamed him 'David Armani' for his taste in designer clothes. Throughout 2008 he had made a series of trips to Mumbai to scout possible targets, gathering detailed information about street layouts, security, the movement of traffic and people, and making videos. Though he described ISI involvement in planning the attack, he testified that the agency's leadership was not involved. Headley was eventually sentenced to thirty-five years. The case made fewer headlines in the US than I had expected. US authorities were reluctant to talk, suggesting there was truth in the reports that he was a double agent.

In 2010 lawyers working for American survivors of Mumbai, and family members of seven of the eight American victims, filed a case in the federal court of New York against ISI and its past and present chief, as well as against LeT. The lead lawyer was James Kreindler, who had successfully sued the Libyan government for $10 million a head compensation for the victims of Pan Am Flight 103, blown up over Lockerbie in 1988. I went to see him in his Manhattan office, and he told me he wanted the same from ISI. He laughed when I asked about evidence implicating ISI. 'The record is replete with evidence of ISI's role in Mumbai going right back to ISI working with al Qaeda to create LeT. It's a complex game they are engaged in – fighting terrorism, working with terrorism, using terrorism … it's layers upon layers, but they have their hand in it all. ISI is really a spider's web of nefarious activities that makes the stuff on *Homeland* look simplistic.'

Would he be able to prove that Major Iqbal was still a serving member of ISI, I wondered. 'They move in and out of the organisation and "retire", but the force is still there,' he replied. He believed Pakistan would pay up rather than have all this exposed before a jury in a New York court.

However, the US government was not ready to abandon its old ally. The court ruled the case out after the State Department submitted a statement to say that ISI enjoyed diplomatic immunity, as it was part of a foreign government.

Kreindler begged to differ: 'ISI has been operating independently from the civilian government for many years, pursuing its own agenda which sometimes is the same as the government and other times quite different.'

The case was resubmitted in 2014, against LeT and its leader Hafiz Saeed. In Pakistan, however, to the frustration of India, LeT remained off-limits. Hafiz Saeed continued to hold rallies and appear at public events and on TV chat shows, even after the Americans put a $10 million bounty on his head in 2012. Its front organisation JuD bought fleets of ambulances, which operated all over the country. The LeT military commander Lakhvi was arrested in Pakistan on 7 December 2008, four days after Indian authorities named him as one of the masterminds of the attack, and he was later indicted with six others. The Pakistan government eventually allowed one of its own civilian intelligence agencies, the Federal Intelligence Agency (FIA), to carry out an investigation into the Mumbai attacks, and LeT's role in them. That came to an abrupt end when the prosecutor Chaudhry Zulfikar Ali was assassinated in broad daylight in Islamabad, his white Toyota Corolla riddled with bullets as he left for work in May 2013. He had been due to appear in court that morning in a case against ex-President Musharraf for failing to provide adequate security for Benazir Bhutto. In March 2015, Islamabad High Court ordered the release of Lakhvi. It was, as Kreindler had said, all 'layers upon layers'.

I asked Pakistan's Foreign Minister Shah Mehmud Qureshi whether he thought the Mumbai attack had been deliberately timed to derail his peace talks. 'Mumbai was a very sad incident and we condemned it and it unfortunately created a hiccup,' he said. He then turned his fire on India. 'What the army and people of Pakistan feel is we have some outstanding issues with India which need resolution. Is the Indian spending on defence justified? They have jacked up spending on defence by 34 per cent in this budget.'

Pakistan had other problems on its hands. In February 2009, two months after the Mumbai attacks, the government agreed a controversial peace deal with Maulana Fazlullah and his Taliban in Swat, and agreed to impose Sharia law in the valley. The Pakistan Taliban thus had their own emirate, and began moving south, closer to the capital.

The Americans were horrified. TV maps showed the Pakistan Taliban just sixty miles from the capital. This was a little misleading, as it might have been sixty miles as the crow flies, but there was the high Malakand Pass in between, and by road it was more like three hours. In testimony to the Foreign Affairs Committee of Congress Hillary Clinton called this an 'existential threat', and accused the Zardari government of 'abdicating to the Taliban and the extremists'.

President Obama tried to reach out directly to Zardari, inviting him to Washington in early May 2009. By then the army had moved into Swat, launching Operation Black Thunderstorm to try to recapture the territory. Many in Washington were arguing that Pakistan was a lost cause. 'Pakistan's pants are on fire,' said Democratic Congressman Gary Ackerman.

While in Washington Zardari had dinner with Zalmay Khalilzad, the American Afghan who had been Bush's Ambassador in Kabul and then Baghdad. Khalilzad was astounded when Zardari told him he believed one of two countries were behind the Pakistan Taliban attacks on his country – either India or the US. He didn't think Indians could be that clever, so it must be the US trying to destabilise Pakistan in order to invade it and seize its nuclear weapons. It was the old argument of ISI.

Swat was eventually recaptured from the Taliban, though only after a third of the population had fled the valley. Fazlullah was surrounded at one point, but after a tussle between ISI and the army he was escorted to the Afghan border, where he disappeared into the mountains of Kunar.

* * *

Throughout Obama's first year in office, American patience with Pakistan continued to be tested. Any attack or attempted attack seemed to link back there. On 19 September 2009 an Afghan-American, Najibullah Zazi, was arrested in Denver, apparently planning to detonate a series of backpacks containing home-made hydrogen-peroxide bombs in the New York subway. He later confessed, and said he had been recruited and trained at an al Qaeda camp in Pakistan.

Obama decided to again reach out to Zardari, writing him a personal letter in which he said using 'proxy groups' would no longer be tolerable. Remembering what Mike McConnell had said about Pakistan's paranoia about being abandoned again, he proposed a more formal long-term strategic partnership.

The letter was hand-delivered by Jim Jones and John Brennan, Obama's counter-terrorism adviser. They explained that to show that the new President was giving more importance to Pakistan, the region would henceforth be referred to as 'PakAf', instead of 'AfPak'. The Pakistanis were horrified. To them that sounded as if Pakistan was the main problem. Qureshi, the Foreign Minister, told me they resented being lumped with Afghanistan at all. 'You can't equate the two countries, our capacities are completely different,' he said. 'This is wrong terminology and should be discontinued.'

Obama's letter referred to Headley and Zazi, warning that if anything happened on US territory there would be a response. If, however, Pakistan cooperated, it could have pretty much anything it wanted. As a start he wanted to increase CIA teams on the ground for joint operations.

When the reply came it was a meandering letter which the White House concluded must have been dictated by ISI. 'We continue to suffer. Pakistan continues to bleed,' it read. 'The proxy war against Pakistan is now in full swing.'

Not knowing what else to do, and not wanting to confront Pakistan head on, the Obama administration resorted to strikes by secret CIA remote-controlled planes firing Hellfire missiles to try to take out militants in the tribal areas. 'Obama started to use drones for lack of strategy in Pakistan,' said David Kilcullen.

As early as the new President's third day in office, 23 January 2009, the first two took place – one in North Waziristan and one in South Waziristan, killing as many as twenty people. The one in the north hit a house which was thought to have four Arabs linked to al Qaeda inside, though locals later claimed it had killed a boy and some teachers. The one in the south killed a tribal leader who was pro-government and his entire family including three children, the youngest just five.

Obama was furious when he was told of the mistake. Yet the drones would become his main weapon in the battle against terrorism – the world's biggest ever secret assassination programme.

While Bush had authorised thirty-six strikes against Pakistan in the whole of 2008, Obama stepped them up to fifty-two in his first year in office. That was just the start.

To provide a carrot as well as a stick, that autumn Congress passed a Bill formulated by Senators John Kerry and Dick Lugar to give Pakistan $7.5 billion in aid over five years. At the last minute a clause was attached stating that the money was dependent on the military not interfering with the democratically elected government. Pakistan's military was predictably furious. General Ehsan ul Haq, the former ISI chief, was in Washington when it was voted, and pointed out the country's flawed democracy and the fact that more than two thirds of Pakistan's MPs do not pay taxes. 'I said to the Americans, "Why don't you stipulate that Prime Ministers need to pay taxes and are democratically elected?"'

Brigadier General Mick Nicholson, who had witnessed the problem on the border at first hand when he commanded forces there in 2006–07, and who returned to Kandahar in 2008, had become Director of the Pakistan/Afghan Coordination Cell at the Pentagon. He thought the large amounts of money being thrown around was one of the problems. 'We Americans approach things as very transactional,' he said. 'It was, "We'll give you $5 billion and pay your bills and you will do this for us."' Chaudhry Nisar Ali, a veteran Pakistani politician whose brother was a general, agreed: 'It's all about dollars and cents. What we want is for the Americans to listen to us.' However, as Nicholson pointed out, 'Then at the same time they were trying to extort money from us on the trucking contract, as all our supplies went through there, and it was Pakistani generals who run the trucking companies – it was a money-making opportunity for them. A Pakistani officer said to me once, "Why don't you just give us the money you're giving to the Afghan army, and we'll take care of things?" I was like, "That's pretty blatant, man. Really, seriously, the way you're taking care of it now?"'

However, as the Pakistanis repeatedly pointed out, they had 100,000 troops on their side of the Durand Line in the tribal areas, and were losing more men than the US. 'They knew how to get to us,' said Nicholson. 'They'd show me pictures of twelve general officers who had been killed and their family members, and told me how militants had even gone into mosques on military bases and killed the children of generals. Then they'd say, "Now you question us and our commitment?" When you see that, that made a believer out of me. When someone comes in and kills your family you are serious about fighting these guys.'

There was another concern. 'When you look at Pakistani society the military is maybe the only institution that can be any kind of guarantor of stability in the whole country,' said Nicholson. 'So you don't want to undermine it too bad. If you do, what happens? Where do the nukes end up?'

Any chance of rapprochement between the US and Pakistan was finished on 30 December 2009 when a Jordanian doctor blew himself up inside an American base in the town of Khost, in south-eastern Afghanistan, killing seven CIA agents.

Humam Khalil al-Balawi, aged thirty-two, had been recruited by Jordanian intelligence that January after being arrested for extreme anti-Western postings on militant websites. The Jordanians believed they had turned him in custody, and he was sent to Pakistan's tribal areas to infiltrate al Qaeda for the CIA by posing as a jihadi. Within six months he claimed to have worked his way into the higher echelons using his medical skills to treat commanders in North Waziristan and ended up as personal doctor to bin Laden's deputy Ayman al Zawahiri, treating him for his diabetes.

This was the first trace of the al Qaeda leadership for years. It seemed too good to be true. So thrilled was the Agency that its Deputy Country Chief travelled from Kabul to Khost, near the border with Pakistan, to meet him. The White House was put on notice to expect a call. It seemed like the first piece of good luck since losing bin Laden in the mountains of Tora Bora.

Balawi was picked up from the border by an Afghan army officer who was in charge of security at the base, FOB Chapman. He was wearing a turban and a large shawl round his shoulders known as a *pattu*. They switched cars in Khost as arranged and drove to the compound, which was surrounded by a high mud wall with watchtowers at each corner. There were two more walls inside with gates to pass through, each with razor wire on top and the last one manned by American soldiers. Astonishingly, given all the security in Afghanistan, Balawi was not searched once.

So excited was the CIA about its source that as the car stopped outside the Agency building and Balawi opened his door, seven CIA agents were waiting to greet him, including the station chief Jennifer Matthews, a mother of three, as well as his Jordanian handler.

As Balawi stepped out, he reached under his *pattu* and detonated his suicide vest with a blinding flash. So powerful was the thirty-pound bomb that it killed Agency operatives fifty feet away, lifted the car off the ground in the blast wave and blew the bomber's turban onto the barbed wire and his head into the parking lot.

It was the Agency's worst loss since 1983 when the US Embassy in Beirut was blown up by a truck bomb. Gary Berntsen, who led the CIA team in Tora Bora, told me the attack had taken out 'decades of experience'. Matthews had been one of the Agency's top experts on al Qaeda.

Afterwards many questions were asked as to how the CIA had let itself be led into such an ambush. Not least because, while supposedly working as a CIA asset, Balawi had continued with his anti-American online postings. The Agency had apparently believed it was good cover.

In fact it seems that in North Waziristan Balawi had linked up with America's old *bête noire* Jalaluddin Haqqani. A week after the attack a video was released showing Balawi alongside Hakimullah Mehsud, who had replaced Baitullah Mehsud as leader of the Pakistan Taliban.

Once again the US urged Pakistan to take action against the Haqqani network; once again Pakistan did nothing.

For CIA Director Leon Panetta this was now personal. No longer trusting ISI at all, he took advantage of the Kerry Lugar package as cover to send in more agents in the guise of aid consultants – a thousand of them, of whom three hundred were outside the ISI radar.

He also unleashed the only weapon he had. In 2010 the CIA more than doubled the number of drone strikes in Pakistan to 122, one every three days.

Locals in the tribal areas said there were so many Reapers and Predators flying overhead that the buzzing sound became part of life. One of the most backward areas on earth had become the main battleground of twenty-first-century warfare. They referred to them as '*bangana*' – Pashto for wasp.

25

Losing the Moral High Ground in Margaritaville

Guantánamo, February 2011

'LADIES AND GENTLEMEN, welcome to Guantánamo Bay!' announced the Air Sunshine pilot as we swooped down over a sparkling turquoise Caribbean fringed with sugary-white beaches that looked as if they belonged in a holiday advert.

From the moment we landed it was clear that this was one of the most surreal places I had ever visited. The door opened to a burst of tropical warmth and dazzling sunlight that had us all reaching for our sunglasses as we stepped down onto the steaming tarmac. A large board at customs proclaimed 'JTF Guantánamo; Honor Bound to Defend Freedom'.

Once outside we took a ferry across a waterway through banks of mangroves, with Jimmy Buffett's holiday calypso 'Margaritaville' playing over the speakers ('Nibblin' on sponge cake, Watching the sun bake ...'). Then we drove through town, past a shopping mall with a banner urging 'Buy Your Flowers and Chocolates for Valentine's Day', and past the only McDonald's on Cuban soil. On the right was an open-air cinema advertising *The Tourist* with Angelina Jolie and Johnny Depp, and a perfect green baseball diamond where men were practising in batting cages.

We were in a little bit of America in communist Cuba. The car radio was switched to Radio Gitmo, and 'Rockin' in Fidel's Backyard' rang out the jingle, followed by 'On an Island With Nowhere to Go'.

The US presence dated from the Spanish–American War in 1898, and the most recent lease, signed in 1934, granted it an indefinite use for $4,085 a year, cheques that Castro always refused to cash.

Now it was prison to some of America's greatest enemies, often referred to as 'the worst of the worst', including KSM, the mastermind of 9/11 whose final hiding place I had visited in Rawalpindi. Also incarcerated there were his fellow plotter Ramzi bin al-Shibh; Abu Zubayda, regarded as a key facilitator; and Abd al Rahim al Nashiri, mastermind of the bombing of the naval ship USS *Cole* in Yemen. Yet, as I had endlessly heard in Afghanistan, there were also many who had simply been in the wrong place at the wrong time, or denounced by tribal enemies and sold for bounties to Americans unfamiliar with tribal rivalries.

As we reached the crest of a small hill a yellow road sign warned us to slow down for iguanas, and we did – the driver explained that there was a $10,000 fine if you hit one. It seemed a strange thing to worry about in a place where human rights had been left behind.

I had wanted to visit 'Gitmo', as it was known, ever since I had moved to the US. Guantánamo was deliberately chosen as a detention centre by the Bush administration because they believed it placed the detainees outside the reach of American laws such as the right to appeal against their imprisonment. It was, said one adviser, 'the legal equivalent of outer space'.

The first twenty prisoners had been brought here from the war in Afghanistan on 11 January 2002, with another ninety shortly after. I was in Afghanistan when the first pictures emerged (taken by a military photographer) of the scarily named Camp X-Ray with its caged inmates in orange jumpsuits and goggles kneeling or on all fours like dogs in a kennel while soldiers trained rifles on them. Wherever I went reporting in Afghanistan and Pakistan, people constantly referred to this humiliating treatment, as well as to atrocities such as Korans being stamped on by guards or thrown down toilets. How could a country that holds itself up as a beacon of liberty do such a thing, they asked.

Camp authorities would later say that they had been given less than a week to build cells for more than a hundred prisoners, and that a new camp had quickly been erected, with running water and proper buildings. But those Camp X-Ray images were indelibly stamped on the world's consciousness, along with reports of brutal interrogations and torture, and international condemnation was swift. A total of 779 men and children, as young as fourteen and as old as eighty-nine, had been through Guantánamo, which had become synonymous with the Bush administration's extra-legal approach.

During his election campaign, Obama had vowed to end what he described as 'a sad chapter in American history'. One of his first acts on taking office was an executive order, signed on 22 January 2009, to close Guantánamo within one year. 'Living our values doesn't make us weaker, it makes us stronger,' he said.

Two years on it was still operating, and 197 prisoners were still there. Obama had other priorities, such as passing affordable healthcare legislation, for which he needed his political capital. Then in his first Congressional elections, in November 2010, he had suffered what he called a 'shellacking', losing control of Congress to the Republicans, who blocked funding for transferring the prisoners to mainland America.

Not only that, but the authorities at Guantánamo were still carrying out the military commissions — where the military are judge, prosecutor, defence and jury — that Obama, the lawyer President, had also vowed to end, denouncing them as 'a legal black hole'. In the two years since he took office there had been only one civilian trial of a Guantánamo detainee. There had been two military commissions, both plea bargains, and a third was about to start, which I had received permission from the Pentagon to attend.

Our small group of journalists were taken first to the MOC, or Media Operations Center, where we were given the ground rules. Basically there were three: we could go nowhere unaccompanied by our military press minders, so we would have to go everywhere as a group; we could photograph almost nothing; and they wouldn't really tell us anything.

The area we were staying in was called 'Camp Justice'. I thought someone was being ironic, but it had been named that for its purpose-built courtrooms. We were billeted in 'Tent City', a double row of cigar-shaped army tents, women in the front and men at the back. At the end of the row were the shower tent and the toilet tent – a row of latrines separated only by canvas and with no doors. The flushing system was so complicated we had to have a briefing on how to operate it.

After we had all got settled we were driven to the NEX, the Navy Exchange supermarket, to buy souvenir Guantánamo T-shirts for us newbies (I resisted the ones printed 'Behavior Modification Instructor') and alcohol supplies for the regulars. We also bought locally bottled water labelled 'Freedom Springs'. Guantánamo was full of ironies. That evening we were taken to Kelly's Irish pub for smokehouse burgers, margaritas with cocktail umbrellas and bottles of Red Stripe. Afterwards it was hard to sleep. The tents were very noisy because of a vast air-conditioning unit pumping out cold air, and I dreamed I was in a hurricane.

Next morning we were taken on a 6.45 a.m. Starbucks run to a café overlooking the bay. Across the water we could see the white guard towers from which the Cubans watch, faced by the plywood towers of the Americans, one of the last vestiges of the Cold War. In between was a minefield. As we downed our cappuccinos, a bugle blast of Reveille came over the loudspeaker, followed by 'The Star Spangled Banner'. Our press officer immediately stood to attention and saluted towards the flag on the hill, staying like that for the entire anthem. She explained that they had to do that at 8 o'clock every morning and evening.

The hearing was starting at 9 a.m., so we were taken back over to Camp Justice, where the trials took place. A $12 million maximum-security courthouse had been specially built on an abandoned landing strip, surrounded by a high fence topped with coils of concertina wire. Snipers take up position on nearby roofs whenever the court is in session, and to enter we had to pass through two x-ray machines. We were allowed nothing inside but notebooks, pens and bottles of water, from which we had to remove the labels in case we had written messages on them.

The viewing gallery was behind a double layer of hurricane glass. There were four rows of seats for journalists, human rights observers and family members, if they could get here. A forty-second delay on the sound system meant any classified information could be redacted by an intelligence officer who listened in and activated a red light whenever anything too sensitive was said.

We watched the lawyers for both sides come in. The room was soon full of uniforms – apart from the judge, a female navy officer. The jury was all military officers and most of the lawyers a mix of army, air force and navy. On the right was the prosecution, the government side, led by Chief Prosecutor Major Myrick, a hefty Marine in green uniform with shaven head. He led a team of eight set out on three benches. On the left was the defence, led by a dark-suited civilian, Howard Cabot, a top Manhattan lawyer working pro bono.

Suddenly a door opened and the accused was brought in. Detainee 707 was Noor Uthman Mohammed, a Sudanese man with a beard the colour of ashes, clad in a pristine white *shalwar kamiz* with white prayer cap and denim jacket. He shuffled into the court-room, wrists secured firmly by American soldiers on either side, then sat, headphones clamped on his head to translate proceedings into Arabic. He was not shackled, but he looked frail, far older than his mid-forties, and beaten down. It had taken him eight and a half years to get his day in court. To do so, he'd had to enter a pre-trial agreement to plead guilty. Before he could enter the courtroom he'd had to sit in a chair called a Body Orifice Security Scanner, to be scanned for hidden metal objects.

The pre-trial agreement meant there was little in the way of courtroom drama – the only thing to be decided was his sentence, and to lighten that he had promised to tell all he knew. Turning supergrass and pleading guilty to war crimes appeared to be the only way out of the world's most notorious prison, where 169 of the 172 inmates were still to come to court.

Asked repeatedly by the judge, speaking slowly in a melodious voice as if to a schoolchild, if he was voluntarily pleading guilty, he stated one word: '*Na'am*' – Arabic for yes. Over and over he was asked. Over and over he replied, '*Na'am.*' Yes, he understood the charges; yes, he had seen the translation; yes, nobody had made him plead guilty.

Before anything further could happen we had the screening of the jury. All were military, and almost all seemed to have served in Iraq or Afghanistan.

The trial started for real on the second day. 'Terrorists are not born, they are made, and the accused has made thousands of them,' was the government's dramatic opening statement from Arthur Gaston, a tall naval commander, resplendent in black uniform with gold epaulettes and buttons. He recounted how in 1994 Noor had arrived in Khalden training camp in Afghanistan, where he gave weapons training to al Qaeda recruits and worked his way up the hierarchy. He had then helped shut it down before 9/11 and moved to a safe house in the Pakistani city of Faisalabad, run by top al Qaeda operative Abu Zubayda. It was there, in a raid in March 2002, that he was picked up along with more than twenty other suspected terrorists, as well as detonators for roadside bombs and a manual that recommended beheading infidels.

His defence admitted that he had been in the camp, but argued that he had never been a member of al Qaeda. Instead they said he was 'little more than a low-level functionary, cooking, running errands', caught up in 'the wrong place at the wrong time'. Born sometime in the 1960s in Port Sudan to a camel herder, Noor had been orphaned at an early age and survived by scavenging and selling things in a market to buy food, and sleeping on relatives' floors. At the market he met pilgrims on their way to cross the Red Sea to Mecca, who told him about Muslim women and children being slaughtered, and the need for jihad. Then, 'out of religious solidarity', he somehow made his way to Afghanistan in 1994, training at Khalden camp then never leaving. First he became an instructor. After a while he stopped doing that and became a kind of camp quartermaster, and mostly it seemed he cooked rice. When

9/11 happened he had decided to return to Sudan, and had gone to stay in Abu Zubayda's safe house in Faisalabad while he waited for papers. Then one night the door was broken down and Pakistanis and Americans poured in.

Captain John Murphy, Chief Prosecutor for the military commissions, insisted that Noor was more than just a footsoldier: 'He was an integral part of Khalden camp, which was a major training facility for al Qaeda providing a pipeline of terrorists.' Those who trained there included Zacharias Moussawi, the so-called 'twentieth hijacker', whose evidence was used against Noor; Mohammed al-Owhali, who took part in bombing the US Embassy in Kenya; and Ahmed Ressan, convicted of participating in the 'Millennium Plot' to bomb Los Angeles Airport in December 1999.

Over the next three days the prosecution mostly told the story of these other men. Noor sat tapping his left foot and staring listlessly to one side. There didn't seem to be any evidence linking him to any attack. The defence pointed out that of 1,050 fingerprints taken on the second storey of Abu Zubayda's house, where the bomb materials were found, not one belonged to Noor. 'Noor is not Osama bin Laden or Ayman al Zawahiri,' said the defence's Howard Cabot. 'He's not the living embodiment of al Qaeda. He's a religious man of limited education who left an impoverished background to go to Afghanistan because of religious duty.'

In Noor's own statement he said that in nine years of US custody, first at Bagram airbase in Afghanistan then at Guantánamo, he had been hooded and chained, subjected to extreme heat and cold and loud music, made to stand for hours, and stripped naked in front of female interrogators. Two of his teeth were knocked out by a guard's rifle-butt. In all those years in custody he had written only one letter home, which was delivered by the Red Cross. 'Please pray for me,' it said. 'I am being held by the Americans.' He appealed to be allowed to return home to stay with his brother Omar, an electrician. In return for a sentence of between ten and fourteen years, he forfeited the right to any appeal about his detention or treatment, and agreed to testify against Abu Zubayda as well as others.

After three days the jury came back with its sentence. Noor rose. Fourteen years, of which he had already served nine. A maximum of thirty-four more months would be in Guantánamo.

Afterwards there were competing press briefings outside the MOC. The government prosecutor declared the verdict a victory that showed the value of the commissions. The human rights observers denounced it as a sham.

Among those observing the proceedings was Mary Cheh, a law professor at George Washington University who was on the board of the National Institute of Military Justice. 'It's a case of no way out, you get one path and that path seems to be to admit guilt to war crimes,' she told me. 'The whole thing was like a kabuki dance where everyone has set roles. I'm sure this is not the way the Obama administration wanted to go.'

Noor would remain in Guantánamo for almost three more years. Finally, on 19 December 2013, he was transferred back to Sudan.

He was one of the lucky ones. In 2009 a taskforce set up by Obama reviewed all the prisoners. It concluded that forty-eight needed to be held indefinitely, on the basis that they were 'too dangerous to release'; thirty-five should be tried; and eighty-nine were being held for no reason and should be released or transferred. Most of them had been there for years. Yet they were still there, because no one knew what to do with them. Fifty-eight of them were Yemenis; it was feared that if they were released they might well join al Qaeda in the Arabian Peninsula (AQAP), which was increasingly seen as the main terrorist threat. Another thirty-one were from countries such as China or Libya, to which it was not safe for them to return. The Obama administration was trying to get third countries to accept them, but with little success. The last to be moved on had been four Uighurs, Chinese Muslims who claimed they had gone to Afghanistan to flee Chinese persecution. They had been given homes in Bermuda in 2009 – perhaps luckier than the six transferred to Albania in 2006.

'The Obama administration is afraid to stand up and say, "Goddamn it, we've got innocent people, we must release them,"' said Thomas Wilner, a lawyer who represented Kuwaiti detainees in Guantánamo. 'He should be ashamed.'

Among those who had been cleared for release yet were still at Guantánamo was a British citizen, Shaker Aamer, a Saudi-born father of five from Battersea who had gone to Afghanistan in summer 2001 to work for a Saudi charity. Like so many Guantánamo prisoners he was not captured on the battlefield but sold for a bounty, and taken first to Bagram and then to Guantánamo. He had been cleared for release by two tribunals yet never freed, some said because if he spoke out about the torture he had witnessed in Bagram it would be potentially explosive.

In Washington I had met Colonel Morris ('Mo') Davis, who had served as Chief Prosecutor at Guantánamo for two years, from 2005 to 2007, then quit in protest. 'Our reputation has been tarnished by what we've done at Guantánamo,' he told me. That week Hillary Clinton had publicly criticised Russia for 'selective prosecution' in the conviction of oil tycoon Mikhail Khodordovsky. 'How does she do that with a straight face when we're keeping people in Gitmo who are never setting foot in a courtroom?' Davis asked.

Indeed, the man who first set up the prison at Guantánamo agreed. Since retiring, Marine Corps General Michael Lehnert had spent much of his time giving talks to schools. 'Guantánamo is a blight on our history,' he said. 'It stands as a recruiting poster for terrorists.'

Of course, the prison was what we journalists all wanted to see in Guantánamo. One afternoon we got our wish. We were presented with glossy press folders declaring 'Guantánamo – Safe, Humane, Legal, Transparent' and showing a photograph of a relaxed inmate walking in the late-afternoon light. Having failed to close the prison, it seemed they were now trying to promote it.

The prison was only about fifteen minutes' drive along Recreation Road. It was located on the edge of the bluff, but designed in such a way that the prisoners had no sight of the sea. The area was surrounded by razor wire, and the gate had the base motto: 'Honor Bound to Defend Freedom'.

The notorious Camp X-Ray, with its open-air cages, was long closed and overgrown with weeds, though surprisingly it had not been destroyed, apparently preserved by court order. Even the plywood interrogation area with its rotting desks and chairs was still there.

Camp X-Ray had been replaced by Camp Delta, a collection of shipping containers and cinderblock buildings. Joseph Hickman, a former Marine who joined the Maryland National Guard after 9/11 hoping to be posted to Afghanistan, ended up at Guantánamo as a prison guard in 2006. He describes going up Tower 1, the supervisors' tower watching over the camps. 'What blew my mind was the noise. Guards were yelling at detainees to shut up and prisoners were screaming back at them "Fuck you America!" Some were standing or lying in their cells yelling at no one – I'd never seen such chaos in a prison.'

He said guards, who were often young navy cooks, would deliberately provoke prisoners. 'They had developed a game called the "Frequent Flyer Program" where they would wake a detainee at midnight, shackle and cuff him then run him from one cell block to the next, put him in an empty cell, take off his cuffs and start the process again until finally back at his original cell. Whichever guards got the fastest time won drinks the next night.'

He also witnessed prisoners being savagely beaten. 'For the first time in uniform I started to feel shame,' he said.[1]

Camp Delta had since been replaced by the three adjoining two-storey concrete buildings we could see – Camps 5 and 6. No one got to see Camp 7, where the worst offenders such as KSM were housed. Indeed, our minders wouldn't even tell us where it was.

We did, however, get a rare peek into Camp 5, for 'non-compliant' prisoners. It seemed impossible to get exact information on Guantánamo, and when I asked our tour guide, the deputy camp commander John Rhodes, for the number of inmates being held in Camp 5 he replied, 'About fifteen.' When I asked what that meant, he replied, 'As low as zero, as many as a hundred.'

For our tour a small, windowless cell with a steel toilet and basin had been laid out with towels, flip-flops, toothbrush and paste, a prayer mat and worry beads – the items an inmate was allowed in the ninety-five-square-foot space. The orange jump-suits had been replaced by white ones unless prisoners were being disciplined for offences such as throwing faeces at guards, in which case they were back in orange. 'We have one prisoner who always wears orange trousers as a fashion statement,' said Rhodes. Each prisoner was allowed eight reading materials. Among the most popular books in the prison library was Harry Potter, though at the time of my visit the prison bestseller was Dan Brown's *Angels and Demons* in Arabic. As for magazines, the favourites were *National Geographic* and car magazines such as *Hot Rod.*

If they were well-behaved the reward was to be given a remote control and allowed four hours of television a week. This could be viewed locked alone in a room sitting in an armchair, feet shackled to the floor.

Through a series of locked gates we were taken to the adjoining Camp 6, the newest prison, completed in 2006, which was at that time home to 'about 125' inmates. This was for 'highly compliant' prisoners who were allowed to live communally in blocks, each with a leader, and only restricted to their cells between midnight and 4 a.m. Rhodes would not tell me which camp the British pris-oner was in.

The favourite prison sport was football, and we could hear a game under way. 'We have some of the best soccer players you'll ever see,' said Rhodes. We didn't see, as the game was being played behind a high fence which we were not allowed through. Instead he took us into a communal rotunda area which had a large TV bolted to the wall. 'Forty-two-inch with twenty-one channels,' he said. The Arab Spring was in full flood, protesters in Cairo's Tahrir Square having forced out President Mubarak. Many of the prison-ers were from the Middle East, and were following events avidly on al Jazeera. They got three newspapers, including *USA Today* – which they called 'USA Last Week', as it arrived a week late. Anything sensitive was blacked out, which appeared to be quite a lot of the front page.

A table had been laid out with recreation items ranging from a book of Sudoku puzzles to a PlayStation 3. 'Prisoners can also take classes,' said Rhodes, adding that the most popular course was art. One detainee only painted roses. I couldn't help noticing that under the tables were shackles. 'It's a soft shackle to put round prisoners' legs for the instructor's safety,' he said.

I had begun to think we were never actually going to see a prisoner. But finally we were allowed a quick look at some in one of the communal living areas. It was weird staring through one-way glass at these bearded men in white jumpsuits, all wearing earphones. They couldn't see us, but they seemed to be staring out, and we caught a glimpse of handwritten protest signs before we were hurriedly moved on.

The previous month an Afghan prisoner had been found dead in the shower after an apparent heart attack. He had been working out 'too hard on the elliptical', we were told.

Rhodes insisted that conditions in Guantánamo had greatly improved. 'I recently agreed a request for chocolate,' he told us. Each prisoner would get a Snickers bar on Mondays and Fridays. He had also moved far more prisoners into the communal blocks – up from a third to 92 per cent – which he said had led to a dramatic reduction in attacks on guards. Though the number of attacks had fallen from more than six hundred in 2009 to a little over a hundred in 2010, that was still two a week. Things were obviously not that good. The fact was, most of these people had probably been picked up for no reason, and now had little hope of ever coming to court. 'Not knowing my future is the worst torture,' Shaker Aamer would write in a letter to his lawyer.[2]

Our press minders were very keen for us to see the prison hospital, where the wonderfully named Drs Sme and Sno proudly showed off the facilities, and glossy posters adorned the walls. They kept pointing out that the camp had 'a higher doctor–patient ratio than in mainland US', and that the treatment was 'far better than most detainees had ever received in their lives'.

We were hurried past the two intensive-care beds inside metal cages. In one room a table was set out with an array of yellow feeding tubes and cans of Ensure liquid nutrient for prisoners on hunger strike. Dr Sme admitted that they had administered between twelve and fifteen cans that morning alone. 'They are just doing it to gain favour with their brothers,' he said. 'It's part of their fight.' The favourite flavour, he told us, was strawberry. He made it sound like giving milk shakes to children. But there was no hiding the fact that being strapped to a chair, having rubber feeding tubes stuck up your nostrils and into your stomach, and being forcibly fed till you vomited was not something one would subject oneself to unless from despair at seeing no way out. Indeed, two years later, in early 2013, reinforcement medics had to be sent to Guantánamo because around two thirds of the prisoners had resorted to hunger strike.

Some people did get out, and the stories they had to tell were not pretty. In Kabul I had met the former Taliban Ambassador to Pakistan, Mullah Abdul Salam Zaeef, the man we journalists had known as 'the Smiling Taliban', who had spent more than three years in Guantánamo.

Zaeef was arrested by ISI in Islamabad and handed over to the Americans, who, he said, took him to Bagram and subjected him to beating and freezing temperatures. He was flown to Guantánamo on 1 July 2002, hooded and chained to other prisoners for the entire thirty-hour journey. By the time they arrived his hands were so swollen that the handcuffs had sunk deep into the flesh, making them hard to open.

He was dressed in one of the notorious orange jumpsuits and taken to the so-called 'Gold Block' of Camp Delta, at that time the only block, where he was put in a small cage, four feet wide and six feet long, with just a metal board to sleep on, a water tap and a toilet. There were no walls, just metal mesh separating the cages. 'It was very uncomfortable having to use the toilet in front of other prisoners,' he said.

They were each issued with two blankets, two towels, a toothbrush and a Koran, but they were so confused about where they were that they prayed in different directions, not knowing where

Mecca was located. If they complained about the lack of food, the following week the menu would be worse.

There were abuses, such as a female guard deliberately throwing a Koran on the ground. Some of the soldiers beat them and tormented them with heavy-metal music, others tried to help. Occasionally they were visited by people from the Red Cross who gave them tea and biscuits; however, Zaeef said they did not trust them.

While he was there a second camp was built, which was known as 'Camp Echo' and which he described as 'a very dark and lonely place'. Prisoners were monitored 24/7 by video cameras, and inside the cells it was impossible to tell if it was night or day. 'No one could hear if you screamed,' he said. There were no books, and even the Korans were taken away.

A third camp was then built, after which he said conditions deteriorated. They were served less food, the quality worsened and their punishment increased. The cages were too small to lie down in; the toilets were visible to all and often blocked, so there was a foetid smell. 'We were not given toilet paper or water to clean ourselves after using the toilet,' he later wrote. 'Only our hands could be used but could not be washed afterwards. The prisoner had to use those same hands to eat his food afterwards. This is how those who claim to defend human rights made us live.'[3]

He said there were daily suicide attempts. There was also violence between the prisoners. Some were thought to be spies and cooperating with the Americans, so others would spit on them, particularly those who abandoned Islam and started wearing crosses in the hope of being released.

Two more camps were built while Zaeef was there. Camp 4 was for those soon to be released, where prisoners lived communally and were allowed to play games and sports and given better food. This was where journalists were taken. There was also Camp 5, away from the others, which word spread was the worst place. 'Each brother who spent time in Camp 5 looked like a skeleton when he was released,' he said.

Many of the prisoners arrested in Pakistan told similar stories – ISI or the police had captured them, and if they could not pay a bribe they were interrogated, beaten and abused, then sold to the Americans. Many had never been to Afghanistan or had any involvement with al Qaeda or the Taliban, but were shoemakers or shepherds. One man was arrested for watching his cattle with his binoculars, another for 'wearing the clothes of a mujahid'. Zaeef said Pakistan was known among the prisoners as 'Majbooristan', the land obliged to fulfil each of America's demands.

Sometimes the prisoners tried to organise, though there was little they could do. In the summer of 2005 disillusionment became so great that there was a mass hunger strike, with at its peak 275 people taking part.

Zaeef was released back to the Afghan government at the end of 2005 because it was thought he could facilitate talks with the Taliban leadership.

One of those who arrived in Guantánamo around the same time as Mullah Zaeef was a Mauritanian called Mohamedou Ould Slahi. He had won a scholarship to Germany, where he had done an engineering degree and also met two of the 9/11 bombers who were living there. After spending two years fighting jihad in Afghanistan from 1990 to 1992, he was picked up in the Mauritanian capital Nouakchott in November 2001, taken to Bagram, then in August 2002 to Guantánamo.

Initially he was believed by camp commanders to be a senior recruiter for al Qaeda, but eventually they concluded he was not involved. Like so many he was never charged, yet never released. 'He reminded me of Forrest Gump,' said Colonel Mo Davis, 'in that there were a lot of noteworthy events in the history of al Qaeda and terrorism, and there was Slahi lurking somewhere in the background.'

Somehow in that hunger-strike summer of 2005 Slahi had managed to write an account of his life in Guantánamo, which was published almost a decade later, after a long battle and 2,500 redactions. The first account by a still-serving prisoner, it recounted sleep deprivation, ice baths, repeated beatings, insults, sexual humiliation and brutal interrogations. He described one particularly painful day in August 2003 when he was dragged from his freezing-cold cell, a bag was pulled over his head, and he was thrown onto a boat with men who made him drink sea water until he vomited.

'My chest was so tightened that I could not breathe properly,' he wrote. 'I c...a...c...n't br...e,' he gasped. 'Suck the air!' shouted one of his captors. His ordeal was just beginning. Slahi was beaten for hours, and ice slipped between his skin and clothes. 'Whenever the ice melted they put in new hard ice cubes. Moreover every once in a while one of the guards smashed me, most of the time in my face ... there is nothing more terrorising than making somebody expect a smash every single heartbeat.'[4]

Guantánamo wasn't the only problem. Prisoners in other facilities were also mistreated. In a Thai restaurant in suburban Bethesda, Maryland, sitting among blue fish-tanks, with Katie Melua crooning 'Crazy' over the speakers, I interviewed a former CIA agent who had a shocking story to tell.

A middle-aged man with a slight paunch under his pink shirt and sand-coloured cargo pants, carrying a dog-eared copy of the works of Plato, Glenn Carle wasn't exactly my image of a spy. Indeed, he told me that a year after 9/11 he was wondering if he would ever be sent on a mission again, after a series of mistakes including leaving a briefcase of documents in a meeting with foreign spies. Then he was called up. His fluent French was required: he was to go and interrogate a captured HVT (high-value target) who it was believed could help locate Osama bin Laden.

Carle was pleased. He had headed the Agency's Afghan department for four years before 9/11, and he and his English wife knew three of those killed in the Twin Towers, including two young women who worked in the Windows on the World restaurant on the top floor. 'I was going to be part of the avenging hidden hand of the CIA,' he said. 'I wanted to interrogate the SOB. I could not wait to look him in the eye and get him to reveal the inner workings of al Qaeda.'

He was told to 'do whatever was necessary' to obtain the information. In other words to use enhanced interrogation techniques, or EIT, such as sleep deprivation, keeping someone in freezing temperatures or standing for long periods, putting them in a confined space with insects, or waterboarding, simulated drowning carried out repeatedly. Carle was shocked. 'We don't do that sort of thing,' he said. 'We do now,' came the reply.

When he questioned the legality of such techniques he was shown a set of memos drafted by John Yoo at the Department of Justice in August 2002 to the CIA and Pentagon that later became known as the 'Torture Memos', and that permitted operatives to move to the 'increased pressure phase'. 'Basically they said, "Do what you want – what the President says is legal is legal."' When Carle brought up the protection of prisoners of war under the Geneva Convention, he was asked, 'Which flag do you serve?'

By then the CIA had established a series of 'black sites' outside US jurisdiction in countries in Eastern Europe and the Middle East where torture was common. One of these was in Morocco, where he was sent.

The prisoner he had been tasked with interviewing was Haji Pacha Wazir, the owner of a network of *hawala* money-transferring agencies in Karachi and the Middle East, who had been kidnapped in the streets of Dubai. The CIA was cock-a-hoop at his capture. They believed he was al Qaeda's top financier – literally bin Laden's banker. 'We can do anything we want,' Carle warned him. 'No one knows where you are. Three thousand of my countrymen are dead, in part because of you.'

Within a week, however, he realised that the man, who he referred to as 'Captus', was not who his bosses thought, and was not even a member of al Qaeda, let alone someone who could lead them to its leader: 'I became convinced he was basically like the train conductor who unknowingly sells a criminal a ticket,' he said. But the more he told Langley they were wrong, the more they insisted he used stronger techniques. 'Be creative, be aggressive, pressure him ...' they said.

Carle admitted to me that in his twenty-three years as a spy, 'I broke laws, I stole, I lied every day about almost everything.' Yet this was going too far. He pointed out that the CIA's own training manual states: 'In general, direct physical brutality creates only resentment, hostility and further defiance.' His cables fell on deaf ears. Langley had Pacha transferred to Afghanistan, hooded and shackled and bundled onto a rendition or 'ghost' flight by agents dressed in black like ninjas. Carle went with him. Their destination was a CIA base near the airport in Kabul, known as 'Hotel California' after the Eagles song featuring the lines 'You can check in any time you like, but you can never leave.'

This was the most notorious of all the black sites. Carle said standard techniques employed there included 'noise, extremes of temperature, sleep deprivation, continuous light or darkness, stripping, hooding – all designed to disorient and psychologically dislocate in the hope of breaking him'. It was miserable for the agents too, with nowhere to go except the dismal Jihadi Bar.

When Pacha still did not provide the information they wanted, they picked up his brother in Germany, who was mentally backward, and interrogated him too.

In December 2002 Carle was told he was being moved on. He spent his last night at Hotel California writing the bluntest cable of his career. In it he again insisted that the assessment that had led to Pacha's rendition had been wrong, and that both men should be freed. Later he discovered it was never sent on by the station chief.

Pacha remained in US custody another eight years – one of the so-called ghost detainees not registered anywhere. He was finally released in 2010, after the Afghan government issued a lawsuit against the US government, and allowed home to Jalalabad.

Back in Langley, Carle watched in silent outrage as President Bush issued a statement in support of the UN Day in support of victims of torture. 'I had lived what we were doing,' he said. 'Our actions soiled what it meant to be American.'

A Senate report on torture, partially released in December 2014, said that it was carried out on a systematic basis on prisoners picked up after 9/11, and was ineffective. It cited examples of slapping, humiliation, exposure to cold, sleep deprivation for as long as seven days, and 'forced rectal feeding', including an anally infused 'lunch tray' of pureed hummus, pasta and nuts. Three prisoners were waterboarded – KSM 183 times, Abu Zubayda at least eighty-three times (he also lost an eye while in custody) and Abd al Rahim al Nashiri an unknown number of times. The Senate investigation found that none of this torture produced any life-saving intelligence. 'This report tells a story of which no American is proud,' it concluded.

Yet no one was punished for what they had done. The only CIA officer who participated in the torture programme to be jailed was the man who blew the whistle on it. John Kiriakou went public on waterboarding in 2007 and was jailed in 2013 – not for the torture, but for disclosing classified information.

Dick Cheney who was Vice President when all this was going on, denounced the Senate report as 'full of crap'. 'I think what needed to be done was done,' he told CNN. 'And I'd do it again in a minute.' It also created a Kafkaesque web. The well-documented use of torture was one of the reasons that cases of Guantánamo prisoners could not come to trial, as the US authorities could not risk opening themselves up to prosecution for their own crimes.

A week after my visit to Guantánamo I interviewed Donald Rumsfeld in a hotel room in New York where he was promoting his memoir, *Known and Unknown*. He was unrepentant about everything, from the war in Iraq to waterboarding. As for Gitmo, he made it sound like a spa. 'I think any honest representation of Guantánamo is it's a properly run facility where people have excellent healthcare, excellent food and athletic opportunities,' he said. 'I remember one Belgian woman who visited and said Guantánamo was vastly better than jails in Belgium. I'm so glad you're interested,' he added, smiling thinly.

26

Chairman Mullen and the Cadillac of the Skies

On board Admiral Mullen's plane, August 2010

THE PROGRAMME HANDED to us on boarding was printed with the enthralling words 'Trip Around the World'. Honolulu–Seoul–New Delhi–Islamabad–Kabul–Kandahar–Baghdad, ran the itinerary: one beach resort, then mostly conflict zones.

Like some latterday emperor, America's top military commander was inspecting his theatres, and I had managed to get invited along.

Travel with military always seemed to involve an ungodly alarm call, and the first pink fingers of dawn were only just lightening the sky when I met up with Admiral Mike Mullen, Chairman of the Joint Chiefs of Staff, and his team at Andrews Airbase outside Washington. Dressed in white Aertex golf shirt and navy tracksuit bottoms, the grey-haired sixty-three-year-old in frameless glasses had the kindly face of a grandfather (he had indeed recently become one).

Mullen was a most unlikely admiral. He grew up in Hollywood, surrounded by movie stars – his parents were publicists – and their kitchen featured in the Quentin Tarantino movie *Pulp Fiction*. However, he wanted to play basketball, and won a sports scholarship to the famous Annapolis Naval School, where he liked the idea of a life on the seas. The first ship he commanded – a tanker – he crashed into a buoy, damaging the propeller.

Chairman Mullen and the Cadillac of the Skies

It obviously didn't hinder his career, for he had risen to the top of the ranks, not just of the navy but the entire military. His spokesman, Captain John Kirby, told me he got up at 3.45 every morning to bench-press 255 pounds – more than twice my weight – while a trainer called Big Dave shouted, 'The baddest chairman ever!'

I'm not sure what I had expected of travelling with the Americans, but this wasn't exactly a luxury trip. Our home for much of the next ten days was Mullen's specially fitted-out C17 military cargo plane which his team jokingly referred to as 'the Cadillac of the Skies'. To my astonishment, when I got inside I found much of the interior taken up by a shiny aluminium Airstream motor home strapped down to the floor. Mullen's staff called this 'the Silver Bullet', and the chairman sat inside like a Queen Bee, speaking to the President on a secure line, conferring with aides bearing files marked 'Top Secret', or occasionally inviting us media in.

Three rows of airline seats had been installed at the front of the plane for his bodyguards, policy advisers, aides, butler, and 'Doc', the doctor. Round the edge were canvas bucket seats for the lesser mortals: his official photographer Chad, me, and the three American journalists accompanying him for the whole trip. There was also a table of constantly replenished chocolate bars and crisps.

Once on board I flicked through the itinerary booklet. Twenty-five thousand miles in ten days was an aerial marathon, particularly as every stop involved endless dinners, meetings with US troops and local top brass. At first I thought some of it was in code, as there were so many acronyms. These turned out to be notes on which uniform should be worn for each occasion – desert casuals, summer whites, business attire, dress uniform (there were no recommendations for female journalists).

I told Mullen it felt like the progress of a Roman Emperor, only by transport plane rather than elephant cavalcade, and he laughed. Pretty much since the founding of America, commentators have drawn parallels between the state of the US and the fall of Rome after five centuries as a superpower. He told me he had just read a book called *Empires of Trust* by historian Thomas Madden, which asked if the US was just another empire of conquest being corrupted by its own power. 'We are not Romans, of course,' said Mullen. 'Our brigade teams are not the legions of old. But we in the US military are likewise held to a high standard. Like the early Romans we are expected to do the right thing, and when we don't, to make it right again. We have learned that trust is the coin of the realm ... Lose the people's trust and we lose the war.'

Mullen was running two wars – in fact five, if you counted the drone campaigns in Pakistan, Yemen and Somalia – all of them in Muslim countries.

The trip provided an astonishing insight into the vast global reach of twenty-first-century America – the US had 301,000 soldiers based in thirty-eight countries – yet the lack of trust in Washington. Wherever we went Mullen handed out specially minted coins as tokens of his visit. Not once did we see passport control or customs – in some places we didn't even need visas (had Afghanistan and Iraq become US territory?). From Seoul to Delhi to Islamabad to Kandahar to Baghdad, Mullen's message, repeated over and over, was 'Trust us, we are committed, we might have been fickle friends in the past but we are not going to abandon you again.'

As far as I could see, no one believed him. 'Are you bringing security or are you bringing violence?' asked a white-bearded elder in Kandahar. 'Why do you get all your intelligence from India?' demanded a young journalist in Pakistan. 'How can you build trust with a country like Pakistan which is a state sponsor of terrorism?' asked an Indian army officer. 'North Korea has 1,200 artillery tubes pointed at us – what is the US doing about it?' questioned a student in Seoul. 'Why can't you make our politicians form a government?' beseeched an Iraqi shopkeeper.

Fortunately the chairman was a patient man. 'We are not magic, we are not all-powerful,' he replied over and over again. 'I know we are the United States, but it does take time. I wish I could throw a switch and everything would be good, it would be over.'

* * *

Chairman Mullen and the Cadillac of the Skies

The trip had a number of aims. Mullen was launching military exercises at a time of new tension on the Korean peninsula after North Korea had torpedoed and sunk a South Korean navy ship. He was also trying to make friends with rising power India – and to reassure it after the Mumbai massacre – while not alienating its traditional enemy Pakistan, an almost impossible balancing act.

In Afghanistan he wanted to check on the surge, the 30,000 extra US troops agreed on by Obama who would all have arrived by the end of the month. He also had to soothe nerves – and Karzai – worried by the change of commander, after the last one had committed professional hara-kiri through *Rolling Stone*. In Iraq, he wanted to make sure everything was on track for the drawdown of US troops to 50,000 by the end of the month, and the handover of command to Iraqi security forces.

Meanwhile his army was overstretched, with suicide rates spiralling. 'We've completely changed from a garrison force to an expeditionary force,' he said. 'Our major units in our army are now in their fifth major about-one-year-long deployment since 2003, with about that much time home in between deployments. So they're pressed; they're tired ... I'm extremely worried about the long-term effects, physically and mentally.'

On his radar screen were the next flashpoints, such as Yemen and Somalia (no one foresaw the Arab Spring, which would kick off with a young fruit-seller setting himself on fire in Tunisia four months later). The places that he said kept him awake at night were Pakistan and Iran. He had no military contacts whatsoever with the latter; nor did he with China, whose own build-up of weapons he said meant he had 'moved from being curious to being genuinely concerned'. As he pointed out, 'Even during the height of the Cold War with the Soviet Union there were always mil to mil contacts.'

At each stop he met generals and politicians, to whom he handed out reassurances along with souvenir pens, paperweights in the form of compasses, and china plates inscribed with his crest. Then it was back on the plane bearing return gifts of boxes of dates and nuts, carpets rolled up and tied with pink tinsel, a statuette of a warrior on a horse, and plaques, most of which would end up in a display cabinet in the Pentagon.

Almost everywhere we landed we encountered another US government plane. In Seoul, Defense Secretary Robert Gates had beaten us to it in what was known as 'the Doomsday Plane', one of four US government 747s equipped to withstand any attack, from nuclear to electromagnetic pulse. Next to land was Hillary Clinton, the Secretary of State. When we got to Delhi we landed alongside the plane of Ambassador Richard Holbrooke, Obama's Special Envoy for Afghanistan and Pakistan. A few weeks earlier he and Mullen had crisscrossed at Brussels airport and held a meeting on the ramp of Mullen's plane.

How on earth did these people conduct policy, I wondered. Gates and Mullen didn't even stop for refuelling: their planes could refuel in mid-air, flying parallel to a tanker plane in a terrifying manoeuvre where the planes flew so close I could see the face of the man operating the nozzle.

After just a few days we had crossed so many time zones that I had lost all sense of what time it was. Almost every night I woke at 3 a.m. local time in a hotel room or military base, wondering where I was as I stared at the time flashing red on a digital clock, just like in the movie *Lost in Translation*.

To help us sleep the plane doctor handed out Ambien in special Pentagon sachets which we grabbed so greedily that he said, 'I feel like a dealer.'

The first stop was Hawaii – a reminder of Pearl Harbor, which the Japanese raided almost seventy years before. When we arrived tourists were catching the last rays of the day on Waikiki beach or enjoying sunset over the Pacific with colourful cocktails decorated with paper umbrellas. We ordered passionfruit mojitos. 'It's all downhill from now,' warned Jim Garamone of the Armed Forces Press Service, a veteran of these trips.

North Korea was said to have missiles targeted on Hawaii, and our next stop was South Korea, where the US still had 28,500 troops stationed. Obama's attempts to persuade Pyongyang to halt its nuclear programme had got nowhere. Instead tensions on the divided peninsula were at their highest for years, the South Koreans outraged at the torpedoing of one of their naval ships, the *Cheonan*, by the communist regime in March, killing forty-six sailors.

Mullen was on his way to sign off on the start of major military exercises involving twenty ships and a hundred planes, designed to show the North not to mess with the South. It was a signal somewhat diluted by the fact that the exercises had been shifted to the East Sea rather than the Yellow Sea, which borders China. 'This is a really critical part of the world,' Mullen said on the flight over. 'When you have an incident like the sinking of the *Cheonan* you worry a great deal what else can happen here. There is nobody in the US or the region that wants to see any kind of conflict break out. But sinking a boat and killing forty-six sailors is completely unacceptable.'

To demonstrate how strongly the US felt, Gates and Clinton were also in Seoul to meet their South Korean opposite numbers. While Mullen made a morale-boosting visit to US troops at Camp Redcloud, the two Secretaries made a provocative trip to the demilitarised zone (DMZ). The three-mile-wide strip was the world's most heavily fortified border, and a stark reminder that for all our focus on the war on terror, the Cold War had not completely gone away. On one side was South Korea, the world's twelfth largest economy, all gleaming office towers, neon screens, adverts for Samsung, its own Disneyland, and bars and restaurants full of fashionably dressed young people with the latest smartphones. On the other was North Korea, the world's most secretive dictatorship, which literally starved its own people while the leadership lived in luxury. More than a million North Koreans were thought to have died of famine in the 1990s.

In the middle of the DMZ was a small blue rectangular building with one door opening to the South and one to the North, and a dividing line running right through it – the Military Armistice Commission. Clinton and Gates went inside, and briefly crossed the line to enter North Korea; or at least the North's side of the building. This made for a dramatic photo opportunity, with a North

Korean soldier staring at them through a window just a few inches away, a thin grey drizzle adding to the atmospherics.

Back in Seoul the pair met up with Mullen to head to a vast memorial plaza and lay wreaths marking the sixtieth anniversary of the start of the Korean War. Thirty-three thousand Americans were killed in the three-year war – which put into perspective the 4,413 in Iraq and the 1,216 by then in Afghanistan.

That evening we all retreated to the hotel bar, where Gates was drinking martinis and reminiscing about the old days in Afghanistan. He told me about sending Stingers to the mujaheddin and having to ship Tennessee mules to carry them in, then finding they weren't strong enough, so they had to import Chinese ones. 'We were just the quartermasters,' he said. 'It was the Pakistanis who were distributing the stuff.' I asked how they knew what was going on. 'We did have our independent sources of information, so if they weren't giving anything to someone we complained. For example, they didn't give any Stingers to Massoud, because he was Tajik. I went to see him, and he'd just killed a Russian officer that day, and presented me with the epaulettes and gun.' I asked Gates if he had met bin Laden. 'Nobody mentioned Osama or Haqqani in those days,' he replied. 'It was all Hekmatyar.' Britain's Foreign Minister David Miliband had been publicly pushing for talks with the Taliban over the previous year, but Gates told me he was reluctant. 'I'm very cautious about this,' he said. 'I think things could turn around in Afghanistan with the surge, and when they do it can happen very quickly, like it did in Anbar. We need to negotiate with them from a position of strength.'

It was clear from my conversations that night that the Americans were not at all happy about what they saw as Britain's freelance efforts at deal-making. 'You guys see everything through the prism of Northern Ireland,' said one. So they were more than amused when it emerged that one of the people the British had been trying to negotiate with, in the belief he was Taliban commander Mullah Mansour, turned out to be not a Taliban at all, but a shopkeeper from Quetta who had fleeced them for hundreds of thousands of pounds.

* * *

Chairman Mullen and the Cadillac of the Skies

The next stop was Delhi in the monsoon season. The skies were swollen with thunderous rainclouds, pavements steaming slightly in the heat, everything green and verdant. It was a dramatic backdrop to the red Lutyens architecture which brought back memories of dancing in the rain on my first trip to India as a student.

Mullen was giving a talk at the National Defence College, a grand white colonial building that had been a British Army mess before independence, a reminder of the days when Britain, not America, was the great imperial power. The entrance hall featured an interesting juxtaposition of a moth-eaten stuffed tiger in a glass case and a bust of Mahatma Gandhi, the great pacifist. We journalists got no further. The generals had decided that 'Mullen's Travelling Media' were not welcome.

When we later got the transcript of Mullen's talk, every single question he had been asked was about Pakistan. 'I know you've been counting my trips to Islamabad,' he had joked to the audience. The Indians did not find it funny. Emotions were still raw eighteen months after the Mumbai massacre, which Indian Home Secretary G.K. Pillai had accused ISI of masterminding.

'We're all very concerned about it happening again, not just the tragedy of losing the people but what it could trigger,' Mullen told me. 'Ten terrorists managed not just to terrorise a city and country but to bring two nuclear-capable countries closer, front and centre, to the possibility of some kind of response, if not to the brink.'

Historically India was close to the Soviet Union, while Pakistan had its on-off marriage with the US. Mullen repeatedly told the Indians that Washington wanted to deepen relations with Delhi. He pointed out that India had the highest number of foreign students in the US – more than 100,000.

At a roundtable of retired officers, the first question was why Mullen had approved extending the tenure of Pakistan's army chief General Kayani, which had just been announced. 'I had nothing to do with it and that's honest truth,' he said, as they all smiled knowingly. They asked why the US gave Pakistan so many weapons. He pointed out the huge disparity between the two countries:

'There isn't a single war game I've taken part in where India doesn't dominate.'

There was little encouragement on Afghanistan. 'We should let Afghanistan slide into what it always was – a black void,' said Professor Bharat Carnad, an expert on nuclear programmes at the Centre for Policy Research. 'The best thing for NATO to do is to get out of Afghanistan and leave them to kill each other, which they're going to do anyway.' 'Most of all do not trust Pakistan, who run with the hare and hunt with the hounds,' warned Commodore Uday Bhaskar, a retired naval commander.

The Indians would have been even more suspicious had they witnessed our arrival in Islamabad the next morning. Astonishingly, this was Mullen's nineteenth trip to Pakistan since taking office two and a half years earlier, and his twentieth meeting with Kayani. We flew into Chaklala airbase, where Kayani was waiting to greet Mullen warmly. The two men had formed a close bond, we were told, helped by the fact that Kayani had studied at US Army Command and General Staff College in Fort Leavenworth.

On the flight Mullen spoke to me about the 'criticality of Pakistan' in turning things round in Afghanistan: 'We can't get at the safe havens that we know exist in Pakistan without their cooperation.' He believed that Kayani was genuinely trying to change things, even though as I pointed out he had been head of ISI from 2004 to 2007, exactly the years when the Taliban were building up in their Pakistani safe havens. 'It seems to me your policy is based on wishful thinking,' I said, 'that somehow hope will triumph over experience.'

Mullen's view appeared to be that some cooperation was better than none. 'Pakistan has captured and killed more terrorists than any country in the world,' he said repeatedly, a Kayani line that ignored the fact that that may be because they trained them. 'It's not easy what Kayani is trying to do, and he needs our help, not our criticism. Say I'm [CIA Director] Leon Panetta and I'm told by the President, "Completely change the CIA." Do you think I'd get that done in a year or two?'

Chairman Mullen and the Cadillac of the Skies

Mullen argued that the US also needed to take responsibility for having abandoned Pakistan in 1990 after the Russians left Afghanistan, and Washington no longer needed ISI to oversee its proxy war. Aid was then abruptly cut off because of Pakistan's nuclear programme, to which the US had previously turned a blind eye. 'We have skin in this,' he admitted, just as Gates had said. He told me he was stunned when in 2008 he spoke to a group of Pakistani War College students at the US Embassy. The majority of questions were about the Pressler Amendment, which was used to cut off Pakistan's aid, even though it had been passed before most of them were born. 'There's not a single junior officer in Pakistan who doesn't know who Senator Pressler is, and there's not a junior officer in the US military who knows who he is,' said Mullen.

However, he admitted he was very worried about proxy groups like Lashkar-e-Toiba and the Haqqani network, which he said were killing more US soldiers than the Taliban. 'I believe the overall strategic approach of ISI needs to change fundamentally. There's a lot I know about ISI and a lot I don't know, and that's true for us as a government. Pakistan is an extraordinarily complex country, and the ISI and military are a big part of that.'

In the months leading up to our trip there had been several examples of that complexity. In January the CIA, acting on a tipoff, had traced a phone to a house in Baldia Town, Karachi, and had passed the information on to the Pakistanis for ISI to carry out a raid. The man inside turned out to be Mullah Abdul Ghani Baradar, deputy to Mullah Omar. Finally a senior Taliban had been arrested – it seemed like a great coup. The story was on the front page of the US press. *Newsweek* called the arrest a 'game changer'. Yet when I spoke to Afghan officials they were livid. Karzai's elder brother Qayum told me Baradar had been negotiating with them. 'This wasn't ISI trying to help – they arrested him to stop talks and as a warning to others,' he fumed.

ISI took Baradar to a detention centre, and refused the CIA access. The Americans began to suspect that the whole thing, including the tipoff, had been a set-up. Pakistan refused to hand him over to Afghanistan, and kept him under house arrest in Karachi. Salahuddin Rabbani, the head of Afghanistan's High Peace Council for negotiating with the Taliban, told me that when he and other Afghan officials finally got access to visit Baradar in 2013 he had clearly been drugged, and couldn't speak.

That wasn't all. On a warm Saturday night in May, a thirty-year-old father of two called Faisal Shahzad tried to bomb Times Square in New York. It was an inept attempt. He left his Nissan Pathfinder parked on Broadway loaded with a poorly constructed bomb made using battery-operated alarm clocks, petrol and bags of fertiliser, rigged it with fireworks, then lit a fuse and caught a train back home to Bridport, Connecticut. Not only did the vehicle fail to detonate, but he had forgotten his keys in the ignition, including that of his house.

He was caught two days later trying to board a plane to Pakistan – once again the trail led back there. Shahzad was the son of a retired Pakistani air force officer, and had got American citizenship after going there to study. He had been trained by the Pakistan Taliban (TTP) in Waziristan. Had the bomb been better constructed many people could have been killed, and the Americans were furious. Panetta flew to Pakistan and warned, 'All bets are off.'

For their part, the Pakistanis were incensed at how Obama had stepped up the drone campaign. Poll after poll showed that Pakistanis considered America more of a threat than terrorists – the most recent, by Pew Survey just before our trip, found that 59 per cent of Pakistanis regarded the US as an enemy.

Mullen's visit, then, came at a sensitive time. According to our booklet, the schedule for the day was to attend a *shura* of Pashtun elders in the tribal areas. We were all looking forward to it. However, Kayani had other ideas. 'Change of plans,' he announced breezily as he greeted Mullen. 'I have a special trip arranged for you.'

'I bet that doesn't involve us,' I said to the other journalists.

Sure enough, Kayani whisked Mullen into his executive Gulfstream jet and took him sightseeing for the day over the tribal areas and into the Himalayas, flying right up to K2, the world's second highest mountain.

We journalists, meanwhile, were taken to the highly fortified US Embassy. There we had a briefing at the Office of Defense Co-Operation with Brigadier General Mike Nagata, who pointed out that Pakistan had almost 140,000 troops in the tribal areas, that it was the longest military campaign in the country's history, and that it had taken thousands of casualties. 'If we had seven infantry divisions within our own borders fighting our own people we'd call that civil war,' he said. 'That doesn't mean we don't have things we'd like Pakistan to do more,' he added.

I pointed out that Pakistan's troops only seemed to go after the Pakistan Taliban, and that even in the recent operation in Swat they had let Maulana Fazlullah escape.

'It's not perfect,' was all Nagata would say. 'But then, my relationship with my wife is not perfect.'

It was about 5 p.m. when Mullen came back to the Ambassador's residence – built after the last one was burned down by students in 1979.

'Kayani has a very nice plane,' he said.

'You probably paid for it,' I replied.

He had, he said, been inhaling cigarette smoke all day. General Kayani is a notorious chain-smoker, who often lights his next cigarette before he has finished the previous one, and he had lit up within ten minutes of their taking off.

Waiting for Mullen was a roundtable with the Pakistani media, at which the questions almost entirely mirrored those the previous night in Delhi. Every one came heavily laced with scepticism. The first set the tone: 'We all keep hearing about Pakistan's role in Mumbai, but what is India doing to avoid another Mumbai?' 'Why do you get all your intelligence from the Indians?' was the next. 'Why are you allowing India to build twenty-seven consulates in Afghanistan?' Every Pakistani I met seemed convinced of this. (In fact there were four, plus an embassy.) And so on.

The only non-India question was one asking for the latest on Osama bin Laden. I found myself doing a double-take at the sudden reminder of the man who started all this, and who till then had not been mentioned. 'I believe he is in Pakistan,' said Mullen, adding, 'But we haven't had any evidence for years.'

'But you have all this sophisticated technology, you can even see a goat from the skies,' argued the journalist.

'Frankly, he's very good at hiding,' shrugged Mullen.

It was clear that the Pakistani media was convinced that the US was leaving Afghanistan the following year. 'We're not running for the exit ... we are there for the long term ... it's just the beginning of a process ...' said Mullen over and over. It was useless. They had heard Obama say that troops would start leaving in July 2011, and would not be swayed.

That night I managed to get out of the Embassy to meet up with some Pakistani friends for supper. I was shocked when one of them declared, 'So ISI has won.' 'What do you mean?' I asked. My friend smiled. 'They said the West wouldn't have the stamina to stay in Afghanistan so we should still back the Taliban, and now they've been proved right.'

Mullen emerged the next morning looking fragile after a dinner with General Kayani which wound up at 1.30 a.m. after 'endless dishes', rounded off with whisky and cigars. We were headed to Afghanistan, with a long day ahead, starting in Jalalabad. From there it was a stunning ride in a Chinook helicopter over the Kunar River to a remote forward operating base, FOB Joyce, in the brown-baked mountains of Kunar in eastern Afghanistan, all jagged peaks under blue, blue sky.

A collection of plywood huts surrounded by wire, the base was less than two miles from the border with Pakistan, and the commander told us they came under attack every day. Mullen met the troops and presented Bronze Stars to two soldiers who had risked their lives to save others pinned down by Taliban fire in an ambush. The regiment had only been there sixty days, and had already lost several soldiers. Just two years before, they had been in Iraq.

Chairman Mullen and the Cadillac of the Skies

One of our escorts from Jalalabad told us that when the recce was being done for our visit, a soldier had been shot in the butt. We did not stay long.

'It's much more kinetic than I expected,' said General John Campbell, who had arrived in June to be regional commander for the east, and had men based in 142 such small FOBs in fourteen provinces. 'We're surging, but the enemy is surging too.'

Next stop was Kabul, where Mullen was expected for lunch with General Petraeus and a series of meetings at ISAF headquarters. He then headed for the US Embassy, complaining on the way, 'I don't get to go to London, Paris, Berlin any more, it's all Baghdad, Kabul, Kandahar and Tikrit.'

The new counter-insurgency strategy had involved a surge of civilians, not just military – in fact the Embassy appeared to have five Ambassadors, and Mullen addressed a gathering of diplomats. 'I realise it's nine years since the attacks which killed 3,000 Americans, but for all intents and purposes this is year one, and starting year two of properly resourcing the war. We don't have a lot of time,' he warned. 'There are a lot of clocks in this business, and they're all working against us.'

Whether the surge would succeed depended very much on our next destination – Kandahar. The former Taliban stronghold was the key city for NATO to control if there was to be any chance of turning the war around.

Since 2006 Kandahar had been under Canadian command, but with only 2,000 troops they never really controlled the area. If they put pressure on one district the Taliban simply moved to another, like squeezing a balloon. The American surge meant there were now 24,000 coalition troops in the south, enough in theory to move into surrounding districts and stay in them, and cut off routes to the Taliban.

Plans for a major offensive had been put on hold, however, after a much-heralded operation to take over the small town of Marja in central Helmand (with a population of just 60,000) had proved far harder than imagined.

Marja had been trumpeted by General McChrystal as an example of his new 'population-centric' COIN strategy, where instead of just taking the town the military would then quickly transfer it to Afghan authority. The idea was that if you could follow up victory with some semblance of authority, services and economic opportunity, locals would turn away from the Taliban. 'We've got a government in a box ready to roll in,' General McChrystal had claimed.

The regional commander for the south-west was a British General, Nick Carter, and it was he who drew up the plans for what became the biggest operation of the war to date. 'It was a completely different way of operating to anything done in the previous three or four years in Helmand, which had all been kinetic clearance operations without any thought to the politics.' The area had been chosen because it – along with nearby Nad-e-Ali – had become a safe haven for Taliban from where they were threatening the British headquarters in Lashkar Gah.

That February, 15,000 US, British, coalition and Afghan troops had launched Operation Moshtarak, which meant 'together', to give the illusion that the Afghan army was actively involved. The US Marines went into Marja while the British secured Nad-e-Ali and the desert up to the canal, all partnered with Afghan troops. But most of the Afghans were from the north, and did not speak Pashto or want to be there. The Marines did not trust them, and complained that most were high on opium or marijuana. 'The Afghan army operating in southern Afghanistan was almost as alien to Afghans in the south as we were,' said General Carter. 'What Pashtuns they had tended to be recruited from the north or east.'

After five days of intense battle they took the town, with the loss of eight Marines, six ANA and around twenty civilians. However, the Taliban disappeared rather than being defeated, and continued to ambush any patrols that ventured outside the town. As for the 'government in a box', this never really materialised. No one from Kabul wanted to come and run Marja, and the man the coalition brought in as District Administrator, Haji Zahir, was completely unfamiliar with Helmand, and had lived in exile in Germany, where it turned out he had spent four years in prison for stabbing his stepson.

'That didn't look good presentationally for the internationals,' admitted Carter. 'Personally I couldn't give a shit whether he'd been in jail anywhere, what mattered was he wasn't very good at wrapping his arms around the elders in Marja and making them feel he was the right bloke to be their Governor. He hadn't spent any time in Helmand and didn't understand the environment.'

Sometimes in Washington I went to the Friday 'shura' held at the Pentagon to discuss AfPak, and the government in a box became a standing joke.

'I didn't like that term,' said Carter. 'It wasn't ever going to be government in a box. This was a population who had lived under a range of different, slightly unpleasant, arrangements for four or five years or more and were utterly unconvinced that anyone was going to provide them any security. Afghans are basically waiting to see who will be in charge tomorrow and tomorrow and the day after. It was fatuous to think within two or three months they would trust their security forces; we needed a year probably to make them feel they were in a good place.'

By May, McChrystal was calling Marja a 'bleeding ulcer'.

If Marja was complicated, Kandahar was far more so. The extra surge troops didn't seem to have dented Taliban pressure on the city – in fact the situation had worsened. Every time troops went out on the main road they were attacked. More than nine years after being forced out, the Taliban seemed poised to overrun their old capital. They were walking around openly in Malajat to the north, and even operating a roadblock inside the city. The trucking companies delivering fuel and supplies to the NATO bases were all having to pay bribes to the Taliban to get through.

McChrystal and Carter had planned major sweeps through several districts, and to ring the city with Baghdad-style biometric controls and walls to filter out insurgents. As part of the new population-centric approach, they flew Karzai into Kandahar in April for a big meeting with elders to inform them of the offensive. Instead he referred to the Taliban as 'brothers', and said the war would never end as long as he was seen as 'a foreign stooge'. When asked whether they wanted the offensive to begin, some elders shouted no, so he insisted to McChrystal that the whole thing be delayed.

The idea of a major offensive was dropped, and Carter came up with a revised plan of ringing the city with police checkpoints, while clearing Kandahar's outlying areas of Taliban. This was just getting under way as we arrived. There was heavy fighting in Malajat and Argandab.

The Governor of Kandahar, Toryalai Wesa, had been a Soviet Commissar, then had lived in exile in Canada. He was an old friend of the Karzai family, and everyone knew the real power in Kandahar was the President's brother Ahmed Wali, who headed the Provincial Council. 'People call him Second President of the South,' said his cousin Izzatullah Wasifi. 'He's more powerful in the south than Karzai is in Kabul.' This presented a conundrum for the international community, given Wali's alleged links with the opium trade, and led to disagreements between McChrystal and his regional commander.

'Stan McChrystal tried very hard to get rid of Ahmed Wali and move him on,' said Carter. 'He thought him nefarious and part of the reason Kandahar was subjected to the kind of level of terrorism it was. I said I'd go along with it if we could prove he was into all this stuff, which we never did.'

As the man on the ground, Carter quickly found it was almost impossible to get anything done without Ahmed Wali. 'I'm absolutely certain that Ahmed Wali was a rich man and absolutely certain he was doing things that would have encouraged people to join the insurgency, but I thought it was better trying to control him and having stability rather than the power vacuum there would be if one had found the excuse for removing him.'

It was, he said, a lesson he had learned from the British removal of Sher Mohammad Akhundzada from Helmand back in 2006: 'You have to take the view in Afghanistan whether sometimes you are better off going with a divisive character who's able to provide some level of stability, and I think in Helmand that it may well have been the case that SMA was a divisive character who was able to bring some stability.' So Ahmed Wali remained, providing what Carter said was often invaluable advice on who was who.

We went to a briefing at which we were shown an incredibly complicated diagram of Kandahar's tribal make-up, for suddenly it seemed the conflict was all about tribes. It made me laugh, remembering how a few years earlier the military had looked at you blankly if you suggested some of the fighting might be tribal rather than Taliban. Now they had gone to the other extreme.

Mullen conferred for a while on Kandahar airfield with Carter, then climbed into a Black Hawk to go to a *shura*. We followed in a Chinook. At least it was billed as a *shura* – in fact only three elders turned up, most clearly figuring it was not worth the risk, given that the Taliban had been assassinating anyone who worked with NATO forces.

The men, all with long grey beards and silken turbans shot through with silver thread, sat at a long table where they looked disparagingly at the green tea served in polystyrene cups and the few biscuits. They had a litany of complaints. 'There are so many problems I don't know where to start,' complained the first. 'Nothing has changed since you were here last except one thing – we didn't want military operations but they have started.'

'I want to talk about security, which is getting worse day by day,' said the second, before taking a large cloth from his pocket and blowing his nose noisily.

'I heard on the radio you came from Pakistan,' said the third. 'Everyone knows the real problem is Pakistan – why aren't you protecting us from them?'

'Pakistan wants a peaceful, stable Afghanistan,' replied Mullen.

'That's not true!' snorted the man with the large cloth. 'Pakistan wants Afghanistan to be a province of Pakistan. You're paying them a lot of money and they just keep sending bad people and explosives here.'

'We all know this,' agreed the third elder. 'As long as you keep sending them millions of dollars this war won't end.'

Once again, July 2011 was high on the agenda. 'If you leave, who's going to help us?' demanded the first elder.

'We're not leaving,' Mullen said again and again. He seemed genuinely moved by the elders, and I realised he probably almost never met real Afghans. 'I wish I could turn the switch and make everything OK.'

'What happened to the switch you had back in 2001?' asked one.

'We thought we'd thrown it,' he replied, 'but we really hadn't, otherwise we wouldn't still be here.'

I had spent too long in Afghanistan to believe these men had taken the risk of attending the meeting without wanting something in return. Sure enough, at the end they handed over a box of grapes, then the third elder asked Mullen to release his son, who was being held in US custody in Bagram. So that was why they came.

If the international community was eventually going to leave without it looking like a defeat, it needed Afghan security forces capable of holding off the Taliban. The US had dramatically stepped up training and was spending $5 billion a year, but we had heard at the base that there was still not a single unit that could operate without foreign help. A British officer responsible for training bomb disposal squads told me he was asked to lower standards (already the lowest in the world) as nobody was passing the course. 'Do you realise the consequences of what you're asking?' he had replied.

Mullen's next stop was to see for himself how the security forces were progressing. We set off in a convoy of heavily armoured MRAPs to visit a police post. The police who greeted us were all wearing different boots, and one with an enormous belly hanging over his belt. They had clearly been practising some kind of drill in Mullen's honour, but they all came to a stop at different times, and when he tried to walk along the row saluting, they crashed into each other.

We climbed up their watchtower looking out over the city, and I noticed that Mullen's skin had taken on a greenish hue. I wondered if it was the heat, the Kayani dinner, or if he was thinking, 'Is this really what we're relying on?'

Chairman Mullen and the Cadillac of the Skies

On the way back children ran out to pelt our vehicles with rocks. The press officer in the front seat had an explanation. 'This shows the children have confidence in the security situation, that they feel they can throw stones,' he said.

I felt sad, thinking how a few years ago I could wander around these streets at will, chatting to people. Once when I got stuck out alone and scared after curfew I had even stayed in one of those mud houses, treated like a princess by the family, who tried to feed me what was probably their entire food stock for the month. Now, seeing the district through the postage-stamp window of the monstrous, heavily armoured vehicle, it seemed very hostile.

We bumped across a filthy canal in which local people were washing and brushing their teeth. Almost ten years into the war most Afghans still didn't have running water or electricity. How on earth could we expect those people to feel they had benefited from the presence of Western troops?

The rest of the day's programme was cancelled. Back at the base I had supper with General Carter, who explained that District 9, where we had been stoned, was full of refugees from Marja who were not overjoyed to have been driven out of their homes.

On the plane out, Mullen fretted, 'There are great expectations on the part of people from the US and the US military, and at the same time there's a reality of what we can do. I'm not a miracle-worker.' To me it all seemed very depressing, yet Mullen said he was 'cautiously optimistic'. 'I think it can be turned,' he insisted. 'This has been a very under-resourced war. We've been through a very thorough review, and I think we understand what we need, we've got the right resources, the leadership to do it, now it's just the execution. I feel as if we're in the same position in Afghanistan as we were in Iraq in 2006–07, when everyone was saying it couldn't be turned around.'

Eventually things were turned around in Kandahar, but it meant using what Carter called 'local solutions' – in other words working with dubious characters.

This meant calling Ahmed Wali Karzai, who called in Abdul

Raziq, commander of the border guards at Spin Boldak. The thirty-year-old was nephew of the commander Mansour Achakzai, who had tugged Colonel Imam's beard in 1994 and ended up being hanged by the Taliban. He was also the leader of one of the biggest forces in the area, with around 3,500 men under his command, basically a mujaheddin militia, mostly from his tribe, the Achakzai. Guarding the border was a highly lucrative post, as they taxed everything coming through, and controlled key drug-smuggling routes; this was said to bring in $5–6 million a month. Not only were they corrupt, but they were reputed to have carried out summary executions of the rival Noorzai tribe.

Carter admits: 'I was very nervous about using them as in 2006 he had allegedly gone on an ethnic-cleansing spree of the Noorzai tribe and I was concerned he might do the same against the Alikozai in Argandab. So we embedded a US special forces company with his gang and they worked hand in glove for several months to minimise any problems.'

As soon as he got the summons from Ahmed Wali, Raziq's men swept in with their wraparound shades, desert-camouflage fatigues and bandoleers of grenades. They cleared Arghandab and Malalajat of Taliban within a few days. Their methods would not have met any human rights codes. However, Carter was impressed: 'Unlike the Afghan army, Abdul Raziq's border police battalion were locals and understood jungle warfare, which Argandab was about, had a very good understanding about how to deal with the IED threat, and were the most effective soldiers the Afghans had.' Afterwards Raziq was promoted to Brigadier General by President Karzai, and hailed as a hero. General Petraeus visited him five times, and he later became Police Chief for Kandahar.

Petraeus's advisor David Kilcullen, one of the world's leading experts on counter-insurgency, was aghast. 'In the eyes of many Afghans the Taliban was a vigilante movement which came about in reaction to the mujaheddin. Then we came in and put exactly the same bunch of arseholes in charge.' Five years later, Carter still insists that using Raziq was the right thing to do. 'We never did hear, and even today haven't heard, of him doing anything out of order. If you go to Kandahar today he is widely respected as Chief of Police, and you don't find people talking about security, but the economy. I think if you go back to 2002 there was a window of opportunity when you could have got rid of these characters, but by 2009–10 you had what you had. I don't think we had time, let alone the capability, to get rid of those characters.'

It was hard to see how using people like Raziq squared with another part of Petraeus's strategy – namely making government accountable and dealing with corruption to try to win over the famed '80 per cent' of Afghans on the fence.

'I think we've learned a lot from Iraq, not just on the military side,' Mullen had said. 'We have the knowledge that security isn't enough – there's got to be action on corruption and the governance piece.'

Under McChrystal, an Anti-Corruption Task Force had been set up at ISAF, a surprising thing for the military to get involved in, but a recognition of the scale of the problem. Sarah Chayes, the former journalist who had run a soap factory in Kandahar and was one of the few foreigners to know the country well, had been brought in as an adviser for McChrystal, then kept on by Petraeus as part of his brains trust, one of what he called his 'Directed Telescopes'. She pointed out that instead of flowing downwards from the government to the people, money was moving upwards in the form of gifts, kickbacks, levies paid to superiors and the purchase of positions. Much of that money then ended up in Dubai. It was not easy to do anything about it, however, as everyone was protected by those above, who feared losing their own source of revenue. 'Ironically the prospect of turning off aid or denying a visa to someone was more complex than the prospect of shooting him.'

In Kabul we had met Yvette Hopkins and an ex-Scotland Yard bobbie called Steve Foster from something called the Afghan Threat Finance Cell, which had been set up to look at exactly how the Taliban was being funded. Every lead they followed seemed to provide evidence that Afghan officials were involved. They found that corruption was systemic, from being shaken down at border crossings to paying to get a job. At least half the population had paid bribes to officials in the previous year, and they estimated bribery to be worth $2.5 billion a year, almost as much as narcotics, and driving many people to the Taliban.

'There's no point going after low-hanging fruit,' said Foster. 'The key is to go after high-level targets to show that no one is immune.' He, supported by the British government, had created an Afghan unit called the Major Crimes Taskforce which was getting training from the FBI, and the previous October they had arrested one such 'untouchable', Brigadier General Saifullah Hakim, head of Kandahar Border Police, after catching him out through a wiretap. He was claiming to have 2,800 staff on his books, and was receiving money for that number, but he actually had only 1,200. He and two others were dividing up the difference every month, as well as looting the relief fund for orphans and widows. They each got seven years.

The morning we met, Hopkins and Foster were very happy, as they had arrested someone from the National Security Council, Mohammad Zia Salehi, a close ally of Karzai. He had been caught on tape soliciting bribes, including a new Toyota for his son, from New Ansari Money Exchange in return for stopping an investigation into the company's role in the large amounts of money being transferred out of the country to Dubai. Though what they had caught him on was relatively minor – the car cost $20,000 – he was thought to be bagman for a vast palace slush fund. Their joy was shortlived. By the end of the day Salehi was released after Karzai intervened with the Attorney General and then even sent a car from the palace to pick Salehi up. The Deputy Attorney General who had issued the arrest warrant was later fired.

Karzai even boasted about his interference. 'Absolutely I intervened ... I intervened very very strongly,' he told Christiane Amanpour on ABC a few weeks later.[1] He complained that the arrest had been carried out in the middle of the night by thirty men with Kalashnikovs – 'exactly reminiscent of the days of the Soviet Union'. In fact Karzai had originally approved the arrest, and the police had first phoned Salehi's number then knocked at his door.

A couple of weeks later Petraeus held a commanders' conference to explain his vision for the campaign. As usual this involved a PowerPoint presentation, and Chayes and her colleagues had provided slides on the importance of going after corruption. To her horror, instead of explaining the new approach, Petraeus focused on slides telling his officers what they knew how to do best: kill the enemy. 'Petraeus even argued against some of our slides.'[2] Chayes went back to Washington.

General Carter said Petraeus had embraced the idea initially, but simply ran out of time. 'I remember when he first took over drawing out on a single sheet of paper the things I thought we needed to do, and one of them was getting after the culture of impunity, as there was no doubt that corruption was part of the insurgency. Ultimately you cannot connect a population to its government if they think that governance is corrupt. The question is whether you have time and commitment to be able to deal with it, and we clearly ran out of time.'

Not long after our trip came the biggest scandal of all – that of the Kabul Bank. In September 2010 it collapsed after $935 million in loans had gone missing, mostly money provided by international donors and some apparently going to fictitious entities. One of the bank's shareholders was Karzai's brother Mahmood, and many government officials had loans. Much of the money had gone to buy property in Dubai, including a series of villas on the man-made archipelago Palm Jumeirah. One of them was owned by Mahmood Karzai, and he invited my family and me there to dinner one evening in March 2011. As we admired his midnight-blue Rolls-Royce parked outside and his waterside view, he pointed out two villas bought by Khlalil Ferozi and Sherkhan Farnood, the bank's chief executives.

Ending the focus on corruption was not the only one of McChrystal's reforms that Petraeus reversed. It was back to business as usual at the Kandahar boardwalk, and the new rules on airstrikes were removed. He took with him as part of his brains trust David Kilcullen, who had been his strategist for the Iraqi troop surge. This time the two men disagreed.

Kilcullen was the only one of Petraeus's immediate staff who had experience of Afghanistan, yet Petraeus never once asked his advice. 'He felt, "I just beat the fuckin' Iraqis, I don't need anyone's advice,"' said Kilcullen. 'I liken it to MacArthur in Korea – he felt, "I've just beaten the Japanese in World War II, so how hard could China be?" They were both still fighting the last war. Afghanistan was a completely different set-up to Iraq, but he never really thought deeply about Afghanistan, he just tried to template across what we had done in Iraq without thinking why it had worked.'

Worse, under pressure from Obama to deliver quickly to meet the 2011 deadline, Petraeus seemed to throw out his own counter-insurgency manual. He upped the number of airstrikes, determined, it seemed, to kill his way to victory.

Soon bombings were running at more than five hundred a month, and night raids quadrupled to around a thousand a month. Petraeus told a Senate hearing in March 2011 that in a typical ninety-day period his forces were killing or capturing 360 insurgent leaders.[3]

President Karzai was distraught about the changes. 'When General Petraeus came things got much worse,' said his Chief of Staff Daudzai. 'It was back to McKiernan's time, but worse. Petraeus called a big meeting and said, "Afghans are boiling water and burning their children's legs just to defame us." Another time he called and threatened us, saying, "Tell Karzai there will be revolution in Kabul and the palace will be shattered."'

Throughout 2011 so many Taliban field commanders were picked off in southern Afghanistan that Kilcullen said the average age fell by ten years. 'Effectively we killed an entire generation of mid-level Taliban, which meant we ended up with younger, more radical guys, and it was even harder to get to a stage where you might bring them to peace.'

When Kilcullen wrote a report criticising the drone attacks as gaining tactical victories but losing the strategic fight, Petraeus tried to have it suppressed.

As the killings went up, so did the number of roadside bombs. President Obama had been warned that the increased number of troops being sent to Afghanistan would lead to increased casualties. However, 2010 was the bloodiest year by far. The deaths of US soldiers in Afghanistan more than tripled, from 155 in 2008 to almost five hundred in 2010. The economic cost was spiralling too – $120 billion in 2010, and $150 billion in 2011 – $5,000 per Afghan, while the economic situation at home in the US was still perilous, with unemployment having risen to 10 per cent. Obama's Vice President and other staff were telling him the surge was a mistake. By early 2011 Gates was saying, 'Obama doesn't believe in his own strategy and doesn't consider the war to be his.'[4]

He wasn't alone. Afghanistan was turning into another Vietnam, only longer. Polls found that 70 per cent of Americans wanted to get out, that just 14 per cent of Americans had a favourable opinion of Afghanistan (only Iran and North Korea fared worse), and most thought the country terminally ungovernable. *Time* magazine ran a cover story calling it 'The Unwinnable War'.[5]

Yet the military kept insisting things could be turned round. Our last stop was Iraq, which had now become the 'other war', from which the US was on its way out.

As in Afghanistan, this war had obviously been a boon for concrete merchants – the route from the airport was lined with high blast walls. Behind some of these, the Americans had opened a new Embassy, the largest and most expensive in the world, costing $750 million to build and almost as big as Vatican City. It housed more than 16,000 employees and had its own food court and shopping mall, swimming pool, basketball court and football pitch as well as apartment blocks.

We were staying on the military base, which the Americans, with no sense of irony, had named 'Camp Victory'. Our rooms were in the once-opulent Al Faw Palace, the former hunting lodge of Saddam's sons Uday and Qusay, overlooking an artificial blue lake which of course had been named 'Victory Lake'. In the reception you could buy Cuban cigars to smoke on the deck.

Within a few weeks, on 1 September, the US was due to officially end its combat mission, drawing its troops down to 50,000 and handing over command to the Iraqis. By the end of the following year the last American soldiers would have left. There was however a problem, particularly given all that Mullen and Petraeus kept saying about the military not being the only side: Iraq had no government. Elections in March had failed to produce a decisive winner. Prime Minister Nouri al-Maliki's Shiite Islamist alliance had won ninety-one seats, and Ayad Allawi's pro-Western secular coalition eighty-nine. Five months on, Iraq still had not formed a government.

Mullen set off on a whirlwind round of meetings with the two rival Shiite politicians Maliki and Allawi, as well as President Jalal Talabani, the Kurdish leader. Each of them told him only they were capable of running the country. Maliki had been Prime Minister since 2006, and had no intention of stepping down. He had spent much of the Saddam years in exile in Damascus then in Iran, and returned in April 2003. He had ended up as Prime Minister after the US Ambassador Zalmay Khalilzad suggested he might form the first government led by Shiites in Iraq since the eighteenth century. The hope had been that he would unify the country, and he had promised to reach out to Sunnis and Kurds. Instead he had used his position to consolidate power for Shiites, and had overseen the grisly execution of Saddam Hussein.

While Mullen was meeting the political leaders, over in parliament the newly elected MPs cancelled an already postponed session and announced that they would not even try to meet again until further notice. They did, however, collect their first monthly salaries – an astonishing $10,000 a month, along with $50,000 for guards and security.

We journalists were taken to 'Camp Prosperity' to meet up with inanely grinning people who appeared to have come from a cult, but in fact were members of the Provincial Reconstruction Team. They told us how important it was to spend 'not just time but *organic* time with sheikhs', and how they had brought in crucial agricultural specialists, 'not just random beekeepers'. One of them even blogged to his family and friends about sheep-dipping.

We also met Scott Hanson, an American pilot in a flying suit with chiselled movie-star looks and a tan to match, who was in charge of training the Iraqi air force 'We have built the air force from zero in 2003 to 6,000,' he began. 'But Iraq already had an air force,' I protested. He looked at me blankly. One of the American journalists poked me in the ribs. 'Haven't you worked out after all this trip that for us Americans history only starts when we arrive?'

When we met up with Mullen again at the end of the day he was eager to declare Iraq a success despite the lack of a government. 'Look at where we are now in Iraq compared to when I was going there in 2006–08, when there was little hope,' he enthused. 'I drove everywhere today, which was a first. We even came through what used to be known as the Highway of Death. Driving through we even got stuck at a roundabout, which just seemed so much more normal than I thought I would ever see. It's stunning.'

It was true that Baghdad no longer resembled a city under siege as it had on my previous visit, when US soldiers were standing guard on every corner. The number of US troops killed was down dramatically – four in the previous month, compared to sixty-six in Afghanistan and to 141 at the high point.

Maybe the war was over for the Americans. However, the bloody civil war between Sunnis and Shiites had been stifled rather than resolved, and for Iraqis the violence was returning. Four hundred and ninety-seven Iraqis had been killed the previous month, the highest for more than two years, and far more than in Afghanistan, where 297 civilians were killed in July. The night before we arrived a suicide bomber detonated a car bomb in Karbala, massacring twenty-five pilgrims on their way into the sacred Shia city. Earlier that day six people were killed in the suicide bombing of the offices of al Arabiya television channel in Baghdad.

Yet Mullen cited Iraq as 'impressive proof' of how his army had learned from its failings and turned itself around. 'It takes visionaries to recognise where we have to go,' he said. 'What is so striking to me is once we figured it out how rapidly we were able to implement. When you consider over an eighteen-month period we went from a no-counter-insurgency approach to where we ended up in Iraq, I think it's a really extraordinary achievement.'

'Aren't you just tackling the branches rather than the root problems?' I suggested.

He agreed. 'The long-term solution is that globally we have got to get to a point where a fourteen- or fifteen-year-old boy has options rather than saying, "I'm going to be a suicide bomber." That means long-term seeking security and prosperity. Dealing with this is going to take a global kind of counter-insurgency that isn't just kinetic, it's the hold and build, providing jobs and education so the fourteen-year-old has other paths, and that needs a vibrant, growing economy.'

Shortly afterwards it was the Iranians who broke the political deadlock. Qassem Suleimani, commander of the elite Quds force of the Iranian Revolutionary Guards, had become a regular visitor to Iraq since the fall of Saddam, and invited a group of Iraqi leaders to the holy city of Qom to celebrate the Eid holiday. There he apparently leant on Moqtada al Sadr to support his old rival Maliki in exchange for ministries. Maliki also agreed to make Jalal Talabani, the pro-Iranian Kurdish leader, President, and to expel all American forces by the end of 2011.

America had lost 4,500 soldiers in Iraq, yet seemed to have handed over the final outcome to the Iranians, the very people Mullen was telling us he regarded as most dangerous (along with Pakistan).

The Americans had planned to leave a few thousand troops in Iraq after the 2011 withdrawal for training, intelligence, and special forces for tracking down insurgents. When he was reconfirmed as Prime Minister, Maliki refused to agree to extend their immunity from prosecution, so they all left. Obama was keen to get out as he had promised before the 2012 election, so did not protest. The Americans were left with no leverage and no intelligence. Within three years Iraq would be the base for the largest jihad of modern times, attracting more fighters than even Afghanistan did back in the 1980s when it all started.

PART IV

GETTING OUT

It may not be very flattering to our amour propre, but I feel sure I am right when I say that the less the Afghans see of us the less they will dislike us.

Secret memo of Lieutenant General Sir Frederick Roberts, 12 May 1880 (during the Second Anglo–Afghan War)

27

Killing bin Laden

Abbottabad, Pakistan, 2 May 2011

THE NIGHT WAS moonless, and the two Ghost Hawk helicopters painted the exact shade of the Pakistani darkness followed the rugged contours of the Pir Panjal mountains, skimming close to avoid radar detection, then abruptly banking right and low towards the town of Abbottabad. On board the first sat a dozen US Navy Seals, crammed together and tense, their superfit bodies bristling with grenades and ammunition, night-vision goggles pulled over their eyes. In the second were eleven Seals and a Pakistani-American CIA interpreter as well as a specially trained tracking dog named Cairo, a Belgian Malinois kitted out in dog body-armour and goggles.

At fifty-six minutes after midnight the words 'Palm Beach' came over the radio, signalling three minutes to landing. Their destination was a three-storey house inside a high white-walled compound which looked just as it did in the photographs they had seen and at the purpose-built mock-up thousands of miles away in a forest in North Carolina, where for the past few weeks they had practised their mission. The commandos gripped their rifles, M4s or MP7s, released a round into the chamber with a metallic click and muttered some final prayers, ready to fast-rope down onto the roof of the building.

Airborne night raids were part of life for these men, but they had never carried out one quite like this. Some took a last look at the leaflets folded in their pockets, on which were printed a series of names, photographs and descriptions of the men and women living in the compound. The gaunt, bearded face on the top – 'age 54, height 6'4 to 6'6, weight 160lbs, eyes brown' – needed no introduction. His codename at US Special Operations Command was 'Crankshaft', but the Seals referred to him as 'Bert', after the tall, thin Muppet in *Sesame Street* (they referred to his portly deputy Ayman al Zawahiri as 'Ernie'). The world knew him as Osama bin Laden, the most wanted man on earth.

Also on the leaflet were three of bin Laden's four wives, seven of his children, two grandchildren and two other men – Ibrahim Said Ahmad Abd al Hamid, known as al Kuwaiti, or 'the Kuwaiti' (he had been born in Pakistan to a Kuwaiti father), and described as a 'courier', his wife and four children, and his brother Abrar with his wife and four children. There were however lots of blank spaces and question marks. Though the house had been watched for months, no one knew exactly what or who they would find inside.

Overhead a Sentinel drone circled 20,000 feet up, sending back live video to officials at CIA headquarters in Virginia and the Situation Room of the White House, to which President Obama had just returned from nine holes of golf at Andrews Air Base, his usual Sunday programme. Among those gathered with him were Admiral Mike Mullen and Secretary of State Hillary Clinton, as well as Vice President Joe Biden and Defense Secretary Bob Gates, both of whom had been sceptical about the operation.

Five minutes behind the strange, humpbacked Ghost Hawks came four more helicopters, Chinooks carrying a quick-reaction force in case anything went wrong. The first was the Command Bird, which bore the commanding officer of Seal Team Six, the elite unit carrying out the raid. The second was the Gun Platform, equipped with three M134 Gatling guns. This would spend the raid hovering three hundred feet above the compound, ready to engage any armoured vehicles or troops that attempted to interfere with the operation, or anyone who tried to flee. A third and fourth helicopter landed in a valley some distance away.

NAME: USAMA BIN LADIN
ALIASES: SHAYKH
SIGNIFICANCE:
POSSIBLE DESCRIPTION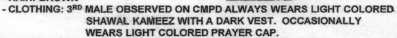

- NATIONALITY: ARAB/SAUDI
- AGE: 54
- HT: 6'4" – 6'6"
- WT: ~160 LBS
- EYES: BROWN
- HAIR: BROWN
- CLOTHING: 3RD MALE OBSERVED ON CMPD ALWAYS WEARS LIGHT COLORED SHAWAL KAMEEZ WITH A DARK VEST. OCCASIONALLY WEARS LIGHT COLORED PRAYER CAP.

FAMILY MEMBERS: CMPD AC1, COURTYARD A, 2ND AND 3RD FLOOR
- 1ST WIFE: AMAL AL FATTAH AL SADAH (28 YRS OLD)
- DAUGHTER: SAFIYAH (9YRS OLD)
* 2 UNIDENTIFIED CHILDREN BORN SINCE 2011 (UNK IF IN "A" COMPOUND

- 2ND WIFE: SIHAM ABDULLAH BIN HUSAYN AL SHARIF (54 YRS OLD)
- SON: KHALID (23 YRS OLD)
- DAUGHTERS: MIRIAM (20 YRS OLD), SUMAYA (16 YRS OLD)

- 3RD WIFE: KHAYRIYA HUSAYN TAHA SABIR aka UMM HAMZA (62 YRS OLD)
- SON: HAMZA (21 YRS OLD)
    - WIFE: MARYAM
    - SON: USAMA (4 YRS OLD)
    - DAUGHTER: KHAYRIYA (1 YR OLD)
* 3RD WIFE KHAYRIYA AND SON RELEASED FROM IRANIAN CUSTODY IN JUL 2010

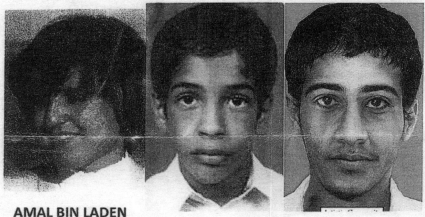

AMAL BIN LADEN
WIFE

KHALID
SON

Mini-guide to the bin Laden compound given to Navy Seals

NAME: IBRAHIM SAID AHMAD ABD AL HAMID
ALIASES: ARSHAD, ASIF KHAN, TARIQ, HAJI NADEEM, SARDAR ASHAD
(OWNER OF AC1)
SIGNIFICANCE: COURIER AND ASSESSED
AS ONE OF 3 INDIVIDUALS
RESPONSIBLE FOR HVT #1s CARE
POSSIBLE DESCRIPTION
 - NATIONALITY: ARAB/KUWAITI
 - AGE: 32
 - HT: 5'9" – 5'11"
 - WT: UNK
 - EYES: UNK
 - HAIR: UNK
 - SKIN: UNK
 - CLOTHING: TYPICALLY A WHITE SHAWAL KAMEEZ
 - OTHER: MOVED FROM MARDAN CITY TO TARGET CMPD IN 2006 WITH
        BROTHER ABRAR
FAMILY MEMBERS: CMPD AC1, COURTYARD C
 - WIFE: MARYAM (31 YRS OLD)
 - SONS: KHALID (5-7 YRS OLD), AHMAD (1-4 YRS OLD), HABIB (18 MONTHS)
 - DAUGHTER: RAHMA (8 YRS OLD)
* WIFE AND KIDS RETURNED TO C CMPD ON 28 APR 2011
 - BROTHER: ABRAR
 - FATHER: AHMAD SAID (DECEASED)
 - MOTHER: HAMIDA AHMAD SAID (46 YRS OLD)

NO PHOTO

NAME: ABRAR AHMAD SAID ABD AL HAMID
ALIASES: ARSHAD, ASIF KHAN,
SARDAR ASHAD (OWNER OF AC1)
SIGNIFICANCE: FACILITATOR FOR HVT #1
POSSIBLE DESCRIPTION
 - NATIONALITY: ARAB/KUWAITI
 - AGE: 33
 - HT: UNK
 - WT: UNK
 - EYES: UNK
 - HAIR: DARK
 - SKIN: UNK
 - CLOTHING: WEARS GLASSES
 - OTHER: MOVED FROM MARDAN CITY TO TARGET CMPD IN 2006 WITH
        BROTHER ABRAR

FAMILY MEMBERS: CMPD AC1, COURTYARD A, FIRST FLOOR
 - WIFE: BUSHRA (~30 YRS OLD)
 - SONS: IBRAHIM (4 MONTHS), ABD AL RAHMAN (1-4 YRS OLD), MUHAMMAD
(6-7 YRS OLD, ATTENDS MADRASSA AWAY FROM FAMILY)
 - DAUGHTER: KHADIJA (1-4 YRS OLD)
 - BROTHER: ABU AHMAD
 - FATHER: AHMAD SAID (DECEASED)
 - MOTHER: HAMIDA AHMAD SAID (46 YRS OLD)

The Ghost Hawks were Black Hawks modified with a skin that meant they barely showed up on radar and made little more sound than a whisper. It was the noise of the Chinooks that woke Aslam Khan, a businessman who lived in the house next door. 'At first I thought it was a tractor ploughing a field,' he said. He looked at his watch and saw it was 1 a.m. 'Then my son told me it was a helicopter.' They ran to the window, but the electricity had gone off. In the darkness and dust thrown up by the rotors they could see nothing. Khan's confusion turned to terror when moments later a blast from his neighbours' courtyard shattered his windows. The explosion, along with the sound of 'seven or eight' gunshots, told him this was not some routine exercise from the nearby military training school, and he started to panic. 'My daughter was very afraid and I took my family and we ran out of the house.'

He was not the only one to be woken. A mile and a half away, near Jalal Baba Park, an IT consultant called Sohaib Athar was jolted awake by the whirr of helicopters. He instantly reached for his phone and tweeted, 'Helicopter hovering above Abbottabad at 1 a.m. (a rare event).' The thirty-three-year-old had recently moved from Lahore, fed up with its frequent bombings, to what he thought was a safe, sleepy town, so he was not best pleased. 'Go away helicopter – before I take out my giant swatter,' he added, followed by, 'A huge window-shaking bang here in Abbottabad Cantt [cantonment]. I hope it's not the start of something nasty.' For the next half-hour Athar continued to post about everything he heard on Twitter, without the faintest clue that his musings were the world's first public record of Osama bin Laden's final moments. The realisation hit him only when he got up on Monday morning and switched on the TV. 'Uh-oh, now I'm the guy who live-blogged the Osama raid without knowing it,' he typed.

The bang he had heard had been the Seals blasting their way into the compound. That had not been part of the plan, but the first Stealth helicopter, codenamed 'Razor 1', had been caught in a downdraught in warmer than expected air, and lost altitude too quickly as it tried to land in the compound. Its tail caught the concrete wall and broke off the rotor, forcing the pilot to crash-land, nose jammed down into the dirt. The Seals quickly climbed out of the side doors, rifles at the ready.

Not knowing what had happened, the pilot of the second helicopter pulled back. The plan had been for Razor 2 to hover over the roof of the house so the Seals could rappel down and surprise bin Laden while he slept. Instead it landed outside the compound and they used explosives to blast the metal gate.

The Seals dashed through the hole. At the end of the drive they saw a small, shoebox-shaped guesthouse. A man ran out waving an AK47. This was Ibrahim, the courier. Before he could take aim they shot him, then ran towards the main house. Ibrahim's brother Abrar rushed out with an AK47 and his wife Bushra. Both were shot.

Meanwhile the Seals from the first helicopter had run inside the house and were going from room to room, not knowing if the place was booby-trapped. As one group headed up the stairs they encountered bin Laden's twenty-three-year-old son Khalid, and shot him dead. At the top a man's head poked out from behind a curtain to see what the commotion was. Through their night-vision goggles the Americans could see it was bin Laden. Two women rushed out, presumably bin Laden's two elder wives, and the Seal who was point-man of the team moved to block their way with his body, even though they could have been wearing suicide vests. Two other Seals, Rob O'Neill and Matt Bissonnette, followed bin Laden into the bedroom.

His youngest wife Amal screamed and threw herself in front of him. Bin Laden's AK47 was by the side of the bed, but before he could reach for it one Seal shoved Amal aside, and the other fired a shot, grazing her in the calf. The two men were less than two feet away from bin Laden as they fired at him – 'bap, bap' – a kill shot to the head, near the left eye, blowing out the back of the brain and cutting the spinal cord, followed by a second to the chest. The al Qaeda leader crumpled to the floor as he was shot a third time.

The Seals took photos for identification, then dragged the body out of the house and loaded it into a nylon body bag. It was then taken onto the helicopter, where a medic took swabs for DNA confirmation that it was indeed bin Laden.

On the audio feed the Seal team commander gave the agreed codeword, 'Geronimo,' then repeated 'Geronimo EKIA' – Enemy Killed in Action. Back in the Situation Room at the White House there were gasps. 'We got him,' said Obama quietly.

While this was going on, other Seals were running through the house gathering up papers, five computers and more than a hundred thumb drives. Altogether these contained more than 6,000 documents that intelligence officials would refer to as a 'treasure trove' which they hoped might stop further attacks. Another team went to the damaged helicopter and smashed the avionics, then wired it up with explosives so no one could steal the technology. As soon as the Chinook and the surviving Black Hawk had lifted off the timer was triggered to blow it up, though its tail remained embedded in the wall.

The tension was not over, however, for Operation Neptune's Spear was not yet finished – the Seals still had to get out of Pakistan.

The Americans were both relieved and astonished by the lack of Pakistani response. Back in January, when the Seal Team Six commander was first flown to a secret underground bunker and told to prepare for a raid on a 'high-value individual', bin Laden's location had been described as a 'non-permissive environment' for American forces. The commander initially assumed this meant Iran. Pakistan, after all, was an ally.

However, relations had deteriorated even further at the start of the year when a CIA contractor called Raymond Davis shot dead two Pakistanis in Lahore who had been following him. Davis had been trying to penetrate Pakistani militant factions like LeT, and the two men had approached him at an intersection on a black motorbike with their guns trained on him. He took out his Glock pistol and shot them through his car window.

When Davis was arrested the police found that his camera, which was in the car, had photographs of military installations. This was regarded by Pakistanis as proof of widely reported rumours in the media that the CIA was sending a vast secret army to Pakistan.

Davis claimed that he worked at the American Consulate as 'a consultant', and Obama said he was a diplomat. Clearly no normal diplomat would be carrying a Glock, and the ISI chief General Pasha was furious when Leon Panetta insisted, 'He's not one of ours.' Davis was kept in a Lahore prison which had a reputation for people dying in unexplained circumstances.

The crisis continued for two months, worsening when the widow of one of the dead men committed suicide. Eventually the US admitted that Davis was working for the CIA, and paid 200 million rupees (about £1.44 million) in blood money, enabling him to be flown out.

The very next day, 17 March, the CIA launched a massive drone attack in North Waziristan, killing at least forty people attending a tribal meeting. It was as if they were saying, 'We can do what we like in your country.' I was in the office of General Athar Abbas, spokesman for the Pakistani military, when the news came in on all of his many TV screens. He was furious.

By the time of the Abbottabad raid then, six weeks later, there was so little trust between the two countries that there was no way the Americans were going to inform Pakistan's civilian or military leadership about it. So great was thought to be the likelihood that Pakistan's military would tip off bin Laden that the US had preferred to take the risk that the Pakistanis would think they had been invaded by India and shoot the helicopters down. It was to mitigate against that that the Stealth helicopters were used, while a navy electronic-warfare aircraft called a Prowler created a corridor for them to fly through that would not show up, and generated the fake impression of an intruder elsewhere.

Of course the helicopter crash alerted attention. General Kayani, the Pakistani army chief, was awoken and informed of it, and contacted the head of the air force. They were baffled. Pakistan had a sophisticated radar system to protect against incursions from enemy India, and they had no idea how it had been breached.

While the Pakistanis were scrambling two F16 jets to the wrong destination, the American helicopters were already carrying bin Laden's body to Jalalabad. There, in a hangar, the Seals were met by their boss Admiral William McRaven, head of JSOC, Joint Special Operations Command, and the female CIA agent code-named 'Maya' who had been fundamental to the search. Her headquarters in Langley had already confirmed from photographs, using facial-recognition technology, that it was bin Laden, but McRaven stretched out the corpse to measure it. Only then did he realise nobody had a tape measure.

Back in bed, General Kayani was woken at 5 a.m. by a phone call from his friend Admiral Mullen – by then the two men had met twenty-seven times in the previous two years – telling him what had happened. It was the first official communication of bin Laden's killing.

Seven thousand miles away in the US capital, Americans watching Donald Trump's *The Celebrity Apprentice* on what was for them still Sunday evening were surprised to see a newsflash around 10.30 p.m. Eastern Time that President Obama was to address the nation. Major newspapers were called by the White House and told to 'Hold the front page.'

I was at home with my family, and we had just finished dinner with my mother, who had arrived from England that afternoon. As we speculated about what had happened, the last thing we thought about was Osama bin Laden – the al Qaeda leader had been hidden so long that he had dropped off radar screens.

A revolution was under way in Libya, the latest in the Arab Spring, and NATO jets had been bombing regime targets, so some journalists thought perhaps the Libyan dictator Colonel Muammar Gaddafi had been killed. But that seemed an unlikely reason for the US President to give a late-night address to the nation – Obama had been reluctant even to get involved with Libya.

It was Twitter, not traditional media, that first broke the news to the world. Keith Urbahn, a former Chief of Staff to Donald Rumsfeld, tweeted at 10.24 p.m.: 'So I am told by a reputable person that they have killed Osama bin Laden. Hot damn.'

Word started to spread, and fifty-seven million Americans tuned in to hear Obama just over an hour later. Standing at a podium on a red carpet in front of the East Room, he announced, 'Tonight, I can report to the American people and to the world that the United States has conducted an operation that killed Osama bin Laden, the leader of al Qaeda, and a terrorist who's responsible for the murder of thousands of innocent men, women and children. A small team of Americans carried out the operation with extraordinary courage and capability. No Americans were harmed. They took care to avoid civilian casualties. After a firefight, they killed Osama bin Laden and took custody of his body.'

Nine years, seven months and twenty-two days after 9/11, the world's most expensive manhunt had been brought to an end with a thirty-eight-minute operation. Contrary to what Obama had said, there had been no firefight. In fact one of the Seals would later say that only twelve shots were fired in the entire operation.

Jubilant crowds gathered outside the White House, chanting 'USA, USA!' and 'CIA! CIA!' One placard read 'Obama 1 Osama 0'. Most of those there were students from the nearby George Washington University who should have been revising for their yearly exams, and who had grown up under the shadow of 9/11. Pilots on domestic airliners, al Qaeda's weapon of choice against America, announced the news to cheers from passengers.

For the Obama administration the first challenge was what to do with the corpse. Conscious of the damage done to the reputation of the US by Abu Ghraib and Guantánamo, it had been drummed into the Seals that there should be no disrespecting the body, no kicking it or any triumphal photos. After consultation with the Saudis it was flown to an American warship, the USS *Carl Vinson*, in the Gulf just off Pakistan. There it was wrapped in a white burial shroud laden with weights, Muslim rites were administered, and at around 2 a.m. DC time it was tossed into the Arabian Sea.

Amid all the celebration there was a nagging doubt. For almost ten years the US had been fighting a bloody war in Afghanistan, the aim of which officials had repeatedly said was to 'disrupt, dismantle and defeat al Qaeda'. Two million American soldiers had been deployed in Afghanistan and Iraq, and more than 100,000 of them were still engaged in Afghan valleys and plains, from Helmand in the south-west to Mazar-i-Sharif in the north. By contrast, Pakistan, where bin Laden had found refuge, was meant to be Washington's ally, and had received more than $20 billion in civilian and military aid over the last ten years.

In Obama's speech he mentioned Pakistan several times, but was careful with his words. 'Over the years, I've repeatedly made clear that we would take action within Pakistan if we knew where bin Laden was. That is what we've done. But it's important to note that our counter-terrorism cooperation with Pakistan helped lead us to bin Laden and the compound where he was hiding.'

Within a few days many people would be asking the same question: How on earth had bin Laden been living for more than five years in an army garrison city, on army-managed land, down the road from Pakistan's top military academy, just fifty miles from the country's capital?

I spent the next few days in Washington, where everyone seemed to want to give their version of events, leaking so many details that the CIA complained they were compromising future operations. Then I flew to Islamabad to try to get some answers.

I landed in a nation in shock. Not shock that the al Qaeda leader had been living with his family in a house so close to the capital, but that America had carried out a brazen raid on their territory, particularly after US–Pakistan relations had been poisoned so much over the Raymond Davis affair.

I headed for the Marriott, which had been rebuilt after the 2008 bombing and looked more like a fort than a hotel – indeed, it was claimed to be the most protected hotel on earth. There I had lunch with one of the country's most senior diplomats, Riaz Khokar, who had been Musharraf's Foreign Secretary from 2002 to 2005, and previously Ambassador to Washington. 'People are very disappointed – they are all asking, how could the US do this to us?' he said. 'In the mosques on Friday nobody was talking about anything else. My butcher today said America has invaded us, and I have no answer to that. The US has got a huge trophy, but it has left a huge crater of distrust.'

Eventually I managed to get him to address the key question – how could bin Laden have been living in Abbottabad without ISI being aware of it? 'Intelligence agencies wouldn't be intelligence agencies if they didn't engage in monkey business,' he replied. 'But what benefit did Pakistan have in keeping bin Laden? He was a liability, he declared war on Pakistan. Would we do that for $1.5 billion a year?'

Also in the Pakistani capital at the time was Marc Grossman, who had become US Special Representative for Afghanistan and Pakistan after the sudden death of Richard Holbrooke. He described the atmosphere as 'surreal', and later told Husain Haqqani, Pakistan's Ambassador to Washington, that he felt Pakistani officials and the rest of the world seemed to exist in 'parallel universes'. 'As Pakistan's Ambassador to the US at the time, I could not tell Grossman that I agreed with him,' said Haqqani. 'But like many Pakistanis who worry about their country's future, I have often noted my compatriots' tendency to live in a world all our own.'

Another old friend, Nusrat Javed, who hosted a nightly television phone-in show, was so frustrated that all the calls were only about the 'outrageous attack by the US' that he got a journalist friend to call in pretending to be a member of the public and ask, 'How on earth was the world's most wanted terrorist living in our midst?' Even though the friend had called the programme not from his own phone but from a phone-box in a market, he was quickly contacted by ISI and warned, 'We know who you are and what you did.'

As usual, conspiracy theorists took over. Many people simply refused to believe that bin Laden had been living in Abbottabad. One national daily, the *Pakistan Observer*, ran a front-page story claiming that he had died years before, and his body kept in a fridge at Bagram airbase: 'The body of frozen Osama was brought to Abbottabad by a helicopter under the most sophisticated and hi-tech operation and taken to the upper storey of the building. A commando immediately sprayed a blood-like solution on his face to establish that the leader of al Qaeda was killed on the spot.'[1] According to this story, the raid had been faked by the CIA to embarrass Pakistan, enable the US to hasten the withdrawal of its forces from Afghanistan, and boost Obama's election prospects for the following year.

Many people I met again told me the old story I'd heard so often in 2001: that bin Laden wasn't behind 9/11 in the first place, but that Mossad had carried out the attacks as an excuse to launch an American-Israeli crusade against the Islamic world.

I was of course eager to see bin Laden's house, so on my second day I headed off to Abbottabad, a two-hour drive from the capital. I had been there before, and remembered it as a genteel green town in the foothills of the Himalayas at the start of the Silk Road to China. The town was founded in 1853 by a British officer, James Abbott, who penned odes to the 'sweet Abbottabad air'. Until the Obama raid it was mostly known for its good schools and golf courses.

I had forgotten how much of a garrison town it was. As I drove in, I passed the pennant of one regiment after another – 'Home of the Pathans', 'Home of the Baluch' ... – as well as the Army Boys' School and the Combined Military Hospital. Road signs requested, 'Please Keep the Cantonment Clean'. I took a right turn for the Kakul Military Academy, the West Point of Pakistan, which had an army checkpoint and a sign warning 'Restricted'. Just before the checkpoint was a turn-off to the right, past a deserted strip of land, to Bilal Town, where bin Laden had been living.

House No. 3, Street 8A, Garga Road, was easy to find. The White House had described it as 'a luxury one million dollar mansion, about eight times the size of neighbouring houses'. It was indeed large, and was surrounded by twelve-foot-high walls topped with concertina wire – but so were many houses in the area: Pashtuns often live in fortified houses because of feuds, and local people had just assumed the two brothers in the house were smugglers.

The area had been cordoned off by police and plain-clothes men, but I managed to convince them to let me through. The compound was a strange triangular shape – the CIA believed it had been designed to thwart surveillance – and a hole had been blasted through the front wall, where the Seals had gone in. The helicopter rotor fin had been removed: Pakistan had handed it over to the Chinese, to annoy the Americans.

Inside the walls stood the three-storey house. It was strange looking up at this place where the world's most wanted man had lived for nearly six years, never coming out except for walks around the garden. The top floor had windows on only one side and a terrace with a seven-foot wall, and it was there that bin Laden had stayed with his youngest wife, Amal, a Yemeni he had married in 2000 when she was just seventeen, and who had since had five children. Two of them were born in the local hospital in Abbottabad, the Interior Minister Rehman Malik told me.

On the second floor lived his other wives, both Saudi – his second and eldest wife, Khairiah, by then in her sixties, and the mother of his twenty-year-old son Hamza, who had two children of his own; and third wife Siham, mother of Khalid. Khairiah had been under house arrest in Tehran after 9/11, but somehow in 2010 she had travelled the 1,500 miles from there to Abbottabad. Both she and Siham were well educated, with doctorates, and gave lessons to the children every day.

The house certainly wasn't a million-dollar luxury property. Indeed, although bin Laden was the son of a billionaire, for many years he had lived an austere life. His first wife, Najwa, who left him, had complained that when they lived in Sudan in the early 1990s he refused to have air conditioning or toys for their children. The Abbottabad house had no air conditioning and just a few gas heaters, so it must have been unbearably hot in summer and bitterly cold in winter.

The family were quite self-sufficient. They kept chickens for eggs and cows in sheds for milk, and grew vegetables. Two goats were delivered to the house every week and slaughtered for meat, and there was a supply of cooking oil and Quaker oats for porridge.

Local people had been warned off not to talk, but some neighbours nervously exchanged a few words. No one had ever seen bin

Laden or any of the children. They told me that if a local child accidentally hit a cricket ball over the compound's wall and knocked at the gate they would not be allowed in, but would be given money to buy a new one.

Only two men ever came out of the compound – Arshad and Tariq Khan, as they were known locally. Their real names were Ibrahim Abu Ahmed ('al Kuwaiti') and his brother Abrar. A local shopkeeper told me he sold them John Player cigarettes, which they bought in singles, suggesting they had little money. It was the brothers who had bought the land in 2005 and built the house, and they lived in a separate house in the compound with their own wives and children. They and the bin Ladens moved in sometime in 2006. No one seemed to know where bin Laden had been between fleeing Tora Bora in December 2001 and then, though he apparently lived for a while in Swat until the 2005 earthquake.

Bin Laden's self-imposed confinement in the Abbottabad compound must have felt very restrictive for a man who loved the outdoor life, riding horses and striding over mountains. His only exercise was walks in the garden, which had a tarpaulin over it so he could not be seen from above. He also wore a cowboy hat to cover his face.

What did he do all day? Only seventeen of the thousands of documents retrieved from inside the compound were later made public, but these showed that he had more control over al Qaeda than had been thought. 'Bin Laden was far more operationally active and hands-on than we realised,' Obama's counter-terrorism czar John Brennan told me. He wrote letters to al Qaeda affiliates such as al Shabaab in Somalia and AQAP in Yemen, and called for suggestions for the tenth anniversary of 9/11. He compiled an annual review, the last of which, in October 2010, was upbeat about Afghanistan, where he wrote that the Americans had suffered 'the worst year since they invaded', and predicted that economic pressure would mount on the Obama administration to withdraw. He was, however, suffering his own financial woes. Like the CEO of a company, he had a financial division, and this seemed to be cash-strapped. Allowances were slashed, and he asked for receipts for everything, even thumb drives costing a few pounds.

It was also clear that the drone programme was having a serious impact on the organisation's ability to move around or to organise major new attacks on the West – the last had been the London bombings in July 2005. He advised followers in Pakistan's tribal regions not to travel except on overcast days, 'when the clouds are heavy', or to meet in tunnels. 'I am leaning towards getting most of our brothers out of the area,' he wrote.

'We know from the material from the compound that OBL himself recognised they were being pummelled,' said Brennan. 'He wanted to carry out more attacks, but his commanders were saying, "Your aspirations outweigh your capabilities."'

A week after the raid, US officials released a video found in the house of a white-bearded bin Laden huddled on the floor in a brown blanket in front of a cheap TV set, using a remote control to watch news clips about himself. They also revealed that they had found packets of 'Just for Men' black hair dye, which he was using to cover up his grey hair and beard. It was hardly the final image the world's most media-conscious terrorist leader would have chosen.

What was most astonishing was not the size or the appearance of the house, but its location. Not only was Abbottabad a military town not far from Pakistan's capital, but the house was on land managed by the military and literally just a few hundred yards from the country's most prestigious military academy. General Musharraf said he used to go running past the house. General Nadeem Taj, his close ally, and head of ISI from 2007 to 2008, had been commandant of the academy in 2006, the year bin Laden moved there. The army chief General Kayani had addressed cadets at their annual passing-out parade. US special forces had even been based there for training in 2008.

The other odd thing was that bin Laden was not living like a man who might one day have to flee at a moment's notice. He had no guards and no escape route, no Tora Bora-style tunnels. He lived as if he thought he was protected, and expected to be forewarned of any danger. The only precautions the Americans found were a few hundred euros and two phone numbers sewn into his pyjamas. Letters taken from the house and later released talked of 'our trusted Pakistani brothers', suggesting he was in touch with local militant groups.

Just as few believed it was possible for so many militant organisations and terror groups to exist in Pakistan unless major elements in the state machinery were protecting them, Brennan said, 'It's inconceivable that he didn't have a support network in Pakistan helping him.'

Tracking down bin Laden was an incredible coup for the CIA. The Agency was under something of a cloud, having been caught flat-footed by the Arab Spring, misjudged Saddam's supposed weapons of mass destruction leading to the ill-judged invasion of Iraq, and tried to justify the use of torture in interrogating detainees.

A few years earlier, in 2006, I had done a story about the hunt for bin Laden, and it was clear then that many in the Agency thought it had reached a dead end. They had taken to referring to bin Laden as 'Elvis'. Under fire for botched intelligence assessments about WMD in Iraq and the use of 'enhanced interrogation techniques', Agency morale was low.

However, the bin Laden cell did not give up, and a few things had caught their attention. Other senior al Qaeda figures had been apprehended while living in Pakistani cities, not in caves as popularly thought. The last senior figure to be caught, Abu Faraj al Libbi, picked up in May 2005, had been waiting at a shop in Mardan (not far from Abbottabad), which was a drop point for a 'designated courier' of bin Laden.

It was well known that bin Laden had stopped using phones and the internet, because these were easily intercepted and had led to others being caught. The CIA knew he used foot messengers, and around 2007 started focusing on trying to find these human carrier-pigeons. 'We had cued onto the notion of the network being the holy grail to burrow into al Qaeda's senior leadership,' said Juan Zarate, who was Deputy National Security Adviser for

Terrorism in the second term of the Bush administration. 'We had enough information to suggest there were a couple of trusted couriers being used by OBL.'

The problem was, they didn't know who they were. They first heard the name 'al Kuwaiti' in 2003, from the interrogations in Guantánamo of a Saudi called Mohamed al Qahtani. Qahtani was supposed to be the twentieth 9/11 hijacker, but had been refused entry to the US by an eagle-eyed customs official at Orlando airport, suspicious of his one-way ticket. He was picked up fleeing from Tora Bora in December 2001 and sent to Guantánamo, where he initially claimed he had gone to Afghanistan because of his love of falconry. Someone made the connection to the man who had been turned away at Orlando, and for a period of forty-eight days starting in November 2002 he was interrogated and tortured, subjected to sleep deprivation and freezing temperatures and forced to listen to loud music by performers including Christina Aguilera.[2] At some point he mentioned the name 'Abu Ahmed al Kuwaiti', but that was just one of hundreds of names being entered into a massive database. The name came up again in the interrogations of other detainees, including an al Qaeda lieutenant, Hassan Gul, who said al Kuwaiti was close to KSM and al Libbi. When KSM was questioned about him during his endless waterboarding sessions he described him as 'retired', which seemed odd. Al Libbi said he had never heard of al Kuwaiti. Investigators wondered if the two men were deliberately steering them away from him. However, they could not track him down, and thought he might be dead.

By 2009 the NSA was blanket monitoring phone calls in the region, and someone else on the Agency's radar in the Gulf made a phone call to a man they realised was al Kuwaiti. The man asked what al Kuwaiti was up to. 'I'm back with the people I was with before,' he replied. There was a pause on the line, then the friend said, 'May God facilitate.'

At the time numerous phone conversations were being intercepted in the area with the help of ISI. The CIA did not share the significance of al Kuwaiti with the Pakistani agency. They tracked his phone down to north-west Pakistan, but they could not pin down his location. Knowing his phone could be used to trace him, al Kuwaiti only put its batteries in and switched it on when he was at least ninety minutes away from Abbottabad. But then in August 2010 a Pakistani asset working for the CIA tracked him to Peshawar, and followed his white Suzuki jeep to the compound.

As soon as they saw the pictures of the house in Abbottabad the CIA team were intrigued. The house was well-fortified, and strangely had no phone or internet connection. Locals said the occupants burned their own rubbish. The CIA became convinced that someone important was hiding there, and started monitoring it with an overhead drone.

The difficulty was knowing what was going on inside the house. One agent came up with the idea of staging a fake polio drive, using a Pakistani physician, Dr Shakil Afridi, so they could obtain samples of blood from the children living there. They never managed to get any.

They also set up a safe house to monitor comings and goings, and a blimp overhead. From this they saw that a tall man often walked in the garden. They nicknamed him 'the Pacer'. When they measured his shadow they found that he was over six feet tall.

Excitement in the unit started to mount. Though they had no actual sighting of bin Laden's face, they became convinced that he was there. CIA Director Leon Panetta told Obama that this was the best 'window of opportunity' since Tora Bora.

Biden and Gates were sceptical. Both men recalled 'Black Hawk Down', the 1993 débâcle in Somalia when two US helicopters were shot down, as well as the failed helicopter mission to rescue hostages from Iran in 1980.

Though he had to admit the chances were only 'fifty-fifty', the usually cautious President took the riskiest decision of his administration. On Friday, 29 April 2011, while much of the world was watching the royal wedding between Prince William and Kate Middleton at Westminster Abbey, he called McRaven. 'It's a go,' he said.

* * *

Obama's gamble paid off, but for Pakistan the discovery of bin Laden had opened up an enormous can of worms. How could ISI, which monitored everything we journalists did, not know that the world's most wanted man was living under its nose? Pakistan's intelligence service was either 'complicit or incompetent', declared Panetta. Neither was a good place to be. Most people assumed the former. Musharraf after all had once said Pakistan's military was so strong that 'Not a single rifle bolt can go missing without us knowing.'[3]

I asked former Republican Congressman Pete Hoekstra, who as Chair of the House Committee on Intelligence from 2004 to 2007 had been privy to intelligence from the region, for his view. 'Finding bin Laden in Pakistan was not exactly a *Casablanca* moment: "Shock! There's gambling in the casino!"' he said. 'I believe there were people in ISI and the military who knew he was there. The question is, how high up does it go?'

Some even speculated that there was a bin Laden desk inside ISI, run by some of the old ideologues, though most believe it more likely that he was protected by one of the militant groups close to the agency.

Lieutenant General Asad Durrani, who ran ISI in the 1990s and later served as Ambassador to Germany and Saudi Arabia, said it was possible the agency did know, and were planning to reveal Osama's whereabouts when it suited it. 'The idea was at the right time his location would be revealed,' he told the BBC's *Hardtalk*. 'And the right time would be when you can get the necessary quid pro quo – if you have someone like Osama bin Laden you are not going to simply hand him over to the United States. Double game is the norm. I think it was Lord Robertson, former Secretary General of NATO, who said, "If you can't ride two horses, don't join the circus." Statecraft isn't about following a linear path, you play so many games, you keep so many balls in the air.'[4]

'Who was hiding him is the $64 million question,' said Bruce Riedel, the former CIA analyst who headed Obama's AfPak review. 'He lived in Pakistan nine years, moved at least three times, was having kids like a twenty-year-old, and his wife gets out of whatever detention in Iran and knows how to find him. We also know he was communicating with LeT and Hafiz Saeed. There are three options: ISI were clueless; or they knew exactly where he was and were protecting him; or something in between – they knew he was somewhere in Pakistan, and his friends in LeT and other militant groups were communicating with him and protecting him.'

There was outrage in the US Congress, which over the years had voted so many billion dollars in aid to Pakistan. Dana Rohrabacher, a Republican Congressman from California, spoke for many when he called for aid to be cut off: 'They were playing us for suckers all along. I used to be Pakistan's best friend on the Hill but I now consider Pakistan to be an unfriendly country to the US. We're giving money to someone who obviously is working against the national security interests of our own country. They've been arming these people [Taliban] to kill our troops, they've been building nukes at our expense and now we know they have been giving aid and comfort to bin Laden. We were snookered. For a long time we bought into this vision that Pakistan's military were a moderate force. In fact the military is in alliance with radical militants.'

Once again, as with the assassination of Benazir Bhutto, there were a lot of coincidences. Yet no smoking gun was found linking ISI to bin Laden. 'There's a very powerful circumstantial case, but in the end that's all it was,' said Riedel. David Kilcullen, the counter-terrorism expert, agreed: 'Let's assume they knew where bin Laden was in 2002 and gave him up. Then they don't get the money and influence and are seen as a basket case by the international community. They had every interest in the world to preserve al Qaeda, not destroy it.' He went further: 'I went from thinking they were playing both sides to thinking they were backing the other side to realising they *are* the other side.'

Over the following years I asked everyone I met who had access to the intelligence trove, but all insisted that nothing had been found. I wondered if people were lying. After all, as Riedel pointed out, if the Obama administration did find a smoking gun which proved Pakistani complicity, that would be a political nightmare.

'What would you do then?' he asked. 'When we say to the Pakistanis, "You've got to stop allowing IEDs being made in your backyard or else," what is the "or else"? We're not going to go to war with them, that's for sure. There's no credible "or else", and Pakistan knows that.' Referring to how the Libyan revolution might have had a very different outcome had Libyan leader Colonel Gaddafi not previously handed over his nuclear weapons programme in a 2003 deal with the US and the British, he said, 'The Pakistanis watched what happened to Gaddafi, and said, "That won't happen to us because we kept our nukes."'

In fact Pakistan had been quietly ramping up its programme, doubling its stockpile of bombs to more than a hundred; by the time of the bin Laden raid it had overtaken Britain and France to be the world's fifth largest nuclear power.

Once again the prevailing view was that Pakistan was too dangerous to cut off. Before I went back to Washington I met a very senior ISI official. 'You know we built up our nuclear arsenal against India, but now they turn out to be very useful in our dealings with America,' he said, smiling like a Bond villain.

Inside Pakistan, some believed that the humiliation of ISI provided an unprecedented opportunity for the civilian government to finally exert authority over the military. 'The game is up,' proclaimed the *Daily Times*, arguing that 'Pakistan's military cannot afford to play its usual double game any more' of supporting militant groups. It also called for parliamentary scrutiny of the military and ISI budgets.

Farahnaz Ispahani, an MP and spokesperson for President Zardari, told me she had gone to him saying, 'This is our chance.' She suggested that he announce a commission of inquiry. He did nothing, then the next day she read in the press that General Kayani had announced the military's own commission. 'We lost the chance,' she said.

General Pasha and General Kayani, as chiefs of ISI and the army, went to explain themselves in an unprecedented closed-door session of parliament on 13 May 2011. Pasha told the MPs he took responsibility, and offered to resign, but Kayani refused. He described the agency's 'key role in safeguarding the country' since its beginning, and warned that criticising the army and ISI would be 'against the national interest'.

Nothing happened. After the session Dr Firdous Awan, the Information Minister, told the press that parliament was aware of the 'critical times' being faced by the military, and had agreed to stand united behind it. 'They should be assured that they are not alone and the whole nation is behind them,' she said.

Surprisingly, it was only the opposition leader Nawaz Sharif who spoke out – a man who had started his political career as a protégé of the army, placed in power by General Zia. This was, he said, 'a historic opportunity [for the government] of tilting the power in favour of civilians'. He added, 'It is time for the agencies to work within their constitutional ambit instead of subverting the constitution, toppling governments, running parallel administrations and controlling foreign policy.'

The government did nothing. The day after the bin Laden raid, the Prime Minister Yusuf Raza Gilani took off for Paris.

I was told that ISI had a series of videos implicating Ministers in everything from accepting kickbacks to footage of the wife of one of them gambling large sums in a London casino, which they threatened to release.

The army and ISI were fighting back. My Pakistani mobile was bombarded with text messages. 'Brothers come to Islamabad Press Club at 4 p.m. to rally to express solidarity with Pakistan army and ISI which have become targets of false propaganda by enemies of Pakistan,' read one. 'CIA failed to learn about Pearl Harbor; CIA failed to warn Americans about 9/11; CIA gave false info of WMD in Iraq; Long Live Pakistan Army,' read another. The name of the CIA station chief in Pakistan was leaked by ISI to press. A number of people were arrested, including the doctor who led the fake polio-vaccination drive aimed at flushing out bin Laden. He was later sentenced to thirty-three years in prison.

I began to feel as if I was living in a parallel universe. I went to see General Hamid Gul, and reminded him how he had spoken to me after KSM's capture in Rawalpindi about the advantages of 'hiding in plain sight'. 'Yes, of course,' he replied. 'No one would have expected Osama living in a town with twenty children.' For a moment I thought we were agreeing. Then he continued, 'But it wasn't bin Laden. He died a long time back, 2004 I think. The Americans just wanted an excuse to blacken the name of Pakistan and hide the fact they botched this thing up. 9/11 happened on CIA's watch. What about the WMD in Iraq? Now this confusion in Afghanistan. Don't the CIA know that the Afghan Taliban is not the same as al Qaeda? So many bloody failures. It's very convenient to blame Pakistan ISI. This humiliating and dishonouring Pakistan after all the services we rendered is shocking. We shouldn't be surprised. Remember, it was the Americans who blew up Zia, you were here then. As General Ayub said, "It may be dangerous to be America's enemy, but to be America's friend is fatal."'

There were enough unexplained disappearances in Pakistan for it to be obvious that investigating links between ISI and al Qaeda was highly dangerous.

It was my birthday while I was in Pakistan, and a friend held a party for me to which a number of Pakistani journalists came, bearing colourful bunches of gladioli, for it was that time of year. Of course the only topic was bin Laden's killing and who had been protecting him. Everyone warned me off investigating. One brave exception was Saleem Shahzad from the *Asia Times*, who had written before about the link between ISI and al Qaeda. Two weeks later, on Sunday, 29 May, the forty-year-old father of three was abducted in broad daylight in Islamabad on his way to do a TV interview. Two days later his body was found on a canal bank in Mandi Bahauddin, about eighty miles away, bruised and battered. He had been beaten to death. 'Any journalist here that doesn't believe that it's our intelligence agencies?' tweeted Mohammad Hanif. Saleem had told colleagues a year earlier that he had received threats from ISI. Admiral Mullen told journalists in Washington a few weeks later, 'It was sanctioned by the government.'

Pakistan had become the most dangerous place on earth to be a journalist. Nine were killed that year, and nobody brought to justice. Anyone who had worked in journalism in Pakistan was only too familiar with ISI control. Whenever there was a major story, editors were given 'guidance' on what line to take. Nobody could afford not to listen. TV and radio stations were dependent on licences from the regulatory body PEMRA, which could be revoked, and newspapers on print from the government as well as advertising.

I had first realised the extent of this control when I was deported in 1990, and journalists I'd considered friends wrote astonishing scurrilous stories about me 'entertaining' local politicians in the Holiday Inn. 'How could you write this?' I asked them later. 'You knew none of it was true.' They shrugged. 'We had no choice, you know that.' In the Zia years under censorship, papers often appeared with stories blacked out and there was only state-controlled TV. Under Musharraf it became much more sophisticated. He had allowed private TV channels, and a slew had opened, so it looked to be free. But they depended on the government to stay on air, and ISI encouraged the media to whip up the anti-American frenzy over drones and 'violation of sovereignty', even though Musharraf had actually agreed to the programme.

Kamran Shafi, a former army officer and diplomat turned journalist, described relations between the media and the authorities as 'wheels within wheels, shadows within shadows, mirrors within mirrors'. As an outspoken commentator, he regularly received threats, phone calls telling him, 'You are dead ... you will be shot and dragged on the streets.' When he called in print for ISI to be headed by a civilian, shots were fired outside his home.

'When you work as a journalist in Pakistan you feel Big Brother is watching you all the time,' said another friend, Malik Siraj Akbar, who set up the first online newspaper in his home province of Baluchistan. 'If you host or help a foreign journalist then you should prepare to be called by ISI. They will immediately call you an "enemy of the state" and threaten you with dire consequences. Many journalists in our ranks are on the ISI payroll, and you don't know who among your own colleagues or bosses, which makes it difficult to openly express your opinion even at the press club or social gatherings. It's very hard to bring an end to ISI's domination as long as top politicians and journalists willingly serve as paid agents of ISI.'

He was subjected to years of harassment and threats for writing about 'disappearances' in Baluchistan, and was eventually forced to flee the country in October 2011 and seek asylum in the US. The harassment started in the summer of 2007, when he was forcibly picked up from the Quetta Press Club and taken to the military cantonment. 'I was questioned for several hours by a Major and Colonel who had marked stories with green highlighter and demanded to know my sources of funding for my paper, and warned me to stop writing about disappearances.'

That was the first of many sessions. Another time he was intercepted by an agent at the hotel in Lahore where he was staying on the way to a conference in India to speak on Baluchistan. 'He warned me of dire consequences if I went. When I returned the same agent was waiting for me at Lahore airport with a couple of other men. I immediately grabbed the German organiser of the conference, who had travelled back on the same plane.'

The threatening sessions did not stop, and his website was frequently blocked. Worst of all were the untraceable phone calls. 'When an anonymous caller tells you the colour of your T-shirt or comments on your new haircut, fear grips more deeply,' he said. These were not idle threats. 'I lost a dozen journalist friends in one year in Baluchistan.'

Nor was size any protection. In 2013 when the country's most-watched TV channel, Geo, dared to suggest that ISI might have been involved in an assassination attempt on its highest-profile anchor, Hamid Mir, ISI called for the channel to be taken off the air, and it was. The message got through. Instead of supporting Geo, other channels lined up to attack it.

* * *

The killing of bin Laden did not improve the situation in Afghanistan. The month after his death a group of militants in suicide vests and armed with RPGs and grenades burst into the Intercontinental Hotel in Kabul while a wedding party was under way. They held guests under siege for five hours as police and commandos battled to take control, supported by NATO helicopters overhead. At least twenty people were killed. In July a US helicopter was shot down in Wardak, around forty-five miles from Kabul, killing thirty US soldiers. Then, in the same area, a massive truck bomb was driven into a base on 10 September, killing five Afghans and injuring ninety-six people, including seventy-seven Americans. This was followed by a twenty-hour siege on the highly guarded US Embassy and ISAF headquarters in Kabul on 13 September. If it wasn't quite the spectacular bin Laden had been calling for to mark the ten years since 9/11, it showed the ability to get into the heart of the capital, and there was plenty of carnage.

US officials said phones recovered from the scene had been used to call numbers associated with the Haqqani network and ISI. Admiral Mullen was just about to retire, and finally lost patience with the country he had tried so hard to befriend. Before stepping down, he told the Senate Armed Services Committee that he had evidence these attacks were carried out by the Haqqani network with the cooperation of ISI. He then launched an unprecedented attack on Pakistan: 'Extremist organisations serving as proxies of the government of Pakistan are attacking Afghan troops and civilians as well as US soldiers. The Haqqani network for one acts as a veritable arm of ISI. By exporting violence they have eroded their internal security ... undermined their international credibility and threatened their economic wellbeing.'

The year after the bin Laden raid, Pakistan bulldozed the Abbottabad house to try to obliterate his memory. His wives and children were flown to Saudi Arabia. His son Hamza, who was not at the house that night, was never found.

Pakistan launched its own investigation into the affair, the Abbottabad Commission. Its report, published in 2013, said 'collective incompetence and negligence' by the intelligence agencies was the main reason bin Laden remained undetected. However, it could not rule out some degree of 'plausibly deniable' support at 'some level outside formal structures of the intelligence establishment'. Among the testimony was a statement by the ISI chief General Pasha insisting, 'the main agenda of the CIA was to have the ISI declared a terrorist organisation'.

Killing bin Laden ended up being the most memorable achievement of the first term of the Obama administration. When the President later met Admiral McRaven, he presented him with a tape measure mounted on a plaque. Then he flew to Fort Campbell in Kentucky to personally thank Seal Team Six and the helicopter pilots. They presented him with a framed American flag that had been on the rescue Chinook, inscribed with the words 'For God and country, Geronimo'.

He did not ask who had fired the fatal shot. Despite the Seal cult of secrecy, two men who were in Abbottabad that night would later go public – Matt Bissonnette, who in his book *No Easy Day* claimed to have fired one of the two shots, if not the fatal one; and Rob O'Neill, who claimed he was the actual shooter.[5]

With bin Laden dead and the Obama administration claiming there were only a hundred al Qaeda left in Afghanistan, it was reasonable to question why NATO still needed 150,000 troops there, continuing a war which by then had cost 1,500 American lives.

Less than two months after the raid, Obama announced his timetable for the withdrawal of the rest of the troops from Afghanistan. On 22 June 2011 he made another, less dramatic, address to the nation. Declaring that 'the tide of war is receding', he said he was speeding up the pullout from the surge, and would completely hand over security to the Afghans in 2014. This was against the advice of Petraeus and his generals, but Obama had other priorities. 'Over the last decade we have spent a trillion dollars on war at a time of rising debt and hard economic times,' he said. 'Now we must invest in America's greatest resource – our people.'

Within hours President Nicolas Sarkozy of France said he would start withdrawing the 4,000-strong French contingent. On 6 July David Cameron announced that he was starting to bring back UK troops, from 9,500 to 9,000 in the first year, then all those who remained by the end of 2014. Whatever the situation on the ground in Afghanistan, the war was coming to an end for the West. People began to talk of 'Afghan goodenough'.

'We will not try to make Afghanistan a perfect place,' said Obama.

Postscript:

War Never Leaves You

Kabul, November 2014

OF COURSE, IN the end I went back. I missed Afghanistan with a yearning that I could not explain – in a way that was deep and anguished, like the lament of an ancient mariner for a troubled sea. I had an adorable clapboard house in Washington, with a rocking chair on the porch and a white picket fence, where every day a yellow school bus came to collect my son, just like in American movies, and I had a great job and wonderful friends. Yet part of me was somewhere else entirely, dreaming of pomegranate pips shining red as rubies. If I drove through Rock Creek Park with my roof down the scent of the pines reminded me of the mountains of Paktia. In my big American house I had a walk-in wardrobe, its shelves piled with silk scarves in bright colours like magenta pink and peacock blue, each one with a memory. I missed squatting uncomfortably on village floors drinking green tea and listening to fantastical stories of ancient feuds. I never remembered the bad bits.

It was by then the thirteenth year of war. After years of being told each year that *that* year was *the* critical year, 2014 really was. The world had lost patience with Afghanistan, and by the end of the year most of the foreign troops would be gone. Obama might call it 'transitioning out', Cameron handing over to an 'Afghan army and police force capable of taking care of their own security', but the reality was that the might of NATO had failed to defeat the Taliban, and the West was on the retreat.

As 2014 dawned, my Afghan friends worried about what would happen – particularly the women, who had once believed the world cared passionately about their fate. In January I went back to Kabul. It wasn't the same. On the evening of Friday, 17 January, the night before I boarded my flight, a suicide bomber walked up to the door of a Lebanese restaurant called Taverna du Liban, one of the most popular eating places for expats in Kabul. It was on the next road to where I stayed, and was my favourite restaurant, with its little garden where one could smoke apple-scented *shisha* as waiters brought alcohol in teapots and endless baskets of warm Arab bread, all presided over by the owner Kamal, sitting at a corner table, smoking broodily like a French actor and dispensing slices of his famous chocolate cake. Over the years I had watched his security transform from a breezy rattan fence to stark concrete walls and a steel door opening to a tunnel in which guards searched diners for weapons. That did not stop the bomber, who blew himself up at the entrance at around 7 o'clock on a busy Friday evening, blasting a hole as two gunmen shot the guards. They then ran in and went from table to table shooting diners, leaving twenty-one dead, including two Americans and two British, and a newlywed Afghan couple.

This was the first time foreign civilians in Afghanistan had been targeted on such a scale. I was used to flying into places as sane people were flying out, but I knew that if I'd gone to Kabul one day earlier I would have been eating there, and I felt the leaden taste of fear. My foreboding only increased as I breakfasted on the way in Dubai with an old ISI contact who warned me for the first time, 'Be careful, they will kill more foreigners.'

He was right. On 11 March a Swedish radio journalist was shot dead in broad daylight on Street 15, the same street as the friends' house where I stayed, and just one block away. Ten days later, again on a Friday, the Afghan weekend, terrorists managed to walk into the Serena Hotel with pistols in their shoes, even though the hotel had been highly guarded since its 2008 attack.

They entered the busy brunch buffet and began firing. The nine people left dead included Sardar Ahmed, a very popular local reporter for AFP, and his wife and two small children. Only their baby son Abuzar survived, found among the carnage miraculously alive although he had been shot in the head. Sardar was one of us.

I had never really known Kabul as a place of fear before. There was a not entirely welcome diversion on the flight when the Afghan woman next to me asked me to look after her baby while she went to the bathroom, then did not come back. Five minutes passed, then ten, then twenty. The baby started grizzling ominously, then crying, then wailing, and would not stop. I looked around desperately for a dummy or a toy but there was nothing, so I walked up and down the aisle jiggling the child, much to the amusement of the Afghan men seated all around. I supposed one of them was the father.

The familiar excitement as the plane flew low over the mountains of the Hindu Kush with their icy winter veins of snow and rock was tempered by the recent attacks – and what might await. I landed to find the city on lockdown and roads closed off, so it was hours before I could get to my friends' house.

Yet it was still good to be back, seeing what had and hadn't changed in the city. The traffic was more chaotic than ever, and street children wandered among the cars selling gum and phone cards, chanting 'No mother, no father,' along with widows begging in tattered blue burqas. I smiled at the crocodile lines of girls going to school in uniform with white scarves on their heads and bookbags on their backs. The school on the hill still had no toilets, and some of the children were still having lessons in freezing tents. Kabul River was still filthy, though the nearby District 1 police station by the money bazaar in the old city was run by a woman – Afghanistan's first female police chief. New places had opened, including the Kim Kardashian Ice-Cream Shop, a fake Top Man and a Chevy showroom (run by a Brit who had been persuaded to move from Bournemouth). In the windows of barber shops pictures of Cristiano Ronaldo had replaced *Titanic* posters of Leonardo diCaprio as the favoured haircut.

Almost everyone seemed to be on a phone, sometimes two, and there were smartphone shops everywhere. The country which at the time of 9/11 had been so cut off from the rest of the world that few people there had known what the Twin Towers were, and the only way to communicate was via a cumbersome satellite phone on a roof, now had seventeen million mobiles. Even in remote villages in the poorest province of Samargand I met elders who told me they were on Facebook.

I was staying with friends from the *Wall Street Journal*, and, determined not to give in to fear, we kept going out at night to the few restaurants still open. It wasn't really fun being the only diners. One Friday morning I was having breakfast in the Flower Café with a few Afghans and the manager asked me to leave, even though we were the only customers. 'People know there is a foreigner in here,' he said.

And the attacks didn't stop. Occasionally the 'duck and cover' alarm would go off at the US Embassy as RPGs were fired down from a nearby hill, and we debated whether to go into the basement safe room. One afternoon we heard a blast not far away. Soon a message came that an aid-agency guesthouse was under attack. Throughout the afternoon we could hear the pop and crackle of gunfire while the guesthouse was under siege.

After that the Afghan security service, NDS, closed down restaurants and guesthouses, saying it couldn't protect them. Even the old Gandamack was closed. Foreigners renting houses were all building safe rooms. Our own security plan was more of a hope than a plan – the idea was that if the Taliban invaded we would run onto the roof, throw a ladder across to the neighbouring house and climb across without getting shot.

Then we got the most chilling call of all – Anja Niedringhaus, a German photographer who had been travelling to Afghanistan for years, had been shot dead. She and her AP colleague Kathy Gannon, who I'd known for twenty-five years, had gone to Khost, and were sitting in the back of a car in a protected convoy of election workers when one of the policemen supposed to be protecting them shouted 'Allahu Akbar' and opened fire through their car window. Anja was killed and Kathy badly injured.

We sat around stunned. There was no pretending any more that Afghanistan was somehow different from other conflicts, or that we old-timers were different. People who had dedicated their lives to showing the real situation of Afghans were being killed.

My Afghan friends were equally nervous, for the attacks were not the only reason for uncertainty. Though the international mission was due to finish at the end of 2014, everyone knew the Afghan forces were not ready to take over. The plan was for some foreign troops to stay on doing training, advising and providing intelligence, along with special forces who were still hunting for bad guys. For this to happen, Karzai needed to sign a bilateral strategic agreement, or BSA, with the Americans. He had approved the draft agreement and then convened a *loya jirga* in November which not only approved it but asked for more American bases. Then, to everyone's shock, he refused to sign.

Without the BSA, the US and NATO troops would all leave, and billions of dollars in aid would disappear, not least the $5 billion a year for paying Karzai's army. Nobody could understand his objection. Every Afghan I met said they wanted it signed.

During my first week back, Karzai held a press conference. It was a one-hour rant against America – anyone would have thought it was the enemy, not the Taliban. 'We can't sacrifice the lives of our people, the sons of the land, for the US,' he raged. 'It's better that they leave Afghanistan and we face whatever is in our destiny.' He compared the BSA to the Gandamak Treaty of 1879, which is viewed as one of the most humiliating moments in Afghan history, ceding Pashtun lands to the British, as well as control of foreign policy.

At the end of the press conference we chatted, and he invited me to come back for an interview. My tape recorder would have to be delivered to the palace twenty-four hours in advance so it could be security vetted. This time the guards didn't even let me take in a pen, but provided me a Bic biro.

Postscript

Since we had last met, Karzai had aged, for he had been through tragedy – Ahmed Wali had been shot dead in Kandahar in July 2011 by his own long-time head of security, who was then killed. More happily, Karzai had become a father for the second time; he had a photograph of his two-year-old daughter by his desk.

Elections were due in a few months, which he could not contest, so I supposed this was the last time I would see him in that office, where I had found him shivering after the fall of the Taliban. I asked him to sum up those twelve or so years. His left eye twitched. 'In the words of Shelley, the great British poet, "I met murder on the way",' he replied. What did he mean? He looked at me and slowly and deliberately repeated the line. 'I met murder on the way.'

The poem was a condemnation of the 'Peterloo Massacre' of 1819, when British cavalry charged a group of demonstrators in Manchester. Was he accusing the US of murder?

'This whole twelve years was one of constant pleading with America to treat the lives of Afghan civilians as lives of people,' he said. 'They did not work with me, they worked against me, they systematically waged a psychological war on our people. Do you know that just between July and November 2010, General Petraeus carried out 3,500 bombardments?'

I shook my head.

'Three thousand five hundred aerial bombs. That's unbelievable, shocking! Who were they trying to win the war against? The Afghan people? So truly, relations went wrong because I met murder on the way.' He told me he and Obama had not spoken for seven months, not since a video conference the previous June in which, he said, 'frank words were exchanged'. They had met again at the funeral of Nelson Mandela in December, but he said they did not speak.

The morning of our interview he had deliberately antagonised the US by releasing thirty-seven of the eighty-eight prisoners the Americans had just handed over from US custody in Bagram. ISAF officials responded with media briefings to say that these men were dangerous. Karzai would go even further a few weeks later, on

International Women's Day. Addressing a gathering he said, 'Afghan men shouldn't test their strength against women. If they're so strong they should go test it against America.'

I asked why he wouldn't sign the BSA. 'It's a monumental decision,' he replied. 'I cannot just gamble.' He told me he had asked his Ambassador in London to bring him the text of the negotiations between Mortimer Durand and King Abdur Rahman over the Durand Line. 'Under pressure our kings signed things and all turned out to be disastrous for Afghanistan,' he said. 'Under pressure if I do the same today I don't know the consequences.'

So it was all about history. After years of being seen as a puppet of the West, Karzai did not want to be remembered as the ruler who signed for the presence of foreign troops. He was often mocked by the Taliban as a latterday Shah Shuja, the exiled Afghan ruler who was restored to the throne by the British in 1839 and slaughtered once they left.

He said he wouldn't sign unless the US brought the Taliban to the table for peace talks. They'd been trying to do that the last few years with no success, I pointed out, so why would the Taliban talk now, when foreign forces were leaving?

'You know where their safe havens are,' he said. 'I have never worked as hard with any country or any issue in my life as trying to improve relations with Pakistan.' He told me that when he had met Musharraf in his last year of government in 2007 and the suicide bombs had started in Pakistan, he told him: 'Mr President, if there's an explosion in Afghanistan my mind goes straight to ISI. But when there's a suicide bomb in Pakistan of course it can't be ISI – you don't blow up your own home. So what's going on? Now it seems with each day passing the government of Pakistan has less power to control things, which is not good for us and not good for them.'

Indeed, even Colonel Imam had been killed, kidnapped in the tribal areas and then shot in the head by a masked man overseen by Hakimullah Mehsud, the head of the TTP, who shouted 'Allahu Akbar!' The whole thing had been filmed and distributed on DVDs.

Karzai clearly believed there was some kind of conspiracy between America, Pakistan and Britain, which I found hard to follow. 'Even when we were in Peshawar during the jihad we knew the Americans were helping the radicals,' he said. 'That's where it all started.'

From outside came the sound of children playing. We went to the window. It was his son Mirwais and two cousins. Soon Karzai would be able to spend more time with them. He smiled. 'Twelve years is too long,' he said.

So many lives had been lost, and so much money spent. Had it all been a waste? 'In general terms the US–led mission in terms of bringing security has not been successful,' he said. 'Particularly in Helmand.'

'Are you saying it would have been better if the British had never gone to Helmand?' I asked.

'I guess so,' he replied, nodding slowly. 'Yes.'

As always when I felt down in Afghanistan, I went to Herat. The city looked thriving, so different from 2001, when shops were bare and everything bleak. There was a new glass-fronted hotel, even if it was surrounded by blast walls, the ancient citadel had been restored, and I even spotted a woman driver.

The Iranian border was less than a hundred miles away, and Iranian influence was everywhere. The cherry jam, soft cheese and juice at breakfast were all Iranian, as was the TV programme always on in the corner of the hotel restaurant. The bookshop I had spotted along the road only sold Iranian literature, and the Imam Khomeini Relief Committee was providing loans for building houses. There was a new library where the books bore portraits of Iran's supreme leader Ayatollah ali Khameini and a new Shiite mosque.

I went to see old Sultan Hamidy in his glass shop by the Big Mosque. A man was squatting outside with a small brown quail with speckled feathers in a wooden cage. 'For fighting,' he said as I looked at it.

Inside the shop, Sultan Hamidy was sitting as if he had been waiting for me. He invited me to sit with him among all the dusty treasures, and a boy appeared with a blue enamel teapot, two glasses and a dish of diamond-shaped sugar crystals. With his long white beard Sultan Hamidy looked older than Father Time. I realised I had no idea how old he was, so I asked him, though Afghans often don't know their exact age. 'I'm seventy-three and have been sitting here fifty-five years seeing many things,' he replied. 'The worst time was when the Russians came and I had to close the shop and drive a taxi.' Once he had whispered the names of the dead as he blew his magical glass into shape, but then they became too many. 'War never leaves this land,' he said. 'Now again business is very bad because foreigners have gone.'

The boy came back with more tea. 'I am training my grandson as my father trained me,' said Sultan Hamidy. They still used the same glass-blowing technique as hundreds of years ago. We sat silent for a while, and the wails of the muezzin rose from the Big Mosque and a car pulled up across the road. The man with the fighting quail gestured to Sultan Hamidy's son, who came in and told me urgently, 'Sorry, you must leave.'

Was it really a threat? Who knew? A few months later two Finnish women aid workers driving through the area in a taxi were shot dead by gunmen on motorbikes.

Next I went for tea with the warlord who had first taken me to Herat many years before. Ismael Khan had been Minister of Water and Power since being ousted as Governor, and had clearly prospered. He was living in a three-storey marble house, white and pillared as a wedding cake, lit by hundreds of lightbulbs, unlike most of the country, and guarded by his fashion militia in sharply-cut camouflage. Inside Ismael looked serene in his white prayer cap, long white tunic of the crispest cotton, and long snowy-white beard. He was holding court with a group of elders, telling them how to vote in the coming elections. 'They just wanted advice,' he smiled, his tiny currant eyes crinkling, when I suggested that did not seem very democratic.

He dispensed with the elders and led me into his garden, past supplicants who tried to kiss his hem and past his private zoo, a pen of peacocks and deer and a large, dusty ostrich. 'I love animals,' he said unexpectedly. Having zoos seemed fashionable among warlords, though I expected Ismael to have something more fearsome than an ostrich. The President's cousin Hashmat Karzai in Kandahar had a lion, though that wouldn't save him when assassins came a few months later.

We sat in a glass conservatory full of plants and talked about the future. He was gloomy. 'The international community shouldn't have taken the guns from our mujaheddin,' he said. 'In this area I was responsible for more than 100,000 mujaheddin across five provinces. We should bring them back. Without security there is nothing.'

From outside came the scream of a peacock. I remembered the Peacock Room in the Arg Palace where the Taliban had painstakingly painted out all the birds' faces. 'In these years foreigners have come and gone,' he shrugged. 'Most come for short times. They want facts and dates, things which are not our way. We can converse all our lifetimes, but you will not understand.'

He stood up suddenly. 'You must visit our Jihad Museum,' he said.

I had never heard of a jihad museum, so I took his advice, and on a chill morning drove to the northern edge of town. There, on a hill, stood a domed rotunda covered in engraved alabaster interspersed with turquoise and lapis tiles and surrounded by a sort of weapons park with a MiG fighter jet on a pedestal, two helicopters and an array of tanks and machine guns. I was met outside by a man in a suit who introduced himself as Abdul Wahab Qattali, better known as General Wahab, the warlord-turned-businessman who had paid for the museum.

He showed me that the inscriptions on the alabaster were the names of 2,100 of the 45,000 Afghans killed in Herat alone. He himself had joined the jihad at nineteen, and spent fourteen years fighting first against Russians then Najibullah. 'We lost 550 people from our area,' he said.

Inside the museum were tall glass display cases of guns and ammunition, one just for AK47s, one of 82mm anti-tank bullets made in China, one with old British Lee Enfields. A long corridor had been turned into a garish gallery of warlords in gilt-framed portraits like renaissance kings. All the old gang were there – Hekmatyar, Sayyaf, Rabbani, Abdul Haq, a pensive Ahmat Shah Massoud against the sunset, and Ismael Khan particularly resplendent. Only Dostum was missing, for he had been on the other side.

Lastly I was taken up the steps to the cupola. This had been given over to a grisly 360-degree diorama depicting the course of the Soviet occupation in clay models. It started with a scene of the Herat uprising against the Soviet presence, women throwing stones and a boy with a catapult, then moved on to mujaheddin raiding a flag from a Soviet tank, various scenes of bloodshed, and ended with a line of Russian tanks leaving. General Wahab flicked a switch and started a sound-and-light show, complete with gunfire.

'What are you thinking?' he asked anxiously. 'Astonishing,' I replied. The whole thing was a triumphalist shrine to defeating a superpower. And it turned out that the weapons were not the only booty. 'We have an actual Russian!' proclaimed General Wahab. Our guide Sheikh Abdullah, a shuffling man with a pale face and bushy henna-red beard, turned out to be an ex-KGB officer whose real name was Khakimov Bakhretdin. 'We captured him in Shindand around thirty years ago and then he joined us!' said General Wahab.

In a halting way, Abdullah explained that he had been born in Uzbekistan to a Ukrainian mother and a Russian father, joined the Soviet army and entered the KGB, then was sent to fight in Herat. He did not have a clue what he was going into, though his sister and brother-in-law were stationed there. 'We were a company of a hundred volunteers,' he said. 'Our problem was, we didn't understand the area so we just destroyed everything – walls, villages …' He had, he said, killed fourteen mujaheddin and captured another twenty-six. Then one day they went into a village they thought mujaheddin were using as a base. The place turned out to be deserted, but early the next morning the mujaheddin attacked, and Bakhretdin was shot in the head. He tried to escape, running into the forest, but they shot him in the back and he fell unconscious, abandoned by his fleeing comrades. 'When I came round a local doctor with a white beard was cleaning the blood and I saw I was in a local house. I was really afraid as we had all heard the stories of terrible things the mujaheddin did. We'd rather be killed than captured.'

Instead they looked after him. The doctor took out the bullet, and when he had recovered his hosts told him to convert to Islam. 'I was scared, I didn't know how. When they talked about Mohammed I thought he was a judge who would come and decide if I would be killed.' One night he dreamed of a very old man coming and sitting next to him and telling him to say '*Hamdullah*' – Praise be to God. When he woke up and lit the oil lamp no one was there. The next morning he told his captors to bring the imam, and he converted.

After that he ended up fighting alongside them against the Russians. 'To start with they didn't trust me, but then one night I went to an Afghan army post and told them I was a Russian and my car had broken down, so they let me in. Then I hit the guards and stole their guns. After that I fought with the mujaheddin until the Russians left.' He ended up marrying an Afghan woman and became a faith healer, changing his name to Sheikh Abdullah. When General Wahab completed the Jihad Museum, he immediately hired him.

Recently he had been tracked down by a Veterans' Commission from Moscow looking for 263 missing Soviets who had never come back from the war. He told them he did not want to leave. Instead he recorded a video message to his mother, who promptly dropped dead of shock.

'When he dies he will be buried here in the museum,' said General Wahab. 'Then we will have a dead Russian instead of a live one, which will also be good.'

After Abdullah/Bakhretdin had finished his story, General Wahab took me into a meeting room hung with lacy curtains. A long table covered with a plastic tablecloth had been set out with bowls of apples and cucumbers, and sharp knives. Waiting there was another man in a suit whom he introduced as General Asis Asiri. 'Also from the other side!' said Wahab.

'Seventeen years I was in the Afghan army, the communist army,' explained General Asiri. He had been trained by the Russian army and sent for six months to Leningrad for officer training. 'Look!' He rolled up his shirt to show raised, vivid scars. 'Wahab and I have scars from each other. Yet now we are like brothers.'

'Now working for me too,' said General Wahab, who had clearly done well from the presence of foreign troops, even if he grumbled about them endlessly. His company, the Faizi group, carried out security and construction – the two most lucrative legal industries in Afghanistan – and had 3,000 workers at one point, building the road from Herat to Lashkar Gah and providing its security and repairs for ten years. Recently the government had taken over responsibility, so he had cut his staff to five hundred.

Asiri was disparaging about the state of the Afghan army, which was supposed to keep the Taliban at bay once the foreign troops had left. 'The international community has not done enough for the Afghan army. When the Russians left we had five hundred active tanks just in Herat, an air force with warplanes and helicopters; now they have nothing, how can they fight the Taliban?'

'Anyway, the point of the museum is to show the young generation they should not go back to fighting,' said Wahab. 'We've had thirty-five years of fighting.' It was also clearly a warning to other superpowers not to make the same mistake.

Looking at this, you wondered why anyone in their right mind would invade Afghanistan. This was a question I had asked the Russian Ambassador, Andrey Avetisyan, a man so passionate about the Beatles that his mobile ringtone was 'Yellow Submarine' and he kept in a glass cabinet the *White Album* that his father had smuggled back from England when he was a boy. No one in his town had ever heard Western music, so they had all passed it round.

No diplomat knew Afghanistan better than Andrey. He spoke fluent Pashto, and had first been posted there in 1984 during the occupation. He had closed his Embassy and taken the Soviet flag down when Najibullah fell in 1992, and had then come back again.

'If the West had been interested in learning from our experience they could have done much better,' he said. 'Like us they thought they could be finished quickly. We would have told them Afghanistan is a place where it's easy to come but takes long to get out.'

Neither the British nor the Americans had ever bothered going to see him.

As well as the museum, General Wahab had built Herat's first amusement park, and that evening he invited me there for dinner in his restaurant. We sat upstairs in a kind of glass pavilion laid with a kingly spread of tureens of coloured rice and bowls of chicken and mutton curry and plates of aubergine with yoghurt. 'Also Britisher food!' said Wahab, pointing to an unappetising plate of macaroni cheese. The other guests included the Russian guide from the museum, the communist General Asiri, some of Wahab's ex-mujaheddin and a few former British and American military men who had gone into private security and were now working for him. It seemed like a *dramatis personae* of the wars. 'We're only missing Mullah Omar,' I joked.

The park was busy, for that day was the Persian holiday *Sizdah Bedar* to mark the beginning of spring, the thirteenth day of *Nowruz*, or Persian New Year. By tradition people picnic outside on that day, to celebrate the victory of light over darkness and of the angel of rain over the demon of drought. It was a warm, velvety night with a crescent moon, and down below I could see crowds strolling about or going for rides in swan boats on a murky lake. On the grass all around families had gathered to cook kebabs or drink tea.

General Wahab took me down for a walk, and everyone invited me to join them or to become their Facebook friend. One of those who waved me over most eagerly was a girl in jeans and a bright orange scarf whose face was beaming with happiness. She told me her name was Nasima, and that she was twenty-one and studying English literature and computing at Herat University. Her dream, she said, was 'to work in an office with my own desk'. Sitting with her were her six sisters, her mother, and a male cousin who had come as their escort, as their father disapproved of the excursion. It was the first time they had been to the park. 'We were scared but we came,' she said. 'Now seeing all these people makes me so happy and hopeful that Afghanistan will be good.' Next time, she said, they might even go on a swan boat.

'We could do that now!' I said. 'I'll take you all.'

She shook her head. 'This time it would be too much.'

Nasima was part of a generation who had grown up after the Taliban – Afghanistan was a very young country, with 70 per cent of the population under thirty – and chatting to her it was clear that she wanted the same as young people all over the world – a job, a loving family and a home. Afghanistan had changed, but there was still some way to go. She looked with envy across from the family section to the ferris wheel. 'Women can't go there,' she said.

I didn't want to leave Herat, particularly for a Kabul on edge, but I had to get back for the election. As before there was a raft of candidates, though in the end only eight ran. The main contenders were Karzai's fifty-three-year old Tajik former Foreign Minister Dr Abdullah Abdullah, and two Pashtuns – Dr Ashraf Ghani, sixty-five, the former Finance Minister and World Bank official who had been living in Washington; and Zulmay Rassoul, Karzai's National Security Adviser, who had been reluctantly persuaded to stand by the President, although at the age of seventy he mostly wanted to play golf.

The Taliban had vowed to disrupt the election, so the 'ring of steel' of security checkpoints around Kabul, which had previously been less than effective, had been stepped up. Many roads had been closed, including all those into the city. The day before the vote, security officials had switched their posts so there could be no collusion with Taliban.

Even so, I did not sleep much that night, so ominous was the feeling that something bad was coming. On election morning I breakfasted early and waited for the first blast. Instead, everything was quiet. When I ventured outside to visit some polling stations, the mood felt almost holiday-like. Large numbers of people had bravely come out to vote, including Turaj Rais, grandson of the Kabul bookseller Shah Mohammad who had risked his life hiding books from the Taliban, and cousin of Sardar Ahmad, the AFP journalist killed a couple of months earlier. 'I am voting in his memory,' Turaj told me. 'They killed Sardar, but by voting we prove to the terrorists they can never kill the hopes of the Afghan people.'

There was more violence in some of the provinces, but even so about six million people voted, 57 per cent of the electorate. One of the biggest problems was polling stations running out of ballot papers.

As predicted, no candidate got more than 50 per cent of the vote, but Abdullah was the clear leader, with a 900,000-vote margin over Ghani. There would be a second round in a couple of months.

I left feeling positive. Maybe, for the first time in history, Afghanistan was going to have a peaceful transition after all those bloody murders in the past. The international community breathed a collective sigh of relief, Cameron and Obama issuing congratulatory statements to the Afghan people.

On the plane out I bumped into Mahmoud Karzai. When I said how well things had gone, he shook his head. 'Wait and see,' he counselled. 'My brother is up to something.'

He was right, we had celebrated too soon. The second round of voting in June showed an even larger turnout of eight million, confounding most observers. In particular there was an incredible increase of 1.9 million votes for Ghani, putting him ahead of Abdullah by more than a million votes. Ghani claimed this was the result of a successful campaign to mobilise the Pashtun vote, but Abdullah cried foul, accusing him of ballot-stuffing. In some eastern provinces, such as Paktika, the turnout had been an unbelievable 96 per cent. The Secretary of the Independent Election Commission had to resign after Abdullah leaked phone calls of him asking officials to 'Take sheep to the mountains, stuff them and bring them back' – code, he said, for ballot-stuffing for the Ghani camp.

Just as in 2009, for months there was deadlock. John Kerry, who had resolved the last election, flew in again in his new guise as US Secretary of State. However, world attention had moved on. Bin Laden might be dead and al Qaeda Central mortally wounded, but new, even more deadly terrorists were emerging. That summer a group called ISIS swept across northern Iraq and by mid-June had seized Samarra, where once I had picnicked, Mosul, and Saddam's home town of Tikrit as the US-trained Iraqi forces fled south. The lightning attacks were remarkably similar to those by which the Taliban had once taken Afghanistan. It also seized the oil hub of Kirkuk, which along with an estimated $429 million looted from Mosul's central bank[1] made it the richest terror group on earth, easily outdoing the Taliban and al Qaeda. On 29 June, the first day of the holy month of Ramadan, ISIS announced its new name, Islamic State, and formally declared the establishment of a Caliphate across the Middle East, as far as Spain, under the leadership of Abu Bakr al Baghdadi. It called on all Muslims to join it.

Having been elected as the man who would take America out of Iraq, on 7 August 2014 President Obama gave another address to the nation, announcing that the US had once again launched airstrikes there. The aim was to rescue a community of minority Yazidis trapped on a mountain by ISIS and facing genocide. Then, as ISIS forces moved to within twenty-five miles of Baghdad in September, the American airstrikes were expanded to go after militants. The US was joined by other nations, including the UK. Soon there were more airstrikes in Iraq than in Afghanistan. By the start of 2015 both countries would be sending back soldiers.

The group had its roots in Afghanistan, where the Jordanian Abu Musab al-Zarqawi had cut his teeth before heading to Iraq and creating al Qaeda in Iraq. The US-led invasion of Afghanistan after 9/11 had meant the loss of Afghanistan as host of a planned future caliphate and he had fled to Iran with al Qaeda military strategist Saif al-Adel where they discussed relocating to Iraq. 'This [would be] our historic opportunity by the means of which perhaps we would be able to establish the Islamic State,' Adel wrote of the plan.

Yet it was how the West reacted that made this a reality. As Cole Bunzel, an expert on ISIS at Princeton University points out, the US invasion of Iraq played into their hands to make this a serious possibility,[2] and in 2005 bin Laden's deputy Ayman Zawahiri wrote to Zarqawi encouraging him to set up an Islamic state in Iraq.

But the al Qaeda core leadership were horrified at the Jordanian's methods. After Zarqawi personally beheaded and murdered prisoners, and released this on video tape, he was rebuked by Zawahiri, who wrote that other Muslims 'will never find [the images] palatable'.[3] Shortly after that he was killed in 2006 by McChrystal's Death-Star Unit, and the group went underground and was eventually taken over by al Baghdadi.

Once the US troops left Iraq in 2011, it regrouped, gaining support from Sunni groups who felt alienated by the staunchly Shiite Iraqi Prime Minister Nouri al-Maliki. In some of the American prisons in Iraq like Camp Bucca, extremist Islamists had got to know former disgruntled Ba'athist officers expert in military strategy – a deadly combination.

It also moved into neighbouring Syria, where a revolt against President Bashar al-Assad had rapidly descended into civil war. Assad's brutal repression of his people, combined with the West's failure to support moderate groups, made Syria fertile ground, and it changed its name to ISIS – Islamic State in Iraq and Syria.

With the West focused on trying to persuade Assad into exile, the rise of ISIS caught it by surprise. And just as Afghanistan had in its time, Syria and Iraq became the *cause célèbre* of the Muslim world. By the end of 2014, not only did ISIS control a third of Iraq and a third of Syria – an area the size of Britain – but it had attracted an estimated 20,000 foreign fighters from outside, making it the largest jihad of modern times.[4] Seven hundred were from the UK.

It seemed a frightening replay of history. The Afghan generation of fighters had, after all, gone on to form the core of al Qaeda, spawn 9/11 and turn up in just about every conflict in the Muslim world, fighting in Bosnia, Algeria, Chechnya, Somalia, Iraq and Libya.

ISIS was a whole new level of evil. They beheaded aid workers and journalists they had taken hostage, and burned alive a captured Jordanian pilot, even asking on Twitter for suggestions of new ways to kill hostages.

That wasn't even all. Libya was being fought over by rival militias including some former al Qaeda, and in northern Nigeria a militant group called Boko Haram was sweeping through schools, cutting the throats of boys and abducting girls from their dormitories, and had declared its own Caliphate.

While all this was distracting attention from Afghanistan, it also made it more urgent not to abandon the country in the way Iraq had been. This meant installing a new President who could sign the BSA, enabling some American troops to stay. Eventually, after a protracted recount in which many of the votes for both sides were discounted, a deal was finally reached in September under which Ghani would be President and Abdullah 'Chief Executive'. After all the West's emphasis on democracy – and $149 million spent by the international community on the elections[5] – the results were not released. They had also ended with the country's most brutal warlord, General Dostum, as Vice President.

At the joint swearing-in, Abdullah looked grim. Few believed the arrangement could work. It would be months before they even agreed a cabinet.

British troops ended their fourth war in Afghanistan at the end of October 2014. Just five hundred soldiers would stay in Kabul as part of a new mission called 'Resolute Support'. Some would be special forces still hunting bad guys, some would be advisers in the Ministries of Defence and Interior, and some would run the officer-training academy known as 'Sandhurst in the Sand'. We would also bring some over to the actual Sandhurst, including sons of some of the old-time warlords like Atta.

Before the troops left, Prime Minister David Cameron made his fourteenth visit to Afghanistan, where he talked of the 'very high cost' of the war, which had taken 453 British lives. He admitted the fight wasn't over: 'If our great-grandfathers were fighting against the Prussian domination of Europe, if our grandfathers were fighting fascism, if our fathers were fighting the Cold War against communism, then I am afraid to say that this struggle against Islamic extremism and terrorism is the struggle of our generation,' he told soldiers at Camp Bastion.[6]

In Afghanistan at least, it would not be our problem any more. Keeping out the Taliban would be the responsibility of the Afghan security forces. By then they numbered 352,000, cost between $4 and $6 billion a year, and the departing forces were falling over each other to say how good they were. Yet more than 5,000 Afghan soldiers had been killed in 2014 alone – more than the entire coalition death toll of the war – an untenable loss. So many had also deserted that the Defence Ministry dropped 36,000 names from the roll.

The Americans left 10,000 troops – more than they originally intended, and allowed to engage against the Taliban rather than just train and advise as originally planned – but insisted that they would all be out by 2016. Altogether there would be 12,000 NATO troops.

The British had initially intended to leave Camp Bastion away from the glare of the media, hoping perhaps to exit with no one back home noticing. In the end they'd realised that that would look like sneaking away. I had to lobby, plead, cajole and threaten to be one of the handful of British journalists to witness the end, as I had been there at the beginning.

The closure was carefully choreographed so the media would focus on the spectacle, and not on what it meant. The last commander, Brigadier Rob Thomson, insisted it was not a withdrawal or a retreat, but 'a deliberate, responsible and measured handover to the Afghans'.

Not everyone was convinced. David Davis, the Conservative MP who had once served with the Territorial SAS, pointed out that Britain had lost more than twice as many lives in Afghanistan as the 179 in Iraq, and told me he believed there should be a public inquiry. 'We're in the sort of war where we don't know the endgame, and if you go in not knowing the objectives you can't achieve them,' he said. 'But if you look at all the possible aims – removing an ungoverned space in which extremists can prosper, destroying the Taliban, putting in place a working democracy, destroying the drug trade, improving the lives of women, stabilising Pakistan – in all those things we failed, and in some cases went backward.'

Unsurprisingly, it is not a view shared by General Nick Carter, the man who had sorted out Kandahar and who went on to become head of the British Army in 2014. 'I don't think it has been a waste of blood and treasure. What I say to people who have lost loved ones there or been wounded is that I think Afghanistan as a whole is a better place than it was in 2002, whether you measure by infrastructure, what the economy has done, healthcare, education … That's not to say there are not an awful lot of things still wrong with it – it's immensely corrupt, its economy is unsustainable, it has serious challenges in terms of relations with its neighbours, it's still very insecure and there are still not equal opportunities for people in many places.'

Schools and clinics, I pointed out, were never the reason we were told we were going into Afghanistan – it was supposed to be for our own national security – and surely the experience has left us less safe: you only have to look at the security outside Carter's own Whitehall office, which was not there thirteen years ago. He insists, 'It is not an unreasonable argument to make that the threat that did emerge from AfPak is less now than it once was.' But he agrees that we are less safe, that his job is a lot more complicated than that of his predecessors prior to 9/11, and that some of that may be our own fault. 'I think the most important lesson I learned from all of this is before you get involved in these problems it's very important you have an understanding what the nature of the problem is, and then set your level of ambition accordingly. When we went into Helmand we didn't understand at all what we were going into, we didn't understand the politics on the ground, what was crime, criminality, insurgency; we didn't understand the tribal dynamics, and we were too ambitious.'

The failures in Iraq and Afghanistan had angered the public at home in Britain and the US, and left political leaders with a reluctance to engage anywhere. Not that they could do so effectively if they wanted to. The Pentagon planned to scale the US Army back to its lowest level since before World War II. As for Britain, defence cuts prompted by the financial crisis meant that by 2018 Carter's entire army would fit in Wembley stadium, with seats to spare – falling from 102,000 in 2010 to 82,500, the difference in theory made up by reserves. The air force had half the number of combat planes it had had five years ago, selling off its entire fleet of Harriers. Carter insisted the British Army was still fit for purpose. 'It depends on what your national appetite is, what your government wants you to do. I would judge our army as being capable of fielding a division (as we did to the Gulf in 1990 and Iraq in 2003), and that to my mind is the benchmark against which you set the credibility of an army.'

Nevertheless, Obama and Cameron would stand by as more than 200,000 people were killed in Syria and Vladimir Putin started to redraw the map of Europe, annexing Crimea from Ukraine. In 2013 Obama had gone back to West Point military academy and outlined a new strategy for fighting terror, questioning the wisdom of large-scale military occupations that stirred local resentment and carried a heavy cost back home. He recalled announcing the surge there in 2009, and said that four of those in the audience that day had been killed, and many more wounded. 'I believe America's security demanded those deployments,' he said. 'But I am haunted by those deaths. I am haunted by those wounds.'

I returned to Kabul under its new double-headed government. It was odd to see all the pictures of Karzai gone. People had grown tired of his endless fights with the US, and there was a sense of relief and a hope of starting anew. A small amusement park had just opened in Kabul, and on the Friday holiday I found people queuing up to get in. They swapped stories of how the new President Ghani was shaking everything up, sacking people who were late to meetings, turning up to check on hospitals in the middle of the night, for he slept only four hours.

His was no easy task. He told me he had been left no money by the previous government, and had inherited a presidency with a staff of 1,700, when he only needed two hundred. 'The problem is if I sack them they will join the Taliban,' he said. After a brief lull the attacks restarted.

His wife Rula, a Lebanese Christian, was out and about, unlike the invisible Mrs Karzai, and had set up a First Lady office. Yet women were scared. A female rapper I had interviewed kept calling me in terror because she was receiving so many threats after appearing on television, and was even being spat on by fellow music students at Kabul University. A woman MP who had often been held up as a model of progress by the West started crying in the middle of an interview. To my horror she told me she was being regularly raped by a provincial Governor, but could do nothing about it as he was threatening the life of her son, and had taken photos of her naked on his phone which he would release if she went public. 'It will be me ruined, not him,' she said. I tried to convince her to tell someone, but the Governor had helped the new President get elected, and I knew in my heart that she was right. Sometimes I wondered what we had done.

One morning I went for coffee at Karzai's new house. The $8 million palace he had built in the Arg, intending to move into it, had been given to Abdullah, so Karzai and his family had moved into what used to be the compound for the United Nations Development Programme. He was sitting holding court with his former Foreign Minister Dr Spanta and several other familiar faces. In his farewell speech he had again blamed the US and Pakistan for Afghanistan's situation. He had thanked Germany and Japan, and not mentioned the British.

'I've been thinking back over the last twelve years,' he said. 'Why were the Western press against me? It was your governments, wasn't it?'

'That's ridiculous!' I said. 'Our governments have nothing to do with what we write.'

He shook his head. I knew he was referring to the *New York Times*, which he believed the Obama administration had deliberately fed with material damaging to him.

'You've spent too much time in Pakistan,' I replied. 'Besides, you got great media at the beginning. Remember, you were "the most stylish man on the planet".'

'No,' he replied. 'That was just my clothes, and they weren't even mine. You called me "the Mayor of Kabul". I wasn't Mayor of Kabul, I was President of the whole country, and I kept it all together.'

The night was falling quickly, and just as they always had in Afghanistan, the foreigners were going away.

It was time for me to go home too. Before I left I went to the bazaar to buy a dented pomegranate, and the shopkeeper charged me one hundred afghanis – more than a pound – which we both knew was too much. Winter was coming and it was turning cold, rain turning to sleet and roads turning to mud. Traffic had come to a halt, and the area I was being driven through was full of black and green flags. People were handing out cups of hot milk and sugar. I'd never seen this in Kabul before – it was *ashura*, the Shiite time of sorrow.

The traffic spluttered forward in fits and starts. Suddenly I realised we were in Interior Ministry Road. '*Tawaqof!*' I commanded the driver. 'Stop!' He tried to tell me he was not allowed to stop, that it was a dangerous place, but I was in foreign-correspondent mode and was already out of the car.

Round the corner was the Mustafa Hotel, and at its doorway was standing Shabuddin, the tall Uzbek guard, just as he had been when we were so happy to find the hotel in 2001. His face lit up in recognition.

'How is everyone?' I asked.

'Not good,' he replied. 'You know we say the devil fell in Kabul when he was cast out of heaven.' He told me that after the hotel's manager Wais Faizi died, his father died of grief, then his brother Mustafa borrowed a lot of money from 'Northern Alliance people' and could not repay it, so they came at night and put him in Pul-i-Charki prison. The hotel had then been divided between creditors into three separate parts. 'Just one floor is owned by fourteen different people,' said Shabuddin. 'There's still a picture of you and Wais in his car upstairs. That was such a happy day, he always called you his sister.'

I asked him to take me to see the photograph, but Shabuddin shook his head. 'It's not like before. It's bad people staying.'

'What about the pigeons?' I asked. 'Are they still there in the courtyard?'

'Yes,' he replied. 'Only a few, as no one feeds them or flies them. People have TV now and Facebook instead of pigeons and kites.'

Round the corner I could see my driver was being moved on by the police, and was gesturing angrily for me to come. But I didn't want to leave.

Now when I looked up at the Bala Hissar a white blimp flew over the top, a strange clash of centuries.

'You foreigners always just pass through,' said Shabuddin. 'We don't know what will happen. But I am happier you came than if you had not.'

I felt happy and sad all at once. As the last US commander, General Joseph Anderson, lowered the US flag in Kabul in December, he said, 'I don't know if I'm pessimistic or optimistic.' Like him, I didn't know what would happen. It felt like that moment before the shadows expire, when the day is over but no one knows what the night will bring.

Kabul airport was the same old teeth-gritting battle, dragging my bags, heavy with body armour, through the four baggage checks and five body checks carried out by the over-made-up, over-zealous women in their cubicles with their kettles and small TVs.

In the last one before I entered the actual terminal building I braced myself for the inevitable squeezing, but this time it was a light touch. 'You have children?' the woman asked as she examined my lipstick. I took a photo out of my wallet, and she asked if she could keep it, as they always did. I was leaving, so I agreed. It amused me that my son's pictures, from baby to teenager, were stuck up in random Afghan homes all over the country.

'Good you go home, family,' she said. 'Here not good.'

'Not just here,' I said. My son, who was a baby all that time ago when 9/11 happened, would soon be going off to college. I had grown up at a time of peace, but he was already accustomed to a world where you could be killed by fanatical strangers in a tube train in London, a coffee bar in Sydney or a magazine office in Paris. Soon I would be going to a new war, or a new old one, perhaps to Iraq, that new breeding ground for jihad. It seemed to me that the international community no longer knew how to bring conflicts to an end.

'I think Americans have learned it's harder to end wars than it is to begin them,' Obama had recently said in the White House's Rose Garden.

I climbed the stairway to the plane, looking out over the line of sixteen abandoned Italian transport planes that the US had ordered for the Afghan air force. They had cost $486 million, and were headed for the scrapyard because they were unsuitable for Afghanistan's high altitude. At the entrance to the plane I stopped, and unbidden tears ran down my cheeks. 'You are scared of the Afghan plane?' asked the young Afghan woman at my side who I'd shared biscuits with in the terminal, and who was headed back to Turkey with her sister. 'No,' I shook my head.

'Are you scared of Ebola?' she asked.

'No!' I replied, smiling through my tears. 'I am just sad.'

She looked confused, and I shook my head. It would take a whole book to explain. Sad because I really believed that things didn't have to be like this. Sad for all the hopes there once were, and for the lessons we did not learn from our ancestors and others who had tried to tame these lands before. Sad for all those lives lost or damaged. For the soldier Luke McCulloch, for Wais 'the Fonz of Kabul', for Nadia the poet, for Benazir, for all the tens of thousands of people killed in Afghanistan and Pakistan since 9/11, and the hundreds of thousands in Iraq and Syria.

Sad that I didn't know how to help the women we left behind. Sad that thousands of schools were still being blown up in Pakistan, which despite everything had not stopped allowing the snakes in its garden. Sad that no Western leader took on Saudi Arabia, which had funded many of these jihadi movements, exported the Wahhabi ideology through madrassas, and fifteen of the nineteen hijackers on 9/11. Sad that the poppy fields of Afghanistan had become an unstoppable tide, poisoning the world's streets in even greater numbers. Sad that $1 trillion had been spent in Afghanistan, yet its children still went to school in tents. Sad that because of what had happened we wouldn't intervene again even when hundreds of thousands were killed. Sad that those sixty words drawn up in the White House in haste after 9/11 had indeed, as Congresswoman Barbara Lee feared, led to open-ended war. Most of all sad because I wasn't sure we had learned anything.

Maybe we hadn't been chased out as in previous wars, but Afghanistan would always be remembered as a failure, in the same breath as Vietnam and Gallipoli. Maybe, as in Iraq, we would all be back, for the Taliban were out there waiting.

As we flew away, the shadow of the plane over the Hindu Kush, glowing red in the late afternoon, I looked down over Kabul and knew I would miss it so. I could not have lived through this and just walked away. I have tried my best in this book to explain who did what and why, but this is a story with few heroes. I knew that for the rest of my life, whenever I met someone else who had lived those days I would feel an urgent need to talk to them. Pomegranates and plots and petty feuds were all in my blood now.

Acknowledgements

NOT MANY CORRESPONDENTS get to cover the same two countries for 28 years, let alone two wars fought in the same country by different superpowers. This book has been such a labour of love and war that it took me a long while actually to sit down and write it. First because I didn't want to stop reporting, and then perhaps because I didn't want to feel I was saying goodbye; and I hope it isn't.

Anyone who has managed to navigate their way into my study over the last year will have seen pile upon pile of notebooks – I have gone through every single one since 1987, except for one lost in a ditch under fire in Helmand in the summer of 2006. On the way I reencountered many old friends, some of whom later turned up in unexpected places, good or bad.

If I thanked all the people who had helped me on three different continents it would fill another book, and this one is already long enough, for these have been two long wars. Many of them are mentioned in these pages, a few are not to protect them, but I hope they know who they are and how deeply grateful I am.

When I nervously walked into Benazir Bhutto's London flat in July 1987 to do an interview as a young intern for the *Financial Times*, I never imagined how she would change my life. I will be forever grateful for the unexpected wedding invitation that landed on my doormat a few months later. Though we had our differences at times, she was a loyal friend whose assassination was a tragic

Acknowledgements

loss for Pakistan. Her wonderful press spokesman Bashir Riaz became a dear friend as have her confidantes Wajid Shamsul Hasan and the ever-stylish Sherry Rehman.

When I was first starting out as a young journalist in Peshawar with a pack of handwritten letters of introduction, the late Fateh Arbab and his family could not have welcomed me more warmly. Sadly, their own grandson had a less welcoming experience when he came to study in England after 9/11, which makes me sad.

Nusrat Javed, Husain Haqqani and Farahnaz Ispahani, Javed and Rita, Tariq Islam and Yasmin, Jugnu and Najam, Dr Shahid, Nadeem and Sehyr Saigol, Aga Siraj Durrani, the Soomro family, Imran Khan and the Sharif brothers have all been incredibly generous with time and hospitality over the years. My dear friend Dr Umar accompanied me on many adventures. Basir has explained many mysteries.

A succession of Pakistan's military spokesmen have arranged trips and patiently explained the army's stance to me from the late Brigadier Siddiq Salik, killed with General Zia, through Generals Shaukat Sultan, Rashid Qureshi, Athar Abbas up to Asim Bajwa – the British MOD could learn something from them.

When I moved to Peshawar to cover the mujaheddin fighting the Soviets in Afghanistan, I met a young spokesman called Hamid Karzai who became a close friend. I also spent many fascinating afternoons talking to Abdul Haq, and his death was a great loss. I would like to thank all the mujaheddin I travelled with in those days. Hamid Gilani and his family were always helpful and thanks to Abdullah Abdullah for explaining many things over the years.

After 9/11, my Afghan 'brother' Wais looked after me at his hotel Mustafa, and Kabul has never been the same without him.

Particular thanks to Fayez, Ziauddin Mojadeddi, Habiba, Jamil Karzai and Commander Muslim as well as former ambassador Dr Daud Yaar in London. I am humbled by Sarah Fane, founder of Afghan Connection, who is building her forty-third school in Afghanistan while the rest of us just talk – or write – about it.

Reporting would have been a lot less fun without the company of friends including Dominic Medley, whose many 'I'll be back' parties

Acknowledgements

I have attended; Griff, Norine Macdonald, Alistair Leithead, Nick Lunt, David Loyn, Simi Jan, Paula Bronstein and Lally Snow. Above all to my 'family' in Kabul – the *Wall Street Journal* gang Yaroslav, Nathan and Margherita – for your hospitality, insight, conversation and amazing food during some of the hardest days in Kabul.

Many British ambassadors in Kabul and Islamabad have given generously of their insight and dinner tables, going back to Sir Nicholas Barrington in Islamabad to most recently Sir Dickie Stagg in Kabul.

Though the MOD could hardly be accused of being helpful to journalists, many military officers have been generous with their time over the years. In particular I would like to thank General Nick Carter, the current army chief, who knows Afghanistan better than any other senior officer; General Sir David Richards, retired chief of defence staff, who really cared about making a difference – and his amazing wife Caroline who helps build schools in Afghanistan; Major General Mark Carleton-Smith for being honest; and many members of 3 Para from the summer of 2006, Major Will Pike, Lt. Col. Giles Timms, and last but not least Major Paddy Blair for making sure I was still alive to tell the tale.

A number of senior American officers have given their time and insight over the years, in particular Admiral Mike Mullen, Gen James Mattis, and Gen 'Mick' Nicholson – it was wonderful to see him and another old Kabul friend Norine get married.

I'd like to thank all troops with whom I have been embedded over the years both British and American. Heartfelt thanks too to Wesley Bauguess, widow of Major Larry Bauguess, for speaking for the first time of her loss and kindly providing photographs.

When I lived in Washington DC, many gave kindly of their time including Mark and Judy Siegel, Ali Jalali, Ambassadors Sayed Tayeb Jawaz and Zalmay Khalilzad, Bruce Riedel, Glenn Carle, Mike Scheuer and David Kilcullen.

I rarely get to travel with a photographer these days but over the years I have been lucky to work with two amazing photographers – Justin Sutcliffe and Paul Hackett – and some of their work appears in this book.

Acknowledgements

Enormous thanks to my editors during these years – Dominic Lawson at the *Sunday Telegraph*, then John Witherow and Martin Ivens at the *Sunday Times*, for encouraging me, giving me space and caring about the story, and their deputies Bob Tyrer and Sarah Baxter and foreign editors Sean Ryan, Peter Conradi and deputy Graham Paterson, always a friendly voice on the phone. I was very lucky to have an inspirational first foreign editor, Jurek Martin of the *Financial Times*, who trusted in me when I was just starting out.

Serendipity led me to Bran Symondson for the stunning cover image taken in front of 'Mount Doom' in Musa Qala, and I am hugely grateful to Julian Humphries, the art director at William Collins, for turning it into this beautiful cover.

My agent David Godwin has always been supportive and a good friend and knows what this book means to me.

I am extremely lucky to have once more as my editor the fabulous Arabella Pike, who was incredibly patient as I kept insisting it wasn't the right time to do the book then incredibly encouraging when it was. She, more than anyone, has turned this book into what it is and was like a mother tigress in protecting me from the tyranny of deadlines. Thanks as well to my meticulous copy-editor Robert Lacey, and to Stephen Guise for seeing the book safely through the production process.

I am delighted to have the lovely publicity director Helen Ellis again handling the book's journey into the outside world – there is no one better.

A big hug to all my friends, particularly Ronke, who have lived through this, and, above all, my wonderful husband and son, who have had to share their wife and mother not just with a book but with two foreign countries.

Last but not least my parents, who saw me off to that wedding in Karachi from which I never really returned.

London, March 2015

Notes

The Leaving
1. US Commission on Terrorist Attacks estimate
2. King Abdullah on CNN, March 2015
3. UNDP report for Afghanistan, 2013
4. Interview with author, London 2014

Chapter 1: Rule Number One
1. Lady Florentia Sale's diary
2. Lieutenant James Rattray, 1837
3. Interview with Jonathan Powell, London 2009
4. Interview with Dr Abdullah Abdullah, Washington DC
5. *No Higher Honor* by Condoleezza Rice, p.62

Chapter 2: Sixty Words
1. *Air Power Against Terror – America's Conduct of Operation Enduring Freedom*, Rand National Defense Institute, pp.78–80

Chapter 3: Making – and Almost Killing – a President
1. Interviews with Jason Amerine, Washington DC
2. Interviews with Hamid Karzai, Kabul, October 2004
3. Interview with James Dobbins, Washington DC
4. Interview with Francesc Vendrell, London 2014
5. Interview with Asadullah and Izzatullah Wasifi, Kabul July 2009

6. Interview with Dr Abdullah Abdullah
7. Brahimi article in *Washington Post*, 7 December 2008
8. *Bush at War* by Bob Woodward, p.310
9. *Decision Points* by George W. Bush, p.207
10. Lieutenant James Rattray, 1837

Chapter 5: Losing bin Laden – the Not So Great Escape

1. Bin Laden video aired on al Jazeera 3 November 2001
2. *Growing Up Bin Laden: Osama's Wife and Son Take Us Inside Their Secret World* by Najwa and Omar bin Laden and Jean Sasson, St Martin's Press 2009
3. *First In* by Gary Schroen
4. Interview with Anas, London 2003
5. *Charlie Wilson's War* by George Crile, p.262
6. Interview with Dr Umar Farooq, Islamabad 2001
7. Interview with Richard Armitage, Virginia 2010
8. *Growing Up Bin Laden* by Najwa and Omar bin Laden and Jean Sasson
9. Interview with Gary Berntsen, New York
10. Interview with Hayatullah, Dubai 2004
11. Special forces history
12. Dalton Fury, testimony to Senate Foreign Affairs Committee
13. Frontier Crimes Regulation, 1901
14. Interview with General Ali Aurakzai, London December 2004
15. Interview with Haji Zahir, Jalalabad 2004
16. Interviews with Mike Scheuer, Washington DC 2007 and 2009
17. Interview with Gul Agha Sherzai, Governor's Palace, Jalalabad, October 2006

Chapter 6: A Tale of Two Generals

1. *In the Line of Fire* by Pervez Musharraf
2. Interview with Richard Armitage, Washington DC
3. Interview with Wendy Chamberlin, Washington DC
4. Interview with Chaudhry Nisar Ali, London February 2015

5. Interview with Sir David Manning, London 2009
6. *Ghost Wars* by Steve Coll
7. Interview with General Zia-ul-Haq, Army House, Rawalpindi, August 1988
8. *First Family*, Pakistani Television Corporation, 2006
9. *My Life with the Taliban* by Mullah Zaeef
10. Interview with Husain Haqqani
11. Interview with Bob Grenier, London 2009
12. Interview with General Moinuddin Haider

Chapter 7: Taliban Central

1. Muttawakil was later released to live in a government guesthouse in Kabul as part of a reconciliation programme to try to win over so-called 'moderate Taliban'
2. Later FBI vein-matching established that the actual killer was Khalid Sheikh Mohammad, or 'KSM'

Chapter 8: Merchants of Ruin – the Return of the Warlords

1. 'Killing You is Very Easy for Us: Human Rights Abuses in Southeastern Afghanistan', Human Rights Watch, July 2003

Chapter 9: Theatre of War

1. Syed Shahid Hussein would rise to number two in the World Bank, the highest position possible for a non-American, as well as serving as Zulfikar Ali Bhutto's chief economic adviser
2. See 2002 interview by Dr Bina D'Costa with Australian doctor Geoffrey Davis who helped many rape victims through abortions
3. *Pakistan: Between Mosque and Military* by Husain Haqqani, p.220
4. Harkat-ul-Jihad-al-Islami later merged with Harkat-ul-Mujaheddin to become Harkat ul Ansar
5. *Daughter of The East* by Benazir Bhutto, 2007
6. Told to the author by Benazir Bhutto. See also *Deception* by Adrian Levy and Cathy Scott-Clark, p.208 and p.224

7. *Shadow War: The Untold Story of Jihad in Kashmir* by Arif Jamal, pp.108–13

Chapter 10: A Tale of Two Wars
1. See for example his message broadcast on al Jazeera on 3 November 2001

Chapter 11: Voting With Mullah Omar
1. An account of this meeting is given by Mullah Abdul Salam Zaeef, Taliban Ambassador to Pakistan at the time of 9/11, in his memoir *My Life with the Taliban,* p.65
2. A UK government statement on 17 November 2004 said that the 'government does not accept its central conclusion', pointing out that Iraqi Ministry of Health figures were 8,853 civilians killed and 15,517 wounded
3. Interview with the author, Washington 2009
4. *In the Line of Fire* by Pervez Musharraf

Chapter 12: Ambush
1. *Danger Close* by Stuart Tootal, p.24

Chapter 13: Bringing Dolphins to Helmand
1. Interview with Brigadier Ed Butler, London 2008
2. Field Notes Afghanistan, General Staff India, 2nd edition, 1915
3. *An Intimate War: An Oral History of the Helmand Conflict* by Mike Martin is excellent on Helmand's tribal rivalries and how the US and British forces failed to understand them
4. Richard Williams writing in *The Times,* 27 October 2014
5. See Parliamentary Report on Opium Production 2001–07
6. Interview with Mohammad Daud, Kabul 24 October 2014
7. UK officials discuss transition, cable, 24 March 2006 (on WikiLeaks)
8. Interview with Lt Col Tootal, London 20 July 2008

Chapter 14: Tethered Goats

1. Inquest, Oxford, 15 February 2008
2. *Danger Close* by Stuart Tootal, p.72
3. *Taking Command* by Gen David Richards, p.208 (diary entry for 10 June 2006)
4. Oral evidence to House of Commons Defence Committee, 29 March 2011
5. Like *An Intimate War* by Mike Martin, *War Comes to Garmser* by Carter Malkasian is excellent on the tribal dynamics of Helmand
6. *Taking Command* by Gen David Richards, p.204

Chapter 15: The President in His Bloody Palace

1. 'Afghanistan at a Crossroads: Challenges, Opportunities and a Way Ahead', report by Marin Strmecki, 17 August 2006
2. *Duty* by Robert Gates, p.202
3. Interview with Gen David Richards, September 2014
4. *Duty* by Robert Gates, p.201
5. Interview with Franz-Michael Melbin, Kabul April 2014

Chapter 16: Whose Side Are You On?

1. Interview with Hamid Mir, Marriott Hotel, Islamabad, November 2006
2. Interview with Richard Codrington, London
3. *Decision Points* by George W. Bush, p.214
4. See *The Taliban I Know* by Sami-ul-Haq
5. *Cables from Kabul* by Sherard Cowper-Coles, p.69
6. 'Info About Situation in Lowgar & Kabul', ISAF report, 21 May 2007; published by WikiLeaks 2010
7. Interview with Christine Fair, 18 December 2014
8. Fair says she had already told the UN she would only serve four months of a six-month contract, and that she was not fired
9. From 2005 to 2006, suicide attacks increased from twenty-seven to 139, roadside bombings from 783 to 1,677

10. *Duty* by Robert Gates, p.199
11. Ibid., p.200
12. Interview with Wesley Bauguess, 24 February 2015

Chapter 17: The Snake Bites Back
1. *Rising Tides* by Liam Fox, p.61

Chapter 18: The Weathermen of Kandahar
1. Robert Gates, 7 October 2008
2. Interview with Gen Richards, London September 2014
3. 'The Madrassa Menace', *Friday Times*, 21 January 2011
4. McNeill interview on PBS, 21 May 2009
5. Interview with Colonel Charles Mayo, 6 January 2015
6. 'America's Afghan Victims', *The Nation*, 20 September 2013

Chapter 19: We'll Always Have Kabul
1. Arrested in 2004 and imprisoned in Pul-i-Charkhi, 'Tora Bora Jack' was pardoned by President Karzai in 2007, and died in Mexico in 2012
2. Gen Daniel Menard, commander of Canadian troops in Kandahar 2009–10, was sent home in disgrace in May 2010 after he was caught having sex with a subordinate
3. National Environmental Protection Agency (NEPA) report, 2009, which describes Kabul as one of the most polluted cities in the world

Chapter 21: Meeting Colonel Imam
1. *The Wars of Afghanistan* by Peter Tomsen, p.535
2. *My Life with the Taliban* by Abdul Salam Zaeef

Chapter 22: The View From Washington
1. *Duty* by Robert Gates, p.298
2. *Obama's Wars* by Bob Woodward, p.301
3. *Cables from Kabul* by Sherard Cowper-Coles, p.148
4. Ibid., p.239
5. Interview with Hamid Karzai, Kabul 19 July 2009

6. By the time RAF Lyneham closed in 2011 the coffins of 345 men and women had passed through it
7. *Face the Nation*, 30 March 2009
8. *Duty* by Robert Gates, p.353
9. *Washington Post*, 21 September 2009
10. *Obama's Wars* by Bob Woodward

Chapter 23: All About the Politics
1. Interview with Umer Daudzai, Islamabad 10 May 2011

Chapter 25: Losing the Moral High Ground in Margaritaville
1. *Murder at Camp Delta* by Joseph Hickman, Simon & Schuster 2015
2. Shaker Aamer blog post, related in a letter to his lawyer Clive Stafford Smith, 14 February 2014
3. *My Life with the Taliban* by Mullah Zaeef
4. *Guantánamo Diary* by Mohamedou Slahi

Chapter 26: Chairman Mullen and the Cadillac of the Skies
1. *This Week*, ABC, 15 August 2010
2. *Thieves of State* by Sarah Chayes, p.154
3. Senate Armed Services Committee, 15 March 2011
4. *Duty* by Robert Gates
5. *Time* magazine, 24 October 2011

Chapter 27: Killing bin Laden
1. 'Dead Osama was Brought Into Abbottabad and Killed', *Pakistan Observer*, 12 May 2011
2. Mohamed al Qahtani, WikiLeaks, The Guantánamo Files, www.wikileaks.org/wikileaksgitmo/prisoner/63.html
3. Musharraf on *Good Morning America*, 23 September 2009
4. Interview with al Jazeera, January 2015. *Head to Head*, recorded 10 February 2015 to air April 2015. Interview with Sarah Montague on BBC *Hardtalk*, 11 February 2015
5. 'The Shooter', *Esquire* magazine, March 2013

Postscript: War Never Leaves You

1. The figure was given by Atheel ak Nujaifi, regional Governor of Nineveh
2. 'From Paper State to Caliphate: The Ideology of the Islamic State' by Cole Bunzel, Brookings Center for Middle East Policy, 2015
3. Ayman al Zawahiri wrote a letter to Zarqawi in 2005
4. According to figures collated by Peter Neumann, director of the International Centre for the Study of Radicalisation at Kings College London, more than 20,000 travelled to Syria and Iraq
5. EU Election Assessment Team report on elections. 16.7 per cent was contributed by the UK
6. David Cameron at Camp Bastion, 3 October 2014

Select Bibliography

Bergen, Peter L. *Manhunt: The Ten-Year Search for Bin Laden: From 9/11 to Abbottabad.* London: Bodley Head, 2012

Berntsen, Gary, and Ralph Pezzullo. *Jawbreaker: The Attack on Bin Laden and Al Qaeda: A Personal Account by the CIA's Key Field Commander.* New York: Crown, 2005

Bhutto, Benazir. *Daughter of the East: An Autobiography* (revised). London: Pocket Books, 2008

Bhutto, Benazir. *Reconciliation: Islam, Democracy and the West.* New York: Harper, 2008

Bishop, Patrick. *3 Para.* London: HarperPress, 2007

Bissonnette, Matt, and Kevin Maurer. *No Easy Day: The Firsthand Account of the Mission That Killed Osama Bin Laden.* New York: Dutton, 2012

Blehm, Eric. *The Only Thing Worth Dying For: How Eleven Green Berets Forged a New Afghanistan.* New York: Harper, 2010

Braithwaite, Rodric. *Afgantsy: The Russians in Afghanistan, 1979–89.* Oxford: Oxford UP, 2011

Bush, George W. *Decision Points.* New York: Crown, 2010

Chandrasekaran, Rajiv. *Little America: The War Within the War for Afghanistan.* New York: Knopf, 2012

Chayes, Sarah. *Thieves of State: Why Corruption Threatens Global Security.* New York: W.W. Norton, 2015

Select Bibliography

Coll, Steve. *Ghost Wars: The Secret History of the CIA, Afghanistan, and bin Laden, from the Soviet Invasion to September 10, 2001.* New York: Penguin Press, 2004

Cowper-Coles, Sherard. *Cables from Kabul: The Inside Story of the West's Afghanistan Campaign.* London: HarperPress, 2011

Dalrymple, William. *Return of a King: The Battle for Afghanistan.* London: Bloomsbury, 2013

Docherty, Leo. *Desert of Death: A Soldier's Journey from Iraq to Afghanistan.* London: Faber & Faber, 2007

Fergusson, James. *A Million Bullets: The Real Story of the British Army in Afghanistan.* London: Bantam, 2008

Fox, Liam. *Rising Tides: Facing the Challenges of a New Era.* London: Heron, 2013

Gall, Carlotta. *The Wrong Enemy: America in Afghanistan, 2001–2014.* Boston: Houghton Mifflin Harcourt, 2014

Gates, Robert Michael. *Duty: Memoirs of a Secretary at War.* London: W.H. Allen, 2014

Grey, Stephen. *Operation Snake Bite.* London: Penguin, 2009

Haqqani, Husain. *Pakistan: Between Mosque and Military.* Washington, DC: Carnegie Endowment for International Peace, 2005

Haqqani, Husain. *Magnificent Delusions: Pakistan, the United States, and an Epic History of Misunderstanding.* New York: PublicAffairs, 2013

Hussein, Zahid. *The Scorpion's Tail.* New York: Free, 2010

Kilcullen, David. *Out of the Mountains: The Coming Age of the Urban Guerrilla.* London: Hurst, 2013

Laden, Najwa bin, Omar bin Laden, and Jean P. Sasson. *Growing up Bin Laden: Osama's Wife and Son Take Us Inside Their Secret World.* New York: St. Martin's, 2009

Ledwidge, Frank. *Investment in Blood: The Real Cost of Britain's Afghan War.* n.p.: Yale UP, 2013

Levy, Adrian, and Cathy Scott-Clark. *Deception.* London: Atlantic Books, 2007

Levy, Adrian, and Cathy Scott-Clark. *The Siege.* London: Penguin, 2013

Select Bibliography

Loyn, David. *Butcher and Bolt.* London: Hutchinson, 2008

McDermott, Terry, and Josh Meyer. *The Hunt for KSM: Inside the Pursuit and Takedown of the Real 9/11 Mastermind, Khalid Sheikh Mohammed.* New York: Little, Brown, 2012

Malkasian, Carter. *War Comes to Garmser: Thirty Years of Conflict on the Afghan Frontier.* London: Hurst, 2013

Martin, Mike. *An Intimate War: An Oral History of the Helmand Conflict.* London: Hurst, 2014

Muñoz, Heraldo. *Getting Away With Murder.* New York: W.W. Norton, 2014

Musharraf, Pervez. *In the Line of Fire: A Memoir.* New York: Free, 2006

Rice, Condoleezza. *No Higher Honor: A Memoir of My Years in Washington.* New York: Crown, 2011

Richards, David. *Taking Command.* London: Headline, 2014

Riedel, Bruce O. *Deadly Embrace: Pakistan, America, and the Future of the Global Jihad.* Washington, D.C.: Brookings Institution, 2011

Rumsfeld, Donald. *Known and Unknown: A Memoir.* New York: Sentinel, 2011

Sale, Florentia. *Lady Sale's Afghanistan.* Leonaur, 2009

Schroen, Gary C. *First In: An Insider's Account of How the CIA Spearheaded the War on Terror in Afghanistan.* New York: Presidio/Ballantine, 2005

Siddiqa, Ayesha. *Military Inc.: Inside Pakistan's Military Economy.* London: Pluto, 2007

Slahi, Mohamedou Ould. *Guantánamo Diary.* New York: Little, Brown, 2015

Smith, Graeme. *The Dogs Are Eating Them Now.* Toronto: Knopf Canada, 2013

Tomsen, Peter. *The Wars of Afghanistan: Messianic Terrorism, Tribal Conflicts, and the Failures of Great Powers.* New York: PublicAffairs, 2011

Tootal, Stuart. *Danger Close.* London: John Murray, 2009

Woodward, Bob. *Bush at War.* New York: Simon & Schuster, 2002

Select Bibliography

Woodward, Bob. *Plan of Attack*. New York: Simon & Schuster, 2004

Woodward, Bob. *Obama's Wars*. New York: Simon & Schuster, 2010

Zaeef, Abdul Salam, Alex Strick Van Linschoten, and Felix Kuehn. *My Life with the Taliban*. New York: Columbia UP, 2010

Illustration Credits

Illustration Credits

Page 6: © Chris Hondros/Getty Images (top); Aamir Qureshi/ AFP/Getty Images (bottom)
Page 7: © the author (top and bottom)
Page 8: © Brooks Kraft/Corbis

Section Three
Page 1: © Johannes Eisele/AFP/Getty Images
Page 2: © Justin Sutcliffe (top and bottom)
Page 3: © Shah Marai/AFP/Getty Images (top); © Justin Sutcliffe (bottom)
Page 4: © Ahmad Jamshid/AP/Press Association Images (top); © the author (bottom)
Page 5: © Justin Sutcliffe (top and bottom)
Pages 6–7: © Justin Sutcliffe
Page 6: © the author (bottom)
Page 7: © Ben Birchall/PA Wire/Press Association Images (bottom)
Page 8: © Justin Sutcliffe (top and bottom)

Index

Index

Index

Index

Index

Chechnya, 90, 170, 590
Cheh, Mary, 500
Cheney, Dick, 126, 336, 511
chess, 18
Chicago, O'Hare airport, 484
Chile, 142
China, 500, 515
Churchill, Winston, 191, 235
CIA
  admiration for bin Laden, 78–9
  and Afghanistan, 29–31, 33–6, 39–40
  and arrest of KSM, 175–6
  and Balawi ambush, 490–1
  and Baradar arrest, 521–2
  and Bhutto assassination, 367
  drone strikes, 488–9, 492
  expansion of operations in Pakistan, 468–9, 488–9
  and hunt for bin Laden, 82, 84, 86, 92–5, 132
  and Iranian revolution, 101
  and Kandahar Strike Force, 254
  and Karzai government, 141–2, 323, 344
  and killing of bin Laden, 549–53, 555–6, 559–61, 566, 570
  and 9/11 attacks, 22–3, 565
  and Pakistani agencies, 28, 105, 111, 333, 402
  and Pearl kidnapping, 126
  purged under Carter, 442
  secret assassination programme, 219
  'special activities division', 196
  support for Hekmatyar, 329
  torture and 'black sites', 508–11, 557
  and US–Soviet proxy war, 435, 443–4, 446–9, 451–2
  and warlords, 135, 137, 140
Clinton, Bill, 92, 101, 115
Clinton, Hillary, 458, 476–7, 487, 501, 516–17, 544
Codrington, Richard, 335, 399
collective punishments, 218
Colombia, 253
Commanders' Emergency Response Programs (CERPs), 267

consultancies, international, 142–3
Cordesman, Antony, 460
corruption, 470–3, 533–5
Cowper-Coles, Sherard, 341, 391–2, 394, 399, 403, 461, 478
Crimea, Russian annexation of, 594
Crocker, Ryan, 333
Crombie, Susan, 240
Crumpton, Hank, 86–7
Curzon, Lord, 390
customs duties, 147–8
'Cyprus group', 51

Dad Mohammad, Mullah, 250
Dadullah, Mullah, 110, 250
Dailey, Major General Dell, 82, 86
Daily Times, 564
Daisy Cutter bombs, 39, 85
Damana, 50
Dannatt, General Richard, 286
Daoud, Sardar Mohammad, 305, 308, 312, 440, 442
D'Arcy, Corporal Matt, 231–4
Dargai barracks bombing, 338–9
Darul Uloom Haqqania, 340
Daud, General Daud, 138
Daud, Engineer Mohammad, 249, 251, 255, 261, 274–5, 280–1, 289, 295, 324, 392
Daudzai, Umer, 324, 470, 473, 536
Davis, Colonel ('Colonel D'), 187–9
Davis, David, 592–3
Davis, Major General Dickie, 10
Davis, Lanny, 115
Davis, Colonel Morris ('Mo'), 501, 507
Davis, Colonel Rodney, 178
Davis, Raymond, 549–50, 553
De Adam Khan, 384
deer, Karzai's, 321, 323
Deerans, Private Kyle, 226, 231–3, 236
Dell, Chris, 393
Delta Force, 84–5, 91, 94, 196–7
DFID, 240, 255, 264, 268, 277, 286, 290, 400
Diana, Princess of Wales, 100
Dilawar (taxi driver), 186

Index

Index

Index

Index

Index

Index

Index

Index

Index

Index

Index

Index

Index

Index

Index

Index